Langenscheidt Universal Dictionary

Norwegian

Norwegian – English
English – Norwegian

Langenscheidt

Heike Pleisteiner
Lexicographical work: Howard Atkinson, Martin Fellermayer, Stuart Fortey, Heike Pleisteiner, Heike Richini, Robin Sawers, Karin Weindl

This dictionary has been created with the help of dictionary databases owned by HarperCollins Publishers Ltd.

1. Auflage 2025 (1,01 - 2025)

www.langenscheidt.com

Print: Publikum d.o.o

ISBN 978-3-12-614015-7

Contents
Innhold

Preface

In selecting the vocabulary and phrases for this dictionary, the editors have had the traveller's needs foremost in mind. This book will prove a useful companion to casual tourists and business travellers alike who appreciate the reassurance a small and practical dictionary can provide. It offers them – as well as beginners and students – all the basic vocabulary they will have to encounter and have to use, giving the key words and expressions to allow them to cope in everyday situations.

This dictionary is designed to slip into pocket or purse, and thus have a role as a handy companion at all times.

Besides just about everything you normally find in dictionaries, there are these bonuses:

- simplified pronunciation after each foreign-word entry, making it easy to read and enunciate words whose spelling may look forbidding
- useful information on how to tell the time and how to count, on conjugating irregular verbs, commonly seen abbreviations and converting to the metric system, in addition to basic phrases.

While no dictionary of this size can pretend to completeness, we are confident this dictionary will help you get most out of your trip abroad.

Forord

I valget av ordforråd og uttrykk til denne ordboken har vi først og fremst tatt sikte på å dekke den reisendes behov. Denne boken vil derfor være en god følgesvenn for både turister og forretningsreisende som setter pris på den tryggheten en hendig ordbok gir. Også de som vil lære språket, nybegynnere såvel som viderekomne, finner her det grunnleggende ordforråd de vil komme i berøring med, dertil nøkkelord og -uttrykk som gjør det mulig å klare seg i dagligdagse situasjoner.

Ordboken er laget for å kunne tas med i en veske eller lomme. Vi håper at den ved sitt praktiske format vil tiltale mange og være til god hjelp i alle situasjoner.

Foruten alt det en ordbok vanligvis inneholder, finner du følgende bonustillegg:

- imitasjon av uttalen etter hver oppføring på fremmedspråket, noe som gjør det enkelt å lese ordet og å bruke ord med en komplisert stavemåte
- en rekke praktiske opplysninger som tallord, vanlige forkortelser, hvordan man angir klokkeslett, bøyning av uregelmessige verb, samt et avsnitt med nyttige uttrykk.

Det sier seg selv at en ordbok av dette format ikke kan gjøre krav på å være fullstendig. Allikevel er vi overbevist om at denne ordboken vil være til uvurderlig hjelp når det gjelder å få det beste ut av utenlandseisen din.

Introduction

This dictionary has been designed to take account of your practical needs. Unnecessary linguistic information has been avoided. The entries are listed in alphabetical order, regardless of whether the entry is printed in a single word or in two or more separate words. As the only exception to this rule, a few idiomatic expressions are listed alphabetically as main entries by the most significant word of the expression. When an entry is followed by sub-entries, such as expressions and locutions, these are also listed in alphabetical order*.

Each main-entry word is followed by a phonetic transcription (see guide to pronunciation). Following the transcription, the part of speech of the entry word is indicated, whenever applicable. If an entry word is used as more than one part of speech, the translations are grouped together after the respective part of speech.

In the regular indefinite plural, both common, masculine and neuter nouns take an *-(e)r* ending. Exceptions: masculine nouns ending in *-er* take *~e* (e.g.: arbeider, pl arbeidere), and monosyllabic neuter nouns remain unchanged (e.g.: barn, pl barn).

All irregular plural forms of nouns not conforming to these rules are given in brackets after the part of speech.

Whenever an entry word is repeated in irregular forms or sub-entries, a tilde (~) is used to represent the full word. In plurals of long words, only the part that changes is written out fully, whereas the unchanged part is represented by a hyphen (-).

Entry word:	Plural:
mus *c* (pl ~)	mus
vidunder *nt* (pl ~, ~e)	vidunder, vidundere
antibiotikum *nt* (pl -ka)	antibiotika

An asterisk (*) in front of a verb indicates that it is irregular. For more detail, refer to the list of irregular verbs.

---

* Note that the Norwegian alphabet comprises 29 letters; æ, ø and å are considered independent characters and come after z, in that order.

Veiledning

Ved utarbeidelsen av denne ordboken har vi først og fremst tatt sikte på å gjøre den så praktisk og anvendelig som mulig. Mindre viktige språklige opplysninger er utelatt. Oppslagsordene står i alfabetisk rekkefølge uansett om uttrykket skrives i ett ord, med bindestrek, eller i to eller flere ord. Det eneste unntaket fra denne regelen er noen få idiomatiske uttrykk, som du vil finne under det meningsbærende ordet. Når et oppslagsord følges av flere sammensetninger eller uttrykk, er også disse satt i alfabetisk rekkefølge.

Hvert hovedoppslagsord er fulgt av lydskrift (se Uttale), og vanligvis av ordklasse. I fall et oppslagsord tilhører flere ordklasser, er oversettelsene gruppert sammen etter de respektive ordklassene.

Dersom et substantiv har uregelmessig flertallsform, er denne angitt. I tilfeller der det kan oppstå tvil, har vi gitt eksempler på bruken.

Bølgestrek (~) er brukt som gjentagelsestegn for oppslagsordet når dette forekommer senere i artikkelen (f.eks. ved uregelmessig flertallsform, sammensatte ord, etc.).

Når det gjelder uregelmessig flertallsform av sammensatte ord, er bare den delen som forandres, skrevet helt ut; en kort strek (–) står for den uforandrede delen.

En stjerne (*) foran et verb betyr at verbet er uregelmessig. Bøyningsmønstret finner du i listen over uregelmessige verb.

I denne ordboken har vi anvendt vanlig engelsk stavemåte. Alle ord som må regnes som amerikanske, er merket *Am* (se listen over forkortelser).

Guide to Pronunciation

Each main entry in this part of the dictionary is followed by a phonetic transcription which shows you how to pronounce the words. This transcription should be read as if it were English. It is based on Standard British pronunciation, though we have tried to take account of General American pronunciation also. Below, only those letters and symbols are explained which we consider likely to be ambiguous or not immediately understood.

The syllables are separated by hyphens, and stressed syllables are printed in *italics*.

Of course, the sounds of any two languages are never exactly the same, but if you follow carefully our indications, you should be able to pronounce the foreign words in such a way that you'll be understood. To make your task easier, our transcriptions occasionally simplify slightly the sound system of the language while still reflecting the essential sound differences.

Consonants

g	always hard, as in **g**o
kh	quite like **h** in **h**uge, but with the tongue raised a little higher
r	rolled in the front of the mouth, except in south-western Norway, where it's pronounced in the back of the mouth
s	always hard, as in **s**o

The consonants **d, l, n, s, t,** if preceded by **r**, are generally pronounced with the tip of the tongue turned up well behind the upper front teeth. The **r** then ceases to be pronounced.

Vowels and Diphthongs

aa	long **a**, as in c**a**r, without any **r**-sound
ah	a short version of **aa**; between **a** in c**a**t and **u** in c**u**t
aw	as in r**aw** (British pronunciation)
æ	like **a** in c**a**t
ææ	a long **æ**-sound
eh	like **e** in g**e**t
er	as in oth**er**, without any **r**-sound
ew	a "rounded **ee**-sound". Say the vowel sound **ee** (as in s**ee**), and while saying it, round your lips as for **oo** (as in s**oo**n), without moving your tongue; when your lips are in the **oo** position, but your tongue in the **ee** position, you should be pronouncing the correct sound
igh	as in s**igh**
o	always as in h**o**t (British pronunciation)
ou	as in l**ou**d
ur	as in f**ur**, but with rounded lips and no **r**-sound

1) A bar over a vowel symbol (e.g. $\overline{\textbf{ew}}$) shows that this sound is long.
2) Raised letters (e.g. $^{\textbf{y}}$**aa**, **ew**$^{\textbf{ee}}$) should be pronounced only fleetingly.

Tones

In Norwegian there are two "tones": one is rising, the other consists of a falling pitch followed by a rise. As these tones are complex and very hard to copy, we do not indicate them, but mark their position as stressed.

Uttale

I denne delen av ordboken er hvert stikkord fulgt av internasjonal lydskrift (IPA). Hvert enkelt tegn i denne fonetiske skriften står for en bestemt lyd. Tegn som her ikke er nærmere forklart, uttales omtrent som de tilsvarende norske bokstavene.

Konsonanter

ð	en slags lespende, stemt **s**-lyd; uttales med tungespissen løftet mot overtennene
g	alltid som i **g**å, aldri som i **g**i
k	alltid som i **k**u, aldri som i **k**inn
ŋ	som **ng** i la**ng**
r	en stemt **r**-lyd som dannes ved at tungebladet heves mot den bakre del av gommene
ʃ	som **sj** i øst- og nordnorsk **sj**ø
θ	en slags lespende, stemmeløs **s**-lyd
w	som **o** i **o**st, men meget svak
z	stemt **s**-lyd
ʒ	stemt **sj**-lyd

Merk: Transkripsjonen [sj] skal alltid uttales som en **s** fulgt av en **j**-lyd, ikke som i øst- og nordnorsk **sj**ø.

Vokaler

ɑː	som **a** i f**a**r
æ	omtrent som **æ** i l**æ**rd
ʌ	omtrent som **a** i k**a**tt
e	som i t**e**legram
ɛ	som **e** i p**e**nn
ə	som **e** i gat**e**
ɔ	som **o** i t**o**lv
u	som **o** i **o**st

1) Et kolon [ː] etter en vokal angir lang vokallyd.
2) Noen franske låneord har nasalert vokal (dvs. at ved uttalen går luften ut både gjennom munn og nese); dette er angitt med en tilde over vokalen (f. eks. [ã]).

Diftonger

En diftong består av to vokaler hvorav den ene er sterk (betont) og den andre svak (ubetont), og uttales som en glidende lyd som bare utgjør én stavelse, som f. eks. **ei** i st**ei**n. I engelske diftonglyder er det alltid den andre vokalen som er svak. Dersom diftongen etterfølges av en [ə] medfører dette en ytterligere svekkelse av den andre vokalen.

Trykk

Tegnet ['] står foran den trykksterke stavelsen, [ˌ] foran stavelser med bitrykk.

Amerikansk uttale

Lydskriften her i boken følger britisk uttale. Selv om amerikansk uttale varierer sterkt fra den ene delen av USA til den annen, kan en sette opp visse regler for forskjellen mellom amerikansk og britisk uttale. Her er noen av dem:

1) I motsetning til på britisk engelsk uttales **r** både når den etterfølges av konsonant og på slutten av ord.
2) I mange ord (f. eks. *ask*, *castle*, *laugh*, osv.) blir [ɑː] til [æ].
3) Lyden [ɔ] uttaler amerikanerne som [ɑ] eller [ɔː].
4) I ord som *duty*, *tune*, *new*, osv. utelates ofte [j]-lyden som på britisk engelsk går forut for [uː].
5) Mange ord har trykkforskyvning i forhold til britisk uttale.

Abbreviations
Forkortelser

adjective	*adj*	adjektiv
adverb	*adv*	adverb
American	*Am*	amerikansk
article	*art*	artikkel
common gender	*c*	felleskjønn
conjunction	*conj*	konjunksjon
masculine	*m*	hankjønn
noun	*n*	substantiv
noun (American)	*nAm*	substantiv (amerikansk)
neuter	*nt*	intetkjønn
numeral	*num*	tallord
past tense	*p*	imperfektum
plural	*pl*	flertall
plural (American)	*plAm*	flertall (amerikansk)
past participle	*pp*	perfektum partisipp
present tense	*pr*	presens
preposition	*prep*	preposisjon
pronoun	*pron*	pronomen
verb	*v*	verb
verb (American)	*vAm*	verb (amerikansk)

Norwegian – English
Norsk – Engelsk

A

-a (*aa*) *art* the
abbedi (ah-ber-*dee*) *nt* abbey
abonnement (ah-boo-ner-*mahngng*) *nt* subscription
abonnent (ah-boo-*nehnt*) *m* subscriber
abort (ah-*bott*) *m* abortion; miscarriage
abort-tilhenger (ah-*bott* til-hehng-er) *c* (pl -e) pro life
abortmotstander (ah-*bott*-moot-stahnd-er) *c* (pl -e) pro choice
absolutt (ahp-soo-*lewtt*) *adj* very, sheer; *adv* absolutely
abstrakt (ahp-*strahkt*) *adj* abstract
absurd (ahp-*sewrd*) *adj* absurd
adapter (ah-*dap*-terr) *m* adaptor
addisjon (ah-di-*shoon*) *m* addition
adekvat (ah-deh-*kvaat*) *adj* adequate
adel (*aa*-derl) *m* nobility
adelig (aa-der-li) *adj* belonging to nobility
adgang (*aad*-gahng) *m* admission, entrance, admittance, entry; ~ **forbudt** no entry, no admittance
adjektiv (*ahd*-[y]ehk-tiv) *nt* adjective
adkomst (*aad*-komst) *m* access
***adlyde** (*aad*-lew-der) *v* obey
administrasjon (ahd-mi-ni-strah-*shoon*) *m* administration
administrerende (ahd-mi-ni-*stray*-rer-ner) *adj* administrative; executive
adoptere (ah-doop-*tay*-rer) *v* adopt
adressat (ahd-reh-*saat*) *m* addressee
adresse (ah-*drehss*-ser) *c* address
adressere (ahd-reh-*say*-rer) *v* address
advare (*aad*-vaa-rer) *v* caution, warn
advarsel (*aad*-vah-sherl) *m* (pl -sler) warning
adverb (ahd-*værb*) *nt* adverb
advokat (ahd-voo-*kaat*) *m* lawyer, barrister; solicitor,

attorney
affektert (ah-fehk-*tāyt*) *adj* affected
affære (ah-*fææ*-rer) *m* affair
Afrika (*aaf*-ri-kah) Africa
afrikaner (ahf-ri-*kaa*-nerr) *m* African
afrikansk (ahf-ri-*kaansk*) *adj* African
aftensmat (*ahf*-terns-maat) *m* supper
agent (ah-*gehnt*) *m* agent
agentur (ah-gehn-*tēwr*) *nt* agency
aggressiv (*ah*-greh-seev) *adj* aggressive
agn (ahngn) *nt* bait
agurk (ah-*gewrk*) *m* cucumber
AIDS (ayds) AIDS
airbag (*ehr*-bæg) *m* airbag
akademi (ah-kah-day-*mee*) *nt* academy
akkompagnere (ah-koom-pahn-ʸ*āy*-rer) *v* accompany
akkreditiv (ah-kreh-di-*teev*) *nt* letter of credit
akkurat (ah-kew-*raat*) *adj* just; exact; *adv* exactly
aksel (*ahk*-serl) *m* (pl aksler) axle
akselerere (*ahk*-ser-ler-*rāy*-rer) *v* accelerate
aksent (ahk-*sahngng*) *m* accent
akseptere (ahk-sehp-*tāy*-rer) *v* accept
aksje (*ahk*-sher) *m* share, stock
aksjon (ahk-*shōōn*) *m* action
akt (ahkt) *m* act; nude
akte (*ahk*-ter) *v* esteem
aktelse (*ahk*-terl-ser) *m* respect; esteem
akterspeil (*ahk*-ter-shpayl) *nt* (pl ~) stern, rear
aktiv (*ahk*-tiv) *adj* active
aktivitet (ahk-ti-vi-*tāyt*) *m* activity
aktuell (ahk-tew-*ehll*) *adj* topical; current
akutt (ah-*kewtt*) *adj* acute
akvarell (ahk-vah-*rehll*) *m* watercolo(u)r
alarm (ah-*lahrm*) *m* alarm
alarmere (ah-lahr-*māy*-rer) *v* alarm
albue (*ahl*-bēw-er) *m* elbow
album (*ahl*-bewm) *nt* album
alder (*ahl*-derr) *m* (pl ~e, aldrer) age
alderdom (*ahl*-der-dom) *m* old age, age
aldri (*ahl*-dri) *adv* never
alene (ah-*lāy*-ner) *adv* alone; only
ale opp (*aa*-ler) *breed, raise
alfabet (ahl-fah-*bāyt*) *nt* alphabet
algebra (*ahl*-geh-brah) *m* algebra
Algerie (ahl-sheh-*ree*) Algeria
algerier (ahl-*shāy*-ri-err) *m* Algerian
algerisk (ahl-*shāy*-risk) *adj* Algerian
alkohol (ahl-koo-*hōōl*) *m*

alcohol, *colloquial* booze
alkoholholdig (ahl-koo-*hōōl*-hol-di) *adj* alcoholic; **alkoholholdige drikker** spirits
all (ahll) *adj* all
allé (ah-*lāy*) *m* avenue
allerede (ah-ler-*rāy*-der) *adv* already
allergi (ahl-ær-*gee*) *m* allergy
allianse (ah-li-*ahng*-ser) *m* alliance
allierte (ah-li-*āy*-ter) *pl* Allies *pl*
allikevel (ah-*lee*-ker-vehl) *conj* yet
allmektig (*ahl*-mehk-ti) *adj* omnipotent
allmenn (*ahl*-māyn) *adj* public; general
alltid (*ahl*-ti) *adv* always; ever; **for ~** forever, for ever
allting (*ahl*-ting) *pron* everything
alm (ahlm) *m* elm
almanakk (ahl-mah-*nahkk*) *m* diary
alminnelig (ahl-*min*-ner-li) *adj* plain, customary, common
alt (ahlt) *pron* everything; *adj* all; *m* alto
alter (*ahl*-terr) *nt* (pl altre) altar
alternativ (ahl-*tæ*-nah-teev) *nt* alternative
altfor (*ahlt*-for) *adv* too
altså (*ahlt*-so) *adv* consequently
alv (ahlv) *m* elf
alvor (*ahl*-vor) *nt* seriousness, gravity
alvorlig (ahl-*vaw*-li) *adj* serious, bad, grave
ambassade (ahm-bah-*saa*-der) *m* embassy
ambassadør (ahm-bah-sah-*dūrr*) *m* ambassador
ambisiøs (ahm-bi-si-*ūrss*) *adj* ambitious
ambulanse (ahm-bew-*lahng*-ser) *m* ambulance
Amerika (ah-*māy*-ri-kah) America
amerikaner (ah-meh-ri-*kaa*-nerr) *m* American
amerikansk (ah-meh-ri-*kaansk*) *adj* American
ametyst (ah-mer-*tewst*) *m* amethyst
amme (*ahm*-mer) *v* nurse
amnesti (ahm-ner-*stee*) *nt* amnesty
amulett (ah-mew-*lehtt*) *m* lucky charm, charm
analfabet (ahn-nahl-fah-*bāyt*) *m* illiterate
analyse (ahn-ah-*lēw*-ser) *m* analysis
analysere (ahn-ah-lew-*sāy*-rer) *v* analyse
analytiker (ahn-ah-*lewt*-ti-kerr) *m* analyst
ananas (*ahn*-nah-nahss) *m* pineapple
anarki (ahn-ahr-*kee*) *nt* anarchy
anatomi (ahn-ah-too-*mee*) *m* anatomy

anbefale (*ahn*-beh-faa-ler) *v* recommend
anbefaling (*ahn*-beh-faa-ling) *c* recommendation
and (ahnn) *c* (pl ender) duck
ane (*aa*-ner) *v* suspect, guess
anelse (*aa*-nerl-ser) *m* notion; suspicion
anemi (ahn-eh-*mee*) *m* anaemia
anerkjenne (*ahn*-nær-kheh-ner) *v* recognize, acknowledge
anerkjennelse (*ahn*-nær-kheh-nerl-ser) *m* recognition
anfall (*ahn*-fahl) *nt* (pl ~) fit
anfører (*ahn*-fūr-rerr) *m* leader
anførselstegn (*ahn*-fur-sherls-tayn) *pl* quotation marks
anger (*ahng*-ngerr) *m* repentance
***angi** (*ahn*-ʸee) *v* indicate
angre (*ahng*-rer) *v* regret, repent
angrep (*ahn*-grāyp) *nt* (pl ~) attack; raid
***angripe** (*ahn*-gree-per) *v* attack, assault
angst (ahngst) *m* fright
***angå** (*ahn*-gaw) *v* concern
angående (*ahn*-gaw-erner) *prep* regarding, about, as regards, concerning
ankel (*ahng*-kerl) *m* (pl ankler) ankle
anker (*ahng*-kerr) *nt* (pl ankre) anchor
anklage[1] (*ahn*-klaa-ger) *v* accuse, charge
anklage[2] (*ahn*-klaa-ger) *m* charge
anklagede (*ahn*-klaa-ger-der) accused
***ankomme** (*ahn*-ko-mer) *v* arrive
ankomst (*ahn*-komst) *m* arrival
ankomsttid (*ahn*-komst-teed) *c* time of arrival
anledning (ahn-*lāyd*-ning) *m* chance, opportunity; ***ha ~ til** afford
anlegg (*ahn*-lehg) *nt* (pl ~) aptitude; construction
anliggende (*ahn*-li-ger-ner) *nt* affair, concern
anmassende (*ahn*-mah-ser-ner) *adj* presumptuous
anmelde (*ahn*-meh-ler) *v* report; review
anmeldelse (*ahn*-meh-lerl-ser) *m* review
anmode (*ahn*-mōō-der) *v* request
anmodning (*ahn*-mōōd-ning) *m* request
anneks (ah-*nehks*) *nt* annex
annektere (ah-nehk-*tāy*-rer) *v* annex
annen (*aa*-ern) *num* second; *pron* other
annerledes (*ahn*-ner-lāy-derss) *adv* otherwise; *adj* different
annetsteds (*aa*-ern-stehss) *adv* elsewhere
annonse (ah-*nong*-ser) *m*

advertisement
annullere (ah-new-*lay*-rer) *v* cancel; recall
anonym (ah-noo-*newm*) *adj* anonymous
ansatt (*ahn*-saht) *m* (pl ~e) employee
***anse** (*ahn*-say) *v* consider, regard
anseelse (*ahn*-say-erl-ser) *m* reputation
anselig (ahn-*say*-li) *adj* considerable, substantial
***ansette** (*ahn*-seh-ter) *v* engage
ansikt (*ahn*-sikt) *nt* face
ansiktskrem (*ahn*-sikts-kraym) *m* face cream
ansiktstrekk (*ahn*-sikts-trehk) *nt* feature
ansjos (ahn-*shooss*) *m* anchovy
anskaffe (*ahn*-skah-fer) *v* *buy, *get
anskaffelse (*ahn*-skah-ferl-ser) *m* purchase
anspennelse (*ahn*-speh-nerl-ser) *m* strain
anspent (*ahn*-spehnt) *adj* tense
anspore (*ahn*-spoo-rer) *v* incite
anstendig (ahn-*stehn*-di) *adj* decent
anstendighet (ahn-*stehn*-di-hayt) *c* decency
anstrengelse (*ahn*-strayng-erl-ser) *m* effort, strain
anstrenge seg (*ahn*-streh-nger) labo(u)r; try
anstøt (*ahn*-sturt) *nt* (pl ~) offense *Am*, offence
anstøtelig (*ahn*-sturt-eli) *adj* offensive
ansvar (*ahn*-svahr) *nt* liability, responsibility
ansvarlig (ahn-*svaa*-li) *adj* liable, responsible; **~ for** in charge of
***anta** (*ahn*-taa) *v* assume, suppose; guess
antakelig (ahn-*taa*-ker-li) *adj* presumable
antall (*ahn*-tahl) *nt* (pl ~) number; quantity
antenne (ahn-*tehn*-ner) *c* aerial
antibiotikum (ahn-ti-bi-*oo*-ti-kewm) *nt* (pl -ka) antibiotic
antikk (ahn-*tikk*) *adj* antique
antikvitet (ahn-ti-kvi-*tayt*) *m* antique
antikvitetshandler (ahn-ti-kvi-*tayts*-hahnd-lerr) *m* antique dealer
antipati (ahn-ti-pah-*tee*) *m* dislike
antyde (*ahn*-tew-der) *v* indicate; imply; hint
antydning (*ahn*-tew-dning) *m* hint
anvende (*ahn*-veh-ner) *v* employ, apply; utilize
anvendelig (ahn-*vehn*-ner-li) *adj* usable
anvendelse (*ahn*-veh-nerl-ser) *m* application
anvise (*ahn*-vee-ser) *v*

indicate
ape (*aa*-per) *c* monkey
aperitiff (ah-peh-ri-*tiff*) *m* aperitif
apotek (ah-poo-*tāyk*) *nt* pharmacy, chemist's; drugstore *nAm*
apoteker (ah-poo-*tāy*-kerr) *m* chemist
apparat (ah-pah-*raat*) *nt* apparatus; machine; appliance; gadget
appell (ah-*pehll*) *m* appeal
appelsin (ah-perl-*seen*) *m* orange
appetitt (ah-per-*titt*) *m* appetite
appetittlig (ah-per-*tit*-li) *adj* appetizing
appetittvekker (ah-per-*tit*-veh-kerr) *m* appetizer
applaudere (ahp-lou-*dāy*-rer) *v* clap, applaud
applaus (ah-*plouss*) *m* applause
aprikos (ahp-ri-*kōōss*) *m* apricot
april (ah-*preel*) April
araber (ah-*raa*-berr) *m* Arab
arabisk (ah-*raa*-bisk) *adj* Arab
arbeid (*ahr*-bay) *nt* labo(u)r, work; employment
arbeide (ahr-*bay*-der) *v* work
arbeider (ahr-*bay*-derr) *m* labo(u)rer, worker, workman
arbeidsbesparende (*ahr*-bayss-beh-spaa-rer-ner) *adj* labo(u)r-saving
arbeidsdag (*ahr*-bayss-daag) *m* working day
arbeidsformidling (*ahr*-bayss-for-mid-ling) *c* employment exchange
arbeidsgiver (*ahr*-bayss-ʸee-verr) *m* employer
arbeidsledig (*ahr*-bayss-lāy-di) *adj* unemployed, jobless
arbeidsledighet (*ahr*-bayss-lāy-di- hāyt) *c* unemployment
arbeidsløs (*ahr*-bayss-lūrss) *adj* unemployed, jobless
arbeidsløshet (*ahr*-bayss-lūrss-hāyt) *c* unemployment
arbeidstillatelse (*ahr*-bayss-ti-laa-terl-ser) *m* work permit; labor permit *Am*
arbeidsnarkoman (*ahr*-bayss-nahr-kōō-*mahn*) *c* workaholic
areal (ah-reh-*aal*) *nt* area
Argentina (ahr-gern-*tee*-nah) Argentina
argentiner (ahr-gern-*tee*-nerr) *m* Argentinian
argentinsk (ahr-gern-*teensk*) *adj* Argentinian
argument (ahr-gew-*mehnt*) *nt* argument
argumentere (ahr-gew-mehn-*tāy*-rer) *v* argue
ark (ahrk) *nt* sheet
arkade (ahr-*kaa*-der) *m*

arcade
arkeolog (ahr-keh-oo-*lawg*) *m* archaeologist
arkeologi (ahr-keh-oo-loo-*gee*) *m* archaeology
arkitekt (ahr-ki-*tehkt*) *m* architect
arkitektur (ahr-ki-tehk-*tewr*) *m* architecture
arkiv (ahr-*keev*) *nt* archives *pl*
arm (ahrm) *m* arm; **arm i arm** arm-in-arm
armbånd (*ahrm*-bon) *nt* (pl ~) bracelet
armbåndsur (*ahrm*-bons-ewr) *nt* (pl ~) wrist-watch
armé (ahr-*may*) *m* army
aroma (ah-*roo*-mah) *m* aroma
arr (ahrr) *nt* scar
arrangere (ah-rahng-*shay*-rer) *v* arrange
arrestasjon (ah-reh-stah-*shoon*) *m* arrest, capture
arrestere (ah-reh-*stay*-rer) *v* arrest
art (ahtt) *m* species
artikkel (ah-*tik*-kerl) *m* (pl artikler) article
artisjokk (ah-ti-*shokk*) *m* artichoke
artistisk (ah-*tiss*-tisk) *adj* artistic
arv (ahrv) *m* inheritance
arve (*ahr*-ver) *v* inherit
arvelig (*ahr*-ver-li) *adj* hereditary
arving (*ahr*v-ing) *m* heir; heiress
asbest (ahss-*behst*) *m* asbestos
asfalt (*ahss*-fahlt) *m* asphalt
Asia (*aa*-si-ah) Asia
asiat (ah-si-*aat*) *m* Asian
asiatisk (ah-si-*aa*-tisk) *adj* Asian
aske (*ahss*-ker) *c* ash
askebeger (*ahss*-ker-bay-gerr) *nt* (pl -gre) ashtray
asparges (ah-*spahr*-gerss) *m* (pl ~) asparagus
aspekt (ah-*spehkt*) *nt* aspect
aspirin (ahss-pi-*reen*) *m* aspirin
assistanse (ah-si-*stahng*-ser) *m* assistance
assistent (ah-si-*stehnt*) *m* assistant
astma (*ahst*-mah) *m* asthma
astronomi (ah-stroo-noo-*mee*) *m* astronomy
asyl (ah-*sewl*) *nt* asylum
at (ahtt) *conj* that
ateist (ah-teh-*ist*) *m* atheist
Atlanterhavet (aht-*lahn*-terr-haa-ver) Atlantic
atlet (aht-*layt*) *m* athlete
atmosfære (aht-mooss-*fææ*-rer) *m* atmosphere
atom (ah-*toom*) *nt* atom; **atom-** atomic
atskillelse (*aat*-shi-lerl-ser) *m* separation
atskillige (aht-*shil*-li-er) *adj* several
atskilt (*aat*-shilt) *adj* separate; *adv* apart
atspredelse (*aat*-spray-derl-ser) *m* amusement,

diversion; recreation
atten (*aht*-tern) *num* eighteen
attende (*aht*-terner) *num* eighteenth
atter (*aht*-terr) *adv* again
attest (ah-*tehst*) *m* certificate
attestere (ah-tehs-*tāy*-rer) *v* attest
attraksjon (ah-trahk-*shōōn*) *m* attraction
attråverdig (*aht*-raw-vær-di) *adj* desirable
aubergine (o-behr-*sheen*) *m* eggplant
auditorium (ou-di-*tōō*-ri-ewm) *nt* (pl -ier) auditorium
august (ou-*gewst*) August
auksjon (ouk-*shōōn*) *m* auction
Australia (ou-*straa*-li-ah) Australia
australier (ou-*straa*-li-err) *m* Australian
australsk (ou-*straalsk*) *adj* Australian
autentisk (ou-*tehn*-tisk) *adj* authentic
automat (ou-too-*maat*) *m* slot machine; vending machine
automatisering (ou-too-mah-ti-*sāy*-ring) *c* automation
automatisk (ou-too-*maa*-tisk) *adj* automatic
automobilklubb (ou-too-moo-*beel*-klewb) *m* automobile club
autorisasjon (ou-too-ri-sah-*shōōn*) *m* authorization
autoritet (ou-too-ri-*tāyt*) *m* authority
autoritær (ou-too-ri-*tæær*) *adj* authoritarian
av (aav) *prep* by, of, for, with, from; *adv* off, **~ og til** sometimes, occasionally
avansert (ah-vahng-*sāyt*) *adj* advanced
avbestille (*aav*-beh-sti-ler) *v* cancel
avbestilling (*aav*-beh-sti-ling) *c* cancellation
avbetale (*aav*-beh-tah-ler) *v* *pay on account; *pay instalments on
avbetalingskjøp (*aav*-beh-tah-lings-khūrp) *nt* (pl ~) hire purchase, *Am* instalment plan
***avbryte** (*aav*-brēw-ter) *v* interrupt
avbrytelse (*aav*-brēwt-erl-ser) *m* interruption
avdekke (*aav*-deh-ker) *v* uncover
avdeling (ahv-*dāy*-ling) *c* department; division, section
avdrag (*aav*-draag) *nt* (pl ~) instalment
aveny (ah-ver-*nēw*) *m* avenue
avfall (*aav*-fahl) *nt* rubbish, refuse, garbage, litter
avfatte (*aav*-fah-ter) *v*

*draw up; compose
avføringsmiddel (*aav*-fūr-rings-mi-derl) *nt* (pl -midler) laxative
avgang (*aav*-gahng) *m* departure
avgangstid (*aav*-gahngs-teed) *c* time of departure
avgifter (*aav*-ʸif-terr) *pl* dues *pl*
***avgjøre** (*aav*-ʸūr-rer) *v* decide
avgjørelse (*aav*-ʸūr-rerl-ser) *m* decision
avgud (*aav*-gēwd) *m* idol
avhandling (*aav*-hahnd-ling) *c* essay, treatise
avhengig (*aav*-heh-ngi) *adj* dependant
avhente (*aav*-hehn-ter) *v* collect, fetch
***avholde seg fra** (*aav*-ho-ler) abstain from
avis (ah-*veess*) *c* newspaper
aviskiosk (ah-*veess*-khosk) *m* newsstand
avlang (*aav*-lahng) *adj* oblong
avleiring (*aav*-lay-ring) *c* deposit
avlevere (*aav*-leh-vāy-rer) *v* deliver
avling (*ahv*-ling) *c* harvest, crop
avløp (*aav*-lūrp) *nt* (pl ~) drain
avløse (*aav*-lūr-ser) *v* relieve
avreise (*aav*-ray-ser) *c* departure
avrundet (*aav*-rew-nert) *adj* rounded
avsende (*aav*-seh-ner) *v* dispatch, dispatch
avsender (*aav*-seh-nerr) *m* sender
avsides (*aav*-see-derss) *adj* out of the way, remote
avskaffe (*aav*-skah-fer) *v* abolish
avskjed (*aav*-shāyd) *m* parting; resignation
avskjedige (*aav*-shāy-di-er) *v* dismiss, fire
avskjedssøknad (*aav*-shāyds-*sūrk*-nah) *m* resignation
avskrekke (*aav*-skrehk-ker) *v* discourage
avsky[1] (*aav*-shēw) *v* hate, dislike, detest
avsky[2] (*aav*-shēw) *m* dislike, disgust
avskyelig (ahv-*shēw*-er-li) *adj* hideous, horrible, disgusting
avslag (*aav*-shlaag) *nt* (pl ~) refusal; discount, reduction
avslapning (*aav*-shlahp-ning) *m* relaxation
avslappet (*aav*-shlah-pert) *adj* easy-going; relaxed
avslutning (*aav*-shlewt-ning) *m* ending
avslutte (*aav*-shlew-ter) *v* stop, finish; settle
avsløre (*aav*-shlūr-rer) *v* reveal; expose
avsløring (*aav*-shlūr-ring) *c*

revelation
***avslå** (*aav*-shlaw) *v* refuse
avsnitt (*aav*-snit) *nt* (pl ~) paragraph; passage
avspark (*aav*-spahrk) *nt* kick-off
avstamning (*aav*-stahm-ning) *m* origin
avstand (*aav*-stahn) *m* distance; space; way
avstandsmåler (*aav*-stahns-maw-lerr) *m* range finder
avstemning (*aav*-stehm-ning) *m* vote
***avta** (*aav*-taa) *v* decrease
avtale (*aav*-taa-ler) *m* agreement, engagement; date, appointment
avtrekker (*aav*-treh-kerr) *m* trigger
avtrykk (*aav*-trewk) *nt* (pl ~) print
avveksling (*aav*-vehks-ling) *c* variation
avvente (*aa*-vehn-ter) *v* await
avverge (*aa*-vær-ger) *v* prevent
***avvike** (*aa*-vee-ker) *v* deviate
avvise (*aa*-vee-ser) *v* reject

B

babord (*baa*-boor) port
baby (*bay*-bi) *m* baby
babybag (*bay*-bi-bæg) *m* carry-cot
bacon (*bay*-kern) *nt* bacon
bad (baad) *nt* bath, bathroom
bade (*baa*-der) *v* bathe; swim
badebukse (*baa*-der-book-ser) *c* swimming-trunks *pl*, bathing suit
badedrakt (*baa*-der-drahkt) *c* swimsuit, swimming suit *Am*, bathing suit
badehette (*baa*-der-heh-ter) *c* bathing cap
badehåndkle (*baa*-der-hong-kler) *nt* (pl -lær) bath towel
badekåpe (*baa*-der-kaw-per) *c* bathrobe
badested (*baa*-der-stay) *nt* seaside resort
badevakt (*baa*-der-vakt)*c*pool attendant
badeværelse (*baa*-der-væl-ser) *nt* bathroom
badstue (*bahss*-tewer) *c* sauna
bagasje (bah-*gaa*-sher) *m* luggage, baggage
bagasjehylle (bah-*gaa*-sher-hew-ler) *c* luggage rack
bagasjeoppbevaring (bah-*gaa*-sher-oop-ber-*vaa*-ring) *c* left luggage office; *Am* baggage deposit office
bagasjerom (bah-*gaa*-sher-

room) *nt* (pl ~) boot; *nAm* trunk
bagasjevogn (bah-*gah*-sher-vongn) *c* luggage van
bak (baak) *prep* behind; *adv* behind; *m* bottom
bake (*baa*-ker) *v* bake
baker (*baa*-kerr) *m* baker
bakeri (bah-ker-*ree*) *nt* bakery
bakgrunn (*baak*-grewn) *m* background
bakhold (*baak*-hol) *nt* (pl ~) ambush
bakke (*bahk*-ker) *m* hill; earth
bakketopp (*bahk*-ker-top) *m* hilltop
baklengs (*baak*-lehngs) *adv* backwards
baklykt (*baak*-lewkt) *c* rear light
baklys (*baak*-lēwss) *nt* (pl ~) tail-light
bakside (*baak*-see-der) *c* rear; reverse
bakterie (bahk-*tāy*-ri-er) *m* bacterium
bakvaskelse (*baak*-vahss-kerl-ser) *m* slander
bakverk (*baak*-værk) *nt* bakegoods; **finere ~** pastry
balanse (bah-*lahng*-ser) *m* balance
balkong (bahl-*kongng*) *m* balcony; dress circle
ball (bahll) *m* ball; *nt* ball
ballett (bah-*lehtt*) *m* ballet
ballong (bah-*longng*) *m* balloon
banan (bah-*naan*) *m* banana
bandasje (bahn-*daa*-sher) *m* bandage
bande (*bahn*-der) *m* gang
bane (*baa*-ner) *m* track
bank (bahngk) *m* bank; *m/nt* tap; ***sette i banken** deposit
banke (*bahng*-ker) *v* knock, tap
bankett (bahng-*kehtt*) *m* banquet
bankhvelv (bahngk-vehlv) *nt* (pl ~) vault
bankkonto (*bahng*-kon-too) *m* (pl ~er, -ti) bank account
banne (*bahn*-ner) *v* curse, *swear
banner (*bahn*-nerr) *nt* (pl ~, ~e) banner
banning (*bahn*-ning) *c* curse
bar (baar) *adj* bare, naked; neat; *m* bar, saloon
barberblad (bahr-*bāyr*-blaa) *nt* (pl ~) razor blade
barbere seg (bahr-*bāy*-rer) shave
barberhøvel (bahr-*bair*-*hur*-verl) *m* (pl -vler) safety razor, razor
barberkost (bahr-*bāyr*-koost) *m* shaving brush
barbermaskin (bahr-*bāyr*-mah-sheen) *m* electric razor, shaver
barberskum (bahr-*bāyr*-skoomm) *nt* shaving foam
bare (*baarer*) *adv* only,

merely
bark (bahrk) *m* bark
barm (bahrm) *m* bosom
barmhjertig (bahrm-*ʸæ*-ti) *adj* merciful
barmhjertighet (bahrm-*ʸæ*-ti-hayt) *c* mercy
barn (baan) *nt* child; kid; **foreldreløst ~** orphan
barnebarn (*baa*-ner-baan) *nt* grandchild
barnehage (*baa*-ner-haa-ger) *m* kindergarten
barnepike (*baa*-ner-pee-ker) *m* nurse
barnevakt (*baa*-ner-vahkt) *c* babysitter
barnevogn (*baa*-ner-voangn) *c* pram; baby carriage *Am*
barneværelse (*baa*-ner-vææ-rerl-ser) *nt* nursery
barokk (bah-*rokk*) *adj* baroque
barometer (bah-roo-*may*-terr) *nt* (pl -tre) barometer
barriere (bah-ri-*ææ*-rer) *m* barrier; crash barrier
barsk (bahshk) *adj* bleak; tough
bart (bahtt) *m* moustache
bartender (*baa*-tehn-derr) *m* bartender
baryton (*bahr*-ri-ton) *m* baritone
basar (bah-*saar*) *m* fair
base (*baa*-ser) *m* base
basere (bah-*say*-rer) *v* base
basilika (bah-*see*-li-kah) *m* basilica
basill (bah-*sill*) *m* germ
basis (*baa*-siss) *m* basis, base
bass (bahss) *m* bass
bastard (bah-*stahrd*) *m* bastard
batteri (bah-ter-*ree*) *nt* battery
***be** (bay) *v* ask; beg; pray
bebo (beh-*boo*) *v* inhabit
beboelig (beh-*boo*-er-li) *adj* habitable, inhabitable
beboer (beh-*boo*-err) *m* occupant, inhabitant
bebreide (beh-*bray*-der) *v* blame, reproach
bebreidelse (beh-*bray*-derl-ser) *m* blame, reproach
bedervelig (beh-*dær*-ver-li) *adj* perishable
***bedra** (beh-*draa*) *v* deceive
bedrag (beh-*draag*) *nt* (pl ~) deceit
bedrageri (beh-drah-ger-*ree*) *nt* fraud
bedre (*bayd*-rer) *adj* better; superior
bedrift (beh-*drift*) *m* concern; feat
bedring (*bayd*-ring) *c* recovery
bedrøvelig (beh-*drur*-ver-li) *adj* sad, dreary
bedrøvet (beh-*drur*-vert) *adj* sad
bedyre (beh-*dew*-rer) *v* affirm
bedømme (beh-*durm*-mer) *v* judge
bedøvelse (beh-*dur*-verl-

ser) *m* anaesthesia
bedøvelsesmiddel (beh-*dūr*-verl-serss-mi-derl) *nt* (pl -midler) anaesthetic
bedårende (beh-*daw*-rer-ner) *adj* enchanting
befale (beh-*faa*-ler) *v* command
befaling (beh-*faa*-ling) *c* order, command
befalshavende (beh-*faals*-haa-ver-ner) *m* commander
befolkning (beh-*folk*-ning) *m* population
befrielse (beh-*free*-erl-ser) *m* liberation
befruktning (beh-*frewkt*-ning) *m* conception; fertilization
begavelse (beh-*gaa*-verl-ser) *m* talent, faculty
begavet (beh-*gaa*-vert) *adj* gifted, talented; clever, brilliant
begeistret (beh-*gayss*-trert) *adj* keen, enthusiastic
begge (behg-ger) *pron* both; either
begivenhet (beh-*ʸee*-vern-hayt) *c* event, happening
begjær (beh-*ʸæær*) *nt* desire; lust
begjære (beh-*ʸææ*-rer) *v* desire
begrave (beh-*graa*-ver) *v* bury
begravelse (beh-*graa*-verl-ser) *m* funeral; burial
begrense (beh-*grehn*-ser) *v* limit
begrenset (beh-*grehn*-sert) *adj* limited
begrep (beh-*grayp*) *nt* notion, idea
***begripe** (beh-*gree*-per) *v* *see, *understand
begunstige (beh-*gewns*-ti-er) *v* favo(u)r
begynne (beh-*ʸewn*-ner) *v* start, commence, *begin; **~ igjen** recommence
begynnelse (beh-*ʸewn*-nerl-ser) *m* beginning; **i begynnelsen** at first; originally
***begå** (beh-*gaw*) *v* commit
behagelig (beh-*haa*-ger-li) *adj* agreeable, pleasing, enjoyable
behandle (beh-*hahnd*-ler) *v* handle, treat
behandling (beh-*hahnd*-ling) *c* treatment
***beholde** (beh-*hol*-ler) *v* *keep
beholder (beh-*hol*-lerr) *m* container
behov (beh-*hoov*) *nt* (pl ~) need; want
behøve (beh-*hūr*-ver) *v* need; demand
behå (*beh*-ho) *m* bra
beige (baysh) *adj* beige
bein (bayn) *nt* (pl ~) leg; bone
beinskinne (*bayn*-shi-ner) *c* splint
beite (*bay*-ter) *nt* pasture; *v* graze

bekjempe (beh-*khehm*-per) *v* combat
bekjenne (beh-*kheh*-ner) *v* confess
bekjent (beh-*khehnt*) *m* acquaintance
***bekjentgjøre** (beh-*khehnt*-ʸūr-rer) *v* announce
bekjentgjørelse (beh-*khehnt*-ʸūr-rerl-ser) *m* announcement; bulletin
bekk (behkk) *m* stream, brook
bekken (*behk*-kern) *nt* pelvis
beklage (beh-*klaager*) *v* regret
beklagelse (beh-*klaa*-gerl-ser) *m* regret
beklager! (beh-*klaa*-gerr) sorry!
bekrefte (beh-*krehf*-ter) *v* confirm; acknowledge; affirm
bekreftelse (beh-*krehf*-terl-ser) *m* confirmation
bekreftende (beh-*krayf*-ter-ner) *adj* affirmative
bekvem (beh-*kvehmm*) *adj* comfortable; easy, convenient
bekvemmelighet (beh-*kvehm*-mer-li-hāyt) *c* comfort
bekymre seg (beh-*khewm*-rer) worry; **bekymre seg om** care about
bekymret (beh-*khewm*-rert) *adj* concerned, worried
bekymring (beh-*khewm*-ring) *c* anxiety, worry; concern, care
belastning (beh-*lahst*-ning) *m* load, strain
beleilig (beh-*lay*-li) *adj* convenient
beleiring (beh-*lay*-ring) *c* siege
Belgia (*behl*-gi-ah) Belgium
belgier (*behl*-gi-err) *m* Belgian
belgisk (*behl*-gisk) *adj* Belgian
beliggende (beh-*lig*-ger-ner) *adj* situated
beliggenhet (beh-*lig*-gern-hāyt) *c* location, site
belte (*behl*-ter) *nt* belt
belyse (beh-*lēw*-ser) *v* illuminate
belysning (beh-*lēwss*-ning) *m* lighting, illumination
belønne (beh-*lurn*-ner) *v* reward
belønning (beh-*lurn*-ning) *c* reward; prize
beløp (beh-*lūrp*) *nt* (pl ~) amount
***beløpe seg til** (beh-*lūr*-per) amount to
bemerke (beh-*mær*-ker) *v* note, notice; remark
bemerkelsesverdig (beh-*mær*-kerl-serss-vær-di) *adj* noticeable, remarkable
bemerkning (beh-*mærk*-ning) *m* remark
benekte (beh-*nehk*-ter) *v* deny
benektende (beh-*nehk*-ter-

ner) *adj* negative
benevnelse (beh-*nehv*-nerl-ser) *m* name, designation, denomination
benk (behngk) *m* bench
bensin (behn-*seen*) *m* fuel, petrol; gas *nAm*, gasoline *nAm*; **blyfri ~** unleaded petrol
bensinpumpe (behn-*seen*-poom-per) *c* petrol pump; fuel pump *Am*
bensinstasjon (behn-*seen*-stah-shoon) *m* service station, petrol station, filling station; gas station *Am*
bensintank (behn-*seen*-tahngk) *m* petrol tank, gas tank *Am*
benytte (beh-*newt*-ter) *v* use, make use of
benådning (beh-*nawd*-ning) *m* pardon
beordre (beh-*or*-drer) *v* order
beredt (beh-*reht*) *adj* prepared
beregne (beh-*ray*-ner) *v* calculate
berettiget (beh-*reht*-ti-ert) *adj* justified
berg (bærg) *nt* mountain
berglendt (*bærg*-lehnt) *adj* mountainous
berolige (beh-*roo*-li-er) *v* reassure, calm down
beroligende (beh-*roo*-li-er-ner) *adj* restful; **~ middel** sedative, tranquillizer
bero på (beh-*roo*) depend on
beruset (beh-*rew*-sert) *adj* intoxicated, drunk
beryktet (beh-*rewk*-tert) *adj* notorious
berømmelse (beh-*rurm*-merl-ser) *m* fame, glory, celebrity
berømt (beh-*rurmt*) *adj* famous
berøre (beh-*rur*-rer) *v* touch
berøring (beh-*rur*-ring) *c* touch
besatt (beh-*sahtt*) *adj* possessed
beseire (beh-*say*-rer) *v* conquer
***besette** (beh-*seht*-ter) *v* occupy
besettelse (beh-*seht*-terl-ser) *m* obsession
besittelse (beh-*sit*-terl-ser) *m* possession
beskatning (beh-*skaht*-ning) *m* taxation
beskjed (beh-*sher*) *m* message
beskjeden (beh-*shay*-dern) *adj* modest
beskjedenhet (beh-*shay*-dern-hayt) *c* modesty
beskjeftige (beh-*shehf*-ti-er) *v* employ, occupy
beskjeftigelse (beh-*shehf*-ti-erl-ser) *m* employment, occupation
***beskrive** (beh-*skree*-ver) *v* describe
beskrivelse (beh-*skree*-

verl-ser) *m* description
beskylde (beh-*shewl*-ler) *v* accuse
beskytte (beh-*shewt*-ter) *v* protect
beskyttelse (beh-*shewt*-terl-ser) *m* protection
***beslaglegge** (beh-*shlaag*-leh-ger) *v* confiscate
beslektet (beh-*shlehk*-tert) *adj* related
beslutning (beh-*shlewt*-ning) *m* decision
besluttsom (beh-*shlewt*-som) *adj* resolute
best (behst) *adj* best
bestanddel (beh-*stahn*-da͞yl) *m* element, ingredient
bestefar (*behss*-ter-faar) *m* (pl -fedre) grandfather, granddad
besteforeldre (*behss*-ter-fo-rehl-drer) *pl* grandparents *pl*
bestemme (beh-*stehm*-mer) *v* define, determine; designate, destine
bestemmelse (beh-*stehm*-merl-ser) *m* regulation
bestemmelsessted (beh-*stehm*-merl-serss-sta͞y) *nt* destination
bestemor (*behss*-ter-mo͞or) *m* (pl -mødre) grandmother
bestemt (beh-*stehmt*) *adj* definite; resolute
***bestige** (beh-*stee*-ger) *v* ascend; mount
bestikk (beh-*stikk*) *nt* cutlery; silverware *nAm*
***bestikke** (beh-*stik*-ker) *v* corrupt, bribe
bestikkelse (beh-*stik*-kerl-ser) *m* corruption, bribery; bribe
bestille (beh-*stil*-ler) *v* order; book, engage, reserve
bestilling (beh-*stil*-ling) *c* order; booking; **laget på ~** made to order
bestrebelse (beh-*stra͞y*-berl-ser) *m* effort
***bestride** (beh-*stree*-der) *v* dispute
bestyre (beh-*ste͞w*-rer) *v* manage
bestyrer (beh-*stew*-rer) *m* manager
***bestå** (beh-*staw*) *v* exist; pass a test; **~ av** consist of
besvare (beh-*svaa*-rer) *v* answer
besvime (beh-*svee*-mer) *v* faint
besvær (beh-*svææ*r) *nt* trouble, inconvenience
besværlig (beh-*svææ*-li) *adj* inconvenient
besøk (beh-*sūrk*) *nt* (pl ~) call, visit
besøke (beh-*sūr*-ker) *v* call on, visit
besøkende (beh-*sūr*-ker-ner) *m* visitor
besøkstid (beh-*sūrks*-teed) *c* visiting hours
betagende (beh-*taa*-ger-

ner) *adj* moving; beautiful
betalbar (beh-*taal*-bahr) *adj* due; payable
betale (beh-*taa*-ler) *v* *pay
betaling (beh-*taa*-ling) *c* payment
betegnende (beh-*tay*-ner-ner) *adj* characteristic
betenkt (beh-*tehngkt*) *adj* uneasy
betennelse (beh-*tehn*-nerl-ser) *m* inflammation; ***gå ~ i** *become septic
betingelse (beh-*ting*-ngerl-ser) *m* term; stipulation
betingelsesløs (beh-*ting*-ngerl-serss-lūrss) *adj* unconditional
betinget (beh-*ting*-ngert) *adj* conditional
betjene (beh-*tʸāy*-ner) *v* attend on; serve
betjening (beh-*tʸāy*-ning) *c* service
betong (beh-*tongng*) *m* concrete
betoning (beh-*tōō*-ning) *c* accent
betrakte (beh-*trahk*-ter) *v* consider, regard; view, watch; **i betraktning av** considering
betraktelig (beh-*trahk*-ter-li) *adj* considerable
betro (beh-*trōō*) *v* confide in
betvile (beh-*tvee*-ler) *v* query, doubt
bety (beh-*tēw*) *v* *mean
betydelig (beh-*tēw*-der-li) *adj* considerable
betydning (beh-*tēwd*-ning) *m* sense; importance; ***være av ~** matter
betydningsfull (beh-*tēwd*-nings-fewl) *adj* important; significant
beundre (beh-*ewn*-drer) *v* admire
beundrer (beh-*ewn*-drerr) *m* fan
beundring (beh-*ewn*-dring) *c* admiration
bevare (beh-*vaa*-rer) *v* *keep; *uphold
bevege (beh-*vāy*-ger) *v* move
bevegelig (beh-*vāy*-ger-li) *adj* mobile
bevegelse (beh-*vāy*-gerl-ser) *m* motion, movement
bever (*bāy*-verr) *m* beaver
beverte (beh-*væ*-ter) *v* entertain, treat
bevilge (beh-*veel*-ger) *v* extend, grant; allow
bevis (beh-*veess*) *nt* proof, evidence; token
bevise (beh-*vee*-ser) *v* prove; demonstrate, *show
bevisst (beh-*vist*) *adj* conscious
bevissthet (beh-*vist*-hāyt) *c* consciousness
bevisstløs (beh-*vist*-lūrss) *adj* unconscious
bevitne (beh-*vit*-ne) *v* attest
bevokte (beh-*vok*-ter) *v* watch, guard
bevæpne (beh-*vāyp*-ner) *v*

arm
bevæpnet (beh-*vāyp*-nert) *adj* armed
bibel (*bee*-berl) *m* (pl bibler) bible
bibliotek (bi-bli-oo-*tāyk*) *nt* library
bidrag (*bee*-draag) *nt* (pl ~) contribution; allowance
bie (*bee*-er) *c* bee
bielv (*bee*-ehlv) *c* tributary
bifalle (*bee*-fah-ler) *v* consent; applaud
biff (biff) *m* steak
bikube (*bee*-kew-ber) *m* beehive
bil (beel) *m* automobile, car
bilde (*bil*-der) *nt* picture, image
bildemelding (*bil*-der-*mehl*-ling) *c* photo message
bile (*bee*-ler) *v* motor
bilhorn (*beel*-hōōn) *nt* (pl ~) hooter
bilisme (bi-*liss*-mer) *m* motoring
bilist (bi-*list*) *m* motorist
biljard (bil-*ʸaad*) *m* billiards *pl*
bille (*bil*-ler) *m* beetle; bug
billedhogger (*bil*-lerd-ho-gerr) *m* sculptor
billett (bi-*lehtt*) *m* ticket
billettautomat (bi-*lehtt*-ou-too-maat) *m* ticket machine
billettkontor (bi-*leht*-koon-tōōr) *nt* box office
billettluke (bi-*leht*-lew-ker) *c* box office window
billettpris (bi-*leht*-preess) *m* fare; admission fee
billig (*bil*-li) *adj* cheap, inexpensive
billigbok (*bil*-li-bōōk) *c* paperback
bilpanser (*beel*-pahn-serr) *nt* bonnet; hood *nAm*
bilran (*bēēl*-rahn) *c* carjacking
bilutleie (*beel*-oot-lay-er) *c* car hire; car rental *Am*
bind (binn) *nt* volume; sanitary napkin *Am*, sanitary towel
***binde** (*bin*-ner) *v* *bind; tie; ~ **sammen** bundle
bindestrek (*bin*-ner-strāyk) *m* hyphen
biologi (bi-oo-loo-*gee*) *m* biology
biologisk nedbrytbar (bēē-oo-*lōō*-isk nayd-*brēwt*-bahr) *adj* biodegradable
bipolar (bee-poo-*lāār*) *adj* bipolar
biskop (*biss*-kop) *m* bishop
***bistå** (*bee*-staw) *v* assist, aid
bit (beet) *m* bit, piece; scrap, morsel; bite
***bite** (*bee*-ter) *v* *bite
bitter (*bit*-terr) *adj* bitter
bjelke (*bʸehl*-ker) *m* beam
bjelle (*bʸehl*-ler) *c* small bell
bjørk (bʸurrk) *c* birch
bjørn (bʸūrn) *m* bear
bjørnebær (*bʸūr*-ner-bæær)

nt (pl ~) blackberry
Blackberry® (*blæk*-bahr-ee) *c* Blackberry®
blad (blaa) *nt* leaf; blade
bladgull (*blaa*-gewl) *nt* gold leaf
bladsalat (*blaa*-sah-laht) *m* lettuce
blakk (blahkk) *adj* broke
blande (*blahn*-ner) *v* mix; **~ seg inn i** interfere with
blandet (*blahn*-nert) *adj* mixed
blanding (*blahn*-ning) *c* mixture
blank (blahngk) *adj* glossy; blank
blankett (blahng-*kehtt*) *m* form
blant (blahnt) *prep* amid; among; **~ annet** among other things
bleie (*blay*-er) *c* nappy; diaper *nAm*
blek (blayk) *adj* pale
bleke (*blay*-ker) *v* bleach
blekk (blehkk) *nt* ink
blekksprut (*blehk*-sprewt) *m* octopus
blekne (*blayk*-ner) *v* fade; *grow pale
blemme (*blehm*-mer) *c* blister
blende (*blehn*-ner) *v* blind
blendende (*blehn*-ner-ner) *adj* glaring
***bli** (blee) *v* *become, *be, *get, *grow; stay; **~ igjen** remain
blikk (blikk) *nt* glance, look; **kaste et ~** glance
blind (blinn) *adj* blind
blindgate (*blin*-gaa-ter) *c* cul-de-sac
blindtarm (*blin*-tahrm) *m* appendix
blindtarmbetennelse (*blin*-tahrm-beh-teh-nerl-ser) *m* appendicitis
blinklys (*blingk*-lewss) *nt* (pl ~) trafficator; blinker *nAm*
blitzlampe (*blits*-lahm-per) *c* flash bulb
blod (bloo) *nt* blood
blodforgiftning (*bloo*-for-yift-ning) *m* blood poisoning
blodkar (*bloo*-kaar) *nt* (pl ~) blood vessel
blodomløp (*bloo*-oom-lurp) *nt* (pl ~) circulation
blodtrykk (*bloo*-trewk) *nt* (pl ~) blood pressure
blogg (*blawg*) *c* blog
blokk (blokk) *c* block
blokkere (blo-*kay*-rer) *v* block
blomkål (*blom*-kawl) *m* cauliflower
blomst (blomst) *m* flower, blossom
blomsterbed (*blom*-sterr-behd) *nt* (pl ~) flowerbed
blomsterforretning (*blom*-sterr-for-reht-ning) *c* flower shop
blomsterhandler (*blom*-sterr-hahnd-lerr) *m* florist
blomsterløk (*blom*-sterr-

lurk) *m* bulb
blomstre (*blom*-strer) *v* flower, blossom
blond (blonn) *adj* fair, blond
blondine (blon-*dee*-ner) *c* blonde
***blottlegge** (*blott*-leh-ger) *v* expose
bluse (*blew*-ser) *c* blouse
bly (blew) *nt* lead
blyant (*blew*-ahnt) *m* pencil
blyantspisser (*blew*-ahnt-spi-serr) *m* pencil sharpener
blyg (blewg) *adj* timid
blære (*blææ*-rer) *c* bladder
blø (blur) *v* *bleed
blødning (*blurd*-ning) *m* h(a)emorrhage
bløt (blurt) *adj* mellow
bløte (*blur*-ter) *v* soak
***bløtgjøre** (*blurt*-[y]ur-rer) *v* soften
blå (blaw) *adj* blue; **blått merke** bruise
blåse (*blaw*-ser) *v* *blow; **~ opp** inflate
blåsende (*blaw*-ser-ner) *adj* gusty
blåskjell (*blo*-shehl) *nt* (pl ~) mussel
bo (boo) *v* live, reside
bobil (*boo*-beel) *m* camper, caravan
boble (*bob*-ler) *c* bubble
bok (book) *c* (pl bøker) book
bokbind (*book*-bin) *nt* (pl ~) binding
bokføre (*book*-fur-rer) *v* enter, book
bokhandel (*book*-hahn-derl) *m* (pl -dler) bookstore
bokhandler (*book*-hahnd-lerr) *m* bookseller
boks (boks) *m* can, tin
bokse (*bok*-ser) *v* box
boksekamp (*bok*-ser-kahmp) *m* boxing match
bokstav (book-*staav*) *m* letter; **stor ~** capital letter
boksåpner (*boks*-awp-nerr) *m* can opener
bolig (*boo*-li) *m* house, residence
Bolivia (boo-*lee*-vi-ah) Bolivia
bolivianer (boo-li-vi-*aa*-nerr) *m* Bolivian
boliviansk (boo-li-vi-*aansk*) *adj* Bolivian
bolle (*bol*-ler) *m* bowl; basin; bun
bolt (bolt) *m* bolt
bom (boomm) *m* barrier; miss
bombardere (boom-bah-*day*-rer) *v* bomb
bombe (*boom*-ber) *c* bomb
bomme (*boom*-mer) *v* miss
bompenger (*boomm*-peh-ngerr) *pl* toll
bomull (*boom*-mewl) *m* cotton; **bomulls-** cotton
bomullsfløyel (*boom*-mewls-flur[ew]-erl) *m* velveteen
bomvei (*boom*-vay) *m*

turnpike *nAm*
bonde (*boon*-ner) *m* (pl bønder) peasant, farmer
bondegård (*boon*-ner-gawr) *m* farm
bondekone (*boon*-ner-ko͞o-ner) *c* farmer's wife
bong (bong) *m* voucher
bopel (*bo͞o*-pa͞yl) *m* domicile
bor (borr) *nt* drill
bord (bo͞or) *nt* table
bordell (boo-*dehll*) *m/nt* brothel
bordtennis (*bo͞o*-teh-niss) *m* ping-pong, table tennis
bore (*bo͞o*-rer) *v* bore, drill; **~plattform** drilling platform
borg (borg) *c* castle
borger (*bor*-gerr) *m* citizen; **borger-** civic
borgerlig (*bor*-ger-li) *adj* middle-class
borgermester (*bor*-ger-mehss-terr) *m* (pl -tre) mayor
bort (boott) *adv* away; ***gå ~** *leave, *go away
borte (*boot*-ter) *adv* gone; off
bortenfor (*boot*-tern-for) *adv* beyond; *prep* off; beyond
bortsett fra (*boot*-seht) apart from
bosatt (*bo͞o*-saht) *adj* resident
boss (boss) *m* boss
bot (bo͞ot) *c* (pl bøter) fine
botanikk (boo-tah-*nikk*) *m* botany
botemiddel (*bo͞o*-ter-mi-derl) *nt* (pl -midler) remedy
bowlingbane (*bov*-ling-baa-ner) *m* bowling alley
bra (braa) *adj* good; *colloquial* super; **bra!** all right!
brann (brahnn) *m* fire
brannalarm (*brahn*-nah-lahrm) *m* fire alarm
brannmann (*brahn*-mahn) *m* firefighter
brannmannskap (*brahn*-mahn-skaap) *nt* firefighter
brannmur (*brahn*-me͞wr) *c* firewall
brannsikker (*brahn*-si-kerr) *adj* fireproof
brannslokker (*brahn*-shloo-kerr) *m* fire extinguisher
brannsår (*brahn*-sawr) *nt* (pl ~) burn
branntrapp (*brahn*-trahp) *c* fire escape
brannvesen (*brahn*-va͞y-sern) *nt* fire brigade
Brasil (brah-*seel*) Brazil
brasilianer (brah-si-li-*aa*-nerr) *m* Brazilian
brasiliansk (brah-si-li-*aansk*) *adj* Brazilian
bratt (brahtt) *adj* steep
bred (bra͞y) *adj* wide, broad
bredbånd (*brehd*-bawn) *nt* broadband
bredd (brehdd) *m* shore, bank; embankment

bredde (*brehd*-der) *m* width, breadth
breddegrad (*brehd*-der-graad) *m* latitude
***brekke** (brehk-ker) *v* fracture; **~ seg** vomit
brekkjern (*brehk*-ʸæn) *nt* crowbar
bremse (*brehm*-ser) *c* brake; *v* slow down
bremselys (*brehm*-ser-lewss) *pl* brake lights
bremsetrommel (*brehm*-ser-troo-merl) *m* (pl -tromler) brake drum
***brenne** (*brehn*-ner) *v* *burn
brennemerke (*brehn*-ner-mær-ker) *nt* brand; stigma
brennpunkt (*brehn*-poongkt) *nt* focus
brensel (*brehn*-sherl) *nt* fuel
brenselolje (*brehn*-sherl-ol-ʸer) *c* fuel oil
brett (brehtt) *nt* tray
brette (*breht*-ter) *v* fold; **~ ut** unfold
brev (brayv) *nt* letter; **rekommandert ~** registered letter
brevpapir (*brayv*-pah-peer) *nt* notepaper
brevveksle (*brayvehk*-shler) *v* correspond
brevveksling (*brayvehk*-shling) *c* correspondence
brikke (*brik*-ker) *c* chip; piece
briller (*bril*-lerr) *pl* spectacles, glasses
***bringe** (*bring*-nger) *v* *bring; **~ tilbake** *bring back
bringebær (*bring*-nger-bæær) *nt* (pl **~**) raspberry
bris (breess) *m* breeze
***briste** (*briss*-ter) *v* *burst
brite (*brit*-ter) *m* Briton
britisk (*brit*-tisk) *adj* British
bro (broo) *c* bridge
brodere (broo-*day*-rer) *v* embroider
broderi (broo-der-*ree*) *nt* embroidery
brokk (brokk) *m*/*nt* hernia
***brolegge** (*broo*-leh-ger) *v* pave
bronkitt (broong-*kitt*) *m* bronchitis
bronse (*brong*-sher) *m* bronze; **bronse-** bronze
bror (broor) *m* (pl brødre) brother
brorskap (*broosh*-kaap) *m*/*nt* fraternity, brotherhood
brosje (*brosh*-sher) *c* brooch
brosjyre (bro-*shew*-rer) *m* brochure
brud (brewd) *c* bride
brudd (brewdd) *nt* fracture, break
bruddstykke (*brewd*-stew-ker) *nt* fragment
brudgom (*brewd*-gom) *m* (pl **~**mer) groom, bridegroom
bruk (brewk) *m* use
brukbar (*brewk*-baar) *adj*

useful
bruke (*brew*-ker) *v* apply, use; *spend; ~ **opp** use up
bruker (*brew*-kerr) *m* user
bruksanvisning (*brewks*-ahn-viss-ning) *m* directions for use
brukt (brewkt) *adj* second--hand
brumme (*broom*-mer) *v* growl
brun (brewn) *adj* brown; tanned
brunette (brew-*neht*-ter) *m* brunette
brunfarge (*brewn*-fahr-ger) *m* suntan
brus (brewss) *m* fizz; *m* lemonade; soft drink *Am*
bruse (*brew*-ser) *v* roar
brusk (brewsk) *m* cartilage
brutal (brew-*taal*) *adj* brutal
brutto (*brewt*-too) *adj* gross
bry (brew) *v* trouble; *nt* bother; ~ **seg** bother; ~ **seg om** mind; care for
brydd (brewdd) *adj* embarrassed; ***gjøre ~** embarrass
brygge (*brewg*-ger) *v* brew
bryggeri (brew-ger-*ree*) *nt* brewery
bryllup (*brewl*-lewp) *nt* wedding
bryllupsdag (*brewl*-lewps-daag) *m* anniversary
bryllupsreise (*brewl*-lewps-ray-ser) *c* honeymoon
brysom (*brew*-som) *adj*
bryst (brewst) *nt* chest, breast; bosom
brystholder (*brewst*-ho-lerr) *m* bra
brystkasse (*brewst*-kah-ser) *c* chest
brystsvømming (*brewst*-svur-ming) *c* breaststroke
***bryte** (*brew*-ter) *v* *break; ~ **sammen** collapse
bryter (*brew*-terr) *m* switch
brød (brur) *nt* bread; loaf; **ristet ~** toast
brøkdel (*brurk*-dayl) *m* fraction
brøl (brurl) *nt* roar
brøle (*brur*-ler) *v* roar
brønn (brurnn) *m* well
bråk (brawk) *nt* din; fuss
bu (bew) *c* booth
bud (bewd) *nt* messenger; bid; **sende ~ etter** *send for
budsjett (bewd-*shehtt*) *nt* budget
bue (*bew*-er) *m* bow; arch
bueformet (*bew*-er-for-mert) *adj* arched
buegang (*bew*-er-gahng) *m* arcade
buet (*bew*-ert) *adj* curved
bukett (bew-*kehtt*) *m* bouquet, bunch
bukk (bookk) *m* buck
bukke (*book*-ker) *v* bow; ~ **under** succumb
bukse (*book*-ser) *c* trousers *pl*; pants *plAm*
buksedrakt (*book*-ser-drahkt) *c* pant suit
buksedress (*book*-ser-

drehss) *m* pant suit
bukseseler (*book*-ser-sa͞y-lerr) *pl* braces *pl*; suspenders *plAm*
buksesmekk (*book*-ser-smehk) *m* fly
bukt (bookt) *c* bay
buktet (*book*-tert) *adj* winding
bulder (*bewl*-derr) *nt* noise
bulgarer (bewl-*gaa*-rerr) *m* Bulgarian
Bulgaria (bewl-*gaa*-ri-ah) Bulgaria
bulgarsk (bewl-*gaashk*) *adj* Bulgarian
bulk (bewlk) *m* dent
bunad (*boo*-nahd) *m* (Norwegian) national costume, national dress
bunke (*boong*-ker) *m* batch
bunn (bewnn) *m* bottom
bunnfall (*bewn*-fahl) *nt* (pl ~) deposit; sediment
bunt (bewnt) *m* bundle
bunte (*bewn*-ter) *v* bundle
buntmaker (*bewnt*-maa-kerr) *m* furrier
bur (be͞wr) *nt* cage
***burde** (*be͞w*-der) *v* *ought to
busk (bewsk) *m* bush; shrub
buss (bewss) *m* bus; coach
butikk (bew-*tikk*) *m* shop; boutique
butikkeier (bew-*tikk-ay*-err) *m* tradeswoman, tradesman
butikkselger (bew-*tikk*-sehl-gerr) *m* shop assistant
butt (bewtt) *adj* blunt
by (be͞w) *m* town, city; **by-** urban
***by** (be͞w) *v* bid
byfolk (*be͞w*-folk) *pl* townspeople *pl*
bygd (bewgd) *c* village
bygg (bewgg) *nt* barley; building
bygge (*bewg*-ger) *v* construct, *build
byggekunst (*bewg*-ger-kewnst) *m* architecture
bygning (*bewg*-ning) *m* construction, building
byll (bewll) *m* abscess, boil
byrde (*bewrr*-der) *m* burden; charge
byrå (bew-*raw*) *nt* agency
byråkrati (bew-ro-krah-*tee*) *nt* bureaucracy
byste (*bewss*-ter) *c* bust
bytte (*bewt*-ter) *v* exchange, swap; *nt* exchange
bær (bæær) *nt* berry
bærbar PC (*bæær*-baar *peh*-seh) *c* laptop
***bære** (*bææ*-rer) *v* carry, *bear; support
bærer (*bææ*-rerr) *m* porter
bøddel (*burd*-derl) *m* (pl bødler) executioner
bøk (bu͞rk) *m* beech
bølge (*burl*-ger) *c* wave
bølgelengde (*burl*-ger-lehng-der) *c* wave-length
bølget (*burl*-gert) *adj* wavy
bølle (*burl*-ler) *m* brute
bøllete (*burl*-ler-ter) *adj* rowdy

bønn (burnn) *m* prayer
bønne (*burn*-ner) *c* bean
***bønnfalle** (*burn*-fah-ler) *v* beg
bør (būrr) *c* load
børs (būrsh) *m* stock exchange
børste (*bursh*-ter) *v* brush; *m* brush
bøyd (bur[ew]d) *adj* bent
bøye (*bur*ew-er) *v* *bend; *m* buoy; ~ **seg** *bend down
bøyelig (*bur*ew-er-li) *adj* flexible, supple
bøyning (*bur*ew-ning) *m* bend
både ... og (*baw*-der aw) both … and
bål (bawl) *nt* bonfire
bånd (bonn) *nt* band; ribbon; tape; leash
bås (bawss) *m* booth
båt (bawt) *m* boat

C

campe (kæm-*per*) *v* camp
camping (*kæm*-ping) *m* camping
campinggjest (*kæm*-ping-[y]ehst) *m* camper
campingplass (*kæm*-ping-plahss) *m* camping site
campingvogn (*kæm*-ping-vongn) *c* caravan; trailer *nAm*
Canada (*kahn*-nah-dah) Canada
CD (*seh*-deh) *m* CD
CD-ROM (seh-deh-*romm*) *m* CD-ROM
CD-spiller (*seh*-deh-*spil*-ler) *c* CD player
celle (*sehl*-ler) *c* cell
cello (*chel*-lo, *sel*-lo) *m* cello
celsius (*sehl*-si-ewss) centigrade
cembalo (*shehm*-bah-loo) *m* harpsichord
centimeter (*sehn*-ti-māy-terr) *m* (pl ~) centimeter *Am*, centimetre
champagne (shahm-*pahn*-[y]er) *m* champagne
charterflygning (*chaa*-terr-flēwg-ning) *m* charter flight
Chile (*chee*-ler) Chile
chilener (chi-*lāy*-nerr) *m* Chilean
chilensk (chi-*lāynsk*) *adj* Chilean
cirka (*seer*-kah) *adv* approximately
clutch (klurch) *m* clutch
cocktail (*kok*-tayl) *m* cocktail
Colombia (koo-*loom*-bi-ah) Colombia
colombianer (koo-loom-bi-*aa*-nerr) *m* Colombian
colombiansk (koo-loom-bi-*aansk*) *adj* Colombian
container (koon-*tay*-nerr)

m container
cricket (*kri*-kertt) *m* cricket
cruise (krēwss) *nt* (pl ~) cruise
Cuba (*kēw*-bah) Cuba

D

da (daa) *conj* when; *adv* then
daddel (*dahd*-derl) *m* (pl dadler) date
dag (daag) *m* day; **i ~** today; **om dagen** by day; **per ~** per day
dagbok (*daag*-book) *c* (pl -bøker) diary
daggry (*daa*-grēw) *nt* daybreak, dawn
daglig (*daag*-li) *adj* everyday, daily
dagligdags (*daag*-li-dahks) *adj* ordinary
dagligstue (*daag*-li-stēw-er) *c* living room
dagsavis (*dahks*-ahveess) *c* daily newspaper
dagslys (*dahks*-lēwss) *nt* daylight
dagsorden (*dahk*-so-dern) *m* agenda
dagspa (*daag*-spaa) *c* day spa
dagstur (*dahks*-tēwr) *m* day trip
dal (daal) *m* valley
dam (dahmm) *m* (pl ~mer) pond; pool
dame (*daa*-mer) *c* lady
dameundertøy (*daa*-mer-ew-ner-tur[ew]) *nt* lingerie
damp (dahmp) *m* steam, vapo(u)r
dampskip (*dahmp*-sheep) *nt* (pl ~) steamer
damspill (*dahm*-spil) *nt* (pl ~) draughts; checkers *plAm*
Danmark (*dahn*-mahrk) Denmark
dans (dahns) *m* dance
danse (*dahn*-ser) *v* dance
dansk (dahnsk) *adj* Danish
danske (*dahn*-sker) *m* Dane
dask (dahsk) *m* smack
datamaskin (*daa*-tah-mah-*sheen*) *m* computer
dato (*daa*-too) *m* date
datter (*daht*-terr) *c* (pl døtre) daughter
de (dee) *pron pl* (c den, nt det) those, they
debatt (deh-*baht*) *m* debate, discussion
debattere (deh-bah-*tāy*-rer) *v* argue, discuss
debet (*dāy*-bert) *m* debit
debetkort (*dāy*-bert-kott) *nt* debit card
defekt (deh-*fehkt*) *m* fault; *adj* faulty
definere (deh-fi-*nāy*-rer) *v* define
definisjon (deh-fi-ni-*shoon*)

m definition
deg (day) *pron* yourself; you
deig (day) *m* batter, dough
deilig (*day*-li) *adj* enjoyable, delicious; pleasant
dekk (dehkk) *nt* tire, tyre; deck; **øverste ~** main deck
dekke (*dehk*-ker) *v* cover
deklarasjon (dehk-lah-rah-*shōōn*) *m* declaration
deklarere (dehk-lah-*rāy*-rer) *v* declare
dekorasjon (deh-koo-rah-*shōōn*) *m* decoration
del (dāyl) *m* part; share
dele (*dāy*-ler) *v* divide; share; **~ seg** fork; **~ ut** *deal
delegasjon (deh-leh-gah-*shōōn*) *m* delegation
delikat (deh-li-*kaat*) *adj* delicate
delikatesse (deh-li-kah-*tehss*-ser) *m* delicatessen
deling (*dāy*-ling) *c* division
***delta** (*dāyl*-taa) *v* participate
deltakelse (*dāyl*-taa-kerl-ser) *m* participation
deltakende (*dāyl*-taa-ker-ner) *adj* sympathetic
deltaker (*dāyl*-taa-kerr) *m* participant
delvis (*dāyl*-veess) *adv* partly; *adj* partial
dem (dehmm) *pron* them
demning (*dehm*-ning) *m* dam; dike
demokrati (deh-moo-krah-*tee*) *nt* democracy
demokratisk (deh-moo-*kraa*-tisk) *adj* democratic
demonstrasjon (deh-moon-strah-*shōōn*) *m* demonstration
demonstrere (deh-moon-*strāy*-rer) *v* demonstrate
den (dehnn) *pron* (nt det, pl de) it; that
denne (*dehn*-ner) *pron* (nt dette) this; *adj* this
dens (dehnns) *pron* its
deodorant (deh-oo-doo-*rahnt*) *m* deodorant
departement (deh-pah-ter-*mahngng*) *nt* department; ministry
deponere (deh-poo-*nāy*-rer) *v* deposit
depositum (deh-*pōō*-si-tewm) *nt* (pl -ta) deposit
depresjon (deh-preh-*shōōn*) *m* depression
deprimere (deh-pri-*māy*-rer) *v* depress
deprimerende (deh-pri-*māy*-rer-ner) *adj* depressing
deprimert (deh-pri-*māyt*) *adj* depressed
deputert (deh-pew-*tāyt*) *m* deputy
der (dæær) *adv* there; **~ borte** over there
dere (*dāy*-rer) *pron* you, yourselves
deres (*dāy*-rerss) *pron* your, yours; their, theirs
derfor (*dær*-for) *adv* therefore

dersom (*dæ*-shom) *conj* if, in case
desember (deh-*sehm*-berr) December
desertere (deh-sæ-*tāy*-rer) *v* desert
desimalsystem (deh-si-*maal*-sewss-tāym) *nt* decimal system
desinfisere (dehss-sin-fi-*sāy*-rer) *v* disinfect; **desinfiserende middel** disinfectant
dessert (deh-*sæær*) *m* dessert; sweet
dessuten (*deh*-sēw-tern) *adv* moreover, also, furthermore, besides
dessverre (dehss-*vær*-rer) *adv* unfortunately
det (dāy) *pron* (c den, pl de) it; that
detalj (deh-*tahl*ʸ) *m* detail
detaljert (deh-tahl-ʸ*āyt*) *adj* detailed
detaljhandel (deh-*tahl*ʸ-hahn-derl) *m* (pl -dler) retail trade
detektiv (*deht*-tehk-teev) *m* detective
dets (dehtts) *pron* its
devaluere (deh-vah-lew-*āy*-rer) *v* devalue
devaluering (deh-vah-lew-*āy*-ring) *c* devaluation
diabetes (di-ah-*bāy*-terss) *m* diabetes
diabetiker (di-ah-*bāy*-ti-kerr) *m* diabetic
diagnose (di-ahg-*nōō*-ser) *m* diagnosis; **stille en ~** diagnose
diagonal (di-ah-goo-*naal*) *m* diagonal; *adj* diagonal
diagram (di-ah-*grahmm*) *nt* (pl ~mer) chart, graph, diagram
dialekt (di-ah-*lehkt*) *m* dialect
diamant (di-ah-*mahnt*) *m* diamond
diaré (di-ah-*rāy*) *m* diarrh(o)ea
diesel (*dee*-serl) *m* diesel
diett (di-*ehtt*) *m* diet
difteri (dif-ter-*ree*) *m* diphtheria
digital (di-gīī-*tahl*) *adj* digital
digital prosjektør (di-gīī-*tahl* proo-*shek*-turr) *c* digital projector
digitalbilde (di-gīī-*tahl-bil*-der) *nt* digital photo
digitalkamera (di-gīī-*tahl-kaa*-mer-rah) *nt* digital camera
dikt (dikt) *nt* poem
diktator (dik-*taa*-toor) *m* dictator
dikter (*dik*-terr) *m* poet
diktere (dik-*tāy*-rer) *v* dictate
dimensjon (di-mehn-*shōōn*) *m* size; dimension
din (deen) *pron* your, yours
dine (*dee*-ner) *pron* your, yours
diplom (di-*plōōm*) *nt* certificate, diploma

diplomat (dip-loo-*maat*) *m* diplomat
direksjon (deer-ehk-*shōōn*) *m* board of directors
direkte (di-*rehk*-ter) *adj* direct
direktiv (di-rehk-*teev*) *nt* directive; direction
direktør (di-rehk-*tūrr*) *m* executive, manager, director
dirigent (di-ri-*gehnt*) *m* conductor
dirigere (di-ri-*gāy*-rer) *v* conduct
dirre (*deer*-rer) *v* tremble
dis (deess) *m* mist, haze
disig (*dee*-si) *adj* hazy; misty
disiplin (di-si-*pleen*) *m* discipline
disk (disk) *m* counter
diskonto (diss-*kon*-too) *m* bank rate
diskstasjon (disk-stah-*shōōn*) *c* disk drive
diskusjon (diss-kew-*shōōn*) *m* discussion; argument
diskutere (diss-kew-*tāy*-rer) *v* discuss; argue
disponibel (diss-poo-*nee*-berl) *adj* available
disposisjon (diss-poo-si-*shōōn*) *m* disposal
disse (*diss*-ser) *pron* these
distrikt (diss-*trikt*) *nt* district
dit (deet) *adv* there
diverse (di-*væsh*-sher) *adj* miscellaneous, various
djerv (dʸærv) *adj* fearless, bold
djevel (*dʸāy*-verl) *m* (pl -vler) devil
do (doo) *m*/*nt colloquial* toilet
dobbel (*dob*-berl) *adj* double
dobbeltseng (*dob*-berlt-sehng) *c* double bed
dokk (dokk) *m* dock
***dokksette** (*dok*-seh-ter) *v* dock
doktor (*dok*-toor) *m* doctor
dokument (doo-kew-*mehnt*) *nt* certificate, document
dokumentmappe (doo-kew-*mehnt*-mah-per) *c* attaché case, briefcase
dollar (*dol*-lar) *m* dollar, *colloquial* buck
dom (domm) *m* (pl ~mer) judgment; verdict, sentence
domfellelse (*dom*-feh-lerl-ser) *m* conviction
domfelt (*dom*-fehltt) *m* (pl ~e) convict
dominere (doo-mi-*nāy*-rer) *v* dominate
domkirke (*dom*-kheer-ker) *c* cathedral
dommer (*dom*-merr) *m* judge; magistrate; umpire
domstol (*dom*-stōōl) *m* court, law court
donasjon (doo-nah-*shōōn*) *m* donation
dongeribukse (*dongh*-ri-book-se) *c* jeans
dose (*dōō*-ser) *m* dose

dott (dott) *m* wisp; tuft; wad
doven (*daw*-vern) *adj* lazy
***dra** (draa) *v* pull; travel, *go; **~ av sted** *set out
drake (*draa*-ker) *m* kite; dragon
drakt (drahkt) *c* costume
dram (drahmm) *m* drink of liquor
drama (*draa*-mah) *nt* drama
dramatisk (drah-*maa*-tisk) *adj* dramatic
drap (draap) *nt* manslaughter, homicide
dreie (*dray*-er) *v* turn, resolve
dreining (*dray*-ning) *m* turn
drenere (dreh-*nāy*-rer) *v* drain
drepe (*drāy*-per) *v* kill
dress (drehss) *m* suit
dressere (dreh-*sāy*-rer) *v* train
dressjakke (*drehss*-ʸahk-ker) *c* jacket
dreven (*drāy*-vern) *adj* skilled, clever
drikk (drikk) *m* drink; beverage; **alkoholfri ~** soft drink
***drikke** (*drik*-ker) *v* *drink
drikkelig (*drik*-ker-li) *adj* drinkable
drikkepenger (*drik*-ker-peh-ngerr) *pl* tip, gratuity
drikkevann (*drik*-ker-vahn) *nt* drinking water
drink (dringk) *m* drink
dristig (*driss*-ti) *adj* bold, daring; risky
dristighet (*driss*-ti-hāyt) *c* daring
dritt (dritt) *m vulgar* crap
***drive frem** (*dree*-ver) propel
drivhus (*dreev*-hewss) *nt* (pl ~) greenhouse
drivkraft (*dreev*-krahft) *c* driving force
dronning (*droan*-ning) *c* queen
drosje (*drosh*-sher) *c* cab, taxi
drosjeholdeplass (*drosh*-sher-ho-ler-plahss) *m* taxi rank; taxi stand *Am*
drosjesjåfør (*drosh*-sher-sho-fūrr) *m* cab driver, taxi driver
druer (*drēw*-err) *pl* grapes *pl*
drukne (*drook*-ner) *v* *be drowned; drown
dryppe (*drewp*-per) *v* drip
drøm (drurmm) *m* (pl ~mer) dream
drømme (*drurm*-mer) *v* *dream
dråpe (*draw*-per) *m* drop
du (dēw) *pron* you
due (*dēw*-er) *c* pigeon
duft (dewft) *m* scent
dugg (dewgg) *m* dew
duk (dēwk) *m* table-cloth
dukke (*dewk*-ker) *v* dive; *c* doll
dukketeater (*dewk*-ker-teh-*aa*-terr) *nt* (pl ~, -tre) puppet-show
dum (doomm) *adj* stupid,

dumb; foolish, silly
dun (dēwn) *nt* down
dunke (*doong*-ker) *v* thump, bump
dunkel (*doong*-kerl) *adj* dim
dur (dēwr) *m* roar; major
dusin (dew-*seen*) *nt* (pl ~) dozen
dusj (dewshsh) *m* shower
duskregn (*dewsk*-rehngn) *nt* drizzle
DVD (*deh*-veh-deh) *c* DVD
DVD-rom (*deh*-veh-deh-*rawm*) *c* (pl ~mer) DVD--rom
dverg (dværg) *m* dwarf
dybde (*dewb*-der) *m* depth
dyd (dēwd) *m* virtue
dykke (*dewk*-ker) *v* dive
dykkermaske (*dew*-ker-*mahss*-ker) *c* goggles *pl*
dyktig (*dewk*-ti) *adj* able, capable, skil(l)ful
dyktighet (*dewk*-ti-hāyt) *c* ability, skill
dynamo (dew-*naa*-moo) *m* dynamo
dyne (*dēw*-ner) *c* eiderdown
dyp (dēwp) *adj* deep; low
dypfryser (*dēwp*-frēw-serr) *m* deep-freeze
dypfryst mat (*dēwp*-frewst maat) frozen food
dypsindig (*dēwp*-sin-di) *adj* profound
dyr (dēwr) *nt* beast, animal; *adj* expensive
dyrebar (*dēw*-rer-baar) *adj* precious; dear
dyrekretsen (*dēw*-rer-kreht-sern) zodiac
dyrke (*dewr*-ker) *v* raise, cultivate, *grow
dyrlege (*dēwr*-lāy-ger) *m* veterinary surgeon
dyster (*dewss*-terr) *adj* gloomy, somber *Am*, sombre
dytt (dewtt) *m* push
dø (dūr) *v* die
død (dūr) *adj* dead; *m* death
dødelig (*dūr*-der-li) *adj* mortal, fatal
dødsfall (*durts*-fahl) *nt* (pl ~) death
dødsstraff (*durt*-strahf) *m* death penalty
døgn (durngn) *nt* twenty--four hours
dømme (*durm*-mer) *v* sentence; judge
døpe (*dūr*-per) *v* baptize, christen
dør (dūrr) *c* door
dørslag (*dūr*-shlaag) *nt* (pl ~) strainer
dørvokter (dūrr-vok-terr) *m* door-keeper
døv (dūrv) *adj* deaf
dåd (dawd) *m* exploit, achievement
dåkalv (*daw*-kahlv) *m* fawn
dåp (dawp) *m* christening, baptism
dårlig (*daw*-li) *adj* ill, bad; poor; ~ **luft** stale air

E

ebbe (*ehb*-ber) *m* ebb

e-billett (*e̅h̅*-bi-*lehtt*) *c* e-ticket

Ecuador (ehk-vah-*dawr*) Ecuador

ecuadorianer (ehk-vah-do-ri-*aa*-nerr) *m* Ecuadorian

ed (a̅y̅d) *m* oath, vow

edderkopp (*ehd*-derr-kop) *m* spider

eddik (*ehd*-dik) *m* vinegar

edel (*a̅y̅*-derl) *adj* noble

edelstein (*a̅y̅*-derl-sta̅y̅n) *m* gem, precious stone

edru (*a̅y̅d*-re̅w̅) *adj* sober

effekt (eh-*fehkt*) *m* effect

effektiv (*ehf*-fehk-tiv) *adj* effective; efficient

eføy (*a̅y̅*-fur^{ew}) *m* ivy

egen (*a̅y̅*-gern) *adj* own; peculiar, odd

egenskap (*a̅y̅*-gern-skaap) *m* quality, characteristic

egentlig (*a̅y̅*-gernt-li) *adv* really

egg (ehgg) *nt* egg

eggeplomme (*ehg*-ger-plo-mer) *c* yolk, egg yolk

egn (ayn) *m* region

egnet (*ay*-nert) *adj* convenient, suitable, fit

egoisme (eh-goo-*iss*-mer) *m* selfishness

Egypt (eh-*gewpt*) Egypt

egypter (eh-*gewp*-terr) *m* Egyptian

egyptisk (eh-*gewp*-tisk) *adj* Egyptian

ei (a̅y̅) *art* a; *num* one

eie (*ay*-er) *v* own; possess, *nt* possession; **eiendeler** belongings *pl*

eiendom (*ay*-ern-dom) *m* (pl ~mer) property; estate; premises *pl*

eiendommelig (ay-ern-*dom*-li) *adj* peculiar; quaint

eiendommelighet (ay-ern-*dom*-li-ha̅y̅t) *c* peculiarity

eiendomsmegler (*ay*-ern-doms-mehg-lerr) *m* house-agent; realtor *nAm*

eier (*ay*-err) *m* owner, proprietor

eik (ayk) *c* oak

eike (*ay*-ker) *m* spoke

eikenøtt (*ay*-ker-nurt) *c* acorn

ekkel (*ehk*-kerl) *adj* nasty

ekko (*ehk*-koo) *nt* echo

ekorn (*ehk*-koon) *nt* squirrel

eksakt (ehk-*sahkt*) *adj* exact

eksamen (ehk-*saa*-mern) *m* exam *colloquial*, examination; ***ta ~** graduate

eksem (ehk-*sa̅y̅m*) *m/nt* eczema

eksempel (ehk-*sehm*-perl) *nt* (pl -pler) example, instance; **for ~** for instance,

for example
eksemplar (ehk-sehm-*plaar*) *nt* specimen; copy
eksentrisk (ehk-*sehn*-trisk) *adj* eccentric
eksil (ehk-*seel*) *nt* exile
eksistens (ehk-si-*stehns*) *m* existence
eksistere (ehk-si-*stāy*-rer) *v* exist
eksklusiv (*ehks*-klew-seev) *adj* exclusive
eksos (ehk-*sōōss*) *m* exhaust gases
eksospotte (ehk-*sōōss*-po-ter) *c* silencer; muffler *nAm*
eksosrør (ehk-*sōōss*-rūrr) *nt* (pl ~) exhaust pipe
eksotisk (ehk-*soo*-tisk) *adj* exotic
ekspedisjon (ehk-sper-di-*shōōn*) *m* expedition
ekspansjon (ehk-spang-*shōōn*) *m* expansion
ekspeditør (ehk-sper-di-*tūrr*) *m* shop assistant, salesman
eksperiment (ehk-speh-ri-*mehnt*) *nt* experiment
eksperimentere (ehk-speh-ri-mehn-*tāy*-rer) *v* experiment
ekspert (ehk-*spæt*) *m* expert
eksplodere (ehk-sploo-*dāy*-rer) *v* explode, blow up
eksplosiv (ehk-sploo-*seev*) *adj* explosive
eksplosjon (ehk-sploo-*shōōn*) *m* blast, explosion
eksponere (ehk-spoo-*nāy*-rer) *v* expose
eksponering (ehk-spoo-*nāy*-ring) *c* exposure
eksportere (ehk-spo-*tāy*-rer) *v* export
ekspress- (ehk-*sprehss*) express
ekstase (ehk-*staa*-ser) *m* ecstasy
ekstra (*ehk*-strah) *adj* additional, extra; spare
ekstravagant (ehk-strah-vah-*gahnt*) *adj* extravagant
ekstrem (ehk-*strāym*) *adj* extreme
ekte (*ehk*-ter) *adj* genuine, authentic, true; *v* marry
ektemann (*ehk*-ter-mahn) *m* (pl -menn) husband
ektepar (*ehk*-ter-paar) *nt* married couple
ekteskap (*ehk*-teh-skaap) *nt* matrimony, marriage
ekvator (ehk-*vaa*-toor) *m* equator
elastisk (eh-*lahss*-tisk) *adj* elastic
eldre (*ehl*-drer) *adj* older; elderly; **eldst** eldest
elefant (eh-ler-*fahnt*) *m* elephant
eleganse (eh-ler-*gahng*-ser) *m* elegance
elegant (eh-ler-*gahnt*) *adj* elegant
elektriker (eh-*lehk*-tri-kerr) *m* electrician
elektrisitet (eh-lehk-tri-si-*tāyt*) *m* electricity

elektrisk (eh-*lehk*-trisk) *adj* electric
elektronisk (eh-lehk-*troo*-nisk) *adj* electronic
element (eh-ler-*mehnt*) *nt* element
elementær (eh-ler-mehn-*tæær*) *adj* primary
elendig (eh-*lehn*-di) *adj* miserable
elendighet (eh-*lehn*-di-hayt) *c* misery
elev (eh-*layv*) *m* pupil
elfenbein (*ehl*-fern-bayn) *nt* ivory
elg (ehlg) *m* moose, elk
eliminere (eh-li-mi-*nay*-rer) *v* eliminate
eller (*ehl*-lerr) *conj* or; **enten ... eller** either ... or; **om ... eller** whether ... or
ellers (*ehl*-lersh) *adv* otherwise; else
elleve (*ehl*-ver) *num* eleven
ellevte (*ehl*-lerf-ter) *num* eleventh
elske (*ehl*-sker) *v* love
elsker (*ehl*-skerr) *m* lover
elskerinne (ehl-sker-*rin*-ner) *c* mistress
elsket (*ehl*-skert) *adj* beloved
elskling (*ehlsk*-ling) *m* sweetheart
elv (elv) *c* river
elvebredd (*el*-ver-brehd) *m* river bank, riverside
elvemunning (*el*-ver-mew-ning) *m* estuary
emalje (eh-*mahl*-ʸer) *m* enamel
emaljert (eh-mahl-*ʸayt*) *adj* enamelled
embete (*ehm*-ber-ter) *nt* civil service office
embetsmann (*ehm*-berts-mahnn) *m* (pl -menn) civil servant
emblem (ehm-*blaym*) *nt* emblem
emigrant (eh-mi-*grahnt*) *m* emigrant
emigrasjon (eh-mi-grah-*shoon*) *m* emigration
emne (*ehm*-ner) *nt* topic, theme
en (ayn) *art* a; *num* one; **-en** the *art*
enakter (*ayn*-ahk-terr) *m* one-act play
ende (*ehn*-ner) *m* end
endelig (*ehn*-der-li) *adv* finally; eventually
endestasjon (*ehn*-ner-stah-shoon) *m* terminal
endetarm (*ehn*-ner-tahrm) *m* rectum
endossere (ahng-do-*say*-rer) *v* endorse
endre (*ehn*-drer) *v* alter; modify
endring (*ehn*-dring) *c* alteration; change
eneforhandler (*ay*-ner-for-hahnd-lerr) *m* sole distributor
energi (eh-nær-*gee*) *m* power, energy
energisk (eh-*nær*-gisk) *adj* energetic

eneste (*ay̅*-nerss-ter) *adj* sole, only
enestående (*ay̅*-ner-sto-er-ner) *adj* exceptional, unique; singular
eng (ehngng) *c* meadow
engangs- (*ay̅n*-gahngs) disposable
engel (*ehng*-ngerl) *m* (pl engler) angel
engelsk (*eh*-ngerlsk) *adj* English
engelskmann (*eh*-ngerlsk-mahn) *m* (pl -menn) Englishman; Briton
England (*ehng*-lahn) England
engroshandel (ahng-*graw*-hahn-derl) *m* (pl -dler) wholesale-trade
engstelig (*ehng*-ster-li) *adj* anxious; afraid
engstelse (*ehng*-sterl-ser) *m* fear
enhet (*ay̅n*-hay̅t) *m* unity; unit
enhver (ehn-*vær*) *pron* anyone; everybody, everyone
enig (*ay̅*-ni) *adj* unanimous, agreed; ***være ~** agree
enke (*ehng*-ker) *c* widow
enkel (*ehng*-kerl) *adj* simple; plain; single
enkelt (*ehng*-kerlt) *adj* individual
enkelte (*ehng*-kerl-ter) *pron* some
enkeltperson (*ehng*-kerlt-pæ-sho͞on) *m* individual
enkeltrom (*ehng*-kerlt-room) *nt* (pl ~) single room
enkemann (*ayng*-ker-mahn) *m* (pl -menn) widower
enn (ehnn) *conj* than
ennå (*ehn*-naw) *adv* yet
enorm (eh-*norm*) *adj* enormous; huge, immense, gigantic
ensartet (*ay̅n*-saa-tert) *adj* uniform
ensidig (*ay̅n*-see-di) *adj* one-sided
ensom (*ay̅n*-som) *adj* lonely
enstemmig (*ay̅n*-steh-mi) *adj* unanimous
entall (*ay̅n*-tahl) *nt* singular
entrénøkkel (ahng-*tray̅*-nur-kerl) *m* (pl -nøkler) latchkey
entreprenør (ahng-trer-preh-*nu̅rr*) *m* contractor
entusiasme (ehn-tew-si-*ahss*-mer) *m* enthusiasm
entusiastisk (ehn-tew-si-*ahss*-tisk) *adj* enthusiastic
enveiskjøring (*ay̅n*-vayss-khu̅r-ring) *c* one-way traffic
epidemi (eh-pi-der-*mee*) *m* epidemic
epilepsi (eh-pi-lehp-*see*) *m* epilepsy
epilog (eh-pi-*lawg*) *m* epilogue
episk (*ay̅*-pisk) *adj* epic
episode (eh-pi-*so͞o*-der) *m* episode
eple (*ehp*-ler) *nt* apple
epos (*ay̅*-pooss) *nt* epic

e-post (*ay̅*-poost) *m* e-mail
erfare (ær-*faa*-rer) *v* experience
erfaren (ær-*faa*-rern) *adj* experienced
erfaring (ær-*faa*-ring) *c* experience
ergerlig (*ær*-ger-li) *adj* annoying
ergre (*ær*-grer) *v* annoy; irritate
ergrelse (*ær*-grerl-ser) *m* annoyance
erindre (eh-*rin*-drer) *v* recall
erindring (eh-*rin*-dring) *c* remembrance
erkjenne (ær-*khehn*-ner) *v* acknowledge; confess, admit
erklære (ær-*klææ*-rer) *v* declare; state
erklæring (ær-*klææ*-ring) *c* declaration, statement
erme (*ær*-mer) *nt* sleeve
erobre (æ-*roo̅b-rer*) *v* conquer; capture
erobrer (æ-*roo̅b*-rerr) *m* conqueror
erobring (æ-*roo̅b*-ring) *c* conquest; capture
erstatning (æ-*shtaht*-ning) *m* indemnity; substitute
erstatte (æ-*shtaht*-ter) *v* replace, substitute
ert (ætt) *c* pea
erte (*æ*-ter) *v* tease
erverve (ær-*vær*-ver) *v* acquire; obtain
ervervelse (ær-*vær*-verl-ser) *m* acquisition
esel (*ay̅*-serl) *nt* (pl esler) donkey
eske (*ehss*-ker) *c* box
eskorte (ehss-*kot*-ter) *m* escort
eskortere (ehss-ko-*tay̅*-rer) *v* escort
essay (*ehss*-say) *nt* (pl ~, ~s) essay
essens (eh-*sehns*) *m* essence
et (ay̅t) *art* a; *num* one; **-et** the *art*
etablere (eh-tah-*blay̅*-rer) *v* establish
etappe (eh-*tahp*-per) *m* stage, leg
etasje (eh-*taa*-sher) *m* stor(e)y, floor; **første ~** ground floor
eter (*ay̅*-terr) *m* ether
etikett (eh-ti-*kehtt*) *m* label
Etiopia (eh-ti-*oo̅*-pi-ah) Ethiopia
etiopier (eh-ti-*oo̅*-pi-err) *m* Ethiopian
etiopisk (eh-ti-*oo̅*-pisk) *adj* Ethiopian
etsteds (eht-*stehss*) *adv* somewhere
etter (*eht*-terr) *prep* after; **~ at** after
etterforske (*eht*-terr-fosh-ker) *v* investigate
etterforskning (*eht*-terr-foshk-ning) *m* inquiry, investigation
***etterfølge** (*eht*-terr-fur-ler) *v* succeed

etterkommer (*eht*-terr-ko-merr) *m* descendant
***etterlate** (*eht*-ter-laa-ter) *v* *leave behind; *leave
etterligne (*eht*-ter-ling-ner) *v* copy, imitate
etterligning (*eht*-ter-ling-ning) *c* imitation
ettermiddag (*eht*-terr-mi-dah) *m* afternoon; **i ~** this afternoon
etternavn (*eht*-ter-nahvn) *nt* (pl ~) family name, surname
etterpå (*eht*-terr-paw) *adv* afterwards
ettersende (*eht*-ter-sheh-ner) *v* forward
ettersom (*eht*-ter-shom) *conj* as, because
etterspore (*eht*-ter-shpoo-rer) *v* trace
etterspørsel (*eht*-ter-shpur-sherl) *m* demand
etui (eh-tew-*ee*) *nt* case
EU (eh-ew) EU
euro (*ou*-roo) *m* Euro
Europa (ou-*roo*-pah) Europe
europeer (ou-roo-*pay*-err) *m* European
europeisk (ou-roo-*pay*-isk) *adj* European
evakuere (eh-vah-kew-*ay*-rer) *v* evacuate
evangelium (eh-vahng-*gay*-li-ewm) *nt* (pl -ier) gospel
eventuell (eh-vehn-tew-*ehll*) *adj* possible
eventyr (*ay*-vern-tewr) *nt* (pl ~) fairytale; tale; adventure
evig (*ay*-vi) *adj* eternal
evighet (*ay*-vi-hayt) *c* eternity
evne (*ehv*-ner) *c* faculty, gift; ability, capacity
evolusjon (eh-voo-lew-*shoon*) *m* evolution

F

fabel (*faa*-berl) *m* (pl fabler) fable
fabrikant (fahb-ri-*kahnt*) *m* manufacturer
fabrikk (fahb-*rikk*) *m* works *pl*, mill, plant, factory
fabrikkere (fahb-ri-*kay*-rer) *v* manufacture
faen (*fah*-ahrn) *colloquial* damn!
fag (faag) *nt* profession
fagforening (*faag*-fo-reh-ning) *c* trade union; union
fagmann (*faag*-mahnn) *m* (pl -menn) expert
fakkel (*fahk*-kerl) *m* (pl fakler) torch
faks (fahks) *m* fax; **sende en ~** send a fax
faktisk (*fahk*-tisk) *adv* as a matter of fact, really, actually, in effect, in fact;

adj actual, factual
faktor (*fahk*-toor) *m* factor
faktum (*fahk*-tewm) *nt* (pl -ta) fact
faktura (fahk-*tew*-rah) *m* invoice
fakturere (fahk-tew-*ray*-rer) *v* bill
fakultet (fah-kewl-*tayt*) *nt* faculty
fald (fahll) *m* hem
falk (fahlk) *m* hawk
fall (fahll) *nt* fall; **i alle ~** at any rate; **i hvert ~** anyway, at any rate
***falle** (*fahl*-ler) *v* *fall; **~ sammen med** coincide; ***la ~** drop
falleferdig (*fahl*-ler-fæ-di) *adj* ramshackle
fallitt (fah-*litt*) *adj* bankrupt
falme (*fahl*-mer) *v* fade
falsk (fahlsk) *adj* false
familie (fah-*mee*-li-er) *m* family
familiær (fah-mi-li-*æær*) *adj* familiar
fanatisk (fah-*naa*-tisk) *adj* fanatical
fang (fahng) *nt* lap
fange (*fahng*-nger) *v* capture; *catch; *m* prisoner; ***ta til ~** capture
fangenskap (*fahng*-ngern-skaap) *nt* imprisonment
fangst (fahngst) *m* catch
fantasi (fahn-tah-*see*) *m* fantasy, imagination, fancy
fantasifoster (fahn-tah-*seefooss*-terr) *nt* illusion
fantastisk (fahn-*tahss*-tisk) *adj* fantastic
fantom (fahn-*toom*) *nt* phantom
far (faar) *m* (pl fedre) father; dad
fare (*faa*-rer) *m* peril, danger; risk
farfar (*fahr*-faar) *m* (pl -fedre) grandfather
farge (*fahr*-ger) *m* colo(u)r; dye; *v* dye; **~ av** discolo(u)r
fargeblind (*fahr*-ger-blin) *adj* colo(u)r-blind
fargerik (*fahr*-ger-reek) *adj* colo(u)rful; gay
farget (*fahr*-gert) *adj* colo(u)red
farlig (*faa*-li) *adj* dangerous
farmakologi (fahr-mah-koo-loo-*gee*) *m* pharmacology
farmor (*fahr*-moor) *c* (pl -mødre) grandmother
fart (fahtt) *m* rate, speed; **i full ~** in a hurry; **saktne farten** slow down; **øke farten** accelerate
fartsgrense (*fahts*-grehn-ser) *c* speed limit
fartsmåler (*fahts*-maw-lerr) *m* speedometer
fartøy (*faa*-tur[ew]) *nt* vessel
fasade (fah-*saa*-der) *m* façade
fasan (fah-*saan*) *m* pheasant
fascisme (fah-*shiss*-mer) *m* fascism
fascist (fah-*shist*) *m* fascist

fascistisk (fah-*shiss*-tisk) *adj* fascist
fase (*faa*-ser) *m* stage, phase
fast (fahst) *adj* firm; fixed; permanent; *adv* tight
fastboende (*fahst*-boo-er-ner) *m* (pl ~) resident
***fastholde** (*fahst*-ho-ler) *v* insist
fastland (*fahst*-lahn) *nt* mainland
***fastsette** (*fahst*-seh-ter) *v* determine; stipulate
***fastslå** (*fahst*-shlo) *v* establish; ascertain
fat (faat) *nt* dish; cask, barrel
fatal (fah-*taal*) *adj* fatal
fatning (*faht*-ning) *m* composure
fatøl *nt* draught beer
fatte (*faht*-ter) *v* *understand, grasp
fattig (*faht*-ti) *adj* poor
fattigdom (*faht*-ti-dom) *m* poverty
fattigslig (*faht*-tik-sli) *adj* poor
favoritt (fah-voo-*ritt*) *m* favo(u)rite
fe (fay) *m* fairy
feber (*fay*-berr) *m* fever
feberaktig (*fay*-berr-ahk-ti) *adj* feverish
februar (feh-brew-*aar*) February
fedme (*fehd*-mer) *m* obesity
fedreland (*fay*-drer-lahn) *nt* native country
feie (*fay*-er) *v* *sweep
feig (fayg) *adj* cowardly
feiging (*fay*-ging) *m* coward
feil (fayl) *m* (pl ~) fault, error, mistake; *adj* incorrect; ***ta ~** *be mistaken
feilaktig (fayl-*ahk*-ti) *adj* mistaken
feile (*fay*-ler) *v* err
feilfri (*fayl*-free) *adj* faultless
feiltakelse (*fayl*-taa-kerl-ser) *m* mistake, error
feiltrinn (*fayl*-trin) *nt* slip
feire (*fay*-rer) *v* celebrate
feiring (*fay*-ring) *c* celebration
fekte (*fehk*-ter) *v* fence
fele (*fai*-ler) *c* fiddle
felg (fehlg) *m* rim
felle (*fehl*-ler) *c* trap
felles (*fehl*-lerss) *adj* common; joint; **i fellesskap** jointly
fellesprosjekt *nt* joint venture
felt (fehlt) *nt* field
feltkikkert (*fehlt*-khi-kert) *m* field glasses
feltseng (*fehlt*-sehng) *c* camp bed; cot *nAm*
fem (fehmm) *num* five
feminin (feh-mi-*neen*) *adj* feminine
femte (*fehm*-ter) *num* fifth
femten (*fehm*-tern) *num* fifteen
femtende (*fehm*-ter-ner) *num* fifteenth

femti (*fehm*-ti) *num* fifty
fengsel (*fehng*-sherl) *nt* (pl -sler) jail, prison
fengsle (*fehng*-shler) *v* imprison; fascinate
ferdig (*fææ*-di) *adj* finished
ferdselsåre (*færd*-serls-*aw*-rer) *c* thoroughfare
ferge (*fær*-ger) *c* ferry-boat
ferie (*fay*-ri-er) *m* vacation, holiday; **på ~** on holiday
ferieleir (*fay*-ri-er-layr) *m* holiday camp
feriested (*fay*-ri-er-stay) *nt* holiday resort
ferje (*fær*-[y]er) *c* ferry-boat
fersk (fæshk) *adj* fresh
fersken (*fæsh*-kern) *m* peach
ferskvann (*fæshk*-vahn) *nt* fresh water
fest (fehst) *m* feast, party
feste (*fehss*-ter) *v* attach, fasten; **~ med nål** pin
festeinnretning (*fehss*-ter-in-reht-ning) *m* fastener
festival (fehss-ti-*vaal*) *m* festival
festlig (*fehst*-li) *adj* festive
festning (*fehst*-ning) *m* fortress; stronghold
fet (fayt) *adj* fat, obese
fett (fehtt) *nt* grease, fat
fetter (*feht*-terr) *m* cousin
fettet (*feht*-tert) *adj* greasy
fettfri (*fehtt*-free) *adj* fat free
fettholdig (*feht*-hol-di) *adj* fatty
fettsuging (*fehtt*-sewg-ing) *c* liposuction

fiasko (fi-*ahss*-koo) *m* failure
fiber (*fee*-berr) *m* (pl fibrer) fibre
fiende (*fee*-ern-der) *m* enemy
fiendtlig (*fee*-ern-tli) *adj* hostile
figur (fi-*gewr*) *m* figure
fik (feek) *m* slap, blow
fike (*fee*-ker) *v* slap
fiken (*fee*-kern) *m* fig
fiks (fiks) *adj* smart
fil (feel) *m* file; lane
filial (fi-li-*aal*) *m* branch
filipens (fi-li-*pehns*) *m* acne
Filippinene (fi-li-*pee*-ner-ner) Philippines *pl*
filippinsk (fi-li-*peensk*) *adj* Philippine
fille (*fil*-ler) *c* rag
film (film) *m* movie, film
filme (*fil*-mer) *v* film
filmkamera (*film*-kaa-mer-rah) *nt* camera
filmlerret (*film*-*lær*-rert) *nt* screen
filosof (fi-loo-*soof*) *m* philosopher
filosofi (fi-loo-soo-*fee*) *m* philosophy
filt (filt) *m* felt
filter (*fil*-terr) *nt* (pl -tre) filter
fin (feen) *adj* fine
finanser (fi-*nahng*-serr) *pl* finances *pl*
finansiell (fi-nahng-si-*ehll*) *adj* financial
finansiere (fi-nahng-si-*ay*-

rer) *v* finance
finger (*fing*-ngerr) *m* (pl -gre) finger
fingeravtrykk (*fing*-ngerr-ahv-trewk) *nt* (pl ~) fingerprint
fingerbøl (*fing*-ngerr-burl) *nt* (pl ~) thimble
finhakke (*feen*-hah-ker) *v* mince
finke (*fing*-ker) *m* finch
Finland (*fin*-lahn) Finland
finmale (*feen*-maa-ler) *v* *grind
finne[1] (*fin*-ner) *m* Finn
***finne**[2] (*fin*-ner) *v* *find; ~ **igjen** recover; ~ **skyldig** convict; ~ **sted** *take place
finsk (finsk) *adj* Finnish
fint! (feent) all right!, okay!
fiol (fi-*o͞ol*) *m* violet
fiolett (fi-oo-*lehtt*) *adj* violet
fiolin (fi-oo-*leen*) *m* violin
fire (*fee*-rer) *num* four
firfisle (*feer*-fis-ler) *c* lizard
firma (*feer*-mah) *nt* firm, company
fisk (fisk) *m* fish
fiske (*fiss*-ker) *v* fish; angle
fiskebein (*fiss*-ker-bayn) *nt* bone, fishbone
fiskeforretning (*fiss*-ker-fo-reht-ning) *c* fish shop
fiskegarn (*fiss*-ker-gaan) *nt* (pl ~) fishing net
fiskekort (*fiss*-ker-kot) *nt* (pl ~) fishing license *Am*, fishing licence
fiskekrok (*fiss*-ker-kro͞ok) *m* fishing hook
fisker (*fiss*-kerr) *m* fisherman
fiskeredskap (*fiss*-ker-rehss-kaap) *nt* fishing tackle
fiskeri (fiss-ker-*ree*) *nt* fishing industry
fiskesnøre (*fiss*-ker-snūr-rer) *nt* fishing line
fiskestang (*fiss*-ker-stahng) *c* (pl -stenger) fishing rod
fiskeutstyr (*fiss*-ker-ewt-stēwr) *nt* fishing gear
fjell (f^y^ehll) *nt* mountain
fjellendt (*f^y^ehl*-lent) *adj* mountainous
fjellkjede (*f^y^ehl*-khāy-der) *m* mountain range
fjellklatring (*f^y^ehl*-klaht-ring) *c* mountaineering
fjerde (*f^y^ææ*-rer) *num* fourth
fjern (f^y^ææn) *adj* far, distant, remote, far-off
fjerne (*f^y^ææ*-ner) *v* *take away, remove
fjerning (*f^y^ææ*-ning) *c* removal
fjernkontroll (*f^y^ǣǣn*-koon-troll) *c* remote control
fjernsyn (*f^y^ææn*-sēwn) *nt* television, *colloquial* telly
fjernsynsapparat (*f^y^ææn*-sēwn-sah-pah-raat) *nt* television set
fjollet (*f^y^ol*-lert) *adj* foolish
i fjor (ee f^y^o͞or) last year
fjord (f^y^o͞or) *m* fjord
fjorten (*f^y^oot*-tern) *num* fourteen; ~ **dager** fortnight

fjortende (*f*ʸ*oot*-ter-ner) *num* fourteenth
fjær (fʸær) *c* (pl ~) feather; spring
fjære (fʸææ-rer) *c* low tide
fjæring (*f*ʸ*ææ*-ring) *c* suspension
fjærkre (*f*ʸ*æær*-kray) *nt* (pl ~) fowl, poultry
flagg (flahgg) *nt* flag
flakke (*flahk*-ker) *v* wander
flamingo (flah-*ming*-goo) *m* flamingo
flamme (*flahm*-mer) *m* flame
flanell (flah-*nehll*) *m* flannel
flaske (*flahss*-ker) *c* bottle; flask
flaskehals (*flahss*-ker-hahls) *m* bottleneck
flaskeåpner (*flahss*-ker-awp-nerr) *m* bottle opener
flass (flahss) *nt* dandruff
flat (flaat) *adj* flat; plane
flekk (flehkk) *m* spot, stain; speck, blot
flekke (*flehk*-ker) *v* stain
flekket (*flehk*-kert) *adj* spotted
flekkfjerner (*flehk*-fʸæ-nerr) *m* stain remover
flere (*flay*-rer) *adj* several; **flest** most
flerkinoanlegg (*flayr*-khee-noo-ahn-*lehgg*) *nt* multiplex (theater)
flertall (*flay*-tahl) *nt* majority; plural
flid (fleed) *m* diligence
flink (flingk) *adj* clever, skil(l)ful, smart
flintstein (*flint*-stayn) *m* flint
flis (fleess) *c* chip; tile
flittig (*fli*-ti) *adj* diligent; industrious
flo (floo) *m* flood
flokk (flokk) *m* herd, flock; bunch
flott (flott) *adj* swell; *colloquial* super
flottør (flo-*turr*) *m* float
flue (*flew*-er) *c* fly
flukt (flewkt) *c* escape
fluktstol (*flewkt*-stool) *m* deck chair
fly (flew) *nt* aeroplane, airplane *nAm*
***fly** (flew) *v* *fly
flybensin (*flew*-behn-seen) *m* kerosene
flygel (*flew*-gerl) *nt* (pl -gler) grand piano
flykaptein (*flew*-kahp-tayn) *m* captain
flykte (*flewk*-ter) *v* escape, flee
flyktig (*flewk*-ti) *adj* casual
flyktning (*flewkt*-ning) *m* refugee
flyndre (*flewnd*-rer) *c* sole
flyplass (*flew*-plahss) *m* airport, airfield
flyselskap (*flew*-sehl-skaap) *nt* airline
***flyte** (*flew*-ter) *v* flow; float
flytende (*flew*-ter-ner) *adj* fluent; fluid, liquid
flyttbar (*flewt*-baar) *adj*

movable
flytte (*flewt*-ter) *v* move
flytur (*flew*-tewr) *m* flight
flyulykke (*flew*-ew-lew-ker) *c* plane crash
flyvert (*flew*-væt) *m* steward
flyvertinne (*flew*-væ-ti-ner) *c* stewardess
fløte (*flur*-ter) *m* cream
fløteaktig (*flur*-ter-ahk-ti) *adj* creamy
fløyel (*flur*ew-erl) *m* velvet
fløyte (*flur*ew-ter) *c* flute; whistle
flå (flaw) *v* fleece
flåte (*flaw*-ter) *m* raft; fleet; navy
fnise (*fnee*-ser) *v* giggle
foajé (foo-ah-*ʸay*) *m* foyer, lobby
fold (foll) *m* crease, fold
folde (*fol*-ler) *v* fold; **~ sammen** fold; **~ ut** *v* unfold
foldekniv (*fol*-ler-kneev) *m* clasp-knife
folk (folk) *nt* people, nation; *pl* people; **folke-** popular; national
folkedans (*fol*-ker-dahns) *m* folk dance
folkemengde (*fol*-ker-mehng-der) *m* crowd
folkerik (*fol*-ker-reek) *adj* populous
folkeslag (fol-ker-*shlaag*) *nt* (pl ~) people
folkevise (*fol*-ker-vee-ser) *c* folk song
folklore (folk-*law*-rer) *m* folklore
fond (fonn) *nt* fund
fondsbørs (*fons*-bursh) *m* stock exchange
fondsmarked (*fons*-mahr-kerd) *nt* stock market
fonetisk (foo-*nay*-tisk) *adj* phonetic
for[1] (forr) *conj* for; *prep* for; **~ hånden** available; **~ å** in order to, to
fôr[2] (foor) *nt* lining; fodder
forakt (for-*ahkt*) *m* scorn, contempt
forakte (for-*ahk*-ter) *v* despise, scorn
foran (*for*-rahn) *prep* before, ahead of, in front of
forandre (for-*ahn*-drer) *v* change; vary, alter
forandring (for-*ahn*-dring) *c* variation, change; alteration
foranledning (*for*-rahn-layd-ning) *m* occasion
foranstaltning (*for*-rahn-stahlt-ning) *m* measure
forargelse (for-*ahr*-gerl-ser) *m* indignation
forbanne (for-*bahn*-ner) *v* curse
forbause (for-*bou*-ser) *v* astonish; amaze, surprise
forbauselse (for-*bou*-serl-ser) *m* astonishment; amazement
forbausende (for-*bou*-ser-ner) *adj* astonishing; amazing
forbedre (for-*bayd*-rer) *v*

improve
forbedring (for-*bāyd*-ring) *c* improvement
forbehold (*for*-ber-hol) *nt* qualification; reservation
forberede (*for*-ber-rāy-der) *v* prepare
forberedelse (*for*-ber-rāy-derl-ser) *m* preparation
forberedende (*for*-ber-rāy-der-ner) *adj* preliminary
forbi (for-*bee*) *prep* past, beyond, past; ***gå ~** pass by
***forbinde** (for-*bin*-ner) *v* connect, link, join; dress; associate
forbindelse (for-*bin*-nerl-ser) *m* connection; relation, reference
forbipasserende (for-*bee*-pah-sāy-rer-ner) *m* (pl ~) passer-by
***forbli** (for-*blee*) *v* remain
forbløffe (for-blurf-fer) *v* astonish
forbokstav (*for*-book-staav) *m* initial
forbruk (*for*-brēwk) *nt* expenditure; consumption
forbruke (*for*-brēw-ker) *v* consume
forbruker (*for*-brēw-kerr) *m* consumer
forbrytelse (for-*brēw*-terl-ser) *m* crime
forbryter (for-*brēw*-terr) *m* criminal
forbrytersk (for-*brēw*-tershk) *adj* criminal
forbud (*for*-bēwd) *nt* (pl ~) prohibition
forbudt (for-*bewtt*) *adj* prohibited; **forbikjøring forbudt** no passing *Am*
forbund (*for*-bewn) *nt* (pl ~) league, union; **forbunds-**federal
forbundsfelle (*for*-bewns-feh-ler) *m* associate
forbundsstat (*for*-bewn-staat) *m* federation
***forby** (for-*bēw*) *v* *forbid, prohibit
fordampe (fo-*dahm*-per) *v* evaporate
fordel (*fo*-dāyl) *m* benefit, advantage, profit; ***ha ~ av** benefit; **til ~ for** for the benefit of
fordelaktig (*fo*-dāyl-ahk-ti) *adj* advantageous
fordele (fo-*dāy*-ler) *v* divide
fordi (fo-*dee*) *conj* as, because; since
fordom (*fo*-dom) *m* (pl ~mer) prejudice
fordreid (fo-*drayd*) *adj* crooked, twisted
fordring (*fod*-ring) *c* claim
***fordrive** (fo-*dree*-ver) *v* expel; chase
fordum (*fo*-dewm) *adv* formerly
fordømt (fo-*dømt*) *adv* damned; *colloquial* bloody
fordøye (fo-*durew*-er) *v* digest
fordøyelig (fo-*durew*-er-li) *adj* digestible
fordøyelse (fo-*durew*-erl-

ser) *m* digestion; **dårlig ~** indigestion
forebygge (*faw*-rer-bew-ger) *v* prevent
forebyggende (*faw*-rer-bew-ger-ner) *adj* preventive
foredrag (*faw*-rer-draag) *nt* (pl ~) lecture
***foregi** (*faw*-rer-^{y}ee) *v* pretend
***foregripe** (*faw*-rer-gree-per) *v* anticipate
foregående (*faw*-rer-gaw-er-ner) *adj* preceding, previous
***forekomme** (*faw*-rer-ko-mer) *v* occur
forelder (for-*ehl*-derr) *m* parent
foreldet (for-*ehl*-dert) *adj* out of date
foreldre (for-*ehl*-drer) *pl* parents *pl*
***forelegge** (*faw*-rer-leh-ger) *v* present
forelesning (*faw*-rer-lāyss-ning) *m* lecture
forelsket (for-*ehl*-skert) *adj* in love
foreløpig (*faw*-rer-lūr-pi) *adj* provisional, temporary
forene (for-*āy*-ner) *v* join, unite
forening (for-*āy*-ning) *c* association; club, society
forent (for-*āynt*) *adj* joint; **De forente stater** (di for-*āyn*-ter *staa*-terr) the States, United States
***foreskrive** (*faw*-rer-skree-ver) *v* prescribe
***foreslå** (*faw*-rer-shlaw) *v* propose, suggest
***forespørre** (*faw*-rer-spur-rer) *v* inquire, query, enquire
forespørsel (*faw*-rer-spur-sherl) *m* (pl -sler) inquiry, query, enquiry
forestille (*faw*-rer-sti-ler) *v* represent; **~ seg** conceive; imagine, fancy
forestilling (*faw*-rer-sti-ling) *c* show, performance; idea, conception
foretak (*faw*-rer-taak) *nt* undertaking; concern
***foretrekke** (*faw*-rer-treh-ker) *v* prefer; **å ~** preferable
forfader (*for*-faa-derr) *m* (pl -fedre) ancestor
forfallen (for-*fahl*-lern) *adj* dilapidated
forfalske (for-*fahl*-sker) *v* counterfeit, forge
forfalskning (for-*fahlsk*-ning) *m* fake
forfalt (for-*fahlt*)*adj*overdue
forfatter (for-*faht*-terr) *m* author, writer
forfengelig (for-*fehng*-nger-li) *adj* vain
forferdelig (for-*fæ*-der-li) *adj* awful, dreadful, frightful, terrible
forfremme (for-*frehm*-mer) *v* promote
forfremmelse (for-*frehm*-

merl-ser) *m* promotion
forfriske (for-*friss*-ker) *v* refresh
forfriskende (for-*friss*-ker-ner) *adj* refreshing
forfriskning (for-*frisk*-ning) *m* refreshment
***forfølge** (for-*furl*-ler) *v* pursue, chase
forføre (for-*fūr*-rer) *v* seduce
forgasser (for-*gahss*-serr) *m* carburettor
forgifte (for-*ʸif*-ter) *v* poison
forgjenger (*for*-ʸeh-ngerr) *m* predecessor
forgjeves (for-*ʸāy*-verss) *adv* in vain; *adj* vain
forglemmelse (for-*glehm*-merl-ser) *m* oversight
forgrunn (*for*-grewn) *m* foreground
forgylt (for-*ʸewlt*) *adj* gilt
i forgårs (ee *for*-gosh) the day before yesterday
***forgå seg** (for-*gaw*) offend
forhandle (for-*hahnd*-ler) *v* negotiate
forhandler (for-*hahnd*-lerr) *m* dealer
forhandling (for-*hahnd*-ling) *c* negotiation
forhastet (for-*hahss*-tert) *adj* rash; premature
forhenværende (*for*-hehn-vææ-rer-ner) *adj* former
forhindre (*for*-hin-drer) *v* prevent; inhibit
forhold (*for*-hol) *nt* (pl ~) relation; affair
forholdsmessig (*for*-hols-meh-si) *adj* proportional
forhør (*for*-hūrr) *nt* (pl ~) interrogation, examination
forhøre (for-*hūr*-rer) *v* interrogate; ~ **seg** inquire
på forhånd (po *for*-hon) in advance
forhåndsbetalt (*for*-hons-beh-tahlt) *adj* prepaid
forhåndsvisning (*for*-hons-visning) *m*preview
forkaste (for-*kahss*-ter) *v* reject, turn down
forkjemper (*for*-khehm-perr) *m* champion
forkjærlighet (*for*-khææ-li-hāyt) *c* preference
forkjølelse (for-*khūr*-lerl-ser) *m* cold; ***bli forkjølet** *catch a cold
forkjørsrett (*for*-khūrsh-reht) *m* right of way
forklare (for-*klaa*-rer) *v* explain
forklaring (for-*klaa*-ring) *c* explanation
forkle (*for*-kler) *nt* (pl -lær) apron
forkledning (for-*klāyd*-ning) *m* disguise
forkle seg (for-*klāy*) disguise
forkorte (for-*kot*-ter) *v* shorten
forkortelse (for-*ko*-terl-ser) *m* abbreviation
forlange (fo-*lahng*-nger) *v* demand

***forlate** (fo-*laa*-ter) *v* check out, *leave; desert
forleden (fo-*lāy*-dern) *adv* recently
forlegen (fo-*lāy*-gern) *adj* embarrassed; ***gjøre ~** embarrass
forlegenhet (fo-*lāy*-gern-hāyt) *c* embarrassment
***forlegge** (fo-*leh*-ger) *v* *mislay
forlegger (*fo*-leh-gerr) *m* publisher
forlenge (fo-*lehng*-nger) *v* lengthen; extend
forlengelse (fo-*lehng*-ngerl-ser) *m* extension
forlovede (fo-*law*-ver-der) *m* fiancé; fiancée
forlovelse (fo-*law*-verl-ser) *m* engagement
forlovelsesring (fo-*law*-verl-serss-ring) *m* engagement ring
forlovet (fo-*law*-vert) *adj* engaged
forlystelse (fo-*lewss*-terl-ser) *m* entertainment, amusement
***forløpe** (fo-*lūr*-per) *v* pass
form (form) *c* form, shape
formalitet (for-mah-li-*tāyt*) *m* formality
formane (for-*maa*-ner) *v* urge
formann (*for*-mahn) *m* (pl -menn) president, chairman, chairwoman; foreman
format (for-*maat*) *nt* size
forme (*for*-mer) *v* shape, model, form
formel (*for*-merl) *m* (pl -mler) formula
formell (for-*mehll*) *adj* formal
formiddag (*for*-mi-dah) *m* morning
formiddagsmat (*for*-mi-dahks-maat) *m* lunch
forminske (for-*min*-sker) *v* lessen
formodning (for-*mōōd*-ning) *m* guess
formue (*for*-moo-er) *m* fortune
formynder (for-*mewn*-derr) *m* guardian
formynderskap (for-*mewn*-der-shkaap) *nt* custody
formørkelse (for-*murr*-kerl-ser) *m* eclipse
formål (*for*-mawl) *nt* (pl ~) purpose, objective, object
formålstjenlig (*for*-mawls-t^{y}āyn-li) *adj* appropriate
fornavn (*fo*-nahvn) *nt* (pl ~) first name, Christian name
fornemme (fo-*nehm*-mer) *v* perceive
fornemmelse (fo-*nehm*-merl-ser) *m* perception; sensation
fornuft (fo-*newft*) *m* reason, sense
fornuftig (fo-*newf*-ti) *adj* reasonable, sensible
fornybar (fo-*nēw*-bāar) *adj* renewable
fornye (fo-*nēw*-er) *v* renew

fornærme (fo-*nær*-mer) *v* offend; insult
fornærmelse (fo-*nær*-merl-ser) *m* offense *Am*, offence; insult
fornøyd (for-*nurewd*) *adj* pleased; glad
fornøyelse (fo-*nur*ew-erl-ser) *m* pleasure
forpakte bort (for-*pahk*-ter bot) lease
forpaktning (for-*pahkt*-ning) *m* lease
forplikte (for-*plik*-ter) *v* oblige; **~ seg** engage; ***være forpliktet til** *be obliged to
forpliktelse (for-*plik*-terl-ser) *m* engagement
forresten (fo-*rehss*-tern) *adv* besides; by the way
forretning (fo-*reht*-ning) *c* store, shop; business
forretninger (fo-*reht*-ningerr) *pl* business; **i ~** on business
forretningskvinne (fo-*reht*-nings-kvin-ner) *c* businesswoman
forretningsmann (fo-*reht*-nings-mahn) *m* (pl -menn) businessman
forretningsmessig (fo-*reht*-nings-meh-si) *adj* business-like
forretningsreise (fo-*reht*-nings-ray-ser) *c* business trip
forretningssenter (fo-*reht*-ning-sehn-terr) *nt* (pl -trer) shopping centre, mall *nAm*
forrett (*for*-reht) hors d'œuvre
forrige (*for*-ʸer) *adj* previous, last, past
forræder (fo-*rāy*-derr) *m* traitor
forræderi (fo-reh-der-*ree*) *nt* treason
forråd (*foar*-rawd) *nt* (pl ~) supply
forråde (fo-*raw*-der) *v* betray
forsamling (fo-*shahm*-ling) *c* assembly, rally
forseelse (fo-*shāy*-erl-ser) *m* offense *Am*, offence, misdemeanour
forsere (fo-*shāy*-rer) *v* force
forside (*fo*-shee-der) *c* front
forsikre (fo-*shik*-rer) *v* assure; insure
forsikring (fo-*shik*-ring) *c* insurance
forsikringspolise (fo-*shik*-rings-poo-lee-ser) *m* insurance policy
forsikringspremie (fo-*shik*-rings-prāy-mi-er) *m* premium
forsiktig (fo-*shik*-ti) *adj* careful, cautious; gentle; wary; ***være ~** watch out
forsiktighet (fo-*shik*-ti-hāyt) *c* caution, precaution
forsinke (fo-*shing*-ker) *v* delay
forsinkelse (fo-*shing*-kerl-ser) *m* delay
forsinket (fo-*shing*-kert) *adj*

overdue
forskjell (*fo*-shehl) *m* distinction, difference; ***gjøre ~** distinguish
forskjellig (fo-*shehl*-li) *adj* different, unlike, distinct; ***være ~** vary, differ
forskning (*foshk*-ning) *m* research
forskole (*fo*-shkōō-ler) *m* kindergarten
forskrekke (fo-*shkrehk*-ker) *v* frighten; ***bli forskrekket** *be frightened
forskrekkelig (fo-*shkrehk*-ker-li) *adj* frightful
forskudd (*fo*-shkewd) *nt* (pl ~) advance; **betale på ~** advance; **på ~** in advance
forslag (*fo*-shlaag) *nt* (pl ~) proposal, suggestion, proposition; motion
forsoning (fo-*shōō*-ning) *c* reconciliation
***forsove seg** (fo-*shaw*-ver) *oversleep
forsprang (*fo*-shprahng) *nt* (pl ~) lead
forstad (*fo*-shtaad) *m* (pl -steder) suburb; **forstads-** suburban
forstand (fo-*shtahnn*) *m* reason; brain, wits *pl*, intellect
forstavelse (*fo*-shtaa-verl-ser) *m* prefix
forstmann (*fosht*-mahn) *m* (pl -menn) forester
forstoppelse (fo-*shtop*-perl-ser) *m* constipation
forstue (fo-*shtēw*-er) *v* sprain
forstuing (fo-*shtēw*-ing) *c* sprain
forstyrre (fo-*shtewr*-rer) *v* disturb; *upset
forstyrrelse (fo-*shtewr*-rerl-ser) *m* disturbance
forstørre (fo-*shturr*-rer) *v* enlarge; magnify
forstørrelse (fo-*shturr*-rerl-ser) *m* enlargement
forstørrelsesglass (fo-*shturr*-rerl-serss-glahss) *nt* (pl ~) magnifying glass
***forstå** (fo-*shtaw*) *v* *understand; *see
forståelse (fo-*shtaw*-erl-ser) *m* understanding
forsvar (*fo*-shvaar) *nt* defense *Am*, defence
forsvare (fo-*shvaa*-rer) *v* defend
forsvarstale (*fo*-shvaa-sh-taa-ler) *m* plea
***forsvinne** (fo-*shvin*-ner) *v* disappear, vanish
forsvunnet (fo-*shvewn*-nert) *adj* lost
forsyne (fo-*shēw*-ner) *v* provide, furnish, supply; **~ med** furnish with
forsyning (fo-*shēw*-ning) *c* stock
forsøk (*fo*-shūrk) *nt* (pl ~) try, attempt; trial; experiment
forsøke (fo-*shūr*-ker) *v* try, attempt
forsømme (fo-*shurm*-mer)

v neglect; fail
forsømmelse (fo-*shurm*-merl-ser) *m* neglect
fort (foott) *adv* quickly
***forta seg** (fo-*taa*) *wear away
fortau (*fo*-tou) *nt* (pl ~) pavement; sidewalk *nAm*
fortauskant (*fo*-touss-kahnt) *m* curb
***fortelle** (fo-*tehl*-ler) *v* *tell; relate
fortelling (fo-*tehl*-ling) *c* story, tale
forte seg (*foot*-ter) hurry
fortid (*fo*-teed) *c* past
fortjene (fo-*tʸay*-ner) *v* deserve, merit
fortjeneste (fo-*tʸay*-nerss-ter) *m* profit, gain; merit
fortred (fo-*trayd*) *m* harm, mischief
fortrinnsrett (*fo*-trins-reht) *m* priority
fortryllelse (fo-*trewl*-lerl-ser) *m* spell
fortryllende (fo-*trewl*-ler-ner) *adj* charming
***fortsette** (*fot*-seh-ter) *v* continue; *keep on, carry on, *go on, proceed, *go ahead
fortsettelse (*fot*-seh-terl-ser) *m* sequel
fortvile (fo-*tvee*-ler) *v* despair
fortvilet (fo-*tvee*-lt) *adj* desperate
fortynne (fo-*tewn*-ner) *v* dilute
forundre (for-*ewn*-drer) *v* amaze
forundring (for-*ewn*-dring) *c* wonder
forurense (*for*-rew-rehn-ser) *v* pollute
forurensning (*for*-rew-rehns-ning) *m* pollution
forurolige (*for*-rew-roo-li-er) *v* alarm
foruroligende (*for*-rew-roo-li-er-ner) *adj* scary
foruten (for-*ew*-tern) *prep* besides
forutgående (*for*-rewt-gaw-er-ner) *adj* prior
forutsatt at (*for*-ewt-sahtt ahtt) provided that, supposing that
***forutse** (*for*-rewt-say) *v* anticipate
***forutsi** (*for*-rewt-see) *v* predict, forecast
forutsigelse (*for*-rewt-see-erl-ser) *m* prediction
forvaltende (for-*vahl*-ter-ner) *adj* administrative
forvaltningsrett (for-*vahlt*-nings-reht) *m* administrative law
forvandle (for-*vahnd*-ler) *v* transform; **forvandles til** turn into
forvaring (for-*vaa*-ring) *c* custody
forveksle (for-*vehk*-shler) *v* *mistake, confuse
forventning (for-*vehnt*-ning) *m* expectation
forvirre (for-*veer*-rer) *v*

confuse
forvirret (for-*veer*-rert) *adj* confused
forvirring (for-*veer*-ring) *c* confusion; disturbance; muddle
forårsake (*for*-ro-shaa-ker) *v* cause
foss (foss) *m* waterfall
fossestryk (*foss*-ser-strewk) *nt* (pl ~) rapids *pl*
fot (foot) *m* (pl føtter) foot; **til fots** on foot, walking
fotball (*foot*-bahl) *m* soccer; football
fotballkamp (*foot*-bahl-kahmp) *m* football match
fotbrems (*foot*-brehms) *m* foot brake
fotgjenger (*foot*-ʸehng-err) *m* pedestrian
fotgjengerovergang (*foot*-ʸayng-err-aw-verr-gahng) *m* crossing, pedestrian crossing; crosswalk *nAm*
fotoforretning (*foo*-too-fo-reht-ning) *c* camera shop
fotograf (foo-too-*graaf*) *m* photographer
fotografere (foo-too-grah-*fay*-rer) *v* photograph
fotografering (foo-too-grah-*fay*-ring) *c* photography
fotografi (foo-too-grah-*fee*) *nt* photograph, photo
fotografiapparat (foo-too-grah-*fee*-ah-pah-raat) *nt* camera
fotokopi (*foot*-too-koo-pee) *m* photocopy
fotokopiere (*foo*-too-koo-pee-*ay*-rer) *v* photocopy
fottur (*foot*-tewr) *m* hike
fra (fraa) *prep* from; out of; as from; **~ og med** from, as from
fradrag (*fraa*-draag) *nt* (pl ~) deduction; rebate
fraflytte (*fraa*-flew-ter) *v* vacate
frakk (frahkk) *m* coat, overcoat
frakt (frahkt) *c* cargo, freight
frankere (frahng-*kay*-rer) *v* stamp
franko (*frahng*-koo) *adv* post-paid
Frankrike (*frahngk*-ree-ker) France
fransk (frahnsk) *adj* French
franskmann (*frahnsk*-mahn) *m* (pl -menn) Frenchman
fraråde (*fraa*-raw-der) *v* dissuade from
frastøtende (*fraa*-stūr-ter-ner) *adj* revolting, repellent, repulsive
***frata** (*fraa*-taa) *v* deprive of
***fratre** (*fraa*-tray) *v* resign
fravær (*fraa*-væær) *nt* (pl ~) absence
fraværende (*fraa*-vææ-rer-ner) *adj* absent
fred (frayd) *m* peace
fredag (*fray*-dah) *m* Friday
fredelig (*fray*-der-li) *adj* peaceful

frekk (frehkk) *adj* insolent, bold, *colloquial* cheeky
frekkhet (*frehk*-hay̅t) *c* impertinence
frekvens (freh-*kvehns*) *m* frequency
frelse (*frehl*-ser) *v* redeem, save; *m* salvation
frem (frehmm) *adv* forward
fremad (*frehm*-maad) *adv* forward
fremadstrebende (*frehm*-maad-stray̅-ber-ner) *adj* go-ahead
***frembringe** (*frehm*-bri-nger) *v* effect
fremdeles (frehm-*day̅*-lerss) *adv* still
fremgang (*frehm*-gahng) *m* prosperity
fremgangsmåte (*frehm*-gahngs-maw-ter) *m* approach; method, process, procedure
***fremgå** (*frehm*-gaw) *v* appear
fremkalle (*frehm*-kah-ler) *v* develop
fremme (*frehm*-mer) *v* promote
fremmed (*frehm*-merd) *adj* strange; foreign; *m* stranger
fremover (*frehm*-maw-verr) *adv* onwards, ahead
fremragende (*frehm*-raa-ger-ner) *adj* outstanding, excellent
fremskritt (*frehm*-skrit) *nt* (pl ~) progress; advance; ***gjøre ~** *get on, advance
fremstille (*frehm*-sti-ler) *v* produce
fremstående (*frehm*-staw-er-ner) *adj* distinguished
fremtid (*frehm*-tee) *c* future
fremtidig (*frehm*-tee-di) *adj* future
fremtoning (*frehm*-too̅-ning) *m* appearance
***fremtre** (*frehm*-tray̅) *v* appear
fremtredende (*frehm*-tray̅-der-ner) *adj* outstanding, distinguished
fremvise (*frehm*-vee-ser) *v* exhibit
fri (free) *adj* free
fribillett (*free*-bi-leht) *m* free ticket
frifinnelse (*free*-fi-nerl-ser) *m* acquittal
frigjørelse (*free*-[y]u̅r̅-rerl-ser) *m* emancipation
frihet (*free*-hay̅t) *c* freedom, liberty
friidrett (*free*-id-reht) *m* athletics *pl*
friksjon (frik-*shoo̅n*) *m* friction
frikvarter (*free*-kvah-tay̅r) *nt* break; recess *nAm*
frimerke (*free*-mær-ker) *nt* postage stamp, stamp
frimerkeautomat (*free*-mær-ker-ou-too-maat) *m* stamp machine
frisk (frisk) *adj* well; **bli ~** recover
frist (frist) *m* term

friste (*friss*-ter) *v* tempt
fristelse (*friss*-terl-ser) *m* temptation
frisyre (fri-*sew*-rer) *m* hair-do
frisør (fri-*surr*) *m* hairdresser
***frita** (*free*-taa) *v* exempt; ~ **for** discharge of
fritak (*free*-taak) *nt* exemption
fritatt (*free*-taht) *adj* exempt
fritid (*free*-teed) *c* spare time; leisure
frivillig[1] (*free*-vi-li) *adj* voluntary
frivillig[2] (*free*-vi-li) *m* (pl ~e) volunteer
frokost (*froo*-kost) *m* breakfast
from (fromm) *adj* pious
frontlys (*front*-lewss) *nt* (pl ~) headlamp, headlight
frontrute (*front*-rew-ter) *c* windscreen; windshield *nAm*
frosk (frosk) *m* frog
frossen (*fross*-sern) *adj* frozen
frost (frost) *m* frost
frotté (fro-*tay*) *m* towel(l)ing, terry(cloth)
frue (*frew*-er) *c* madam; mistress
frukt (frewkt) *m* fruit
fruktbar (*frewkt*-baar) *adj* fertile
frukthage (*frewkt*-haa-ger) *m* orchard
fruktsaft (*frewkt*-sahft) *m* squash
fryd (frewd) *m* delight, joy
frykt (frewkt) *m* fear, dread
frykte (*frewk*-ter) *v* fear, dread
fryktelig (*frewk*-ter-li) *adj* terrible, dreadful
frynse (*frewn*-ser) *c* fringe
fryse (*frew*-ser) *v* *freeze
***fryse** (*frew*-ser) *v* *freeze
fryseboks (*frew*-ser-boks) *m* freezer
frysepunkt (*frew*-ser-pewngt) *nt* freezing point
fryser (*frew*-serr) *m* freezer
frysevæske (*frew*-ser-vehss-ker) *c* antifreeze
frø (frur) *nt* seed
fugl (fewl) *m* bird
fukte (*fook*-ter) *v* moisten, damp
fuktig (*fook*-ti) *adj* wet, damp, humid, moist
fuktighet (*fook*-ti-hayt) *c* damp, humidity, moisture
fuktighetskrem (*fook*-ti-hayts-kraym) *m* moisturizing cream
full (fewll) *adj* full; drunk
fullende (*fewl*-leh-ner) *v* accomplish, complete, finish
fullføre (*fewl*-fur-rer) *v* complete
fullkommen (*fewl*-ko-mern) *adj* perfect
fullkommenhet (*fewl*-ko-mern-hayt) *c* perfection
fullsatt (*fewl*-saht) *adj* full up

fullstappet (*fewl*-stah-pert) *adj* chockfull
fullstendig (fewl-*stehn*-di) *adv* altogether, *adj* total; utter, whole, complete
fundament (fewn-dah-*mehnt*) *nt* base
fundamental (fewn-dah-mehn-*taal*) *adj* fundamental
fungere (fewng-*gay*-rer) *v* work
funklende (*foongk*-ler-ner) *adj* sparkling
funksjon (fewngk-*shoon*) *m* function; operation
funksjonshemmet (fewngk-*shoons*-hemmert) *m* disabled
fure (*few*-rer) *m* groove
furu (*few*-rew) *c* pine
fusjon (few-*shoon*) *m* fusion; merger
fusjonere (few-shoon-*ay*-rer) *v* fusion; merge
fy! (few) shame!
fyldig (*fewl*-di) *adj* bulky; plump
fylke (*fewl*-ker) *nt* province
fyll (fewll) *nt* filling
fylle (*fewl*-ler) *v* fill; **~ opp** fill up; **~ ut** fill in; fill out *Am*
fyllepenn (*fewl*-ler-pehn) *m* fountainpen
fylt (fewlt) *adj* stuffed
fyr (fewr) *m* chap, fellow
fyring (*few*-ring) *c* heating
fyrstikk (*fewsh*-tik) *m* match
fyrstikkeske (*fewsh*-ti-kehss-ker) *c* match-box
fyrtårn (*few*-tawn) *nt* (pl ~) lighthouse
fysiker (*few*-si-kerr) *m* physicist
fysikk (few-*sikk*) *m* physics
fysiologi (few-si-oo-loo-*gee*) *m* physiology
fysisk (*few*-sisk) *adj* physical
føde (*fur*-der) *c* nourishment
fødested (*fur*-der-stayd) *nt* place of birth
fødsel (*furt*-serl) *m* (pl -sler) birth; childbirth
fødselsdag (*furt*-serls-daag) *m* birthday
fødselsveer (*furt*-serls-vay-err) *pl* labo(u)r pains
født (furtt) *adj* born
følbar (*furl*-baar) *adj* tangible
føle (*fur*-ler) *v* *feel
følelig (*fur*-ler-li) *adj* perceptible
følelse (*fur*-lerl-ser) *m* sensation, feeling; emotion
følelsesløs (*fur*-lerl-serss-lurss) *adj* numb
følesans (*fur*-ler-sahns) *m* touch
følge (*furl*-ler) *m* consequence; result; *v* følge ***holde ~ med** *keep up with
***følge** (*furl*-ler) *v* follow, accompany
følgende (*furl*-ger-ner) *adj*

subsequent, following
følsom (*fūrl*-som) *adj* sensitive
før (fūrr) *conj* before; *prep* before
føre (*fūr*-rer) *v* *lead, conduct
fører (*fūr*-rerr) *m* leader; driver, conductor
førerhund (*fūr*-rerr-hewn) *m* guide dog
førerkort (*fūr*-rerr-kot) *nt* (pl ~) driving licence, driver's license *Am*
førerskap (*fūr*-rer-shkaap) *nt* leadership
først (fursht) *adv* at first; **~ og fremst** especially, essentially
første (*fursh*-ter) *num* first; *adj* foremost, primary
førstehjelp (*fursh*-ter-ʸehlp) *c* first aid
førstehjelpsskrin (*fursh*-ter-ʸehlp-skreen) *nt* first aid kit
førstehjelpsstasjon (*fursh*-ter-ʸehlp-stah-shōōn) *m* first aid post
førsteklasses (*fursh*-ter-klah-serss) *adj* first-class, first-rate
førsterangs (*fursh*-ter-rahngs) *adj* first-rate
førti (*furt*-ti) *num* forty
føydal (fur^ew^-*daal*) *adj* feudal
få (faw) *adj* few
***få** (faw) *v* *get; obtain, receive; *have; **~ til å** cause to
fårekjøtt (*faw*-rer-khurtt) *nt* mutton

G

gaffel (*gahf*-ferl) *m* (pl gafler) fork
gal (gaal) *adj* wrong, false; mad, crazy
galge (*gahl*-ger) *m* gallows *pl*
galle (*gahl*-ler) *m* bile, gall
galleblære (*gahl*-ler-blææ-rer) *c* gall bladder
galleri (gah-ler-*ree*) *nt* gallery
gallestein (*gahl*-ler-stayn) *m* gallstone
galopp (gah-*lopp*) *m* gallop
galskap (*gaal*-skaap) *m* madness
gammel (*gahm*-merl) *adj* ancient, old; aged; **gammelt brød** stale bread
gammeldags (*gahm*-merl-dahks) *adj* ancient, old-fashioned; quaint
gang[1] (gahng) *m* time; **en ~** once; some time, some day; **en ~ til** once more; **for en gangs skyld** for once; **gang på gang** time and again; ***gå i ~ med**

*undertake; **med en ~** straight away; **nok en ~** once more
gang[2] (gahngng) *m* aisle; hallway
gangsti (*gahng*-sti) *m* footpath
ganske (*gahn*-sker) *adv* quite, fairly, pretty, rather
gap (gaap) *nt* mouth, throat
garantere (gah-rahn-*tāy*-rer) *v* guarantee
garanti (gah-rahn-*tee*) *m* guarantee
garasje (gah-*raa*-sher) *m* garage
garderobe (gahr-der-*rōō*-ber) *m* (pl ~) wardrobe; checkroom *nAm*, cloakroom
garderobeskap (gahr-der-*rōō*-ber-skaap) *nt* (pl ~) wardrobe, closet *nAm*
gardin (gah-*deen*) *m*/*nt* curtain
garn (gaan) *nt* yarn, knitting wool; net
gartner (*gaht*-nerr) *m* gardener
gasje (*gaa*-sher) *m* pay, salary
gass (gahss) *m* gas
gasskomfyr (*gahss*-koom-few) *m* gas cooker
gassovn (*gahss*-ovnn) *m* gas oven
gasspedal (*gahss*-peh-daal) *m* accelerator
gassverk (*gahss*-værk) *nt* gasworks
gate (*gaa*-ter) *c* street, road
gatekryss (*gaa*-ter-krewss) *nt* (pl ~) crossroads
gave (*gaa*-ver) *c* present, gift
gavekort (*gāāv*-er-kott) *nt* (pl ~) gift card
gavl (gahvl) *m* gable
gavmild (*gaav*-mil) *adj* liberal, generous
gavmildhet (*gaav*-mil-hāyt) *c* generosity
gebiss (geh-*biss*) *nt* denture, false teeth
geit (ʸayt) *c* goat
gelé (sheh-*lāy*) *m* jelly
gelender (geh-*lehn*-derr) *nt* (pl -dre) railing, rail
gemen (geh-*māyn*) *adj* foul, mean
general (geh-ner-*raal*) *m* general
generasjon (geh-ner-rah-*shōōn*) *m* generation
generator (geh-ner-*raa*-toor) *m* generator
generell (sheh-ner-rehll) *adj* universal, general
generøs (sheh-ner-*rūrss*) *adj* generous
geni (sheh-*nee*) *nt* genius
genser (*gehn*-serr) *m* sweater, jersey, pullover, sweatshirt
geografi (geh-oo-grah-*fee*) *m* geography
geologi (geh-oo-loo-*gee*) *m* geology
geometri (geh-oo-meh-*tree*) *m* geometry

gest (shehst) *m* gesture
gestikulere (gehss-ti-kew-*lay*-rer) *v* gesticulate
gevinst (geh-*vinst*) *m* prize
gevær (geh-*vææ*r) *nt* rifle, gun
***gi** (*y*ee) *v* *give; ~ **etter** indulge, *give in; ~ **opp** *v* *give up; ~ **seg** *give in
gift (*y*ift) *c* poison
gifte seg (*yif*-ter) marry
giftig (*yif*-ti) *adj* toxic, poisonous
gikt (*y*ikt) *c* gout
gips (*y*ips) *m* plaster
gir (geer) *nt* gear; **skifte ~** change gear
girkasse (*geer*-kah-ser) *c* gear-box
girstang (*gee*-shtahng) *c* (pl -stenger) gear lever
gissel (*giss*-serl) *nt* (pl gisler) hostage
gitar (gi-*taar*) *m* guitar
gjedde (*yayd*-der) *c* pike
gjeld (*y*ehll) *c* debt
***gjelde** (*yehl*-ler) *v* concern, apply
gjelle (*yehl*-ler) *c* gill
gjemme (*yehm*-mer) *v* *hide
gjenforene (*yehn*-fo-ray-ner) *v* reunite
gjeng (*y*ehngng) *m* gang
gjenlyd (*yehn*-lewd) *m* echo
gjennom (*yehn*-noom) *prep* through; ***gå ~** pass through
gjennombløte (*yehn*-noom-blur-ter) *v* soak
gjennombore (*yehn*-noom-boo-rer) *v* pierce
***gjennomgå** (*yehn*-noom-gaw) *v* *go through, suffer
gjennomreise (*yehn*-noom-ray-ser) *c* passage
gjennomsiktig (*yehn*-noom-sik-ti) *adj* sheer, transparent
gjennomsnitt (*yehn*-noom-snit) *nt* (pl ~) average, mean; **i ~** on the average
gjennomsnittlig (*yehn*-noom-snit-li) *adj* average, medium
gjennomtrenge (*yehn*-noom-treh-nger) *v* penetrate
gjennvinnbar (*yenn*-vinn-bahr) *adj* recyclable
gjenopplivelse (*yehn*-noop-lee-verl-ser) *m* revival
***gjenoppta** (*yehn*-nop-taa) *v* resume
gjensidig (*yehn*-see-di) *adj* mutual
gjenstand (*yehn*-stahn) *m* object; article
***gjenta** (*yehn*-taa) *v* repeat
gjentakelse (*yehn*-taa-kerl-ser) *m* repetition
gjerde (*yææ*-der) *nt* fence
gjerne (*yææ*-ner) *adv* willingly, gladly
gjerning (*yææ-ning*) *c* deed
gjerrig (*yær*-ri) *adj* stingy
gjespe (*yehss*-per) *v* yawn
gjest (*y*ehst) *m* guest
gjesteværelse (*yehss*-ter-

vææ-rerl-ser) *nt* guest room
gjestfri (*ʸehst*-free) *adj* hospitable
gjestfrihet (*ʸehst*-fri-hāyt) *c* hospitality
gjeter (*ʸāy*-terr) *m* shepherd
gjette (*ʸeht*-ter) *v* guess
gjær (ʸæær) *m* yeast
gjære (*ʸææ*-rer) *v* ferment
gjø (ʸūr) *v* bark, bay
gjødsel (*ʸurt*-serl) *c* manure, dung
gjøk (ʸūrk) *m* cuckoo
***gjøre** (*ʸūr*-rer) *v* *do
glad (glaa) *adj* cheerful, glad, joyful, happy; ***være ~ i** love
glans (glahns) *m* gloss
glansløs (*glahns*-lūrss) *adj* mat
glass (glahss) *nt* glass; **glass-** glass
glassmaleri (*glahss*-maa-ler-ree) *nt* stained glass window
glasur (glah-*sēwr*) *m* icing, frosting
glatt (glahtt) *adj* slippery; smooth
glede (*glāy*-der) *c* gladness, joy, delight; *v* please, delight; ***ha ~ av** enjoy; **med ~** gladly
glemme (*glehm*-mer) *v* *forget
glemsom (*glehm*-som) *adj* forgetful
***gli** (glee) *v* *slide, glide; skid, slip
glidefly (*glee*-der-flēw) *nt* (pl ~) glider
glidelås (*glee*-der-lawss) *m* zip, zipper
glimrende (*glim*-rer-ner) *adj* splendid
glimt (glimt) *nt* flash; glimpse
glinse (*glin*-ser) *v* *shine
glis (gleess) *nt* grin
glise (glee-ser) *v* grin
global oppvarming (glōō-*bāal* oop-*vahrm*-ing *c* global warming
globalisere (glōō-*bāal*-ee-*sāyr*-eh) *v* globalize
globalisering (glōō-*bāal*-ee-*shēer*-ing) *c* globalization
globalt posisjonsystem (glōō-*bahlt* poo-sish-*oons*-sews-*taym*) *nt* (pl ~mer) global positioning system (GPS)
globus (*glōō*-bewss) *m* globe
glød (glūrd) *m* glow
gløde (*glūr*-der) *v* glow
***gni** (gnee) *v* rub
gnist (gnist) *m* spark
gobelin (goo-beh-*lehngng*) *nt* tapestry
god (gōō) *adj* good; kind
godkjenne (*gōō*-kheh-ner) *v* approve of, approve
godkjennelse (*gōō*-kheh-nerl-ser) *m* approval
godlynt (*gōō*-lewnt) *adj* good-humo(u)red
godmodig (gōō-*mōō*-di)

adj good-tempered, good-natured
***godskrive** (*goo*-skree-ver) *v* credit
godstog (*goots*-tawg) *nt* (pl ~) goods train; freight train *Am*
godsvogn (*goots*-vongn) wag(g)on*m* (goods)wagon; freight car *Am*
godt (gott) *adv* well
godter (*got*-terr) *pl* candy *nAm*, sweets
***godtgjøre** (*got*-ʸur-rer) *v* *make good
godtgjørelse (*got*-ʸur-rerl-ser) *m* remuneration
godtroende (*goo*-troo-er-ner) *adj* credulous
godvilje (*goo*-vil-ʸer) *m* goodwill
golf (golf) *m* golf; gulf
golfbane (*golf*-baa-ner) *m* golf links, golf course
gondol (gon-*dool*) *m* gondola
grad (graad) *m* degree; grade; **i den ~** so
gradvis (*graad*-veess) *adv* gradually; *adj* gradual
grafisk (*graa*-fisk) *adj* graphic; **~ fremstilling** diagram
gram (grahmm) *nt* gram
grammatikk (grah-mah-*tikk*) *m* grammar
grammatisk (grah-*maa*-tisk) *adj* grammatical
gran (graan) *c* fir tree
granitt (grah-*nitt*) *m* granite
granne (*grahn*-ner) *m* neighbo(u)r
grapefrukt (*grayp*-frewkt) *c* grapefruit
grasiøs (grah-si-*urss*) *adj* graceful
gratis (*graa*-tiss) *adj* free, gratis; free of charge
gratulasjon (grah-tew-lah-*shoon*) *m* congratulation
gratulere (grah-too-*lay*-rer) *v* congratulate
grav (graav) *c* tomb, grave
grave (*graa*-ver) *v* *dig; **~ ned** bury
gravere (grah-*vay*-rer) *v* engrave
gravid (grah-*veed*) *adj* pregnant
gravlund (*graav*-lewn) *m* cemetery
gravstein (*graav*-stayn) *m* tombstone, gravestone
gravør (grah-*vurr*) *m* engraver
gre (greh) *v* comb
grei (gray) *adj* nice; **det er greit** that's fine; OK
greie (gray-er) *v* cope
greker (*gray*-kerr) *m* Greek
gren (grayn) *c* branch
grense (*grehn*-ser) *c* limit, bound, boundary; frontier, border
grenseløs (*grehn*-ser-lurss) *adj* unlimited
grep (grayp) *nt* grasp; clutch, grip
gresk (graysk) *adj* Greek
gress (grehss) *nt* grass

gresshoppe (*grehss*-ho-per) *c* grasshopper
gressløk (*grehss*-lurk) *m* chives *pl*
gressplen (*grehss*-playn) *m* lawn
gresstrå (*greh*-straw) *nt* (pl ~) blade of grass
greve (*gray*-ver) *m* earl, count
grevinne (greh-*vin*-ner) *c* countess
grevskap (*grayv*-skaap) *nt* county
gribb (gribb) *m* vulture
grille (*gril*-ler) *v* grill; barbecue
grind (grinn) *c* gate
***gripe** (*gree*-per) *v* *take, *catch, grasp, seize, grip; **~ inn** intervene, interfere
gris (greess) *m* pig
grisk (grisk) *adj* greedy
griskhet (*grisk*-hayt) *c* greed
grop (groop) *c* pit
grossist (groos-*sist*) *m* wholesale dealer
grotte (*grot*-ter) *c* cave, grotto
grov (grawv) *adj* coarse, gross
grovsmed (*grawv*-smay) *m* blacksmith
gru (grew) *m* horror
grundig (*grewn*-di) *adj* thorough
grunn[1] (grewnn) *m* ground; reason; cause; **på ~ av** owing to, because of, for, on account of
grunn[2] (grewnn) *adj* shallow
grunnlag (*grewn*-laag) *nt* (pl ~) basis; basics
***grunnlegge** (*grewn*-leh-ger) *v* found
grunnleggende (*grewn*-leh-ger-ner) *adj* basic
grunnlov (*grewn*-lawv) *m* constitution
grunnsetning (*grewn*-seht-ning) *m* principle
grunntall (*grewn*-tahll) *nt* cardinal number
gruppe (*grewp*-per) *c* group; party
gruppere (grew-*pay*-rer) *v* classify
grus (grewss) *m* gravel, grit
grusom (*grew*-som) *adj* cruel, harsh; terrible, horrible, grim
gruve (*grew*-ver) *c* pit, mine
gruvearbeider (*grew*-ver-ahr-bay-derr) *m* miner
gruvedrift (*grew*-ver-drift) *c* mining
gryte (*grew*-ter) *c* pot
grøft (grurft) *c* ditch
grønn (grurnn) *adj* green; **grønt kort** green card
grønnsak (*grurn*-saak) *c* vegetable
grønnsakhandler (*grurn*-saak-hahnd-lerr) *m* greengrocer; vegetable man
grøt (grurt) *m* porridge
grå (graw) *adj* grey
grådig (*graw*-di) *adj* greedy

***gråte** (*graw*-ter) *v* *weep, cry
gud (gewd) *m* god
guddommelig (gew-*dom*-mer-li) *adj* divine
gudfar (*gew*-faar) *m* (pl -fedre) godfather
gudinne (gew-*din*-ner) *c* goddess
gudstjeneste (*gewts*-tʸay-nerss-ter) *m* worship, service
guide (gighd) *m* guide
gul (gewl) *adj* yellow
gull (gewll) *nt* gold
gullsmed (*gewl*-smay) *m* jeweller, goldsmith
gulrot (*gewl*-root) *c* (pl -røtter) carrot
gulsott (*gewl*-sot) *m* jaundice
gulv (gewlv) *nt* floor
gulvteppe (*gewlv*-teh-per) *nt* carpet
gummi (*gewm*-mi) *m* rubber, gum
gunstig (*gewn*-sti) *adj* favo(u)rable; cheap
gurgle (*gewr*-gler) *v* gargle
gutt (gewtt) *m* boy; lad
guvernør (gew-veh-*nurr*) *m* governor
gyldig (ʸ*ewl*-di) *adj* valid
gyllen (ʸ*ewl*-lern) *adj* golden
gymnastikk (gewm-nah-*stikk*) *m* physical education, PE; gymnastics *pl*
gymnastikksal (gewm-nah-*stik*-saal) *m* gymnasium
gynekolog (gew-ner-koo-*lawg*) *m* gynaecologist
gynge (ʸ*ewng*-nger) *v* rock
gys (ʸewss) *nt* shudder
gøy (gurᵉʷ) *m* / *nt* fun
gøyal (*gur*ew-ahl) *adj* amusing
***gå** (gaw) *v* *go, walk; pull out; **~ bort** *leave, *go away; pass away; **~ forbi** pass by; **~ forut for** precede; **~ fottur** hike; **~ fra borde** disembark; **~ gjennom** pass through; **~ hjem** *go home; **~ igjennom** *go through; **~ i land** land; **~ inn** enter, *go in; **~ med på** agree; **~ ned** descend; **~ om bord** embark; **~ over** cross; **~ sin vei** depart; **~ tilbake** *get back; **~ til verks** proceed; **~ ut** *go out; **~ videre** *go ahead, *go on
i går (i-*gawr*) yesterday
gårdsplass (*gawsh*-plahss) *m* backyard, courtyard
gås (gawss) *c* (pl gjess) goose
gåsehud (*gaw*-ser-hewd) *c* goose flesh
gåte (*gaw*-ter) *c* puzzle, enigma, riddle
gåtefull (*gaw*-ter-fewl) *adj* mysterious

H

***ha** (haa) *v* *have; **~ noe imot** mind; **~ på seg** *wear; **~ det!** bye-bye
hage (*haa*-ger) *m* garden
hagl (hahgl) *nt* hail; buckshot
hai (high) *m* shark
haike (*high*-ker) *v* hitchhike
haiker (*high*-kerr) *m* hitchhiker
hake (*haa*-ker) *c* chin
hakke (*hahk*-ker) *v* chop
hale (*haa*-ler) *m* tail
hallo! (hah-*l͞o͞o*) hello!
halm (hahlm) *m* straw
halmtak (*hahlm*-taak) *nt* (pl ~) thatched roof
hals (hahls) *m* throat, neck
halsbrann (*hahls*-brahn) *m* heartburn
halsbånd (*hahls*-bon) *nt* (pl ~) collar
halsesyke (*hahl*-ser-s͞e͞w-ker) *m* sore throat
halskjede (*hahls*-kh͞ay-der) *nt* necklace
halt (hahlt) *adj* lame
halte (*hahl*-ter) *v* limp
halv (hahll) *adj* half; **halv-** semi-
halvdel (*hahl*-d͞ayl) *m* half
halvere (hahl-*v͞ay*-rer) *v* halve
halvsirkel (*hahl*-seer-kerl) *m* (pl -kler) semicircle
halvt (hahlt) *adv* half
halvtid (*hahl*-teed) *c* half time
halvveis (*hahl*-vayss) *adv* halfway
halvøy (*hahl*-lur[ew]) *c* peninsula
ham (hahmm) *pron* him
hamburger (*hahmm*-bur-gerr) *m* hamburger, beefburger, burger
hammer (*hahm*-merr) *m* hammer
hamp (hahmp) *m* hemp
han (hahnn) *pron* he, him; **hann-** male
handel (*hahn*-derl) *m* (pl -dler) commerce, business, trade; deal; ***drive ~** trade; **handels-** commercial
handelsmann (*hahn*-derls-mahn) *m* (pl -menn) tradesman
handelsrett (*hahn*-derls-reht) *m* commercial law
handelsvare (*hahn*-derls-vaa-rer) *m* merchandise
handikap (*hahn*-di-kapp) *nt* handicap
handle (*hahnd*-ler) *v* shop; act; **~ med** *deal with
handlebag (*hahnd*-ler-bæg) *m* shopping bag
handlende (*hahnd*-ler-ner) *m* (pl ~) dealer
handling (*hahnd*-ling) *c* action, act, deed; plot
hane (*haa*-ner) *m* cock
hans (hahns) *pron* his

hanske (*hahn*-sker) *m* glove
hard (haar) *adj* hard
harddisk (*haar*-disk) *m* hard disk
hardnakket (*haanah*-kert) *adj* obstinate
hare (*haa*-rer) *m* hare
harmoni (hahr-moo-*nee*) *m* harmony
harpe (*hahr*-per) *c* harp
harsk (hahshk) *adj* rancid
hasselnøtt (*hahss*-serl-nurt) *c* hazelnut
hast (hahst) *m* haste
hastig (*hahss*-ti) *adj* hasty
hastighet (*hahss*-ti-ha̅y̅t) *c* speed
hastverk (*hahst*-værk) *nt* hurry
hat (haat) *nt* hatred, hate
hate (*haa*-ter) *v* hate, detest
hatt (hahtt) *m* hat
haug (hou) *m* pile, heap; mound
hauk (houk) *m* hawk
hav (haav) *nt* ocean
havmåke (*haav*-maw-ker) *c* seagull
havn (hahvn) *c* port, harbour
havnearbeider (*hahv*-ner-ahr-bay-derr) *m* docker
havneby (*hahv*-ner-be̅w̅) *m* seaport
havre (*hahv*-rer) *m* oats *pl*
hebraisk (heh-*braa*-isk) *nt* Hebrew
hedensk (*ha̅y̅*-dernsk) *adj* pagan, heathen
heder (*ha̅y̅*-derr) *m* glory
hederlig (*ha̅y̅*-der-li) *adj* honourable
hedning (*ha̅y̅d*-ning) *m* pagan, heathen
hedre (*ha̅y̅*-drer) *v* honour
heftig (*hehf*-ti) *adj* severe, violent, fierce
hegre (*ha̅y̅*-grer) *m* heron
hei (hay) *c* heath
heis (hayss) *m* lift; elevator *nAm*
heise (*hay*-ser) *v* hoist
heisekran (*hay*-ser-kraan) *m* crane
hekk (hehkk) *m* hedge
hekle (*hehk*-ler) *v* crochet
heks (hehks) *c* witch
hel (ha̅y̅l) *adj* entire, whole
helbrede (*hehl*-bra̅y̅-der) *v* cure, heal
helbredelse (*hehl*-bra̅y̅-derl-ser) *m* recovery, cure
heldig (*hehl*-di) *adj* lucky, fortunate
heldigvis (*hehl*-di-vis) *adv* luckily, fortunately
hele (*ha̅y̅*-ler) *nt* whole; **i det ~** altogether
helg (hehlg) *c* weekend
helgen (*hehl*-gern) *m* saint
helgenskrin (*hehl*-gern-skreen) *nt* (pl ~) reliquary
helikopter (hehll-ee-*kopp*-terr) *nt* helicopter
helkornbrød (*ha̅y̅l*-ko̅o̅n-bru̅r̅) *nt* (pl ~) wholemeal bread
hell (*hehll*) *nt* luck
Hellas (*hehl*-lahss) Greece
helle (*hehl*-ler) *v* pour; slope

heller (*hehl*-lerr) *adv* sooner, rather
hellig (*hehl*-li) *adj* holy, sacred
helligbrøde (*hehl*-li-brūr-der) *m* sacrilege
helligdag (*hehl*-li-daag) *m* holiday, Sunday
helligdom (*hehl*-li-dom) *m* (pl ~mer) shrine
helling (*hehl*-ling) *c* gradient
helse (*hehl*-ser) *c* health
helseattest (*hehl*-ser-ah-tehst) *m* health certificate
helt[1] (hehlt) *m* hero
helt[2] (hāyt) *adv* wholly, entirely, quite, completely
heltinne (hehlt-*inn*-ner) *c* heroine
helvete (*hehl*-ver-ter) *nt* hell
hemme (*hehm*-mer) *v* inhibit
hemmelig (*hehm*-li) *adj* secret
hemmelighet (*hehm*-li-hāyt) *c* secret
hemorroider (heh-moo-*ree*-derr) *pl* piles *pl*, haemorrhoids *pl*
hende (*hehn*-ner) *v* happen, occur
hendelse (*hehn*-nerl-ser) *m* incident, happening, occurrence
hendig (*hehn*-di) *adj* handy
***henge** (*hehng*-nger) *v* *hang
hengebro (*hehng*-nger-brōō) *c* suspension bridge
hengekøye (*hehng*-nger-kur[ew]-er) *c* hammock
hengelås (*heh*-nger-lawss) *m* padlock
henger (*hehng*-ngerr) *m* hanger
hengiven (*hehn*-[y]ee-vern) *adj* affectionate
hengivenhet (*hehn*-[y]ee-vern-hāyt) *c* affection
hengsel (*hehng*-sherl) *nt* (pl -sler) hinge
henne (*hehn*-ner) *pron* her
hennes (*hehn*-nerss) *pron* her, hers
henrettelse (*hehn*-reh-terl-ser) *m* execution
henrivende (*hehn*-ree-ver-ner) *adj* adorable, delightful, enchanting
henrykt (*hehn*-rewkt) *adj* delighted
hensikt (*hehn*-sikt) *m* intention, purpose, design; ***ha til ~** intend
henstand (*hehn*-stahn) *m* respite
hensyn (*hehn*-sēwn) *nt* regard; **med ~ til** as regards, regarding
hensynsfull (*hehn*-sēwns-fewl) *adj* considerate
hensynsfullhet (*hehn*-sēwns-fewl-hāyt) *c* consideration
hente (*hehn*-ter) *v* fetch; *get, pick up, collect
henvende seg til (*hehn*-veh-ner) address

henvise til (*hehn*-vee-ser) refer to
henvisning (*hehn*-veess-ning) *m* reference
her (hæær) *adv* here
heretter (*hææ*-reh-terr) *adv* from now on
herkomst (*hæær*-komst) *m* origin
herlig (*hææ*-li) *adj* wonderful, lovely, delightful
hermetikk (hær-mer-*tikk*) *m* tinned food
hermetikkboks (hær-mer-*tik*-boks) *m* tin; can *nAm*
hermetikkåpner (hær-mer-*tik*-awp-nerr) *m* tin opener
hermetisere (hær-mah-ti-*sāy*-rer) *v* preserve
herre (*hær*-rer) *m* gentleman
herredømme (*hær*-rer-dur-mer) *nt* dominion
herregård (*hær*-rer-gawr) *m* mansion, manor house
herretoalett (*hær*-rer-too-ah-leht) *nt* men's room
herske (*hæsh*-ker) *v* reign, rule
hersker (*hæsh*-kerr) *m* sovereign
hertug (*hæt*-tewg) *m* duke
hertuginne (hæ-tew-*gin*-ner) *c* duchess
hes (hāyss) *adj* hoarse
hest (hehst) *m* horse
hestekraft (*hehss*-ter-krahft) *c* (pl -krefter) horsepower
hestesko (*hehss*-ter-skōō) *m* (pl ~) horseshoe
hesteveddeløp (*hehss*-ter-veh-der-lūrp) *nt* (pl ~) horserace
het (hāyt) *adj* hot
hete (*hāy*-ter) *m* heat
***hete** (*hāy*-ter) *v* *be called
heteroseksuell (*hāy*-ter-roo-sehk-sew-ehl) *adj* heterosexual
hette (*heht*-ter) *c* hood
heve (*hāy*-ver) *v* raise; *draw, cash
hevelse (*hāy*-verl-ser) *m* swelling
hevn (hehvn) *m* revenge
hi (hee) *nt* den
hierarki (hi-eh-rahr-*kee*) *nt* hierarchy
hikke (*hik*-ker) *m* hiccup
hilse (*hil*-ser) *v* greet; salute; **~ på** say hello to
hilsen (*hil*-sern) *m* greeting
himmel (*him*-merl) *m* (pl himler) sky; heaven
hindre (*hin*-drer) *v* hinder, impede
hindring (*hin*-dring) *c* obstacle, impediment
hinsides (*heen*-see-derss) *prep* beyond
hint (hinnt) *nt* hint; *v* **~e** hint
hiphop (*hipp*-hopp) *c* hip--hop
hissig (*hiss*-si) *adj* hot--tempered, quick-tempered
historie (hiss-*tōō*-ri-er) *c* history

historiker (hiss-*too*-ri-kerr) *m* historian
historisk (hiss-*too*-risk) *adj* historic, historical
hittegods (*hit*-ter-goots) *nt* lost and found
hittegodskontor (*hit*-ter-goots-koon-toor) *nt* lost property office
hittil (*heet*-til) *adv* so far
hjelm (ʸehlm) *m* helmet
hjelp (ʸehlp) *c* aid, assistance, help; relief
***hjelpe** (ʸ*ehl*-per) *v* help, aid; support, assist
hjelper (ʸ*ehl*-perr) *m* helper
hjelpsom (ʸehlp-som) *adj* helpful
hjem (ʸehmm) *nt* home
hjemlengsel (ʸ*ehm*-lehng-serl) *m* homesickness
hjemme (ʸ*ehm*-mer) *adv* at home
hjemmelaget (ʸ*ehm*-mer-laa-gert) *adj* home-made
hjemover (ʸ*ehm*-maw-verr) *adv* homeward
hjemreise (ʸ*ehm*-ray-ser) *c* return journey
hjerne (ʸ*ææ*-ner) *m* brain
hjernerystelse (ʸ*ææ*-ner-rewss-terl-ser) *m* concussion
hjerte (ʸ*æt*-ter) *nt* heart
hjerteanfall (ʸ*æt*-ter-ahn-fahl) *nt* (pl ~) heart attack
hjerteklapp (ʸ*æt*-ter-klahp) *m* palpitation
hjertelig (ʸ*æt*-li) *adj* cordial, hearty
hjerteløs (ʸ*æt*-ter-lurss) *adj* heartless
hjort (ʸott) *m* deer
hjul (ʸewl) *nt* wheel
hjørne (ʸ*ur*-ner) *nt* corner
hode (*hoo*-der) *nt* head; **på hodet** upside down
hodepine (*hoo*-der-pee-ner) *c* headache
hodepute (*hoo*-der-pew-ter) *c* pillow
hoff (hoff) *nt* court
hofte (*hof*-ter) *c* hip
hold (holl) *nt* stitch
***holde** (*hol*-ler) *v* *hold; *keep; **~ oppe** *hold up; **~ opp med** stop; **~ på** *hold; **~ på med** *keep at; **~ seg borte fra** *keep away from; **~ seg fast** *hold on; **~ tilbake** keep back, *withhold **~ ut** *keep up; *bear, endure; **~ utkikk etter** watch for
holdeplass (*hol*-ler-plahss) *m* stop
holdning (*hold*-ning) *m* position, attitude
Holland (*hol*-lahn) Holland
hollandsk (*hol*-lahnsk) *adj* Dutch
hollender (*hol*-lehn-derr) *m* Dutchman
homofil (hoo-moo-*feel*) *adj* homosexual, gay *colloquial*; lesbian
honning (*hon*-ning) *m* honey
honorar (hoo-noo-*raar*) *nt* fee

hop (ho͞op) *m* lot; heap
hopp (hopp) *nt* jump, leap, hop
hoppe[1] (*hop*-per) *v* jump; skip, hop; *leap; **~ over** skip
hoppe[2] (*hop*-per) *c* mare
hore (*ho͞o*-rer) *c* whore
horisont (hoo-ri-*sont*) *m* horizon
horisontal (hoo-ri-son-*taal*) *adj* horizontal
horn (ho͞on) *nt* horn
hornorkester (*ho͞o*-nor-kehss-terr) *nt* (pl -tre) brass band
hos (hooss) *prep* with; at
hospital (hooss-pi-*taal*) *nt* hospital
hoste (*hooss*-ter) *v* cough; *m* cough
hotell (hoo-*tehll*) *nt* hotel
hov (ho͞ov) *m* hoof
hoved- (*ho͞o*-verd) capital, cardinal, chief, main, primary, principal
hovedgate (*ho͞o*-verd-gaa-ter) *c* main street
hovedkvarter (*ho͞o*-verd-kvah-tāyr) *nt* headquarters *pl*
hovedledning (*ho͞o*-verd-lāyd-ning) *m* mains *pl*
hovedsakelig (*ho͞o*-verd-saa-ker-li) *adv* mainly
hovedstad (*ho͞o*-verd-staad) *m* (pl -steder) capital
hovedvei (*ho͞o*-verd-vay) *m* thoroughfare, main road
hoven (*haw*-vern) *adj* snooty
hovmester (*hawv*-mehss-terr) *m* (pl -tre) head waiter
hovmodig (hov-*mo͞o*-di) *adj* haughty; proud
hud (hēwd) *c* skin
hudfarge (*hēwd*-fahr-ger) *m* complexion
hukommelse (hew-*kom*-merl-ser) *m* memory
hul (hēwl) *adj* hollow
hule (*hēw*-ler) *c* cave, cavern
hull (hewll) *nt* hole
hulrom (*hēwl*-room) *nt* (pl ~) cavity
humle (*hoom*-ler) *c* bumblebee; *m* hops
hummer (*hoom*-merr) *m* lobster
humor (*hēw*-moor) *m* humo(u)r
humoristisk (hew-moo-*riss*-tisk) *adj* humorous
humpet (*hoom*-pert) *adj* bumpy
humør (hew-*mūrr*) *nt* mood; spirits
hun (hewnn) *pron* she; **hunn-** female
hund (hewnn) *m* dog
hundehus (*hewn*-ner-hēwss) *nt* (pl ~) kennel
hunderem (*hewn*-ner-rehmm) *c* (pl ~mer) lead
hundre (*hewn*-drer) *num* hundred
hurtig (*hewt*-ti) *adj* fast,

quick, rapid
hurtigtaster (*hewt*-ti-tahs-ter) *c* (pl ~e) speed dial(ing)
hurtigtog (*hewt*-ti-tawg) *nt* (pl ~) through train, express train
hus (hewss) *nt* house; **hus-** domestic
husarbeid (*hewss*-ahr-bayd) *nt* housework
husbåt (*hewss*-bawt) *m* houseboat
husdyr (*hewss*-dewr) *nt* (pl ~) domestic animal
huse (*hew*-ser) *v* lodge
huseier (*hewss*-ay-err) *m* landlord
hushjelp (*hewss*-ʸerlp) *c* maid, housemaid
husholderske (*hewss*-ho-lersh-ker) *m* housekeeper
husholdning (*hewss*-hol-ning) *m* housekeeping
huske (*hewss*-ker) *v* remember; recollect; *swing; *m* swing
huslærer (*hewss*-lææ-rerr) *m* tutor
husmor (*hewss*-moor) *c* (pl -mødre) housewife
husrom (*hewss*-room) *nt* accommodation; **skaffe ~** accommodate
husstand (*hew*-stahn) *m* household
husvert (*hewss*-vӕt) *m* landlord, landlady
hutre (*hewt*-rer) *v* shiver
hva (vaa) *pron* what; **~ enn** whatever; **~ som helst** anything
hval (vaal) *m* whale
hvelv (vehlv) *nt* arch
hvelving (*vehl*-ving) *m* vault
hvem (vehmm) *pron* who; **~ som enn** whoever; **~ som helst** anybody; **til ~** whom
hver (vӕӕr) *adj* every, each
hverandre (vӕ-*rahn*-drer) *pron* each other
hverdag (*vӕӕ*-daag) *m* weekday
hvete (*vay*-ter) *m* wheat
hvetebolle (*vay*-ter-bo-ler) *m* bun
hvetebrødsdager (*vay*-ter-brurss-daa-gerr) *pl* honeymoon
hvile (*vee*-ler) *v* rest; *m* rest
hvilehjem (*vee*-ler-ʸehm) *nt* (pl ~) rest home
hvilken (*vil*-kern) *pron* which; **~ som helst** whichever; **hvilke som helst** any
hvin (veen) *nt* shriek
hvis (viss) *conj* if; in case
hviske (*viss*-ker) *v* whisper
hvisking (*viss*-king) *c* whisper
hvit (veet) *adj* white
hvitløk (*veet*-lurk) *m* garlic
hvitting (*vit*-ting) *m* whiting
hvor (voor) *adv* where; how; **~ enn** wherever; **~ mange** how many; **~ mye** how much; **~ som helst** anywhere

hvordan (*voo*-dahn) *adv* how

hvorfor (*voor*-for) *adv* why; what for

hyggelig (*hewg*-ger-li) *adj* pleasant, enjoyable

hygiene (hew-gi-*a̅y̅*-ner) *m* hygiene

hygienisk (hew-gi-*a̅y̅*-nisk) *adj* hygienic

hykler (*hewk*-lerr) *m* hypocrite

hykleri (hewk-ler-*ree*) *nt* hypocrisy

hyklersk (*hewk*-lehshk) *adj* hypocritical

hyl (he̅w̅l) *nt* scream, yell

hyle (*he̅w̅*-ler) *v* scream, yell

hylle (*hewl*-ler) *c* shelf; *v* *pay tribute to

hyllest (*hewl*-lerst) *m* homage, tribute

hymne (*hewm*-ner) *m* hymn

hypotek (hew-poo-*ta̅y̅k*) *nt* mortgage

hyppig (*hewp*-pi) *adj* frequent

hyppighet (*hewp*-pi-ha̅y̅t) *c* frequency

hyssing (*hewss*-sing) *m* twine

hysterisk (hewss-*ta̅y̅*-risk) *adj* hysterical

hytte (*hewt*-ter) *c* cabin, hut; chalet, lodge; cottage

hæl (hæl) *m* heel

høflig (*hurf*-li) *adj* polite, civil

høne (*hu̅r̅*-ner) *c* hen

hørbar (*hu̅r̅r*-baar) *adj* audible

høre (*hu̅r̅*-rer) *v* *hear

hørsel (*hursh*-sherl) *m* hearing

høst (hurst) *m* autumn; fall *nAm*

høste (*hurss*-ter) *v* gather

høvding (*hurv*-ding) *m* chieftain

høvisk (*hu̅r̅*-visk) *adj* courteous

høy[1] (hur^{ew}) *adj* tall, high; loud

høy[2] (hur^{ew}) *nt* hay

høyde (*hur*ew-der) *m* height; altitude, rise

høydepunkt (*hur*ew-der-poongt) *nt* zenith, height

høyderygg (*hur*ew-der-rewgg) *m* ridge

høyere (*hur*ew-er-rer) *adj* superior, higher

høyland (*hur*ew-lahn) *nt* (pl ~) uplands *pl*

høylydt (*hur*ew-lewt) *adj* loud

høyre (*hur*ew-rer) *adj* right; right-hand; **på ~ side** right-hand

høyrød (*hur*ew-ru̅r̅) *adj* crimson

høysesong (*hur*ew-seh-song) *m* peak season, high season

høyslette (*hur*ew-shleh-ter) *c* plateau

høysnue (*hur*ew-snew-er) *m* hay fever

høyst (hur^{ew}st) *adv* at most

høyt (hur^{ew}t) *adv* aloud

høytalertelefon (*hurew-taal-er-tel-e-foon*) *c* speaker phone
høytidelig (hur^ew^-*tee*-der-li) *adj* solemn
høyttaler (*hurew-taa-lerr*) *m* loud-speaker
høyvann (*hurew-vahn*) *nt* high tide
hån (hawn) *m* mockery, scorn
hånd (honn) *c* (pl hender) hand; ***ta ~ om** attend to
håndarbeid (*hon*-nahr-bayd) *nt* needlework; handwork
håndbagasje (*hon*-bah-gaa-sher) *m* hand luggage; hand baggage *Am*
håndbok (*hon*-book) *c* (pl -bøker) handbook, manual
håndbrems (*hon*-brehms) *m* hand-brake
håndflate (*hon*-flaa-ter) *c* palm
håndfull (*hon*-fewl) *m* handful
håndholdt (hon-*holt*) *adj* hand held
håndjern (*hon*-^y^æen) *pl* handcuffs *pl*
håndkle (*hong*-kler) *nt* (pl -lær) towel
håndkrem (*hon*-kraym) *m* hand cream
håndlaget (*hon*-laa-gert) *adj* hand-made
håndledd (*hon*-lehd) *nt* (pl ~) wrist
håndskrift (*hon*-skrift) *c* handwriting
håndtak (*hon*-taak) *nt* (pl ~) handle
håndtere (hon-*tay*-rer) *v* handle
håndterlig (hon-*tay*-li) *adj* manageable
håndtrykk (*hon*-trewk) *nt* (pl ~) handshake
håndvask (*hon*-vahsk) *m* wash-basin; hand wash
håndverk (*hon*-værk) *nt* (pl ~) handicraft
håndveske (*hon*-vehss-ker) *c* bag, handbag
håne (*haw*-ner) *v* mock
håp (hawp) *nt* hope
håpe (*haw*-per) *v* hope
håpefull (*haw*-per-fewl) *adj* hopeful
håpløs (*hawp*-lurss) *adj* hopeless
håpløshet (*hawp*-lurss-hayt) *c* despair
hår (hawr) *nt* hair
hårbalsam (*hawr*-bahl-sahm) *m* conditioner
hårbørste (*hawr*-bursh-ter) *m* hairbrush
håret (*haw*-rert) *adj* hairy
hårfrisyre (*hawr*-fri-sew-rer) *m* hair-do
hårgelé (*hawr*-sheh-*lay*) *m* hair gel
hårklipp (*hawr*-klip) *m* haircut
hårlakk (*haw*-lahk) *m* hair spray
hårskill (*haw*-shil) *m* parting

hårspenne (*haw*-shpeh-ner) *c* hair-pin; bobby pin *Am*

hårtørrer (*haw*-turr-rerr) *m* hairdrier, hairdryer

I

i (ee) *prep* in; for, at

***iaktta** (i-*ahk*-tah) *v* observe, watch

iakttakelse (i-*ahk*-taa-kerl-ser) *m* observation

ibenholt (*ee*-bern-holt) *m*/*nt* ebony

idé (i-*day*) *m* idea

ideal (i-deh-*aal*) *nt* ideal

ideell (i-deh-*ehll*) *adj* ideal

identifisere (i-dehn-ti-fi-*say*-rer) *v* identify

identifisering (i-dehn-ti-fi-*say*-ring) *c* identification

identisk (i-*dehn*-tisk) *adj* identical

identitet (i-dehn-ti-*tayt*) *m* identity

identitetskort (i-dehn-ti-*tayts*-kot) *nt* (pl ~) identity card, ID

idiom (i-di-*oom*) *nt* idiom

idiomatisk (i-di-oo-*maa*-tisk) *adj* idiomatic

idiot (i-di-*oot*) *m* idiot

idiotisk (i-di-*oo*-tisk) *adj* idiotic

idol (i-*dool*) *nt* idol

idrettsmann (*eed*-rehts-mahn) *m* (pl -menn) sportsman

idrettskvinne (*eed*-rehts-*kvin*-ner) *c* sportswoman

ifølge (i-*furl*-ger) *prep* according to

igjen (i-[y]*ehnn*) *adv* again

ignorere (ig-noo-*ray*-rer) *v* ignore

ikke (*ik*-ker) *adv* not

ikke-røyker (*ik*-ker-*rurew*-kerr) *m* non-smoker

ikon (i-*koon*) *m*/*nt* icon

ild (ill) *m* fire

ildfast (*il*-fahst) *adj* fireproof, ovenproof

ildsfarlig (*ils*-faa-li) *adj* inflammable

ildsted (*il*-stayd) *nt* hearth

illegal (*il*-leh-gaal) *adj* illegal

illeluktende (*il*-ler-look-ter-ner) *adj* smelly

illevarslende (*il*-ler-vahsh-ler-ner) *adj* sinister, ominous

illusjon (i-lew-*shoon*) *m* illusion

illustrasjon (i-lew-strah-*shoon*) *m* illustration; picture

illustrere (i-lew-*stray*-rer) *v* illustrate

imens (i-*mehns*) *adv* meanwhile, in the meantime

imidlertid (i-*mid*-ler-ti) *adv*

though; in the meantime
imitasjon (i-mi-tah-*shoon*) *m* imitation
imitere (i-mi-*tay*-rer) *v* imitate
immigrant (i-mi-*grahnt*) *m* immigrant
immigrasjon (i-mi-grah-*shoon*) *m* immigration
immigrere (i-mi-*gray*-rer) *v* immigrate
immun: *gjøre ~ (*ʸur*-rer i-*mewn*) immunize
immunitet (i-mew-ni-*tayt*) *m* immunity
imperium (im-*pay*-ri-ewm) *nt* (pl -ier) empire
imponere (im-poo-*nay*-rer) *v* impress
imponerende (im-poo-*nay*-rer-ner) *adj* impressive, imposing
import (im-*pott*) *m* import
importavgift (im-*pot*-taav-ʸift) *c* import duty
importere (im-po-*tay*-rer) *v* import
importvarer (im-*pot*-vaa-rerr) *pl* imported goods
importør (im-po-*turr*) *m* importer
impotens (im-poo-*tehns*) *m* impotence
impotent (im-poo-*tehnt*) *adj* impotent
improvisere (im-proo-vi-*say*-rer) *v* improvise
impuls (im-*pewls*) *m* impulse
impulsiv (*im*-pewl-seev) *adj* impulsive
imøtekommende (i-*mur*-ter-ko-mer-ner) *adj* obliging
indeks (*in*-dehks) *m* index
inder (*in*-derr) *m* Indian
India (*in*-di-ah) India
indianer (in-di-*aa*-nerr) *m* Indian
indiansk (in-di-*aansk*) *adj* Indian
indirekte (*in*-di-rehk-ter) *adj* indirect
indisk (*in*-disk) *adj* Indian
individ (in-di-*veed*) *nt* individual
individuell (in-di-vi-dew-*ehll*) *adj* individual
Indonesia (in-doo-*nay*-si-ah) Indonesia
indonesier (in-doo-*nay*-si-err) *m* Indonesian
indonesisk (in-doo-*nay*-sisk) *adj* Indonesian
indre (*in*-drer) *adj* internal; inside, inner
industri (in-dew-*stree*) *m* industry
industriell (in-dew-stri-*ehll*) *adj* industrial
industriområde (in-dew-*stree*-om-raw-der) *nt* industrial area
infanteri (in-fahn-ter-*ree*) *nt* infantry
infeksjon (in-fehk-*shoon*) *m* infection
infinitiv (in-*fin*-ni-teev) *m* infinitive
infisere (in-fi-*say*-rer) *v*

infect
inflasjon (in-flah-*shōōn*) *m* inflation
influensa (in-flew-*ehn*-sah) *m* flu, influenza
informasjon (in-for-mah-*shōōn*) *m* information
informasjonskontor (in-for-mah-*shōōns*-koon-*tōōr*) *nt* inquiry office, information bureau
informere (in-for-*māy*-rer) *v* inform
inline rulleskøyter (inn-*læin* rew-ler-shurew-ter) *pl* Rollerblade
infrarød (*in*-frah-rūr) *adj* infra-red
ingefær (*ing*-nger-fæær) *m* ginger
ingen (*ing*-ngern) *pron* nobody, no one; none; *adj* no; **~ av dem** neither
ingeniør (in-shern-*ʸurr*) *m* engineer
ingensteds (*ing*-ngern-stehss) *adv* nowhere
ingenting (*ing*-ngern-ting) *pron* nil, nothing
ingrediens (ing-greh-di-*ehns*) *m* ingredient
initiativ (i-nit-si-ah-*teev*) *nt* initiative
injeksjon (in-ʸehk-*shōōn*) *m* injection
inkludert (in-klew-*dāyt*) *adj* included; **alt ~** all included
inklusive (*in*-klew-seever) *adv* inclusive
inkompetent (*in*-kom-per-tehnt) *adj* incompetent
inn (inn) *adv* in; **~ i** into
innbefatte (*in*-beh-fah-ter) *v* comprise, include
innbille seg (*in*-bi-ler) imagine
innbilsk (*in*-bilsk) *adj* conceited
innbilt (*in*-bilt) *adj* imaginary
innblande (*in*-blah-ner) *v* involve
innblandet (*in*-blah-nert) *adj* concerned, involved
innblanding (*in*-blah-ning) *c* interference
innbringende (*in*-bri-nger-ner) *adj* profitable
innbrudd (*in*-brewd) *nt* burglary
innbruddstyv (*in*-brewds-tēwv) *m* burglar
***innby** (*in*-bēw) *v* ask; invite
innbydelse (in-*bēw*-derl-ser) *m* invitation
innbygger (*in*-bew-gerr) *m* inhabitant
inndele (*in*-dāy-ler) *v* *break down, divide into
inne (*in*-ner) *adv* indoors; inside
***innebære** (*in*-ner-bææ-rer) *v* imply
innehaver (*in*-ner-haa-verr) *m* owner, bearer
***inneholde** (*in*-ner-ho-ler) *v* contain
innen (*in*-nern) *prep* inside; within
innendørs (*in*-nern-dūrsh)

adj indoor
innenfor (*in*-nern-for) *prep* inside; within
innenlands (*in*-nern-lahns) *adj* domestic
innfall (*in*-fahl) *nt* (pl ~) idea; whim; brain wave
innfatning (*in*-faht-ning) *m* frame
innflytelse (*in*-flew̄-terl-ser) *m* influence
innflytelsesrik (*in*-flew̄-terl-serss-reek) *adj* influential
innfødt (*in*-furt) *m* (pl ~e) native
innføre (*in*-fur̄-rer) *v* import; introduce; initiate
innførsel (*in*-fur-sherl) *m* import
innførselstoll (*in*-fur-sherls-tol) *m* duty
inngang (*in*-gahng) *m* entrance, entry; way in
inngangspenger (*in*-gahngs-peh-ngerr) *pl* entrance fee
innhold (*in*-hol) *nt* contents *pl*
innholdsfortegnelse (*in*-hols-fo-tay-nerl-ser) *m* table of contents
inni (*in*-ni) *adv prep* within; inside
innkassere (*in*-kah-sa̅y̅-rer) *v* collect
innledende (*in*-la̅y̅-der-ner) *adj* preliminary
innledning (*in*-la̅y̅d-ning) *m* introduction
innlemme (*in*- la̅y̅m -mer) *v* integrate
innlysende (*in*-lew̄-ser-ner) *adj* obvious
innover (*in*-naw-verr) *adv* inwards
innpakning (*in*-pahk-ning) *m* packing, wrapping
innpakningspapir (*in*-pahk-nings-pah-peer) *nt* wrapping paper
innrede (*in*-reh-der) *v* furnish; decorate
innredning (*in*-reh-dning) *m* furnishing, decoration
innrette (*in*-reht-ter) *v* arrange
innretning (*in*-reht-tning) *m* facilities; gadget
innrømme (*in*-rur-mer) *v* acknowledge, admit
innsamler (*in*-sahm-lerr) *m* collector
innsats (*in*-sahts) *m* achievement; contribution; stake
innsatt (*in*-saht) *m* (pl ~e) prisoner
***innse** (*in*-sa̅y̅) *v* realize, *see
innside (*in*-see-der) *c* inside; interior
innsikt (*in*-sikt) *m* insight
innsirkle (*in*-seer-kler) *v* encircle
innsjø (*in*-shu̅r̅) *m* lake
innskipning (*in*-ship-ning) *m* embarkation
innskrenkning (*in*-skrehngk-ning) *m*

reduction, restriction
***innskrive** (*in*-skree-ver) *v* list, enter, register; ~ **seg** register
***innskyte** (*in*-shew-ter) *v* insert
innskytelse (*in*-shew-terl-ser) *m* impulse
innsprøyte (*in*-sprur^{ew}-ter) *v* inject
innstendig (in-*stehn*-di) *adj* urgent
inntekt (*in*-tehkt) *c* income, earnings
inntektsskatt (*in*-tehkt-skaht) *m* income tax
inntil (*in*-til) *conj* until, till; *prep* till
inntreden (*in*-tray-dern) *m* entrance
inntrengende (*in*-treh-nger-ner) *adj* pressing
inntrykk (*in*-trewk) *nt* impression; ***gjøre ~ på** impress
innvende (*in*-veh-ner) *v* object; ~ **mot** object to
innvendig (*in*-vehn-di) *adv* within
innvending (*in*-veh-ning) *c* objection
innviklet (*in*-vik-lert) *adj* complex, complicated
innvilge (*in*-vil-ger) *v* grant
innvoller (*in*-vo-lerr) *pl* insides, entrails
innånde (*in*-no-ner) *v* inhale
insekt (*in*-sehkt) *nt* insect; bug *nAm*
insektmiddel (*in*-sehkt-mi-derl) *nt* (pl -midler) insecticide, insect repellent
insinuere (in-si-new-ay-rer) *v* hint, insinuate
insistere (in-si-*stay*-rer) *v* insist
inskripsjon (in-skrip-*shoon*) *m* inscription
inspeksjon (in-spehk-*shoon*) *m* inspection
inspektør (in-spayk-*turr*) *m* inspector
inspirere (in-spi-*ray*-rer) *v* inspire
inspisere (in-spi-*say*-rer) *v* inspect
installasjon (in-stah-lah-*shoon*) *m* installation
installere (in-stah-*lay*-rer) *v* install
instinkt (in-*stingt*) *nt* instinct
institusjon (in-sti-tew-*shoon*) *m* institution
institutt (in-sti-*tewtt*) *nt* institution, institute
instruktør (in-strewk-*turr*) *m* instructor
instrument (in-strew-*mehnt*) *nt* instrument
instrumentbord (in-strew-*mehnt*-boor) *nt* (pl ~) dashboard
intakt (in-*tahkt*) *adj* intact; unbroken
integrere (in-teh-*grey*-rer) *v* integrate
intellekt (in-teh-*lehkt*) *nt*

intellect
intellektuell (in-teh-lehk-tew-*ehll*) *adj* intellectual
intelligens (in-teh-li-*gehns*) *m* intelligence
intelligent (in-teh-li-*gehnt*) *adj* intelligent; clever
intens (in-*tehns*) *adj* intense
interessant (in-ter-reh-*sahngng*) *adj* interesting
interesse (in-ter-*rehss*-ser) *m* interest
interessere (in-ter-reh-*sāy*-rer) *v* interest
interessert (in-ter-reh-*sāyt*) *adj* interested
internasjonal (*in*-ter-nah-shoo-naal) *adj* international
Internett (*in*-terr-nett*l*) Internet
intervall (in-terr-*vahl*) *nt* interval
intervju (in-terr-*v[y]ew*) *nt* interview
intet (*in*-tert) *nt* nothing
intetkjønn (*in*-tert-khurn) neuter
intetsigende (*in*-tert-see-er-ner) *adj* insignificant, petty
intim (in-*teem*) *adj* intimate
intrige (in-*tree*-ger) *m* intrigue
introduksjonsskriv (in-troo-dewk-*shōōn*-skreev) *nt* (pl ~) letter of recommendation
introdusere (in-troo-dew-*sāy*-rer) *v* introduce
invadere (in-vah-*dāy*-rer) *v* invade
invasjon (in-vah-*shōōn*) *m* invasion
investere (in-vehss-*tāy*-rer) *v* invest
investering (in-vehss-*tāy*-ring) *c* investment
invitere (in-vi-*tāy*-rer) *v* invite
Irak (i-*raak*) Iraq
iraker (i-*raa*-kerr) *m* Iraqi
irakisk (i-*raa*-kisk) *adj* Iraqi
Iran (i-*raan*) Iran
iraner (i-*raa*-nerr) *m* Iranian
iransk (i-*rahnsk*) *adj* Iranian
Irland (*eer*-lahn) Ireland
ironi (i-roo-*nee*) *m* irony
ironisk (i-*rōō*-nisk) *adj* ironical
irritabel (i-ri-*taa*-berl) *adj* irritable
irritere (i-ri-*tāy*-rer) *v* irritate; annoy
irriterende (i-ri-*tāy*-rer-ner) *adj* annoying
irsk (eeshk) *adj* Irish
is (eess) *m* ice
isbre (*eess*-brāy) *m* glacier
iskald (*eess*-kahl) *adj* freezing
iskrem (*eess*-krāym) *m* ice cream
Island (*eess*-lahn) Iceland
islandsk (*eess*-lahnsk) *adj* Icelandic
islending (*eess*-leh-ning) *m* Icelander
isolasjon (i-soo-lah-*shōōn*) *m* isolation; insulation
isolator (i-soo-*laa*-toor) *m*

insulator
isolere (i-soo-*lay*-rer) *v* insulate; isolate
isolert (i-soo-*layt*) *adj* isolated
Israel (*eess*-rah-ehl) Israel
israeler (iss-rah-*ay*-lerr) *m* Israeli
israelsk (iss-rah-*aylsk*) *adj* Israeli
istedenfor (i-*stay*-dern-for) *prep* instead of
isvann (*eess*-vahn) *nt* iced water
især (i-*sæær*) *adv* especially
Italia (i-*taa*-li-ah) Italy
italiener (i-tah-li-*ay*-nerr) *m* Italian
italiensk (i-tah-li-*aynsk*) *adj* Italian
iver (*ee*-verr) *m* zeal
ivrig (*eev*-ri) *adj* zealous; anxious, eager

J

ja (ʸaa) yes; **~ vel!** well!; OK!
jade (*ʸaa*-der) *m* jade
jage (*ʸaa*-ger) *v* hunt, chase; **~ bort** chase
jakke (*ʸahk*-ker) *c* jacket
jakt (ʸahkt) *c* hunt; chase
jakte (*ʸahk*-ter) *v* hunt
jamre (*ʸahm*-rer) *v* moan
januar (ʸah-new-*aar*) January
Japan (*ʸaa*-pahn) Japan
japaner (ʸah-*paa*-nerr) *m* Japanese
japansk (*ʸaa*-pahnsk) *adj* Japanese
japp (*yahpp*) *c* yuppie
jeg (ʸay) *pron* I
jekk (ʸehkk) *m* jack
jeksel (*ʸehk*-serl) *m* (pl -sler) molar
jente (*ʸehn*-ter) *c* girl
jern (ʸææn) *nt* iron
jernbane (*ʸææn*-baa-ner) *m* railway; railroad *nAm*
jernbaneferje (*ʸææn*-baa-ner-fær-ʸer) *c* train ferry
jernbaneovergang (*ʸææn*-baa-ner-aw-verr-gahng) *m* crossing
jernbanevogn (*ʸææn*-baa-ner-vongn) *c* coach
jernvarehandel (*ʸææn*-vaa-rer-hahn-derl) *m* (pl -dler) hardware store
jernvarer (*ʸææn*-vaa-rerr) *pl* hardware
jersey (*ʸæsh*-shi) *m* jersey
jetfly (*ʸeht*-flew) *nt* (pl ~) jet
jetlag (*ʸett*-læg) *c* jet lag
jevn (ʸehvn) *adj* level; smooth, even
jo (ʸoo) *adv* yes; certainly; **jo … jo** the … the
jobb (ʸobb) *m* job
jockey (*ʸok*-ki) *m* jockey
jod (ʸodd) *m* iodine
jogge (*ʸogg*-er) *v* go

jogging, go running
joggesko (*y*ogg-er-skōō) *pl* running shoes; sneakers; tennis shoes
jolle (*yol*-ler) *c* dinghy
jomfru (*yom*-frēw) *c* virgin
jonglere (*y*on-*gler*-rer) *v* juggle
jonglør (*yon*-glūr) *m* juggler
jord (*y*ōōr) *c* earth; ground, soil
Jordan (*yoo*-dahn) Jordan
jordaner (*y*oo-*daa*-nerr) *m* Jordanian
jordansk (*y*oo-*daansk*) *adj* Jordanian
jordbruk (*yōōr*-brēwk) *nt* agriculture
jordbunn (*yōōr*-bewn) *m* soil
jordbær (*yōōr*-bæær) *nt* (pl ~) strawberry
jordklode (*yōōr*-klōō-der) *m* globe
jordmor (*yōōr*-mōōr) *c* (pl -mødre) midwife
jordskjelv (*yōōr*-shehlv) *m* / *nt* (pl ~) earthquake
jordsmonn (*yōōsh*-mon) *nt* soil
journalist (shoo-nah-*list*) *m* journalist
journalistikk (shoor-nah-li-*stikk*) *m* journalism
jubileum (*y*ew-bi-*lāy*-ewm) *nt* (pl -eer) jubilee; anniversary
jukse (*yook*-ser) *v* cheat
jul (*y*ewl) *c* Christmas, Xmas; **gledelig ~!** Merry Christmas!
juli (*yew*-li) July
juling (*yew*-ling) *c* spanking
jungel (*yoong*-ngerl) *m* jungle
juni (*yew*-ni) June
junior (*yew*-ni-oor) *adj* junior
juridisk (*y*ew-*ree*-disk) *adj* legal
jurisdiksjon (*y*ew-ris-dik-*shōōn*) *m* jurisdiction
jurist (*y*ew-*rist*) *m* lawyer
jury (*yew*-ri) *m* jury
justere (*y*ewss-*tāy*-rer) *v* adjust
juvel (*y*ew-*vāyl*) *m* gem
jøde (*yūr*-der) *m* Jew
jødisk (*yūr*-disk) *adj* Jewish

K

kabaret (kah-bah-*ray*) *m* cabaret
kabel (*kaa*-berl) *m* (pl kabler) cable; **~-TV** cable tv
kabelfjernsyn (*kaa*-berl-f*y*ææn-sēwn) *nt* cable television
kabin (kah-*been*) *m* cabin
kabinett (kah-bi-*nehtt*) *nt* cabinet
kafé (kah-*fay*) *m* café

kafeteria (kah-feh-*tāy*-ri-ah) *m* cafeteria; self-service restaurant
kaffe (*kahf*-fer) *m* coffee
kaffein (kah-feh-*een*) *m* caffeine
kaffeinfri (kah-feh-*een*-free) *adj* decaffeinated
kaffetrakter (*kahf*-fer-trahk-terr) *m* percolator
kai (kigh) *c* dock, quay
kajakk (kah-*yahkk*) *m* kayak
kake (*kaa*-ker) *c* cake
kaki (*kaa*-ki) *m* khaki
kald (kahll) *adj* cold
kalender (kah-*lehn*-derr) *m* (pl -drer) calendar
kalk (kahlk) *m* lime
kalkulator (*kahl*-koo-lah-toor) *m* calculator
kalkun (kahl-*kēwn*) *m* turkey
kalle (*kahl*-ler) *v* call, name
kalori (kah-loo-*ree*) *m* calorie
kalsium (*kahl*-si-ewm) *nt* calcium
kalv (kahlv) *m* calf
kalvekjøtt (*kahl*-ver-khurt) *nt* veal
kalveskinn (*kahl*-ver-shin) *nt* (pl ~) calf skin
kam (kahmm) *m* (pl ~mer) comb
kamerat (kah-mer-*raat*) *m* friend, buddy
kamp (kahmp) *m* fight, battle, combat; struggle; match
kampanje (kahm-*pahn*-ʸer) *m* campaign
kanadier (kah-*naa*-di-err) *m* Canadian
kanadisk (kah-*naa*-disk) *adj* Canadian
kanal (kah-*naal*) *m* channel, canal; **Den engelske ~** English Channel
kanarifugl (kah-*naa*-ri-fēwl) *m* canary
kandidat (kahn-di-*daat*) *m* candidate
kanel (kah-*nāyl*) *m* cinnamon
kanin (kah-*neen*) *m* rabbit
kano (*kaa*-noo) *m* canoe
kanon (kah-*nōōn*) *m* gun
kanskje (*kahn*-sher) *adv* perhaps, maybe
kant (kahnt) *m* edge, verge, rim, border
kantine (kahn-*tee*-ner) *c* canteen
kaos (*kaa*-oss) *nt* chaos
kaotisk (kah-*ōō*-tisk) *adj* chaotic
kapasitet (kah-pah-si-*tāyt*) *m* capacity
kapell (kah-*pehll*) *nt* chapel
kapellan (kah-peh-*laan*) *m* chaplain
kapital (kah-pi-*taal*) *m* capital
kapitalanbringelse (kah-pi-*taal*-ahn-bri-ngerl-ser) *m* investment
kapitalisme (kah-pi-tah-*liss*-mer) *m* capitalism
kapitulasjon (kah-pi-tew-

lah-*shōōn*) *m* capitulation
kapp (kahpp) *nt* cape
kappe (*kahp*-per) *c* coat, cloak
kappløp (*kahp*-lūrp) *nt* race
kapre (*kaap*-rer) *v* hijack
kaprer (*kaap*-rerr) *m* hijacker
kapsel (*kahp*-serl) *m* (pl -sler) capsule
kaptein (kahp-*tayn*) *m* captain
kar (kaar) *nt* vessel; *m* guy
karakter (kah-rahk-*tāyr*) *m* character; mark
karakterisere (kah-rahk-teh-ri-*sāy*-rer) *v* characterize
karakteristisk (kah-rahk-teh-*riss*-tisk) *adj* characteristic
karaktertrekk (kah-rahk-*tāy*-trehk) *nt* (pl ~) characteristic
karamell (kah-rah-*mehll*) *m* caramel
karantene (kah-rahn-*tāy*-ner) *m* quarantine
karat (kah-*raat*) *m* carat
kardinal (kahr-di-*naal*) *m* cardinal
karneval (*kaa*-ner-vahl) *nt* carnival
karosseri (kah-ro-ser-*ree*) *nt* bodywork; body *nAm*
karpe (*kahr*-per) *m* carp
karri (*kahr*-ri) *m* curry
karriere (kah-ri-*ææ*-rer) *m* career
kart (kahtt) *nt* map
kartong (kah-*tongng*) *m* carton; **kartong-** cardboard
karusell (kah-rew-*sehll*) *m* merry-go-round
kaserne (kah-*sææ*-ner) *m* barracks *pl*
kasino (kah-*see*-noo) *nt* casino
kasjmir (kahsh-*meer*) *m* cashmere
kasse (*kahss*-ser) *c* pay desk; crate
kassere (kah-*sāy*-rer) *v* discard
kasserer (kah-*sāy*-rerr) *m* cashier; treasurer; teller *nAm*
kasserolle (kah-ser-*rol*-ler) *m* saucepan
kassett (kah-*sett*) *m* cassette
kassettspiller (kah-*sett*-spi-lerr) *m* recorder
kast (kahst) *nt* throw, cast
kastanje (kah-*stahn*-[y]er) *m* chestnut
kaste (*kahss*-ter) *v* *cast, *throw; toss; ~ **opp** vomit
katakombe (kah-tah-*koom*-ber) *m* catacomb
katalog (kah-tah-*lawg*) *m* catalogue
katarr (kah-*tahrr*) *m* catarrh
katastrofal (kah-tah-stroo-*faal*) *adj* disastrous
katastrofe (kah-tah-*strōō*-fer) *m* catastrophe, calamity, disaster
katedral (kah-ter-*draal*) *m* cathedral

kategori (kah-ter-goo-*ree*) *m* category
kateter (kah-*tāy*-terr) *nt* (pl -tre) desk; catheter
katolsk (kah-*tōōlsk*) *adj* catholic
katt (kahtt) *m* cat
kausjon (kou-*shōōn*) *m* bail, security; guarantee
kaviar (kah-vi-*aar*) *m* caviar
keiser (*kay*-serr) *m* emperor
keiserdømme (*kay*-ser-dur-mer) *nt* empire
keiserinne (kay-ser-*rin*-ner) *c* empress
keiserlig (*kay*-ser-li) *adj* imperial
keivhendt (*khayv*-hehnt) *adj* left-handed
kelner (*kehl*-nerr) *m* waiter, waitress
kenguru (*kehng*-gew-rew) *m* kangaroo
kennel (*kehn*-nerl) *m* kennel
Kenya (*kehn*-ʸah) Kenya
keramikk (kheh-rah-*mikk*) *m* ceramics *pl*; pottery
kikke (*khik*-ker) *v* peep
kikkert (*khik*-kert) *m* binoculars *pl*
kilde (*khil*-der) *m* fountain, source, well, spring; **kildesortering** *c* waste separation
kile (*khee*-ler) *v* tickle; *m* wedge
kilo (*khee*-loo) *m*/*nt* kilogram
kilometer (*khil*-loo-māy-terr) *m* (pl ~) kilometer *Am*, kilometre
kilometertall (*khil*-loo-māy-ter-tahl) *nt* (pl ~) distance in kilometres (*Am* kilometers)
kim (kheem) *m* germ
Kina (*khee*-nah) China
kineser (khi-*nāy*-serr) *m* Chinese
kinesisk (khi-*nāy*-sisk) *adj* Chinese
kinn (khinn) *nt* cheek
kinnbein (*khin*-bayn) *nt* (pl ~) cheek-bone
kinnskjegg (*khin*-shehg) *nt* sideburns *pl*, whiskers *pl*
kino (*khee*-noo) *m* cinema, pictures; movies *plAm*, movie theater *Am*
kiosk (khosk) *m* kiosk
kirke (*kheer*-ker) *c* church; chapel
kirkegård (*kheer*-ker-gawr) *m* graveyard, churchyard
kirketårn (*kheer*-ker-tawn) *nt* (pl ~) steeple
kirsebær (*khish*-sher-bæær) *nt* (pl ~) cherry
kirurg (khi-*rewrg*) *m* surgeon
kirurgi (khi-rewg-*ee*) *c*: **rekonstruktiv ~** reconstructive surgery
kiste (*khiss*-ter) *c* chest; coffin
kjede (*khāy*-deh) *v* bore
kjedelig (*khāy*-der-li) *adj* dull, boring

kjeft (khehft) *m* mouth
kjeks (khehks) *m* (pl ~) cookie; biscuit
kjele (*khay*-ler) *m* kettle
kjelke (*khæl*-ker) *m* sledge, sleigh
kjeller (*khehl*-lerr) *m* cellar
kjelleretasje (*khehl*-lerr-eh-taa-sher) *m* basement
kjemi (kheh-*mee*) *m* chemistry
kjemisk (*khay*-misk) *adj* chemical
kjempe (*khehm*-per) *v* combat, *fight, struggle, battle; *m* giant
kjenne (*khehn*-ner) *v* *know; ~ **igjen** recognize
kjennelse (*khehn*-nerl-ser) *m* verdict
kjennemerke (*khehn*-ner-mær-ker) *nt* feature
kjenner (*khehn*-nerr) *m* connoisseur
kjennetegn (*khehn*-ner-tayn) *nt* (pl ~) characteristic
kjennetegne (*khehn*-ner-tay-ner) *v* mark, characterize
kjennskap (*khehn*-skaap) *nt* knowledge
kjent (khehnt) *adj* noted
kjepphest (*khehp*-hehst) *m* hobby-horse
kjerne (*khææ*-ner) *m* pip; heart, essence, core, nucleus; **kjerne-** nuclear
kjernehus (*khææ*-ner-hewss) *nt* (pl ~) fruit core
kjernekraft (*khææ*-ner-krahft) *c* nuclear energy
kjerre (*khær*-rer) *c* cart
kjertel (*khæt*-terl) *m* (pl -tler) gland
kjetting (*kheht*-ting) *m* chain
kjeve (*khay*-ver) *m* jaw
kjole (*khoo*-ler) *m* gown, dress; frock; **lang** ~ robe
kjæledyr (*khay*-ler-dewr) *nt* (pl ~) pet
kjælenavn (*khay*-ler-nahvn) *nt* (pl ~) nickname
kjær (khæær) *adj* dear
kjæreste (*khææ*-rerss-ter) *m* darling, girlfriend, boyfriend
kjærlig (*khææ*-li) *adj* affectionate
kjærlighet (*khææ*-li-hayt) *c* love
kjærlighetshistorie (*khææ*-li-hayts-hiss-too-ri-er) *c* love story
kjøkken (*khurk*-kern) *nt* kitchen
kjøkkenhage (*khurk*-kern-haager) *m* kitchen garden
kjøkkenhåndkle (*khurk*-kern-hong-kler) *nt* (pl -lær) kitchen towel
kjøkkenredskap (*t*[y]*urk*-kehn-reh-skaap) *nt* utensil
kjøkkensjef (*khurk*-kern-shayf) *m* chef
kjøl (khurl) *m* keel
kjøleskap (*khur*-ler-skaap) *nt* (pl ~) refrigerator, fridge

kjølig (*khur*-li) *adj* chilly, cool
kjønn (khurnn) *nt* sex; gender; **kjønns-** genital
kjønnssykdom (*khurn-sewk*-dom) *m* venereal disease
kjøp (khurp) *nt* purchase; **godt ~** bargain
kjøpe (*khur*-per) *v* purchase, *buy
kjøper (khur-perr) *m* purchaser, buyer
kjøpesenter (*khur*-per-senterr) *nt* shopping centre, mall *nAm*
kjøpesum (*khur*-per-sewm) *m* (pl ~mer) purchase price
kjøpmann (*khurp*-mahn) *m* (pl -menn) shopkeeper; trader, merchant
***kjøpslå** (*khurp*-shlo) *v* bargain
kjøre (*khur*-rer) *v* *drive; *ride; **~ forbi** *overtake; pass *vAm*; **~ for fort** *speed
kjørebane (*khur*-rer-baa-ner) *m* carriageway; roadway *nAm*
kjøretur (*khur*-rer-tewr) *m* drive
kjøretøy (*khur*-rer-tur[ew]) *nt* vehicle
kjøtt (khurtt) *nt* meat; flesh
klage (*klaa*-ger) *v* complain; *m* complaint
klagebok (*klaa*-ger-book) *c* (pl -bøker) complaints book
klamre (*klahm*-rer) *v*: **~ seg til** cling to
klandre (*klahn*-drer) *v* blame
klang (klahngng) *m* tone; sound
klappe (*klahp*-per) *v* clap, applaud
klar (klaar) *adj* clear; serene; ready; ***ha klart for seg** realize; **~ over** aware
***klargjøre** (*klaar*-[y]ur-rer) *v* elucidate, clarify
***klarlegge** (*klaar*-leh-ger) *v* clarify
klart (*klaart*) *adv* certainly
klasse (*klahss*-ser) *c* class; form
klassekamerat (*klahss*-ser-kah-mer-raat) *m* class--mate
klasseværelse (*klahss*-ser-vææ-rerl-ser) *nt* classroom
klassifisere (klah-si-fi-*say*-rer) *v* classify, class
klassisk (*klahss*-sisk) *adj* classical
klatre (*klaht*-rer) *v* climb
klatring (*klaht*-ring) *c* climb
klausul (*klou*-sewl) *m* clause
kle (klay) *v* *become; suit; **~ av seg** undress; **~ på seg** dress; **~ seg** dress; **~ seg om** change
klebe (*klay*-beh) *v* *stick
klebrig (*klayb*-ri) *adj* sticky
klem (klehm) *m* (pl ~mer) hug
klemme (*klehm*-mer) *v*

squeeze; cuddle, hug
klenge (*klehng*-er) *v* cling
klenodie (kleh-*nōō*-di-er) *nt* gem
kleshenger (*klāyss*-heh-ngerr) *m* coat hanger
klesskap (*klāy*-skaap) *nt* (pl ~) wardrobe, closet *nAm*
klient (kli-*ehnt*) *m* client
klikk (klik) *m* set, clique; *nt* click
klikke (klik-ker) *v* click; **~ på plass** click into place
klima (*klee*-mah) *nt* climate
klinikk (kli-*nikk*) *m* clinic
klinkekule (*kling*-ker-kōō-ler) *c* marble
klippe (*klip*-per) *v* *cut; *m* cliff, rock; **~ av** *cut off
klistre (*kliss*-trer) *v* paste; cling; **~merke** *nt* sticker
klo (klōō) *c* (pl klør) claw
kloakk (kloo-*ahkk*) *m* sewer
klok (klōōk) *adj* clever, wise
klokke (*klok*-ker) *c* clock; bell; **klokken ...** at ... o'clock
klokkerem (*klok*-ker-rehm) *c* (pl ~mer) watch-strap
klokkespill (*klok*-ker-spil) *nt* chimes *pl*
klone (*klōō*-neh) *v* clone
kloning (*kloon*-ing) *c* clone
klor (klōōr) *m* chlorine
kloss (kloss) *m* block
klosset (*kloss*-sert) *adj* awkward, clumsy
kloster (kloss-terr) *nt* (pl -tre) convent, monastery, cloister
klovn (klovn) *m* clown
klubb (klewbb) *m* club
klubbe (*klewb*-ber) *c* club
klukke (*klook*-*ker*) *v* chuckle
klump (kloomp) *m* lump
klumpet (*kloom*-pert) *adj* lumpy
klut (klēwt) *m* cloth
***klype** (*klēw*-per) *v* pinch
klær (klæær) *pl* clothes *pl*
klø (klūr) *v* itch
kløe (*klūr*-er) *m* itch
kløft (klurft) *c* chasm, cleft
kløver (*klurv*-verr) *m* clover
kløyve (*klur*ew-ver) *v* *split
knagg (knahgg) *m* peg
knapp (knahpp) *m* button; *adj* scarce
knappe (*knahp*-per) *v* button; **~ opp** unbutton
knappenål (*knahp*-per-nawl) *c* pin
knapphet (*knahp*-hāyt) *c* scarcity, shortage
knapphull (*knahp*-hewl) *nt* buttonhole
knapt (knahpt) *adv* scarcely
kne (knāy) *nt* (pl knær) knee
kneipe (*knay*-per) *c* pub
***knekke** (*knehk*-ker) *v* crack; break
knekt (knehkt) *m* knave
knele (*knāy*-ler) *v* *kneel
knep (knāyp) *nt* trick
kneskål (*knāy*-skawl) *c* kneecap
knipetang (*knee*-per-tahng) *c* (pl -tenger) pincers *pl*

knipling (*knip*-ling) *m* lace
knirke (*kneer*-ker) *v* creak
kniv (kneev) *m* knife
knoke (*knōō*-ker) *m* knuckle
knopp (knopp) *m* bud
knott (knott) *m* knob
knulle (*knewl*-ler) *v vulgar* fuck
knurre (*knewr*-rer) *v* grumble
knuse (knēwser) *v* *break; smash
knust (knēwst) *adj* broken
knute (*knēw*-ter) *m* knot
knutepunkt (*knēw*-ter-poongt) *nt* junction
knytte (*knēw*-ter) *v* tie, knot; **~ til** attach to; **~ opp** untie
knyttneve (*knewt*-nāy-ver) *m* fist
knyttneveslag (*knewt*-nāy-ver-shlaag) *nt* (pl **~**) punch
koagulere (koo-ah-gew-*lāy*-rer) *v* coagulate
kobbe (*kob*-ber) *m* seal
kode (*kōō*-der) *m* code
koffert (*koof*-fert) *m* case, suitcase; trunk
kokain (koo-kah-*een*) *m*/*nt* cocaine
koke (*kōō*-ker) *v* boil
kokebok (*kōō*-ker-bōōk) *c* (pl -bøker) cookery book; cookbook *nAm*
kokk (kokk) *m* cook
kokosnøtt (*kook*-kooss-nurt) *c* coconut
koldtbord (*kolt*-bōōr) *nt* (pl **~**) buffet
kolje (*kol*-ʸer) *c* haddock
kolle (*kol*-ler) *m* hill, peak
kollega (koo-*lāy*-gah) *m* colleague
kolleksjon (kol-lerk-*shōōn*) *n* collection *m*
kollektiv (*kol*-lerk-teev) *adj* collective
kollidere (koo-li-*dāy*-rer) *v* collide, crash
kollisjon (koo-li-*shōōn*) *m* crash, collision
koloni (koo-loo-*nee*) *m* colony
kolonne (koo-*lon*-ner) *m* column
kolossal (koo-loo-*saal*) *adj* enormous, tremendous
koma (*kōō*-mah) *m* coma
kombinasjon (koom-bi-nah-*shōōn*) *m* combination
kombinere (koom-bi-*nāy*-rer) *v* combine
komedie (koo-*māy*-di-er) *m* comedy
komfort (koom-*fawr*) *m* comfort
komfortabel (koom-fo-*taa*-berl) *adj* comfortable
komfyr (koom-*fēwr*) *m* cooker; stove
komiker (*kōō*-mi-kerr) *m* comedian
komisk (*kōō*-misk) *adj* funny, comic
komité (koo-mi-*tāy*) *m* committee
komma (*kom*-mah) *nt* comma

komme (*kom*-mer) *nt* coming
***komme** (*kom*-mer) *v* *come; **~ an på** depend; **~ over** *come across; **~ på** *think of; **~ seg** recover; **~ tilbake** return
kommende (*kom*-mer-ner) *adj* oncoming
kommentar (koo-mehn-*taar*) *m* comment
kommentere (koo-mehn-*tāy*-rer) *v* comment
kommersiell (koo-mæ-shi-*ehll*) *adj* commercial
kommisjon (koo-mi-*shōōn*) *m* commission
kommode (koo-*mōō*-der) *m* chest of drawers; bureau *nAm*
kommunal (koo-mew-*naal*) *adj* municipal
kommune (koo-*mēw*-ner) *m* local authority, municipality
kommunestyre (koo-*mēw*-ner-stēw-rer) *nt* local council
kommunikasjon (koo-mew-ni-kah-*shōōn*) *m* communication
kommuniké (koo-mew-ni-*kāy*) *nt* communiqué
kommunisme (koo-mew-*niss*-mer) *m* communism
kommunist (koo-mew-*nist*) *m* communist
kompakt (koom-*pahkt*) *adj* compact
kompani (koom-pah-*nee*) *nt* company
kompanjong (koom-pahn-*ʸongng*) *m* partner, associate
kompass (koom-*pahss*) *m* / *nt* compass
kompensasjon (koom-pehn-sah-*shōōn*) *m* compensation
kompensere (koom-pehn-*sāy*-rer) *v* compensate
kompetent (koom-per-*tehnt*) *adj* qualified; capable
kompleks (koom-*plehks*) *nt* complex
komplett (koom-*pleht*t) *adj* complete
kompliment (koom-pli-*mahngng*) *m* compliment
komplimentere (koom-pli-mehn-*tāy*-rer) *v* compliment
komplisert (koom-pli-*sāyt*) *adj* complicated
komplott (koom-*plott*) *nt* plot
komponist (koom-poo-*nist*) *m* composer
komposisjon (koom-poo-si-*shōōn*) *m* composition
kompromiss (koom-proo-*miss*) *nt* compromise
kondisjon (koon-di-*shōōn*) *m* physical fitness
konditori (koon-di-too-*ree*) *nt* pastry shop
kondom (koon-*dom*) *nt* condom
kone (*kōō*-ner) *c* wife

konfekt (koon-*fehkt*) *m* chocolate
konferanse (koon-fer-*rahng*-ser) *m* conference
konfidensiell (koon-fi-dehn-si-*ehll*) *adj* confidential
konfiskere (koon-fiss-*kāy*-rer) *v* confiscate
konflikt (koon-*flikt*) *m* conflict
konfrontere (kon-fron-*tāy*-rer) *v* face, confront
konge (*kong*-nger) *m* king
kongelig (*kong*-nger-li) *adj* royal
kongerike (*kong*-nger-ree-ker) *nt* kingdom
kongress (kong-*grehss*) *m* congress
konjakk (kon-*ʸahkk*) *m* cognac
konklusjon (koong-klew-*shōōn*) *m* conclusion
konkret (koong-*krāyt*) *adj* concrete
konkurranse (koong-kew-*rahng*-ser) *m* contest, competition; rivalry
konkurrent (koong-kew-*rehnt*) *m* rival, competitor
konkurrere (koong-kew-*rāy*-rer) *v* compete
konkurs (koong-*kēwsh*) *adj* bankrupt
konsekvens (kon-ser-*kvehns*) *m* consequence
konsentrasjon (koon-sehn-trah-*shōōn*) *m* concentration
konsentrere (koon-sehn-*trāy*-rer) *v* concentrate
konsert (koon-*sætt*) *m* concert
konsertsal (koon-*sæt*-saal) *m* concert hall
konservativ (koon-*sær*-vah-teev) *adj* conservative
konservatorium (koon-sær-vah-*tōō*-ri-ewm) *nt* (pl -ier) music academy
konservere (kon-sær-*vāy*-rer) *v* preserve
konservering (kon-sær-*vāy*-ring) *c* preservation
konsesjon (koon-seh-*shōōn*) *m* license *Am*, licence; concession
konsis (koon-*seess*) *adj* concise
konstant (koon-*stahnt*) *adj* constant; even
konstatere (koon-stah-*tāy*-rer) *v* note; diagnose, ascertain
konstruere (koon-strew-*āy*-rer) *v* construct
konstruksjon (koon-strewk-*shōōn*) *m* construction
konsul (*kon*-sewl) *m* consul
konsulat (kon-sew-*laat*) *nt* consulate
konsultasjon (kon-sewl-tah-*shōōn*) *m* consultation
konsum (koon-*sewm*) *nt* consumption
konsument (koon-sew-*mehnt*) *m* consumer
konsumere (koon-sew-

meh-rer) *v* consume
kontakt (koon-*tahkt*) *m* touch, contact
kontakte (koon-*tahk*-ter) *v* contact
kontaktlinser (koon-*tahkt*-lin-serr) *pl* contact lenses
kontanter (koon-*tahn*-terr) *pl* cash
kontinent (koon-ti-*nehnt*) *nt* continent
kontinental (koon-ti-nehn-*taal*) *adj* continental
kontinuerlig (koon-ti-new-*ay*-li) *adj* continuous
konto (*kon*-too) *m* (pl ~er, -ti) account
kontor (koon-*toor*) *nt* office
kontortid (koon-*too*-teed) *c* office hours, business hours
kontra (*kon*-trah) *prep* versus
kontrakt (koon-*trahkt*) *m* contract; agreement; pact
kontrast (koon-*trahst*) *m* contrast
kontroll (koon-*troll*) *m* control; inspection
kontrollere (koon-troo-*lay*-rer) *v* verify, check, control
kontrollør (koon-troo-*lurr*) *m* supervisor
kontroversiell (kon-troo-væ-shi-*ehll*) *adj* controversial
kontur (kon-*toor*) *m* outline
konversasjon (koon-væ-shah-*shoon*) *m* conversation
konvolutt (koon-voo-*lewtt*) *m* envelope
kooperativ (koo-*op*-rah-teev) *adj* co-operative
koordinasjon (koo-o-di-nah-*shoon*) *m* co--ordination
kopi (koo-*pee*) *m* copy
kopiere (koo-pi-*ay*-rer) *v* copy
kople (kop-ler) *v* connect; ~ **til** connect
kopp (kopp) *m* cup
kopper (*kop*-perr) *pl* smallpox; *nt* copper
kor (koor) *nt* choir
korall (koo-*rahll*) *m* coral
kordfløyel (*kawd*-flur[ew]-erl) *m* corduroy
kork (kork) *m* cork; stopper
korketrekker (*kor*-ker-treh-kerr) *m* corkscrew
korn (koon) *nt* grain, corn
kornåker (*koo*-naw-kerr) *m* (pl -krer) cornfield
korpulent (kor-pew-*lehnt*) *adj* stout, corpulent
korrekt (koo-*rehkt*) *adj* correct
korrespondanse (koo-rer-spoon-*dahng*-ser) *m* correspondence
korrespondent (koo-rer-spoon-*dehnt*) *m* correspondent
korridor (koo-ri-*door*) *m* corridor
korrigere (koo-ri-*gay*-rer) *v* correct
korrupt (koo-*rewpt*) *adj*

corrupt
kors (koshsh) *nt* cross
korsett (ko-*shehtt*) *nt* corset
korsfeste (kosh-*fehss*-ter) *v* crucify
korsfestelse (kosh-*fehss*-terl-ser) *m* crucifixion
korstog (*kosh*-tawg) *nt* (pl ~) crusade
korsvei (*kosh*-vay) *m* road fork
kort (kott) *adj* short; brief; *nt* card
kortfattet (*kot*-fah-tert) *adj* brief
kortslutning (*kot*-slewt-ning) *m* short circuit
kortstokk *m* pack
kortvarig (*kot*-vaa-ri) *adj* momentary
koselig (*kōō*-ser-li) *adj* cosy; nice
kosmetika (koss-meh-*tikk*) *pl* cosmetics *pl*
kost[1] (kost) *m* fare; **~ og losji** room and board, bed and board, board and lodging
kost[2] (koost) *m* broom
kostbar (*kost*-baar) *adj* expensive; precious
koste (*koss*-ter) *v* *cost
kostfri (*kost*-free) *adj* free of charge
kostnad (*kost*-nah) *m* cost
kotelett (ko-ter-*lehtt*) *m* chop
krabbe (*krahb*-ber) *v* crawl; *c* crab
kraft (krahft) *c* (pl krefter) force; energy, power
kraftig (*krahf*-ti) *adj* strong
kraftverk (*krahft*-værk) *nt* power station
krage (*kraa*-ger) *m* collar
kragebein (*kraa*-ger-bayn) *nt* (pl ~) collarbone
krampe (*krahm*-per) *m* cramp; clamp
krampetrekning (*krahm*-per-trehk-ning) *m* convulsion
kran (kraan) *c* crane; tap
krangel (*krahng*-ngerl) *m*/*nt* (pl -gler) dispute, row, quarrel
krangle (*krahng*-ler) *v* quarrel
krater (*kraa*-terr) *nt* crater
kratt (krahtt) *nt* scrub
krav (kraav) *nt* demand, claim; requirement
kreativ (*kreh*-atieev) *adj* creative
kreditor (*krāy*-di-toor) *m* creditor
kreditt (kreh-*ditt*) *m* credit
kredittkort (kreh-*dit*-kot) *nt* (pl ~) credit card
kreere (kreh-*āy*-rer) *v* create
kreft (krehft) *m* cancer
krem (krāym) *m* cream
kremere (kreh-*māy*-rer) *v* cremate
kremgul (*krāy*-m-gēwl) *adj* cream
krenke (*krehng*-ker) *v* offend, injure; trespass
krenkelse (*krehng*-kerl-ser) *m* violation

krenkende (*krehng*-ker-ner) *adj* offensive
kresen (*kraȳ*-sern) *adj* particular
krets (krehts) *m* ring, circle
kretsløp (*krehts*-lūrp) *nt* (pl ~) cycle
kreve (*kraȳ*-ver) *v* require, claim; charge
krig (kreeg) *m* war
krigsfange (*kriks*-fah-nger) *m* prisoner of war
krigsmakt (*kriks*-mahkt) *c* armed forces
krigsskip (*krik*-sheep) *nt* warship
krim (kri-m) *m* detective story
kriminalitet (kri-mi-nah-li-*taȳt*) *m* criminality
kriminell (kri-mi-*nehll*) *adj* criminal
kringkaste (*kring*-kahss-ter) *v* *broadcast
kringkasting (*kring*-kahss-ting) *c* broadcast
krise (*kree*-ser) *c* crisis
kristen[1] (*kriss*-tern) *m* (pl -tne) Christian
kristen[2] (*kriss*-tern) *adj* Christian
Kristus (*kriss*-tewss) Christ
kritiker (*kree*-ti-kerr) *m* critic
kritikk (kri-*tikk*) *m* criticism
kritisere (kri-ti-*saȳ*-rer) *v* criticize
kritisk (*kree*-tisk) *adj* critical
kritt (kritt) *nt* chalk
kro (kroo) *c* pub, tavern
krok (krook) *m* hook
kroket (*kroo*-kert) *adj* crooked
krokodille (kroo-koo-*dil*-ler) *c* crocodile
kronblad (*kroon*-blaa) *nt* (pl ~) petal
krone (*kroo*-ner) *c* crown; *v* crown
kronisk (*kroo*-nisk) *adj* chronic
kronologisk (kroo-noo-*law*-gisk) *adj* chronological
kropp (kropp) *m* body
krukke (*krook*-ker) *c* jar; pitcher
krum (kroomm) *adj* curved
krumning (*kroom*-ning) *m* bend; curve
krus (krewss) *nt* mug
krusifiks (krew-si-*fiks*) *nt* crucifix
krutt (krewtt) *nt* gunpowder
krybbe (*krewb*-ber) *c* manger
krydder (*krewd*-derr) *nt* (pl ~) spice
krydderier (krew-der-*ree*-err) *pl* spices
krydret (*krewd*-rert) *adj* spiced, spicy
krykke (*krewk*-ker) *c* crutch
krympe (*krewm*-per) *v* *shrink
krympefri (*krewm*-per-free) *adj* shrinkproof
krypdyr (*krewp*-dewr) *nt* (pl ~) reptile
***krype** (*krew*-per) *v* *creep

kryss (krewss) *nt* cross
krysse (*krewss*-ser) *v* cross
krysse av (*krewss*-ser) tick off
krystall (krew-*stahll*) *m/nt* crystal; **krystall-** *adj* crystal
krøll (krurll) *m* curl
krølle (*krurl*-ler) *v* curl; crease
krøllet (*krurl*-lert) *adj* curly
kråke (*kraw*-ker) *c* crow
ku (kēw) *c* (pl ~er, kyr) cow
kubaner (kew-*baa*-nerr) *m* Cuban
kubansk (kew-*baansk*) *adj* Cuban
kubbe (*kewb*-ber) *m* log
kube (*kēw*-ber) *m* cube
kul[1] (kēwl) *m* lump
kul[2] (kēwl) *adj colloquial* super, cool
kulde (*kewl*-ler) *c* cold
kuldegysning (*kewl*-ler-gēwss-ning) *m* chill
kule (*kēw*-ler) *c* bullet; sphere
kulepenn (*kēw*-ler-pehn) *m* ballpoint pen, Biro
kull (kewll) *nt* coal; litter
kult (kēwlt) *adj colloquial* super, cool
kultivert (kewl-ti-*vāyt*) *adj* cultured
kultur (kewl-*tēwr*) *m* culture
kun (kewnn) *adv* only
kunde (*kewn*-der) *m* client, customer
***kunne** (*kewn*-ner) *v* *can, *be able to; *may, *might
***kunngjøre** (*kewn*-ʸūr-rer) *v* announce; proclaim
kunngjøring (*kewn*-ʸūr-ring) *c* announcement; notice
kunst (kewnst) *m* art; **~ og håndverk** arts and crafts; **skjønne kunster** fine arts
kunstakademi (*kewnst*-ah-kah-deh-mee) *nt* art school
kunstferdig (*kewnst*-fææ-di) *adj* elaborate
kunstgalleri (*kewnst*-gah-ler-ree) *nt* gallery, art gallery
kunsthistorie (*kewnst*-hiss-tōo-ri-er) *c* art history
kunsthåndverk (*kewnst*-hon-værk) *nt* (pl ~) handicraft
kunstig (*kewn*-sti) *adj* artificial
kunstner (*kewnst*-nerr) *m* artist
kunstnerisk (*kewnst*-ner-risk) *adj* artistic
kunstsamling (*kewnst*-sahm-ling) *c* art collection
kunstutstilling (*kewnst*-ewt-sti-ling) *c* art exhibition
kunstverk (*kewnst*-værk) *nt* work of art
kupé (kew-*pāy*) *m* compartment
kupert (kew-*pāyt*) *adj* hilly
kupong (kew-pongng) *m* coupon
kuppel (*kewp*-perl) *m* (pl kupler) dome
kur (kēwr) *m* cure

kurs (kēwsh) *nt* course; *m* course
kursted (*kēw*-shtāy) *nt* spa
kurv (kewrv) *m* basket; hamper
kurve (*kewr*-ver) *m* curve
kusine (kew-*see*-ner) *c* cousin
kusma (*kewss*-mah) *m* mumps
kutt (kewtt) *nt* cut
kuvertavgift (kew-*vææ*-raav-^{y}ift) *c* cover charge
kuøye (*kēw*-ur^{ew}-er) *nt* porthole
kvadrat (kvah-*draat*) *nt* square
kvadratisk (kvah-*draa*-tisk) *adj* square
kvaksalver (*kvahk*-sahl-verr) *m* quack
kvalifikasjon (kvah-li-fi-kah-*shōōn*) *m* qualification
kvalifisere seg (kvah-li-fi-*sāy*-rer) qualify
kvalifisert (kvah-li-fi-*sāyt*) *adj* qualified
kvalitet (kvah-li-*tāyt*) *m* quality
kvalm (kvahlm) *adj* sick
kvalme (*kvahl*-mer) *m* nausea; sickness
kvantitet (kvahn-ti-*tāyt*) *m* quantity
kvart (kvahtt) quarter
kvartal (kvah-*taal*) *nt* quarter; house block *Am*; **kvartals-** quarterly
kvarter (kvah-*tāyr*) *nt* quarter of an hour; district; quarter
kveg (kvāyg) *nt* cattle *pl*
kveite (*kvay*-ter) *c* halibut
kveld (kvehll) *m* evening
kvele (*kvāy*-ler) *v* choke; strangle
kveles (*kvāy*-lerss) *v* choke
kveste (*kvehss*-ter) *v* injure
kvestelse (*kvehss*-terl-ser) *m* injury
kvikksølv (*kvik*-surl) *nt* mercury
kvinne (*kvin*-ner) *c* woman
kvinnelege (*kvin*-ner-lāy-ger) *m* gynaecologist
kvise (*kvee*-ser) *c* pimple
kvist (kvist) *m* twig
kvitt (kvit) *adj*: **bli ~** get rid of
kvittering (kvi-*tāy*-ring) *c* receipt
kvote (*kvōō*-ter) *m* quota
kylling (*khewl*-ling) *m* chicken
kyndig (*khewn*-di) *adj* skilled, skil(l)ful
kysk (khewsk) *adj* chaste
kyss (khewss) *nt* kiss
kysse (*khewss*-ser) *v* kiss
kyst (khewst) *m* coast; seashore, shore, seaside
kø (kūr) *m* line; queue; ***stå i ~** queue; stand in line *Am*
kølle (*kurl*-ler) *c* club; mallet
køye (*kur*ew-er) *c* bunk
kål (kawl) *m* cabbage
kåpe (*kaw*-per) *c* coat
***la** (laa) *v* *let; allow to; **~ være** *keep off

L

laboratorium (lah-boo-rah-*too*-ri-ewm) *nt* (pl -ier) laboratory
labyrint (lah-bew-*rint*) *m* labyrinth; maze
ladning (*lahd*-ning) *m* charge
lag (laag) *nt* layer; team
lage (*laa*-ger) *v* *make
lagerbeholdning (*laa*-gerr-beh-hold-ning) *m* stock
lagerbygning (*laagerr*-bewg-ning) *m* store house, warehouse
lagerplass (*laa*-gerr-plahss) *m* depot
lagre (*laag*-rer) *v* store; stock
lagring (*laag*-ring) *c* storage
lagune (lah-*gew*-ner) *m* lagoon
laken (*laa*-kern) *nt* sheet
lakk (lahkk) *m* varnish, lacquer
lakkere (lah-*kay*-rer) *v* varnish
lakris (*lahk*-riss) *m* liquorice
laks (lahks) *m* salmon
laktose (lahk-*toos*-er) *c* lactose
laktoseintolerant (lahk-*toos*-er-inn-tool-er-*ahnkt*) *adj* lactose intolerant
lam (lahmm) *nt* lamb; *adj* lame
lamme (*lahm*-mer) *v* paralyse
lammekjøtt (*lahm*-mer-khurt) *nt* lamb
lampe (*lahm*-per) *c* lamp
lampeskjerm (*lahm*-per-shærm) *m* lampshade
land (lahnn) *nt* country, land; ***gå i ~** disembark, land; **i ~** ashore; **på landet** in the country
landbruk (*lahn*-brewk) *nt* agriculture
lande (*lahn*-ner) *v* land
landemerke (*lahn*-ner-mær-ker) *nt* landmark
landflyktig *m* (pl ~e) exile
landgang (*lahn*-gahng) *m* gangway
landlig (*lahn*-li) *adj* rural
landområde (lahnn-om-*raw*-der) *nt* country
landsby (*lahns*-bew) *m* village
landsens (*lahn*-serns) *adj* rustic
landskap (*lahn*-skaap) *nt* scenery, landscape
landsmann (*lahns*-mahn) *m* (pl -menn) countryman
landsted (*lahn*-stay) *nt* country house
landstryker (*lahn*-strew-kerr) *m* tramp
lang (lahngng) *adj* long; tall
langs (lahngs) *prep* past, along; **på ~** lengthways

langsom (*lahng*-som) *adj* slow
langvarig (*lahng*-vaa-ri) *adj* longlasting
lapp (lahp) *m* patch, scrap, note
larm (lahrm) *m* noise
last (lahst) *c* freight, cargo, load; bulk
laste (*lahss*-ter) *v* charge, load
laste opp (*lahss*-ter awpp) *v* upload
lastebil (*lahss*-ter-beel) *m* lorry; truck *nAm*
lasterom (*lahss*-ter-room) *nt* (pl ~) hold
lat (laat) *adj* idle; lazy
***late som** (*laa*-ter somm) pretend
***late til** (*laa*-ter till) seem
Latin-Amerika (lah-*teen*-ah-mày-ri-kah) Latin America
latinamerikansk (lah-*tee*-nah-mày-ri-kaansk) *adj* Latin-American
latter (*laht*-terr) *m* laughter, laugh
latterlig (*laht*-ter-li) *adj* ridiculous; ludicrous
***latterliggjøre** (*laht*-ter-li-ʸūr-rer) *v* ridicule
lav (laav) *adj* low
lavland (*laav*-lahn) *nt* (pl ~) lowlands *pl*
lavsesong (*laav*-seh-song) *m* low season
lavtrykk (*laav*-trewk) *nt* (pl ~) low pressure; depression
lavvann (*laa*-vahn) *nt* low tide
***le** (lāy) *v* laugh
ledd[1] (lehdd) *nt* joint; **gått av ~** dislocated
ledd[2] (lehdd) *nt* link
lede (*lāy*-der) *v* *lead, head
ledelse (*lāy*-derl-ser) *m* management, administration; lead
ledende (*lāy*-der-ner) *adj* leading
ledig (*lāy*-di) *adj* vacant, unoccupied
ledning (*lāyd*-ning) *m* flex; electric cord
ledsager (*lāyd*-saa-gerr) *m* companion
legal (leh-*gaal*) *adj* legal
legalisering (leh-gah-li-*sāy*-ring) *c* legalization
legasjon (leh-gah-*shōōn*) *m* legation
legat (leh-*gaat*) *nt* legacy
lege (*lāy*-ger) *m* physician, doctor; *v* cure, heal; **allmennpraktiserende ~** general practitioner
legekontor (*lāy*-ger-koon-tōōr) *nt* surgery
legeme (*lāy*-ger-mer) *nt* body
legemiddel (*lāy*-ger-mi-derl) *nt* (pl -midler) remedy, medicine
legevitenskap (*lāy*-ger-vee-tern-skaap) *m* medical science
legg (lehgg) *m* calf

***legge** (*lehg*-ger) *v* *put, *lay; pave; **~ igjen** *leave; **~ sammen** add; **~ seg** *go to bed; **~ seg ned** *lie down
lei av (lay) fed up with, tired of
leie (*lay*-er) *v* hire, rent, lease; *m* rent; **~ ut** *let; lease; **til ~** for hire
leieboer (*lay*-er-b*oo*-err) *m* lodger, tenant
leiegård (*lay*-er-gawr) *m* block of flats; apartment house *Am*
leiekontrakt (*lay*-er-koon-trahkt) *m* tenancy agreement
lei for (lay) sorry
leilighet (*lay*-li-hayt) *c* flat, apartment *nAm*; occasion, opportunity
leir (layr) *m* camp
leire (*lay*-rer) *c* clay
lek (layk) *m* play
leke (*lay*-ker) *v* play
lekeplass (*lay*-ker-plahss) *m* recreation ground, playground
leketøy (*lay*-ker-tur[ew]) *nt* toy
leketøysforretning (*lay*-ker-tur[ew]ss-fo-reht-ning) *c* toyshop
lekk (lehkk) *adj* leaky
lekkasje (leh-*kaa*-sher) *m* leak
lekke (*lehk*-ker) *v* leak
lekker (*lehk*-kerr) *adj* delicious, nice
lekkerbisken (*lehk*-kerr-biss-kern) *m* delicacy
lekmann (*layk*-mahn) *m* (pl -menn) layman
leksikon (*lehk*-si-kon) *nt* (pl ~, ~er, -ka) encyclop(a)edia
leksjon (lehk-*shoon*) *m* lesson
lektor (*lehk*-toor) *m* master, teacher
lem (lehmm) *nt* (pl ~mer) limb
lene seg (*lay*-ner) *v* *lean
lenestol (*lay*-ner-stool) *m* armchair; easy chair
lengde (*lehng*-der) *c* length
lengdegrad (*lehng*-der-graad) *m* longitude
lenge (*lehng*-er) *adv* long
lengsel (*lehng*-serl) *m* (pl -sler) longing; wish
lengte etter (*lehng*-ter) long for
lenke (*lehn*-ker) *c* link
leppe (*lehp*-per) *c* lip
leppepomade (*lehp*-per-poo-maa-der) *m* lip balm
leppestift (*lehp*-per-stift) *m* lipstick
lerke (*lær*-ker) *c* lark
lerret (*lær*-rert) *nt* canvas; screen
lesbisk (*les*-bisk) *adj* lesbian
lese (*lay*-ser) *v* *read
leselampe (*lay*-ser-lahm-per) *c* reading lamp
leselig (*lay*-ser-li) *adj* legible

lesesal (*lay*-ser-saal) *m* reading room
lesning (*layss*-ning) *m* reading
lesse av (*lehss*-ser) discharge, unload
lete etter (*lay*-ter) look for, search; hunt for
leting (*lay*-ting) *c* search
lett (lehtt) *adj* light; easy; gentle
lette (*leht*-ter) *v* *take off
lettelse (*leht*-terl-ser) *m* relief
letthet (*leht*-hayt) *c* ease
leve (*lay*-ver) *v* live
levebrød (*lay*-ver-brur) *nt* livelihood, living
levende (*lay*-ver-ner) *adj* alive, live
lever (*lehv*-verr) *c* liver
leveranse (leh-ver-*rahng*-ser) *m* delivery
levere (leh-*vay*-rer) *v* deliver
levering (leh-*vay*-ring) *c* delivery; supply
levestandard (*lay*-ver-stahn-dahr) *m* standard of living
levetid (*lay*-ver-teed) *c* lifetime
levning (*lehv*-ning) *m* remnant
li (lee) *c* hillside
libaneser (li-bah-*nay*-serr) *m* Lebanese
libanesisk (li-bah-*nay*-sisk) *adj* Lebanese
Libanon (*lee*-bah-non) Lebanon
liberal (li-beh-*raal*) *adj* liberal
Liberia (li-*bay*-ri-ah) Liberia
liberier (li-*bay*-ri-err) *m* Liberian
liberisk (li-*bay*-risk) *adj* Liberian
***lide** (*lee*-der) *v* suffer
lidelse (*lee*-derl-ser) *m* suffering
lidenskap (*lee*-dern-skaap) *m* passion
lidenskapelig (lee-dern-*skaa*-per-li) *adj* passionate
liga (*lee*-gah) *m* league
***ligge** (*lig*-ger) *v* *lie
lighter (*ligh*-terr) *m* lighter
lik[1] (leek) *adj* alike, like; equal; ***være ~** equal
lik[2] (leek) *nt* corpse
like (*lee*-ker) *v* *be fond of, fancy, like; *adv* equally, as; *adj* even
likedan (*lee*-ker-dahn) *adv* alike; *adj* alike
likefrem (*lee*-ker-frehm) *adj* direct; simple
likegyldig (*lee*-ker-ʸewl-di) *adj* indifferent; careless
likeledes (*lee*-ker-lay-derss) *adv* likewise; also
likesinnet (*lee*-ker-si-nert) *adj* like-minded
likestrøm (*lee*-ker-strurm) *m* direct current
likeså (*lee*-ker-so) *adv* likewise
likevekt (*lee*-ker-vehkt) *m*

balance
likevel (*lee*-ker-vehl) *adv* yet, however; still
likhet (*leek*-hāyt) *c* equality; resemblance, similarity
likne (*lik*-ner) *v* resemble
liknende (*lik*-ner-ner) *adj* similar
liksom (*lik*-som) *conj* like, as
liktorn (*leek*-tōōn) *m* corn
likør (li-*kūrr*) *m* liqueur
lilje (*lil*-ʸer) *c* lily
lilla (*lil*-lah) *adj* purple, mauve, violet
lillefinger (*lil*-ler-fi-ngerr) *m* (pl -gre) little finger
lim (leem) *nt* gum, glue
limbånd (*leem*-bon) *nt* (pl ~) adhesive tape
limett (li-*mehtt*) *m* lime
limonade (li-moo-*naa*-der) *m* lemonade
lind (linn) *m* lime
lindetre (*lin*-der-trāy) *nt* (pl -trær) limetree
lindre (*lin*-drer) *v* relieve
lindring (*lin*-dring) *c* relief
line (*lee*-ner) *c* line
linjal (lin-*ʸaal*) *m* ruler
linje (*lin*-ʸer) *c* line; extension
linse (*lin*-ser) *c* lens
lintøy (*leen*-turᵉʷ) *nt* linen
lisens (li-*sehns*) *m* license *Am*, licence
lisse (*liss*-ser) *c* lace
list (list) *c* cunning, ruse
liste (*liss*-ter) *c* list
lite (*lee*-ter) *adj* little
liten (*lee*-tern) *adj* (pl små) small, little; short; petty, minor; **bitte** ~ tiny, minute
liter (*lee*-terr) *m* (pl ~) liter *Am*, litre
litt (litt) *pron* some
litteratur (li-ter-rah-*tēwr*) *m* literature
litterær (li-ter-*rææг*) *adj* literary
liv (leev) *nt* life
livbelte (*leev*-behl-ter) *nt* lifebelt
livfull (*leev*-fewl) *adj* vivid
livlig (*liv*-li) *adj* lively, brisk
livmor (*leev*-mōōr) *c* womb
livsfarlig (*lishs*-faa-li) *adj* perilous
livsforsikring (*lifs*-fo-shik-ring) *c* life insurance
livvakt (*lee*-vahkt) *m* bodyguard
lodd (lodd) *m* destiny, lot
loddrett (*lod*-reht) *adj* perpendicular
loft (loft) *nt* attic
logikk (loo-*gikk*) *m* logic
logisk (*lōō*-gisk) *adj* logical
lojal (loo-*ʸaal*) *adj* loyal
lokal (loo-*kaal*) *adj* local
lokalisere (loo-kah-li-*sāy*-rer) *v* locate
lokaltog (loo-*kaal*-tawg) *nt* (pl ~) local train
lokk (lokk) *nt* cover, lid, top
lokomotiv (loo-koo-moo-*teev*) *nt* engine, locomotive
lomme (*loom*-mer) *c* pocket
lommebok (*loom*-mer-bōōk) *c* (pl -bøker) wallet,

pocketbook
lommekalkulator (*loom*-mer-*kahl*-koo-lah-too) *m* (pocket) calculator
lommekniv (*loom*-mer-kneev) *m* penknife, pocket-knife
lommelykt (*loom*-mer-lewkt) *c* torch, flash-light
lommeregner (*loom*-mer-*ray*-nerr) *m* (pocket) calculator
lommetørkle (*loom*-mer-turr-kler) *nt* (pl -lær) handkerchief
lord (lord) *m* lord
los (lo͞oss) *m* pilot
losji (loo-*shee*) *nt* accommodation, lodgings *pl*
loslitt (*lo͞o*-shlit) *adj* threadbare
losse (*loss*-ser) *v* discharge
lotteri (lo-ter-*ree*) *nt* lottery
lov (lawv) *m* law; permission; ***ha ~ til** *be allowed to
love (*law*-ver) *v* promise
lovlig (*lawv*-li) *adj* lawful, legitimate
lubben (*lewb*-bern) *adj* plump
lue (*le͞wer*) *c* cap
luft (lewft) *c* air; sky; **luft-** pneumatic
lufte (*lewf*-ter) *v* air; ventilate; **~ ut** ventilate
lufthavn (*lewft*- hahvn) *c* airport
luftig (*lewf*-ti) *adj* airy
luftkondisjonering (*lewft*-koon-di-shoo-nāy-ring) *c* air conditioning
luft-kondisjonert (*lewft*-koon-di-shoo-nāyt) *adj* air--conditioned
luftpost (*lewft*-post) *m* airmail
luftsyke (*lewft*-se͞w-ker) *m* air-sickness
lufttett (*lewf*-teht) *adj* airtight
lufttrykk (*lewft*-trewkk) *nt* (pl ~) atmospheric pressure
lugar (lew-*gaar*) *m* cabin
luke (*le͞w*-ker) *c* hatch
lukke (*look*-ker) *v* close, *shut; **~ opp** unlock
lukket (*look*-kert) *adj* closed, shut
luksuriøs (lewk-sew-ri-*u͞rss*) *adj* luxurious
luksus (*lewk*-sewss) *m* luxury
lukt (lookt) *c* odo(u)r, smell
lukte (*look*-ter) *v* *smell
lumbago (loom-*baa*-goo) *m* lumbago
lund (lewnn) *m* grove
lune (*le͞w*-ner) *nt* mood, humo(u)r
lunge (*loong*-nger) *c* lung
lungebetennelse (*loong*-nger-beh-teh-nerl-ser) *m* pneumonia
lunken (*loong*-kern) *adj* lukewarm, tepid
lunsj (lurnsh) *m* luncheon, dinner, lunch

lunte (*lewn*-ter) *c* fuse
lur (lēwr) *m* nap; *adj* smart, cunning
lus (lēwss) *c* (pl ~) louse
ly (lēw) *nt* shelter, cover; ***gi ~** shelter
lyd (lēwd) *m* sound; noise
lydbånd (*lēwd*-bonn) *nt* (pl ~) tape
***lyde** (*lēw*-der) *v* sound
lydig (*lēw*-di) *adj* obedient
lydighet (*lēw*-di-hāyt) *c* obedience
lydpotte (*lēwd*-po-ter) *c* silencer; muffler *nAm*
lydtett (*lēw*-d-teht) *adj* soundproof
lykke (*lewk*-ker) *c* happiness, fortune; **~ til!** good luck!
lykkelig (*lewk*-li) *adj* happy
lykkes (*lewk*-kerss) *v* manage, succeed
lykkønskning (*lewk*-kurnsk-ning) *m* congratulation
lykt (lewkt) *c* lantern
lyn (lēwn) *nt* lightning
lyng (lewngng) *m* heather
lynmelding (*lēwn*-mehl-ling) *c* instant message
lys (lēwss) *nt* light; *adj* light; pale; **skarpt ~** glare
lysbilde (*lēwss*-bil-der) *nt* slide
lysende (*lēw*-ser-ner) *adj* luminous
lyserød (*lēw*-ser-rūr) *adj* pink
lyshåret (*lēwss*-haw-rert) *adj* fair
lyskaster (*lēwss*-kahss-terr) *m* searchlight
lyske (*lewss*-ker) *m* groin
lysmåler (*lēwss*-maw-lerr) *m* exposure meter
lysning (*lēwss*-ning) *m* clearing
lyspære (*lēwss*-pææ-rer) *c* light bulb
lyst (lewst) *c* desire; zest; ***ha ~ til** *feel like, fancy
lystbåt (*lewst*-bawt) *m* yacht
lystig (*lewss*-ti) *adj* cheerful, jolly
lystspill (*lewst*-spil) *nt* (pl ~) comedy
lytt (lewtt) *adj* noisy
lytte (*lewt*-ter) *v* listen; eavesdrop
lytter (*lewt*-terr) *m* listener
***lyve** (*lēw*-wer) *v* lie, *tell a lie
lær (læær) *nt* leather; **lær-** leather
lærd (læærd) *adj* scholarly
lære (*lææ*-rer) *v* *learn; *teach; *c* teachings *pl*; **~ utenat** memorize
lærebok (*lææ*-rer-bōōk) *c* (pl -bøker) textbook
lærer (*lææ*-rerr) *m* master, teacher, schoolmaster, schoolteacher
lærerik (*lææ*-rer-reek) *adj* instructive
lærling (*læær*-ling) *m* apprentice; trainee
løfte (*lurf*-ter) *v* lift; *nt* vow; promise

løgn (lur^ewn) *c* lie
løk (lurk) *m* onion
løkke (*lurk*-ker) *c* loop
lønn (lurnn) *m* salary, pay, wages *pl*; maple
lønne (*lurn*-ner) *v* *pay; **~ seg** *be worthwhile
lønnsom (*lurn*-som) *adj* profitable
lønnstaker (*lurns*-taa-kerr) *m* employee
lønnstillegg (*lurns*-ti-lehg) *nt* (pl ~) *pay rise; raise *nAm*
løp (lūrp) *nt* course
***løpe** (*lūr*-per) *v* *run
løper (*lūr*-perr) *m* runner
lørdag (*lūr*-dah) *m* Saturday
løs (lūrss) *adj* loose
løse (*lūr*-ser) *v* solve; unfasten; **~ opp** *undo
løsepenger (*lūr*-ser-peh-ngerr) *pl* ransom
løsne (lurss-ner) *v* unfasten, detach; loosen
løsning (*lūrss*-ning) *m* solution
løve (*lūr*-ver) *m* lion
løvetann (*lūr*-ver-tahn) *c* dandelion
lån (lawn) *nt* loan
låne (*law*-ner) *v* borrow; **~ bort** *lend
lår (lawr) *nt* thigh
lås (lawss) *m* lock
låse (*law*-ser) *v* lock; **~ inne** lock up; **~ opp** unlock
låve (*law*-ver) *m* barn

M

madrass (mahd-*rahss*) *m* mattress
mage (*maa*-ger) *m* stomach; belly; **mage-** gastric
mager (*maa*-gerr) *adj* lean, thin
magesår (*maa*-ger-sawr) *nt* (pl ~) gastric ulcer
magi (mah-*gee*) *m* magic
magisk (*maa*-gisk) *adj* magic
magnetisk (mahng-*nāy*-tisk) *adj* magnetic
mai (migh) May
mais (mighss) *m* maize; corn *nAm*
maiskolbe (*mighss*-kol-ber) *m* corn on the cob
major (mah-^y*ōōr*) *m* major
makrell (mah-*krehll*) *m* mackerel
makt (mahkt) *c* might, power; rule
maktesløs (*mahk*-terss-lūrss) *adj* powerless
malaria (mah-*laa*-ri-ah) *m* malaria
Malaysia (mah-*ligh*-si-ah) Malaysia
malaysier (mah-*ligh*-s^yerr) *m* Malay
malaysisk (mah-*ligh*-sisk) *adj* Malaysian
male (*maa*-ler) *v* paint;

*grind
maler (*maa*-lerr) *m* painter
maleri (mah-ler-*ree*) *nt* picture, painting
malerisk (*maa*-ler-risk) *adj* picturesque
malerskrin (*maa*-ler-shkreen) *nt* (pl ~) paint--box
maling (*maa*-ling) *c* paint
malm (mahlm) *m* ore
malplassert (*maal*-plah-sa͞yt) *adj* misplaced
mamma (*mahm*-mah) *f*mom, mommy
man (mahnn) *pron* one
mandag (*mahn*-dah) *m* Monday
mandarin (mahn-dah-*reen*) *m* tangerine, mandarin
mandat (mahn-*daat*) *nt* mandate
mandel (*mahn*-derl) *m* (pl -dler) almond
mandler (*mahn*-dlerr) *pl* tonsils *pl*; **betente ~** tonsilitis
manerer (mah-*na͞y*-rerr) *pl* manners *pl*
manesje (mah-*na͞y*-sher) *m* ring
manet (mah-*na͞yt*) *m* jelly--fish
mange (*mahng*-nger) *pron* many; much
mangel (*mahng*-ngerl) *m* (pl -gler), want, lack, deficiency; shortage
mangelfull (*mahng*-ngerl-fewl) *adj* faulty, defective
mangle (*mahng*-ler) *v* fail, lack
manglende (*mahng*-ler-ner) *adj* missing, lacking
mani (mah-*nee*) *m* craze
manikyr (mah-ni-*ke͞wr*) *m* manicure
manikyrere (mah-ni-kew-*ra͞y*-rer) *v* manicure
mann (mahnn) *m* (pl menn) man; husband
mannekeng (mah-ner-*kehngng*) *m* model
mannskap (*mahn*-skaap) *nt* crew
mansjett (mahn-*shehtt*) *m* cuff
mansjettknapper (mahn-*sheht*-knah-perr) *pl* cuff links *pl*
manuskript (mah-noo-*skript*) *nt* manuscript
marg (mahrg) *m* margin; marrow
margarin (mahr-gah-*reen*) *m* margarine
marine- (mah-*ree*-ner) naval
maritim (mah-ri-*teem*) *adj* maritime
mark (mahrk) *m* worm; *c* field
marked (*mahr*-kerd) *nt* market
markere (mahr-*ka͞y*-rer) *v* mark; score
marmelade (mahr-mer-*laa*-der) *m* marmalade
marmor (*mahr*-moor) *m* marble

marokkaner (mah-ro-*kaa*-nerr) *m* Moroccan
marokkansk (mah-ro-*kaansk*) *adj* Moroccan
Marokko (mah-*rok*-koo) Morocco
mars (mahshsh) March
marsj (mahshsh) *m* march
marsjere (mah-*shāy*-rer) *v* march
marsjfart (*mahsh*-faht) *c* cruising speed
marsvin (*maa*-shveen) *nt* (pl ~) guinea pig
martyr (*maa*-tēwr) *m* martyr
mas (maass) *nt* fuss
maske (*mahss*-ker) *c* mask; mesh
maskin (mah-*sheen*) *m* machine, engine
maskineri (mah-shi-ner-ree) *nt* machinery
maskinskade (mah-*sheen*-skaa-der) *m* breakdown
maskulin (*mahss*-kew-leen) *adj* masculine
massasje (mah-*saa*-sher) *m* massage
masse (*mahss*-ser) *m* bulk
masseproduksjon (*mahss*-ser-proo-dewk-shōōn) *m* mass production
massere (mah-*sāy*-rer) *v* massage
masseødeleggelsesvåpen (*mahs*-ser-urd-eh-leh-gel-sehs-*vāwp*-ehn) *nt* (pl ~) WMD
massiv (mah-*seev*) *adj* massive; solid
massør (mah-*sūrr*) *m* masseur
mast (mahst) *c* mast
mat (maat) *m* food; **lage ~** cook
mate (*maa*-ter) *v* *feed
matematikk (mah-ter-mah-*tikk*) *m* mathematics
matematisk (mah-ter-*maa*-tisk) *adj* mathematical
materiale (mah-ter-ri-*aa*-ler) *nt* material
materiell (mah-ter-ri-*ehll*) *adj* material
matforgiftning (*maat*-for-ʸift-ning) *m* food poisoning
matlyst (*maat*-lewst) *c* appetite
matolje (*maat*-ol-ʸer) *c* salad-oil
matt (mahtt) *adj* mat, dull, dim
matte (*maht*-ter) *c* mat
matvareforretning (*maat*-vaa-rer-fo-reht-ning) *c* grocer's
matvarehandler (*maat*-vaa-rer-hahnd-lerr) *m* grocer
matvarer (*maat*-vaa-rerr) *pl* foodstuffs *pl*, groceries *pl*
maur (mour) *m* ant
mausoleum (mou-soo-*lāy*-ewm) *nt* (pl -eer) mausoleum
med (māy) *prep* with; by; **~ mindre** unless
medalje (meh-*dahl*-ʸer) *m* medal
***medbringe** (*māy*-bri-nger)

v *bring
meddele (*māy*-dāy-ler) *v* communicate, inform; notify
meddelelse (*māy*-dāy-lerl-ser) *m* information, communication
medfødt (*māy*-furt) *adj* inborn
medfølelse (*māyd*-fūr-lerl-ser) *m* sympathy
medfølende (*māyd*-fūr-leh-ner) *adj* sympathetic
medisin (meh-di-*seen*) *m* medicine; drug
medisinsk (meh-di-*seensk*) *adj* medical
meditere (meh-di-*tāy*-rer) *v* meditate
medlem (*māyd*-lehm) *nt* (pl ~mer) member, associate
medlemskap (*māyd*-lehm-skaap) *nt* membership
medlidenhet (mehd-*lee*-dern-hāyt) *c* pity; ***ha ~ med** pity
medregne (*māyd*-ray-ner) *v* include, count in
medvirkning (*māyd*-veerk-ning) *m* co-operation
meg (may) *pron* me, myself
meget (*māy*-gert) *adv* very; far
megle (*mehg*-ler) *v* mediate
megler (*mehg*-lerr) *m* mediator; broker
meieri (may-er-*ree*) *nt* dairy
meisel (*may*-serl) *m* (pl -sler) chisel
mekaniker (meh-*kaa*-ni-kerr) *m* mechanic
mekanisk (meh-*kaa*-nisk) *adj* mechanical
mekanisme (meh-kah-*niss*-mer) *m* mechanism
meksikaner (mehks-i-*kaa*-nerr) *m* Mexican
meksikansk (mehks-i-*kaansk*) *adj* Mexican
mektig (*mehk*-ti) *adj* powerful, mighty
mel (māyl) *nt* flour
melankoli (meh-lahng-koo-*lee*) *m* melancholy
melde (*mehl*-ler) *v* report; bid; **~ seg** report
melding (*mehl*-ling) *c* report
melk (mehlk) *c* milk
melkaktig (*mehl*-kahk-ti) *adj* milky
mellom (*mehl*-lom) *prep* between; among
mellommann (*mehl*-loo-mahn) *m* (pl -menn) intermediary
mellomrom (*mehl*-loom-room) *nt* (pl ~) space
mellomspill (*mehl*-loom-spil) *nt* (pl ~) interlude
mellomste (*mehl*-loom-ster) *adj* middle
mellomtid (*mehl*-loom-teed) *c* interim; **i mellomtiden** meanwhile
melodi (meh-loo-*dee*) *m* tune; melody
melodisk (meh-*lōō*-disk) *adj* tuneful
melodrama (meh-loo-*draa*-

mah) *nt* melodrama
melon (meh-*loon*) *m* melon
membran (mehm-*braan*) *m* diaphragm
memorandum (meh-moo-*rahn*-dewm) *nt* (pl -da) memo
men (mehnn) *conj* but; only
mene (*māy*-ner) *v* *mean; consider
mened (*māyn*-āyd) *m* perjury
mengde (*mehng*-der) *m* lot, amount, mass; crowd
menighet (*māy*-ni-hāyt) *c* congregation
mening (*māy*-ning) *m* opinion; meaning, sense
meningsløs (*māy*-nings-lurss) *adj* meaningless, senseless
meningsmåling (*māy*-nings-maw-ling)*c* poll
menneske (*mehn*-sker) *nt* human being, man
menneskehet (*mehn*-sker-hāyt) *c* humanity, mankind
menneskelig (*mehn*-sker-li) *adj* human
mens (mehns) *conj* while
menstruasjon (mehn-strew-ah-*shoon*) *m* menstruation
mental (mehn-*taal*) *adj* mental
meny (meh-*new*) *m* menu
mer (māyr) *adj* more; **litt ~** some more
merkbar (*mærk*-baar) *adj* perceptible, noticeable
merke[1] (*mær*-ker) *v* mark; *nt* tick, mark; brand
merke[2] (*mær*-ker) *v* sense; notice; ***legge ~ til** notice
merkelapp (*mær*-ker-lahp) *m* tag; ***sette ~ på** label
merkelig (*mær*-ker-li) *adj* funny, queer
merknad (*mærk*-nah) *m* note
merkverdig (mærk-*vær*-di) *adj* curious, strange
meslinger (*mehsh*-li-ngerr) *pl* measles
messe (*mehss*-ser) *m* Mass
messing (*mehss*-sing) *m* brass
mester (*mehss*-terr) *m* (pl ~e, -trer) master; champion
mesterverk (*mehss*-terr-vayrk) *nt* masterpiece
mestre (*mehss*-trer) *v* cope
metall (meh-*tahll*) *nt* metal; **metall-** metal
metalltråd (meh-*tahl*-traw) *m* wire
meter (*māy*-terr) *m* (pl ~) metre
metode (meh-*too*-der) *m* method
metodisk (meh-*too*-disk) *adj* methodical
metrisk (*māyt*-risk) *adj* metric
Mexico (*mehk*-si-koo) Mexico
middag (*mid*-dah) *m* dinner; midday; **spise ~** dine

middel (*mid*-derl) *nt* (pl midler) means
middelalderen (*mid*-derl-ahld-rern) Middle Ages
middelaldersk (*mid*-derl-ahl-dershk) *adj* mediaeval
Middelhavet (*mid*-derl-haa-vert) Mediterranean
middelklasse (*mid*-derl-klah-ser) *c* middle class
middelmådig (*mid*-derl-maw-di) *adj* average, commonplace
middels (*mid*-derls) *adj* medium
midje (*mid*-ʸer) *c* waist
midlertidig (*mid*-ler-tee-di) *adj* temporary
midnatt (*mid*-nahtt) *c* midnight
midte (*mit*-ter) *m* midst, middle
midtpunkt (*mit*-poongt) *nt* center *Am*, centre
midtsommer (*mit*-so-merr) *m* midsummer
migrene (mig-*ray*-ner) *m* migraine
mikrobølgeovn (*mik*-roo-burl-ge-ovnn) *m* microwave oven
mikrofon (mik-roo-*foon*) *m* microphone
mikser (*mik*-serr) *m* mixer
mild (mill) *adj* mild; gentle
milestein (*mee*-ler-stayn) *m* milestone
militær- (mi-li-*tæær*) military
miljø (mil-*ʸur*) *nt* milieu; environment
miljøvern (mil-*ʸur*-vææn) *nt* environmental protection
milliard (mil-*ʸard*) *m* billion
million (mil-*ʸoon*) *m* million
millionær (mil-ʸoo-*næær*) *m* millionaire
min (meen) *pron* my
mindre (*min*-drer) *adv* less; *adj* minor; **ikke desto ~** nevertheless
mindretall (*min*-drer-tahll) *nt* (pl ~) minority
mindreverdig (*min*-drer-vær-di) *adj* inferior
mindreårig (*min*-drer-aw-ri) *m* (pl ~e) minor
mineral (mi-ner-*raal*) *nt* mineral
mineralvann (mi-ner-*raal*-vahn) *nt* mineral water; soda (pop); lemonade
miniatyr (mi-ni-ah-*tewr*) *m* miniature
minibank (*miin*-i-bahnk) *c* automatic teller machine (ATM)
minimum (*mee*-ni-moom) *nt* (pl -ima) minimum
mink (mingk) *m* mink
minke (*ming*-ker) *v* decrease
minne (*min*-ner) *nt* remembrance, memory; **~ på** remind
minnes (*min*-nerss) *v* recall
minnesmerke (*min*-nerss-mær-ker) *nt* monument
minnestein (*min*-nerstayn) *m* memorial

minneverdig (*min*-ner-vær-di) *adj* memorable
minoritet (mi-noo-ri-*tayt*) *m* minority
minske (*min*-sker) *v* lessen, reduce, decrease
minst (minst) *adj* least; *adv* at least; **i det minste** at least
minus (*mee*-newss) *adv* minus
minutt (mi-*newtt*) *nt* minute
mirakel (mi-*raa*-kerl) *nt* (pl -kler) miracle
mirakuløs (mi-rah-kew-*lurss*) *adj* miraculous
misbillige (*miss*-bi-li-er) *v* disapprove
misbruk (*miss*-brewk) *nt* abuse, misuse
misdannet (*miss*-dahn-nert) *adj* deformed
misfornøyd (*miss*-fo-nur[ew]d) *adj* discontented
***misforstå** (*miss*-fo-shtaw) *v* *misunderstand
misforståelse (*miss*-fo-*shtaw*-erl-ser) *m* misunderstanding
mislike (*miss*-lee-ker) *v* dislike
mislykkes (*miss*-lew-kerss) *v* fail
mislykket (*miss*-lew-kert) *adj* unsuccessful
mistanke (*miss*-tahng-ker) *m* suspicion
miste (*miss*-ter) *v* miss; *lose
mistenke (*miss*-tehng-ker) *v* suspect
mistenkelig (miss-*tehng*-ker-li) *adj* suspicious
mistenksom (miss-*tehngk*-som) *adj* suspicious
mistenksomhet (*miss*-*tehngk*-som-hayt) *c* suspicion
mistenkt (*miss*-tehngt) *m* suspect
mistro (*miss*-troo) *v* mistrust
mistroisk (*miss*-troo-isk) *adj* distrustful
misunne (mi-*sewn*-ner) *v* envy; grudge
misunnelig (mi-*sewn*-li) *adj* envious
misunnelse (*mi*-*sewn*-nerl-ser) *m* envy
mobil (moo-*beel*) *adj* mobile
mobil(-telefon) (moo-*beel*-(teh-ler-foon)) *m* cellphone, mobile (phone)
modell (moo-*dehll*) *m* model
modellere (moo-der-*lay*-rer) *v* model
modem (*moo*-dem)*nt* modem
moden (*moo*-dern) *adj* ripe, mature
modenhet (*moo*-dern-hayt) *c* maturity
moderat (moo-der-*raat*) *adj* moderate
moderne (moo-*dææ*-ner) *adj* modern; fashionable; trendy

modifisere (moo-di-fi-*sāy*-rer) *v* modify
modig (*mōō*-di) *adj* courageous, brave, plucky
moll (*moll*) *m* minor
molo (*mōō*-loo) *m* jetty
molte (*mol*-ter) *c* cloudberry
moms (merverdiomsetningsavgift) (*mooms*) *m* purchase tax, turnover tax, sales tax
monark (moo-*nahrk*) *m* monarch, ruler
monarki (moo-nahr-*kee*) *nt* monarchy
monolog (moo-noo-*lawg*) *m* monologue
monopol (moo-noo-*pōōl*) *nt* monopoly
monoton (moo-noo-*tōōn*) *adj* monotonous
monter (*moon*-terr) *m* (pl -trer) show-case
monument (moo-new-*mehnt*) *nt* monument
moped (moo-*pāyd*) *m* moped; motorbike *nAm*
mor (mōōr) *c* (pl mødre) mother
moral (moo-*raal*) *m* morality; moral
moralsk (moo-*raalsk*) *adj* moral
mord (moord) *nt* assassination, murder
morder (*moor*-derr) *m* murderer
more (*mōō*-rer) *v* amuse; entertain
morfar (*moor*-faar) *m* (pl -fedre) grandfather
morfin (moor-*feen*) *m* morphine
morgen (*maw*-ern) *m* morning; **i ~** tomorrow; **i morges** this morning
morgenavis (*maw*-ern-ah-veess) *c* morning paper
morgenkåpe (*maw*-ern-kaw-per) *c* dressing gown
morgenutgave (*maw*-ern-ēwt-gaa-ver) *c* morning edition
mormor (*moor*-mōōr) *c* (pl -mødre) grandmother
moro (*moor*-roo) *c* fun
morsmål (*mōōsh*-mawl) *nt* mother tongue, native language
morsom (*moosh*-shom) *adj* enjoyable, entertaining; humorous
mort (moot) *m* roach
mosaikk (moo-sah-*ikk*) *m* mosaic
mose (*mōō*-ser) *m* moss; *v* mash
moské (mooss-*kāy*) *m* mosque
moskito (mooss-*kee*-too) *m* mosquito
mot[1] (mōōt) *prep* against; towards
mot[2] (mōōt) *nt* courage; **ta motet fra** *v* discourage
motbydelig (moot-*bēw*-der-li) *adj* disgusting, revolting
mote (*mōō*-ter) *m* fashion
motell (moo-*tehll*) *nt* motel

motgang (*mo͞ot*-gahng) *m* adversity, hardship

motiv (moo-*teev*) *nt* motive; pattern

motivere (moo-tee-*va͞y*-rer)) *v* motivate

motor (*mo͞o*-toor) *m* motor, engine

motorbåt (*mo͞o*-toor-bawt) *m* motor-boat

motorstopp (*mo͞o*-toor-stop) *m*/*nt* (pl ~) breakdown

motorsykkel (*mo͞o*-toor-sew-kerl) *m* (pl -sykler) motor-cycle

motorvei (*mo͞o*-toor-vay) *m* motorway; highway *nAm*

motsatt (*mo͞ot*-saht) *adj* opposite, contrary; reverse; **det motsatte** the contrary

motsetning (*mo͞ot*-seht-ning) *m* contrast; reverse

***motsette seg** (*mo͞ot*-seh-ter) oppose

***motsi** (*mo͞ot*-see) *v* contradict

motstand (*mo͞ot*-stahn) *m* resistance

motstander (*mo͞ot*-stahn-derr) *m* opponent

motstridende (*mo͞ot*-stree-der-ner) *adj* contradictory

motsvarende (*mo͞ot*-svaa-rer-ner) *adj* equivalent

***motta** (*mo͞o*-taa) *v* receive; accept

mottakelse (*mo͞o*-taa-kerl-ser) *m* reception, receipt

motto (*moot*-too) *nt* motto

motvilje (*mo͞ot*-vil-ʸer) *m* aversion, dislike, antipathy

mugg (mewgg) *m* mildew

mugge (*mewg*-ger) *c* jug

muggen (*mewg*-gern) *adj* mouldy

muldyr (*mewl*-de͞wr) *nt* (pl ~) mule

mulesel (*mewl*-a͞y-serl) *nt* (pl -sler) mule

mulig (*me͞w*-li) *adj* possible; eventual; realizable

muligens (*me͞w*-li-erns) *adv* perhaps

mulighet (*me͞w*-li-ha͞yt) *c* possibility

mulkt (mewlkt) *c* fine

multe (*mool*-ter) *c* cloudberry

multikulturell (mo͞ol-ti-*kewl*-tewr-*ehll*) *adj* multicultural

multiplex (*mo͞ol*-ti-plehks) *c* multiplex

multiplikasjon (mool-ti-pli-kah-*sho͞on*) *m* multiplication

multiplisere (mool-ti-pli-*sa͞y*-rer) *v* multiply

munk (moongk) *m* monk

munkeorden (*moong*-ker-*or*-dern) *m* monastic order

munn (mewnn) *m* mouth

munning (*mewn*-ning) *m* outlet; estuary; muzzle

munnvann (*mewn*-vahn) *nt* mouthwash

munter (*mewn*-terr) *adj* merry, gay

muntlig (*mewnt*-li) *adj* oral, verbal
mur (mewr) *m* brick wall
mure (*mew*-rer) *v* *lay bricks
murer (*mew*-rerr) *m* bricklayer
murpuss (*mewr*-pewss) *m* plaster
murstein (*mew*-shtayn) *m* brick
mus (mewss) *c* (pl ~) mouse; **~matte** *c* mouse pad
museum (mew-*say*-ewm) *nt* (pl -eer) museum
musikal (mew-si-kaarl) *m* musical
musikalsk (mew-si-*kaalsk*) *adj* musical
musiker (*mew*-si-kerr) *m* musician
musikk (mew-*sikk*) *m* music
musikkinstrument (mew-*sikk*-in-strew-mehnt) *nt* musical instrument
musikkspill (mew-*sikk*-spil) *nt* (pl ~) musical comedy
muskatnøtt (mewss-*kaat*-nurt) *c* nutmeg
muskel (*mewss*-kerl) *m* (pl -kler) muscle
muskuløs (mewss-kew-*lurss*) *adj* muscular
muslim (mewss-*lim*) *m* Muslim
musserende (mew-*say*-rer-ner) *adj* sparkling
mutter (*mewt*-terr) *m* (pl ~e, mutrer) nut
mye (*mew*-er) *adj* much; *adv* much; **like ~** as much
mygg (mewgg) *m* (pl ~) mosquito
myggnett (*mewg*-neht) *nt* (pl ~) mosquito net
myk (mewk) *adj* supple, smooth, soft; tender
mynde (*mewn*-der) *m* greyhound
myndig (*mewn*-di) *adj* of age
myndighet (*mewn*-di-hayt) *c* authority; **utøvende ~** executive; **myndigheter** authorities *pl*
mynt (mewnt) *m* coin
mynte (*mewn*-ter) *c* mint
myntenhet (*mewnt*-ayn-hayt) *m* monetary unit
myr (mewr) *c* swamp, bog
myrde (*mewr*-der) *v* murder
mysterium (mewss-*tay*-ri-ewm) *nt* (pl -ier) mystery
mystisk (*mewss*-tisk) *adj* mysterious
myte (*mew*-ter) *m* myth
mytteri (mew-ter-*ree*) *nt* mutiny
møbler (*murb*-lerr) *pl* furniture
møblere (murb-*lay*-rer) *v* furnish
møll (murll) *m* (pl ~) moth
mølle (*murl*-ler) *c* mill
mønster (*murn*-sterr) *nt* (pl -tre) pattern
mør (murr) *adj* tender
mørk (murrk) *adj* obscure,

dark
mørke (*murr*-ker) *nt* dark; gloom
møte (*mūr*-ter) *v* encounter, *meet; *nt* encounter, meeting; appointment
møtende (*mūr*-ter-ner) *adj* oncoming
møtested (*mūr*-ter-stāy) *nt* meeting place
måke (*maw*-ker) *c* gull
mål (mawl) *nt* measure; goal; target; tongue, language
målbevisst (*mawl*-beh-vist) *adj* determined
måle (*maw*-ler) *v* measure
målebånd (*maw*-ler-bon) *nt* (pl ~) tape measure
måleinstrument (*maw*-ler-in-strew-mehnt) *nt* gauge
måler (*maw*-lerr) *m* meter
målestokk (*maw*-ler-stok) *m* scale
mållinje (*mawl*-lin-^{y}er) *c* finish
målløs (*mawl*-lūrss) *adj* speechless
målmann (*mawl*-mahn) *m* (pl -menn) goalkeeper
måltid (*mawl*-teed) *nt* meal
måne (*maw*-ner) *m* moon
måned (*maw*-nerd) *m* month
månedlig (*maw*-nerd-li) *adj* monthly
måneskinn (*maw*-ner-shin) *nt* moonlight
måte (*maw*-ter) *m* fashion, way, manner; **på hvilken som helst** ~ any way; **på ingen** ~ by no means
***måtte** (*mot*-ter) *v* *must, *have to; *be bound to; need, need to

N

nabo (*naa*-boo) *m* neighbo(u)r
nabolag (*naa*-boo-laag) *nt* (pl ~) vicinity, neighbo(u)rhood
naiv (nah-*eev*) *adj* naïve
naken (*naa*-kern) *adj* nude, bare, naked
nakke (*nahk*-ker) *m* nape of the neck
narkoman (nahr-koo-*mahn*) *m* drug addict
narkose (nahr-*kōō*-ser) *m* narcosis
narkotika (nahr-*kōō*-ti-kah) *m* (pl ~) drug; **narkotisk middel** narcotic
narre (*nahr*-rer) *v* fool
nasjon (nah-*shōōn*) *m* nation
nasjonal (nah-shoo-*naal*) *adj* national
nasjonaldrakt (nah-shoo-*naal*-drahkt) *c* national dress
nasjonalisere (nah-shoo-

nah-li-*sāy*-rer) *v* nationalize
nasjonalitet (nah-shoo-nah-li-*tāyt*) *m* nationality
nasjonalpark (nah-shoo-*naal*-pahrk) *m* national park
nasjonalsang (nah-shoo-*naal*-sahng) *m* national anthem
natt (nahtt) *c* (pl netter) night; **i ~** tonight; **om natten** by night
nattergal (*naht*-terr-gaal) *m* nightingale
nattklubb (*naht*-klewb) *m* cabaret, nightclub
nattkrem (*naht*-krāym) *m* night cream
nattlig (*naht*-li) *adj* nightly
natt-takst (*naht*-tahkst) *m* night rate
natt-tog (*naht*-tawg) *nt* (pl ~) night train
natur (nah-*tewr*) *m* nature
naturlig (nah-*tēw*-li) *adj* natural
naturligvis (nah-*tēw*-li-veess) *adv* of course, naturally
naturskjønn (nah-*tēw*-shurn) *adj* scenic
naturvitenskap (nah-*tewr*-vee-tern-skaap) *m* natural science
navigasjon (nah-vi-gah-*shōōn*) *m* navigation
navigere (nah-vi-*gāy*-rer) *v* navigate
navle (*nahv*-ler) *m* navel
navn (nahvn) *nt* name; **i ...s ~** on behalf of, in the name of
nebb (nehbb) *nt* beak
ned (nāyd) *adv* down; downstairs
nedbetale (*nāyd*-beh-taa-ler) *v* *pay off
nedbetaling (*nāyd*-beh-taa-ling) *c* down payment
nedbør (*nāyd*-būrr) *m* precipitation
nede (*nāy*-der) *adv* below, downstairs
nedenfor (*nāy*-dern-for) *prep* under, below
nedenunder (*nāy*-dern-ew-nerr) *adv* underneath
nederlag (*nāy*-der-laag) *nt* (pl ~) defeat
Nederland (*nāy*-der-lahn) the Netherlands
nederlandsk (*nāy*-der-lahnsk) *adj* Dutch
nederlender (*nāy*-der-leh-nerr) *m* Dutchman
nedgang (*nāyd*-gahng) *m* decrease; depression
nedkomst (*nāyd*-komst) *m* delivery
nedlasting (nayd-*lahs*-ting) *c* download
nedover (*nāy*-do-verr) *adv* down, downwards
nedre (*nāyd*-rer) *adj* inferior, lower
nedrivning (*nāyd*-reev-ning) *m* demolition
nedslått (*nāyd*-shlot) *adj* down

nedstemt (*nā̄yd*-stehmt) *adj* depressed
nedstigning (*nāyd*-steeg-ning) *m* descent
nedtrykt (*nāyd*-trewkt) *adj* depressed
negativ (*nāy*-gah-teev) *adj* negative; *nt* negative
negl (nayl) *m* nail
neglefil (*nay*-ler-feel) *c* nail file
neglelakk (*nay*-ler-lahk) *m* nail polish
neglesaks (*nay*-ler-sahks) *c* nail scissors *pl*
nei (nay) no
nekte (*nehk*-ter) *v* deny
nemlig (*nehm*-li) *adv* namely
neppe (*nehp*-per) *adv* hardly
nerve (*nær*-ver) *m* nerve
nervøs (nær-*vūrss*) *adj* nervous
nese (*nāy*-ser) *c* nose
neseblod (*nāy*-ser-bloo) *nt* nosebleed
nesebor (*nāy*-ser-boor) *nt* (pl ~) nostril
nesevis (*nāy*-ser-veess) *adj* impertinent
neshorn (*nāyss*-hoon) *nt* (pl ~) rhinoceros
neste (*nehss*-ter) *adj* next; following
nesten (*nehss*-tern) *adv* nearly, almost
nestleder (*nehsst-lāyd*-err) *c* (pl ~e) executive assistant
nett (nehtt) *nt* net; Internet; *adj* neat
netthinne (*neht*-hi-ner) *c* retina
netto (*neht*-too) *adv* net
nettopp (*neht*-top) *adv* just
nettsted (*nehtt*-stay) *nt* (pl ~er) website
nettverk (*neht*-værk) *nt* network
nettverksbygging (*neht*-værks-*bewgg*-ing) *c* networking
nevne (*nehv*-ner) *v* mention
nevralgi (nehv-rahl-*gee*) *m* neuralgia
nevrose (nehv-*roo*-ser) *m* neurosis
nevø (neh-*vūr*) *m* nephew
ni (nee) *num* nine
niende (*nee*-er-ner) *num* ninth
niese (ni-*āy*-ser) *c* niece
nifs (nifs) *adj* creepy
Nigeria (ni-*gāy*-ri-ah) Nigeria
nigerianer (ni-geh-ri-*aa*-nerr) *m* Nigerian
nigeriansk (ni-geh-ri-*aansk*) *adj* Nigerian
nikk (nikk) *nt* nod
nikke (*nik*-ker) *v* nod
nikkel (*nik*-kerl) *m* nickel
nikotin (ni-koo-*teen*) *m* nicotine
nitten (*nit*-tern) *num* nineteen
nittende (*nit*-ter-ner) *num* nineteenth
nitti (*nit*-ti) *num* ninety
nivellere (ni-ver-*lāy*-rer) *v*

level
nivå (ni-*vaw*) *nt* level
noe (*nōō*-er) *pron* something
noen (*nōō*-ern) *pron* somebody, someone; some; ~ **gang** ever
nok (nokk) *adv* enough
nokså (*nok*-so) *adv* fairly, somewhat
nominasjon (noo-mi-nah-*shōōn*) *m* nomination
nominell (noo-mi-*nehll*) *adj* nominal
nominere (noo-mi-*nāy*-rer) *v* nominate
nonne (*non*-ner) *c* nun
nonsens (*non*-serns) *nt* nonsense
nord (nōōr) *m* north
nordlig (*nōō*-li) *adj* north, northern
nordmann (*noor*-mahn) *m* (pl -menn) Norwegian
Nordpolen (*nōōr*-pōō-lern) North Pole
nordvest (noor-*vehst*) *m* north-west
nordøst (noor-*urst*) *m* north-east
Norge (*nor*-ger) Norway
norm (norm) *m* standard
normal (noor-maal) *adj* normal; regular
norsk (noshk) *adj* Norwegian
nota (*nōō*-tah) *m* bill
notar (noo-*taar*) *m* notary
notat (noo-*taat*) *nt* note
notere (noo-*tāy*-rer) *v* note
notis (noo-*teess*) *m* note
notisblokk (noo-*teess*-blok) *c* note pad
notisbok (noo-*teess*-bōōk) *c* (pl -bøker) notebook
november (noo-*vehm*-berr) November
null (newll) *nt* zero, nought
nummer (*noom*-merr) *nt* (pl numre) number; act
nummerskilt (*noom*-mer-shilt) *nt* registration plate; licence plate *Am*
nummervisning (*nomm*-ehr-*vēēss*-nee-ning) *c* caller id
ny (nēw) *adj* new; recent
nyanse (new-*ahng*-ser) *m* nuance; shade
nybegynner (*nēw*-beh-[y]ew-nerr) *m* beginner; learner
nybygger (*nēw*-bew-gerr) *m* pioneer
nyhet (*nēw*-hāyt) *c* news; **nyheter** *pl* news
nykke (*newk*-ker) *nt* whim
nylig (*nēw*-li) *adv* recently, lately
nynne (*newn*-ner) *v* hum
nyre (*nēw*-rer) *c* kidney
***nyse** (*nēw*-ser) *v* sneeze
nysgjerrig (new-*shær*-ri) *adj* curious; inquisitive; nosy *colloquial*
nysgjerrighet (new-*shær*-ri-hāyt) *c* curiosity
***nyte** (*nēw*-ter) *v* enjoy
nytelse (*nēw*-terl-ser) *m* enjoyment
nytte (*newt*-ter) *c* utility,

use; *v* *be of use
nytteløs (*newt*-ter-lūrss) *adj* idle
nyttig (*newt*-ti) *adj* useful
nyttår (*newt*-tawr) *nt* New Year
Ny-Zealand (nēw-*sāy*-lahn) New Zealand
nær (nææ) *adv* near; *adj* close, near
nærende (*nææ*-rer-ner) *adj* nourishing, nutritious
nærhet (*nææ*r-hāyt) *c* vicinity
næring (*nææ*r-ing) *c* nourishment; industry; economy; **næringsliv** economy
nærliggende (*nææ*-li-ger-ner) *adj* neighbo(u)ring, nearby
nærme seg (*nær*-mer) approach
nærsynt (*nææ*-shewnt) *adj* short-sighted
nærvær (*nææ*r-vææ) *nt* presence
nød (nūrd) *c* misery, distress
nøde (*nūr*-der) *v* compel; ***være nødt til** *be obliged to
nødsignal (*nūrd*-sing-naal) *nt* distress signal
nødssituasjon (*nūrd*-si-tew-ah-shōōn) *m* emergency
nødstilfelle (*nūrds*-til-feh-ler) *nt* emergency
nødtvunget (*nūrd*-tvoo-ngert) *adv* by force
nødutgang (*nūrd*-ēwt-gahng) *m* emergency exit
nødvendig (nurd-*vehn*-di) *adj* necessary
nødvendighet (nurd-*vehn*-di-hāyt) *c* necessity, need
nøkkel (*nurk*-kerl) *m* (pl nøkler) key
nøkkelhull (*nurk*-kerl-hewl) *nt* keyhole
nøktern (*nurk*-tern) *adj* down-to-earth, sober
nøle (*nūr*-ler) *v* hesitate
nøtt (nurtt) *c* nut
nøtteknekker (*nurt*-ter-kneh-kerr) *m* nutcrackers *pl*
nøtteskall (*nurt*-ter-skahl) *nt* (pl ~) nutshell
nøyaktig (nur[ew]-*ahk*-ti) *adj* accurate, precise, exact; careful
nøyaktighet (nur[ew]-*ahk*-ti-hāyt) *c* correctness
nøye seg med (*nur*ew-er) *make do with
nøytral (nur[ew]-*traal*) *adj* neutral
nå[1] (naw) *v* reach; *catch; *make
nå[2] (naw) *adv* now; **~ og da** occasionally, now and then
nåde (*naw*-der) *m* mercy, grace
nål (nawl) *c* needle
nåletre (*naw*-ler-trāy) *nt* (pl -rær) firtree
når (norr) *adv* when; *conj* when; **~ enn** whenever
nåtid (*naw*-teed) *c* present

nåtildags (*naw*-til-dahks) *adv* nowadays

nåværende (*naw*-vææ-er-ner) *adj* current, present

O

oase (oo-*aa*-ser) *m* oasis
obduksjon (ob-dewk-*shōōn*) *m* autopsy
oberst (*ōō*-bersht) *m* colonel
objekt (oob-*ʸehkt*) *nt* object
objektiv (ob-ʸehk-*teev*) *adj* objective
obligasjon (ob-li-gah-*shōōn*) *m* bond
obligatorisk (oob-li-gah-*tōō*-risk) *adj* obligatory, compulsory
observasjon (op-sehr-vah-*shōōn*) *m* observation
observatorium (op-sehr-vah-*tōō*-ri-ewm) *nt* (pl -ier) observatory
observere (op-sehr-*vāy*-rer) *v* observe
offensiv (*of*-fahng-seev) *adj* offensive; *m* offensive
offentlig (*of*-fernt-li) *adj* public
***offentliggjøre** (*o*-fernt-li-ʸūr-rer) *v* publish
offentliggjørelse (*of*-fernt-li-ʸūr-rerl-ser) *m* publication
offer (*of*-ferr) *nt* (pl ofre) victim; casualty; sacrifice
offiser (o-fi-*sāyr*) *m* (pl ~er) officer
offisiell (o-fi-si-*ehll*) *adj* official
ofre (*of*-rer) *v* sacrifice
ofte (*of*-ter) *adv* frequently, often
og (o) *conj* and
også (*oss*-so) *adv* also; as well, too
okkupasjon (o-kew-pah-*shōōn*) *m* occupation
okse (*ook*-ser) *m* ox
oksekjøtt (*ook*-ser-khurt) *nt* beef
oksygen (ok-sew-*gāyn*) *nt* oxygen
oktober (ok-*tōō*-berr) October
olabukse (*ōō*-lah-book-se) *c* jeans
oliven (oo-*lee*-vern) *m* (pl ~, ~er) olive
olivenolje (oo-*lee*-vern-ol-ʸer) *c* olive oil
olje (*ol*-ʸer) *c* oil
oljebrønn (*ol*-ʸer-brurn) *m* oil well
oljefilter (*ol*-ʸer-fil-terr) *nt* (pl -tre) oil filter
oljemaleri (*ol*-ʸer-maa-ler-ree) *nt* oil painting
oljeraffineri (*ol*-ʸer-rah-fi-ner-ree) *nt* oil refinery
oljet (*ol*-ʸert) *adj* oily
oljetrykk (*ol*-ʸer-trewk) *nt* (pl ~) oil pressure

om (oomm) *prep* round; about; in; *conj* whether, if
om bord (om bo͞or) aboard
omdanne (*oom*-dah-ner) *v* transform
omdreining (*om*-dray-ning) *m* revolution
omegn (*oom*-mayn) *m* surroundings *pl*
omelett (oo-mer-*lehtt*) *m* omelette
omfang (*oom*-fahng) *nt* extent
omfangsrik (*oom*-fahngs-reek) *adj* big, bulky, extensive
omfatte (*oom*-fah-ter) *v* comprise, include
omfattende (*oom*-fah-ter-ner) *adj* comprehensive, extensive
omfavne (*oom*-fahv-ner) *v* embrace, hug
omfavnelse (*oom*-fahv-nerl-ser) *m* embrace
omgang (*oom*-gahng) *m* round; half time
***omgi** (*oom*-ʸee) *v* encircle, circle, surround
omgivelser (*oom*-ʸee-verl-serr) *pl* environment; setting
***omgå** (*oom*-gaw) *v* by-pass
omgående (*oom*-gaw-er-ner) *adj* prompt
***omgås** (*oom*-gawss) *v* associate with; **~ med** mix with
omhyggelig (oom-*hew*-ger-li) *adj* careful, thorough
omkjøring (*oom*-khūr-ring) *c* detour, diversion
***omkomme** (*oom*-ko-mer) *v* perish
omkostninger (*oom*-kost-ni-ngerr) *pl* expenses *pl*
omkring (oom-*kringng*) *prep* round, around; *adv* about
omkringliggende (om-*kring*-li-ger-ner) *adj* surrounding
omløp (*oom*-lūrp) *nt* circulation; orbit
omregne (*oom*-ray-ner) *v* convert
omregningstabell (*oom*-ray-nings-tah-behll) *m* conversion chart
omringe (*oom*-ri-nger) *v* encircle, circle, surround
omriss (*oom*-riss) *nt* (pl ~) contour, outline; **gi et ~ av** outline
område (*oom*-raw-der) *nt* zone, area, territory, region; sphere
omsetning (*oom*-seht-ning) *m* turnover
omslag (*oom*-shlaag) *nt* reverse; sleeve, jacket
omslutte (*oom*-*shlewt*-ter) *v* envelop
omsorg (*oom*-sorg) *c* care
omstendighet (oom-*stehn*-di-hāyt) *c* condition, circumstance
omstridt (*oom*-strit) *adj* controversial
omtale (*oom*-taa-ler) *m*

mention
omtanke (*oom*-tahng-ker) *m* consideration
omtenksom (oom-*tehngk*-som) *adj* thoughtful
omtrent (oom-*trehnt*) *adv* approximately; about
omtrentlig (oom-*trehnt*-li) *adj* approximate
omvei (*oom*-vay) *m* detour
omvende (*oom*-veh-ner) *v* convert
ond (oonn) *adj* wicked, ill, evil
ondartet (*oon*-naa-tert) *adj* malignant
onde (*oon*-der) *nt* evil
ondsinnet (*oon*-si-nert) *adj* evil
ondskapsfull (*oon*-skaaps-fewl) *adj* vicious, spiteful, malicious
onkel (*oong*-kerl) *m* (pl onkler) uncle
onsdag (*oons*-dah) *m* Wednesday
onyks (*o͞o*-newks) *m* onyx
opal (oo-*paal*) *m* opal
opera (*oo*-per-rah) *m* opera; opera house
operasjon (oo-per-rah-*sho͞on*) *m* surgery, operation
operatør (oo-per-rah-*tu͞rr*) *m* operator
operere (oo-per-*ra͞y*-rer) *v* operate
opp (oopp) *adv* up
oppblåsbar (*oop*-blawss-baar) *adj* inflatable
oppdage (*oop*-daa-ger) *v* discover, detect; notice
oppdagelse (*oop*-daa-gerl-ser) *m* discovery
oppdikte (*oop*-dik-ter) *v* invent
***oppdra** (*oop*-draa) *v* educate; *bring up; raise; rear
oppdrag (*oop*-draag) *nt* (pl ~) assignment
oppdragelse (*oop*-draa-gerl-ser) *m* up-bringing
oppdrette (*oop*-dreh-ter) *v* *breed
oppfatning (*oop*-faht-ning) *m* opinion, view
oppfatte (*oop*-fah-ter) *v* conceive
***oppfinne** (*oop*-fi-ner) *v* invent
oppfinnelse (*oop*-fi-nerl-ser) *m* invention
oppfinner (*oop*-fi-nerr) *m* inventor
oppfinnsom (oop-*fin*-som) *adj* inventive
oppfostre (*oop*-foost-rer) *v* educate; *bring up; raise; rear
oppføre (*oop*-fu͞r-rer) *v* construct; **~ seg** act, behave
oppførelse (*oop*-fu͞r-rerl-ser) *m* show; construction
oppførsel (*oop*-fur-sherl) *m* conduct, behavio(u)r
oppgave (*oop*-gaa-ver) *c* duty; task; exercise
***oppgi** (*oop*-[y]ee) *v* declare;

*give up
opphav (*oop*-haav) *nt* origin
opphisse (*oop*-hi-ser) *v* excite
opphisselse (*oop*-hi-serl-ser) *m* excitement
opphisset (*oop*-hi-sert) *adj* excited
opphold (*oop*-hol) *nt* (pl ~) stay
***oppholde seg** (*oop*-ho-ler) stay
oppholdstillatelse (*oop*-hols-ti-laa-terl-ser) *m* residence permit
opphøre (*oop*-hūr-rer) *v* finish, cease, discontinue, expire, end
oppkalle (*oop*-kahl-ler) *v* name after
opplag (*oop*-laag) *nt* (pl ~) edition
opplagt (*oop*-lahkt) *adj* fit; self-evident
oppleve (*oop*-lāy-ver) *v* experience
opplyse (*oop*-lēw-ser) *v* inform; illuminate
opplysning (*oop*-lēwss-ning) *m* information
oppløp (*oop*-lūrp) *nt* (pl ~) riot
oppløse (*oop*-lūr-ser) *v* dissolve
oppløselig (oop-*lūr*-ser-li) *adj* soluble
oppløsning (*oop*-lūrss-ning) *m* solution
oppmerksom (oop-*mærk*-som) *adj* attentive; ***være ~** *pay attention; ***være ~ på** attend to, *pay attention to
oppmerksomhet (oop-*mærk*-som-hāyt) *c* notice, attention
oppmuntre (*oop*-mewn-trer) *v* encourage; cheer up
oppnå (*oop*-naw) *v* achieve, attain
oppnåelig (oop-*naw*-er-li) *adj* attainable; obtainable
opponere (oo-poo-*nāy*-rer) *v* oppose
opposisjon (oo-poo-si-*shōōn*) *m* opposition
oppover (*oop*-paw-verr) *adv* up, upwards
oppreist (*oop*-rayst) *adj* erect
opprette (*oop*-reh-ter) *v* found; institute
***opprettholde** (*oop*-reht-ho-ler) *v* maintain
oppriktig (oop-*rik*-ti) *adj* sincere, honest
oppringning (*oop*-ring-ning) *m* call
opprinnelig (oop-*rin*-ner-li) *adj* original, initial
opprinnelse (oop-*rin*-nerl-ser) *m* origin, source
opprør (*oop*-rūrr) *nt* (pl ~) revolt, rebellion; ***gjøre ~** revolt
opprørende (*oop*-rūr-rer-ner) *adj* revolting
opprørt (*oop*-rūrt) *adj* *upset
oppsiktsvekkende (*oop*-sikts-veh-ker-ner) *adj*

sensational, striking
oppskrift (*oop*-skrift) *c* recipe
oppslag (*oop*-slag) *nt* bulletin
oppslagstavle (oop-shlaks-*tahv*-ler) *c* message board
oppspore (*oop*-spōō-rer) *v* trace
oppstand (*oop*-stahn) *m* rising, rebellion, revolt
oppstigning (*oop*-steeg-ning) *m* ascent; rise
oppstyr (*oop*-stēwr) *nt* fuss
***oppstå** (*oop*-staw) *v* *arise
oppsyn (*oop*-sēwn) *nt* (pl ~) supervision
oppsynsmann (*oop*-sēwns-mahn) *m* (pl -menn) warden
***oppta** (*oop*-taa) *v* *take up; occupy
opptak[1] (*oop*-taak) *nt* (pl ~) recording
opptak[2] (*oop*-taak) *nt* admission
opptatt (*oop*-taht) *adj* busy, engaged; occupied
opptog (*oop*-tawg) *nt* (pl ~) procession
opptre (*oop*-trāy) *v* perform
opptreden (*oop*-trāy-dern) *m* appearance
oppvakt (*oop*-vahkt) *adj* bright
oppvarte (*oop*-vah-ter) *v* wait on
oppvask (*oop*-vahsk) *m* washing-up; dirty dishes
oppvaskmaskin (*oop*-vahsk-mah-sheen) *m* dishwasher
oppvise (*oop*-vee-ser) *v* exhibit, show
oppå (*oop*-po) *prep* on top of
optiker (*oop*-ti-kerr) *m* optician
optimisme (oop-ti-*miss*-mer) *m* optimism
optimist (oop-t-*mist*) *m* optimist
optimistisk (oop-ti-*miss*-tisk) *adj* optimistic
oransje (oo-*rahng*-sher) *adj* orange
ord (ōōr) *nt* word
ordbok (*ōōr*-bōōk) *c* (pl -bøker) dictionary
orden (*o*-dern) *m* order; **i ~** in order
ordentlig (*o*-dernt-li) *adj* tidy; neat
ordforråd (*ōōr*-fo-rawd) *nt* vocabulary
ordinær (o-di-*nær*) *adj* vulgar
ordliste (*ōōr*-liss-ter) *c* word list
ordne (*oord*-ner) *v* arrange, settle; sort; fix
ordning (*oord*-ning) *c* arrangement, method; settlement
ordre (*oord*-rer) *m* order
ordspill (*ōōr*-spil) *nt* (pl ~) pun
ordspråk (*ōōr*-sprawk) *nt* (pl ~) proverb
ordstrid (*ōōr*-streed) *m*

dispute
ordveksling (*o͞o͞r*-vehk-shling) *c* argument
organ (or-*gaan*) *nt* organ
organisasjon (or-gah-ni-sah-*sho͞o͞n*) *m* organization
organisere (or-gah-ni-*sa̅y̅*-rer) *v* organize
organisk (or-*gaa*-nisk) *adj* organic
orgel (*or*-gerl) *nt* (pl orgler) organ
orientalsk (o-ri-ehn-*taalsk*) *adj* oriental
Orienten (o-ri-*ehn*-tern) Orient
orientere seg (o-ri-ehn-*ta̅y̅*-rer) orientate
original (o-ri-gi-*naal*) *adj* original
orkan (or-*kaan*) *m* hurricane
orke (*or*-ker) *v* sustain
orkester (or-*kehss*-terr) *nt* (pl -tre) orchestra; band
orkesterplass (or-*kehss*-terr-plahss) *m* stall; orchestra seat *Am*
ornament (o-nah-*mehnt*) *nt* ornament
ornamental (o-nah-mehn-*taal*) *adj* ornamental
ortodoks (o-too-*doks*) *adj* orthodox
oss (oss) *pron* us, ourselves
ost (oost) *m* cheese
outsource (*awt*-sour-ser) *v* outsource
ouverture (oo-ver-*te̅w̅*-rer) *m* overture
oval (oo-*vaal*) *adj* oval
ovenfor (*aw*-vern-for) *prep* above, over; *adv* above, overhead
ovenpå (*aw*-vern-paw) *adv* upstairs
over (*aw*-verr) *prep* across, over; *adv* over; **over-** upper; **~ ende** down, over
overall (*aw*-ver-rol) *m* overalls *pl*
overalt (o-ver-*rahlt*) *adv* everywhere, throughout
overanstrenge (*aw*-ver-rahn-streh-nger) *v* strain; **~ seg** overwork
overbevise (*aw*-verr-beh-vee-ser) *v* convince, persuade
overbevisning (*aw*-verr-beh-veess-ning) *m* conviction, persuasion
overdreven (*aw*-dra̅y̅-vern) *adj* extravagant, excessive
***overdrive** (*aw*-ver-dree-ver) *v* exaggerate; magnify; overdo
overdrivelse (*aw*-verr-driv-erl-ser) *m* exaggeration
overenskomst (*aw*-ver-rehns-komst) *m* settlement, agreement
overensstemmelse (*aw*-ver-rehns-steh-merl-ser) *m* agreement; **i ~ med** in accordance with, according to
overfall (*aw*-verr-fahl) *nt* (pl ~) attack; robbery; hold-up
overfart (*aw*-verr-faht) *m*

crossing, passage
overfladisk (*aw*-verr-flaa-disk) *adj* superficial
overflate (*aw*-verr-flaa-ter) *c* surface
overflod (*aw*-verr-flōōd) *m* abundance; plenty
overflødig (*aw*-verr-flūr-di) *adj* superfluous; redundant
overfor (*aw*-verr-for) *prep* opposite, facing; towards
overfylt (*aw*-verr-fewlt) *adj* crowded
overføre (*aw*-verr-fūr-rer) *v* transfer; remit
overgang (*aw*-verr-gahng) *m* transition
***overgi seg** (*aw*-verr-ʸee) surrender
overgivelse (*aw*-verr-ʸee-verl-ser) *m* surrender
overgrodd (*aw*-verr-grood) *adj* overgrown
***overgå** (*aw*-verr-gaw) *v* exceed, *outdo
overhale (*aw*-verr-haa-ler) *v* overhaul
overhodet (o-verr-*hōō*-der) *adv* at all
overlagt (*aw*-ver-lahkt) *adj* deliberate
***overlate** (*aw*-ver-laa-ter) *v* *leave to; entrust
overlegen (*aw*-ver-lāy-gern) *adj* superior, haughty
overleve (*aw*-ver-lāy-ver) *v* survive
overlærer (*aw*-ver-lææ-rerr) *m* headmaster, head teacher
overmodig (*aw*-verr-mōō-di) *adj* presumptuous
overoppsyn (*awv*-err-op-sēwn) *nt* supervision
overraske (*aw*-ver-rahss-ker) *v* surprise
overraskelse (*aw*-ver-rahss-kerl-ser) *m* surprise
***overrekke** (*aw*-ver-reh-ker) *v* hand, *give
overrumple (*aw*-ver-roomp-ler) *v* *catch
***overse** (*aw*-ver-shāy) *v* overlook
***oversette** (*aw*-ver-sheh-ter) *v* translate
oversettelse (*aw*-ver-sheh-terl-ser) *m* translation; version
oversetter (*aw*-ver-sheh-terr) *m* translator
overside (*aw*-ver-shee-der) *c* top side, top
oversikt (*aw*-ver-shikt) *m* survey
oversjøisk (*aw*-ver-shūr-isk) *adj* overseas
***overskride** (*aw*-ver-shkree-der) *v* exceed
overskrift (*aw*-ver-shkrift) *c* heading; headline
overskudd (*aw*-ver-shkewd) *nt* (pl ~) surplus
overskyet (*aw*-ver-shēw-ert) *adj* overcast, cloudy
overspent (*aw*-ver-shpehnt) *adj* overstrung
overstrømmende (*aw*-ver-shtrur-mer-ner) *adj* exuberant

oversvømmelse (*aw*-ver-shvur-merl-ser) *m* flood
***overta** (*aw*-ver-taa) *v* *take over
overtale (*aw*-ver-taa-ler) *v* persuade
overtrekk (*aw*-ver-trehkk)*nt* overdraft
overtrett (*aw*-ver-trehtt) *adj* over-tired
overtro (*aw*-ver-tro͞o) *c* superstition
overveie (*aw*-verr-vay-er) *v* consider; deliberate
overveielse (*aw*-verr-vay-erl-ser) *m* consideration; deliberation
overvekt (*aw*-verr-vehkt) *c* overweight; predominance
overvelde (*aw*-verr-veh-ler) *v* overwhelm
***overvinne** (*aw*-verr-vi-ner) *v* *overcome; defeat
***overvære** (*aw*-verr-vææ-rer) *v* attend
overvåke (*awv*-err-vaw-ker) *v* supervise; patrol
overvåking (*awv*-err-vaw-king)*c*surveillance
ovn (ovnn) *m* stove, furnace
ozon (oo-so͞on) *nt* ozone

P

padde (*pahd*-der) *c* toad
padleåre (*pahd*-ler-aw-rer) *c* paddle
Pakistan (pah-ki-*staan*) Pakistan
pakistaner (pah-ki-*staa*-nerr) *m* Pakistani
pakistansk (pah-ki-*staansk*) *adj* Pakistani
pakke[1] (*pahk*-ker) *c* package, parcel
pakke[2] (*pahk*-ker) *v* pack; **~ inn** wrap; envelop **~ ned** pack up; **~ opp** unpack, unwrap
pakkhus (*pahk*-he͞wss) *nt* (pl ~) warehouse
pakt (pahkt)*c*pact
palass (pah-*lahss*) *nt* palace
palme (*pahl*-mer) *m* palm
panel (pah-*na͞yl*) *nt* panel
panelverk (pah-*na͞yl*-værk) *nt* panelling
panikk (pah-*nikk*) *m* scare, panic
panne (*pahn*-ner) *c* forehead; pan
panser (*pahn*-serr) *nt* bonnet; hood *nAm*
pant (pahnt) *m* deposit
pantelån (*pahn*-ter-lawn) *nt* mortgage
pantelåner (*pahn*-ter-lawnerr) *m* pawnbroker
***pantsette** (*pahnt*-seh-ter) *v* pawn
papegøye (pah-per-*gur*ew-er) *m* parrot; parakeet
papir (pah-*peer*) *nt* paper; **papir-** paper

papirhandel (pah-*peer*-hahn-derl) *m* (pl -dler) stationer's
papirkniv (pah-*peer*-kneev) *m* paper knife
papirkurv (pah-*peer*-kewrv) *m* wastepaper basket
papirlommetørkle (pah-*peer*-loo-mer-turr-kler) *nt* (pl -lær) tissue
papirpose (pah-*peer*-pōō-ser) *m* paper bag
papirserviett (pah-*peer*-sær-vi-eht) *m* paper napkin
papirvarer (pah-*peer*-vaa-rerr) *pl* stationery
papp (pahpp) *m* cardboard
pappa (*pahp*-pah) *m* dad, daddy
par (paar) *nt* pair; couple
parabol (pah-rah-*bōōl*) *c* satellite dish
parade (pah-*raa*-der) *m* parade
parabolantenne (pah-raa-bōōl-ahn-*tehn*-ner) *c* satellite dish
paradis (pah-raa-*dis*) *nt* paradise
parafin (pah-rah-*feen*) *m* paraffin
parallell (pah-rah-*lehll*) *m* parallel; *adj* parallel
paraply (pah-rah-*plēw*) *m* umbrella
parasoll (pah-rah-*soll*) *m* sunshade
parat (pah-*raat*) *adj* ready
parfyme (pahr-*fēw*-mer) *m* perfume
park (pahrk) *m* park; **offentlig parkanlegg** public garden
parkere (pahr-*kāy*-rer) *v* park
parkering (pahr-*kāy*-ring) *c* parking; **~ forbudt** no parking
parkeringsavgift (pahr-*kāy*-rings-aav-ʸift) *c* parking fee
parkeringslys (pahr-*kāy*-rings-lēwss) *nt* (pl ~) parking light
parkeringsplass (pahr-*kāy*-rings-plahss) *m* car park; parking lot *Am*
parkeringssone (pahr-*kāy*-ring-sōō-ner) *c* parking zone
parkometer (pahr-koo-*māy*-terr) *nt* (pl ~, -tre) parking meter
parlament (pahr-lah-*mehnt*) *nt* parliament; **parlamentarisk** *adj* parliamentary
parlør (pah-*lūrr*) *m* phrase book
parti (pah-*tee*) *nt* party; side
partisk (*paa*-tisk) *adj* partial
partner (*paat*-nerr) *m* partner; associate
parykk (pah-*rewkk*) *m* wig
pasient (pah-si-*ehnt*) *m* patient
pasifisme (pah-si-*fiss*-mer) *m* pacifism
pasifist (pah-si-*fist*) *m* pacifist

pasifistisk (pah-si-*fiss*-tisk) *adj* pacifist
pass (pahss) *nt* passport; mountain pass
passasje (pah-*saa*-sher) *m* passage
passasjer (pah-sah-*shayr*) *m* passenger
passasjerbåt (pah-sah-*shayr*-bawt) *m* liner
passe (*pahss*-ser) *v* fit, suit; tend; look after; **~ på** mind, *take care of; **~ seg for** mind, look out; **~ til** match
passende (*pahss*-ser-ner) *adj* appropriate, convenient, adequate; proper, just
passere (pah-*say*-rer) *v* pass
passfoto (*pahss*-foo-too) *nt* (pl ~) passport photograph
passiv (*pahss*-seev) *adj* passive
passkontroll (*pahss*-koon-trol) *m* passport control
passord (*pahss*- *oor*) *m* password
pasta (*pahss*-tah) *m* paste; noodles
patent (pah-*tehnt*) *nt* patent
pater (*paa*-terr) *m* Father
patriot (paht-ri-*oot*) *m* patriot
patron (paht-*roon*) *m* cartridge
patrulje (paht-*rewl*-*y*er) *m* patrol
patruljere (pah-trewl-*yay*-rer) *v* patrol
pattedyr (*paht*-ter-dewr) *nt* (pl ~) mammal
pause (*pou*-ser) *m* pause; intermission, interval
pave (*paa*-ver) *m* pope
paviljong (pah-vil-*yoangng*) *m* pavilion
peanøtt (*pee*-ah-nurt) *c* peanut
pedal (peh-*daal*) *m* pedal
peis (payss) *m* fireplace
peke (*pay*-ker) *v* point
pekefinger (*pay*-ker-fi-ngerr) *m* (pl -grer) index finger
pelikan (peh-li-*kaan*) *m* pelican
pels (pehls) *m* fur
pelskåpe (*pehls*-kaw-per) *c* fur coat
pen (payn) *adj* good--looking, handsome, pretty; fine, nice
pendler (*pehnd*-lerr) *m* commuter
pengeanbringelse (*pehng*-nger-ahn-bri-ngerl-ser) *m* investment
pengepung (*pehng*-nger-poong) *m* purse
penger (*pehng*-ngerr) *pl* money
pengeseddel (*pehng*-nger-seh-derl) *m* (pl -sedler) banknote
pengeskap (*pehng*-nger-skaap) *nt* (pl ~) safe
pengeutpresning (*pehng*-nger-ewt-prehss-ning) *m*

blackmail; **presse penger av** blackmail
penicillin (peh-ni-si-*leen*) *nt* penicillin
penn (pehnn) *m* pen
pensel (*pehn*-serl) *m* (pl -sler) paint-brush, brush
pensjon (pahng-*shōōn*) *m* pension; board; retirement; **full ~** full board, board and lodging, bed and board; **gå av med ~** retire
pensjonat (pahng-shoo-*naat*) *nt* boarding-house, guest-house, pension
pensjonatskole (pahng-shoo-*naat*-skōō-ler) *m* boarding school
pensjonert (pahng-shoo-*nāyt*) *adj* retired
pepper (*pehp*-perr) *m* pepper
peppermynte (peh-perr-*mewn*-ter) *c* peppermint
pepperrot (*pehp*-per-rōōt) *c* horseradish
per, pr. (pær) *prep* per
perfeksjon (pær-fehk-*shōōn*) *m* perfection
perfekt (pær-*fehkt*) *adj* perfect; faultless
periode (peh-ri-*ōō*-der) *m* period
periodevis (peh-ri-*ōō*-der-veess) *adj* periodical
perle (*pææ*-ler) *c* pearl, bead
perlekjede (*pææ*-ler-khāy-der) *nt* beads *pl*
perlemor (*pææ*-ler-mōōr) *nt* mother of pearl
perm (pærm) *m* cover
permisjon (pær-mi-*shōōn*) *m* leave; permit
perrong (peh-*rongng*) *m* platform
perser (*pæsh*-sherr) *m* Persian
Persia (*pæsh*-shi-ah) Persia
persienne (pæ-shi-*ehn*-ner) *m* blind, shutter
persille (pæ-*shil*-ler) *c* parsley
persisk (*pæsh*-shisk) *adj* Persian
person (pæ-*shōōn*) *m* person; **per ~** per person
personale (pæ-shoo-*naa*-ler) *nt* personnel, staff
personlig (pæ-*shōōn*-li) *adj* personal; private
personlighet (pæ-*shōōn*-li-hāyt) *c* personality
persontog (pæ-*shōōn*-tawg) *nt* (pl ~) passenger train
perspektiv (pæsh-pehk-*teev*) *nt* perspective
pertentlig (pæ-*tehnt*-li) *adj* precise
pese (*pāy*-ser) *v* pant
pessimisme (peh-si-*miss*-mer) *m* pessimism
pessimist (peh-si-*mist*) *m* pessimist
pessimistisk (peh-si-*miss*-tisk) *adj* pessimistic
petisjon (peh-ti-*shōōn*) *m* petition
petroleum (peht-*rōō*-leh-

ewm) *m* petroleum; kerosene
pianist (piah-*nist*) *m* pianist
piano (pi-*aa*-noo) *nt* piano
pigg (pigg) *m* spike; peak
pigge (*pigg*-ger) *v* spike; prod
piggtråd (*pigg*-traw) *m* barbed wire
pikant (pi-*kahnt*) *adj* savo(u)ry
pike (*pee*-ker) *m* girl
pikenavn (*pee*-ker-nahvn) *nt* (pl ~) maiden name
pikkolo (*pik*-koo-loo) *m* bellboy
piknik (*pik*-nik) *m* picnic; ***dra på ~** picnic
pil (peel) *c* arrow; willow
pilegrim (*pil*-grim) *m* pilgrim
pilegrimsreise (*pil*-grims-ray-ser) *m* pilgrimage
pille (*pil*-ler) *c* pill
pilot (pi-*lōōt*) *m* pilot
pimpstein (*pimp*-stayn) *m* pumice stone
pine (*pee*-ner) *v* torment; *c* torment
pingvin (ping-*veen*) *m* penguin
PIN kode (*pinn-kōō*-der) *c* PIN; personal identification number
pinlig (*peen*-li) *adj* embarrassing, awkward
pinnsvin (*pin*-sveen) *nt* (pl ~) hedgehog
pinse (*pin*-ser) *c* Pentecost
pinsett (pin-*sehtt*) *m* tweezers *pl*
pipe (*pee*-per) *c* pipe
pipetobakk (*pee*-per-too-bahk) *m* pipe tobacco
pisk (pisk) *m* whip
pistol (piss-*tōōl*) *m* pistol
pittoresk (pi-too-*rehsk*) *adj* picturesque
plage (*plaa*-ger) *v* bother; *m* nuisance
plagg (plahgg) *nt* garment
plakat (plah-*kaat*) *m* poster, placard
plan (plaan) *m* scheme, project, plan; map; *nt* level; *adj* even, flat, level
planet (plah-*nāyt*) *m* planet
planetarium (plah-neh-*taa*-ri-ewm) *nt* (pl -ier) planetarium
planke (*plahng*-ker) *m* board, plank
***planlegge** (*plaan*-leh-ger) *v* plan
planovergang (*plaa*-naw-verr-gahng) *m* level crossing
plantasje (plahn-*taa*-sher) *m* plantation
plante (*plahn*-ter) *m* plant; *v* plant
planteskole (*plahn*-ter-skōōler) *m* nursery
plass (plahss) *m* square; room; seat
plassere (plah-*sāy*-rer) *v* *put, *lay
plaster (*plah*-sterr) *nt* (pl ~, -tre) plaster
plastikk (plahss-*tikk*) *m*

plastic; **plastikk-** plastic
plate (*plaa*-ter) *c* plate; sheet; record
platespiller (*plaa*-ter-spi-lerr) *m* record player
platina (*plaa*-ti-nah) *m* platinum
pleie (*play*-er) *v* *be in the habit of; nurse
pleieforeldre (*play*-er-fo-rehl-drer) *pl* foster parents *pl*
pleiehjem (*play*-er-ʸehm) *nt* (pl ~) foster-home
plettfri (*pleht*-free) *adj* spotless, stainless
plikt (plikt) *c* duty
plog (ploog) *m* plough
plombe (*ploom*-ber) *m* filling
plomme (*ploom*-mer) *c* plum
plugge inn (*plewg*-er-in) plug in
plukke (*plook*-ker) *v* pick
pluss (plewss) *adv* plus
plutselig (*plewt*-ser-li) *adj* suddenly; sudden
plyndring (*plewn*-dring) *c* robbery
plystre (*plewss*-trer) *v* whistle
pløye (*plur*ew-er) *v* plough
poengsum (po-*ehng*-sewm) *m* (pl ~mer) score
poesi (poo-eh-*see*) *m* poetry
pokal (poo-*kaal*) *m* cup
Polen (*poo*-lern) Poland
polere (poo-*lay*-rer) *v* polish
polio (*poo*-li-oo) *m* polio
polise (poo-*lee*-ser) *m* policy
politi (poo-li-*tee*) *nt* police *pl*
politibetjent (poo-li-*tee*-beh-tʸehnt) *m* policeman, policewoman
politiker (poo-*lee*-ti-kerr) *m* politician
politikk (poo-li-*tikk*) *m* politics; policy
politisk (poo-*lee*-tisk) *adj* political
politistasjon (poo-li-*tee*-stah-shoon) *m* police station
polsk (poolsk) *adj* Polish
polstre (*pol*-strer) *v* upholster
pommes frites (pom fritt) chips; French fries *Am*
ponni (*pon*-ni) *m* pony
popmusikk (*pop*-mew-sik) *m* pop music
populær (poo-pew-*læær*) *adj* popular
porselen (poo-sher-*layn*) *nt* china, porcelain
porsjon (poo-*shoon*) *m* portion; helping
port (poott) *m* gate
portier (poo-ti-*æær*) *m* (pl ~er) doorman
portner (*poot*-nerr) *m* porter
porto (*poot*-too) *m* postage
portrett (poot-*rehtt*) *nt* portrait
Portugal (*poo*-tew-gahl)

Portugal
portugiser (poo-tew-*gee*-serr) *m* Portuguese
portugisisk (poo-tew-*gee*-sisk) *adj* Portuguese
pose (*pōō*-ser) *m* bag
posisjon (poo-si-*shōōn*) *m* position; station
positiv (*pōō*-si-teev) *adj* positive
post (post) *m* mail, post; item; **ledig ~** vacancy; **poste restante** poste restante
postbud (*post*-bēwd) *nt* (pl ~) postman
poste (*poss*-ter) *v* mail, post
postei (*poewss*-tei) *m* pasty
poster (*poewss*-terr) *m* poster
postkasse (*post*-kah-ser) *c* pillar-box, letter-box; mailbox *nAm*
postkontor (*post*-koon-tōōr) *nt* post-office
postkort (*post*-kot) *nt* (pl ~) postcard
postnummer (*post*-noo-merr) *nt* (pl -numre) zip code *Am*
postvesen (*post*-vāy-sern) *nt* postal service
pote (*pōō*-ter) *m* paw
potet (poo-*tāyt*) *m* potato; **~stappe** *c* mashed potatoes
praksis (*prahk*-siss) *m* practice
prakt (prahkt) *m* splendo(u)r
praktfull (*prahkt*-fewl) *adj* magnificent, gorgeous, splendid
praktisere (prahk-ti-*sāy*-rer) *v* practise
praktisk (*prahk*-tisk) *adj* practical; **~ talt** practically
prat (praat) *m*/*nt* chat
prate (*praa*-ter) *v* chat
preke (*prāy*-ker) *v* preach
preken (*prāy*-kern) *m* sermon
prekestol (*prāy*-ker-stōōl) *m* pulpit
premie (*prāy*-mi-er) *m* prize
preposisjon (preh-poo-si-*shōōn*) *m* preposition
presang (preh-*sahngng*) *m* gift, present
presentasjon (preh-sahng-tah-*shōōn*) *m* introduction, presentation
presentere (preh-sahng-*tāy*-rer) *v* present, introduce
president (preh-si-*dehnt*) *m* president
presis (preh-*seess*) *adj* punctual, precise
press (prehss) *nt* pressure
presse (*prehss*-ser) *v* press; squeeze; *c* press
pressekonferanse (*prehss*-ser-koon-feh-rahng-ser) *m* press conference
presserende (preh-*sāy*-rer-ner) *adj* urgent, pressing
prest (prehst) *m* clergyman, parson; rector, minister; **katolsk ~** priest

prestasjon (prehss-tah-*shōōn*) *m* feat, achievement
prestegård (*prehss*-ter-gawr) *m* vicarage, parsonage
prestere (prehss-*tāy*-rer) *v* achieve
prestisje (prehss-*tee*-sher) *m* prestige
prevensjonsmiddel (preh-vahng-*shōōns*-mi-derl) *nt* (pl -midler) contraceptive
prikk (prik) *m* dot
primær (pri-*mæær*) *adj* primary
prins (prins) *m* prince
prinsesse (prin-*sehss*-ser) *c* princess
prinsipp (prin-*sipp*) *nt* principle
prioritet (pri-oo-ri-*tāyt*) *m* priority
pris (preess) *m* cost, price; charge, rate; award
prisfall (*preess*-fahl) *nt* drop in price, slump
prisliste (*preess*-liss-ter) *c* price list
privat (pri-*vaat*) *adj* private
privatliv (pri-*vaat*-leev) *nt* privacy
privilegere (pri-vi-leh-*gāy*-rer) *v* favo(u)r
privilegium (pri-vi-*lāy*-gi-ewm) *nt* (pl -ier) privilege
problem (proo-*blāym*) *nt* problem; question
produksjon (proo-dook-*shōōn*) *m* production; output
produkt (proo-*dewkt*) *nt* product; produce
produsent (proo-dew-*sehnt*) *m* producer
produsere (proo-dew-*sāy*-rer) *v* produce
profesjon (proo-feh-*shōōn*) *m* profession
profesjonell (proo-feh-shoo-*nehll*) *adj* professional
professor (proo-*fehss*-soor) *m* professor
profet (proo-*fāyt*) *m* prophet
program (proo-*grahmm*) *nt* (pl ~mer) programme
programvare (proo-*grahmm*-vaarer) *m* software
progressiv (*proog*-reh-seev) *adj* progressive
promenade (proo-mer-*naa*-der) *m* promenade
pronomen (proo-*nōō*-mern) *nt* pronoun
propaganda (proo-pah-*gahn*-dah) *m* propaganda
propell (proo-*pehll*) *m* propeller
proporsjon (proo-poo-*shōōn*) *m* proportion
prosent (proo-*sehnt*) *m* percent
prosentsats (proo-*sehnt*-sahts) *m* percentage
prosesjon (proo-seh-*shōōn*) *m* procession
prosess (proo-*sehss*) *m*

process
prosjekt (proo-*shehkt*) *nt* project
prosjektør (proo-shehk-*tūrr*) *m* spotlight
prospekt (proo-*spehkt*) *nt* prospectus
prospektkort (proo-*spehkt*-kot) *nt* (pl ~) picture postcard, postcard
prostituert (proo-sti-tew-*āyt*) *m* prostitute
protein (proo-teh-*een*) *nt* protein
protest (proo-*tehst*) *m* protest
protestantisk (proo-ter-*stahn*-tisk) *adj* Protestant
protestere (proo-ter-*stāy*-rer) *v* protest; object
protokoll (proo-too-*koll*) *m* record
proviant (proo-vi-*ahnt*) *m* provisions *pl*
provins (proo-*vins*) *m* province
provinsiell (proo-vin-si-*ehll*) *adj* provincial
prute (*prew*-ter) *v* bargain
prøve (*prūr*-ver) *v* try, attempt; try on; rehearse; *c* specimen; test; rehearsal
prøverom (*prūr*-ver-room) *nt* (pl ~) fitting room
psykiater (sew-ki-*aa*-terr) *m* psychiatrist
psykisk (*sēw*-kisk) *adj* psychic
psykoanalytiker (sew-koo-ah-nah-*lewt*-ti-kerr) *m* analyst, psychoanalyst
psykolog (sew-koo-*lawg*) *m* psychologist
psykologi (sew-koo-loo-*gee*) *m* psychology
psykologisk (sew-koo-*law*-gisk) *adj* psychological
publikum (*pewb*-li-kewm) *nt* audience, public
publisitet (pewb-li-si-*tāyt*) *m* publicity
pudder (*pewd*-derr) *nt* powder
puff (pewff) *nt* push
pule (*pew*-ler) *v vulgar* fuck
puls (pewls) *m* pulse
pulsåre (*pewls*-aw-rer) *c* artery
pult (pewlt) *m* desk
pumpe (*poom*-per) *v* pump; *c* pump
pund (pewnn) *nt* pound
pung (poongng) *m* purse; pouch
punkt (poongt) *nt* point; item
punktering (poong-*tāy*-ring) *c* puncture, blow-out; flat tyre
punktert (poong-*tāyt*) *adj* punctured
punktlig (*poongt*-li) *adj* punctual
punktum (*pewng*-tewm) *nt* full stop, period, dot
pur (pēwr) *adj* sheer
purpurfarget (*pewr*-pewr-fahr-gert) *adj* purple
pusekatt (*pēw*-ser-kaht) *m* pussy-cat

pusle (*pewsh*-ler) *v* potter; busy oneself
puslespill (*pewsh*-ler-spil) *nt* (pl ~) jigsaw puzzle
pusse (*pewss*-ser) *v* polish
pussig (*pewss*-si) *adj* funny
pust (pewst) *m* breath
puste (*pewss*-ter) *v* breathe; ~ **ut** expire, exhale
pute (*pēw*-ter) *c* cushion; pillow; pad
putevar (*pēw*-ter-vaar) *nt* (pl ~) pillow-case
putte (*pewt*-ter) *v* *put
pyjamas (pew-*shaa*-mahss) *m* pyjamas *pl*
pynt (pewnt) *m* decoration
pynte (*pewn*-ter) *v* decorate
pytt (pewtt) *m* puddle
pære (*pææ*-rer) *c* pear
pæreholder (*pææ*-rer-hoa-lerr) *m* socket
pølse (*purl*-ser) *c* sausage
på (paw) *prep* upon, on, at; to
***pådra seg** (*paw*-draa) contract
påfallende (*paw*-fah-ler-ner) *adj* striking
påfugl (*paw*-fēwl) *m* peacock
påkrevd (*paw*-krehvd) *adj* requisite
pålegg (*paw*-lehg) *nt* (pl ~) rise; sandwich spread, cold cuts
***pålegge** (*paw*-lehg-er) *v* raise, charge
pålitelig (po-*lee*-ter-li) *adj* sound, reliable, trustworthy
påske (*pawss*-ker) *c* Easter
påskelilje (*pawss*-ker-lil-ʸer) *c* daffodil
påskjønne (*paw*-shur-ner) *v* appreciate
påskudd (*paw*-skewd) *nt* (pl ~) pretext, pretence
***påstå** (*paw*-staw) *v* claim
***påta seg** (*paw*-taa) *take charge of
påvirke (*paw*-veer-ker) *v* affect, influence

R

rabalder (rah-*bahl*-derr) *nt* racket
rabarbra (rah-*bahr*-brah) *m* rhubarb
rabatt (rah-*bahtt*) *m* discount, rebate
rabies (*raa*-bi-ehss) *m* rabies
racket (*rehk*-ket) *m* racket
rad (raad) *m* row
radering (rah-*dāy*-ring) *c* etching
radiator (rah-di-*aa*-toor) *m* radiator
radikal (rah-di-*kaal*) *adj* radical
radio (*raa*-di-oo) *m* radio
radius (*raa*-di-ewss) *m* (pl

-ier) radius
raffineri (rah-fi-ner-*ree*) *nt* refinery
rak (raak) *adj* straight
rake (*raa*-ker) *c* rake
rakett (rah-*kehtt*) *m* rocket
ramme (*rahm*-mer) *c* frame; *v* *hit
rampe (*rahm*-per) *c* ramp
ran (raan) *nt* robbery
rand (rahnn) *m* (pl render) brim
rane (*raa*-ner) *v* rob
rang (rahngng) *m* rank
ransake (*rahn*-saa-ker) *v* search
ransel (*rahn*-serl) *m* (pl -sler) satchel
ransmann (*raans*-mahn) *m* (pl -menn) robber
rap (ræp) *c* rap
rapphøne (*rahp*-hūr-ner) *c* partridge
rapport (rah-*pott*) *m* report
rapportere (rah-po-*tāy*-rer) *v* report
rar (raar) *adj* odd
rase (*raa*-ser) *m* race; breed; *v* rage; **rase-** racial
rasende (*raa*-ser-ner) *adj* mad, furious
raseri (raa-ser-*ree*) *nt* rage, anger
rasjon (rah-*shōōn*) *m* ration
rask (rahsk) *adj* swift, fast; *nt* trash
raspe (*rahss*-per) *v* grate
rastløs (*rahst*-lūrss) *adj* restless
rastløshet (*rahst*-lūrss-hāyt) *c* unrest
ratt (rahtt) *nt* steering wheel
rattstamme (*raht*-stah-mer) *m* steering column
rav (raav) *nt* amber
ravn (rahvn) *m* raven
reagere (reh-ah-ga***y*-rer) *v* react
reaksjon (reh-ahk-*shōōn*) *m* reaction
realisere (reh-ah-li-*sāy*-rer) *v* realize
realistisk (reh-ah-*liss*-tisk) *adj* matter-of-fact
redaktør (reh-dahk-*tūrr*) *m* editor
redd (rehdd) *adj* afraid; ***være ~** *be afraid
redde (*rehd*-der) *v* rescue, save
reddik (*rehd*-dik) *m* radish
rede (*rāy*-der) *nt* nest
redegjørelse (*rāy*-der-ʸūr-rerl-ser) *m* account
redigere (reh-dig-*ehrer*) *v* edit
redning (*rehd*-ning) *m* rescue
redsel (*reht*-serl) *m* (pl -sler) terror, horror
redselsfull (*reht*-serls-fewl) *adj* awful, horrible
redskap (*rehss*-kaap) *nt* utensil, tool
reduksjon (reh-dewk-*shōōn*) *m* reduction
redusere (reh-dew-*sāy*-rer) *v* reduce
referanse (reh-fer-*rahng*-ser) *m* reference

referat (reh-fer-raat) *nt* minutes
refill (ri-*fill*) *m* (pl ~) refill
refleks (reh-*flehks*) *m* reflection
reflektere (rehf-lehk-*tāy*-rer) *v* reflect
reflektor (reh-*flehk*-toor) *m* reflector
Reformasjonen (reh-for-mah-*shōō*-nern) the Reformation
refundere (reh-fewn-*dāy*-rer) *v* refund
regatta (reh-*gaht*-tah) *m* regatta
regel (*rāy*-gerl) *m* (pl regler) rule; regulation; **som ~** in general, as a rule
regelmessig (*rāy*-gerl-meh-si) *adj* regular
regent (reh-*gehnt*) *m* ruler
regi (reh-*shee*) *m* direction, staging
regime (reh-*shee*-mer) *nt* régime
regional (reh-gi-oo-*naal*) *adj* regional
regissere (reh-shi-*sai*-rer) *v* direct
regissør (reh-shi-*sūrr*) *m* director
register (reh-*giss*-terr) *nt* (pl ~, -tre) index
registrere (reh-gi-*strāy*-rer) *v* record
registrering (reh-gi-*strāy*-ring) *c* registration
registreringsnummer (reh-gi-*strāy*-rings-noo-merr) *nt* (pl -numre) registration number; licence number *Am*
regjere (reh-*ʸāy*-rer) *v* govern, rule
regjering (reh-*ʸāy*-ring) *c* government; rule
regjeringstid (reh-*ʸāyrings*-teed) *c* reign
regn (rayn) *nt* rain
regnbue (*rayn*-bēw-er) *m* rainbow
regne[1] (*ray*-ner) *v* rain
regne[2] (*ray*-ner) *v* reckon; **~ ut** calculate
regnfrakk (*rayn*-frahk) *m* raincoat, mackintosh
regnfull (*rayn*-fewl) *adj* rainy
regning (*ray*-ning) *c* arithmetic; bill; check *nAm*
regnskur (*rayn*-skōōr) *m* shower
regulere (reh-gew-*lāy*-rer) *v* regulate
regulering (reh-gew-*lāy*-ring) *c* regulation; brace
rehabilitering (reh-hah-bi-li-*tāy*-ring) *c* rehabilitation
reinsdyr (*rayns*-dēwr) *nt* (pl ~) reindeer
reise[1] (*ray*-ser) *v* travel; *c* voyage, journey, trip; **~ bort** depart
reise[2] (*ray*-ser) *v* erect; **~ seg** *rise
reisebyrå (*ray*-ser-bew-raw) *nt* travel agency, travel agent

reiseforsikring (*ray*-ser-fo-shik-ring) *c* travel insurance
reisehåndbok (*ray*-ser-hon-book) *c* (pl -bøker) travel guide
reisende (*ray*-ser-ner) *m* (pl ~) travel(l)er
reiseplan (*ray*-ser-plaan) *m* itinerary
reiserute (*ray*-ser-rew-ter) *c* itinerary
reisesjekk (*ray*-ser-shehk) *m* travel(l)er's cheque
reiseutgifter (*ray*-ser-ewt-ʸif-terr) *pl* travelling expenses
reke (*ray*-ker) *c* shrimp; prawn
rekke (*rehk*-ker) *c* rank, file; chain
***rekke** (*rehk*-ker) *v* pass, *catch
rekkefølge (*rehk*-ker-fur-ler) *m* sequence, order
rekkevidde (*rehk*-ker-vi-der) *c* reach; range
rekkverk (*rehk*-værk) *nt* railing
reklame (reh-*klaa*-mer) *m* advertising; commercial
rekommandere (reh-koo-mahn-*day*-rer) *v* register
rekord (reh-koord) *m* record
rekreasjon (rehk-reh-ah-*shoon*) *m* recreation
rekreasjonssenter (reh-kreh-ah-*shoon*-sehn-terr) *nt* (pl -trer) recreation centre (*Am* center)
rekrutt (rehk-*rewtt*) *m* recruit
rektangel (rehk-*tahng*-ngerl) *nt* (pl -gler) oblong, rectangle
rektangulær (rehk-tahng-gew-*læær*) *adj* rectangular
rektor (*rehk*-toor) *m* headmaster, principal
relativ (*rehl*-lah-teev) *adj* comparative, relative
relieff (reh-li-*ehff*) *nt* relief
religion (reh-li-gi-*oon*) *m* religion
religiøs (reh-li-gi-*urss*) *adj* religious
relikvie (reh-*leek*-vi-er) *m* relic
rem (rehmm) *c* (pl ~mer) strap
remisse (reh-*miss*-ser) *m* remittance
ren (rayn) *adj* clean; pure; **gjøre rent** clean
rengjøring (*rayn*-ʸur-ring) *c* cleaning
rengjøringsmiddel (*rayn*-ʸur-rings-mi-derl) *nt* (pl -midler) detergent
rennestein (*rehn*-ner-stayn) *m* gutter
rense (*rehn*-ser) *v* clean
rensemiddel (*rehn*-ser-mi-derl) *nt* (pl -midler) cleaning fluid
renseri (rehn-ser-*ree*) *nt* dry cleaner's
renslig (*rayn*-shli) *adj* clean, cleanly

rente (*rehn*-ter) *c* interest
rep (rāyp) *nt* rope
reparasjon (reh-pah-rah-*shōōn*) *m* reparation, repair
reparere (reh-pah-*rāy*-rer) *v* repair; mend, fix
repertoar (reh-peh-too-*aar*) *nt* repertory
reporter (reh-*paw*-terr) *m* reporter
representant (reh-preh-sern-*tahnt*) *m* agent
representasjon (reh-preh-sern-tah-*shōōn*) *m* representation
representativ (reh-preh-*sehn*-tah-teev) *adj* representative
representere (reh-preh-sern-*tāy*-rer) *v* represent
reproduksjon (reh-proo-dewk-*shōōn*) *m* reproduction
reprodusere (reh-proo-dew-*sāy*-rer) *v* reproduce
republikansk (reh-pewb-li-*kaansk*) *adj* republican
republikk (reh-pew-*blikk*) *m* republic
resepsjon (reh-sehp-*shōōn*) *m* reception office
resepsjonist (reh-sehp-*shōōn-ist*) *m* receptionist
resept (reh-*sehpt*) *m* prescription
reservasjon (reh-sær-vah-*shōōn*) *m* reservation, booking
reserve (reh-*sær*-ver) *m* reserve; **reserve-** spare
reservedekk (reh-*sær*-ver-dehk) *nt* (pl ~) spare tyre
reservedel (reh-*sær*-ver-dāyl) *m* spare part
reservehjul (reh-*sær*-ver-ʸēwl) *nt* (pl ~) spare wheel
reservere (reh-sær-*vāy*-rer) *v* reserve; book
reservert (reh-sær-*vāyt*) *adj* reserved
reservoar (reh-sær-voo-*aar*) *nt* reservoir
resirkulerbar (*reh*-seer-kew-*lāyr*-bahr) *adj* recyclable
resirkulere (*reh*-seer-kew-*lāy*-rer) *v* recycle
resonnere (reh-soo-*nāy*-rer) *v* reason
respekt (rehss-*pehkt*) *m* esteem, respect; regard
respektabel (rehss-pehk-*taa*-berl) *adj* respectable
respektere (rehss-pehk-*tāy*-rer) *v* respect
respektiv (*rehss*-pehk-teev) *adj* respective
rest (rehst) *m* rest; remainder, remnant
restaurant (rehss-tew-*rahngng*) *m* restaurant
resterende (rehss-*tāy*-rer-ner) *adj* remaining
resultat (reh-sewl-*taat*) *nt* result; outcome, issue
resultere (reh-sewl-*tāy*-rer) *v* result
resymé (reh-sew-*māy*) *nt* résumé

retning (*reht*-ning) *m* direction; way
retningslinje (*rehtt*-nings-lin-ʸer) *c* guideline
retningsnummer (*rehtt*-nings-noom-merr) *nt* area code
rett[1] (rehtt) *m* dish, course
rett[2] (rehtt) *m* law, justice; *adj* right; appropriate; *adv* straight; ***ha ~** *be right; **~ frem** straight on, straight ahead
rette[1] (*reht*-ter) *v* correct; **med ~** rightly
rette[2] (*reht*-ter) *v* direct; **~ mot** aim at
rettelse (*reht*-terl-ser) *m* correction
rettergang (*reht*-terr-gahng) *m* trial
rettferdig (reht-*fær*-di) *adj* just, fair, right
rettferdiggjøre (reht-*fær*-di-ʸūr-rer) *v* justify
rettferdighet (reht-*fær*-di-hāyt) *c* justice
rettighet (*reht*-ti-hāyt) *c* right
rettslig (*reht*-shli) *adj* legal
rettssak (*reht*-saak) *c* lawsuit, trial
returnere (reh-tewr-*nāy*-rer) *v* *send back
reumatisme (rehv-mah-*tiss*-mer) rheumatism
rev (rāyv) *m* fox; *nt* reef
revers (reh-*væshsh*) *m* reverse
revidere (reh-vi-*dāy*-rer) *v* revise
revisjon (reh-vi-*shōōn*) *m* revision
revolusjon (reh-voo-lew-*shōōn*) *m* revolution
revolusjonær (reh-voo-lew-shoo-*næær*) *adj* revolutionary
revolver (reh-*vol*-verr) *m* gun, revolver
revy (reh-*vew*) *m* revue
revyteater (reh-*vew*-teh-aa-terr) *nt* (pl ~, -tre) music hall
ribbein (*rib*-bayn) *nt* (pl ~) rib
ridder (*rid*-derr) *m* knight
***ride** (*ree*-der) *v* *ride
rideskole (*ree*-der-skōō-ler) *m* riding school
ridning (*reed*-ning) *m* riding
rift (rift) *c* tear
rik (reek) *adj* wealthy, rich
rikdom (*reek*-dom) *m* (pl ~mer) wealth, riches *pl*
rike (*reeker*) *nt* kingdom
rikelig (*ree*-ker-li) *adj* plentiful; abundant
rikelighet (*reek*-li-hāyt) *c* plenty
riksvei (*riks*-vay) *m* highway
riktig (*rik*-ti) *adj* correct, just, right; proper; *adv* rather
rim (reem) *nt* rhyme
rimelig (*ree*-mer-li) *adj* reasonable
ring (ringng) *m* ring
ringe (*ring*-nger) *v* *ring; *adj* small; *v* call; ring up,

phone; call up *Am*
ringeakt (*ring*-nger-ahkt) *m* contempt, disdain
ringeklokke (*ring*-nger-klo-ker) *c* doorbell, bell
ringvei (*ring*-vay) *m* by-pass
rips (rips) *m* (pl ~) (red)currant
ris (reess) *m* rice
risikabel (ri-si-*kaa*-berl) *adj* risky; precarious, critical
risikere (ri-si-*kay*-rer) *v* risk
risiko (*riss*-si-koo) *m* risk; hazard, chance
risp (risp) *nt* scratch
rispe (*riss*-per) *v* scratch
rist (rist) *c* grate
riste (*riss*-ter) *v* roast; *shake; toast
rival (ri-*vaal*) *m* rival
rivalisere (ri-vah-li-*say*-rer) *v* rival
rivalitet (ri-vah-li-*tayt*) *m* rivalry
***rive** (*ree*-ver) *v* *tear; **~ i stykker** rip; **~ ned** demolish
rivjern (*reev*-ʸæn) *nt* (pl ~) grater
ro[1] (roo) *m* quiet; **falle til ~** calm down; **roe seg** calm down; **~ og mak** leisure
ro[2] (roo) *v* row
robust (roo-*bewst*) *adj* robust
robåt (*roo*-bawt) *m* rowing boat
rogn (rongn) *c* roe
rolig (*roo*-li) *adj* quiet, calm, tranquil; serene
rom (roomm) *nt* room, chamber; space
roman (roo-*maan*) *m* novel
romanforfatter (roo-*maan*-for-faht-terr) *m* novelist
Romania (roo-*maa*-ni-ah) Rumania
romantisk (roo-*mahn*-tisk) *adj* romantic
romerbad (*roo*-merr-baad) *nt* (pl ~) Turkish bath
romersk-katolsk (*roo*-mersh-kah-toolsk) *adj* Roman Catholic
romferge (*room*-fær-ger), **romferje** (*room*-fær-ʸer) *c* space shuttle
romme (*room*-mer) *v* contain
rommelig (*room*-mer-li) *adj* spacious, roomy; large
rop (roop) *nt* call, cry; shout
rope (*roo*-per) *v* cry, call; shout
ror (roor) *nt* helm, rudder
rorgjenger (*roor*-ʸeh-ngerr) *m* helmsman
rormann (*roor*-mahn) *m* (pl -menn) helmsman
ros (rooss) *m* glory, praise
rosa (*roo*-sah) *adj* rose
rose (*roo*-ser) *c* rose; *v* praise
rosenkrans (*roo*-sern-krahns) *m* beads *pl*, rosary
rosenkål (*roo*-sern-kawl) *m* sprouts *pl*
rosin (roo-*seen*) *c* raisin
rot[1] (root) *c* (pl røtter) root
rot[2] (root) *nt* muddle, mess

rote (*roo*-ter) *v* muddle; ~ **til** mess up
rotte (*rot*-ter) *c* rat
rouge (roosh) *m* rouge
rovdyr (*rawv*-dewr) *nt* (pl ~) beast of prey
ru (rew) *adj* rough; harsh
rubin (rew-*been*) *m* ruby
rubrikk (rew-*brikk*) *m* column
ruin (rew-*een*) *m* ruins
rulett (rew-*lehtt*) *m* roulette
rull (rewll) *m* roll
rulle (*rewl*-ler) *v* roll
rullegardin (*rewl*-ler-gah-deen) *m/nt* blind
rulleskøyteløping (rewl-ler-shur[ew]-ter-lurp-ing) *c* roller-skating
rullestein (*rewl*-ler-stayn) *m* boulder
rullestol (*rewl*-ler-stool) *m* wheelchair
rulletrapp (*rewl*-ler-trahp) *c* escalator
rumener (roo-*may*-nerr) *m* Rumanian
rumensk (roo-*maynsk*) *adj* Rumanian
rumpeballe (*room*-per-bah-ler) *m* buttock
rund (rewnn) *adj* round
runde (*rewn*-der) *m* round; lap
rundhåndet (*rewn*-ho-nert) *adj* generous
rundkjøring (*rewn*-khur-ring) *c* roundabout
rundreise (*rewn*-ray-ser) *c* tour
rundspørring (*rewn*-spur-ring) *c* enquiry; poll
rundstykke (*rewn*-stew-ker) *nt* roll; bun *nAm*
rundt (rewnt) *prep* about; *adv* around
rushtid (*rursh*-teed) *m* rush hour, peak hour
russer (*rewss*-serr) *m* Russian
russisk (*rewss*-sisk) *adj* Russian
Russland (*rewss*-lahn) Russia
rust (rewst) *m* rust
rusten (*rewss*-tern) *adj* rusty
rustning (*rewst*-ning) *m* armour
rute (*rew*-ter) *c* check; pane; route
ruteplan (*rew*-ter-plaan) *m* schedule
rutine (rew-*tee*-ner) *m* routine
rutsjebane (*rewt*-sher-baa-ner) *m* slide
rydde opp (*rewd*-der) tidy up
rydde vekk (*rewd*-der vehkk) *put away
rye (*rew*-er) *c* rug
rygg (rewgg) *m* back
rygge (*rewg*-ger) *v* reverse
ryggrad (*rewg*-raad) *m* spine, backbone
ryggsekk (*rewg*-sehk) *m* knapsack, rucksack
ryggsmerter (*rewg*-smæ-terr) *pl* backache
rykk (rewkk) *nt* wrench, tug

rykte (*rewk*-ter) *nt* rumour; reputation, fame
rynke (*rewng*-ker) *c* wrinkle; crease
ryste (*rewss*-ter) *v* *shake
rytme (*rewt*-mer) *m* rhythm
rytter (*rewt*-terr) *m* horseman, rider
rød (rūr) *adj* red
rødbete (*rūr*-bāy-ter) *c* beetroot
rødme (*rurd*-mer) *v* blush
rødspette (*rūr*-speh-ter) *c* plaice
rødstrupe (*rūr*-strēw-per) *m* robin
røkelse (*rūr*-kerl-ser) *m* incense
rømling (*rurm*-ling) *m* runaway
rømme[1] (*rurm*-mer) *m* sour cream
rømme[2] (*rurm*-mer) *v* escape, flee
røntgenbilde (*rurnt*-kern-bil-der) *nt* X-ray
røntgenfotografere (*rurnt*-kern-foo-too-grah-fāy-rer) *v* X-ray
røpe (*rūr*-per) *v* *give away
rør (rūrr) *nt* tube, pipe; cane
røre (*rūr*-rer) *v* touch; stir; **~ seg** move
rørende (*rūr*-rer-ner) *adj* touching
rørlegger (*rūr*-leh-gerr) *m* plumber
røyk (rur^ewk) *m* smoke
røyke (*rur*ew-ker) *v* smoke; **røyking forbudt** no smoking
røykekupé (*rur*ew-ker-kew-pāy) *m* smoking compartment, smoker
røyker (*rur*ew-kerr) *m* smoker
røykfri (*rur*^ew*k*-frēe) *adj* smoke-free
rå (raw) *adj* raw
råd (rawd) *nt* advice; counsel, council; ***ha ~ til** *can afford
råde (*raw*-der) *v* advise
rådgiver (*rawd*-^yee-verr) *m* counsellor
rådhus (*rawd*-hēwss) *nt* (pl ~) town hall
rådslagning (*rawd*-shlaag-ning) *m* deliberation
***rådslå** (*rawd*-shlaw) *v* deliberate
rådsmedlem (*rawds*-māyd-lerm) *nt* (pl ~mer) councillor
***rådspørre** (*rawd*-spur-rer) *v* consult
råmateriale (*raw*-mah-ter-ri-aa-ler) *nt* raw material
råtten (*rot*-tern) *adj* rotten

S

safe (sayf) *m* safe
safir (sah-*feer*) *m* sapphire
saft (sahft) *c* juice
saftig (*sahf*-ti) *adj* juicy
sag (saag) *c* saw
sagbruk (*saag*-broōk) *nt* (pl ~) sawmill
sagflis (*saag*-fleess) *c* sawdust
sak (saak) *c* matter, cause; case; issue
sakfører (*saak*-fūr-rerr) *m* solicitor
sakkyndig (*saak*-khewn-di) *adj* expert
saks (sahks) *c* scissors *pl*
sakte (*sahk*-ter) *adj* slow
sal (saal) *m* hall; saddle
salat (sah-*laat*) *m* salad, lettuce
saldo (*sahl*-doo) *m* balance
salg (sahlg) *nt* sale; **til salgs** for sale
salgbar (*sahlg*-baar) *adj* saleable
salme (*sahl*-mer) *m* hymn
salmiakk (sahl-mi-*ahkk*) *m* ammonia
salong (sah-*longng*) *m* salon; lounge, drawing room
salt (sahlt) *nt* salt; *adj* salty
saltkar (*sahlt*-kaar) *nt* (pl ~) salt cellar, salt shaker *Am*
salve (*sahl*-ver) *c* ointment
samarbeid (*sahm*-mahr-bayd) *nt* co-operation
samarbeide (*sahm*-mahr-bay-der) *v* collaborate
samarbeidsvillig (*sahm*-mahr-bayds-vi-li) *adj* co-operative
same (*saa*-mer) *m* Saami (aborigines of Northern Scandinavia)
samfunn (*sahm*-fewn) *nt* (pl ~) society; community; **samfunns-** social
samle (*sahm*-ler) *v* collect, gather; assemble; compile; **~ inn** collect
samler (*sahm*-lerr) *m* collector
samles (*sahm*-lerss) *v* gather
samling (*sahm*-ling) *c* collection
samme (*sahm*-mer) *adj* same
sammen (*sahm*-mern) *adv* together
sammendrag (*sahm*-mern-draag) *nt* (pl ~) summary
sammenføye (*sahm*-mern-fur^ew-er) *v* join
sammenheng (*sahm*-mern-hehng) *m* connection; coherence
sammenkomst (*sahm*-mern-komst) *m* meeting, assembly
sammenligne (*sahm*-mern-

ling-ner) *v* compare
sammenligning (*sahm*-mern-ling-ning) *m* comparison; **uten ~** by far
sammensetning (*sahm*-mern-seht-ning) *m* composition
sammensmeltning (*sahm*-mern-smehlt-ning) *m* merger
sammenstille (*sahm*-mern-sti-ler) *v* combine
sammenstøt (sahm-mern-stūrt) *nt* (pl ~) collision
sammensvergelse (*sahm*-mern-svær-gerl-ser) *m* plot
sammensverge seg (*sahm*-mern-svær-ger) conspire
sammentreff (sahm-mern-trehf) *nt* (pl ~) coincidence
samordne (*sahm*-mor-dner) *v* co-ordinate
samtale (*sahm*-taa-ler) *m* talk, conversation; discussion
samtale venter (*sahm*-tāa-ler *vehn*-ter) *c* call waiting
samtidig[1] (*sahm*-tee-di) *adj* simultaneous; contemporary; *adv* simultaneously
samtidig[2] (*sahm*-tee-di) *m* (pl ~e) contemporary
samtykke (*sahm*-tew-ker) *v* consent; *nt* consent
samvittighet (sahm-*vit*-ti-hāyt) *c* conscience
sanatorium (sah-nah-*tōo*-ri-ewm) *nt* (pl -ier) sanatorium
sand (sahnn) *m* sand
sandal (sahn-*daal*) *m* sandal
sanddyne (*sahn*-dēw-ner) *c* dune
sandet (*sahn*-nert) *adj* sandy
sandpapir (*sahn*-pah-peer) *nt* sandpaper
sang (sahngng) *m* song
sanger (*sahng*-ngerr) *m* vocalist, singer
sanitetsbind (sah-ni-*tāyts*-bin) *nt* (pl ~) sanitary towel
sanitær (sah-ni-*tææ r*) *adj* sanitary
sann (sahnn) *adj* true
sannferdig (sahn-*fær*-di) *adj* truthful
sannhet (*sahn*-hāyt) *c* truth
sannsynlig (sahn-*sēwn*-li) *adj* probable, likely
sannsynligvis (sahn-*sēwn*-li-veess) *adv* probably
sans (sahns) *m* sense
sardin (sah-*deen*) *m* sardine
satellitt (sah-ter-*litt*) *m* satellite; **~-TV** satellite tv
satellittoverføring (sah-ter-*litt*-aw-verr-fūr-ing) *c* satellite television
satelittradio (sah-ter-*litt*-*rah*-di-ōo) *c* satelite radio
sateng (sah-*tehngng*) *m* satin
sau (sou) *m* sheep
Saudi-Arabia (*sou*-di-ah-rah-bi-ah) Saudi Arabia
saudiarabisk (*sou*-di-ah-raa-bisk) *adj* Saudi

Arabian
saus (souss) *m* sauce
savn (sahvn) *nt* lack
savne (*sahv*-ner) *v* miss; lack; **savnet person** missing person
scene (*sāy*-ner) *m* stage; scene; shot
***se** (sāy) *v* *see; look; notice; **~ opp** look out; **~ på** look at; **~ ut** look
sebra (*sāyb*-rah) *m* zebra
seder (*sāy*-derr) *pl* customs; morals
sedvane (*sāyd*-vaa-ner) *m* usage
sedvanlig (sehd-*vaan*-li) *adj* customary
seer (*sāy*-err) *m* spectator
seg (say) *pron* himself, herself, itself, oneself; themselves
segl (sayl) *nt* seal
seier (*say*-err) *m* victory
seig (say) *adj* tough
seil (sayl) *nt* sail
seilbar (*sayl*-baar) *adj* navigable
seilbåt (*sayl*-bawt) *m* sailing boat
seilduk (*sayl*-dēwk) *m* canvas
seile (*say*-ler) *v* sail
seilforening (*sayl*-fo-rāy-ning) *c* yacht club
seilsport (*sayl*-spot) *m* yachting
sekk (sehkk) *m* sack
sekretær (sehk-rer-*tæær*) *m* secretary; clerk
seks (sehks) *num* six
seksjon (sehk-*shōōn*) *m* section
seksten (*sayss*-tern) *num* sixteen
sekstende (*sayss*-ter-ner) *num* sixteenth
seksti (*sehks*-ti) *num* sixty
seksualitet (sehk-sew-ah-li-*tāyt*) *m* sexuality
seksuell (sehk-sew-*ehll*) *adj* sexual
sekund (seh-*kewnn*) *nt* second
sekundær (seh-kewn-*dæær*) *adj* secondary; subordinate
sel (sāyl) *m* seal
***selge** (*sehl*-ler) *v* *sell
selleri (seh-ler-*ree*) *m* celery
selskap (*sehl*-skaap) *nt* party, company; society
selskapsantrekk (*sehl*-skaap-sahn-trehk) *nt* (pl ~) evening dress
selters (*sehl*-tersh) *m* soda water
selv (sehll) *pron* myself, yourself, herself, himself, itself, oneself, ourselves, yourselves, themselves; self, selves; **~ om** though, although
selvbetjening (*sehl*-beh-tʸāy-ning) *c* self-service
selvbetjeningsvaskeri (*sehl*-beh-tʸāy-nings-vahss-ker-ree) *nt* launderette
selvfølgelig (sehl-*furl*-ger-li) *adv* naturally, of course

selvgod (*sehl*-goo) *adj* conceited
selvisk (*sehl*-visk) *adj* selfish
selvmord (*sehl*-moord) *nt* (pl ~) suicide
selvmordsangrep (sehl-morts-*ahn*-grāyp) *nt* (pl ~) suicide attack
selvmordsbomber (sehl-morts-*boom*-ber) *c* (pl ~e) suicide bomber
selvopptatt (*sehl*-lop-taht) *adj* self-centered *Am*, self-centred
selvstendig (sehl-*stehn*-di) *adj* independent; self-employed
selvstyre (*sayl*-stēw-rer) *nt* self-government
selvstyrt (*sehl*-stēwt) *adj* autonomous
sement (seh-*mehnt*) *m* cement
semikolon (seh-mi-*kōō*-lon) *nt* semi-colon
sen (sāyn) *adj* late; **for sent** too late; **senere** afterwards
senat (seh-*naat*) *nt* senate
senator (seh-*naa*-toor) *m* senator
sende (sehn-ner) *v* *send; transmit; **~ av sted** dispatch, *send off; **~ bort** dismiss; **~ tilbake** *send back
sendemann (*sehn*-ner-mahn) *m* (pl -menn) envoy
sender (*sehn*-nerr) *m* transmitter
sending (*sehn*-ning) *c* consignment; transmission
sene (*sāy*-ner) *c* sinew, tendon
seng (sehngng) *c* bed
sengeteppe (*sehng*-nger-teh-per) *nt* bedspread
sengetøy (*sehng*-nger-tur[ew]) *nt* bedding
senil (seh-*neel*) *adj* senile
senit (*sāy*-nit) *nt* zenith
senke (*sehng*-ker) *v* lower
sennep (*sehn*-nerp) *m* mustard
sensasjon (sehn-sah-*shōōn*) *m* sensation
sensasjonell (sehn-sah-shoo-*nehll*) *adj* sensational
sensur (sehn-*sēwr*) *m* censorship
sentimental (sehn-ti-mehn-*taal*) *adj* sentimental
sentral (sehn-*traal*) *adj* central
sentralbord (sehn-*traal*-bōōr) *nt* (pl ~) switchboard
sentralfyring (sehn-*traal*-fēw-ring) *c* central heating
sentralisere (sehn-trah-li-*sāy*-rer) *v* centralize
sentralstasjon (sehn-*traal*-stah-shōōn) *m* central station
sentrum (*sehn*-trewm) *nt* (pl -ra) town center *Am*, town centre, center *Am*, centre
separat (seh-pah-*raat*) *adv* apart, separately
separere (seh-pah-*rāy*-rer) *v* separate

september (sehp-*tehm*-berr) September
septisk (*sehp*-tisk) *adj* septic
seremoni (seh-reh-moo-*nee*) *m* ceremony
serie (*sa̅y̅*-ri-er) *m* series, sequence
seriøs (seh-ri-*u̅r̅ss*) *adj* serious
servere (sær-*va̅y̅*-rer) *v* serve
serveringsavgift (sær-*va̅y̅*-ring-saav-ʸift) *c* service charge
serviett (sær-vi-*ehtt*) *m* napkin, serviette
servise (sær-*vee*-ser) *nt* dinner service
servitør (sær-vi- *thu̅r̅*) *m* waiter, waitress
sesjon (seh-*sho̅o̅n*) *m* session
sesong (seh-*songng*) *m* season; **utenfor sesongen** off season
sesongkort (seh-*song*-kot) *nt* (pl ~) season ticket
sete (*sa̅y̅*-ter) *nt* seat; chair
setning (*seht*-ning) *m* sentence
sett (sehtt) *nt* set
***sette** (*seht*-ter) *v* *lay, place, *set; **~ i gang** launch; **~ inn** insert; **~ i stand** enable; **~ opp** *make up; *draw up; **~ på** turn on; **~ sammen** compose, assemble; **~ seg** *sit down
severdighet (sa̅y̅-*vær*-di-ha̅y̅t) *c* sight; scenic place
sex (sehks) *m* sex
shorts (shawts) *m* (pl ~) shorts *pl*
***si** (see) *v* *say, *tell
siamesisk (si-ah-*ma̅y̅*-sisk) *adj* Siamese
side (*see*-der) *c* page; side; **på den andre siden** across; **på den andre siden av** across, beyond; **til ~** aside; **til siden** sideways; aside; **ved siden av** next to, beside
sidegate (*see*-der-gaa-ter) *c* sidestreet
siden (*see*-dern) *adv* since; *prep* since; *conj* since; **for ... siden** ago
siffer (*sif*-ferr) *nt* (pl ~, sifre) digit
sigar (si-*gaar*) *m* cigar
sigarett (si-gah-*rehtt*) *m* cigarette
sigarettetui (si-gah-*reht*-teh-tew-ee) *nt* cigarette case
sigarettobakk (si-gah-*reht*-too-bahk) *m* cigarette tobacco
signal (sing-naal) *nt* signal
signalement (sing-nah-ler-*mahngng*) *nt* description
signalere (sing-nah-*la̅y̅*-rer) *v* signal
signatur (sing-nah-*te̅w̅r*) *m* signature
sikker (*sik*-kerr) *adj* secure, safe; certain, sure

sikkert (*sik*-kerrt) *adv* certainly
sikkerhet (*sik*-kerr-hāyt) *c* security, safety
sikkerhetsbelte (*sik*-kerr-hāyts-behl-ter) *nt* seat belt, safety belt
sikkerhetsforanstaltning (*sik*-kerr-hāyts-fo-rahn-stahlt-ning) *m* precaution
sikkerhetsnål (*sik*-kerr-hāyts-nawl) *c* safety pin
sikkert (*sik*-kert) *adv* surely; **helt ~** without fail
sikre seg (*sik*-rer) secure
sikring (*sik*-ring) *c* fuse
sikt (sikt) *m* visibility
sikte[1] (*sik*-ter) *nt* aim; ***ta ~ på** aim at
sikte[2] (*sik*-ter) *v* aim; **~ på** aim at
sil (seel) *m* sieve, strainer
sild (sill) *c* (pl **~**) herring
sile (*see*-ler) *v* strain
silke (*sil*-ker) *m* silk
simpel (*sim*-perl) *adj* common; vulgar
simpelthen (*sim*-pehlt-hehn) *adv* simply
simulere (si-mew-*lāy*-rer) *v* simulate
sindig (*sin*-di) *adj* sedate, soberminded
sink (singk) *m* zinc
sinke (*sing*-ker) *v* impede
sinn (sinn) *nt* mind
sinne (*sin*-ner) *nt* anger, temper
sinnsbevegelse (*sins*-beh-vāy-gerl-ser) *m* emotion
sinnsforvirring (*sins*-for-vi-ring) *c* insanity
sinnssyk (*sin*-sēwk) *adj* insane, mad, crazy
sint (sint) *adj* cross, angry
sirene (si-*rāy*-ner) *c* siren
siriss (si-*riss*) *m* cricket
sirkel (*seer*-kerl) *m* (pl -kler) circle
sirkulasjon (seer-kew-lah-*shōōn*) *m* circulation
sirkus (*seer*-kewss) *nt* circus
sirup (*seer*-rewp) *m* syrup
sist (sist) *adj* last
siste (*siss*-ter) *adj* ultimate; **i det ~** lately
sitat (si-*taat*) *nt* quotation
sitere (si-*tāy*-rer) *v* quote
sitron (si-*trōōn*) *m* lemon
***sitte** (*sit*-ter) *v* *sit
sitteplass (*sit*-ter-plahss) *m* seat
situasjon (si-tew-ah-*shōōn*) *m* position, situation
siv (seev) *nt* rush, reed
sivil (si-*veel*) *adj* civil; civilian
sivilisasjon (si-vi-li-sah-*shōōn*) *m* civilization
sivilisert (si-vi-li-*sāyt*) *adj* civilized
sivilperson (si-*veel*-pæ-shōōn) *m* civilian
sivilrett (si-*veel*-reht) *m* civil law
sjakk (shahkk) *m* chess; **sjakk!** check!
sjakkbonde (*shahk*-boo-ner) *m* (pl -bønder) pawn
sjakkbrett (*shahk*-breht) *nt*

(pl ~) chessboard; checkerboard *nAm*
sjal (shaal) *nt* shawl
sjalu (shah-*lew*) *adj* jealous; envious
sjalusi (shah-lew-*see*) *m* jealousy
sjampinjong (shahm-pin-*yongng*) *m* mushroom
sjampo (*shahm*-poo) *m* shampoo
sjanse (*shahng*-ser) *m* chance
sjargong (shaa-*gongng*) *m* slang; jargon
sjarlatan (*shaa*-lah-tahn) *m* quack
sjarm (shahrm) *m* charm; glamour, attraction
sjarmerende (shahr-*may*-rer-ner) *adj* charming
sjef (shayf) *m* manager, boss, chief
sjekk (shehkk) *m* cheque; check *nAm*
sjekke (*shehk*-ker) *v* check
sjel (shayl) *c* soul
sjelden (*shehl*-dern) *adv* rarely, seldom; *adj* rare, uncommon, infrequent
sjenere (sheh-*nay*-rer) *v* embarrass
sjenert (sheh-*nayt*) *adj* shy
sjenerthet (sheh-*nayt*-hayt) *c* timidity
sjetong (sheh-*tong*) *m* token
sjette (*sheht*-ter) *num* sixth
sjofel (*shoof*-erl) *adj* mean
sjokk (shokk) *nt* shock
sjokkere (sho-*kay*-rer) *v* shock
sjokkerende (sho-*kay*-rer-ner) *adj* shocking
sjokolade (shoo-koo-*laa*-der) *m* chocolate
sju (shew) *num* seven
sjuende (*shew*-er-ner) *num* seventh
sjusket (*shewss*-kert) *adj* slovenly
sjø (shur) *m* sea
sjøfugl (*shur*-fewl) *m* sea-bird
sjøkart (*shurkaht*) *nt* chart
sjømann (*shur*-mahn) *m* (pl -menn) sailor, seaman
sjøpinnsvin (*shur*-pin-sveen) *nt* (pl ~) sea urchin
sjøreise (*shur*-ray-ser) *c* cruise
sjørøver (*shur*-rur-verr) *m* pirate
sjøsetning (*shur*-seht-ning) *m* launching
sjøsyk (*shur*-sewk) *adj* seasick
sjøsyke (*shur*-sew-ker) *m* seasickness
sjøvann (*shur*-vahn) *nt* sea water
sjåfør (sho-*furr*) *m* chauffeur
skade (*skaa*-der) *m* injury, damage; harm, mischief; *v* *hurt, harm, injure; damage
skadelig (*skaa*-der-li) *adj* harmful, hurtful
skadeserstatning (*skaa*-

der-sææsh-taht-ning) *m* compensation, indemnity
skadet (*skaa*-dert) *adj* injured
skaffe (*skahf*-fer) *v* provide, furnish
skaft (skahft) *nt* handle
skala (*skaa*-lah) *m* scale
skall (skahll) *nt* shell; skin
skalldyr (*skahl*-dēwr) *nt* (pl ~) shellfish
skalle (*skahl*-ler) *m* skull
skallet (*skahl*-lert) *adj* bald
skam (skahmm) *c* shame, disgrace
skamfull (*skahm*-fewl) *adj* ashamed
skamme seg (*skahm*-mer) *be ashamed
skandale (skahn-*daa*-ler) *m* scandal
skandinav (skahn-di-*naav*) *m* Scandinavian
Skandinavia (skahn-di-*naa*-vi-ah) Scandinavia
skandinavisk (skahn-di-*naa*-visk) *adj* Scandinavian
skanne (*skahn*-ner) *v* scan
skanner (*skahn*-nerr) *c* (pl ~e) scanner
skap (skaap) *nt* cupboard; closet; locker
skape (*skaaper*) *v* create
skapende (*skaa*-pene) *adj* creative
skapning (*skaap*-ning) *m* creature
skarlagenrød (skah-*laa*-gern-rur) *adj* scarlet
skarp (skahrp) *adj* sharp; keen; bright
skatt (skahtt) *m* treasure; tax; darling
skattefri (*skaht*-ter-free) *adj* tax-free
***skattlegge** (*skaht*-leh-ger) *v* tax
ski (shee) *c* (pl ~) ski; ***gå på ~** ski
skibukse (*shee*-book-ser) *c* ski pants
skifer (*shee*-ferr) *m* slate
skift (shift) *nt* shift
skifte (*shif*-ter) *v* switch; change
skiftenøkkel (*shif*-ter-nur-kerl) *m* (pl -nøkler) monkey wrench *Am*
skiheis (*shee*-hayss) *m* ski lift
skihopp (*shee*-hop) *nt* (pl ~) ski jump
skikk (shikk) *m* custom
skikkelse (*shi*-kerl-ser) *m* figure
skille (*shil*-ler) *v* separate, part; divide
skilles (*shil*-lerss) *v* divorce
skillevegg (*shil*-ler-vehg) *m* partition
skillevei (*shil*-ler-vay) *m* road fork
skilpadde (*shil*-pah-der) *c* turtle
skilsmisse (*shils*-mi-ser) *m* divorce
skiløper (*shee*-lūr-perr) *m* skier
skiløping (*shee*-lūr-ping) *c* skiing

skimte (*shim*-ter) *v* glimpse
skinke (*shing*-ker) *c* ham
skinn (shinn) *nt* skin; hide; glare; **semsket ~** suede; **skinn-** leather
skinne¹ (*shin*-ner) *v* *shine
skinne² (*shin*-ner) *c* rail; track
skinnende (*shin*-ner-ner) *adj* bright
skinnhellig (*shin*-heh-li) *adj* hypocritical
skip (sheep) *nt* boat, ship
skipe (*shee*-per) *v* ship
skipsfart (*ships*-faht) *m* navigation, navigation; shipping
skipsreder (*ships*-rāy-derr) *m* shipowner
skipsverft (*ships*-værft) *nt* shipyard
skisse (*shiss*-ser) *c* sketch
skissere (shi-*sāy*-rer) *v* sketch
skistaver (*shee*-staa-verr) *pl* ski sticks; ski poles *Am*
skistøvler (*shee*-sturv-lerr) *pl* ski boots
skitt (shitt) *m* dirt
skitten (*shit*-tern) *adj* filthy, dirty, foul; soiled
skive (*shee*-ver) *c* disc; slice
skiveprolaps (*shee*-ver-pro-lahps) *m* slipped disc
skje¹ (shāy) *v* occur, happen
skje² (shāy) *c* spoon
skjebne (*shāyb*-ner) *m* destiny, fate; fortune, luck
skjebnesvanger (*shāyb*-ner-svah-ngerr) *adj* fatal
skjefull (*shāy*-fewl) *m* spoonful
skjegg (shehgg) *nt* beard
skjelett (*sheh-lehtt*) *nt* skeleton
skjell (shehll) *nt* shell, sea--shell; scale
skjelle (*shehl*-ler) *v* scold; **~ ut** call names
skjelne (*shehl*-ner) *v* distinguish
***skjelve** (*shehl*-ver) *v* tremble, shiver
skjeløyd (*shāyl*-ur^ew^d) *adj* cross-eyed
skjema (*shāy*-mah) *nt* scheme; form
skjemme bort (*shehm*-mer boot) *spoil
skjenke (*shehng*-ker) *v* pour; donate
skjenne på (*shehn*-ner) *v* scold
skjerf (shærf) *nt* scarf
skjerm (shærm) *m* screen
skjermbrett (*shærm*-breht) *nt* folding screen
skjev (shāyv) *adj* slanting
skjorte (*shoot*-ter) *c* shirt
skjul (shēwl) *nt* cover
skjule (*shēw*-ler) *v* *hide, conceal
skjær (shæær) *adj* sheer; *nt* rock
***skjære** (*shææ*-rer) *v* *cut; carve; **~ av** *cut off; **~ i** carve; **~ ned** *cut; **~ ut** carve
skjødesløs (*shūr*-derss-lūrss) *adj* careless

skjønn (shurnn) *adj* wonderful, lovely
skjønne (*shurn*-ner) *v* *understand, *see
skjønnhet (*shurn*-hāyt) *c* beauty
skjønnhetspleie (*shurn*-hāyts-play-er) *m* beauty treatment
skjønnhetssalong (*shurn*-hāyt-sah-long) *m* beauty parlo(u)r, beauty salon
skjønt (shurnt) *conj* though, although
skjør (shūrr) *adj* fragile
skjørt (shurtt) *nt* skirt
skjøteledning (*shūr*-ter-lāyd-ning) *m* extension cord
skli (sklee) *v* slip
sko (skōō) *m* (pl ~) shoe
skog (skōōg) *m* wood, forest
skogkledd (*skōōg*-klehd) *adj* wooded
skogsområde (*skoogs*-oom-raw-der) *nt* woodland
skokrem (*skōō*-krāym) *m* shoe polish
skole (*skōō*-ler) *m* school; **videregående ~** secondary school
skolebestyrer (*skōō*-ler-beh-stēw-rerr) *m* principal
skolegutt (*skōō*-ler-gewt) *m* schoolboy
skolepike (*skōō*-ler-pee-ker) *m* schoolgirl
skolisse (*skōō*-li-ser) *c* shoe-lace
skomaker (*skōō*-maa-kerr) *m* shoemaker
skorpe (*skor*-per) *c* crust
skorstein (*skosh*-tayn) *m* chimney
skotsk (skotsk) *adj* Scottish
Skottland (*skot*-lahn) Scotland
skotøy (*skōō*-tur[ew]) *nt* footwear
skotøyforretning (*skōō*-tur[ew]-fo-reht-ning) *c* shoe shop
skramme (*skrahm*-mer) *c* scratch
skrap (skraap) *nt* junk
skrape (*skraa*-per) *v* scrape, scratch
skravle (*skrahv*-ler) *v* chat
skravlebøtte (*skrahv*-ler-bur-ter) *c* chatterbox
skredder (*skrehd*-derr) *m* tailor
skreddersydd (*skrehd*-der-shewd) *adj* tailor-made
skrekk (skrehkk) *m* fright
skrekkelig (skreh-ker-li) *adj* horrible, grim
skrell (skrehll) *nt* peel
skrelle (*skrehl*-ler) *v* peel
skremme (*skrehm*-mer) *v* scare, terrify
skremmende (*skrehm*-mer-ner) *adj* terrifying
skremt (skrehmt) *adj* frightened
skrifte (*skrif*-ter) *v* confess
skriftemål (*skrif*-ter-mawl) *nt* (pl ~) confession
skriftlig (*skrift*-li) *adj* in

writing; written
skrik (skreek) *nt* scream, cry
***skrike** (*skree*-ker) *v* shout, scream, cry; shriek
skritt (skritt) *nt* step, pace, move
***skrive** (*skree*-ver) *v* *write; **~ inn** book; **~ ned** *write down; **~ på data** type; **~ seg inn** check in; **~ ut** print out
skriveblokk (*skree*-ver-blok) *c*; writing pad
skrivebord (*skree*-ver-boor) *nt* desk, bureau
skrivemaskin (*skree*-ver-mah-sheen) *m* typewriter
skrivemaskinpapir (*skree*-ver-mah-sheen-pah-peer) *nt* typing paper
skrivepapir (*skree*-ver-pah-peer) *nt* writing paper
skriver (*skree*-verr) *m* printer
skru (skrew) *v* screw; **~ av** turn off; **~ på** turn on
skrubbe (*skrewb*-ber) *v* scrub
skrubbsår (*skrewb*-sawr) *nt* (pl ~) graze
skrue (*skrew*-er) *m* screw
skruestikke (*skrew*-er-sti-ker) *m* clamp
skrujern (*skrew*-ʸææn) *nt* (pl ~) screw-driver
skrukke (*skrook*-ker) *v* crease
skrunøkkel (*skrew*-nur-kerl) *m* (pl -nøkler) wrench
***skryte** (*skrew*-ter) *v* boast
skrøne (*skrur*-ner) *v* *tell tall tales
skrøpelig (*skrur*-per-li) *adj* fragile
skrå (skraw) *adj* slanting
skråne (*skraw*-ner) *v* slant
skrånende (*skraw*-ner-ner) *adj* sloping, slanting
skråning (*skraw*-ning) *m* incline, slope
skudd (skewdd) *nt* shot
skuddår (*skewd*-dawr) *nt* (pl ~) leap year
skue (*skoo*-er) *nt* sight
skuespill (*skew*-er-spil) *nt* (pl ~) drama
skuespiller (*skew*-er-spi-lerr) *m* actor, actress *m*; comedian
skuespillforfatter (*skew*-er-spil-for-fah-terr) *m* playwright
skuff (skooff) *m* drawer
skuffe (*skewf*-fer) *v* disappoint; ***være skuffet** *be disappointed
skuffelse (*skewf*-ferl-ser) *m* disappointment
skulder (*skewl*-derr) *c* (pl -drer) shoulder
skulke (*skewl*-ker) *v* play truant
***skulle** (*skewl*-ler) *v* *shall; *should
skulptur (skewlp-*tewr*) *m* sculpture
skum (skoomm) *nt* foam, lather
skumgummi (*skoom*-gew-

mi) *m* foam rubber
skumme (*skoom*-mer) *v* foam
skumring (*skoom*-ring) *c* twilight
skur (skēwr) *nt* shed; *m* shower
skurd (skewrd) *m* carving
skurk (skewrk) *m* bastard, villain, rascal
skvette (*skveht*-ter) *v* splash
sky (shēw) *c* cloud; *adj* shy
skyet (*shēw*-ert) *adj* cloudy
skyffel (*shewf*-ferl) *m* (pl skyfler) shovel
skygge (*shewg*-ger) *m* shadow, shade
skyggefull (*shewg*-ger-fewl) *adj* shady
skyggelue (*shewg*-er-*lew*-er) *c* cap
skyhet (*shēw*-hāyt) *c* shyness
skyld (shewll) *c* blame, guilt
skylde (*shewl*-ler) *v* owe
skyldig (*shewl*-di) *adj* guilty; due; ***være ~** owe
skylle (*shewl*-ler) rinse
skylling (*shewl*-ling) *c* rinse
skynde seg (*shewn*-ner) hurry, hasten
skyskraper (*shēw*-skraa-perr) *m* skyscraper
***skyte** (*shēw*-ter) *v* fire, *shoot
skyteskive (*shēw*-ter-shee-ver) *c* mark, target
***skyve** (*shēw*-ver) *v* push
skyvedør (*shēw*-ver-dūrr) *c* sliding door
skøyeraktig (*skur*ew-er-rahk-ti) *adj* mischievous
skøyte (*shur*ew-ter) *c* skate; ***gå på skøyter** skate
skøytebane (*shur*ew-ter-baa-ner) *m* skating rink
skøyteløping (*shur*ew-ter-lūr-ping) *c* skating
skål (skawl) *c* saucer; *m* toast
sladder (*shlahd*-derr) *m* gossip
sladre (*shlahd*-rer) *v* gossip
slag (shlaag) *nt* blow; smash; breed; battle; lapel
slaganfall (*shlaagahn*-fahl) *nt* (pl ~) stroke
slagord (*shlaa*-gōor) *nt* (pl ~) slogan
slags (shlahks) *m*/*nt* sort; **alle ~** all sorts of
slakter (*shlahk*-terr) *m* butcher
slange (*shlahng*-nger) *m* snake
slang (shlahng) *m* slang
slank (shlahngk) *adj* slender, slim
slanke seg (shlahng-ker) slim
slapp (shlahpp) *adj* limp
slappe av (*shlahp*-per) relax
slave (*shlaa*-ver) *m* slave
slede (*shlāy*-er) *m* sleigh, sledge
sleip (shlayp) *adj* slippery
slekt (shlehkt) *m* family; relatives
slektning (*shlehkt*-ning) *m*

relation, relative
slem (shlehmm) *adj* naughty, bad
slenge (*shlehng*-nger) *v* *throw
slentre (*shlehn*-trer) *v* stroll
slepe (*shlay*-per) *v* haul, drag
slepebåt (*shlay*-per-bawt) *m* tug
slette (*shleht*-ter) *c* plain
slettvar (*shleht*-vaar) *m* brill
slik (shleek) *pron* such; *adv* thus, so, such; **~ at** so that; **~ som** such as
slikke (*shlik*-ker) *v* lick, lap
slips (shlips) *nt* tie, necktie
***slite** (*shlee*-ter) *v* labo(u)r; **~ ut** wear out
sliten (*shlee*-tern) *adj* weary, worn out
slitt (shlitt) *adj* worn
slokke (*shlook*-ker) *v* *put out, extinguish
slott (shlott) *nt* castle
slu (shlew) *adj* sly, cunning
sludder (*shlewd*-derr) *nt* rubbish
sluke (*shlew*-ker) *v* swallow
slukt (shlewkt) *m* gorge
slum (shlewmm) *m* slum
slump (shloomp) *m* chance; **på ~** by chance
slurk (shlewrk) *m* sip
slurvet (*shlewr*-vert) *adj* sloppy
sluse (*shlew*-ser) *m* lock
slutning (*shlewt*-ning) *m* conclusion; end
slutt (shlewtt) *m* finish, end; **til ~** at last; eventually
slutte (*shlewt*-ter) *v* finish, end; quit; **~ seg til** join
sluttresultat (*shlewt*-reh-sewl-taat) *nt* final result
slyngel (*shlewng*-ngerl) *m* (pl -gler) rascal
slør (shlurr) *nt* veil
sløse bort (*shlur*-ser boot) waste
sløseri (shlur-ser-*ree*) *nt* waste
sløv (shlurv) *adj* dull, blunt
sløyfe (*shlur*ew-fer) *c* bow; bow tie
slå (shlaw) *m* bolt
***slå** (shlaw) *v* *strike, *beat, *hit; punch; bruise; dial; **~ av** switch off; **~ hakk i** chip; **~ igjen** slam; **~ i hjel** kill; **~ i stykker** crack; **~ ned** knock down; **~ opp** look up; **~ på** switch on; **~ seg ned** settle down; **~ til** *strike
slående (*shlaw*-er-ner) *adj* striking
***slåss** (shloss) *v* *fight; struggle
smak (smaak) *m* taste; flavo(u)r; ***sette ~ på** flavo(u)r
smake (*smaa*-ker) *v* taste; **~ på** taste
smakløs (*smaak*-lurss) *adj* tasteless
smal (smaal) *adj* narrow
smaragd (smah-*rahgd*) *m* emerald
smart (smaat) *adj* smart, lur

smed (smāy) *m* smith
smekke (*smehk*-ker) *v* smack
smell (smehll) *nt* crack
***smelle** (*smehl*-ler) *v* crack
smelte (*smehl*-ter) *v* melt, thaw
smerte (*smæt*-ter) *m* pain; grief, sorrow
smertefri (*smæt*-ter-free) *adj* painless
smertefull (*smæ*-ter-fool) *adj* painful
smertestillende middel (*smæ*-ter-stil-lene *mid*-del) *nt* painkiller
***smette** (*smeht*-ter) *v* slip
smidig (*smee*-di) *adj* supple
smil (smeel) *nt* smile
smile (*smee*-ler) *v* smile
sminke (*sming*-ker) *c* make--up
smitte (*smit*-ter) *v* infect
smittende (*smi*-ter-ner) *adj* contagious
smittsom (*smit*-som) *adj* infectious, contagious
smoking (*smaw*-king) *m* dinner jacket; tuxedo *nAm*
smug (*smēwg*) *nt* alley, lane
smugle (*smewg*-ler) *v* smuggle
smul (smēwl) *adj* smooth
smule (*smēw*-ler) *m* crumb; bit
smykke (*smewk*-ker) *nt* piece of jewellery (*Am* jewelry)
smør (smurr) *nt* butter
smørbrød (*smūrr*-brūr) *nt* (pl ~) open sandwich
***smøre** (*smūr*-rer) *v* grease; lubricate
smøreolje (*smūr*-rer-ol-ʸer) *c* lubrication oil
smøring (*smūr*-ring) *c* lubrication
små (*smaw*) (pl liten) *adj* small
småbarn (*smaw*-baan) *nt* toddler
smågris (*smaw*-greess) *m* piglet
småkake (*smaw*-kaa-ker) *c* biscuit; cookie *nAm*
smålig (*smaw*-li) *adj* stingy
småpenger (*smaw*-peh-ngerr) *pl* petty cash, change
småstein (*smaw*-stayn) *m* pebble
snakke (*snahk*-ker) *v* *speak, talk
snakkesalig (*snahk*-ker-saa-li) *adj* talkative
snart (snaat) *adv* presently, soon, shortly; **så ~ som** as soon as
snegl (snayl) *m* snail
snekker (*snehk*-kerr) *m* carpenter
snever (*snāy*-verr) *adj* narrow, restricted
sneversynt (*snāy*-ver-shēwnt) *adj* narrow--minded
snikskytter (*sneek*-shew-terr) *m* sniper
snill (snill) *adj* good, nice, kind

snitte (*snit*-ter) *v* *cut, slice
snitsel (*snit*-tsel) *m* cutlet
sno (sn*oo*) *v* twist; **~ seg** *wind
snor (sn*oo*r) *c* string; cord
snorke (*snor*-ker) *v* snore
snorkel (*snor*-kerl) *m* (pl -kler) snorkel
snu (sn*ew*) *v* turn round; **~ om** invert; **~ seg** turn round
snuble (*snewb*-ler) *v* stumble
snurre (*snewr*-rer) *v* *spin
snute (*snew*-ter) *c* snout
***snyte** (*snew*-ter) *v* cheat
snø (sn*ur*) *v* snow; *m* snow
snøskred (*snur*-skr*ay*d) *nt* (pl ~) avalanche
snøslaps (*snur*-shlahps) *nt* slush
snøstorm (*snur*-storm) *m* blizzard, snowstorm
sodavann (*soo*-dah-vahn) *nt* soda water
sofa (*soof*-fah) *m* sofa
software (*sooft*-vehr) *m* software
sogn (songn) *nt* parish
sogneprest (*song*-ner-prehst) *m* rector, vicar
sokk (sokk) *m* sock
sol (s*oo*l) *c* sun
solbrent (*sool*-brehnt) *adj* sunburned
solbriller (*sool*-bri-lerr) *pl* sun-glasses *pl*
solbær (*sool*-bæær) *nt* (pl ~) black-currant
soldat (sool-*daat*) *m* soldier
sole seg (*soo*-ler) sunbathe
solid (soo-*leed*) *adj* solid, firm
solistkonsert (soo-*list*-koon-sæt) *m* recital
sollys (*sool*-l*ew*ss) *nt* sunlight
solnedgang (*sool*-n*ay*-gahng) *m* sunset
sololje (*soo*-lol-ʸer) *c* suntan oil
soloppgang (*soo*-lop-gahng) *m* sunrise
solrik (*sool*-reek) *adj* sunny
solseil (*sool*-sayl) *nt* (pl ~) awning
solskinn (*sool*-shin) *nt* sunshine
solstikk (*sool*-stik) *nt* (pl ~) sunstroke
solsystem (*sool*-sewss-*taym*) *nt* solar system
som (somm) *pron* who, that, which; *conj* as; **~ om** as if
somletog (*soom*-ler-tawg) *nt* (pl ~) slow train; milk train *Am*
sommer (*som*-merr) *m* (pl somrer) summer
sommerfugl (*som*-merr-f*ew*l) *m* butterfly
sommertid (*som*-mer-teed) *c* summer time
sone (*soo*-ner) *c* zone; **trådløs ~** wireless internet hotspot
sopp (sopp) *m* mushroom; toadstool
sorg (sorg) *c* sorrow, grief; mourning

sort (sott) *m* kind, sort
sortere (so-*tāy*-rer) *v* sort, assort
sortiment (so-ti-*mahngng*) *nt* assortment
sosial (soo-si-*aal*) *adj* social
sosialisme (soo-si-ah-*liss*-mer) *m* socialism
sosialist (soo-si-ah-*list*) *m* socialist
sosialistisk (soo-si-ah-*liss*-tisk) *adj* socialist
sosiologi (soo-si-oo-loo-*gee*) *m* sociology
***sove** (*saw*-ver) *v* *sleep
sovende (*saw*-ver-ner) *adj* asleep
sovepille (*saw*-ver-pi-ler) *c* sleeping pill
sovepose (*saw*-ver-pōō-ser) *m* sleeping bag
sovesal (*saw*-ver-saal) *m* dormitory
sovevogn (*saw*-ver-vongn) *c* sleeping car; Pullman
soveværelse (*saw*-ver-vææ-rerl-ser) *nt* bedroom
sovne (*sov*-ner) *v* *fall asleep
spade (*spaa*-er) *m* spade
spalte (*spahl*-ter) *c* column
spandere (spahn-*dāy*-rer) *v* *spend
Spania (*spaa*-ni-ah) Spain
spanier (*spaa*-ni-err) *m* Spaniard
spanjol (spahn-*ʸōōl*) *m* Spaniard
spann (spahnn) *nt* pail, bucket
spansk (spahnsk) *adj* Spanish
spare (*spaa*-rer) *v* save; economize
sparebank (*spaa*-rer-bahngk) *m* savings bank
sparegris (*spaa*-rer-gris) *m* piggy bank
sparepenger (*spaa*-rer-peh-ngerr) *pl* savings *pl*
spark (spahrk) *nt* kick
sparke (*spahr*-ker) *v* kick; ***gi sparken** dismiss
sparsommelig (spaa-*shom*-mer-li) *adj* thrifty, economical
spasere (spah-*sāy*-rer) *v* walk
spaserstokk (spah-*sāy*-shtok) *m* walking stick
spasertur (spah-*sāy*-tēwr) *m* stroll, walk
spedalskhet (speh-*daalsk*-hāyt) *c* leprosy
spedbarn (*spāy*-baan) *nt* (pl ~) infant
speider (*spay*-derr)*m*girl scout; boy scout
speil (spayl) *nt* looking-glass, mirror
speilbilde (*spayl*-bil-der) *nt* reflection
spekulere (speh-kew-*lāy*-rer) *v* speculate
spenne (*spayn*-ner) *c* buckle
spennende (*spehn*-ner-ner) *adj* exciting
spenning (*spehn*-ning) *m* tension; voltage

sperre (*spehr*-rer) *v* block; **~ inne** lock up
spesialisere seg (speh-si-ah-li-*sāy*-rer) specialize
spesialist (speh-si-ah-*list*) *m* specialist
spesialitet (speh-si-ah-li-*tāyt*) *m* speciality
spesiell (speh-si-*ehll*) *adj* particular, special
spesifikk (speh-si-*fikk*) *adj* specific
spidd (spidd) *nt* spit
spiker (*spee*-kerr) *m* (pl ~, -krer) nail
spill (spill) *nt* game
spille (*spil*-ler) *v* play; act
spillemerke (*spil*-ler-mær-ker) *nt* chip
spiller (*spil*-lerr) *m* player
spillkort (*spil*-kot) *nt* (pl ~) playing card
spillopper (spi-*lop*-perr) *pl* mischief
spinat (spi-*naat*) *m* spinach
spindelvev (*spin*-derl-vāyv) *m* (pl ~) spider's web
***spinne** (*spin*-ner) *v* *spin
spion (spi-*ōōn*) *m* spy
spir (speer) *nt* spire
spirituosa (spi-ri-tew-*ōō*-sah) *pl* spirits
spise (*spee*-ser) *v* *eat
spisekart (*spee*-ser-kaht) *nt* menu
spiselig (*spee*-ser-li) *adj* edible
spisesal (*spee*-ser-saal) *m* dining room
spiseskje (*spee*-ser-shāy) *c* tablespoon
spisestue (*spee*-ser-stēw-er) *c* dining room
spisevogn (*spee*-ser-vongn) *c* dining car
spiss (spiss) *adj* pointed, sharp; *m* tip, point
spissborgerlig (*spiss*-bor-ger-li) *adj* bourgeois
spisse (*spiss*-ser) *v* sharpen
splint (splint) *m* splinter
splinter ny (*splin*-terr nēw) brand-new
spole (*spōō*-ler) *m* spool
spor (spōōr) *nt* trace; trail, track
sport (spott) *m* sport
sports og nyttekjøretøy (*spotts*-aw-*newt*-teh-*khur*-er-turew) *nt* (pl ~) SUV
sportsbil (*spotsh*-beel) *m* sports car
sportsklær (*spotsh*-klæær) *pl* sportswear
sprang (sprahng) *nt* jump
spray (spray) *m* atomizer; spray
sprayflaske (*spray*-flahss-ker) *c* atomizer
spre (sprāy) *v* *spread; scatter; *shed
sprekk (sprehkk) *m* crack
***sprekke** (*sprehk*-ker) *v* *burst; crack
sprenge (*sprehng*-er) *v* blow up
sprengstoff (*sprehng*-stof) *nt* explosive
springvann (*spring*-vahn) *nt* (pl ~) fountain

sprit (spreet) *m* liquor
spritapparat (*spree*-tah-pah-raat) *nt* spirit stove
sprut (sprewt) *m* squirt
sprute (sprewt-er) *v* squirt; spray
sprø (sprur) *adj* crisp
sprøyte (*spru*rew-ter) *c* syringe; shot
språk (sprawk) *nt* language
spurv (spewrv) *m* sparrow
spyd (spewd) *nt* spear
spytt (spewtt) *nt* spit
spytte (*spewt*-ter) *v* *spit
spøk (spurk) *m* joke
spøkelse (*spur*-kerl-ser) *nt* ghost; spirit
***spørre** (*spurr*-rer) *v* ask
spørrelek (*spurr*-rer-layk) *m* quiz
spørsmål (*spursh*-mawl) *nt* (pl ~) question; matter, issue
spørsmålstegn (*spursh*-mawls-tayn) *nt* (pl ~) question mark
spå (spaw) *v* predict, tell fortunes
sta (staa) *adj* head-strong, stubborn, pig-headed, obstinate
stabel (*staa*-berl) *m* (pl -bler) stack
stabil (stah-*beel*) *adj* stable
stable (*stahb*-ler) *v* pile
stadig (*staa*-di) *adj* continual, frequent
stadion (*staa*-di-oon) *nt* stadium
stadium (*staa*-di-ewm) *nt* (pl -ier) stage, phase
stakitt (stah-*kitt*) *nt* picket fence
stall (stahll) *m* stable
stallkar (*stahll*-kahrr) *m* groom
stamme (*stahm*-mer) *m* trunk; tribe; *v* stammer
stamcelle (*stahm*-sehl-ler) *c* stem cell
stampe (*stahm*-per) *v* stamp
stand[1] (stahnn) *m* (pl stender) state; ***gjøre i ~** mend; **i ~ til** able
stand[2] (stahnn) *m* stand
standard- (*stahn*-dahr) standard
standhaftig (stahn-*hahf*-ti) *adj* steadfast
stang (stahngng) *c* (pl stenger) bar, pole; rod
stanse (*stahn*-ser) *v* stop, halt, pull up
start (staat) *m* take-off; beginning, start
startbane (*staat*-baa-ner) *m* runway
starte (*staht*-ter) *v* start, *begin
stasjon (stah-*shoon*) *m* station; depot *nAm*
stat (staat) *m* state; **stats-** national
statistikk (stah-ti-*stikk*) *m* statistics *pl*
statsborgerskap (*staats*-bor-ger-shkaap) *nt* citizenship
statskasse (*staats*-kahs-ser) *c* treasury

statsminister (*staats*-mi-niss-terr) *m* (pl ~e, -trer) premier, Prime Minister
statsoverhode (*staat*-saw-verr-hōō-der) *nt* head of state
statsråd (*staats*-rawd) *m* minister
statstjenestemann (*staats*-t^y^āy-ner-ster-mahn) *m* (pl -menn) civil servant
statue (*staa*-tew-er) *m* statue
stave (*staa*-ver) *v* *spell
stavelse (*staa*-verl-ser) *m* syllable
stavemåte (*staa*-ver-maw-ter) *m* spelling
stearinlys (steh-ah-*reen*-lēwss) *nt* (pl ~) candle
stebarn (*stāy*-baan) *nt* (pl ~) stepchild
sted (stāy) *nt* spot, site, place; locality
stedfortreder (*stāy*-fo-trāy-derr) *m* substitute; deputy
stedlig (*stāyd*-li) *adj* local; resident
stefar (*stāy*-faar) *m* (pl -fedre) stepfather
steg (stāyg) *nt* step
steil (stayl) *adj* steep
stein (stayn) *m* stone; **stein-** stone
steinbrudd (*stayn*-brewd) *nt* (pl ~) quarry
steinet (*stay*-nert) *adj* rocky
steintøy (*stayn*-tur^ew^) *nt* stoneware, crockery
steke (*stāy*-ker) *v* fry; roast
stekeovn (*stāy*-ker-ovn) *m* oven
stekepanne (*stāy*-ker-pah-ner) *c* frying pan
stemme (*stehm*-mer) *m* voice; vote; *v* vote; **~ overens** agree
stemmerett (*stehm*-mer-reht) *m* franchise, suffrage
stemning (*stehm*-ning) *m* atmosphere; mood
stemor (*stāy*-mōōr) *c* (pl -mødre) stepmother
stempel (*stehm*-perl) *nt* (pl ~, -pler) stamp; piston
stenge (*stehng*-nger) *v* close; **~ av** turn off; *cut off; **~ inne** *shut in
stengt (stehngt) *adj* closed, shut
stereo (*stāyh*-rāyoo) *m* stereo
stereoanlegg (*stāyh*-rāyoo-ahn-lehg) *nt* stereo (unit)
steril (steh-*reel*) *adj* sterile
sterilisere (steh-ri-li-*sāy*-rer) *v* sterilize
sterk (stærk) *adj* strong; powerful
sti (stee) *m* trail, path
stift (stift) *m* staple
stifte (*stif*-ter) *v* found, institute
stiftelse (*stif*-terl-ser) *m* foundation
stige (*stee*-ger) *m* ladder
***stige** (*stee*-ger) *v* ascend, *rise; **~ av** *get off; **~ opp** ascend; **~ på** *get on
stigning (*steeg*-ning) *m*

increase; ascent
stikk (stikk) *nt* bite, sting; picture, engraving
***stikke** (*stik*-ker) *v* *sting
stikkelsbær (*stik*-kerls-bæær) *nt* (pl ~) gooseberry
stikkontakt (*stik*-koon-tahkt) *m* plug
stikkord (*stikk*-o͞or) *nt* catchword
stikkpille (*stik*-pi-ler) *c* suppository
stil (steel) *m* style; essay
stilk (stilk) *m* stem
stillas (sti-*laass*) *nt* scaffolding
stille (*stil*-ler) *adj* calm, quiet, still; silent; *v* place, *put; ~ **inn** tune in
Stillehavet (*stil*-ler-haa-ver) Pacific Ocean
stillestående (*stil*-ler-staw-er-ner) *adj* stationary
stillferdig (stil-*fææ*di) *adj* quiet
stillhet (*stil*-hāy̅t) *c* silence, quiet
stilling (*stil*-ling) *c* position; job
stimulans (sti-mew-*lahngs*) *m* stimulant
stimulere (sti-mew-*lāy̅*-rer) *v* stimulate
sting (stingng) *nt* stitch
***stinke** (*sting*-ker) *v* *smell, *stink
stipend (sti-*pehnd*) *nt* grant, scholarship
stirre (*steer*-rer) *v* stare, gaze
stiv (steev) *adj* stiff
***stjele** (*st*ʸ*āy̅*-ler) *v* *steal
stjerne (*st*ʸ*ææ*-ner) *c* star
stoff (stoff) *nt* cloth, material, fabric; matter
stokk (stokk) *m* cane, stick
stokke (*stok*-ker) *v* shuffle
stol (sto͞ol) *m* chair
stola (*sto͞o*-lah) *m* stole
stole på (*sto͞o*-ler) trust; rely on
stolpe (*stol*-per) *m* post; pillar
stolt (stolt) *adj* proud
stolthet (*stolt*-hāy̅t) *c* pride
stopp! (stopp) stop!
stoppe (*stop*-per) *v* stop; quit; darn
stor (sto͞or) *adj* great, major, big; large
storartet (*sto͞o*-raa-tert) *adj* superb, grand, terrific
Storbritannia (*sto͞or*-bri-tah-ni-ah) Great Britain
stork (stork) *m* stork
storm (storm) *m* gale; storm
stormagasin (*sto͞or*-mah-gah-seen) *nt* department store
stormfull (*storm*-fewl) *adj* stormy
stormlykt (*storm*-lewkt) *c* hurricane lamp
storslått (*sto͞o*-shlot) *adj* magnificent
Stortinget (*sto͞or*-ti-nger) Norwegian Parliament
stortingsrepresentant (*sto͞o*-tings-reh-preh-sern-*tahnt*) *m* Member of (the

Norwegian) Parliament
straff (strahff) *m* punishment; penalty
straffe (*strahf*-fer) *v* punish
strafferett (*strahf*-fer-reht) *m* criminal law
straffespark (*strahf*-fer-spahrk) *nt* (pl ~) penalty kick
straks (strahks) *adv* instantly, at once, immediately
stram (strahmm) *adj* tight
stramme (*strahm*-mer) *v* tighten; **strammes** to be tightened
strand (strahnn) *c* (pl strender) beach
strebe (*strāy*-ber) *v* aspire; ~ **etter** pursue, aim at
streife omkring (*stray*-fer) roam
streik (strayk) *m* strike
streike (stray-ker) *v* *strike
strek (strāyk) *m* line
strekning (*strehk*-ning) *m* stretch; distance
streng (strehngng) *adj* strict, severe, harsh; *m* string
stress (strehss) *nt* stress
strid (streed) *m* contest; fight, battle, struggle
***strides** (*stree*-derss) *v* dispute
strikk (strikk) *m* rubber band
strikke (*strik*-ker) *v* *knit
strimmel (*strim*-merl) *m* (pl strimler) strip
stripe (*stree*-per) *c* stripe
stripet (*stree*-pert) *adj* striped
strofe (*stroo*-fer) *m* stanza
struktur (strewk-*tewr*) *m* structure; texture, fabric
strupekatarr (*strewper*-kah-tahr) *m* laryngitis
struts (strewts) *m* ostrich
***stryke** (*strew*-ker) *v* iron; *strike; fail an exam
strykefri (*strew*-ker-free) *adj* drip-dry, wash and wear
strykejern (*strew*-ker-ʸææn) *nt* (pl ~) iron
strøm (strurmm) *m* (pl ~mer) electricity; current, stream; **med strømmen** downstream; **mot strømmen** upstream
strømfordeler (*strurm*-fo-dāy-lerr) *m* distributor
strømme (*strurm*-mer) *v* flow, stream
strømpe (*strurm*-per) *c* stocking
strømpebukse (*strurm*-per-book-ser) *c* tights *pl*, panty hose
stråle (*straw*-ler) *m* beam, ray; spout, jet; *v* *shine
strålende (*straw*-ler-ner) *adj* brilliant; glorious
student (stew-*dehnt*) *m* student
studere (stew-*dāy*-rer) *v* study
studium (*stew*-di-oom) *nt* (pl -ier) study; studies
stue (*stew*-er) *c* sitting room

stuert (*stoo*-ert) *m* steward
stum (stewmm) *adj* mute, dumb
stund (stewnn) *c* while
stup (stewp) *nt* precipice
stupe (*stew*-per) *v* dive
stusse (*stewss*-ser) *v* trim
stygg (stewgg) *adj* ugly
stykke (*stewk*-ker) *nt* piece, fragment, lump, part; ***gå i stykker** *break down; **i stykker** broken; **stort ~** chunk
styrbord (*stewr*-boor) starboard
styre (*stew*-rer) *v* direct; steer; *nt* board, direction; government; rule
styrke (*stewr*-ker) *m* power, strength; force; **væpnede styrker** armed forces
styrte (*stewt*-ter) *v* crash; rush, dash
stær (stæær) *m* starling
stø (stur) *adj* steady
stønne (*sturn*-ner) *v* groan
støpejern (*stur*-per-^{y}ææn) *nt* (pl ~) cast iron
størkne (*sturr*-kner) *v* harden
størrelse (*sturr*-rerl-ser) *m* size; **stor ~** outsize
størsteparten (*sturssh*-ter-pah-tern) *m* bulk, the greater part of
støt (sturt) *nt* bump
støtdemper (*sturt*-dehm-perr) *m* shock absorber
støte (*stur*-ter) *v* bump; **~ på** run into, *come across; knock against; **~ sammen** bump
støtfanger (*sturt*-fah-ngerr) *m* bumper
støtte (*sturt*-ter) *v* *hold up; *m* support
støv (sturv) *nt* dust
støvel (*sturv*-verl) *m* (pl -vler) boot
støvet (*stur*-vert) *adj* dusty
støvsuge (*sturv*-sew-ger) *v* hoover; vacuum *vAm*
støvsuger (*sturv*-sew-gerr) *m* vacuum cleaner
støy (stur^{ew}) *m* noise
støyende (*sturew*-er-ner) *adj* noisy
***stå** (staw) *v* *stand; **~ opp** *get up; *rise
stående (*staw*-er-ner) *adj* erect
stål (stawl) *nt* steel; **rustfritt ~** stainless steel
ståltråd (*stawl*-traw) *m* wire
subjekt (sewb-^{y}*ehkt*) *nt* subject
substans (sewb-*stahns*) *m* substance
substansiell (sewb-stahn-si-*ehl*) *adj* substantial
substantiv (*sewp*-stahn-teev) *nt* noun
subtil (sewb-*teel*) *adj* subtle
suge (*sew*-ger) *v* suck
suite (*svit*-ter) *m* suite
sukke (*sewk*-ker) *v* sigh
sukker (*sook*-kerr) *nt* sugar
sukkerbit (*sook*-kerr-beet) *m* lump of sugar
sukkersyke (*sook*-ker-

shew-ker) *m* diabetes
sukkersykepasient (*sook*-ker-shew-ker-pah-si-ehnt) *m* diabetic
sukkertøy (*sook*-ker-tur[ew]) *nt* sweet; candy *nAm*
sukre (*sook*-rer) *v* sweeten
suksess (sewk-*sehss*) *m* success; hit
sult (sewlt) *m* hunger
sulten (*sewl*-tern) *adj* hungry
sum (sewmm) *m* (pl ~mer) sum; amount
summing (*sewm*-ming) *c* buzz
sump (soomp) *m* marsh
sunn (sewnn) *adj* healthy; wholesome
superlativ (sew-*pæl*-lah-teev) *m* superlative
supermarked (*sew*-perr-mahr-kerd) *nt* supermarket
suppe (*sewp*-per) *c* soup
suppeskje (*sewp*-per-shay) *c* soup spoon
suppetallerken (*sewp*-per-tah-lær-kern) *m* soup plate
sur (sewr) *adj* sour
surfe (*sewr*-fer) *v* surf
surfingbrett (*surr*-fing-breht) *nt* surf-board
surstoff (*sew*-shtof) *nt* oxygen
suspendere (sewss-pahng-*day*-rer) *v* suspend
suvenir (sew-ver-*neer*) *m* souvenir
svak (svaak) *adj* weak, feeble; faint; slight
svakhet (*svaak*-hayt) *c* weakness
svale (*svaa*-ler) *c* swallow
svamp (svahmp) *m* sponge
svane (*svaa*-ner) *c* swan
svangerskap (*svahng*-ngerr-skaap) *nt* pregnancy
svar (svaar) *nt* answer, reply; **som ~** in reply
svare (*svaa*-rer) *v* answer, reply; **~ til** correspond
svart (svahtt) *adj* dirty; black
svartebørs (*svaht*-ter-bursh) *m* black market
svarttrost (*svaht*-rost) *m* blackbird
sveise (*svay*-ser) *v* weld
Sveits (svayts) Switzerland
sveitser (*svayt*-serr) *m* Swiss
sveitsisk (*svayt*-sisk) *adj* Swiss
svelge (*svehl*-ger) *v* swallow
svelle (*svehl*-ler) *v* *swell
svensk (svehnsk) *adj* Swedish
svenske (*svehn*-sker) *m* Swede
sverd (sværd) *nt* sword
***sverge** (*svær*-ger) *v* vow, *swear
Sverige (*svær*-[y]er) Sweden
svette (*sveht*-ter) *v* perspire, sweat; *m* perspiration, sweat
***svi** (svee) *v* *burn
svigerdatter (*svee*-gerr-dah-terr) *c* daughter-in-law
svigerfar (*svee*-gerr-faar) *m*

(pl -fedre) father-in-law
svigerforeldre (*svee*-gerr-fo-rehl-drer) *pl* parents-in-law *pl*
svigerinne (svee-ger-*rin*-ner) *c* sister-in-law
svigermor (*svee*-gerr-mo͞or) *c* (pl -mødre) mother-in-law
svigersønn (*svee*-ger-shurn) *m* son-in-law
svikte (*svik*-ter) *v* *let down
svimmel (*svim*-merl) *adj* dizzy, giddy
svimmelhet (*svim*-merl-hāyt) *c* dizziness, giddiness
svindel (*svin*-derl) *m* swindle
svindle (*svin*-dler) *v* swindle
svindler (*svin*-dlerr) *m* swindler
svinekjøtt (*svee*-ner-khurt) *nt* pork
svinelær (*svee*-ner-læær) *nt* pigskin
sving (svingng) *m* turning, bend, turn
svingdør (*sving*-dūrr) *c* revolving door
svinge (*sving*-nger) *v* turn; *swing
sviske (*sviss*-ker) *c* prune
svoger (*svaw*-gerr) *m* (pl ~e, -grer) brother-in-law
svulst (svewlst) *m* tumo(u)r, growth
svær (svæær) *adj* huge
svært (svææt) *adv* very
svømme (*svurm*-mer) *v* *swim
svømmebasseng (*svurm*-mer-bah-sehng) *nt* swimming pool
svømmer (*svurm*-merr) *m* swimmer
svømmevest (*svurm*-me-vest) *m* life jacket
svømming (*svurm*-ming) *c* swimming
swahili (svah-*hee*-li) *m* Swahili
sy (sēw) *v* *sew; ~ **sammen** *sew up
syd (sēwd) *m* south
sydlig (*sēwd*-li) *adj* southerly
Sydpolen (*sēwd*-po͞o-lern) South Pole
syk (sēwk) *adj* sick, ill
sykdom (*sēwk*-dom) *m* (pl ~mer) sickness, illness; disease
sykebil (*sēw*-ker-beel) *m* ambulance
sykehus (*sēw*-ker-hēwss) *nt* (pl ~) hospital
sykepleier (*sēw*-ker-play-er) *m* nurse
sykkel (*sewk*-kerl) *m* (pl sykler) bicycle, cycle, bike
sykle (*sewk*-kler) *v* bicycle, cycle, bike
syklist (sewk-*list*) *m* cyclist
syklus (*sēwk*-lewss) *m* cycle
sylinder (sew-*lin*-derr) *m* (pl ~e, -drer) cylinder
syltetøy (*sewl*-ter-tur^{ew}) *nt* jam
symaskin (*sēw*-mah-sheen)

m sewing machine
symbol (sewm-*bōōl*) *nt* symbol
symfoni (sewm-foo-*nee*) *m* symphony
sympati (sewm-pah-*tee*) *m* sympathy
sympatisk (sewm-*paa*-tisk) *adj* nice
symptom (sewm-*tōōm*) *nt* symptom
syn (sēwn) vision; outlook, view; sight, spectacle
synagoge (sew-nah-*gōō*-ger) *m* synagogue
synd (sewnn) *m* sin; **så synd!** what a pity!; **synes ~ på** pity
synde (*sewnn*-der) *v* sin
syndebukk (*sewn*-der-book) *m* scapegoat
synder (*sewnn*-derr) *m* sinner
synes (*sēw*-nerss) *v* appear, look, seem; **jeg ~** I think; I find
***synge** (*sewng*-nger) *v* *sing
***synke** (*sewng*-ker) *v* *sink
synlig (*sēwn*-li) *adj* visible
synonym (sew-noo-*nēwm*) *nt* synonym
synspunkt (*sēwns*-poongt) *nt* point of view
syntetisk (sewn-*tāy*-tisk) *adj* synthetic
syrer (*sēw*-rerr) *m* Syrian
Syria (*sēw*-ri-ah) Syria
syrisk (*sēw*-risk) *adj* Syrian
system (sewss-*tāym*) *nt* system
systematisk (sewss-teh-*maa*-tisk) *adj* systematic
sytten (*surt*-tern) *num* seventeen
syttende (*surt*-ter-ner) *num* seventeenth
sytti (*surt*-ti) *num* seventy
syv (sēwv) *num* seven
syvende (*sēw*-ver-ner) *num* seventh
sær (sææ̀r) *adj* queer
særdeles (sæ-*dāy*-lerss) *adv* quite
særdeleshet: i ~ (ee sæ-***āy*-lerss-hāyt) in particular
særegen (*sææ*-reh-gern) *adj* particular
særlig (*sææ*r-li) *adv* especially
særskilt (*sææ*-shilt) *adj* separate
søke (*sūr*-ker) *v* *seek, apply
søker (*sūr*-kerr) *m* view--finder
søknad (*sūrk*-nah) *m* application
søle (*sūr*-ler) *v* *spill; *m* mud
sølet (*sūr*-lert) *adj* muddy
sølv (surll) *nt* silver; **sølv-**silver
sølvsmed (*surl*-smāy) *m* silversmith
sølvtøy (*surl*-tur[ew]) *nt* silverware
søm (surmm) *m* (pl ~mer) seam
sømmelig (*surm*-mer-li) *adj*

proper
søndag (*surn*-daa) *m* Sunday
sønn (surnn) *m* son
søppel (*surp*-perl) *nt* garbage, litter
søppelbøtte (*surp*-perl-bur-ter) *c* rubbish bin; waste basket *Am*
søppelkasse (*surp*-perl-kah-ser) *c* dustbin; trash can *Am*
sør (sūr) *m* south
Sør-Afrika (*sūr*-rahf-ri-kah) South Africa
sørge (*surr*-ger) *v* grieve; mourn; **~ for** see to, look after
sørlig (*sūr*-li) *adj* southern
sørvest (surr-*vehst*) *m* south-west
sørøst (surr-*urst*) *m* south--east
søster (*surss*-terr) *c* (pl -tre) sister
søt (sūrt) *adj* sweet
søtsaker (*sūrt*-saa-kerr) *pl* candy *nAm*
søvn (survn) *m* sleep
søvnig (*surv*-ni) *adj* sleepy
søvnløs (*survn*-lūrss) *adj* sleepless
søvnløshet (*survn*-lūrss-hayt) *c* insomnia
søyle (*sure*w-ler) *c* column
så (saw) *adv* so; then; *conj* so, so that; *v* *sow; **~ vel som** as well as; **~ vidt** barely; as much
såkalt (*saw*-kahlt) *adj* so--called
såle (*saw*-ler) *m* sole
sånn (sonn) *adj* such
såpe (*saw*-per) *c* soap
sår (sawr) *nt* wound; ulcer, sore; *adj* sore
sårbar (*sawr*-baar) *adj* vulnerable
såre (*saw*-rer) *v* wound; *hurt
***ta** (taa) *v* *take; **~ bort** *take out; **~ ille opp** resent; *** ~ imot** accept; **~ inn** stay; **~ med** *bring; **~ med seg** *take away; **~ opp** pick up; *bring up; **~ på** *put on; **~ seg av** attend to, *deal with; **~ vare på** *take care of; **~ vekk** *take away

T

tabell (tah-*behll*) *m* chart, table
tablett (tahb-*lehtt*) *m* tablet
tabu (*taa*-bew) *nt* taboo
tak (taak) *nt* roof; ceiling; grip
takk (tahkk) thank you
takke (*tahk*-ker) *v* thank; ***ha å ~ for** owe
takknemlig (tahk-*nehm*-li) *adj* grateful, thankful
takknemlighet (tahk-*nehm*-

li-hāyt) *c* gratitude
taksameter (tahk-sah-*māy*-terr) *nt* (pl ~, -tre) taxi-meter
taksere (tahk-*sāy*-rer) *v* value, estimate
takstein (*taak*-stayn) *m* tile
taktikk (tahk-*tikk*) *m* tactics *pl*
tale (*taa*-ler) *m* speech
talent (tah-*lehnt*) *nt* talent
talerstol (*taa*-ler-shtōōl) *m* pulpit
talkum (*tahl*-kewm) *m* talc powder
tall (tahll) *nt* figure, number
tallerken (tah-*lær*-kern) *m* plate, dish
tallord (*tahl*-lōōr) *nt* (pl ~) numeral
tallrik (*tahl*-reek) *adj* numerous
tam (tahmm) *adj* tame
tampong (tahm-*pongng*) *m* tampon
tang (tahngng) *c* (pl tenger) tongs *pl*, pliers *pl*
tank (tahngk) *m* tank
tankbåt (*tahngk*-bawt) *m* tanker
tanke (*tahng*-ker) *m* thought, idea
tankefull (*tahng*-ker-fewl) *adj* thoughtful
tankestrek (*tahng*-ker-strāyk) *m* dash
tann (tahnn) *c* (pl tenner) tooth
tannbørste (*tahn*-bursh-ter) *m* toothbrush
tannkjøtt (*tahn*-khurt) *nt* gum
tannkrem (*tahnn*-krāym) *m* toothpaste
tannlege (*tahn*-lāy-ger) *m* dentist
tannpasta (*tahn*-pahss-tah) *m* toothpaste
tannpine (*tahn*-pee-ner) *c* toothache
tannpirker (*tahn*-peer-kerr) *m* toothpick
tannregulering (*tahn*-reh-gew-*lāy*-ring) *c* brace
tannverk (*tahn*-værk) *m* toothache
tante (*tahn*-ter) *c* aunt
tap (taap) *nt* loss
tape (*taa*-per) *v* *lose
taper (*taa*-perr) *m* loser
tapet (tah-*pāyt*) *nt* wallpaper
tapper (*tahp*-perr) *adj* brave, courageous
tapperhet (*tahp*-perr-hāyt) *c* courage
tariff (tah-*riff*) *m* rate, tariff
tarm (tahrm) *m* intestine, gut; **tarmer** bowels *pl*, intestines
tast (tahst) *m* key
tastatur (tahsta-*tēwr*) *nt* keyboard
taste (*tahs*-ter) *v* dial, type
tau (tou) *nt* cord
taue (*tou*-er) *v* tow, tug
taus (touss) *adj* silent
tavle (*tahv*-ler) *c* blackboard; board
taxi (*tahk*-si) *m* taxi

te (tāy) *m* tea
teater (teh-*aa*-terr) *nt* (pl ~, -tre) theater *Am*, theatre
teaterstykke (teh-*aa*-ter-shtew-ker) *nt* play
tegn (tayn) *nt* sign, token, signal; indication
tegne (*tay*-ner) *v* *draw; sketch; ~ **opp** design
tegnefilm (*tay*-ner-film) *m* cartoon
tegnestift (*tay*-ner-stift) *m* drawing pin; thumbtack *nAm*
tegning (*tay*-ning) *c* sketch, drawing
tekanne (*tāy*-kah-ner) *c* teapot
tekniker (*tehk*-ni-kerr) *m* technician
teknikk (tehk-*nikk*) *m* technique
teknisk (*tehk*-nisk) *adj* technical
teknisk støtte (*tehk*-nisk *sturt*-ter) *c* technical support
teknologi (tehk-noo-loo-*gee*) *m* technology
teknologisk (tehk-noo-*loo-gee*) *adj* technological
tekopp (*tāy*-kop) *m* teacup
tekst (tehkst) *m* text; subtitle
tekstil (tehk-*steel*) *m*/*nt* textile
telefaks (*teh*-ler-fahks) *m* fax; **sende en ~** send a fax
telefon (teh-ler-*fōōn*) *m* phone, telephone
telefonere (teh-ler-foo-*nāy*-rer) *v* phone
telefonkatalog (teh-ler-*fōōn*-kah-tah-lawg) *m* telephone directory; telephone book *Am*
telefonkiosk (teh-ler-*fōōn*-khosk) *m* telephone booth
telefonkort (teh-ler-*fōōn*-kot)*nt* phone card
telefonrør (teh-ler-*fōōn*-rūrr) *nt* (pl ~) receiver
telefonsamtale (teh-ler-*fōōn*-sahm-taa-ler) *m* telephone call
telefonsentral (teh-ler-*fōōn*-sehn-traal) *m* telephone exchange
telefonsvarer (teh-ler-*fōōn*-*svaa*-rerr) *m* answering machine
telekommunikasjon (*teh*-ler-koo-mewn-ni-kah-*shōōn*) *c* telecommunications
telekort (*tel*-ler-kōōt) *nt* (pl ~) phone card
teleobjektiv (*tāy*-ler-ob-ʸehk-teev) *nt* telephoto lens
telepati (teh-ler-pah-*tee*) *m* telepathy
***telle** (*tehl*-ler) *v* count; ~ **opp** count
telt (tehlt) *nt* tent
tema (*tāy*-mah) *nt* theme
temme (*tehm*-mer) *v* tame
temmelig (*tehm*-mer-li) *adv* rather, pretty, fairly, quite
tempel (*tehm*-perl) *nt* (pl ~,

-pler) temple
temperatur (tehm-per-rah-*tewr*) *m* temperature
tempo (*tehm*-poo) *nt* pace
tendens (tehn-*dehns*) *m* tendency; ***ha ~ til** tend
tenke (*tehng*-ker) *v* *think; **~ over** *think over; **~ på** *think of; **~ seg** imagine, fancy; **~ ut** conceive
tenker (*tehng*-kerr) *m* thinker
tenne (*tehn*-ner) *v* *light
tenning (*tehn*-ning) *c* ignition
tennis (*tehn*-niss) *m* tennis
tennisbane (*tehn*-niss-baa-ner) *m* tennis court
tennissko (*tehn*-ni-skoo) *pl* tennis shoes
tennplugg (*tehn*-plewg) *m* sparking plug
tennspole (*tehn*-spoo-ler) *m* ignition coil
tenåring (*tay*-naw-ring) *m* teenager
teologi (teh-oo-loo-*gee*) *m* theology
teoretisk (teh-oo-*ray*-tisk) *adj* theoretical
teori (teh-oo-*ree*) *m* theory
teppe (*tehp*-per) *nt* blanket; carpet; curtain
terapi (teh-rah-*pee*) *m* therapy
termin (tær-*meen*) *m* term
termometer (tær-moo-*may*-terr) *nt* (pl ~, -tre) thermometer
termosflaske (*tær*-mooss-flahss-ker) *c* thermos flask
termostat (tær-moo-*staat*) *m* thermostat
terning (*tææ*-ning) *m* cube; dice *pl*
terpentin (tær-pehn-*teen*) *m* turpentine
terrasse (tæ-*rahss*-ser) *m* terrace
terreng (tæ-*rehngng*) *nt* terrain
terror (*tær*-roor) *m* terror
terrorisme (tæ-roo-*riss*-mer) *m* terrorism
terrorist (tæ-roo-*rist*) *m* terrorist
terskel (*tæsh*-kerl) *m* threshold
tesalong (*tay*-sah-long) *m* tea-shop
tese (*tay*-ser) *m* thesis
teservise (*tay*-sær-vee-ser) *nt* tea set
teskje (*tay*-shay) *c* teaspoon
test (tehst) *m* test
testamente (tehss-tah-*mehn*-ter) *nt* will
teste (*tehss*-ter) *v* test
tett (tehtt) *adj* dense, thick
tettpakket (*teht*-pah-kert) *adj* crowded
Thailand (*tigh*-lahn) Thailand
thailandsk (*tigh*-lahnsk) *adj* Thai
thailender (*tigh*-leh-nerr) *m* Thai
ti (tee) *num* ten
tid (teed) *c* time; period; **hele tiden** all the time; **i**

tide in time
tidevann (*tee*-der-vahn) *nt* tide
tidlig (*tee*-li) *adj* early; **tidligere** before, former, previous, formerly, *adv* before; past
tidsbesparende (*tits*-beh-spaa-rer-ner) *adj* time--saving
tidsfordriv (*tits*-for-driv) *nt* pastime
tidsskrift (*tit*-skrift) *nt* magazine, periodical, review, journal
tie (*tee*-er) *v* *be silent, *keep quiet
tiende (*tee*-er-ner) *num* tenth
tiger (*tee*-gerr) *m* tiger
tigge (*tig*-ger) *v* beg
tigger (*tig*-gerr) *m* beggar
til (till) *prep* to; for; until, till; **en ~** another; **~ og med** even
tilbake (til-*baa*-ker) *adv* back; ***gå ~** *get back
tilbakebetale (til-*baa*-ker-beh-taa-ler) *v* reimburse, *repay
tilbakebetaling (til-*baa*-ker-beh-taa-ling) *c* repayment, refund
tilbakegang (til-*baa*-ker-gahng) *m* recession
tilbakekalle (til-*baa*-ker-kah-ler) *v* recall
tilbakekomst (til-*baa*-ker-komst) *m* return
tilbakereise (til-*baa*-ker-ray-ser) *c* return journey
tilbakevei (til-*baa*-ker-vay) *m* way back
tilbakevise (til-*baa*-ker-vee-ser) *v* reject
***tilbe** (*til*-bay̅) *v* worship
tilbehør (*til*-beh-hu̅rr) *nt* accessories *pl*
tilberede (*til*-beh-ray̅-der) *v* prepare; cook
***tilbringe** (*til*-bri-nger) *v* *spend
tilbud (*til*-be̅wd) *nt* (pl ~) offer; supply; bid
***tilby** (*til*-be̅w) *v* offer; *bid
tilbøyelig (til-*bur*ew-er-li) *adj* inclined; ***være ~ til** tend to
tilbøyelighet (til-*bur*ew-er-li-hay̅t) *c* inclination, tendency
tildele (*til*-day̅-ler) *v* award; assign to; administer
tilfeldig (til-*fehl*-di) *adj* incidental, accidental, casual
tilfeldighet (til-*fehl*-di-hay̅t) *c* chance, coincidence
tilfeldigvis (til-*fehl*-di-veess) *adv* by chance
tilfelle (*til*-feh-ler) *nt* case, instance; chance; coincidence; **i ~ av** in case of
tilfluktssted (*til*-flewkt-steh) *nt* shelter
tilfreds (til-*frehts*) *adj* content; satisfied
tilfredshet (til-*frehts*-hay̅t) *c* contentment

tilfredsstille (*til*-freht-sti-ler) *v* satisfy
tilfredsstillelse (*til*-freht-sti-lerl-ser) *m* satisfaction
tilfredsstillende (*til*-freht-sti-lerl-ner) *adj* satisfactory
tilfredsstilt (*til*-freht-stilt) *adj* satisfied
tilførsel (*til*-fur-sherl) *m* (pl -sler) supply
tilføye (*til*-fur[ew]-er) *v* add; inflict
tilføyelse (*til*-fur[ew]-erl-ser) *m* addition
tilgang (*til*-gahng) *m* access
***tilgi** (*til*-[y]ee) *v* *forgive
tilgivelse (*til*-[y]ee-verl-ser) *m* pardon
tilgjengelig (til-*[y]ehng*-nger-li) *adj* available; accessible
tilhenger (*til*-heh-ngerr) *m* trailer; supporter
tilhøre (*til*-hūr-rer) *v* belong, belong to
tilhører (*til*-hūr-rerr) *m* auditor
***tilintetgjøre** (ti-*lin*-tert-[y]ūr-rer) *v* destroy; ruin
***tillate** (*til*-laa-ter) *v* permit, allow; ***være tillatt** *be allowed
tillatelse (*til*-laa-terl-ser) *m* permission, authorization; permit; ***gi ~** license
tillegg (*til*-lehg) *nt* (pl ~) supplement; surcharge; annex
tillit (*til*-leet) *m* faith, confidence, trust
tillitsfull (*til*-leets-fewl) *adj* confident
tilpasse (*til*-pah-ser) *v* adapt, suit; adjust; accommodate
tilrettevise (til-*reht*-ter-vee-ser) *v* reprimand
tilråde (*til*-raw-der) *v* recommend
tilsiktet (*til*-sik-tert) *adj* intentional
***tilskrive** (*til*-skree-ver) *v* assign to
tilskudd (*til*-skewd) *nt* (pl ~) subsidy; grant
tilskuer (*til*-skēw-err) *m* spectator
tilsluttet (*til*-shlew-tert) *adj* affiliated
tilstand (*til*-stahn) *m* condition
tilstedeværelse (til-*stāy*-der-vææ-rerl-ser) *m* presence
tilstedeværende (til-*stāy*-der-vææ-rer-ner) *adj* present
tilstrekkelig (til-*streh*-ker-li) *adj* enough, sufficient; adequate; ***være ~** suffice; *do
tilstøtende (*til*-stūr-ter-ner) *adj* neighbo(u)ring, adjacent
***tilstå** (*til*-staw) *v* confess, admit
tilståelse (*til*-staw-erl-ser) *m* confession
tilsvare (*til*-svaa-rer) *v* correspond
tilsvarende (*til*-svaa-rer-

ner) *adj* equivalent
tilsynelatende (til-*sēw*-ner-laa-ter-ner) *adj* apparent
***tilta** (*til*-taa) *v* increase
tiltakende (*til*-taa-ker-ner) *adj* progressive
***tiltrekke** (*til*-treh-ker) *v* attract
tiltrekkende (*til*-treh-ker) *adj* attractive
tiltrekning (*til*-trehk-ning) *m* attraction
time (*tee*-mer) *m* hour; lesson; **hver ~** hourly
timeplan (*ti*-mer-plaan) *m* schedule
timian (*tee*-mi-ahn) *m* thyme
tind (tinn) *m* peak
tine (*tee*-ner) *v* thaw
ting (tingng) *m* (pl ~) thing
tinn (tinn) *nt* pewter, tin
tinning (tin-ning) *m* temple
tirsdag (*teesh*-dah) *m* Tuesday
tispe (*tiss*-per) *c* bitch
tistel (*tiss*-terl) *m* (pl -tler) thistle
tittel (*tit*-terl) *m* (pl titler) title
tiur (*tee*-ēwr) *m* wood grouse
tjene (*t^y^ay*-ner) *v* earn; *make
tjener (*t^y^ay*-nerr) *m* boy, servant, domestic
tjeneste (*t^y^ay*-nerss-ter) *m* favo(u)r; service
tjue (*khēw*-er) *num* twenty
tjuende (*khēw*-er-ner) *num* twentieth
tjære (*khææ*-rer) *c* tar
to (tōō) *num* two
toalett (too-ah-*lehtt*) *nt* bathroom, lavatory, toilet; washroom, rest room *Am*
toalettpapir (too-ah-*leht*-pah-peer) *nt* toilet paper
toalettsaker (too-ah-*leht*-saa-kerr) *pl* toiletry
toalettveske (too-ah-*leht*-vehss-ker) *c* toilet case
tobakk (too-*bahkk*) *m* tobacco
tobakksforretning (too-*bahks*-fo-reht-ning) *c* tobacconist's
todelt (*tōō*-dehlt) *adj* two--piece
tog (tawg) *nt* train, parade
tolk (tolk) *m* interpreter
tolke (*tol*-ker) *v* interpret
toll (toll) *m* customs duty; customs *pl*
tollavgift (*tol*-laav-^y^ift) *c* customs duty
toller (*tol*-lerr) *m* customs officer
tollfri (*toll*-free) *adj* duty--free
tolv (toll) *num* twelve
tolvte (*tol*-ter) *num* twelfth
tom (tomm) *adj* empty
tomat (too-*maat*) *m* tomato
tomme (*tom*-me) *m* inch
tommelfinger (*tom*-merl-fi-ngerr) *m* (pl -gre) thumb
tomt (tomt) *c* grounds, plot
tone (*tōō*-ner) *m* note, tone
tonn (tonn) *nt* ton

topp (topp) *m* summit, top; peak
topplokk (*top*-lok) *nt* (pl ~) cylinder head
torden (*too*-dern) *m* thunder
tordenvær (*too*-dern-væær) *nt* (pl ~) thunderstorm
tordne (*tood*-ner) *v* thunder
***tore** (*too*-rer) *v* dare
torg (torg) *nt* market-place
torn (tōōn) *m* thorn
torsdag (*tawsh*-dah) *m* Thursday
torsk (toshk) *m* (pl ~) cod
tortur (too-*tewr*) *m* torture
torturere (too-tew-*ray*-rer) *v* torture
tosk (tosk) *m* fool
tospråklig (*too*-sprawk-li) *adj* bilingual
total (too-*taal*) *adj* total; overall; utter
totalisator (too-tah-li-*saa*-toor) *m* bookmaker
totalitær (too-tah-li-*tæær*) *adj* totalitarian
totalsum (too-*taal*-sewm) *m* (pl ~mer) total
totalt (too-*taalt*) *adv* completely
tradisjon (trah-di-*shoon*) *m* tradition
tradisjonell (trah-di-shoo-*nehll*) *adj* traditional
trafikk (trah-*fikk*) *m* traffic
trafikk-kork (trah-*fik*-kork) *m* jam, traffic jam
trafikklys (trah-*fik*-lēwss) *nt* (pl ~) traffic light
trafikkraseri (trah-*fikk*-raa-ser-*ree*) *nt* road rage
tragedie (trah-*gay*-di-er) *m* tragedy
tragisk (*traa*-gisk) *adj* tragic
trakt (trahkt) *c* region; funnel
traktat (trahk-*taat*) *m* treaty
traktor (*trahk*-toor) *m* tractor
trang (trahngng) *adj* tight, narrow; *m* urge
transaksjon (trahn-sahk-*shoon*) *m* deal, transaction
transatlantisk (*trahn*-saht-lahn-tisk) *adj* transatlantic
transformator (trahns-for-*maa*-toor) *m* transformer
transpirasjon (trahn-spi-rah-*shoon*) *m* perspiration
transpirere (trahn-spi-*ray*-rer) *v* perspire
transport (trahns-*pott*) *m* transport, transportation
transportabel (trahns-po-*taa*-berl) *adj* portable
transportere (trahns-po-*tay*-rer) *v* transport
trapp (trahpp) *c* stairs *pl*, staircase
travel (*traa*-verl) *adj* busy
travelhet (*traa*-verl-hayt) *c* bustle
***tre** (tray) *v* step; thread
tre[1] (tray) *num* three
tre[2] (tray) *nt* (pl trær) tree; wood; **tre-** wooden
tredje (*trayd*-[y]er) *num* third
***treffe** (*trehf*-fer) *v* *hit; *meet

treg (tra̅yg) *adj* slack
trekant (*tra̅y*-kahnt) *m* triangle
trekantet (*tra̅y*-kahn-tert) *adj* triangular
trekk (trehkk) *nt* move; trait; *m* draught
***trekke** (*trehk*-ker) *v* pull, *draw; upholster; **~ fra** deduct; subtract; **~ opp** *wind; uncork; **~ tilbake** *withdraw; **~ ut** extract
trekning (*trehk*-ning) *m* draw
trekull (*tra̅y*-kewl) *nt* charcoal
trene (*tra̅y*-ner) *v* drill; train
trener (*tra̅y*-nerr) *m* coach; trainer
trenge (*trehng*-nger) *v* need; **~ seg frem** push
trening (*tra̅y*-ning) *c* training
treskjærerarbeid (*tra̅y*-shææ-rerr-ahr-bayd) *nt* wood carving
tresko (*tra̅y*-sko̅o̅) *m* (pl ~) wooden shoe
trett (trehtt) *adj* tired, weary
trette (*treht*-ter) *v* argue, quarrel; tire; *m* quarrel
tretten (*treht*-tern) *num* thirteen
trettende (*treht*-ter-ner) *num* thirteenth; *adj* tiring
tretti (*treht*-ti) *num* thirty
trettiende (*treht*-ti-er-ner) *num* thirtieth
trevle opp (*trehv*-ler) fray
tribune (tri-*be̅w̅*-ner) *m* stand
trick (trikk) *nt* trick
trikk (trikk) *m* tram; streetcar *nAm*
trillebår (*tril*-ler-bawr) *c* wheelbarrow
trinn (trinn) *nt* step
trinse (*trin*-ser) *c* pulley
trist (trist) *adj* sad
triumf (tri-*ewmf*) *m* triumph
triumfere (tri-ewm-*fa̅y*-rer) *v* triumph
triumferende (tri-ewm-*fa̅y*-rer-ner) *adj* triumphant
tro (tro̅o̅) *v* believe; reckon; *c* belief, faith; *adj* faithful
trofast (*tro̅o̅*-fahst) *adj* faithful, true
trolig (*tro̅o̅*-li) *adj* credible
trolldom (*trol*-dom) *m* magic
tromme (*troom*-mer) *c* drum
trommehinne (*troom*-mer-hi-ner) *c* ear-drum
trompet (troom-*pa̅yt*) *m* trumpet
trone (*tro̅o̅*-ner) *c* throne
tropene (*tro̅o̅*-per-ner) *pl* tropics *pl*
tropisk (*tro̅o̅*-pisk) *adj* tropical
tropper (*trop*-perr) *pl* troops *pl*
tross (tross) *prep* in spite of, despite; **til ~ for** in spite of
trost (trost) *m* thrush
true (*tre̅w̅*-er) *v* threaten
truende (*tre̅w̅*-er-ner) *adj*

threatening
trumf (trewmf) *m* trump, trump card
trupp (trewpp) *m* band; company
truse (trēw-ser) *c* briefs *pl*, panties *pl*; underpants *plAm*
trussel (*trewss*-serl) *m* (pl -sler) threat
trygle (*trēw*-ger-ler) *v* plead, beseech, beg
trykk[1] (trewkk) *nt* pressure
trykk[2] (trewkk) *nt* engraving, print
trykk[3] (trewkk) *nt* stress; ***legge ~ på** stress
trykke[1] (*trewk*-ker) *v* press; **~ på** press
trykke[2] (*trewk*-ker) *v* print
trykkende (*trewk*-ker-ner) *adj* stuffy
trykknapp (*trewk*-knahp) *m* push button; press-stud
trykkoker (trewk-kōō-kerr) *m* pressure cooker
tryllekunstner (*trewl*-ler-kewnst-nerr) *m* magician
trøbbel (*trurb*-berl) *nt* trouble
trøffel (*trur*-ferl) *m* truffle
trøst (trurst) *c* comfort
trøste (*trurss*-ter) *v* comfort
trøstepremie (*trurss*-ter-prāy-mi-er) *m* consolation prize
trå (traw) *v* step
tråd (traw) *m* thread
trådløs (*trawd*-lūrss) *adj* wireless
tube (*tēw*-ber) *m* tube
tuberkulose (tew-bær-kew-*lōō*-ser) *m* tuberculosis
tulipan (tew-li-*paan*) *m* tulip; **~-løk** tulip bulb
tull (tewll) *nt* rubbish
tunfisk (*tēwn*-fisk) *m* tuna
tung (toongng) *adj* heavy
tunge (*toong*-nger) *c* tongue
tungnem (*toong*-nehm) *adj* slow
tunika (*tēw*-ni-kah) *m* tunic
Tunisia (tew-*nee*-si-ah) Tunisia
tunisier (tew-*nee*-si-err) *m* Tunisian
tunisisk (tew-*nee*-sisk) *adj* Tunisian
tunnel (tew-*nehll*) *m* tunnel
tur (tēwr) *m* ride, trip; turn
turbin (tewr-*been*) *m* turbine
turbojet (*tewr*-boo-ʸeht) *m* turbojet
turgjenger (*tēwr*-ʸeh-ngerr) *m* walker
turist (tew-*rist*) *m* tourist
turistklasse (tew-*rist*-klah-ser) *c* tourist class
turistkontor (tew-*rist*-koon-tōōr) *nt* tourist office
turisttrafikk (tew-*riss*-trah-fik) *m* tourism
turner (*tew*-nerr) *m* gymnast
turnering (tew-*nāy*-ring) *c* tournament
turnsko (*tēwn*-skōō) *pl* gym shoes; sneakers *plAm*
tur-retur (*tēwr*-reh-tēwr)

round trip
tusen (*tēw*-sern) *num* thousand
tusmørke (*tewss*-murr-ker) *nt* dusk
tut (tēwt) *m* nozzle
tute (*tēw*-ter) *v* hoot; honk *vAm*, toot *vAm*
TV (*te***wehr) *m colloquial* TV
tvang (tvahng) *m* constraint; force
tverr (tværr) *adj* cross
tvert imot (*tvæt* i-*mōōt*) on the contrary
tvert om (*tvæt* om) the other way round
tvetydig (*tvāy*-tēw-di) *adj* ambiguous
tvil (tveel) *m* doubt; **uten ~** without doubt
tvile (*tvee*-ler) *v* doubt
tvillinger (*tvil*-li-ngerr) *pl* twins *pl*
tvilsom (*tveel*-som) *adj* doubtful
***tvinge** (*tving*-nger) *v* force
tvist (tvist) *m* dispute
tydelig (*tēw*-der-li) *adj* clear, distinct, plain; evident, apparent; explicit
tyfus (*tēw*-fewss) *m* typhoid
tygge (*tewg*-ger) *v* chew
tyggegummi (*tewg*-ger-gew-mi) *m* chewing gum
tykk (tewkk) *adj* thick; corpulent, big
tykkelse (*tewk*-kerl-ser) *m* thickness
tykkfallen (*tewk*-fah-lern) *adj* stout
tykne (*tewk*-ner) *v* thicken
tyngde (*tewng*-der) *m* weight
tyngdekraft (*tewng*-der-krahft) *c* gravity
tynge (*tewng*-nger) *v* oppress
tynn (tewnn) *adj* thin; sheer; weak
type (*tēw*-per) *m* type
typisk (*tēw*-pisk) *adj* typical
tyr (tēwr) *m* bull
tyrann (tew-*rahnn*) *m* tyrant
tyrefektning (*tēw*-rer-fehkt-ning) *m* bullfight
Tyrkia (*tewr*-ki-ah) Turkey
tyrkisk (*tewr*-kisk) *adj* Turkish
tysk (tewsk) *adj* German
tysker (*tewss*-kerr) *m* German
Tyskland (*tewsk*-lahn) Germany
tyv (tēwv) *m* thief
tyve (*tēw*-ver) *num* twenty
tyvende (*tēw*-ver-ner) *num* twentieth
tyveri (tēw-ver-*ree*) *nt* robbery, theft
tøffel (*turf*-ferl) *m* (pl tøfler) slipper
tømme (*turm*-mer) *v* empty
tømmer (*turm*-merr) *nt* timber
tømmermenn (*turm*-merr-mehn) *pl* hangover
tømming (*turm*-ming) *c* emptying
tønne (*turn*-ner) *c* cask,

barrel
tørke (*turr*-ker) *c* drought; *v* wipe, dry; **~ av** wipe; **~ bort** wipe
tørkeapparat (*turr*-ker-ah-pah-raat) *nt* dryer
tørr (turrr) *adj* dry
tørst (tursht) *adj* thirsty; *m* thirst
tøvær (*tūr*-vææг) *nt* thaw
tøye (*tur*ew-er) *v* stretch
tøyelig (*tur*ew-er-li) *adj* elastic
tøyelighet (*tur*ew-er-li-hāyt) *c* elasticity
tøyle (*tur*ew-ler) *v* curb; restrain
tå (taw) *c* (pl tær) toe
tåke (*taw*-ker) *c* mist, fog
tåkelykt (*taw*-ker-lewkt) *c* foglamp
tåket (*taw*-kert) *adj* foggy
tålmodig (tol-*mōō*-di) *adj* patient
tålmodighet (tol-*mōō*-di-hāyt) *c* patience
tåpelig (*taw*-per-li) *adj* silly, foolish; crazy
tåre (*taw*-rer) *c* tear
tårn (tawn) *nt* tower

U

uakseptabel (*ēw*-ahk-sep-taabel) *adj* unacceptable
ualminnelig (ew-ahl-*mi*-ner-li) *adj* unusual
uanselig (ew-ahn-*sāy*-li) *adj* inconspicuous, insignificant
uanstendig (*ēw*-ahn-stehn-di) *adj* indecent; obscene
uavbrutt (*ēw*-ahv-brewt) *adj* continuous
uavhengig (*ēw*-ahv-heh-ngi) *adj* independent
uavhengighet (*ēwahv*-heh-ngi-hāyt) *c* independence
ubebodd (*ēw*-beh-bood) *adj* uninhabited
ubeboelig (ēw-beh-*bōō*-er-li) *adj* uninhabitable
ubegrenset (*ēw*-beh-grehn-sert) *adj* unlimited
ubehagelig (*ēw*-beh-haa-ger-li) *adj* disagreeable, unpleasant; nasty
ubekvem (*ēw*-beh-kvehm) *adj* uncomfortable
ubekymret (*ēw*-beh-khewm-rert) *adj* carefree
ubeleilig (*ēw*-beh-lay-li) *adj* inconvenient
ubeleilighet (*ēw*-beh-lay-li-hāyt) *c* inconvenience
ubesindig (*ēw*-beh-sin-di) *adj* rash
ubeskjeden (*ēw*-beh-shāy-dern) *adj* immodest
ubeskyttet (*ēw*-beh-shew-tert) *adj* unprotected
ubestemt (*ēw*-beh-stehmt) *adj* indefinite
ubesvart (*ēw*-beh-svaat) *adj* unanswered

ubetydelig (ew̄-beh-*tew̄*-der-li) *adj* insignificant; slight, petty
ubevisst (*ew*-ber-vist) *adj* unconscious
ubotelig (ew-*bōō*-ter-li) *adj* irreparable
ubåt (*ew*-bawt) *m* submarine
udugelig (ew-*dew̄*-ger-li) *adj* incapable
udyrket (*ew*-dewr-kert) *adj* uncultivated
uegnet (ew̄-ay-nert) *adj* unsuitable, unfit
uekte (ew̄-ehk-ter) *adj* false
uendelig (ew-*ehn*-ner-li) *adj* endless, infinite
uenig: *være ~ (*vææ*-rer ew-*ay*-ni) disagree
uerfaren (ew̄-ær-faa-rern) *adj* inexperienced
ufaglært (ew̄-faag-lææt) *adj* unskilled
uflaks (ew̄-flahks) *m* bad luck
uforklarlig (ew̄-for-*klaa*-li) *adj* unaccountable
uformell (ew̄-for-mehll) *adj* casual, informal
uforskammet (ew̄-fo-shkah-mert) *adj* insolent, impertinent, impudent; rude, *colloquial* cheeky
uforskammethet (ew̄-fo-shkah-mert-hāyt) *c* insolence
uforståelig (ew̄-fo-shtaw-er-li) *adj* puzzling
ufortjent (ew̄-fo-t^{y}āynt) *adj* unearned
ufremkommelig (ew̄-frehm-ko-mer-li) *adj* impassable
ufullkommen (ew̄-fewl-ko-mern) *adj* imperfect
ufullstendig (ew̄-fewl-stehn-di) *adj* incomplete
ufølsom (ew̄-fur-l-som) *adj* insensitive
ufør (ew̄-fūr) *adj* disabled
ugift (ew̄-^{y}ift) *adj* single
ugjenkallelig (ew-^{y}ehn-*kahl*-ler-li) *adj* irrevocable
ugle (*ewg*-ler) *c* owl
ugress (ew̄-grehss) *nt* weed
ugunstig (ew̄-gewn-sti) *adj* unfavo(u)rable
ugyldig (ew̄-^{y}ewl-di) *adj* invalid, void
uhelbredelig (ew̄-hehl-*brāy*-der-li) *adj* incurable
uheldig (ew-*hehl*-di) *adj* unfortunate, unlucky
uheldigvis (ew-*hehl*-di-veess) *adv* unfortunately
uhell (ew̄-hehl) *nt* misfortune; accident; mishap
uhyggelig (ew-*hew*-ger-li) *adj* creepy; ominous
uhøflig (ew-*hurf*-li) *adj* impolite
ujevn (ew̄-^{y}ehvn) *adj* uneven
uke (ew̄-ker) *c* week
ukentlig (ew̄-kernt-li) *adj* weekly
ukjent (ew̄-khehnt) *adj* unknown, unfamiliar
uklar (ew̄-klaar) *adj* obscure, dim

uklok (*ew̄*-klo͞ok) *adj* unwise
uknuselig (ew-*knew̄*-ser-li) *adj* unbreakable
ukvalifisert (*ew̄*-kvah-li-fi-sa͞yt) *adj* unqualified
uleilighet (ew-*lay*-li-ha͞yt) *c* trouble
ulempe (*ew̄*-lehm-per) *m* disadvantage
uleselig (ew-*la͞y*-ser-li) *adj* illegible
ulik (*ew̄*-leek) *adj* unequal, uneven
ulike (*ew̄*-lee-ker) *adj* odd
ull (ewll) *c* wool; **ull-** wool(l)en
ulljakke (*ewl*-[y]ah-ker) *c* sweater, cardigan
ulovlig (*ew̄*-lawv-li) *adj* illegal, unlawful
ultrafiolett (*ewl*-trah-fi-oo-leht) *adj* ultraviolet
ulv (ewlv) *m* wolf
ulykke (*ew̄*-lew-ker) *c* accident, misfortune; calamity, disaster; misery
ulykkelig (ew-*lewk*-ker-li) *adj* unhappy; miserable
ulærd (*ew̄*-læærd) *adj* uneducated
umake (*ew̄*-maa-ker) *m* pains; ***være umaken verd** *be worthwhile
umiddelbart (*ew̄*-mi-derl-baat) *adv* immediately, instantly
umoderne (*ew̄*-moo-dææ-ner) *adj* out of date; old--fashioned
umulig (ew-*mew̄*-li) *adj* impossible
umyndig (*ew̄*-mewn-di) *adj* under age
umåtelig (ew-*maw*-ter-li) *adj* vast, immense
under[1] (*ewn*-derr) *nt* wonder
under[2] (*ewn*-nerr) *prep* below, during, beneath, under; *adv* beneath
underbukse (*ewn*-nerr-book-ser) *c* panties *pl*, drawers, pants *pl*; shorts *plAm*
underdrive (*ewn*-nerr-driver) *v* understate
underdrivelse (*ewn*-nerr-driv-erl-ser) *n* understatement
underernæring (*ewn*-nerr-æ-nææ-ring) *c* malnutrition
undergang (*ewn*-nerr-gahng) *m* ruin, destruction
undergrunnsbane (*ewn*-nerr-grewns-baa-ner) *m* underground; subway *nAm*
***underholde** (*ewn*-nerr-ho-ler) *v* entertain, amuse
underholdende (*ewn*-nerr-ho-ler-ner) *adj* entertaining
underholdning (*ewn*-nerr-hol-ning) *m* entertainment
underjordisk (*ewn*-nerr-[y]oor-disk) *adj* underground
underkaste seg (*ewn*-nerr-kahss-ter) submit
underkue (*ewn*-nerr-kew̄-

er) *v* subject
underlegen (*ewn*-ner-lāy-gern) *adj* inferior
underlig (*ewn*-der-li) *adj* odd, strange, queer; peculiar
underordnet (*ewn*-ner-oord-nert) *adj* subordinate; minor, secondary; additional
underretning (*ewn*-ner-reht-ning) *m* notice
underrette (*ewn*-ner-reh-ter) *v* inform; notify
underskrift (*ewn*-nerr-skrift) *c* signature
underskudd (*ewn*-ner-shkewd) *nt* (pl ~) deficit
understreke (*ewn*-ner-shtrāy-ker) *v* underline; emphasize
understrøm (*ewn*-ner-shtrurm) *m* (pl ~mer) undercurrent
undersøke (*ewn*-ner-shūr-ker) *v* enquire; examine
undersøkelse (*ewn*-ner-shūr-kerl-ser) *m* investigation, enquiry; check-up, examination
undersått (*ewn*-ner-shot) *m* subject
undertegne (*ewn*-ner-tay-ner) *v* sign
undertrykke (*ewn*-ner-trew-ker) *v* oppress, suppress
undertøy (*ewn*-ner-tur[ew]) *pl* underwear
undervanns- (*ewn*-nerr-vahns) underwater
undervise (*ewn*-nerr-vee-ser) *v* *teach; instruct
undervisning (*ewn*-nerr-veess-ning) *c* tuition, instruction
undervurdere (*ewn*-nerr-vew-dāy-rer) *v* underestimate
undre seg (*ewn*-drer) wonder; marvel
ung (oongng) *adj* young
ungarer (*oong*-gaa-rerr) *m* Hungarian
Ungarn (*ewng*-gaan) Hungary
ungarsk (*ewng*-gaashk) *adj* Hungarian
ungdom (*oong*-dom) *m* (pl ~mer) youth; **ungdoms-** juvenile
ungdomsherberge (*oong*-doms-hær-bær-ger) *nt* youth hostel
unge (*oong*-nger) *m* kid
ungkar (*oong*-kaar) *m* bachelor
uniform (ew-ni-*form*) *c* uniform
union (ew-ni-*ōōn*) *m* union
univers (ew-ni-*væshsh*) *nt* universe
universell (ew-ni-væ-*shehll*) *adj* universal
universitet (ew-ni-væ-shi-*tāyt*) *nt* university
***unngå** (*ewn*-gaw) *v* avoid; escape
unnskyld! (*ewn*-shewl) sorry!
unnskylde (*ewn*-shew-ler) *v*

excuse

unnskyldning (*ewn*-shewl-ning) *m* apology, excuse; ***be om ~** apologize

***unnslippe** (*ewn*-shli-per) *v* escape

unntak (*ewn*-taak) *nt* (pl ~) exception

unntaksvis (*ewn*-taaks-vis) *adv* for a change

unntatt (*ewn*-taht) *prep* except

***unnvike** (*ewn*-vee-ker) *v* avoid

***unnvære** (*ewn*-vææ-rer) *v* spare

unyttig (*ew*-new-ti) *adj* useless

unødvendig (*ew*-nurd-vern-di) *adj* unnecessary

unøyaktig (*ew*-nur^{ew}-ahk-ti) *adj* inaccurate

uoffisiell (*ew*-o-fi-si-erl) *adj* unofficial

uopphørlig (*ew*-oop-hur-li) *adv* continually

uorden (*ew*-o-dern) *m* disorder; **i ~** out of order; broken

uordentlig (*ew*-ont-li) *adj* untidy

uoverkommelig (*ew*-o-verr-ko-mer-li) *adj* prohibitive, insurmountable

uovertruffen (*ew*-o-ver-troo-fern) *adj* unsurpassed

upartisk (*ew*-paa-tisk) *adj* impartial

upassende (*ew*-pah-ser-ner) *adj* improper

upersonlig (*ew*-pæ-shoon-li) *adj* impersonal

upopulær (*ew*-poo-pew-lær) *adj* unpopular

upålitelig (*ew*-po-lee-ter-li) *adj* unreliable, untrustworthy

ur (ewr) *nt* watch

uregelmessig (*ew*-ray-gerl-meh-si) *adj* irregular

urett (*ew*-reht) *m* wrong, injustice; ***gjøre ~** wrong; ***ha ~** *be wrong

urettferdig (*ew*-reht-fæ-di) *adj* unfair, unjust

uriktig (ew-*rik*-ti) *adj* incorrect, wrong

urimelig (ew-*ree*-mer-li) *adj* unreasonable; absurd

urin (ew-*reen*) *m* urine

urmaker (*ewr*-maa-kerr) *m* watch-maker

uro (*ew*-roo) *m* unrest

urolig (ew-*roo*-li) *adj* restless; uneasy

urskog (*ew*-shkoog) *m* jungle; primeval forest

urt (ewtt) *c* herb

urtids- (*ew*-tits) ancient

Uruguay (ew-rew-gew-*igh*) Uruguay

uruguayaner (ew-rew-gew-igh-*aa*-nerr) *m* Uruguayan

uruguayansk (ew-rew-gew-igh-*aansk*) *adj* Uruguayan

usann (*ew*-sahn) *adj* untrue

usannsynlig (*ew*-sahn-sewn-li) *adj* improbable, unlikely

usedvanlig (ew-sehd-*vaan*-

li) *adj* uncommon, extraordinary, exceptional
uselvisk (*ew*-sehl-visk) *adj* unselfish
usikker (*ew*-si-kerr) *adj* uncertain; doubtful; unsafe
uskadd (*ew*-skahd) *adj* unhurt; whole
uskadelig (ew-*skaa*-der-li) *adj* harmless
uskikkelig (ew-*shik*-ker-li) *adj* naughty
uskyld (*ew*-shewl) *c* innocence
uskyldig (ew-*shewl*-di) *adj* innocent
uspiselig (ew-*spee*-ser-li) *adj* inedible
ustabil (*ew*-stah-beel) *adj* unstable
ustadig (ew-*staa*-di) *adj* unsteady
ustø (*ew*-stur) *adj* unsteady
usunn (*ew*-sewn) *adj* unhealthy, unsound
usympatisk (*ew*-sewm-paa-tisk) *adj* unpleasant
usynlig (ew-*sewn*-li) *adj* invisible
ut (ewt) *adv* out; ***gå ~** *go out; **~ over** beyond
utad (*ew*-taad) *adv* outwards
utakknemlig (*ew*-tahk-nehm-li) *adj* ungrateful
utbre (*ewt*-bray) *v* expand
utbredelse (*ewt*-bred-ehl-ser) *m* expansion
utbrudd (*ewt*-brewd) *nt* (pl ~) outbreak
***utbryte** (*ewt*-brew-ter) *v* exclaim
utbytte (*ewt*-bew-ter) *nt* benefit; profit; ***ha ~ av** profit
utdanne (*ewt*-dah-ner) *v* educate
utdannelse (*ewt*-dah-nerl-ser) *m* education; background
utdele (*ewt*-day-ler) *v* distribute
utdrag (*ewt*-draag) *nt* (pl ~) extract, excerpt
utdype (*ewt*-dew-per) *v* elaborate
ute (*ew*-ter) *adv* out
***utelate** (*ew*-ter-laa-ter) *v* omit, *leave out
utelukke (*ew*-ter-loo-ker) *v* exclude
utelukkende (*ew*-ter-loo-ker-ner) *adv* solely, exclusively
uten (*ew*-tern) *prep* without
utenat (*ew*-ter-naht) *adv* by heart
utendørs (*ew*-tern-dursh) *adv* outdoors
utenfor (*ew*-tern-for) *prep* outside; *adv* outside
utenkelig (ew-*tehng*-ker-li) *adj* inconceivable
utenlands (*ew*-tern-lahns) *adv* abroad
utenlandsk (*ew*-tern-lahnsk) *adj* alien, foreign
utflukt (*ewt*-flookt) *c* trip, excursion, outing
utfolde (*ewt*-fo-ler) *v*

unfold, display
utfordre (*ewt*-foord-rer) *v* challenge; dare; **utfordrende** challenging, defiant
utforske (*ewt*-fosh-ker) *v* explore
utføre (*ewt*-fur-rer) *v* execute, perform, implement, carry out; export
utførlig (ewt-*fur*-li) *adj* detailed
utførsel (*ewt*-fur-sherl) *m* (pl -sler) export
utgang (*ewt*-gahng) *m* way out, exit; outcome
utgangspunkt (*ewt*-gahngs-poongt) *nt* starting point
utgave (*ewt*-gaa-ver) *c* edition
***utgi** (*ewt*-ʸee) *v* publish; issue; edit
utgift (*ewt*-ʸift) *c* expense; **utgifter** expenditure
utgravning (*ewt*-graav-ning) *m* excavation
***utgyte** (*ewt*-ʸew-ter) *v* *shed
***utholde** (*ewt*-ho-ler) *v* endure
utholdelig (*ewt*-ho-ler-li) *adj* tolerable
utilfreds (*ew*-til-frehts) *adj* dissatisfied
utilfredsstillende (*ew*-til-freht-sti-ler-ner) *adj* unsatisfactory
utilgjengelig (*ew*-til-ʸeh-nger-li) *adj* inaccessible
utilsiktet (*ew*-til-sik-tert) *adj* unintentional
utilstrekkelig (*ew*-til-streh-ker-li) *adj* insufficient; inadequate
utiltalende (*ew*-til-taa-ler-ner) *adj* unpleasant
utjevne (*ewt*-ʸehv-ner) *v* equalize
utkant (*ewt*-kahnt) *m* outskirts *pl*
utkast (*ewt*-kahst) *nt* draft
utkjørsel (*ewt*-khur-sherl) *m* exit, driveway
utkople (*ewt*-kop-ler) *v* disconnect
utlede (*ewt*-lay-der) *v* deduce, infer
utlending (*ewt*-lehn-ing) *m* alien, foreigner
utligne (*ewt*-ling-ner) *v* level
utluftning (*ewt*-lewft-ning) *m* ventilation
utløp (*ewt*-lurp) *nt* (pl ~) expiry
***utløpe** (*ewt*-lur-per) *v* expire
utløpt (*ewt*-lurpt) *adj* expired
utmatte (*ewt*-mah-ter) *v* exhaust
utmattet (*ewt*-mah-tert) *adj* tired
utmerke seg (*ewt*-mær-ker) excel
utmerket (*ewt*-mær-kert) *adj* fine, excellent
utnevne (*ewt*-nehv-ner) *v* appoint
utnevnelse (*ewt*-nehv-nerl-

ser) *m* nomination, appointment
utnytte (*ew̄t*-new-ter) *v* exploit
utpresse (*ew̄t*-preh-ser) *v* extort
utpressing (*ew̄t*-preh-sing) *c* extortion
utregning (*ew̄t*-ray-ning) *c* calculation
utrivelig (ew-*tree*-ver-li) *adj* unpleasant
utro (*ew̄*-troo) *adj* unfaithful
utrolig (ew-*troo*-li) *adj* incredible; amazing
utrop (*ew̄t*-roop) *nt* (pl ~) exclamation
utruste (*ew̄t*-rewss-ter) *v* equip
utrustning (*ew̄t*-rewst-ning) *m* outfit
utsalg (*ew̄t*-sahlg) *nt* (pl ~) sales
utseende (*ew̄t*-sāy-er-ner) *nt* look, appearance; semblance
utsending (*ew̄t*-seh-ning) *m* delegate
***utsette** (*ew̄t*-seh-ter) *v* postpone; expose; **utsatt for** liable to; subject to
utsettelse (*ew̄t*-seh-terl-ser) *m* delay
utside (*ew̄t*-seeer) *c* outside; exterior
utsikt (*ew̄t*-sikt) *m* view; prospect, outlook
utskeielse (*ew̄t*-shay-erl-ser) *m* excess
utskrift (*ew̄t*-skrift) *c* printout
utslett (*ew̄t*-sleht) *nt* rash
utslitt (*ew̄t*-shlit) *adj* worn-out
utsolgt (*ew̄t*-solt) *adj* sold out
utstedelse (*ew̄t*-stāy-derl-ser) *m* issue
utstikker (*ew̄t*-sti-kerr) *m* pier
utstille (*ew̄t*-sti-ler) *v* *show, exhibit; display
utstilling (*ew̄t*-sti-ling) *c* exposition, exhibition, show, display
utstillingsdukke (*ew̄t*-sti-lings-dew-ker) *c* mannequin
utstillingslokale (*ew̄t*-sti-lings-loo-kaa-ler) *nt* showroom
utstillingsvindu (*ew̄t*-sti-lings-vin-dew) *nt* shop-window
utstrakt (*ew̄t*-strahkt) *adj* extensive, broad
utstyr (*ew̄t*-stew̄r) *nt* equipment; kit, gear
utstyre (*ew̄t*-stew̄-rer) *v* equip
utsøkt (*ew̄t*-surkt) *adj* exquisite, select
uttale (*ew̄*-taa-ler) *m* pronunciation; *v* pronounce; **~ galt** mispronounce
uttrykk (*ew̄*-trewk) *nt* (pl ~) expression; phrase; term; ***gi ~ for** express
uttrykke (*ew̄*-trew-ker) *v*

express
uttrykkelig (ew-*trewk*-ker-li) *adj* explicit, express
utvalg (*ēw̄t*-vahlg) *nt* (pl ~) choice, selection; variety, assortment; committee
utvalgt (*ēw̄t*-vahlt) *adj* select
utvandre (*ēw̄t*-vahn-drer) *v* emigrate
utvei (*ēw̄t*-vay) *m* way out; course
utveksle (*ēw̄t*-vehk-shler) *v* exchange
utveksling (*ēw̄t*-vehk-shling) *c* exchange
***utvelge** (*ēw̄t*-vehl-ger) *v* select
utvendig (*ēw̄t*-vehn-di) *adj* external, outward
utvide (*ēw̄t*-vee-der) *v* widen; extend, expand, enlarge
utvidelse (*ēw̄t*-vee-derl-ser) *m* extension; expansion
utvikle (*ēw̄t*-vik-ler) *v* develop
utvikling (*ēw̄t*-vik-ling) *c* development
utvilsomt (ew-*tveel*-somt) *adv* undoubtedly
utvise (*ēw̄t*-vee-ser) *v* expel
utvungenhet (*ēw̄*-tvoo-ngern-hāyt) *c* ease
utydelig (ew-*tēw̄*-der-li) *adj* dim
utøve (*ēw̄*-tūr-ver) *v* exercise
utålelig (ew-*taw*-ler-li) *adj* intolerable
utålmodig (*ēw̄*-tol-mōō-di) *adj* eager, impatient
uunngåelig (ew-ewng-*gaw*-er-li) *adj* unavoidable, inevitable
uunnværlig (ew-ewn-*vææ*-li) *adj* essential
uutholdelig (ew-ewt-*hol*-ler-li) *adj* unbearable
uvanlig (ew-*vahn*-li) *adj* unusual
uvant (*ēw̄*-vahnt) *adj* unaccustomed
uvedkommende (*ēw̄*-vāyd-ko-mer-ner) *m* (pl ~) trespasser
uvel (*ēw̄*-vehl) *adj* unwell
uvennlig (*ēw̄*-vehn-li) *adj* unkind, unfriendly
uventet (*ēw̄*-vehn-tert) *adj* unexpected
uvesentlig (ew-*vāy*-sernt-li) *adj* insignificant
uviktig (*ēw̄*-vik-ti) *adj* unimportant
uvillig (*ēw̄*-vi-li) *adj* unwilling; averse
uvirkelig (*ēw̄*-veer-ker-li) *adj* unreal
uvirksom (*ēw̄*-veerk-som) *adj* idle
uviss (*ew*-viss) *adj* uncertain
uvitende (*ēw̄*-vi-ter-ner) *adj* ignorant
uvurderlig (ēw̄-vew-*dāy*-li) *adj* priceless
uvær (*ew*-væær) *nt* (pl ~) tempest
uærlig (*ēw̄*-ææ-li) *adj* dishonest; crooked
uønsket (*ēw̄*-urn-skert) *adj* undesirable

V

vaffel (*vahf*-ferl) *m* (pl vafler) waffle
vag (vaag) *adj* vague, faint
vakker (*vahk*-kerr) *adj* handsome, fair, beautiful
vakle (*vahk*-ler) *v* falter
vaklende (*vahk*-ler-ner) *adj* shaky
vaksinasjon (vahk-si-nah-*shoon*) *m* inoculation
vaksinere (vahk-si-*nay*-rer) *v* vaccinate, inoculate
vaksinering (vahk-si-*nay*-ring) *c* vaccination
vakt (vahkt) *m* guard; attendant
vaktel (*vahk*-terl) *m* (pl -tler) quail
vaktmester (*vahkt*-mehss-terr) *m* (pl ~e, -trer) caretaker, janitor
vakuum (*vaa*-kewm) *nt* vacuum
valen (*vaa*-lern) *adj* numb
valg (vahlg) *nt* choice, pick; election
valgfri (*vahlg*-free) *adj* optional
valgkrets (*vahlg*-krehts) *m* constituency
valgspråk (*vahlg*-sprawk) *nt* (pl ~) slogan
valmue (*vahl*-mewer) *m* poppy
valnøtt (*vaal*-nurt) *c* walnut
vals (vahls) *m* waltz
valuta (vah-*lewt*-tah) *m* currency
valutakurs (vah-*lewt*-tah-kewsh) *m* rate of exchange, exchange rate
vandre (*vahn*-drer) *v* wander
vandrerhjem (*vahn*-drer-yehmm) *nt* youth hostel
vane (*vaa*-ner) *m* custom, habit
vanilje (vah-*nil*-yer) *m* vanilla
vanlig (*vaan*-li) *adj* common, usual, ordinary, habitual; customary, regular, simple
vanligvis (*vaan*-li-veess) *adv* as a rule, usually
vann (vahnn) *nt* water; **innlagt ~** running water
vannfarge (*vahn*-fahr-ger) *m* watercolo(u)r
vannkopper (*vahn*-ko-perr) *pl* chickenpox
vannkran (*vahn*-kraan) *c* faucet *nAm*
vannmelon (*vahn*-meh-loon) *m* watermelon
vannski (*vahn*-shee) *c* water ski
vannstoff (*vahn*-stof) *nt* hydrogen; **~ hyperoksyd** peroxide
vanntett (*vahn*-teht) *adj* waterproof

vanskapt (*vahn*-skahpt) *adj* deformed
vanskelig (*vahn*-sker-li) *adj* difficult; hard
vanskelighet (*vahn*-sker-li-hāyt) *c* difficulty
vant (vahnt) *adj* accustomed; ***være ~ til** *be used to
vanvidd (*vahn*-vid) *nt* lunacy
vanvittig (*vahn*-vi-ti) *adj* mad
vaporisator (vah-poo-ri-*saa*-toor) *m* atomizer
vare (*vaa*-rer) *v* last; *c* ware
varebil (*vaa*-rer-beel) *m* pick-up van, van, delivery van
varehus (*vaa*-rer-hēwss) *nt* (pl ~) department store
varemerke (*vaa*-rer-mær-ker) *nt* trademark
varemesse (*vaa*-rer-meh-ser) *c* fair
vareopptelling (*vaa*-rer-oop-teh-ling) *c* inventory
vareprøve (*vaarer*-prūr-ver) *c* sample
varer (*vaa*-rerr) *pl* merchandise, wares *pl*, goods *pl*
varetekt (*vaa*-rer-tehkt) *c* custody
variabel (vah-ri-*aa*-berl) *adj* variable
variere (vah-ri-*āy*-rer) *v* vary
variert (vah-ri-*āyt*) *adj* varied
varig (*vaa*-ri) *adj* lasting; permanent
varighet (*vaa*-ri-hāyt) *c* duration
varm (vahrm) *adj* hot, warm
varme (*vahr*-mer) *m* heat, warmth; *v* warm; **~ opp** heat
varmeflaske (*vahr*-mer-flahss-ker) *c* hot-water bottle
varmeovn (*vahr*-mer-ovn) *m* heater
varmepute (*vahr*-mer-pēw-ter) *c* heating pad
varsle (*vahsh*-ler) *v* forecast; notify
vase (*vaa*-ser) *m* vase
vask (vahsk) *m* washing; laundry; sink
vaskbar (*vahsk*-baar) *adj* washable
vaske (*vahss*-ker) *v* wash; **~ opp** wash up
vaskemaskin (*vahss*-ker-mah-sheen) *m* washing machine
vaskepulver (*vahss*-ker-pewl-verr) *nt* washing powder
vaskeri (vahss-ker-*ree*) *nt* laundry
vasse (*vahss*-ser) *v* wade
vatt (vahtt) *m* cotton wool
vatt-teppe *nt* quilt
ved (vāy) *m* firewood; *prep* by; on; **~ siden av** beside, next to
vedde (*vehd*-der) *v* *bet
veddeløp (*vehd*-der-lūrp) *nt*

race
veddeløpsbane (*vehd*-der-lūrps-baa-ner) *m* race--course; racetrack
veddeløpshest (*vehd*-der-lūrps-hehst) *m* race-horse
veddemål (*vehd*-der-mawl) *nt* (pl ~) bet
vedlegg (*vāy*-lehg) *nt* enclosure; attachment
***vedlegge** (*vāy*-leh-ger) *v* attach, enclose
vedlikehold (veh-*lee*-ker-hol) *nt* maintenance, upkeep
vedrøre (*vāy*-rūr-rer) *v* affect
vedrørende (*vāy*-rūr-rer-ner) *prep* with reference to, concerning
***vedta** (*vāy*-taa) *v* adopt, decide
vedvarende (*vāy*-vaa-rer-ner) *adj* permanent
veg (vay) *m* road; way
vegetarianer (veh-ger-tah-ri-*aa*-nerr) *m* vegetarian
vegg (vehgg) *m* wall
veggedyr (*vehg*-ger-dēwr) *nt* (pl ~) bug
vei (vay) *m* road; way; **på ~ til** bound for
veiarbeid (*vay*-ahr-bayd) *nt* road work
veidekke (*vay*-deh-ker) *nt* pavement
veie (*vay*-er) *v* weigh
veikant (*vay*-kahnt) *m* roadside, wayside
veikart (*vay*-kaht) *nt* road map
veikryss (*vay*-krewss) *nt* (pl ~) intersection, junction
veilede (*vay*-lāy-der) *v* direct
veinett (*vay*-neht) *nt* (pl ~) road system
veiskilt (*vay*-shilt) *nt* road sign
veiviser (*vay*-vee-serr) *m* signpost
vekk (vehkk) *adv* off; away
vekke (*vehk*-ker) *v* *wake, *awake
vekkeklokke (*vehk*-ke-klo-ker) *c* alarm-clock
vekselstrøm (*vehk*-serl-strurm) *m* alternating current
vekselvis (*vehk*-sherl-veess) *adv* alternate
veksle (*vehk*-shler) *v* change; exchange
vekslepenger (*vehk*-shler-peh-ngerr) *pl* change
vekslingskontor (*vehk*-shlings-koon-tōor) *nt* money exchange, exchange office
vekst (vehkst) *m* growth
vekt (vehkt) *c* weight; scales *pl*; ***legge ~ på** stress
vektstang (*vehkt*-stahng) *c* (pl -tenger) lever
velbegrunnet (*vehl*-beh-grew-nert) *adj* well--founded
velbehag (*vehl*-beh-haag) *nt* pleasure
veldig (*vehl*-di) *adj* huge;

immense
velferd (*vehl*-fææр) *m* welfare
***velge** (*vehl*-ger) *v* *choose; pick; elect; **~ ut** select
velgjørenhet (*vehl*-ʸūr-rern-hāyt) *c* charity
velhavende (*vehl*-haa-ver-ner) *adj* well-to-do
velkjent (*vehl*-khehnt) *adj* familiar; well-known
velkommen (vehl-*kom*-mern) *adj* welcome; **hilse ~** welcome
velkomst (*vehl*-komst) *m* welcome
vellykket (*vehl*-lew-kert) *adj* successful
velsigne (vehl-*sing*-ner) *v* bless
velsignelse (vehl-*sing*-nerl-ser) *m* blessing
velsmakende (*vehl*-smaa-ker-ner) *adj* tasty, savo(u)ry
velstand (*vehl*-stahn) *m* prosperity
velstående (*vehl*-stawer-ner) *adj* prosperous
velvære (*vehl*-vææ-rer) *nt* comfort
vemmelig (*vehm*-mer-li) *adj* nasty
vemod (*vāy*-mōōd) *nt* sadness
vemodig (*vāy*-mōō-di) *adj* sad
vende (*vehn*-ner) *v* turn; **~ om** turn over; **~ tilbake** return; *go back, turn back
vendepunkt (*vehn*-ner-pewngt) *nt* turning point
vending (*vehn*-ning) *c* turn
Venezuela (veh-neh-sew-*āy*-lah) Venezuela
venezuelaner (veh-neh-sew-eh-*laa*-nerr) *m* Venezuelan
venezuelansk (veh-neh-sew-eh-*laansk*) *adj* Venezuelan
venn (vehnn) *m* (male, female) friend
venne (*vehn*-ner) *v* accustom
venninne (veh-*nin*-ner) *c* (female) friend
vennlig (*vehn*-li) *adj* kind, friendly; **med ~ hilsen, mvh** best regards; yours sincerely
vennligst (*vehn*-likst) please
vennskap (*vehn*-skaap) *nt* friendship
vennskapelig (vehn-*skaa*-per-li) *adj* friendly
venstre (*vehn*-strer) *adj* left; left-hand
vente (*vehn*-ter) *v* wait; expect; **~ på** await
venteliste (*vehn*-ter-liss-ter) *c* waitinglist
ventet (*vehn*-tert) *adj* due
venteværelse (*vehn*-ter-vææ-rerl-ser) *nt* waiting room
ventil (vehn-*teel*) *m* valve
ventilasjon (vehn-ti-lah-*shōōn*) *m* ventilation

ventilator (vehn-ti-*laa*-toor) *m* ventilator
ventilere (vehn-ti-*lay*-rer) *v* ventilate
venting (*vehn*-ting) *m* waiting
veps (vehps) *m* wasp
veranda (væ-*rahn*-dah) *m* veranda
verb (værb) *nt* verb
verd (værd) *nt* worth; ***være ~** *be worth
verden (*vær*-dern) *m* world
verdensberømt (*vær*-derns-beh-rurmt) *adj* world-famous
verdensdel (*vær*-derns-dayl) *m* continent
verdenskrig (*vær*-derns-kreeg) *m* world war
verdensomfattende (*vær*-dern-soom-fah-ter-ner) *adj* global
verdensomspennende (*vær*-dern-soom-speh-ner-ner) *adj* world-wide
verdensrom (*vær*-derns-room) *nt* space
verdi (væædee) *m* value
verdifull (væ-*dee*-fewl) *adj* valuable
verdig (*væ*-di) *adj* dignified; worthy of
verdighet (*væ*-di-hayt) *c* dignity
verdiløs (væ-*dee*-lurss) *adj* worthless
verdipapirer (væ-*dee*-pah-pee-rerr) *pl* stocks and shares
verdisaker (væ-*dee*-saa-kerr) *pl* valuables *pl*
***verdsette** (*værd*-seh-ter) *v* appreciate estimate
verdsettelse (*værd*-seh-terl-ser) *m* appreciation
verk (værk) *m* ache; pus
verke (*vær*-ker) *v* ache
verken ... eller (*vær*-kern ... ehl-err) neither ... nor
verksted (*værk*-stay) *nt* workshop
verktøy (*værk*-tur[ew]) *nt* implement, tool
vern (vææn) *nt* defense *Am*, defence
vernepliktig (*vææ*-ner-plik-ti) *m* conscript
verre (*vær*-rer) *adv* worse; *adj* worse; **verst** worst
vers (væshsh) *nt* verse
versjon (væ-*shoon*) *m* version
vert (vætt) *m* host; landlord
vertikal (væ-ti-*kaal*) *adj* vertical
vertinne (væ-*tin*-ner) *c* hostess; landlady
vertshus (*væts*-hewss) *nt* (pl ~) public house; inn; *m* roadside restaurant
vesen (*vay*-sern) *nt* being; essence
vesentlig (*vay*-sernt-li) *adj* essential; vital
veske (*vehss*-ker) *c* bag
vest (vehst) *m* west; waistcoat; vest *nAm*
vestlig (*vehst*-li) *adj* western, westerly

veterinær (veh-ter-ri-*næær*) *m* veterinary surgeon
vett (vehtt) *nt* brains, sense
vev (vay̅v) *m* loom; *nt* tissue
veve (*vay̅*-ver) *v* *weave
vi (vee) *pron* we
via (*vee*-ah) *prep* via
viadukt (vi-ah-*dewkt*) *m* viaduct
vibrasjon (vi-brah-*shoon*) *m* vibration
vibrere (vi-*bray̅*-rer) *v* vibrate
vid (vee) *adj* wide
vidd (vidd) *nt* wit
vidde (vee-er) *c* plateau
videokamera (*vid*-eoo-kah-meh-raa) *nt* video camera
videokassett (*vid*-eoo-kah-*sehtt*) *m* video cassette
videospiller (*vid*-eoo-spil-lerr) *m* video recorder
videre (*vee*-der-rer) *adj* further; farther; **og så ~** and so on, etcetera
vidstrakt (*vee*-strahkt) *adj* vast, broad
vidunder (vi-*dewn*-derr) *nt* (pl ~, ~e) marvel
vidunderlig (vi-*dewn*-der-li) *adj* wonderful, marvel(l)ous
vie (*vee*-er) *v* marry; devote; dedicate
vielse (*vee*-erl-ser) *m* wedding
vielsesring (*vee*-erl-serss-ring) *m* wedding ring
vifte (*vif*-ter) *c* fan
vifterem (*vif*-ter-rehm) *c* fan belt
vik (veek) *c* inlet, creek
vikle (*vik*-ler) *v* *wind
viktig (*vik*-ti) *adj* important; big, capital
viktighet (*vik*-ti-hay̅t) *c* importance
vilje (*vil*-ʸer) *m* will; **med ~** on purpose
viljestyrke (*vil*-ʸer-stewr-ker) *m* will-power
vilkår (*vil*-kawr) *nt* condition
vilkårlig (vil-*kaw*-li) *adj* arbitrary
vill (vill) *adj* savage, wild; fierce; **gått ~** lost
villa (*vil*-lah) *m* villa
***ville** (*vil*-ler) *v* *will, want
villig (*vil*-li) *adj* willing
vilt (vilt) *nt* game, quarry
vin (veen) *m* wine
vind (vinn) *m* wind
vindebro (*vin*-ner-broo) *c* drawbridge
vindhard (*vin*-haar) *adj* windy
vindkast (*vin*-kahst) *nt* (pl ~) blow, gust
vindmølle (*vin*-mur-ler) *c* windmill
vindu (*vin*-dew) *nt* window
vindusvisker (*vin*-dewss-viss-kerr) *m* windscreen wiper; windshield wiper *Am*
vinge (vingng-er) *m* wing
vink (vingk) *nt* sign
vinkart (*veen*-kaht) *nt* wine list

vinke (*ving*-ker) *v* wave
vinkel (*ving*-kerl) *m* (pl -kler) angle
vinkjeller (*veen*-kheh-lerr) *m* wine cellar
vinmonopol (*veen*-moo-noo-pōōl) *nt* off-licence, *Am* liquor store
***vinne** (*vin*-ner) *v* gain, *win
vinnende (*vin*-ner-ner) *adj* winning
vinner (*vin*-nerr) *m* winner
vinranke (*veen*-rahng-ker) *m* vine
vinter (*vin*-terr) *m* (pl -trer) winter
vintersport (*vin*-ter-shpot) *m* winter sports
vipe (*vee*-per) *c* pewit
vippe (*vip*-per) *c* seesaw
virke (*veer*-ker) *v* work; operate
virkelig (*veer*-ker-li) *adj* actual, real; very, true; substantial; *adv* indeed, really
virkelighet (*veer*-ker-li-hāyt) *c* reality; **i virkeligheten** as a matter of fact
virkemåte (*veer*-ker-maw-ter) *m* mode of operation
virkning (*veerk*-ning) *m* effect
virkningsfull (*veerk*-nings-fewl) *adj* effective, efficient
virkningsløs (*veerk*-nings-lūrss) *adj* inefficient, ineffective
virksom (*veerk*-som) *adj* active
virksomhet (*veerk*-som-hāyt) *c* enterprise, business
virus (*vēēr*-rews) *nt* (pl ~) virus
virvar (*veer*-vahr) *nt* muddle
vis (veess) *adj* wise; *nt* way, manner
visdom (*veess*-dom) *m* wisdom
vise (*vee*-ser) *v* *show; point out; display; **~ frem** *show; **~ seg** appear; prove
visepresident (*vee*-ser-preh-si-dehnt) *m* vice president
visitere (vi-si-*tāy*-rer) *v* search
visitt (vi-*sitt*) *m* call, visit
visittkort (vi-*sit*-kot) *nt* (pl ~) card, business card
viskelær (*viss*-ker-læær) *nt* (pl ~) rubber, eraser
vispe (*viss*-per) *v* whip
viss (viss) *adj* certain
visse (*viss*-ser) *pron* some
visum (*vee*-sewm) *nt* (pl visa) visa
vitamin (vi-tah-*meen*) *nt* vitamin
***vite** (*vee*-ter) *v* *know
vitebegjærlig (*vee*-ter-beh-ʸææ-li) *adj* curious
vitenskap (*vee*-tern-skaap) *m* science
vitenskapelig (*vee*-tern-skaaper-li) *adj* scientific
vitenskapskvinne (*vee*-

tern-skaaps-kvin-ner) *c* (female) scientist
vitenskapsmann (*vee*-tern-skaaps-mahn) *m* (pl -menn) (male) scientist
vitne (*vit*-ner) *nt* witness; *v* testify
vitnesbyrd (*vit*-nerss-bewrd) *nt* certificate
vits (vits) *m* joke
vittig (*vit*-ti) *adj* humorous, witty
vogn (voangn) *c* carriage
vokal (voo-*kaal*) *m* vowel; *adj* vocal
voks (voks) *m* wax
vokse (*vok*-ser) *v* *grow
voksen[1] (*vok*-sern) *m* (pl -sne) adult, grown-up
voksen[2] (*vok*-sern) *adj* adult, grown-up
vokskabinett (*voks*-kah-bi-neht) *nt* waxworks *pl*
vokte seg (*vok*-ter) beware
vold (voll) *m* violence; force
volde (*vol*-ler) *v* cause
voldsom (*vol*-som) *adj* violent
***voldta** (*vol*-taa) *v* rape
voldtekt (*vol*-tekt) *c* rape
vollgrav (*vol*-graav) *c* moat
volt (volt) *m* volt
volum (voo-*lēwm*) *nt* volume
vond (voonn) *adj* bad, painful; evil; ***gjøre vondt** *hurt; ***ha vondt** *have a pain
vorte (*vor*-ter) *c* wart
votter (*vot*-terr) *pl* mittens *pl*
vrak (vraak) *nt* wreck
vrengt (vrehngt) *adj* inside out
***vri** (vree) *v* twist, wrench; **~ om** turn
vridning (*vreed*-ning) *m* twist
vrien (*vree*-ern) *adj* difficult
vrøvle (*vrurv*-ler) *v* talk rubbish
vugge (*vewg*-ger) *c* cradle
vulgær (vewl-*gæær*) *adj* vulgar
vulkan (vewl-*kaan*) *m* volcano
vurdere (vew-*dāy*-rer) *v* evaluate; value, estimate
vurdering (vew-*dāy*-ring) *c* estimate; appreciation
vær (væær) *nt* weather
***være** (*vææ*-rer) *v* *be; **vær så god** here you are
værelse (*vææ*-rerl-ser) *nt* room; **~ med frokost** bed and breakfast
værelsesbetjening (*vææ*-rerl-serss-beh-t^y^āy-ning) *c* room service
værelsestemperatur (*vææ*-rerl-serss-tehm-peh-rah-tewr) *m* room temperature
værmelding (*væær*-meh-ling) *c* weather forecast
væske (*vehss*-ker) *c* fluid
våge (*vaw*-ger) *v* dare; venture
vågemot (*vaw*-ger-mōōt) *nt* guts
våken (*vaw*-kern) *adj* awake

våkne (*vok*-ner) *v* wake up
våningshus (*vaw*-nings-hēw̄ss) *nt* (pl ~) farmhouse
våpen (*vaw*-pern) *nt* (pl ~) arm, weapon
våpenstillstand (*vaw*-pern-still-stann) *m* ceasefire
vår[1] (vawr) *pron* our; ours
vår[2] (vawr) *m* spring; springtime
våt (vawt) *adj* wet; moist

W

watt (vahtt) *m* watt

Y

ydmyk (*ēw̄d*-mēw̄k) *adj* humble
ynde (*ewn*-der) *m* grace
yndig (*ewn*-di) *adj* lovely, graceful
yndling (*ewnd*-ling) *m* favo(u)rite; **yndlings-** pet, favo(u)rite
ynkelig (*ewng*-ker-li) *adj* lamentable
yrke (*ewr*-ker) *nt* trade; occupation
yte (*ēw̄*-ter) *v* yield, produce
ytre (*ewt*-rer) *v* utter; express; *adj* exterior
ytterlig (*ewt*-ter-li) *adj* extreme
ytterligere (*ewt*-ter-li-er-rer) *adj* additional, further
ytterlighet (*ewt*-ter-li-hāȳt) *c* extreme
ytterside (*ewt*-ter-shee-der) *c* outside
ytterst (*ewt*-tersht) *adj* utmost, extreme

Z

zoo (sōō) *m* zoo; **zoologisk hage** zoological gardens
zoologi (soo-loo-*gi*) *m* zoology
zoomlinse (*sōōm*-lin-ser) *c* zoom lens

Æ

ærbødig (ær-*būr*-di) *adj* respectful
ærbødighet (ær-*būr*-di-hāyt) *c* respect
ære (*ææ*-rer) *c* honour; glory; *v* honour
ærefull (*ææ*-rer-fewl) *adj* honourable
ærend (*ææ*-rern) *nt* errand
æresfølelse (*ææ*-rerss-fūr-erl-ser) *m* sense of honour
ærgjerrig (ær-*ʸær*-ri) *adj* ambitious
ærgjerrighet (ær-*ʸær*-ri-hāyt) *c* ambition
ærlig (*ææ*-li) *adj* honest; straight
ærlighet (*ææ*-li-hāyt) *c* honesty
ærverdig (ær-*vær*-di) *adj* venerable

Ø

øde (*ūr*-der) *adj* desert; waste
***ødelegge** (*ūr*-der-leh-ger) *v* wreck; smash; destroy; ruin; *spoil
ødeleggelse (*ūr*-der-leh-gerl-ser) *m* destruction
ødsel (*urt*-serl) *adj* wasteful; lavish
øke (*ūr*-ker) *v* increase; raise
økning (*ūrk*-ning) *m* increase
økologi (ur-koo-loo-*gee*) *m* ecology
økologisk (ur-koo-*loo*-gisk) *adj* ecologic; ecological
økonom (ur-koo-*nōōm*) *m* economist
økonomi (ur-koo-noo-*mee*) *m* economy
økonomisk (ur-koo-*nōō*-misk) *adj* economic; economical
økoturist (*ūr*-koo-tēw-*rist*) *c* eco-tourist
øks (urks) *c* axe
øl (urll) *nt* beer; ale
øm (urmm) *adj* sore; gentle, tender
ønske (*urns*-ker) *v* wish, want, desire; *nt* wish, desire; **~ til lykke** congratulate
ønskelig (*urns*-ker-li) *adj* desirable
øre (*ūr*-rer) *nt* ear
øredobb (*ūr*-rer-dob) *m* earring
øreverk (*ūr*-rer-værk) *m* earache
ørken (*urr*-kern) *m* desert

ørn ($\overline{ur}$n) *c* eagle
ørret (*urr*-rert) *m* trout
øsregn ($\overline{ur}$*ss*-rayn) *nt* downpour
øst (urst) *m* east
Østerrike (*urss*-ter-ree-ker) Austria
østerriker (*urss*-ter-ree-kerr) *m* Austrian
østerriksk (*urss*-ter-reeksk) *adj* Austrian
østers (*urss*-tersh) *m* (pl ~) oyster
østlig (*urst*-li) *adj* eastern
østre (*urst*-rer) *adj* eastern
øve ($\overline{ur}$-ver) *v* exercise; **~ seg** practise
øvelse ($\overline{ur}$*v*-erl-ser) *m* exercise
øverst ($\overline{ur}$-versht) *adj* top
øvre ($\overline{ur}$*v*-rer) *adj* upper
for øvrig (for $\overline{ur}$*v*-ri) moreover
øy (ur[ew]) *c* island
øye (*ur*ew-er) *nt* (pl øyne) eye
øyeblikk (*ur*ew-er-blik) *nt* instant, second, moment
øyeblikkelig (ur[ew]-er-*blik*-li) *adv* instantly, immediately; *adj* immediate
øyenbryn (*ur*ew-ern-br$\overline{ew}$n) *nt* (pl ~) eyebrow
øyenbrynsblyant (*ur*ew-ern-br$\overline{ew}$ns-blew-ahnt) *m* eyebrow pencil
øyenlege (*ur*ew-ern-l$\overline{ay}$-ger) *m* oculist
øyenlokk (*ur*ew-ern-lok) *nt* eyelid
øyenskygge (*ur*ew-ern-shew-ger) *m* eye shadow
øyensverte (*ur*ew-ern-svæ-ter) *c* mascara
øyensynlig (ur[ew]-ern-*s$\overline{ew}$n*-li) *adv* apparently
øyenvippe (*ur*ew-ern-vi-per) *m* eyelash
øyenvitne (*ur*ew-ern-vit-ner) *nt* eye-witness

Å

åbor (*ob*-boor) *m* bass, perch
åk (awk) *nt* yoke
åker (*aw*-kerr) *m* (pl åkrer) field
ål (awl) *m* eel
ånd (onn) *m* spirit; ghost
åndedrett (*on*-der-dreht) *nt* breathing, respiration
åndelig (*on*-der-li) *adj* spiritual
åpen (*aw*-pern) *adj* open
åpenbare (*aw*-pern-baa-rer) *v* reveal
åpenbart (*aw*-pern-baat) *adv* apparently
åpenhjertig (*aw*-pern-[y]æ-ti) *adj* open
åpne (*awp*-ner) *v* open; *undo

åpning (*awp*-ning) *c* opening; breach, gap
åpningstid (*awp*-nings-teed) *c* business hours
år (awr) *nt* year; **per ~** per annum
årbok (*awr*-bo͞ok) *c* (pl -bøker) annual
åre (*aw*-rer) *m* oar; vein
åreknute (*aw*-rer-knew-ter) *m* varicose vein
århundre (*awr*-hewn-drer) *nt* century
årlig (*aw*-li) *adj* yearly, annual
årsak (*aw*-shaak) *c* reason, cause
årsdag (*awsh*-daag) *m* anniversary
årstid (*awsh*-teed) *c* season
årvåken (*awr*-vaw-kern) *adj* vigilant
åtte (*ot*-ter) *num* eight
åttende (*ot*-ter-ner) *num* eighth
åtti (*ot*-ti) *num* eighty

English – Norwegian
Engelsk – Norsk

A

a [ei, ə] *art* (an) en; ei; et *art*
abbey ['æbi] *n* abbedi *nt*
abbreviation [əˌbriːvi'eiʃən] *n* forkortelse *m*
ability [ə'biləti] *n* dyktighet *c*; evne *c*
able ['eibəl] *adj* i stand til, dyktig; ***be ~ to** *være i stand til; *kunne
aboard [ə'bɔːd] *adv* om bord
abolish [ə'bɔliʃ] *v* avskaffe
abortion [ə'bɔːʃən] *n* abort *m*
about [ə'baut] *prep* om; angående; rundt; *adv* omtrent, omkring
above [ə'bʌv] *prep* over; ovenfor; *adv* over; ovenfor
abroad [ə'brɔːd] *adv* utenlands
abscess ['æbses] *n* byll *m*
absence ['æbsəns] *n* fravær *nt*
absent ['æbsənt] *adj* fraværende
absolutely ['æbsəluːtli] *adv* absolutt
abstain from [əb'stein] *avholde seg fra
abstract ['æbstrækt] *adj* abstrakt
absurd [əb'səːd] *adj* urimelig, absurd
abundance [ə'bʌndəns] *n* overflod *m*
abundant [ə'bʌndənt] *adj* rikelig
abuse [ə'bjuːs] *n* misbruk *nt*
academy [ə'kædəmi] *n* akademi *nt*
accelerate [ək'seləreit] *v* akselerere, øke farten
accelerator [ək'seləreitə] *n* gasspedal *m*
accent ['æksənt] *n* aksent *m*; betoning *c*
accept [ək'sept] *v* akseptere, *ta imot, *motta
access ['ækses] *n* tilgang *m*
accessible [ək'sesəbəl] *adj* tilgjengelig
accessories [ək'sesəriz] *pl* tilbehør *nt*
accident ['æksidənt] *n* ulykke *c*, uhell *nt*
accidental [ˌæksi'dentəl] *adj* tilfeldig
accommodate [ə'kɔmədeit] *v* tilpasse; skaffe husrom
accommodation [əˌkɔmə'deiʃən] *n* husrom

nt, losji *nt*
accompany [ə'kʌmpəni] *v* følge; akkompagnere
accomplish [ə'kʌmpliʃ] *v* fullende; fullføre
accordance: in ~ with [in ə'kɔːdəns wið] i overensstemmelse med
according to [ə'kɔːdiŋ tuː] ifølge; i overensstemmelse med
account [ə'kaunt] *n* konto *m*; redegjørelse *m*; **~ for** avlegge regnskap for; **on ~ of** på grunn av
accurate ['ækjurət] *adj* nøyaktig
accuse [ə'kjuːz] *v* beskylde; anklage
accused [ə'kjuːzd] *n* anklagede *m*
accustom [ə'kʌstəm] *v* venne; **accustomed** vant
ache [eik] *v* verke; *n* verk *m*
achieve [ə'tʃiːv] *v* oppnå; prestere
achievement [ə'tʃiːvmənt] *n* prestasjon *m*
acknowledge [ək'nɔlidʒ] *v* erkjenne; innrømme; bekrefte
acne ['ækni] *n* filipens *m*
acorn ['eikɔːn] *n* eikenøtt *c*
acquaintance [ə'kweintəns] *n* bekjent *m*
acquire [ə'kwaiə] *v* erverve
acquisition [ˌækwi'ziʃən] *n* ervervelse *m*
acquittal [ə'kwitəl] *n* frifinnelse *m*
across [ə'krɔs] *prep* over; på den andre siden av; *adv* på den andre siden
act [ækt] *n* handling *c*; akt *m*; nummer *nt*; *v* handle, oppføre seg; spille
action ['ækʃən] *n* handling *c*, aksjon *m*
active ['æktiv] *adj* aktiv; virksom
activewear ['æktivˌweə] *n* sportsklær *pl*
activity [æk'tivəti] *n* aktivitet *m*
actor ['æktə] *n* skuespiller *m*
actress ['æktris] *n* skuespiller *m*
actual ['æktʃuəl] *adj* faktisk, virkelig
actually ['æktʃuəli] *adv* faktisk
acute [ə'kjuːt] *adj* akutt
adapt [ə'dæpt] *v* tilpasse
adaptor [ə'dæptə] *n* adapter *m*
add [æd] *v* *legge sammen; tilføye
addition [ə'diʃən] *n* addisjon *m*; tilføyelse *m*
additional [ə'diʃənəl] *adj* ekstra; ytterligere
address [ə'dres] *n* adresse *c*; *v* adressere; henvende seg til
addressee [ˌædre'siː] *n* adressat *m*
adequate ['ædikwət] *adj* tilstrekkelig; passende, adekvat

adjective ['ædʒiktiv] *n* adjektiv *nt*
adjust [ə'dʒʌst] *v* justere; tilpasse
administer [əd'ministə] *v* bestyre; tildele
administration [əd,mini'streiʃən] *n* administrasjon *m*; ledelse *m*
administrative [əd'ministrətiv] *adj* administrerende; forvaltende; **~ law** forvaltningsrett *m*
admiration [,ædmə'reiʃən] *n* beundring *c*
admire [əd'maiə] *v* beundre
admission [əd'miʃən] *n* adgang *m*; opptak *nt*
admit [əd'mit] *v* *oppta; innrømme, erkjenne
admittance [əd'mitəns] *n* adgang *m*; **no ~** adgang forbudt
adopt [ə'dɔpt] *v* adoptere; *vedta
adorable [ə'dɔːrəbəl] *adj* henrivende
adult ['ædʌlt] *n* voksen *m*; *adj* voksen
advance [əd'vɑːns] *n* fremskritt *nt*; forskudd *nt*; *v* *gjøre fremskritt; betale på forskudd; **in ~** på forhånd, på forskudd
advanced [əd'vɑːnst] *adj* avansert
advantage [əd'vɑːntidʒ] *n* fordel *m*
advantageous [,ædvən'teidʒəs] *adj* fordelaktig
adventure [əd'ventʃə] *n* eventyr *nt*
adverb ['ædvəːb] *n* adverb *nt*
advertisement [əd'vəːtismənt] *n* annonse *m*
advertising ['ædvətaiziŋ] *n* reklame *m*
advice [əd'vais] *n* råd *nt*
advise [əd'vaiz] *v* råde
advocate ['ædvəkət] *n* talsmann *m*
aerial ['ɛəriəl] *n* antenne *c*
aeroplane ['ɛərəplein] *n* fly *nt*
affair [ə'fɛə] *n* anliggende *nt*; affære *m*, forhold *nt*
affect [ə'fekt] *v* påvirke; vedrøre
affected [ə'fektid] *adj* affektert
affection [ə'fekʃən] *n* hengivenhet *c*
affectionate [ə'fekʃənit] *adj* hengiven, kjærlig
affiliated [ə'filieitid] *adj* tilsluttet
affirm [ə'fəːm] *v* bedyre; bekrefte
affirmative [ə'fəːmətiv] *adj* bekreftende
afford [ə'fɔːd] *v* *ha råd til
afraid [ə'freid] *adj* redd, engstelig; ***be ~** *være redd
Africa ['æfrikə] Afrika
African ['æfrikən] *adj*

afrikansk; *n* afrikaner *m*
after ['ɑːftə] *prep* etter; *conj* etter at
afternoon [ˌɑːftə'nuːn] *n* ettermiddag *m*; **this ~** i ettermiddag
afterwards ['ɑːftəwədz] *adv* senere; etterpå
again [ə'gen] *adv* igjen; **~ and again** gang på gang
against [ə'genst] *prep* mot
age [eidʒ] *n* alder *m*; alderdom *m*; **of ~** myndig; **under ~** umyndig
aged ['eidʒid] *adj* gammel
agency ['eidʒənsi] *n* agentur *nt*; byrå *nt*
agenda [ə'dʒendə] *n* dagsorden *m*
agent ['eidʒənt] *n* agent *m*, representant *m*
aggressive [ə'gresiv] *adj* aggressiv
ago [ə'gou] *adv* for … siden
agree [ə'griː] *v* *være enig; *gå med på; stemme overens
agreeable [ə'griːəbəl] *adj* behagelig
agreement [ə'griːmənt] *n* kontrakt *m*; overenskomst *m*, avtale *m*; overensstemmelse *m*
agriculture ['ægrikʌltʃə] *n* jordbruk *nt*
ahead [ə'hed] *adv* fremover; **~ of** foran; ***go ~** *gå videre; **straight ~** rett frem
aid [eid] *n* hjelp *c*; *v* *hjelpe, *bistå
AIDS [eidz] *n* AIDS
aim [eim] *n* sikte *nt*; **~ at** rette mot, sikte på; strebe etter, *ta sikte på
air [ɛə] *n* luft *c*; *v* lufte
airbag ['ɛə bæg] *n* airbag *m*
air conditioning ['ɛəkənˌdiʃəniŋ] *n* luftkondisjonering *c*; **air-conditioned** *adj* luftkondisjonert
airfield ['ɛəfiːld] *n* flyplass *m*
airline ['ɛəlain] *n* flyselskap *nt*
airmail ['ɛəmeil] *n* luftpost *m*
airplane ['ɛəplein] *nAm* fly *nt*
airport ['ɛəpɔːt] *n* lufthavn *c*, flyplass *m*
airsickness ['ɛəˌsiknəs] *n* luftsyke *m*
airtight ['ɛətait] *adj* lufttett
airy ['ɛəri] *adj* luftig
aisle [ail] *n* sideskip *nt*; midtgang *m*
alarm [ə'lɑːm] *n* alarm *m*; *v* alarmere, forurolige; **~ clock** vekkeklokke *c*
album ['ælbəm] *n* album *nt*
alcohol ['ælkəhɔl] *n* alkohol *m*
alcoholic [ˌælkə'hɔlik] *adj* alkoholholdig
ale [eil] *n* øl *nt*
algebra ['ældʒibrə] *n* algebra *m*
Algeria [æl'dʒiəriə] Algerie
Algerian [æl'dʒiəriən] *adj*

algerisk; *n* algerier *m*
alien ['eiliən] *n* utlending *m*; *adj* utenlandsk
alike [ə'laik] *adj* likedan, lik; *adv* likedan
alive [ə'laiv] *adj* levende
all [ɔːl] *adj* all; **~ in** alt inkludert; **~ right!** fint!, årleit; **at ~** overhodet
allergic [ə'ləʒik] *adj* allergisk
allergy ['ælədʒi] *n* allergi *m*
alley ['æli] *n* smug *nt*
alliance [ə'laiəns] *n* allianse *m*
allow [ə'lau] *v* *tillate, bevilge; **~ to** *la; ***be allowed** *være tillatt; ***be allowed to** *ha lov til
allowance [ə'lauəns] *n* bidrag *nt*
almond ['ɑːmənd] *n* mandel *m*
almost ['ɔːlmoust] *adv* nesten
alone [ə'loun] *adv* alene
along [ə'lɔŋ] *prep* langs
aloud [ə'laud] *adv* høyt
alphabet ['ælfəbet] *n* alfabet *nt*
already [ɔːl'redi] *adv* allerede
also ['ɔːlsou] *adv* også; dessuten, likeledes
altar ['ɔːltə] *n* alter *nt*
alter ['ɔːltə] *v* forandre, endre
alteration [ˌɔːltə'reiʃən] *n* forandring *c*, endring *c*
alternate [ɔːl'təːnət] *adj* vekselvis
alternative [ɔːl'təːnətiv] *n* alternativ *nt*
although [ɔːl'ðou] *conj* skjønt
altitude ['æltitjuːd] *n* høyde *m*
alto ['æltou] *n* (pl **~s**) alt *m*
altogether [ˌɔːltə'geðə] *adv* fullstendig; i det hele
always ['ɔːlweiz] *adv* alltid
am [æm] *v* (pr be)
amaze [ə'meiz] *v* forbause, forundre
amazement [ə'meizmənt] *n* forbauselse *m*
amazing [ə'meiziŋ] *adj* forbausende
ambassador [æm'bæsədə] *n* ambassadør *m*
amber ['æmbə] *n* rav *nt*
ambiguous [æm'bigjuəs] *adj* tvetydig
ambition [æm'biʃən] *n* ærgjerrighet *c*
ambitious [æm'biʃəs] *adj* ærgjerrig
ambulance ['æmbjuləns] *n* ambulanse *m*, sykebil *m*
ambush ['æmbuʃ] *n* bakhold *nt*
America [ə'merikə] Amerika
American [ə'merikən] *adj* amerikansk; *n* amerikaner *m*
amethyst ['æmiθist] *n* ametyst *m*
amid [ə'mid] *prep* blant, midt i

ammonia [ə'mouniə] *n* salmiakk *m*
amnesty ['æmnisti] *n* amnesti *nt*
among [ə'mʌŋ] *prep* blant, mellom; **~ other things** blant annet
amount [ə'maunt] *n* mengde *m*; beløp *nt*, sum *m*; **~ to** *beløpe seg til
amuse [ə'mju:z] *v* more, *underholde
amusement [ə'mju:zmənt] *n* fornøyelse *m*, atspredelse *m*
amusing [ə'mju:ziŋ] *adj* morsom, gøyal
anaemia [ə'ni:miə] *n* anemi *m*
anaesthesia [ˌænis'θi:ziə] *n* bedøvelse *m*
anaesthetic [ˌænis'θetik] *n* bedøvelsesmiddel *nt*
analyse ['ænəlaiz] *v* analysere
analysis [ə'næləsis] *n* (pl -ses) analyse *m*
analyst ['ænəlist] *n* analytiker *m*; psykoanalytiker *m*
anarchy ['ænəki] *n* anarki *nt*
anatomy [ə'nætəmi] *n* anatomi *m*
ancestor ['ænsestə] *n* forfader *m*
anchor ['æŋkə] *n* anker *nt*
anchovy ['æntʃəvi] *n* ansjos *m*
ancient ['einʃənt] *adj* gammel; foreldet, gammeldags; urtids-
and [ænd, ənd] *conj* og
angel ['eindʒəl] *n* engel *m*
anger ['æŋgə] *n* sinne *nt*; raseri *nt*
angle ['æŋgəl] *v* fiske; *n* vinkel *m*
angry ['æŋgri] *adj* sint
animal ['æniməl] *n* dyr *nt*
ankle ['æŋkəl] *n* ankel *m*
annex[1] ['æneks] *n* anneks *nt*; tillegg *nt*
annex[2] [ə'neks] *v* annektere
anniversary [ˌæni'və:səri] *n* årsdag *m*, bryllupsdag *m*
announce [ə'nauns] *v* *kunngjøre, *bekjentgjøre
announcement [ə'naunsmənt] *n* kunngjøring *c*, bekjentgjørelse *m*
annoy [ə'nɔi] *v* ergre, irritere
annoyance [ə'nɔiəns] *n* ergrelse *m*
annoying [ə'nɔiiŋ] *adj* ergerlig, irriterende
annual ['ænjuəl] *adj* årlig; *n* årbok *c*
anonymous [ə'nɔniməs] *adj* anonym
another [ə'nʌðə] *adj* en til; en annen
answer ['ɑ:nsə] *v* svare; besvare; *n* svar *nt*
answering machine ['ɑ:nsəriŋ mə'ʃi:n] *n* telefonsvarer *m*
ant [ænt] *n* maur *m*
antibiotic [ˌæntibai'ɔtik] *n*

antibiotikum *nt*
anticipate [æn'tisipeit] *v* *forutse, *foregripe
antifreeze ['æntifri:z] *n* frysevæske *c*
antipathy [æn'tipəθi] *n* motvilje *m*
antique [æn'ti:k] *adj* antikk; *n* antikvitet *m*; ~ **dealer** antikvitetshandler *m*
anxiety [æŋ'zaiəti] *n* bekymring *c*
anxious ['æŋkʃəs] *adj* ivrig; engstelig
any ['eni] *adj* hvilke som helst
anybody ['enibɔdi] *pron* hvem som helst
anyhow ['enihau] *adv* på hvilken som helst måte
anyone ['eniwʌn] *pron* enhver
anything ['eniθiŋ] *pron* hva som helst
anyway ['eniwei] *adv* i hvert fall
anywhere ['eniwεə] *adv* hvor som helst
apart [ə'pɑ:t] *adv* atskilt, separat; ~ **from** bortsett fra
apartment [ə'pɑ:tmənt] *nAm* leilighet *c*; ~ **house** *Am* leiegård *m*
aperitif [ə'perətiv] *n* aperitiff *m*
apologize [ə'pɔlədʒaiz] *v* *be om unnskyldning
apology [ə'pɔlədʒi] *n* unnskyldning *m*
apparatus [ˌæpə'reitəs] *n* apparat *nt*
apparent [ə'pærənt] *adj* tilsynelatende; tydelig
apparently [ə'pærəntli] *adv* åpenbart; øyensynlig
appeal [ə'pi:l] *n* appell *m*
appear [ə'piə] *v* *se ut til, synes; *fremgå; vise seg; *fremtre
appearance [ə'piərəns] *n* fremtoning *m*; utseende *nt*; opptreden *m*
appendicitis [əˌpendi'saitis] *n* blindtarmbetennelse *m*
appendix [ə'pendiks] *n* (pl -dices, -dixes) blindtarm *m*
appetite ['æpətait] *n* matlyst *c*, appetitt *m*
appetizer ['æpətaizə] *n* appetittvekker *m*
appetizing ['æpətaiziŋ] *adj* appetittlig
applause [ə'plɔ:z] *n* applaus *m*
applaud [ə'plɔ:d] *v* applaudere
apple ['æpəl] *n* eple *nt*
appliance [ə'plaiəns] *n* apparat *nt*
application [ˌæpli'keiʃən] *n* anvendelse *m*; søknad *m*
apply [ə'plai] *v* anvende, bruke; søke; *gjelde
appoint [ə'pɔint] *v* utnevne
appointment [ə'pɔintmənt] *n* avtale *m*, møte *nt*; utnevnelse *m*
appreciate [ə'pri:ʃieit] *v* *verdsette; påskjønne

appreciation [ə,priːʃi'eiʃən] *n* vurdering *c*; verdsettelse *m*
apprentice [ə'prentis] *n* lærling *m*
approach [ə'proutʃ] *v* nærme seg; *n* fremgangsmåte *m*
appropriate [ə'proupriət] *adj* formålstjenlig, passende, rett
approval [ə'pruːvəl] *n* godkjennelse *m*; billigelse *m*
approve [ə'pruːv] *v* godkjenne
approximate [ə'prɔksimət] *adj* omtrentlig
approximately [ə'prɔksimətli] *adv* cirka, omtrent
apricot ['eiprikɔt] *n* aprikos *m*
April ['eiprəl] april
apron ['eiprən] *n* forkle *nt*
Arab ['ærəb] *adj* arabisk; *n* araber *m*
arbitrary ['ɑːbitrəri] *adj* vilkårlig
arcade [ɑː'keid] *n* buegang *m*, arkade *m*
arch [ɑːtʃ] *n* bue *m*; hvelv *nt*
archaeologist [,ɑːki'ɔlədʒist] *n* arkeolog *m*
archaeology [,ɑːki'ɔlədʒi] *n* arkeologi *m*
arched [ɑːtʃt] *adj* bueformet
architect ['ɑːkitekt] *n* arkitekt *m*
architecture ['ɑːkitektʃə] *n* byggekunst *m*, arkitektur *m*
archives ['ɑːkaivz] *pl* arkiv *nt*
are [ɑː] *v* (pr be)
area ['ɛəriə] *n* område *nt*; areal *nt*; ~ **code** retningsnummer *nt*
Argentina [,ɑːdʒən'tiːnə] Argentina
Argentinian [,ɑːdʒən'tiniən] *adj* argentinsk; *n* argentiner *m*
argue ['ɑːgjuː] *v* diskutere, debattere, argumentere; trette
argument ['ɑːgjumənt] *n* argument *nt*; diskusjon *m*
***arise** [ə'raiz] *v* *oppstå
arithmetic [ə'riθmətik] *n* regning *c*
arm [ɑːm] *n* arm *m*; våpen *nt*; *v* bevæpne
armchair ['ɑːmtʃɛə] *n* lenestol *m*
armed [ɑːmd] *adj* bevæpnet; ~ **forces** væpnede styrker
armour ['ɑːmə] *n* rustning *m*
army ['ɑːmi] *n* armé *m*
aroma [ə'roumə] *n* aroma *m*
around [ə'raund] *prep* omkring; *adv* rundt
arrange [ə'reindʒ] *v* ordne; arrangere
arrangement [ə'reindʒmənt] *n* ordning *c*
arrest [ə'rest] *v* arrestere; *n* arrestasjon *m*, pågripelse

m
arrival [ə'raivəl] *n* ankomst *m*
arrive [ə'raiv] *v* *ankomme
arrow ['ærou] *n* pil *c*
art [ɑ:t] *n* kunst *m*; kunstferdighet *m*; **~ collection** kunstsamling *m*; **~ exhibition** kunstutstilling *c*; **~ gallery** kunstgalleri *nt*; **~ history** kunsthistorie *c*; **arts and crafts** kunst og håndverk; **~ school** kunstakademi *nt*
artery ['ɑ:təri] *n* pulsåre *c*
artichoke ['ɑ:titʃouk] *n* artisjokk *m*
article ['ɑ:tikəl] *n* gjenstand *m*; artikkel *m*
artificial [ˌɑ:ti'fiʃəl] *adj* kunstig
artist ['ɑ:tist] *n* kunstner *m*
artistic [ɑ:'tistik] *adj* kunstnerisk, artistisk
as [æz] *conj* liksom, som; like; fordi, ettersom; **~ from** fra; fra og med; **~ if** som om
asbestos [æz'bestɔs] *n* asbest *m*
ascend [ə'send] *v* *stige; *stige opp; *bestige
ascent [ə'sent] *n* stigning *m*; oppstigning *m*
ascertain [ˌæsə'tein] *v* konstatere; forvisse seg om, *fastslå
ash [æʃ] *n* aske *c*
ashamed [ə'ʃeimd] *adj* skamfull; ***be ~** skamme seg
ashore [ə'ʃɔ:] *adv* i land
ashtray ['æʃtrei] *n* askebeger *nt*
Asia ['eiʃə] Asia
Asian ['eiʃən] *adj* asiatisk; *n* asiat *m*
aside [ə'said] *adv* til siden, til side
ask [ɑ:sk] *v* *spørre; *be; *innby
asleep [ə'sli:p] *adj* sovende
asparagus [ə'spærəgəs] *n* asparges *m*
aspect ['æspekt] *n* utseende *nt*; aspekt *nt*
asphalt ['æsfælt] *n* asfalt *m*
aspire [ə'spaiə] *v* strebe
aspirin ['æspərin] *n* aspirin *m*
assassination [əˌsæsi'neiʃən] *n* mord *nt*
assault [ə'sɔ:lt] *v* *angripe; *overfalle
assemble [ə'sembəl] *v* samle, *sette sammen
assembly [ə'sembli] *n* forsamling *c*, sammenkomst *m*
assignment [ə'sainmənt] *n* oppdrag *nt*
assign to [ə'sain] *v* tildele; *tilskrive
assist [ə'sist] *v* *bistå, *hjelpe; **~ at** *hjelpe til med
assistance [ə'sistəns] *n* hjelp *c*; assistanse *m*, understøttelse *m*
assistant [ə'sistənt] *n*

assistent *m*
associate¹ [ə'souʃiət] *n* partner *m*, kompanjong *m*; forbundsfelle *m*; medlem *nt*
associate² [ə'souʃieit] *v* *forbinde; **~ with** *omgås
association [əˌsousi'eiʃən] *n* forening *c*
assort [ə'sɔːt] *v* sortere
assortment [ə'sɔːtmənt] *n* utvalg *nt*, sortiment *nt*
assume [ə'sjuːm] *v* *anta, formode
assure [ə'ʃuə] *v* forsikre
asthma ['æsmə] *n* astma *m*
astonish [ə'stɔniʃ] *v* forbløffe, forbause
astonishing [ə'stɔniʃiŋ] *adj* forbausende
astonishment [ə'stɔniʃmənt] *n* forbauselse *m*
astronaut ['æstrənɔːt] *n* astronaut *m*
astronomy [ə'strɔnəmi] *n* astronomi *m*
asylum [ə'sailəm] *n* asyl *nt*
at [æt] *prep* på, hos, i
ate [et] *v* (p eat)
atheist ['eiθiist] *n* ateist *m*
athlete ['æθliːt] *n* idrettsutøver *m*
athletics [æθ'letiks] *pl* friidrett *m*
Atlantic [ət'læntik] Atlanterhavet
ATM [ˌeiti'em] *n* minibank *m*
atmosphere ['ætməsfiə] *n* atmosfære *m*; stemning *m*
atom ['ætəm] *n* atom *nt*
atomic [ə'tɔmik] *adj* atom-
atomizer ['ætəmaizə] *n* sprayflaske *c*; spray *m*, vaporisator *m*
attach [ə'tætʃ] *v* feste; *vedlegge; **attached to** knyttet til
attachment [ə'tætʃmənt] *n* vedlegg *m*
attack [ə'tæk] *v* *angripe; *n* angrep *nt*
attain [ə'tein] *v* oppnå
attainable [ə'teinəbəl] *adj* oppnåelig
attempt [ə'tempt] *v* forsøke, prøve; *n* forsøk *nt*
attend [ə'tend] *v* *overvære; **~ on** betjene; **~ to** *ta hånd om, *ta seg av; *være oppmerksom på
attendance [ə'tendəns] *n* deltakelse *m*
attendant [ə'tendənt] *n* vakt *c*
attention [ə'tenʃən] *n* oppmerksomhet *c*; ***pay ~** *være oppmerksom
attentive [ə'tentiv] *adj* oppmerksom
attest [ə'test] *v* attestere, bevitne
attic ['ætik] *n* loft *nt*
attitude ['ætitjuːd] *n* holdning *m*
attorney [ə'təːni] *n* advokat *m*
attract [ə'trækt] *v* *tiltrekke
attraction [ə'trækʃən] *n*

attraksjon *m*; tiltrekning *m*, sjarm *m*
attractive [ə'træktiv] *adj* tiltrekkende
auction ['ɔ:kʃən] *n* auksjon *m*
audible ['ɔ:dibəl] *adj* hørbar
audience ['ɔ:diəns] *n* publikum *nt*
auditor ['ɔ:ditə] *n* tilhører *m*
auditorium [ˌɔ:di'tɔ:riəm] *n* auditorium *nt*
August ['ɔ:gəst] august
aunt [ɑ:nt] *n* tante *c*
Australia [ɔ'streiliə] Australia
Australian [ɔ'streiliən] *adj* australsk; *n* australier *m*
Austria ['ɔstriə] Østerrike
Austrian ['ɔstriən] *adj* østerriksk; *n* østerriker *m*
authentic [ɔ:'θentik] *adj* autentisk; ekte
author ['ɔ:θə] *n* forfatter *m*
authoritarian [ɔ:ˌθɔri'tɛəriən] *adj* autoritær
authority [ɔ:'θɔrəti] *n* autoritet *m*; myndighet *c*
authorization [ˌɔ:θərai'zeiʃən] *n* tillatelse *m*; autorisasjon *m*
automatic [ˌɔ:tə'mætik] *adj* automatisk; **~ teller** minibank *m*
automation [ˌɔ:tə'meiʃən] *n* automatisering *c*
automobile ['ɔ:təməbi:l] *n* bil *m*; **~ club** automobilklubb *m*
autonomous [ɔ:'tɔnəməs] *adj* selvstyrt
autopsy ['ɔ:tɔpsi] *n* obduksjon *m*
autumn ['ɔ:təm] *n* høst *m*
available [ə'veiləbəl] *adj* tilgjengelig, disponibel, for hånden
avalanche ['ævəlɑ:nʃ] *n* snøskred *nt*
avenue ['ævənju:] *n* aveny *m*; gate *c*
average ['ævəridʒ] *adj* gjennomsnittlig; *n* gjennomsnitt *nt*; **on the ~** i gjennomsnitt
averse [ə'və:s] *adj* uvillig
aversion [ə'və:ʃən] *n* motvilje *m*
avoid [ə'vɔid] *v* *unngå; *unnvike
await [ə'weit] *v* vente på, avvente
awake [ə'weik] *adj* våken
***awake** [ə'weik] *v* vekke
award [ə'wɔ:d] *n* pris *m*; *v* tildele
aware [ə'wɛə] *adj* klar over
away [ə'wei] *adv* bort; ***go ~** reise bort
awful ['ɔ:fəl] *adj* forferdelig, redselsfull
awkward ['ɔ:kwəd] *adj* pinlig; klosset
awning ['ɔ:niŋ] *n* markise *m*
axe [æks] *n* øks *c*
axle ['æksəl] *n* aksel *m*

B

baby ['beibi] *n* baby *m*; ~ **carriage** *Am* barnevogn *c*
babysitter ['beibi,sitə] *n* barnevakt *c*
bachelor ['bætʃələ] *n* ungkar *m*
back [bæk] *n* rygg *m*; *adv* tilbake; ***go ~** vende tilbake
backache ['bækeik] *n* ryggsmerter *pl*
backbone ['bækboun] *n* ryggrad *m*
background ['bækgraund] *n* bakgrunn *m*
backwards ['bækwədz] *adv* baklengs
bacon ['beikən] *n* bacon *nt*
bacterium [bæk'tiːriəm] *n* (pl -ria) bakterie *m*
bad [bæd] *adj* dårlig; alvorlig; slem
bag [bæg] *n* pose *m*; veske *c*, håndveske *c*; reiseveske *c*
baggage ['bægidʒ] *n* bagasje *m*; **~ deposit office** *Am* bagasjeoppbevaring *c*; **hand ~** håndbagasje *m*
bail [beil] *n* kausjon *m*
bait [beit] *n* agn *nt*
bake [beik] *v* bake
baker ['beikə] *n* baker *m*
bakery ['beikəri] *n* bakeri *nt*
balance ['bæləns] *n* likevekt *c*; balanse *m*; saldo *m*
balcony ['bælkəni] *n* balkong *m*
bald [bɔːld] *adj* skallet
ball [bɔːl] *n* ball *m*; ball *nt*
ballet ['bælei] *n* ballett *m*
balloon [bə'luːn] *n* ballong *m*
ballpoint pen ['bɔːlpɔintpen] *n* kulepenn *m*
banana [bə'nɑːnə] *n* banan *m*
band [bænd] *n* orkester *nt*; bånd *nt*
bandage ['bændidʒ] *n* bandasje *m*
bank [bæŋk] *n* bredd *m*; bank *m*; *v* *sette i banken; **~ account** bankkonto *m*
banknote ['bæŋknout] *n* pengeseddel *m*
bank rate ['bæŋkreit] *n* diskonto *m*
bankrupt ['bæŋkrʌpt] *adj* konkurs, fallitt
banner ['bænə] *n* banner *nt*
banquet ['bæŋkwit] *n* bankett *m*
baptism ['bæptizəm] *n* dåp *m*
baptize [bæp'taiz] *v* døpe
bar [bɑː] *n* bar *m*; stang *c*
barbecue ['bɑːbikjuː] *n* grillfest *m*, grilling *c*; *v* grille
barbed wire ['bɑːbd waiə] *n* piggtråd *m*
barber ['bɑːbə] *n* frisør *m*

bare [bɛə] *adj* naken, bar
barely ['bɛəli] *adv* så vidt
bargain ['bɑːgin] *n* godt kjøp; *v* *kjøpslå, prute
baritone ['bæritoun] *n* baryton *m*
bark [bɑːk] *n* bark *m*; *v* gjø
barley ['bɑːli] *n* bygg *m*
barn [bɑːn] *n* låve *m*
barometer [bə'rɔmitə] *n* barometer *nt*
baroque [bə'rɔk] *adj* barokk
barracks ['bærəks] *pl* kaserne *m*
barrel ['bærəl] *n* fat *nt*, tønne *c*
barrier ['bæriə] *n* barriere *m*; bom *m*
barrister ['bæristə] *n* advokat *m*
bartender ['bɑːˌtendə] *n* bartender *m*
base [beis] *n* base *m*, basis *m*; fundament *nt*; *v* basere
baseball ['beisbɔːl] *n* baseball *m*
basement ['beismənt] *n* kjelleretasje *m*
basic ['beisik] *adj* grunnleggende; **basics** *npl* grunnlag *nt* / *pl*
basilica [bə'zilikə] *n* basilika *m*
basin ['beisən] *n* bolle *m*
basis ['beisis] *n* (pl bases) basis *m*, grunnlag *nt*
basket ['bɑːskit] *n* kurv *m*
bass[1] [beis] *n* bass *m*
bass[2] [bæs] *n* (pl ~) åbor *m*
bastard ['bɑːstəd] *n* bastard *m*; skurk *m*
batch [bætʃ] *n* bunke *m*
bath [bɑːθ] *n* bad *nt*; **~ towel** badehåndkle *nt*
bathe [beið] *v* bade
bathing cap ['beiðiŋkæp] *n* badehette *c*
bathing suit ['beiðiŋsuːt] *n* badedrakt *c*; badebukse *c*
bathrobe ['bɑːθroub] *n* badekåpe *c*
bathroom ['bɑːθruːm] *n* bad *nt*, baderværelse *nt*; toalett *nt*
batter ['bætə] *n* deig *m*
battery ['bætəri] *n* batteri *nt*
battle ['bætəl] *n* slag *nt*; kamp *m*, strid *m*; *v* kjempe
bay [bei] *n* bukt *c*; *v* gjø
***be** [biː] *v* *være
beach [biːtʃ] *n* strand *c*; **nudist ~** nudistbadestrand *c*
bead [biːd] *n* perle *c*; **beads** *pl* perlekjede *nt*; rosenkrans *m*
beak [biːk] *n* nebb *nt*
beam [biːm] *n* stråle *m*; bjelke *m*
bean [biːn] *n* bønne *c*
bear [bɛə] *n* bjørn *m*
***bear** [bɛə] *v* *bære; tåle; *holde ut
beard [biəd] *n* skjegg *nt*
bearer ['bɛərə] *n* innehaver *m*
beast [biːst] *n* dyr *nt*; **~ of prey** rovdyr *nt*
beat [biːt] *n* rytme *m*; slag *nt*
***beat** [biːt] *v* *slå

beautiful ['bju:tifəl] *adj* vakker
beauty ['bju:ti] *n* skjønnhet *c*; **~ parlo(u)r** skjønnhetssalong *m*; **~ treatment** skjønnhetspleie *m*
beaver ['bi:və] *n* bever *m*
because [bi'kɔz] *conj* fordi; ettersom; **~ of** på grunn av
***become** [bi'kʌm] *v* *bli; kle
bed [bed] *n* seng *c*; **~ and board** kost og losji, helpensjon *m*; **~ and breakfast** værelse med frokost
bedding ['bediŋ] *n* sengetøy *nt*
bedroom ['bedru:m] *n* soveværelse *nt*
bee [bi:] *n* bie *c*
beech [bi:tʃ] *n* bøk *m*
beef [bi:f] *n* oksekjøtt *nt*
beefburger [bi:fbə:gə] *n* hamburger *m*
beehive ['bi:haiv] *n* bikube *m*
been [bi:n] *v* (pp be)
beer [biə] *n* øl *nt*
beetle ['bi:təl] *n* bille *m*
beetroot ['bi:tru:t] *n* rødbete *c*
before [bi'fɔ:] *prep* før; foran; *conj* før; *adv* tidligere
beg [beg] *v* tigge; *bønnfalle; *be
beggar ['begə] *n* tigger *m*
***begin** [bi'gin] *v* begynne; starte
beginner [bi'ginə] *n* nybegynner *m*
beginning [bi'giniŋ] *n* begynnelse *m*; start *m*
behalf: on ~ of [ɔn bi'hɑ:f ɔv] på vegne av; til fordel for
behave [bi'heiv] *v* oppføre seg
behavio(u)r [bi'heivjə] *n* oppførsel *m*
behind [bi'haind] *prep* bak; *adv* bak
beige [beiʒ] *adj* beige
being ['bi:iŋ] *n* vesen *nt*
Belgian ['beldʒən] *adj* belgisk; *n* belgier *m*
Belgium ['beldʒəm] Belgia
belief [bi'li:f] *n* tro *c*
believe [bi'li:v] *v* tro
bell [bel] *n* klokke *c*; ringeklokke *c*
bellboy ['belbɔi] *n* pikkolo *m*
belly ['beli] *n* mage *m*
belong [bi'lɔŋ] *v* tilhøre
belongings [bi'lɔŋiŋz] *pl* eiendeler
beloved [bi'lʌvd] *adj* elsket
below [bi'lou] *prep* nedenfor; under; *adv* nede
belt [belt] *n* belte *nt*
bench [bentʃ] *n* benk *m*
bend [bend] *n* sving *m*, bøyning *m*; krumning *m*
***bend** [bend] *v* bøye; **~ down** bøye seg
beneath [bi'ni:θ] *prep* under; *adv* under
benefit ['benifit] *n* utbytte

nt; fordel *m*; *v* *ha fordel av
bent [bent] *adj* (pp bend) bøyd
berry ['beri] *n* bær *nt*
beside [bi'said] *prep* ved siden av
besides [bi'saidz] *adv* dessuten; forresten; *prep* foruten
best [best] *adj* best
bet [bet] *n* veddemål *nt*; innsats *m*
***bet** [bet] *v* vedde
betray [bi'trei] *v* forråde
better ['betə] *adj* bedre
between [bi'twi:n] *prep* mellom
beverage ['bevəridʒ] *n* drikk *m*
beware [bi'wɛə] *v* vokte seg
beyond [bi'jɔnd] *prep* hinsides; på den andre siden av; ut over; *adv* bortenfor
bible ['baibəl] *n* bibel *m*
bicycle ['baisikəl] *n* sykkel *m*
bid [bid] *n* bud *nt*; tilbud *nt*
***bid** [bid] *v* *tilby; *by
big [big] *adj* stor; omfangsrik; tykk; viktig
bike [baik] *n colloquial* sykkel *m*; *v* sykle
bile [bail] *n* galle *m*
bilingual [bai'liŋgwəl] *adj* tospråklig
bill [bil] *n* regning *c*, nota *m*; *v* fakturere
billiards ['biljədz] *pl* biljard *m*
billion ['biljən] *n* milliard *m*
***bind** [baind] *v* *binde
binding ['baindiŋ] *n* bokbind *nt*
binoculars [bi'nɔkjələz] *pl* kikkert *m*
biodegradable [ˌbaioudi'greidəbəl] *adj* biologisk nedbrytbar
biology [bai'ɔlədʒi] *n* biologi *m*
bipolar [ˌbai'poulə] *adj* bipolar
birch [bə:tʃ] *n* bjørk *c*
bird [bə:d] *n* fugl *m*
birth [bə:θ] *n* fødsel *m*
birthday ['bə:θdei] *n* fødselsdag *m*
biscuit ['biskit] *n* småkake *c*
bishop ['biʃəp] *n* biskop *m*
bit [bit] *n* bit *m*; smule *m*
bitch [bitʃ] *n* tispe *c*
bite [bait] *n* bit *m*; stikk *nt*
***bite** [bait] *v* *bite
bitter ['bitə] *adj* bitter
black [blæk] *adj* svart; **~ market** svartebørs *m*
blackberry ['blækbəri] *n* bjørnebær *nt*
Blackberry® ['blækbəri] *n* Blackberry *c*
blackbird ['blækbə:d] *n* svarttrost *m*
blackboard ['blækbɔ:d] *n* tavle *c*
blackcurrant [ˌblæk'kʌrənt] *n* solbær *nt*
blackmail ['blækmeil] *n* pengeutpresning *m*; *v*

presse penger av
blacksmith ['blæksmiθ] *n* grovsmed *m*
bladder ['blædə] *n* blære *c*
blade [bleid] *n* blad *nt*; ~ **of grass** gresstrå *nt*
blame [bleim] *n* skyld *c*; bebreidelse *m*; *v* klandre, bebreide
blank [blæŋk] *adj* blank
blanket ['blæŋkit] *n* ullteppe *nt*; teppe *nt*
blast [blɑ:st] *n* eksplosjon *m*
bleach [bli:tʃ] *v* bleke
bleak [bli:k] *adj* ødslig, barsk
***bleed** [bli:d] *v* blø; flå
bless [bles] *v* velsigne
blessing ['blesiŋ] *n* velsignelse *m*
blind [blaind] *n* persienne *m*, rullegardin *c* / *nt*; *adj* blind; *v* blende
blister ['blistə] *n* blemme *c*, gnagsår *nt*
blizzard ['blizəd] *n* snøstorm *m*
block [blɔk] *v* sperre, blokkere; *n* kloss *m*; kvartal *nt*; ~ **of flats** leiegård *m*
blog [blɔg] *n* (Nett)blogg *c*
blond [blɔnd] *adj* blond
blonde [blɔnd] *n* blondine *c*, blond person *m*
blood [blʌd] *n* blod *nt*; ~ **poisoning** blodforgiftning *m*; ~ **pressure** blodtrykk *nt*; ~ **vessel** blodkar *nt*
bloody [blʌdi] *adj* blodig; *colloquial* fordømt
blossom ['blɔsəm] *n* blomst *m*; *v* blomstre
blot [blɔt] *n* flekk *m*
blouse [blauz] *n* bluse *c*
blow [blou] *n* fik *m*, slag *nt*; vindkast *nt*
***blow** [blou] *v* blåse; ~ **up** sprenge; eksplodere
blowout ['blouaut] *n* punktering *c*; utblåsning *m*
blue [blu:] *adj* blå; nedtrykt
blunt [blʌnt] *adj* sløv; butt
blush [blʌʃ] *v* rødme
board [bɔ:d] *n* planke *m*; tavle *c*; oppslagstavle *c*; pensjon *m*; styre *nt*; ~ **and lodging** kost og losji, helpensjon *m*
boardinghouse ['bɔ:diŋhaus] *n* pensjonat *nt*
boarding school ['bɔ:diŋsku:l] *n* pensjonatskole *m*
boast [boust] *v* *skryte
boat [bout] *n* båt *m*, skip *nt*
body ['bɔdi] *n* kropp *m*; legeme *nt*
bodyguard ['bɔdigɑ:d] *n* livvakt *c*
body-work ['bɔdiwə:k] *n* karosseri *nt*
bog [bɔg] *n* myr *c*
boil [bɔil] *v* koke; *n* byll *m*
bold [bould] *adj* dristig; frekk
Bolivia [bə'liviə] Bolivia
Bolivian [bə'liviən] *adj* boliviansk; *n* bolivianer *m*

bolt [boult] *n* slå *c*; bolt *m*
bomb [bɔm] *n* bombe *c*; *v* bombardere
bond [bɔnd] *n* obligasjon *m*
bone [boun] *n* bein *nt*; fiskebein *nt*; *v* skjære ut bein
bonnet ['bɔnit] *n* bilpanser *nt*
book [buk] *n* bok *c*; *v* reservere, bestille; bokføre
booking ['bukiŋ] *n* bestilling *c*, reservasjon *m*
bookmaker ['buk,meikə] *n* totalisator *m*
bookseller ['buk,selə] *n* bokhandler *m*
bookstand ['bukstænd] *n* bokstand *m*
bookstore ['bukstɔː] *n* bokhandel *m*
boot [buːt] *n* støvel *m*; bagasjerom *nt*
booth [buːð] *n* bu *c*; bås *m*
booze [buːz] *n colloquial* alkohol *m*; *v* drikke alkohol
border ['bɔːdə] *n* grense *c*; kant *m*
bore[1] [bɔː] *v* kjede; bore; *n* kjedelig person *m*
bore[2] [bɔː] *v* (p bear)
boring ['bɔːriŋ] *adj* kjedelig
born [bɔːn] *adj* født
borrow ['bɔrou] *v* låne
bosom ['buzəm] *n* barm *m*; bryst *nt*
boss [bɔs] *n* boss *m*, sjef *m*
botany ['bɔtəni] *n* botanikk *m*
both [bouθ] *adj* begge; **both ... and** både ... og
bother ['bɔðə] *v* plage; bry seg; *n* bry *nt*
bottle ['bɔtəl] *n* flaske *c*; **~ opener** flaskeåpner *m*; **hot-water ~** varmeflaske *c*
bottleneck ['bɔtəlnek] *n* flaskehals *m*
bottom ['bɔtəm] *n* bunn *m*; akterspeil *nt*, bak *m*; *adj* underste
bought [bɔːt] *v* (p, pp buy)
boulder ['bouldə] *n* rullestein *m*
bound [baund] *n* grense *c*; ***be ~ to** *måtte; **~ for** på vei til
boundary ['baundəri] *n* grense *c*
bouquet [bu'kei] *n* bukett *m*
bourgeois ['buəʒwaː] *adj* spissborgerlig
boutique [bu'tiːk] *n* butikk *m*
bow[1] [bau] *v* bukke
bow[2] [bou] *n* bue *m*; **~ tie** sløyfe *c*
bowels [bauəlz] *pl* tarmer
bowl [boul] *n* bolle *m*
bowling ['bouliŋ] *n* bowling *m*; **~ alley** bowlingbane *m*
box[1] [bɔks] *v* bokse; **boxing match** boksekamp *m*
box[2] [bɔks] *n* eske *c*
box office ['bɔks,ɔfis] *n* billettluke *c*, billettkontor *nt*
boy [bɔi] *n* gutt *m*; tjener *m*
boyfriend ['bɔifrend] *n*

kjæreste *m*
bra [brɑː] *n* brystholder *m*, behå *m*
brace ['breis] *n* (tann-)regulering *c*
bracelet ['breislit] *n* armbånd *nt*
braces ['breisiz] *pl* bukseseler *pl*;
brain [brein] *n* hjerne *m*; forstand *m*;~ **wave** innfall *nt*
brake [breik] *n* brems *m*; ~ **drum** bremsetrommel *m*; ~ **lights** bremselys *pl*
branch [brɑːntʃ] *n* gren *m*; filial *m*
brand [brænd] *n* merke *nt*; brennemerke *nt*
brand-new [ˌbrænd'njuː] *adj* splinter ny
brass [brɑːs] *n* messing *m*; ~ **band** hornorkester *nt*
brave [breiv] *adj* modig, tapper
Brazil [brə'zil] Brasil
Brazilian [brə'ziljən] *adj* brasiliansk; *n* brasilianer *m*
breach [briːtʃ] *n* åpning *c*
bread [bred] *n* brød *nt*; **wholemeal** ~ helkornbrød *nt*
breadth [bredθ] *n* bredde *m*
break [breik] *n* brudd *nt*; *m* pause *m*; frikvarter *nt*
***break** [breik] *v* *bryte; ~ **down** *gå i stykker; inndele
breakdown ['breikdaun] *n* maskinskade *m*, motorstopp *m* / *nt*
breakfast ['brekfəst] *n* frokost *m*
breast [brest] *n* bryst *nt*
breaststroke ['breststrouk] *n* brystsvømming *c*
breath [breθ] *n* pust *m*
breathe [briːð] *v* puste
breathing ['briːðiŋ] *n* åndedrett *nt*
breed [briːd] *n* rase *m*; slag *nt*
***breed** [briːd] *v* ale opp, oppdrette
breeze [briːz] *n* bris *m*
brew [bruː] *v* brygge
brewery ['bruːəri] *n* bryggeri *nt*
bribe [braib] *v* *bestikke
bribery ['braibəri] *n* bestikkelse *m*
brick [brik] *n* murstein *m*
bricklayer ['brikleiə] *n* murer *m*
bride [braid] *n* brud *c*
bridegroom ['braidgruːm] *n* brudgom *m*
bridge [bridʒ] *n* bro *c*; bridge *m*
brief [briːf] *adj* kort; kortfattet
briefcase ['briːfkeis] *n* dokumentmappe *c*
briefs [briːfs] *pl* truse *c*
bright [brait] *adj* skinnende; oppvakt
brighten ['braitən] *v* lyse opp
brill [bril] *n* slettvar *m*
brilliant ['briljənt] *adj*

strålende; begavet
brim [brim] *n* rand *m*
***bring** [briŋ] *v* *ta med, *bringe; *medbringe; **~ back** *bringe tilbake; **~ up** *oppdra; *ta opp
brisk [brisk] *adj* livlig
Britain ['britən] Britannia
British ['britiʃ] *adj* britisk
Briton ['britən] *n* brite *m*
broad [brɔːd] *adj* bred; utstrakt, vidstrakt; allmenn
broadband ['brɔːdæbænd] *n* bredbånd *nt*
broadcast ['brɔːdkɑːst] *n* sending *c*
***broadcast** ['brɔːdkɑːst] *v* kringkaste
brochure ['brouʃuə] *n* brosjyre *m*
broke[1] [brouk] *v* (p break)
broke[2] [brouk] *adj* blakk
broken ['broukən] *adj* (pp break) knust, i stykker; i uorden
broker ['broukə] *n* megler *m*
bronchitis [brɔŋ'kaitis] *n* bronkitt *m*
bronze [brɔnz] *n* bronse *m*; *adj* bronse-
brooch [broutʃ] *n* brosje *c*
brook [bruk] *n* bekk *m*
broom [bruːm] *n* kost *m*
brothel ['brɔθəl] *n* bordell *nt*
brother ['brʌðə] *n* bror *m*
brother-in-law ['brʌðərinlɔː] *n* (pl brothers-) svoger *m*
brought [brɔːt] *v* (p, pp bring)
brown [braun] *adj* brun
bruise [bruːz] *n* blått merke; *v* *slå
brunette [bruː'net] *n* brunette *m*
brush [brʌʃ] *n* børste *m*; pensel *m*; *v* børste
brutal ['bruːtəl] *adj* brutal
bubble ['bʌbəl] *n* boble *c*
buck [bʌk] *n* bukk *m*; *colloquial* dollar *m*
bucket ['bʌkit] *n* spann *nt*
buckle ['bʌkəl] *n* spenne *c*
bud [bʌd] *n* knopp *m*
buddy ['bʌdi] *n colloquial* kamerat *m*
budget ['bʌdʒit] *n* budsjett *nt*
buffet ['bufei] *n* koldtbord *nt*
bug [bʌg] *n* veggedyr *nt*; bille *m*; insekt *nt*
***build** [bild] *v* bygge
building ['bildiŋ] *n* bygning *m*
bulb [bʌlb] *n* blomsterløk *m*; **light ~** lyspære *c*
Bulgaria [bʌl'gɛəriə] Bulgaria
Bulgarian [bʌl'gɛəriən] *adj* bulgarsk; *n* bulgarer *m*
bulk [bʌlk] *n* last *c*; masse *m*; størsteparten *m*
bulky ['bʌlki] *adj* fyldig, omfangsrik
bull [bul] *n* tyr *m*, okse *m*
bullet ['bulit] *n* kule *c*
bulletin ['bulitin] *n* bekjentgjørelse *m*, oppslag *nt*

bullfight ['bulfait] *n* tyrefektning *m*
bump [bʌmp] *v* støte; støte sammen; dunke; *n* støt *nt*
bumper ['bʌmpə] *n* støtfanger *m*
bumpy ['bʌmpi] *adj* humpet
bun [bʌn] *n* hvetebolle *m*
bunch [bʌntʃ] *n* bukett *m*; flokk *m*
bundle ['bʌndəl] *n* bunt *m*; *v* bunte, *binde sammen
bunk [bʌŋk] *n* køye *c*
buoy [bɔi] *n* bøye *m*
burden ['bə:dən] *n* byrde *m*
bureau ['bjuərou] *n* (pl ~x, ~s) skrivebord *nt*; kommode *m*
bureaucracy [bjuə'rɔkrəsi] *n* byråkrati *nt*
burger [bə:gə] *n* hamburger
burglar ['bə:glə] *n* innbruddstyv *m*
burgle ['bə:gəl] *v* *begå innbrudd
burial ['beriəl] *n* begravelse *m*
burn [bə:n] *n* brannsår *nt*
***burn** [bə:n] *v* *brenne; *svi
***burst** [bə:st] *v* *sprekke; *briste
bury ['beri] *v* begrave; grave ned
bus [bʌs] *n* buss *m*
bush [buʃ] *n* busk *m*
business ['biznəs] *n* forretninger *pl*, handel *m*; virksomhet *c*, forretning *c*; yrke *nt*; **~ card** visittkort *nt*; **~ hours** åpningstid *c*, kontortid *c*; **~ trip** forretningsreise *c*; **on ~** i forretninger
business-like ['biznislaik] *adj* forretningsmessig
businessman ['biznəsmən] *n* (pl -men) forretningsmann *m*
businesswoman ['biznəswumən] *n* (pl -women) forretningskvinne *c*
bust [bʌst] *n* byste *c*
bustle ['bʌsəl] *n* travelhet *c*
busy ['bizi] *adj* opptatt; travel
but [bʌt] *conj* men; dog; *prep* unntatt
butcher ['butʃə] *n* slakter *m*
butter ['bʌtə] *n* smør *nt*
butterfly ['bʌtəflai] *n* sommerfugl *m*; **~ stroke** butterfly *m*
buttock ['bʌtək] *n* rumpeballe *m*
button ['bʌtən] *n* knapp *m*; *v* knappe
***buy** [bai] *v* kjøpe; anskaffe
buyer ['baiə] *n* kjøper *m*
buzz [bʌs] *n* summing *c*
by [bai] *prep* av; med; ved
bye-bye [bai'bai] *colloquial* ha det!
by-pass ['baipɑ:s] *n* ringvei *m*; bypass *m*; *v* *omgå

C

cab [kæb] *n* drosje *c*, taxi *m*
cabaret ['kæbərei] *n* kabaret *m*; nattklubb *m*
cabbage ['kæbidʒ] *n* kål *m*
cab driver ['kæb,draivə] *n* drosjesjåfør *m*, taxisjåfør *m*
cabin ['kæbin] *n* kabin *m*; hytte *c*; omkledningskabin *m*; lugar *m*
cable ['keibəl] *n* kabel *m*; **~ tv** kabelfjernsyn, *nt* kabel-TV *nt*
café ['kæfei] *n* kafé *m*
cafeteria [,kæfə'tiəriə] *n* kafeteria *m*
caffeine ['kæfi:n] *n* kaffein *m*
cage [keidʒ] *n* bur *nt*
cake [keik] *n* kake *c*
calamity [kə'læməti] *n* ulykke *c*, katastrofe *m*
calcium ['kælsiəm] *n* kalsium *nt*
calculate ['kælkjuleit] *v* regne ut
calculation [,kælkju'leiʃən] *n* utregning *c*
calculator ['kælkjuleitə] *n* kalkulator *m*, lommeregner *m*
calendar ['kæləndə] *n* kalender *m*
calf [kɑ:f] *n* (pl calves) kalv *m*; legg *m*; **~skin** kalveskinn *nt*
call [kɔ:l] *v* rope; kalle; ringe opp; *n* rop *nt*; besøk *nt*, visitt *m*; oppringning *m*; ***be called** *hete; **~ names** skjelle ut; **~ on** besøke; **~ up** *Am* ringe opp
call waiting ['kɔ:l‿'weitiŋ] *n* samtale venter *c*
caller ID ['kɔ:lər‿ai'di:] *n* nummervisning *c*
calm [kɑ:m] *adj* stille, rolig; **~ down** berolige; roe seg, falle til ro
calorie ['kæləri] *n* kalori *m*
came [keim] *v* (p come)
camel ['kæməl] *n* kamel *m*
camera ['kæmərə] *n* fotografiapparat *nt*; filmkamera *nt*; **~ shop** fotoforretning *c*
camp [kæmp] *n* leir *m*; *v* campe; **~ bed** feltseng *c*
campaign [kæm'pein] *n* kampanje *m*
camper ['kæmpə] *n* campinggjest *m*; bobil *m*
camping ['kæmpiŋ] *n* camping *m*; **~ site** campingplass *m*
can [kæn] *n* boks *m*; **~ opener** boksåpner *m*
***can** [kæn] *v* *kan
Canada ['kænədə] Canada
Canadian [kə'neidiən] *adj* kanadisk; *n* kanadier *m*
canal [kə'næl] *n* kanal *m*
canary [kə'nɛəri] *n*

kanarifugl *m*
cancel ['kænsəl] *v* annullere; avbestille
cancellation [ˌkænsə'leiʃən] *n* avbestilling *c*
cancer ['kænsə] *n* kreft *m*
candid ['kændid] *adj* åpen, oppriktig
candidate ['kændidət] *n* kandidat *m*
candle ['kændəl] *n* stearinlys *nt*
candy ['kændi] *nAm* sukkertøy *nt*; godter *pl*, søtsaker *pl*
cane [kein] *n* rør *nt*; stokk *m*
canister ['kænistə] *n* boks *m*
canoe [kə'nuː] *n* kano *m*
canteen [kæn'tiːn] *n* kantine *c*
canvas ['kænvəs] *n* lerret *nt*, seilduk *m*
cap [kæp] *n* lue *c*, skyggelue *c*
capable ['keipəbəl] *adj* dyktig, kompetent
capacity [kə'pæsəti] *n* kapasitet *m*; evne *c*
cape [keip] *n* cape *m*; kapp *nt*
capital ['kæpitəl] *n* hovedstad *m*; kapital *m*; *adj* viktig, hoved-; **~ letter** stor bokstav
capitalism ['kæpitəlizəm] *n* kapitalisme *m*
capitulation [kəˌpitju'leiʃən] *n* kapitulasjon *m*
capsule ['kæpsjuːl] *n* kapsel *m*
captain ['kæptin] *n* kaptein *m*; flykaptein *m*
capture ['kæptʃə] *v* fange, *ta til fange; erobre; *n* arrestasjon *m*; erobring *c*
car [kɑː] *n* bil *m*; **~ hire** bilutleie *m*; **~ park** parkeringsplass *m*; **~ rental** *Am* bilutleie *c*
carjacking ['kɑːˌdʒækiŋ] *n* biltyveri *nt*
caramel ['kærəməl] *n* karamell *m*
carat ['kærət] *n* karat *m*
caravan ['kærəvæn] *n* bobil *m*
carburettor [ˌkɑːbju'retə] *n* forgasser *m*
card [kɑːd] *n* kort *nt*; visittkort *nt*
cardboard ['kɑːdbɔːd] *n* papp *m*; *adj* kartong-
cardigan ['kɑːdigən] *n* ulljakke *c*
cardinal ['kɑːdinəl] *n* kardinal *m*; *adj* hoved-; **~ number** grunntall *nt*
care [kɛə] *n* omsorg *c*; bekymring *c*; **~ about** bekymre seg om; **~ for** bry seg om; ***take ~ of** passe på, *ta vare på
career [kə'riə] *n* karriere *m*
carefree ['kɛəfriː] *adj* ubekymret
careful ['kɛəfəl] *adj* forsiktig; omhyggelig, nøyaktig

careless ['kɛələs] *adj* likegyldig, skjødesløs
caretaker ['kɛəˌteikə] *n* vaktmester *m*
cargo ['ka:gou] *n* (pl ~es) last *c*, frakt *c*
carnival ['ka:nivəl] *n* karneval *nt*
carp [ka:p] *n* (pl ~) karpe *m*
carpenter ['ka:pintə] *n* snekker *m*
carpet ['ka:pit] *n* gulvteppe *nt*, teppe *nt*
carriage ['kæridʒ] *n* hestevogn *c*, vogn *c*
carriageway ['kæridʒwei] *n* kjørebane *m*
carrot ['kærət] *n* gulrot *c*
carry ['kæri] *v* *bære; føre; ~ **on** *fortsette; ~ **out** utføre
carrycot ['kærikɔt] *n* babybag *m*
cart [ka:t] *n* kjerre *c*
cartilage ['ka:tilidʒ] *n* brusk *m*
carton ['ka:tən] *n* kartong *m*
cartoon [ka:'tu:n] *n* tegnefilm *m*
cartridge ['ka:tridʒ] *n* patron *m*
carve [ka:v] *v* *skjære; *skjære i, *skjære ut
carving ['ka:viŋ] *n* utskjæring *c*, skurd *m*
case [keis] *n* tilfelle *nt*; sak *c*; koffert *m*; etui *nt*; **attaché** ~ dokumentmappe *c*; **in** ~ hvis
cash [kæʃ] *n* kontanter *pl*; *v* innkassere, heve; ~ **dispenser** minibank *m*
cashier [kæ'ʃiə] *n* kasserer *m*
cashmere ['kæʃmiə] *n* kasjmir *m*
casino [kə'si:nou] *n* (pl ~s) kasino *nt*
cask [ka:sk] *n* fat *nt*, tønne *c*
cassette [kə'set] *n* kassett *m*
cast [ka:st] *n* kast *nt*
***cast** [ka:st] *v* kaste; **cast iron** støpejern *nt*
castle ['ka:səl] *n* slott *nt*, borg *c*
casual ['kæʒuəl] *adj* uformell; tilfeldig, flyktig
casualty ['kæʒuəlti] *n* ulykke *c*; offer *nt*
cat [kæt] *n* katt *m*
catacomb ['kætəkoum] *n* katakombe *m*
catalogue ['kætəlɔg] *n* katalog *m*
catarrh [kə'ta:] *n* katarr *m*
catastrophe [kə'tæstrəfi] *n* katastrofe *m*
***catch** [kætʃ] *v* fange; *gripe; overrumple; nå, *rekke
catchword [kætʃwə:d] *n* stikkord *nt*
category ['kætigəri] *n* kategori *m*
caterer [ˌkeitərər] *n* catering *m*
cathedral [kə'θi:drəl] *n* katedral *m*, domkirke *c*
catheter [kə'θi:dər] *n*

kateter *nt*
catholic ['kæθəlik] *adj* katolsk
cattle ['kætəl] *pl* kveg *nt*
caught [kɔ:t] *v* (p, pp catch)
cauliflower ['kɔliflauə] *n* blomkål *m*
cause [kɔ:z] *v* forårsake; volde; *n* årsak *c*; grunn *m*; sak *c*; **~ to** *få til å
caution ['kɔ:ʃən] *n* forsiktighet *c*; *v* advare
cautious ['kɔ:ʃəs] *adj* forsiktig
cave [keiv] *n* grotte *c*; hule *c*
cavern ['kævən] *n* hule *c*
caviar ['kævia:] *n* kaviar *m*
cavity ['kævəti] *n* hulrom *nt*
CD [si:'di:] *n* CD *m*; **~ player** CD-spiller
CD (-ROM) [si:'di:(rɔm)] *n* CD-ROM *m*
cease [si:s] *v* opphøre
ceasefire [si:sfaiə] *n* våpenstillstand *m*
ceiling ['si:liŋ] *n* tak *nt*
celebrate ['selibreit] *v* feire
celebration [,seli'breiʃən] *n* feiring *c*
celebrity [si'lebrəti] *n* berømmelse *m*
celery ['seləri] *n* selleri *m*
cell [sel] *n* celle *c*
cellar ['selə] *n* kjeller *m*
cellphone ['selfoun] *n* mobil(-telefon) *m*
cement [si'ment] *n* sement *m*
cemetery ['semitri] *n* gravlund *m*
censorship ['sensəʃip] *n* sensur *m*
center ['sentə] *nAm* sentrum *nt*; midtpunkt *nt*
centigrade ['sentigreid] celsius
centimeter *Am*, **centimetre** ['sentimi:tə] *n* centimeter *m*
central ['sentrəl] *adj* sentral; **~ heating** sentralfyring *c*; **~ station** sentralstasjon *m*
centralize ['sentrəlaiz] *v* sentralisere
centre, **center** *Am* ['sentə] *n* sentrum *nt*; midtpunkt *nt*
century ['sentʃəri] *n* århundre *nt*
ceramics [si'ræmiks] *pl* keramikk *m*
ceremony ['serəməni] *n* seremoni *m*
certain ['sə:tən] *adj* sikker; viss
certainly ['sə:tənli] *adv* sikkert; klart
certificate [sə'tifikət] *n* attest *m*; vitnesbyrd *nt*, diplom *nt*, dokument *nt*
chain [tʃein] *n* kjede *nt* , kjetting *m*
chair [tʃεə] *n* stol *m*; sete *nt*
chairman ['tʃεəmən] *n* (pl -men) formann *m*, leder *m*
chairwoman ['tʃεəwumən] *n* (pl -women) formann *m*, leder *m*
chalet ['ʃælei] *n* hytte *c*
chalk [tʃɔ:k] *n* kritt *nt*
challenge ['tʃæləndʒ] *v*

utfordre; *n* utfordring *c*
chamber ['tʃeimbə] *n* rom *nt*
champagne [ʃæm'pein] *n* champagne *m*
champion ['tʃæmpjən] *n* mester *m*; forkjemper *m*
chance [tʃɑ:ns] *n* slump *m*; sjanse *m*, anledning *m*; risiko *m*; tilfelle *nt*; **by ~** tilfeldigvis
change [tʃeindʒ] *v* forandre; veksle; kle seg om; skifte; *n* forandring *c*, endring *c*; småpenger *pl*, vekslepenger *pl*; vekslepenger *pl*; **for a ~** til avveksling; unntaksvis
channel ['tʃænəl] *n* kanal *m*; **English Channel** Den engelske kanal
chaos ['keiɔs] *n* kaos *nt*
chaotic [kei'ɔtik] *adj* kaotisk
chap [tʃæp] *n* fyr *m*
chapel ['tʃæpəl] *n* kapell *nt*, kirke *c*
chaplain ['tʃæplin] *n* kapellan *m*
character ['kærəktə] *n* karakter *m*
characteristic [ˌkærəktə'ristik] *adj* betegnende, karakteristisk; *n* kjennetegn *nt*; karaktertrekk *nt*
characterize ['kærəktəraiz] *v* karakterisere
charcoal ['tʃɑ:koul] *n* trekull *nt*
charge [tʃɑ:dʒ] *v* kreve; *pålegge; anklage; laste; *n* pris *m*; ladning *m*, byrde *m*, belastning *m*; anklage *m*; **free of ~** kostfri; **in ~ of** ansvarlig for; ***take ~ of** *påta seg
charity ['tʃærəti] *n* velgjørenhet *c*
charm [tʃɑ:m] *n* sjarm *m*; amulett *m*
charming ['tʃɑ:miŋ] *adj* sjarmerende
chart [tʃɑ:t] *n* tabell *m*; diagram *nt*; sjøkart *nt*; **conversion ~** omregningstabell *m*
chase [tʃeis] *v* *forfølge; jage bort, *fordrive; *n* jakt *c*
chasm ['kæzəm] *n* kløft *c*
chassis ['ʃæsi] *n* (pl ~) chassis *nt*
chaste [tʃeist] *adj* kysk
chat [tʃæt] *v* prate, skravle; *n* prat *m* / *nt*
chatterbox ['tʃætəbɔks] *n* skravlebøtte *c*
chauffeur ['ʃoufə] *n* sjåfør *m*
cheap [tʃi:p] *adj* billig; gunstig
cheat [tʃi:t] *v* jukse, *snyte
check [tʃek] *v* sjekke, kontrollere; *n* rute *c*; regning *c*; sjekk *m*; **check!** sjakk!; **~ in** sjekke inn; **~ out** sjekke ut
checkbook ['tʃekbuk] *nAm* sjekkhefte *nt*

checkerboard ['tʃekəbɔːd] *nAm* sjakkbrett *nt*
checkers ['tʃekəz] *plAm* damspill *nt*
checkroom ['tʃekruːm] *nAm* garderobe *m*
checkup ['tʃekʌp] *n* undersøkelse *m*
cheek [tʃiːk] *n* kinn *nt*
cheekbone ['tʃiːkboun] *n* kinnbein *nt*
cheeky [tʃiːki] *adj* *colloquial* frekk, uforskammet
cheer [tʃiə] *v* hylle, juble; **~ up** oppmuntre
cheerful ['tʃiəfəl] *adj* lystig, glad
cheese [tʃiːz] *n* ost *m*
chef [ʃef] *n* kjøkkensjef *m*
chemical ['kemikəl] *adj* kjemisk
chemist ['kemist] *n* apoteker *m*; **chemist's** apotek *nt*
chemistry ['kemistri] *n* kjemi *m*
cheque [tʃek] *n* sjekk *m*
cherry ['tʃeri] *n* kirsebær *nt*
chess [tʃes] *n* sjakk *m*
chest [tʃest] *n* bryst *nt*; brystkasse *c*; kiste *c*; **~ of drawers** kommode *m*
chestnut ['tʃesnʌt] *n* kastanje *m*
chew [tʃuː] *v* tygge
chewing gum ['tʃuːiŋgʌm] *n* tyggegummi *m*
chicken ['tʃikin] *n* kylling *m*
chickenpox ['tʃikinpɔks] *n* vannkopper *pl*
chief [tʃiːf] *n* sjef *m*; *adj* hoved-, over-
chieftain ['tʃiːftən] *n* høvding *m*
child [tʃaild] *n* (pl children) barn *nt*
childbirth ['tʃaildbəːθ] *n* fødsel *m*
childhood ['tʃaildhud] *n* barndom *m*
Chile ['tʃili] Chile
Chilean ['tʃiliən] *adj* chilensk; *n* chilener *m*
chill [tʃil] *n* kuldegysning *m*
chilly ['tʃili] *adj* kjølig
chimes [tʃaimz] *pl* klokkespill *nt*
chimney ['tʃimni] *n* skorstein *m*
chin [tʃin] *n* hake *c*
China ['tʃainə] Kina
china ['tʃainə] *n* porselen *nt*
Chinese [tʃai'niːz] *adj* kinesisk; *n* kineser *m*
chip [tʃip] *n* flis *c*; chip *m*; brikke *c*; *v* *slå hakk i, snitte; **chips** pommes frites
chisel ['tʃizəl] *n* meisel *m*
chives [tʃaivz] *pl* gressløk *m*
chlorine ['klɔːriːn] *n* klor *m*
chocolate ['tʃɔklət] *n* sjokolade *m*; konfekt *m*
choice [tʃɔis] *n* valg *nt*; utvalg *nt*
choir [kwaiə] *n* kor *nt*
choke [tʃouk] *v* kveles; kvele; *n* choke *m*
***choose** [tʃuːz] *v* *velge

chop [tʃɔp] *n* kotelett *m*; *v* hakke
Christ [kraist] Kristus
christen ['krisən] *v* døpe
christening ['krisəniŋ] *n* dåp *m*
Christian ['kristʃən] *adj* kristen; **~ name** fornavn *nt*
Christmas ['krisməs] *n* jul *c*
chronic ['krɔnik] *adj* kronisk
chronological [ˌkrɔnə'lɔdʒikəl] *adj* kronologisk
chuckle ['tʃʌkəl] *v* klukke, *le
chunk [tʃʌŋk] *n* stort stykke
church [tʃəːtʃ] *n* kirke *c*
churchyard ['tʃəːtʃjɑːd] *n* kirkegård *m*
cigar [si'gɑː] *n* sigar *m*
cigarette [ˌsigə'ret] *n* sigarett *m*; **~ case** sigarettetui *nt*; **~ lighter** [ˌsigə'retˌlaitə] *n* lighter *m*
cinema ['sinəmə] *n* kino *m*
cinnamon ['sinəmən] *n* kanel *m*
circle ['səːkəl] *n* sirkel *m*; krets *m*; balkong *m*; *v* *omgi, omringe
circulation [ˌsəːkju'leiʃən] *n* sirkulasjon *m*; blodomløp *nt*; omløp *nt*
circumstance ['səːkəmstæns] *n* omstendighet *c*
circus ['səːkəs] *n* sirkus *nt*
citizen ['sitizən] *n* borger *m*
citizenship ['sitizənʃip] *n* statsborgerskap *nt*
city ['siti] *n* by *m*
civic ['sivik] *adj* borger-
civil ['sivəl] *adj* sivil; høflig; **~ law** sivilrett *m*; **~ servant** statstjenestemann *m*
civilian [si'viljən] *adj* sivil; *n* sivilperson *m*
civilization [ˌsivəlai'zeiʃən] *n* sivilisasjon *m*
civilized ['sivəlaizd] *adj* sivilisert
claim [kleim] *v* kreve; *påstå; *n* krav *nt*, fordring *c*
clamp [klæmp] *n* krampe *m*; skruestikke *c*
clap [klæp] *v* klappe, applaudere
clarify ['klærifai] *v* *klarlegge, *klargjøre
class [klɑːs] *n* klasse *c*
classical ['klæsikəl] *adj* klassisk
classify ['klæsifai] *v* gruppere
classmate ['klɑːsmeit] *n* klassekamerat *m*
classroom ['klɑːsruːm] *n* klasseværelse *nt*
clause [klɔːz] *n* klausul *m*
claw [klɔː] *n* klo *c*
clay [klei] *n* leire *c*
clean [kliːn] *adj* ren; *v* rense, gjøre rent
cleaning ['kliːniŋ] *n* rengjøring *c*; **~ fluid** vaskemiddel *nt*
clear [kliə] *adj* klar; tydelig; *v* rydde
clearing ['kliəriŋ] *n* lysning

m
cleft [kleft] *n* kløft *c*
clergyman ['klə:dʒimən] *n* (pl -men) prest *m*
clerk [klɑ:k] *n* sekretær *m*, kontorpersonale *nt*
clever ['klevə] *adj* intelligent; flink, begavet, klok
click [klik] *v* klikke; ~ **into place** klikke på plass
client ['klaiənt] *n* kunde *m*; klient *m*
cliff [klif] *n* klippe *m*
climate ['klaimit] *n* klima *nt*
climb [klaim] *v* klatre; *n* klatring *c*
cling ['kliŋ] *v* klistre, klenge; ~ **to** klamre seg til
clinic ['klinik] *n* klinikk *m*
cloak [klouk] *n* kappe *c*
cloakroom ['kloukru:m] *n* garderobe *m*
clock [klɔk] *n* klokke *c*; **at ... o'clock** klokken / klokka ...
cloister ['klɔistə] *n* kloster *nt*
clone [kloun] *v* klone; *n* kloning *c*
close[1] [klouz] *v* lukke; **closed** *adj* stengt, lukket
close[2] [klous] *adj* nær
closet ['klɔzit] *nAm* skap *nt*; garderobeskap *nt*
close-up ['klousʌp] *n* nærbilde *nt*
cloth [klɔθ] *n* stoff *nt*; klut *m*
clothes [klouðz] *pl* klær *pl*
clothing ['klouðiŋ] *n* klær *pl*
cloud [klaud] *n* sky *c*
cloudberry [klaudbəri] *n* molte *c*, multe *c*
cloudy ['klaudi] *adj* skyet, overskyet
clover ['klouvə] *n* kløver *m*
clown [klaun] *n* klovn *m*
club [klʌb] *n* klubb *m*, forening *c*; kølle *c*, klubbe *c*
clumsy ['klʌmzi] *adj* klosset
clutch [klʌtʃ] *n* clutch *m*; grep *nt*
coach [koutʃ] *n* buss *m*; jernbanevogn *c*; trener *m*
coal [koul] *n* kull *nt*
coarse [kɔ:s] *adj* grov
coast [koust] *n* kyst *m*
coat [kout] *n* frakk *m*, kåpe *c*; kappe *c*; ~ **hanger** kleshenger *m*
cocaine [kou'kein] *n* kokain *m / nt*
cock [kɔk] *n* hane *m*
cocktail ['kɔkteil] *n* cocktail *m*
coconut ['koukənʌt] *n* kokosnøtt *c*
cod [kɔd] *n* (pl ~) torsk *m*
code [koud] *n* kode *m*
coffee ['kɔfi] *n* kaffe *m*
cognac ['kɔnjæk] *n* konjakk *m*
coherence [kou'hiərəns] *n* sammenheng *m*
coin [kɔin] *n* mynt *m*
coincide [ˌkouin'said] *v* *falle sammen med
coincidence [ˌkouin'sidens]

m tilfelle *nt*, tilfeldighet *c*
cold [kould] *adj* kald; *n* kulde *c*; forkjølelse *m*; ***catch a ~** *bli forkjølet
collaborate [kə'læbərait] *v* samarbeide
collapse [kə'læps] *v* *bryte sammen
collar ['kɔlə] *n* halsbånd *nt*; krage *m*
collarbone ['kɔləboun] *n* kragebein *nt*
colleague ['kɔli:g] *n* kollega *m*
collect [kə'lekt] *v* samle; hente, avhente; samle inn
collection [kə'lekʃən] *n* samling *c*; kolleksjon *m*
collective [kə'lektiv] *adj* kollektiv
collector [kə'lektə] *n* samler *m*; innsamler *m*
college ['kɔlidʒ] *n* høyere læreinstitusjon; høyskole *m*
collide [kə'laid] *v* kollidere
collision [kə'liʒən] *n* sammenstøt *nt*, kollisjon *m*
Colombia [kə'lɔmbiə] Colombia
Colombian [kə'lɔmbiən] *adj* colombiansk; *n* colombianer *m*
colonel ['kə:nəl] *n* oberst *m*
colony ['kɔləni] *n* koloni *m*
colo(u)r ['kʌlə] *n* farge *m*; *v* farge
colo(u)r-blind ['kʌləblaind] *adj* fargeblind
colo(u)red ['kʌləd] *adj* farget
colo(u)rful ['kʌləfəl] *adj* fargerik
column ['kɔləm] *n* søyle *c*, spalte *c*; kolonne *m*
coma ['koumə] *n* koma *m*
comb [koum] *v* gre; *n* kam *m*
combat ['kɔmbæt] *n* kamp *m*; *v* bekjempe, kjempe
combination [ˌkɔmbi'neiʃən] *n* kombinasjon *m*
combine [kəm'bain] *v* kombinere; sammenstille
***come** [kʌm] *v* *komme; **~ across** støte på; *komme over
comedian [kə'mi:diən] *n* skuespiller *m*; komiker *m*
comedy ['kɔmədi] *n* komedie *m*, lystspill *nt*
comfort ['kʌmfət] *n* komfort *m*, bekvemmelighet *c*, velvære *nt*; trøst *m*; *v* trøste
comfortable ['kʌmfətəbəl] *adj* bekvem, komfortabel
comic ['kɔmik] *adj* komisk
comics ['kɔmiks] *pl* tegneserie *m*
coming ['kʌmiŋ] *n* komme *nt*; *adj* kommende
comma ['kɔmə] *n* komma *nt*
command [kə'ma:nd] *v* befale; *n* befaling *c*
commander [kə'ma:ndə] *n* befalshavende *m*
commemoration [kəˌmemə'reiʃən] *n* minnefest *m*; **in ~ of** til

minne om
commence [kə'mens] *v* begynne
comment ['kɔment] *n* kommentar *m*; *v* kommentere
commerce ['kɔmə:s] *n* handel *m*
commercial [kə'mə:ʃəl] *adj* handels-, kommersiell; *n* reklame *m*; **~ law** handelsrett *m*
commission [kə'miʃən] *n* kommisjon *m*
commit [kə'mit] *v* *overlate, betro; *begå
committee [kə'miti] *n* komité *m*
common ['kɔmən] *adj* felles; vanlig, alminnelig; simpel
commune ['kɔmju:n] *n* kommune *m*
communicate [kə'mju:nikeit] *v* meddele
communication [kə,mju:ni'keiʃən] *n* kommunikasjon *m*; meddelelse *m*
communism ['kɔmjunizəm] *n* kommunisme *m*
communist ['kɔmjunist] *n* kommunist *m*
community [kə'mju:nəti] *n* samfunn *nt*
commuter [kə'mju:tə] *n* pendler *m*
compact ['kɔmpækt] *adj* kompakt
companion [kəm'pænjən] *n* ledsager *m* ; guide *m*
company ['kʌmpəni] *n* selskap *nt*, firma *nt*
comparative [kəm'pærətiv] *adj* relativ
compare [kəm'pεə] *v* sammenligne
comparison [kəm'pærisən] *n* sammenligning *c*
compartment [kəm'pɑ:tmənt] *n* kupé *m*
compass ['kʌmpəs] *n* kompass *m* / *nt*; passer *m*
compel [kəm'pel] *v* tvinge; nøde
compensate ['kɔmpənseit] *v* kompensere, erstatte
compensation [,kɔmpən'seiʃən] *n* kompensasjon *m*; skadeserstatning *m*
compete [kəm'pi:t] *v* konkurrere
competition [,kɔmpə'tiʃən] *n* konkurranse *m*
competitor [kəm'petitər] *n* konkurrent *m*
compile [kəm'pail] *v* samle
complain [kəm'plein] *v* klage
complaint [kəm'pleint] *n* klage *c*
complete [kəm'pli:t] *adj* fullstendig, komplett; *v* fullende
completely [kəm'pli:tli] *adv* helt, totalt
complex ['kɔmpleks] *n* kompleks *nt*; *adj* innviklet
complexion [kəm'plekʃən]

n hudfarge *m*
complicated ['kɔmplikeitid] *adj* komplisert, innviklet
compliment ['kɔmplimənt] *n* kompliment *m*; *v* komplimentere
compose [kəm'pouz] *v* *sette sammen; komponere
composer [kəm'pouzə] *n* komponist *m*
composition [ˌkɔmpə'ziʃən] *n* komposisjon *m*; sammensetning *m*
comprehensive [ˌkɔmpri'hensiv] *adj* omfattende
comprise [kəm'praiz] *v* innbefatte, omfatte
compromise ['kɔmprəmaiz] *n* kompromiss *nt*
compulsory [kəm'pʌlsəri] *adj* obligatorisk
computer [kɔm'pjutə] *n* datamaskin *m*, PC *m*
conceal [kən'si:l] *v* skjule
conceited [kən'si:tid] *adj* selvgod; innbilsk *colloquial*
conceive [kən'si:v] *v* oppfatte, tenke ut; forestille seg
concentrate ['kɔnsəntreit] *v* konsentrere
concentration [ˌkɔnsən'treiʃən] *n* konsentrasjon *m*
conception [kən'sepʃən] *n* forestilling *c*; befruktning *m*
concern [kən'sə:n] *v* *gjelde, *angå; *n* bekymring *c*; anliggende *nt*; bedrift *m*, foretak *nt*, konsern *nt*
concerned [kən'sə:nd] *adj* bekymret; innblandet
concerning [kən'sə:niŋ] *prep* angående, vedrørende
concert ['kɔnsət] *n* konsert *m*; **~ hall** konsertsal *m*
concession [kən'seʃən] *n* konsesjon *m*
concierge [ˌkɔ̃si'ɛəʒ] *n* portner *m*
concise [kən'sais] *adj* konsis
conclusion [kəŋ'klu:ʒən] *n* konklusjon *m*, slutning *m*
concrete ['kɔŋkri:t] *adj* konkret; *n* betong *m*
concurrence [kəŋ'kʌrəns] *n* overensstemmelse *m*
concussion [kəŋ'kʌʃən] *n* hjernerystelse *m*
condition [kən'diʃən] *n* vilkår *nt*; kondisjon *m*, tilstand *m*; omstendighet *c*
conditional [kən'diʃənəl] *adj* betinget
conditioner [kən'diʃənə] *n* hårbalsam *m*
condom ['kɔndɔm] *n* kondom *nt*
conduct[1] ['kɔndʌkt] *n* oppførsel *m*
conduct[2] [kən'dʌkt] *v* ledsage; dirigere
conductor [kən'dʌktə] *n* leder *m*; dirigent *m*

conference ['kɔnfərəns] *n* konferanse *m*
confess [kən'fes] *v* *tilstå; skrifte; bekjenne
confession [kən'feʃən] *n* tilståelse *m*; skriftemål *nt*
confidence ['kɔnfidəns] *n* tillit *m*
confident ['kɔnfidənt] *adj* tillitsfull
confidential [ˌkɔnfi'denʃəl] *adj* konfidensiell
confirm [kən'fəːm] *v* bekrefte
confirmation [ˌkɔnfə'meiʃən] *n* bekreftelse *m*
confiscate ['kɔnfiskeit] *v* *beslaglegge, konfiskere
conflict ['kɔnflikt] *n* konflikt *m*
confuse [kən'fjuːz] *v* forvirre
confusion [kən'fjuːʒən] *n* forvirring *c*
congratulate [kəŋ'grætʃuleit] *v* gratulere
congratulation [kəŋˌgrætʃu'leiʃən] *n* gratulasjon *m*, lykkønskning *m*
congregation [ˌkɔŋgri'geiʃən] *n* menighet *c*; forsamling *c*
congress ['kɔŋgres] *n* kongress *m*
connect [kə'nekt] *v* *forbinde; kople; kople til
connection [kə'nekʃən] *n* forbindelse *m*; sammenheng *m*
connoisseur [ˌkɔnə'səː] *n* kjenner *m*
conquer ['kɔŋkə] *v* erobre; beseire
conqueror ['kɔŋkərə] *n* erobrer *m*
conquest ['kɔŋkwest] *n* erobring *c*
conscience ['kɔnʃəns] *n* samvittighet *c*
conscious ['kɔnʃəs] *adj* bevisst
consciousness ['kɔnʃəsnəs] *n* bevissthet *c*
conscript ['kɔnskript] *n* vernepliktig *m*
consent [kən'sent] *v* samtykke; bifalle; *n* samtykke *nt*
consequence ['kɔnsikwəns] *n* følge *m*, konsekvens *m*
consequently ['kɔnsikwəntli] *adv* altså
conservative [kən'səːvətiv] *adj* konservativ
consider [kən'sidə] *v* betrakte; overveie; *anse, mene
considerable [kən'sidərəbəl] *adj* betraktelig; betydelig, anselig
considerate [kən'sidərət] *adj* hensynsfull
consideration [kənˌsidə'reiʃən] *n* overveielse *m*; omtanke *m*;

hensyn *nt*
considering [kən'sidəriŋ] *prep* i betraktning av
consignment [kən'sainmənt] *n* sending *c*
consist of [kən'sist] *bestå av
conspire [kən'spaiə] *v* sammensverge seg
constant ['kɔnstənt] *adj* konstant
constipation [ˌkɔnsti'peiʃən] *n* forstoppelse *m*
constituency [kən'stitʃuənsi] *n* valgkrets *m*
constitution [ˌkɔnsti'tju:ʃən] *n* grunnlov *m*
construct [kən'strʌkt] *v* konstruere; bygge, oppføre
construction [kən'strʌkʃən] *n* konstruksjon *m*; oppførelse *m*, bygning *m*
consul ['kɔnsəl] *n* konsul *m*
consulate ['kɔnsjulət] *n* konsulat *nt*
consult [kən'sʌlt] *v* *rådspørre
consultation [ˌkɔnsəl'teiʃən] *n* konsultasjon *m*
consume [kən'sju:m] *v* konsumere, forbruke; *ødelegge
consumer [kən'sju:mə] *n* forbruker *m*
consumption [kən'sumpʃən] *n* forbruk *nt*, konsum *nt*
contact ['kɔntækt] *n* kontakt *m*; *v* kontakte; ~ **lenses** kontaktlinser *pl*
contagious [kən'teidʒəs] *adj* smittsom, smittende
contain [kən'tein] *v* *inneholde; romme
container [kən'teinə] *n* beholder *m*; container *m*
contemporary [kən'tempərəri] *adj* samtidig
contempt [kən'tempt] *n* ringeakt *m*, forakt *m*
content [kən'tent] *adj* tilfreds
contentment [kən'tentment] *n* tilfredshet *c*
contents ['kɔntents] *pl* innhold *nt*
contest ['kɔntest] *n* strid *m*; konkurranse *m*
continent ['kɔntinənt] *n* kontinent *nt*, verdensdel *m*
continental [ˌkɔnti'nentəl] *adj* kontinental
continual [kən'tinjuəl] *adj* stadig; **continually** *adv* uopphørlig
continue [kən'tinju:] *v* *fortsette
continuous [kən'tinjuəs] *adj* uavbrutt, kontinuerlig
contour ['kɔntuə] *n* omriss *nt*
contraceptive [ˌkɔntrə'septiv] *n*

prevensjonsmiddel *nt*
contract[1] ['kɔntrækt] *n* kontrakt *m*
contract[2] [kən'trækt] *v* *pådra seg
contractor [kən'træktə] *n* entreprenør *m*
contradict [ˌkɔntrə'dikt] *v* *motsi
contradictory [ˌkɔntrə'diktəri] *adj* motstridende
contrary ['kɔntrəri] *n* det motsatte; *adj* motsatt; **on the ~** tvert imot
contrast ['kɔntrɑːst] *n* kontrast *m*, motsetning *m*
contribution [ˌkɔntri'bjuːʃən] *n* bidrag *nt*
control [kən'troul] *n* kontroll *m*; *v* kontrollere
controversial [ˌkɔntrə'vəːʃəl] *adj* kontroversiell, omstridt
convenience [kən'viːnjəns] *n* bekvemmelighet *c*
convenient [kən'viːnjənt] *adj* bekvem; passende, egnet, beleilig
convent ['kɔnvənt] *n* nonnekloster *nt*
conversation [ˌkɔnvə'seiʃən] *n* samtale *m*
convert [kən'vəːt] *v* omvende; omregne
convict[1] [kən'vikt] *v* *finne skyldig
convict[2] ['kɔnvikt] *n* domfelt *m*
conviction [kən'vikʃən] *n* overbevisning *m*; domfellelse *m*
convince [kən'vins] *v* overbevise
convulsion [kən'vʌlʃən] *n* krampetrekning *m*
cook [kuk] *n* kokk *m*; *v* lage mat, tilberede
cookbook ['kukbuk] *nAm* kokebok *c*
cooker ['kukə] *n* komfyr *m*; **gas ~** gasskomfyr *m*
cookery book ['kukəribuk] *n* kokebok *c*
cookie ['kuki] *nAm* småkake *c*
cool [kuːl] *adj* kjølig
cooperation [kouˌɔpə'reiʃən] *n* samarbeid *nt*; medvirkning *m*
co-operative [kou'ɔpərətiv] *adj* kooperativ; samarbeidsvillig
coordinate [kou'ɔːdineit] *v* samordne
coordination [kouˌɔːdi'neiʃən] *n* koordinasjon *m*
cope [koup] *v* greie, mestre
copper ['kɔpə] *n* kopper *nt*
copy ['kɔpi] *n* kopi *m*; eksemplar *nt*; *v* kopiere; etterligne
coral ['kɔrəl] *n* korall *m*
cord [kɔːd] *n* tau *nt*; snor *c*
cordial ['kɔːdiəl] *adj* hjertelig

corduroy ['kɔ:dərɔi] *n* kordfløyel *m*
core [kɔ:] *n* kjerne *m*; kjernehus *nt*
cork [kɔ:k] *n* kork *m*
corkscrew ['kɔ:kskru:] *n* korketrekker *m*
corn [kɔ:n] *n* korn *nt*; liktorn *m*; ~ **on the cob** maiskolbe *m*
corner ['kɔ:nə] *n* hjørne *nt*
cornfield ['kɔ:nfi:ld] *n* kornåker *m*
corpse [kɔ:ps] *n* lik *nt*
corpulent ['kɔ:pjulənt] *adj* korpulent; tykk, fyldig
correct [kə'rekt] *adj* korrekt, riktig; *v* rette, korrigere
correction [kə'rekʃən] *n* rettelse *m*
correctness [kə'rektnəs] *n* nøyaktighet *c*
correspond [ˌkɔri'spɔnd] *v* brevveksle; svare til, tilsvare
correspondence [ˌkɔri'spɔndəns] *n* korrespondanse *m*, brevveksling *c*
correspondent [ˌkɔri'spɔndənt] *n* korrespondent *m*
corridor ['kɔridɔ:] *n* korridor *m*
corrupt [kə'rʌpt] *adj* korrupt; *v* *bestikke
corruption [kə'rʌpʃən] *n* bestikkelse *m*
corset ['kɔ:sit] *n* korsett *nt*
cosmetics [kɔz'metiks] *pl* kosmetika *pl*
cost [kɔst] *n* kostnad *m*; pris *m*
***cost** [kɔst] *v* koste
cosy ['kouzi] *adj* koselig
cot [kɔt] *nAm* feltseng *c*
cottage ['kɔtidʒ] *n* hytte *c*
cotton ['kɔtən] *n* bomull *m*; bomulls-; ~ **wool** *n* vatt *m*
couch [kautʃ] *n* sofa *m*
cough [kɔf] *n* hoste *m*; *v* hoste
could [kud] *v* (p can)
council ['kaunsəl] *n* råd *nt*; rådsforsamling *c*
councillor ['kaunsələ] *n* rådsmedlem *nt*
counsel ['kaunsəl] *n* råd *nt*
counsellor ['kaunsələ] *n* rådgiver *m*
count [kaunt] *v* *telle; *telle opp; medregne; *anse; *n* greve *m*
counter ['kauntə] *n* disk *m*
counterfeit ['kauntəfi:t] *v* forfalske
countess ['kauntis] *n* grevinne *c*
country ['kʌntri] *n* land *nt*; landområde *nt*; ~ **house** landsted *nt*
countryman ['kʌntrimən] *n* (pl -men) landsmann *m*
county ['kaunti] *n* grevskap *nt*
couple ['kʌpəl] *n* par *nt*
coupon ['ku:pɔn] *n* kupong *m*
courage ['kʌridʒ] *n*

tapperhet *c*, mot *nt*
courageous [kə'reidʒəs] *adj* tapper, modig
course [kɔːs] *n* kurs *m*; rett *m*; løp *nt*; kurs *nt*; **intensive ~** intensivkurs *nt*; **of ~** naturligvis, selvfølgelig
court [kɔːt] *n* domstol *m*; hoff *nt*; gårdsplass *m*
courteous ['kəːtiəs] *adj* høflig
cousin ['kʌzən] *n* kusine *c*, fetter *m*
cover ['kʌvə] *v* dekke; *n* ly *nt*, skjul *nt*; lokk *nt*; perm *m*; **~ charge** kuvertavgift *c*
cow [kau] *n* ku *c*
coward ['kauəd] *n* feiging *m*
cowardly ['kauədli] *adj* feig
crab [kræb] *n* krabbe *c*
crack [kræk] *n* smell *nt*; sprekk *m*; *v* *smelle; *slå i stykker, *knekke, *sprekke
cracker ['krækə] *nAm* kjeks *m*
cradle ['kreidəl] *n* vugge *c*
cramp [kræmp] *n* krampe *m*
crane [krein] *n* kran *c*
crap [kræp] *n vulgar* dritt *m*
crash [kræʃ] *n* kollisjon *m*; *v* kollidere; styrte; **~ barrier** barriere *m*
crate [kreit] *n* kasse *c*
crater ['kreitə] *n* krater *nt*
crawl [krɔːl] *v* krabbe; *n* crawl *m*
craze [kreiz] *n* mani *m*
crazy ['kreizi] *adj* gal; sinnssyk
creak [kriːk] *v* knirke
cream [kriːm] *n* krem *m*; fløte *m*; *adj* kremgul
creamy ['kriːmi] *adj* fløteaktig
crease [kriːs] *v* skrukke, krølle; *n* fold *m*; rynke *c*; press *m*
create [kri'eit] *v* skape; kreere
creative [kri'eitiv] *adj* kreativ, skapende
creature ['kriːtʃə] *n* skapning *m*
credible ['kredibəl] *adj* troverdig
credit ['kredit] *n* kreditt *m*; *v* *godskrive; **~ card** kredittkort *nt*
creditor ['kreditə] *n* kreditor *m*
credulous ['kredjuləs] *adj* godtroende
creek [kriːk] *n* vik *c*
***creep** [kriːp] *v* *krype
creepy ['kriːpi] *adj* nifs, uhyggelig
cremate [kri'meit] *v* kremere
crew [kruː] *n* mannskap *nt*
cricket ['krikit] *n* cricket *m*; siriss *m*
crime [kraim] *n* forbrytelse *m*
criminal ['kriminəl] *n* forbryter *m*; *adj* forbrytersk, kriminell; **~ law** strafferett *m*
criminality [ˌkrimi'næləti] *n* kriminalitet *m*
crimson ['krimzən] *adj*

høyrød
crisis ['kraisis] *n* (pl crises) krise *c*
crisp [krisp] *adj* sprø
critic ['kritik] *n* kritiker *m*
critical ['kritikəl] *adj* kritisk; risikabel
criticism ['kritisizəm] *n* kritikk *m*
criticize ['kritisaiz] *v* kritisere
crochet ['krouʃei] *v* hekle
crockery ['krɔkəri] *n* steintøy *nt*
crocodile ['krɔkədail] *n* krokodille *c*
crooked ['krukid] *adj* kroket, fordreid; uærlig
crop [krɔp] *n* avling *c*
cross [krɔs] *v* *gå over; *adj* tverr, sint; *n* kors *nt*
cross-eyed ['krɔsaid] *adj* skjeløyd
crossing ['krɔsiŋ] *n* overfart *m*; kryss *nt*; fotgjengerovergang *m*; jernbaneovergang *m*
crossroads ['krɔsroudz] *n* gatekryss *nt*
crosswalk ['krɔswɔ:k] *nAm* fotgjengerovergang *m*
crow [krou] *n* kråke *c*
crowbar ['krouba:] *n* brekkjern *nt*
crowd [kraud] *n* mengde *m*, folkemengde *m*
crowded ['kraudid] *adj* overfylt; tettpakket
crown [kraun] *n* krone *c*; *v* krone
crucifix ['kru:sifiks] *n* krusifiks *nt*
crucifixion [,kru:si'fikʃən] *n* korsfestelse *m*
crucify ['kru:sifai] *v* korsfeste
cruel [kruəl] *adj* grusom
cruise [kru:z] *n* sjøreise *c*, cruise *nt*
crumb [krʌm] *n* smule *m*
crusade [kru:'seid] *n* korstog *nt*
crust [krʌst] *n* skorpe *c*
crutch [krʌtʃ] *n* krykke *c*
cry [krai] *v* *gråte; *skrike; rope; *n* skrik *nt*; rop *nt*
crystal ['kristəl] *n* krystall *m / nt*; *adj* krystall-
Cuba ['kju:bə] Cuba
Cuban ['kju:bən] *adj* kubansk; *n* kubaner *m*
cube [kju:b] *n* kube *m*; terning *m*
cuckoo ['kuku:] *n* gjøk *m*
cucumber ['kju:kəmbə] *n* agurk *m*
cuddle ['kʌdəl] *v* kjæle med; klemme
cuff [kʌf] *n* mansjett *m*; **~ links** *pl* mansjettknapper *pl*
cul-de-sac ['kʌldəsæk] *n* blindgate *c*
cultivate ['kʌltiveit] *v* dyrke
culture ['kʌltʃə] *n* kultur *m*
cultured ['kʌltʃəd] *adj* kultivert
cunning ['kʌniŋ] *adj* slu
cup [kʌp] *n* kopp *m*; pokal *m*

cupboard ['kʌbəd] *n* skap *nt*
curb [kə:b] *n* fortauskant *m*; *v* tøyle
cure [kjuə] *v* helbrede, lege; *n* kur *m*; helbredelse *m*
curiosity [ˌkjuəri'ɔsəti] *n* nysgjerrighet *c*
curious ['kjuəriəs] *adj* vitebegjærlig, nysgjerrig; merkverdig
curl [kə:l] *v* krølle; *n* krøll *m*
curly ['kə:li] *adj* krøllet
currant ['kʌrənt] *n* rips *m*; solbær *nt*
currency ['kʌrənsi] *n* valuta *m*; **foreign ~** utenlandsk valuta
current ['kʌrənt] *n* strøm *m*; *adj* nåværende, aktuell; **alternating ~** vekselstrøm *m*; **direct ~** likestrøm *m*
curry ['kʌri] *n* karri *m*
curse [kə:s] *v* banne; forbanne; *n* banning *c*; forbannelse *m*
curtain ['kə:tən] *n* gardin *m* / *nt*; teppe *nt*
curve [kə:v] *n* kurve *m*; krumning *m*
curved [kə:vd] *adj* krum, buet
cushion ['kuʃən] *n* pute *c*
custody ['kʌstədi] *n* varetekt *c*; forvaring *c*; formynderskap *nt*
custom ['kʌstəm] *n* vane *m*; skikk *m*
customary ['kʌstəməri] *adj* alminnelig, sedvanlig, vanlig
customer ['kʌstəmə] *n* kunde *m*
customs ['kʌstəmz] *pl* toll *m*; **~ duty** tollavgift *c*; **~ officer** toller *m*
cut [kʌt] *n* kutt *nt*
***cut** [kʌt] *v* *skjære; klippe; *skjære ned; **~ off** *skjære av; klippe av; stenge av
cutlery ['kʌtləri] *n* bestikk *nt*
cutlet ['kʌtlət] *n* snitsel *m*
cycle ['saikəl] *n* sykkel *m*; kretsløp *nt*, syklus *m*
cycling ['saikliŋ] *n* sykling *c*
cyclist ['saiklist] *n* syklist *m*
cylinder ['silində] *n* sylinder *m*; **~ head** topplokk *nt*

D

dad [dæd], **daddy** ['dædi] *n* pappa *m*
daffodil ['dæfədil] *n* påskelilje *c*
daily ['deili] *adj* daglig; *n* dagsavis *c*
dairy ['dɛəri] *n* meieri *nt*; melkebutikk *m*
dam [dæm] *n* demning *m*
damage ['dæmidʒ] *n* skade *m*; *v* skade
damn [dæm] *v* forbanne; **~!**

faen *colloquial*
damp [dæmp] *adj* fuktig; *n* fuktighet *c*; *v* fukte
dance [dɑːns] *v* danse; *n* dans *m*
dandelion ['dændilaiən] *n* løvetann *c*
dandruff ['dændrəf] *n* flass *nt*
Dane [dein] *n* danske *m*
danger ['deindʒə] *n* fare *m*
dangerous ['deindʒərəs] *adj* farlig
Danish ['deiniʃ] *adj* dansk; **~ pastry** wienerbrød *nt*
dare [dɛə] *v* *tore, våge; utfordre
daring ['dɛəriŋ] *adj* dristig
dark [dɑːk] *adj* mørk; *n* mørke *nt*
darling ['dɑːliŋ] *n* kjæreste *m*, skatt *m*
darn [dɑːn] *v* stoppe
dash [dæʃ] *v* styrte; *n* tankestrek *m*
dashboard ['dæʃbɔːd] *n* instrumentbord *nt*
data ['deitə] *pl* data *pl*
date[1] [deit] *n* dato *m*; avtale *m*; stevnemøte *nt*; *v* datere; **out of ~** umoderne
date[2] [deit] *n* daddel *m*
daughter ['dɔːtə] *n* datter *c*
daughter-in-law ['dɔːtərinlɔ] *n* (pl daughters-) svigerdatter *c*
dawn [dɔːn] *n* daggry *nt*
day [dei] *n* dag *m*; **by ~** om dagen; **~ trip** dagstur *m*; **per ~** per dag; **the ~ before yesterday** i forgårs
daybreak ['deibreik] *n* daggry *nt*
daylight ['deilait] *n* dagslys *nt*; **~ saving time** sommertid *c*
day spa ['dei‿ˌspɑː] *n* dagspa *c*
dead [ded] *adj* død
deaf [def] *adj* døv
deal [diːl] *n* transaksjon *m*, handel *m*
***deal** [diːl] *v* dele ut; **~ with** *ta seg av; handle med
dealer ['diːlə] *n* forhandler *m*; dealer *m*
dear [diə] *adj* kjær; dyr; dyrebar
death [deθ] *n* død *m*; **~ penalty** dødsstraff *m*
debate [di'beit] *n* debatt *m*
debit ['debit] *n* debet *m*
debit card ['debit‿ˌkɑːd] *n* debetkort *nt*
debt [det] *n* gjeld *c*
decaffeinated [diː'kæfineitid] *adj* kaffeinfri
deceit [di'siːt] *n* bedrag *nt*
deceive [di'siːv] *v* *bedra
December [di'sembə] desember
decency ['diːsənsi] *n* anstendighet *c*
decent ['diːsənt] *adj* anstendig
decide [di'said] *v* *avgjøre
decision [di'siʒən] *n* beslutning *m*, avgjørelse *m*
deck [dek] *n* dekk *nt*; **~**

chair fluktstol *m*
declaration [ˌdeklə'reiʃən] *n* erklæring *c*; deklarasjon *m*
declare [di'klɛə] *v* erklære; *oppgi; deklarere
decorate [ˌdekə'reit] *v* pynte; innrede
decoration [ˌdekə'reiʃən] *n* dekorasjon *m*
decrease [diː'kriːs] *v* minke, minske; *avta; *n* nedgang *m*
dedicate ['dedikeit] *v* vie
deduce [di'djuːs] *v* utlede; avlede; konkludere
deduct [di'dʌkt] *v* *trekke fra
deed [diːd] *n* handling *c*, gjerning *c*
deep [diːp] *adj* dyp
deep-freeze [ˌdiːp'friːz] *n* dypfryser *m*
deer [diə] *n* (pl ~) hjort *m*
defeat [di'fiːt] *v* *overvinne; *n* nederlag *nt*
defective [di'fektiv] *adj* mangelfull
defence, **defense** *Am* [di'fens] *n* forsvar *nt*; vern *nt*
defend [di'fend] *v* forsvare
deficiency [di'fiʃənsi] *n* mangel *m*
deficit ['defisit] *n* underskudd *nt*
define [di'fain] *v* bestemme, definere
definite ['definit] *adj* bestemt
definition [ˌdefi'niʃən] *n* definisjon *m*
deformed [di'fɔːmd] *adj* misdannet, vanskapt
degree [di'griː] *n* grad *m*
delay [di'lei] *v* forsinke; *utsette; *n* forsinkelse *m*; utsettelse *m*
delegate ['deligət] *n* utsending *m*
delegation [ˌdeli'geiʃən] *n* delegasjon *m*
deliberate[1] [di'libəreit] *v* overveie, *rådslå
deliberate[2] [di'libərət] *adj* overlagt
deliberation [diˌlibə'reiʃən] *n* overveielse *m*, rådslagning *m*
delicacy ['delikəsi] *n* lekkerbisken *m*; finfølelse *m*
delicate ['delikət] *adj* delikat
delicatessen [ˌdelikə'tesən] *n* delikatesse *m*; matvareforretning *c*
delicious [di'liʃəs] *adj* deilig, lekker
delight [di'lait] *n* glede *c*, fryd *m*; *v* glede; **I'm ~ed** gleder meg
delightful [di'laitfəl] *adj* henrivende, herlig
deliver [di'livə] *v* levere, avlevere
delivery [di'livəri] *n* levering *c*, leveranse *m*; nedkomst *m*; **~ van** varebil *m*

demand [di'mɑːnd] *v* behøve, forlange; *n* krav *nt*; etterspørsel *m*
democracy [di'mɔkrəsi] *n* demokrati *nt*
democratic [ˌdemə'krætik] *adj* demokratisk
demolish [di'mɔliʃ] *v* *rive ned; *ødelegge
demolition [ˌdemə'liʃən] *n* nedrivning *m*
demonstrate ['demənstreit] *v* bevise; demonstrere
demonstration [ˌdemən'streiʃən] *n* demonstrasjon *m*
den [den] *n* hi *nt*; hule *c*
Denmark ['denmɑːk] Danmark
denomination [diˌnɔmi'neiʃən] *n* benevnelse *m*; trosretning *m*; verdienhet *m*
dense [dens] *adj* tett
dent [dent] *n* bulk *m*
dentist ['dentist] *n* tannlege *m*
denture ['dentʃə] *n* gebiss *nt*
deny [di'nai] *v* benekte; nekte
deodorant [diː'oudərənt] *n* deodorant *m*
depart [di'pɑːt] *v* reise bort, *gå sin vei; *avgå ved døden
department [di'pɑːtmənt] *n* avdeling *c*, departement *nt*; **~ store** stormagasin *nt*, varehus *nt*
departure [di'pɑːtʃə] *n* avreise *c*; avgang *m*
dependant [di'pendənt] *adj* avhengig
depend on [di'pend] bero på; **that depends** det kommer an på
deposit [di'pɔzit] *n* depositum *nt*; pant *m*; bunnfall *nt*, avleiring *c*; *v* deponere
depot ['depou] *n* lagerplass *m*; stasjon *m*
depress [di'pres] *v* tynge ned
depressing [di'presiŋ] *adj* deprimerende
depression [di'preʃən] *n* depresjon *m*; lavtrykk *nt*; nedgang *m*
deprive of [di'praiv] *frata
depth [depθ] *n* dybde *m*
deputy ['depjuti] *n* deputert *m*; stedfortreder *m*
descend [di'send] *v* *gå ned
descendant [di'sendənt] *n* etterkommer *m*
descent [di'sent] *n* nedstigning *m*
describe [di'skraib] *v* *beskrive
description [di'skripʃən] *n* beskrivelse *m*; signalement *nt*
desert[1] ['dezət] *n* ørken *m*; *adj* øde
desert[2] [di'zəːt] *v* desertere; *forlate
deserve [di'zəːv] *v* fortjene
design [di'zain] *v* tegne opp; *n* design *m*; utkast *nt*;

hensikt *m*
designate ['dezigneit] *v* peke ut
desirable [di'zaiərəbəl] *adj* attråverdig, ønskelig
desire [di'zaiə] *n* ønske *nt*; lyst *c*, begjær *nt*; *v* ønske, begjære
desk [desk] *n* skrivebord *nt*; kateter *nt*; pult *m*
despair [di'spɛə] *n* håpløshet *c*; *v* fortvile
despatch [di'spætʃ] *v* avsende
desperate ['despərət] *adj* fortvilet
despise [di'spaiz] *v* forakte
despite [di'spait] *prep* tross
dessert [di'zəːt] *n* dessert *m*
destination [ˌdesti'neiʃən] *n* bestemmelsessted *nt*
destine ['destin] *v* bestemme
destiny ['destini] *n* skjebne *m*, lodd *m*
destroy [di'strɔi] *v* *ødelegge, *tilintetgjøre
destruction [di'strʌkʃən] *n* ødeleggelse *m*; undergang *m*
detach [di'tætʃ] *v* løsne
detail ['diːteil] *n* detalj *m*
detailed ['diːteild] *adj* detaljert, utførlig
detect [di'tekt] *v* oppdage
detective [di'tektiv] *n* detektiv *m*; ~ **story** krim *m*
detergent [di'təːdʒənt] *n* vaskepulver *nt*
determine [di'təːmin] *v* *fastsette, bestemme
determined [di'təːmind] *adj* bestemt
detest [di'test] *v* avsky, hate
detour ['diːtuə] *n* omvei *m*; omkjøring *c*
devaluation [ˌdiːvælju'eiʃən] *n* devaluering *c*
devalue [ˌdiː'væljuː] *v* devaluere
develop [di'veləp] *v* utvikle; fremkalle
development [di'veləpmənt] *n* utvikling *c*
deviate ['diːvieit] *v* *avvike
devil ['devəl] *n* djevel *m*
devote [di'vout] *v* *hengi
dew [djuː] *n* dugg *m*
diabetes [ˌdaiə'biːtiːz] *n* sukkersyke *m*, diabetes *m*
diabetic [ˌdaiə'betik] *n* diabetiker *m*, sukkersykepasient *m*
diagnose [ˌdaiəg'nouz] *v* stille en diagnose; konstatere
diagnosis [ˌdaiəg'nousis] *n* (pl -ses) diagnose *m*
diagonal [dai'ægənəl] *n* diagonal *m*; *adj* diagonal
diagram ['daiəgræm] *n* diagram *nt*; grafisk fremstilling
dial ['daiəl] *n* urskive *c*; *v* slå, taste
dialect ['daiəlekt] *n* dialekt *m*
diamond ['daiəmənd] *n*

diamant *m*
diaper ['daiəpə] *nAm* bleie *c*
diaphragm ['daiəfræm] *n* mellomgulv *nt*
diarrh(o)ea [daiə'riə] *n* diaré *m*
diary ['daiəri] *n* almanakk *m*; dagbok *c*
dictate [dik'teit] *v* diktere
dictator [dik'teitə] *n* diktator *m*
dictionary ['dikʃənəri] *n* ordbok *c*
did [did] *v* (p do)
die [dai] *v* dø
diesel ['di:zəl] *n* diesel *m*
diet ['daiət] *n* diett *m*
differ ['difə] *v* *være forskjellig
difference ['difərəns] *n* forskjell *m*
different ['difərənt] *adj* forskjellig; annerledes
difficult ['difikəlt] *adj* vanskelig; vrien
difficulty ['difikəlti] *n* vanskelighet *c*
***dig** [dig] *v* grave
digest [di'dʒest] *v* fordøye
digestible [di'dʒestəbəl] *adj* fordøyelig
digestion [di'dʒestʃən] *n* fordøyelse *m*
digit ['didʒit] *n* siffer *nt*
digital ['diʒitəl] *adj* digital
digital camera ['didʒitəl‿'kæmərə] *n* digitalkamera *nt*
digital photo ['didʒitəl‿'foutou] *n* digitalbilde *nt*
digital projector ['didʒitəl‿prə'jektə] *n* Digital prosjektør *c*
dignified ['dignifaid] *adj* verdig
dignity ['digniti] *n* verdighet *c*
dilapidated [di'læpideitid] *adj* forfallen
diligence ['dilidʒəns] *n* flid *m*
diligent ['dilidʒənt] *adj* flittig
dilute [dai'lju:t] *v* fortynne
dim [dim] *adj* dunkel, matt; uklar, utydelig
din [din] *v* bråk *nt*
dine [dain] *v* spise middag
dinghy ['diŋgi] *n* jolle *c*
dining car ['dainiŋkɑ:] *n* spisevogn *c*
dining room ['dainiŋru:m] *n* spisestue *c*; spisesal *m*
dinner ['dinə] *n* middag *m*; lunsj *m*, aftensmat *m*; **~ jacket** smoking *m*; **~ service** servise *nt*
diphtheria [dif'θiəriə] *n* difteri *m*
diploma [di'ploumə] *n* diplom *nt*
diplomat ['dipləmæt] *n* diplomat *m*
direct[1] ['direkt] *adj* direkte, likefrem
direct [2] [di'rekt] *v* rette; veilede; styre; regissere
direction [di'rekʃən] *n* retning *m*; direktiv *nt*; regi

m; styre *nt*, veiledning *m*; **directional signal** *Am* retningsviser *m*; **directions for use** bruksanvisning *m*
directive [di'rektiv] *n* direktiv *nt*
director [di'rektə] *n* direktør *m*; regissør *m*
directory [di'rektəri] *n* adressebok *c*; telefonkatalog *m*
dirt [də:t] *n* skitt *m*
dirty ['də:ti] *adj* skitten, svart
disabled [di'seibəld] *adj* funksjonshemmet, ufør
disadvantage [ˌdisəd'vɑ:ntidʒ] *n* ulempe *m*
disagree [ˌdisə'gri:] *v* *være uenig
disagreeable [ˌdisə'gri:əbəl] *adj* ubehagelig
disappear [ˌdisə'piə] *v* *forsvinne
disappoint [ˌdisə'pɔint] *v* skuffe
disappointment [ˌdisə'pɔintmənt] *n* skuffelse *m*
disapprove [ˌdisə'pru:v] *v* misbillige
disaster [di'zɑ:stə] *n* katastrofe *m*; ulykke *c*
disastrous [di'zɑ:strəs] *adj* katastrofal
disc [disk] *n* skive *c*; plate *c*; **slipped ~** skiveprolaps *m*
discard [di'skɑ:d] *v* kassere
discharge [dis'tʃɑ:dʒ] *v* lesse av, losse; **~ of** *frita for
discipline ['disiplin] *n* disiplin *m*
discolo(u)r [di'skʌlə] *v* farge av
disconnect [ˌdiskə'nekt] *v* utkople; *ta ut kontakten
discontented [ˌdiskən'tentid] *adj* misfornøyd
discontinue [ˌdiskən'tinju:] *v* stanse, opphøre
discount ['diskaunt] *n* rabatt *m*, avslag *nt*
discourage ['diskʌrədʒ] *v* *ta motet fra, avskrekke
discover [di'skʌvə] *v* oppdage
discovery [di'skʌvəri] *n* oppdagelse *m*
discuss [di'skʌs] *v* diskutere; debattere
discussion [di'skʌʃən] *n* diskusjon *m*; samtale *m*, debatt *m*
disease [di'zi:z] *n* sykdom *m*
disembark [ˌdisim'bɑ:k] *v* *gå fra borde, *gå i land
disgrace [dis'greis] *n* skam *c*
disguise [dis'gaiz] *v* forkle seg; *n* forkledning *m*
disgust [dis'gʌst] *n* avsky *m*
disgusting [dis'gʌstiŋ] *adj* motbydelig, avskyelig
dish [diʃ] *n* tallerken *m*; fat *nt*; rett *m*; **dirty dishes**

oppvask *m*
dishonest [di'sɔnist] *adj* uærlig
dishwasher [di'swɔʃə] *n* oppvaskmaskin *m*
disinfect [ˌdisin'fekt] *v* desinfisere
disinfectant [ˌdisin'fektənt] *n* desinfiserende middel
disk drive ['disk‿ˌdraiv] *n* diskstasjon *c*
dislike [di'slaik] *v* mislike, avsky; *n* motvilje *m*, avsky *m*, antipati *m*
dislocated ['disləkeitid] *adj* gått av ledd
dismiss [dis'mis] *v* sende bort; *gi sparken, avskjedige
disorder [di'sɔːdə] *n* uorden *m*
dispatch [di'spætʃ] *v* avsende, sende av sted
display [di'splei] *v* utstille; vise; *n* utstilling *c*
disposable [di'spouzəbəl] *adj* engangs-
disposal [di'spouzəl] *n* disposisjon *m*
dispose of [di'spouz] kvitte seg med
dispute [di'spjuːt] *n* ordstrid *m*; krangel *m* / *nt*, tvist *m*; *v* *strides, *bestride
dissatisfied [di'sætisfaid] *adj* utilfreds
dissolve [di'zolv] *v* oppløse
dissuade from [di'sweid] fraråde
distance ['distəns] *n* avstand *m*; strekning *m*; **~ in kilometres (kilometers** *Am*) kilometertall *nt*
distant ['distənt] *adj* fjern
distinct [di'stiŋkt] *adj* tydelig; forskjellig
distinction [di'stiŋkʃən] *n* forskjell *m*
distinguish [di'stiŋgwiʃ] *v* skjelne, *gjøre forskjell
distinguished [di'stiŋgwiʃt] *adj* fremstående
distress [di'stres] *n* nød *c*; bedrøvelse *m*; **~ signal** nødsignal *nt*
distribute [di'stribjuːt] *v* utdele
distributor [di'stribjutə] *n* eneforhandler *m*; strømfordeler *m*
district ['distrikt] *n* distrikt *nt*; kvartal *nt*
disturb [di'stəːb] *v* forstyrre
disturbance [di'stəːbəns] *n* forstyrrelse *m*; forvirring *c*
ditch [ditʃ] *n* grøft *c*
dive [daiv] *v* dukke, stupe
diversion [dai'vəːʃən] *n* omkjøring *c*; atspredelse *m*
divide [di'vaid] *v* dele; fordele; skille
divine [di'vain] *adj* guddommelig
division [di'viʒən] *n* deling *c*; atskillelse *m*; avdeling *c*
divorce [di'vɔːs] *n* skilsmisse *m*; *v* skilles
dizziness ['dizinəs] *n*

svimmelhet *c*
dizzy ['dizi] *adj* svimmel
***do** [du:] *v* *gjøre; *være tilstrekkelig
dock [dɔk] *n* dokk *m*; kai *c*; *v* *dokksette; *legge til kai
docker ['dɔkə] *n* havnearbeider *m*
doctor ['dɔktə] *n* lege *m*; doktor *m*
document ['dɔkjumənt] *n* dokument *nt*
dog [dɔg] *n* hund *m*
doll [dɔl] *n* dukke *c*
dollar [dɔl] *n* dollar *m*
dome [doum] *n* kuppel *m*
domestic [də'mestik] *adj* hus-; innenlands; **~ animal** husdyr *nt*
domicile ['dɔmisail] *n* bopel *m*
dominate [ˌdɔmi'neit] *v* dominere
dominion [də'minjən] *n* herredømme *nt*
donate [dou'neit] *v* skjenke
donation [dou'neiʃən] *n* donasjon *m*
done [dʌn] *v* (pp do)
donkey ['dɔŋki] *n* esel *nt*
donor ['dounə] *n* donator *m*; giver *m*
door [dɔ:] *n* dør *c*; **revolving ~** svingdør *c*; **sliding ~** skyvedør *c*
doorbell ['dɔ:bel] *n* ringeklokke *c*
doorkeeper ['dɔ:ˌki:pə] *n* dørvokter *m*
doorman ['dɔ:mən] *n* (pl -men) portier *m*
dormitory ['dɔ:mitri] *n* sovesal *m*
dose [dous] *n* dose *m*
dot [dɔt] *n* punkt *nt*, punktum *nt*, prikk *m*
double ['dʌbəl] *adj* dobbel; **~ bed** dobbeltseng *c*
doubt [daut] *v* tvile, betvile; *n* tvil *m*; **without ~** uten tvil
doubtful ['dautfəl] *adj* tvilsom; usikker
dough [dou] *n* deig *m*; *colloquial* penger *pl*
down[1] [daun] *adv* ned, nedover; over ende; *adj* nedslått; *prep* nedover, langs; **~ payment** nedbetaling *c*
down[2] [daun] *n* dun *nt*
download ['daunˌloud] *n* nedlasting *c*
downpour ['daunpɔ:] *n* øsregn *nt*
downstairs [ˌdaun'stɛəz] *adv* ned; nede
downstream [ˌdaun'stri:m] *adv* med strømmen
down-to-earth [ˌdauntu'ə:θ] *adj* nøktern
downwards ['daunwədz] *adv* nedover
dozen ['dʌzən] *n* (pl ~, ~s) dusin *nt*
draft [drɑ:ft] *n* utkast *nt*
drag [dræg] *v* slepe
dragon ['drægən] *n* drake *m*
drain [drein] *v* drenere; *n* avløp *nt*
drama ['drɑ:mə] *n* drama *nt*;

skuespill *nt*
dramatic [drə'mætik] *adj* dramatisk
drank [dræŋk] *v* (p drink)
draught [drɑːft] *n* trekk *m*; **~ beer** fatøl *nt*; **draughts** damspill *nt*
draw [drɔː] *n* trekning *m*
***draw** [drɔː] *v* tegne; *trekke; heve; **~ up** avfatte, *sette opp
drawbridge ['drɔːbridʒ] *n* vindebro *c*
drawer ['drɔːə] *n* skuff *m*; **drawers** underbukse *c*
drawing ['drɔːiŋ] *n* tegning *c*; **~ pin** tegnestift *m*; **~ room** salong *m*
dread [dred] *v* frykte; *n* frykt *m*
dreadful ['dredfəl] *adj* fryktelig, forferdelig
dream [driːm] *n* drøm *m*
***dream** [driːm] *v* drømme
dress [dres] *v* kle på; kle på seg, kle seg; *forbinde; *n* kjole *m*
dressing gown ['dresiŋgaun] *n* morgenkåpe *c*
dressmaker ['dres,meikə] *n* skredder *m*
drill [dril] *v* bore; trene; *n* bor *nt*; **drilling platform** boreplattform *nt*
drink [driŋk] *n* drink *m*; drikk *m*
***drink** [driŋk] *v* *drikke
drinking water ['driŋkiŋ,wɔːtə] *n* drikkevann *nt*
drip-dry [,drip'drai] *adj* strykefri
drive [draiv] *n* vei *m*; kjøretur *m*
***drive** [draiv] *v* kjøre; føre
driver ['draivə] *n* fører *m*, sjåfør *m*
driver's license *nAm*, **driving licence** *n* førerkort *nt*
drizzle ['drizəl] *n* duskregn *nt*
drop [drɔp] *v* *la falle; *n* dråpe *m*
drought [draut] *n* tørke *c*
drown [draun] *v* drukne; ***be drowned** drukne
drug [drʌg] *n* narkotika *m*; medisin *m*; **~ addict** narkoman *m*
drugstore ['drʌgstɔː] *nAm* apotek *nt*
drum [drʌm] *n* tromme *c*
drunk [drʌŋk] *adj* (pp drink) full, beruset
dry [drai] *adj* tørr; *v* tørke
dry-clean [,drai'kliːn] *v* rense
dry cleaner's [,drai'kliːnəz] *n* renseri *nt*
dryer ['draiə] *n* tørketrommel *m*, tørkeapparat *nt*
duchess [dʌtʃis] *n* hertuginne *c*
duck [dʌk] *n* and *c*
due [djuː] *adj* ventet; skyldig; forfalt til betaling
dues [djuːz] *pl* avgifter *pl*

dug [dʌg] *v* (p, pp dig)
duke [dju:k] *n* hertug *m*
dull [dʌl] *adj* kjedelig; matt; sløv
dumb [dʌm] *adj* stum; dum
dune [dju:n] *n* sanddyne *c*
dung [dʌŋ] *n* gjødsel *c*
duration [dju'reiʃən] *n* varighet *c*
during ['djuəriŋ] *prep* under, i løpet av
dusk [dʌsk] *n* tusmørke *nt*
dust [dʌst] *n* støv *nt*
dustbin ['dʌstbin] *n* søppelkasse *c*
dusty ['dʌsti] *adj* støvet
Dutch [dʌtʃ] *adj* hollandsk, nederlandsk
Dutchman ['dʌtʃmən] *n* (pl -men) nederlender *m*, hollender *m*
duty ['dju:ti] *n* plikt *m*; oppgave *c*; innførselstoll *m*; **customs ~** tollavgift *c*
duty-free [ˌdju:ti'fri:] *adj* tollfri
DVD [divi'di:] *n* DVD *m*
DVD-ROM ['di:vi:di:'rɔm] *n* DVD-rom *c*
dwarf [dwɔ:f] *n* dverg *m*
dye [dai] *v* farge; *n* farge *m*
dynamo ['dainəmou] *n* (pl ~s) dynamo *m*

E

each [i:tʃ] *adj* hver; **~ other** hverandre
eager ['i:gə] *adj* ivrig, utålmodig
eagle ['i:gəl] *n* ørn *c*
ear [iə] *n* øre *nt*
earache ['iəreik] *n* øreverk *m*
eardrum ['iədrʌm] *n* trommehinne *c*
earl [ə:l] *n* greve *m*
early ['ə:li] *adj* tidlig
earn [ə:n] *v* tjene; fortjene
earnest ['ə:nist] *n* alvor *nt*
earnings ['ə:niŋz] *pl* inntekt *c*
earring ['iəriŋ] *n* øredobb *m*
earth [ə:θ] *n* jord *c*; bakke *m*
earthquake ['ə:θkweik] *n* jordskjelv *m / nt*
ease [i:z] *n* letthet *c*, utvungenhet *c*
east [i:st] *n* øst *m*
Easter ['i:stə] påske *c*
eastern ['i:stən] *adj* østlig, østre
easy ['i:zi] *adj* lett; bekvem; **~ chair** lenestol *m*
easy-going ['i:ziˌgouiŋ] *adj* avslappet
***eat** [i:t] *v* spise
eavesdrop ['i:vzdrɔp] *v* sniklytte
ebony ['ebəni] *n* ibenholt *m / nt*
eccentric [ik'sentrik] *adj* eksentrisk
echo ['ekou] *n* (pl ~es)

gjenlyd *m*, ekko *nt*
eclipse [i'klips] *n* formørkelse *m*
economic [ˌiːkə'nɔmik] *adj* økonomisk
economical [ˌiːkə'nɔmikəl] *adj* økonomisk, sparsommelig
economist [i'kɔnəmist] *n* økonom *m*
economize [i'kɔnəmaiz] *v* spare
economy [i'kɔnəmi] *n* økonomi *m*; næring *c*, næringsliv *nt*
eco-tourist ['iːkouˌtuːrist] *n* økoturist *c*
ecstasy ['ekstəzi] *n* ekstase *m*
Ecuador ['ekwədɔː] Ecuador
Ecuadorian [ˌekwə'dɔːriən] *n* ecuadorianer *m*
eczema ['eksimə] *n* eksem *m / nt*
edge [edʒ] *n* kant *m*
edible ['edibəl] *adj* spiselig
edit ['edit] *v* utgi, redigere
edition [i'diʃən] *n* utgave *c*; opplag *nt*; **morning ~** morgenutgave *c*
editor ['editə] *n* redaktør *m*
educate ['edʒukeit] *v* *oppdra, utdanne
education [ˌedʒu'keiʃən] *n* utdannelse *m*; oppdragelse *m*
eel [iːl] *n* ål *m*
effect [i'fekt] *n* effekt *m*, virkning *m*; *v* *frembringe; **in ~** faktisk
effective [i'fektiv] *adj* effektiv, virkningsfull
efficient [i'fiʃənt] *adj* virkningsfull, effektiv
effort ['efət] *n* anstrengelse *m*; bestrebelse *m*; prestasjon *m*
egg [eg] *n* egg *nt*; **~ yolk** eggeplomme *c*
eggplant ['egplɑːnt] *n* aubergine *m*
Egypt ['iːdʒipt] Egypt
Egyptian [i'dʒipʃən] *adj* egyptisk; *n* egypter *m*
eiderdown ['aidədaun] *n* ederdun *nt*; dyne *c*
eight [eit] *num* åtte
eighteen [ˌei'tiːn] *num* atten
eighteenth [ˌei'tiːnθ] *num* attende
eighth [eitθ] *num* åttende
eighty ['eiti] *num* åtti
either ['aiðə] *pron* den ene eller den andre; **either ... or** enten ... eller
elaborate [i'læbəreit] *v* utdype
elastic [i'læstik] *adj* elastisk; tøyelig; **~ band** strikk *m*
elasticity [ˌelæ'stisəti] *n* tøyelighet *c*
elbow ['elbou] *n* albue *m*
elder ['eldə] *adj* eldre
elderly ['eldəli] *adj* eldre
elect [i'lekt] *v* *velge
election [i'lekʃən] *n* valg *nt*
electric [i'lektrik] *adj* elektrisk; **~ cord** ledning

m; ~ **razor** barbermaskin *m*
electrician [ˌilek'triʃən] *n* elektriker *m*
electricity [ˌilek'trisəti] *n* elektrisitet *m*
electronic [ilek'trɔnik] *adj* elektronisk
elegance ['eligəns] *n* eleganse *m*
elegant ['eligənt] *adj* elegant
element ['elimənt] *n* element *nt*, bestanddel *m*
elephant ['elifənt] *n* elefant *m*
elevator ['eliveitə] *nAm* heis *m*
eleven [i'levən] *num* elleve
eleventh [i'levənθ] *num* ellevte
elf [elf] *n* (pl elves) alv *m*
eliminate [i'limineit] *v* fjerne; avskaffe
elm [elm] *n* alm *m*
else [els] *adv* ellers
elsewhere [ˌel'swεə] *adv* annetsteds
elucidate [i'lu:sideit] *v* *klargjøre
e-mail ['i: meil] *n* e-post *m*; *v* sende (med) e-post
emancipation [iˌmænsi'peiʃən] *n* frigjøring *c*
embankment [im'bæŋkmənt] *n* bredd *m*; demning *m*
embargo [em'bɑ:gou] *n* (pl ~es) beslag *nt*; handelsforbud *nt*
embark [im'bɑ:k] *v* *gå om bord
embarkation [ˌembɑ:'keiʃən] *n* innskipning *m*
embarrass [im'bærəs] *v* *gjøre brydd, *gjøre forlegen; sjenere; **embarrassed** brydd, flau, forlegen; **embarrassing** pinlig; **embarrassment** forlegenhet *c*
embassy ['embəsi] *n* ambassade *m*
emblem ['embləm] *n* emblem *nt*; symbol *nt*
embrace [im'breis] *v* omfavne; *n* omfavnelse *m*
embroider [im'brɔidə] *v* brodere
embroidery [im'brɔidəri] *n* broderi *nt*
emerald ['emərəld] *n* smaragd *m*
emergency [i'mə:dʒənsi] *n* krisesituasjon *m*, nødstilfelle *nt*; ~ **exit** nødutgang *m*
emigrant ['emigrənt] *n* utvandrer *m*
emigrate ['emigreit] *v* utvandre
emigration [ˌemi'greiʃən] *n* emigrasjon *m*
emotion [i'mouʃən] *n* sinnsbevegelse *m*, følelse *m*
emperor ['empərə] *n* keiser *m*
emphasize ['emfəsaiz] *v*

understreke
empire ['empaiə] *n* imperium *nt*, keiserdømme *nt*
employ [im'plɔi] *v* *ansette; anvende
employee [ˌemplɔi'iː] *n* lønnstaker *m*, ansatt *m*
employer [im'plɔiə] *n* arbeidsgiver *m*
employment [im'plɔimənt] *n* beskjeftigelse *m*, arbeid *nt*; ~ **exchange** arbeidsformidling *c*
empress ['empris] *n* keiserinne *c*
empty ['empti] *adj* tom; *v* tømme
enable [i'neibəl] *v***sette i stand
enamel [i'næməl] *n* emalje *m*
enamelled [i'næməld] *adj* emaljert
enchanting [in'tʃɑːntiŋ] *adj* bedårende, henrivende
encircle [in'səːkəl] *v* omringe, *omgi; innsirkle
enclose [iŋ'klouz] *v* *vedlegge
enclosure [iŋ'klouʒə] *n* vedlegg *nt*
encounter [iŋ'kauntə] *v* møte; *n* møte *nt*
encourage [iŋ'kʌridʒ] *v* oppmuntre
encyclop(a)edia [enˌsaiklə'piːdiə] *n* leksikon *nt*
end [end] *n* ende *m*, slutt *m*; *v* slutte; opphøre
ending ['endiŋ] *n* avslutning *m*
endless ['endləs] *adj* uendelig
endorse [in'dɔːs] *v* endossere
endure [in'djuə] *v* *utholde
enemy ['enəmi] *n* fiende *m*
energetic [ˌenə'dʒetik] *adj* energisk
energy ['enədʒi] *n* energi *m*; kraft *c*
engage [iŋ'geidʒ] *v* *ansette; bestille; forplikte seg; **engaged** forlovet; opptatt
engagement [iŋ'geidʒmənt] *n* forlovelse *m*; forpliktelse *m*; avtale *m*; ~ **ring** forlovelsesring *m*
engine ['endʒin] *n* maskin *m*, motor *m*; lokomotiv *nt*
engineer [ˌendʒi'niə] *n* ingeniør *m*
England ['iŋglənd] England
English ['iŋgliʃ] *adj* engelsk
Englishman ['iŋgliʃmən] *n* (pl -men) engelskmann *m*
engrave [iŋ'greiv] *v* gravere
engraving [iŋ'greiviŋ] *n* trykk *nt*; kopperstikk *nt*
enigma [i'nigmə] *n* gåte *c*
enjoy [in'dʒɔi] *v* *nyte, *ha glede av
enjoyable [in'dʒɔiəbəl] *adj* behagelig, hyggelig, morsom; deilig
enjoyment [in'dʒɔimənt] *n* nytelse *m*

enlarge [in'lɑːdʒ] *v* forstørre; utvide
enlargement [in'lɑːdʒmənt] *n* forstørrelse *m*
enormous [i'nɔːməs] *adj* enorm, kolossal
enough [i'nʌf] *adv* nok; *adj* tilstrekkelig
enquire [iŋ'kwaiə] *v* *forespørre; undersøke
enquiry [iŋ'kwaiəri] *n* forespørsel *m*; undersøkelse *m*; rundspørring *c*
enter ['entə] *v* *gå inn, *tre inn i; *innskrive
enterprise ['entəpraiz] *n* virksomhet *c*; driftighet *c*
entertain [ˌentə'tein] *v* *underholde, more; beverte
entertainer [ˌentə'teinə] *n* underholder *m*
entertaining [ˌentə'teiniŋ] *adj* morsom, underholdende
entertainment [ˌentə'teinmənt] *n* underholdning *m*, forlystelse *m*
enthusiasm [in'θjuːziæzəm] *n* entusiasme *m*
enthusiastic [inˌθjuːzi'æstik] *adj* entusiastisk
entire [in'taiə] *adj* hel
entirely [in'taiəli] *adv* helt
entrails ['entreilz] *n* innvoller
entrance ['entrəns] *n* inngang *m*; adgang *m*; inntreden *m*; **~ fee** inngangspenger *pl*
entry ['entri] *n* inngang *m*, adgang *m*; oppføring *c*; **no ~** adgang forbudt
envelop [in'veləp] *v* pakke inn, omslutte
envelope ['envəloup] *n* konvolutt *m*
envious ['enviəs] *adj* sjalu, misunnelig
environment [in'vaiərənmənt] *n* miljø *nt*; omgivelser *pl*; **environmental protection** miljøvern *nt*
envoy ['envɔi] *n* sendemann *m*
envy ['envi] *n* misunnelse *m*; *v* misunne
epic ['epik] *n* epos *nt*; *adj* episk
epidemic [ˌepi'demik] *n* epidemi *m*
epilepsy ['epilepsi] *n* epilepsi *m*
epilogue ['epilɔg] *n* epilog *m*
episode ['episoud] *n* episode *m*
equal ['iːkwəl] *adj* lik; *n* likemann *m*; *v* måle seg med
equality [i'kwɔləti] *n* likhet *c*
equalize ['iːkwəlaiz] *v* utjevne
equally ['iːkwəli] *adv* like

equator [i'kweitə] *n* ekvator *m*
equip [i'kwip] *v* utruste, utstyre
equipment [i'kwipmənt] *n* utstyr *nt*
equivalent [i'kwivələnt] *adj* motsvarende, tilsvarende
eraser [i'reizə] *n* viskelær *nt*
erect [i'rekt] *v* reise; *adj* oppreist, stående
err [əː] *v* feile
errand ['erənd] *n* ærend *nt*
error ['erə] *n* feiltakelse *m*, feil *m*
escalator ['eskəleitə] *n* rulletrapp *c*
escape [i'skeip] *v* *unnslippe; *unngå, flykte; *n* flukt *c*
escort[1] ['eskɔːt] *n* eskorte *m*
escort[2] [i'skɔːt] *v* ledsage
especially [i'speʃəli] *adv* især, først og fremst, særlig
essay ['esei] *n* essay *nt*; stil *m*, avhandling *c*
essence ['esəns] *n* essens *m*; vesen *nt*, kjerne *m*
essential [i'senʃəl] *adj* uunnværlig; vesentlig
essentially [i'senʃəli] *adv* først og fremst
establish [i'stæbliʃ] *v* etablere; *fastslå
estate [i'steit] *n* eiendom *m*
esteem [i'stiːm] *n* aktelse *m*, respekt *m*; *v* akte
estimate[1] ['estimeit] *v* vurdere, taksere, *verdsette
estimate[2] ['estimət] *n* vurdering *c*
estuary ['estʃuəri] *n* elvemunning *m*
etcetera [et'setərə] og så videre
etching ['etʃiŋ] *n* radering *c*
eternal [i'təːnəl] *adj* evig
eternity [i'təːnəti] *n* evighet *c*
ether ['iːθə] *n* eter *m*
Ethiopia [iθi'oupiə] Etiopia
Ethiopian [iθi'oupiən] *adj* etiopisk; *n* etiopier *m*
e-ticket ['iːˌtikət] *n* e-billett *c*
EU ['iː'ju] εʊ, ðen europeiske union *m*
Euro ['juːrou] *n* euro *m*
Europe ['juərəp] Europa
European [ˌjuərə'piːən] *adj* europeisk; *n* europeer *m*
evacuate [i'vækjueit] *v* evakuere
evaluate [i'væljueit] *v* vurdere
evaporate [i'væpəreit] *v* fordampe
even ['iːvən] *adj* jevn, like, plan; konstant; *adv* til og med
evening ['iːvniŋ] *n* kveld *m*; **~ dress** selskapsantrekk *nt*
event [i'vent] *n* begivenhet *c*
eventual [i'ventʃuəl] *adj* mulig; endelig
eventually [i'ventʃuəli] *adv* endelig; til slutt
ever ['evə] *adv* noen gang;

alltid
every ['evri] *adj* hver
everybody ['evri,bɔdi] *pron* enhver
everyday ['evridei] *adj* daglig
everyone ['evriwʌn] *pron* enhver
everything ['evriθiŋ] *pron* alt
everywhere ['evriwɛə] *adv* overalt
evidence ['evidəns] *n* bevis *nt*
evident ['evidənt] *adj* tydelig
evil ['iːvəl] *n* onde *nt*; *adj* ondsinnet, ond
evolution [,iːvə'luːʃən] *n* evolusjon *m*
exact [ig'zækt] *adj* nøyaktig
exactly [ig'zæktli] *adv* akkurat
exaggerate [ig'zædʒəreit] *v* *overdrive
exam [ig'zæm] *colloquial*, **examination**
[ig,zæmi'neiʃən] *n* eksamen *m*; undersøkelse *m*; forhør *nt*
examine [ig'zæmin] *v* undersøke
example [ig'zɑːmpəl] *n* eksempel *nt*; **for ~** for eksempel
excavation [,ekskə'veiʃən] *n* utgravning *m*
exceed [ik'siːd] *v* *overskride; *overgå
excel [ik'sel] *v* utmerke seg
excellent ['eksələnt] *adj* fremragende, utmerket
except [ik'sept] *prep* unntatt
exception [ik'sepʃən] *n* unntak *nt*
exceptional [ik'sepʃənəl] *adj* usedvanlig, enestående
excerpt ['eksəːpt] *n* utdrag *nt*
excess [ik'ses] *n* utskeielse *m*; overdrivelse *m*
excessive [ik'sesiv] *adj* overdreven
exchange [iks'tʃeindʒ] *v* bytte, veksle, utveksle; *n* bytte *nt*; børs *m*; **~ office** vekslingskontor *nt*; **~ rate** valutakurs *m*
excite [ik'sait] *v* opphisse
excited [ik'saitəd] *adj* opphisset
excitement [ik'saitmənt] *n* opphisselse *m*; spenning *m*
exciting [ik'saitiŋ] *adj* spennende
exclaim [ik'skleim] *v* *utbryte
exclamation [,ekskləˈmeiʃən] *n* utrop *nt*
exclude [ik'skluːd] *v* utelukke
exclusive [ik'skluːsiv] *adj* eksklusiv
exclusively [ik'skluːsivli] *adv* utelukkende
excursion [ik'skəːʃən] *n* utflukt *c*
excuse[1] [ik'skjuːs] *n* unnskyldning *m*

excuse² [ik'skjuːz] *v* unnskylde
execute ['eksikjuːt] *v* utføre
execution [ˌeksi'kjuːʃən] *n* henrettelse *m*
executioner [ˌeksi'kjuːʃənə] *n* bøddel *m*
executive [ig'zekjutiv] *adj* administrerende; *n* utøvende makt; direktør *m*
exempt [ig'zempt] *v* *frita; *adj* fritatt
exemption [ig'zempʃən] *n* fritak *nt*
exercise ['eksəsaiz] *n* øvelse *m*; oppgave *c*; *v* øve; utøve
exhale [eks'heil] *v* puste ut
exhaust [ig'zɔːst] *n* eksosrør *nt*; *v* utmatte; **~ gases** eksos *m*
exhibit [ig'zibit] *v* utstille; fremvise, oppvise
exhibition [ˌeksi'biʃən] *n* utstilling *c*
exile ['eksail] *n* eksil *nt*; landflyktig *m*
exist [ig'zist] *v* eksistere
existence [ig'zistəns] *n* eksistens *m*
exit ['eksit] *n* utgang *m*; utkjørsel *m*
exotic [ig'zɔtik] *adj* eksotisk
expand [ik'spænd] *v* utvide; utbre; utfolde
expansion [ik'spænʃən] *n* utbredelse; utvidelse, ekspansjon
expect [ik'spekt] *v* vente
expectation [ˌekspek'teiʃən] *n* forventning *m*
expedition [ˌekspə'diʃən] *n* ekspedisjon *m*
expel [ik'spel] *v* utvise
expenditure [ik'spenditʃə] *n* forbruk *nt*
expense [ik'spens] *n* utgift *c*; **expenses** *pl* omkostninger *pl*, kostnader *pl*
expensive [ik'spensiv] *adj* dyr; kostbar
experience [ik'spiəriəns] *n* erfaring *c*; *v* oppleve, erfare; **experienced** erfaren
experiment [ik'sperimənt] *n* eksperiment *nt*, forsøk *nt*; *v* eksperimentere
expert ['ekspəːt] *n* fagmann *m*, ekspert *m*; *adj* sakkyndig
expire [ik'spaiə] *v* *utløpe, opphøre; utånde; **expired** utløpt
explain [ik'splein] *v* forklare
explanation [ˌeksplə'neiʃən] *n* forklaring *c*
explicit [ik'splisit] *adj* tydelig, uttrykkelig
explode [ik'sploud] *v* eksplodere
exploit [ik'splɔit] *v* utnytte
explore [ik'splɔː] *v* utforske
explosion [ik'splouʒən] *n* eksplosjon *m*
explosive [ik'splousiv] *adj*

eksplosiv; *n* sprengstoff *nt*
export[1] [ik'spɔːt] *v* eksportere, utføre
export[2] ['ekspɔːt] *n* eksport *m*, utførsel *m*
expose [ik'spous] *v* utsette; avsløre; eksponere
exposition [ˌekspə'ziʃən] *n* utstilling *c*
exposure [ik'spouʒə] *n* utsatthet *c*; eksponering *c*; **~ meter** lysmåler *m*
express [ik'spres] *v* uttrykke; *gi uttrykk for, ytre; *adj* ekspress-; uttrykkelig; **~ train** hurtigtog *nt*
expression [ik'spreʃən] *n* uttrykk *nt*
exquisite [ik'skwizit] *adj* utsøkt
extend [ik'stend] *v* forlenge; utvide; bevilge
extension [ik'stenʃən] *n* forlengelse *m*; utvidelse *m*; linje *c*; **~ cord** skjøteledning *m*
extensive [ik'stensiv] *adj* omfangsrik; utstrakt, omfattende
extent [ik'stent] *n* omfang *nt*
exterior [ek'stiəriə] *adj* ytre; *n* utside *c*
external [ek'stəːnəl] *adj* utvendig
extinguish [ik'stiŋgwiʃ] *v* slokke
extort [ik'stɔːt] *v* utpresse
extortion [ik'stɔːʃən] *n* utpressing *c*
extra ['ekstrə] *adj* ekstra
extract[1] [ik'strækt] *v* *trekke ut
extract[2] ['ekstrækt] *n* utdrag *nt*
extradite ['ekstrədait] *v* utlevere en forbryter
extraordinary [ik'strɔːdənri] *adj* usedvanlig
extravagant [ik'strævəgənt] *adj* ekstravagant, overdreven
extreme [ik'striːm] *adj* ekstrem; ytterst, ytterlig; *n* ytterlighet *c*
exuberant [ig'zjuːbərənt] *adj* overstrømmende
eye [ai] *n* øye *nt*; **~ shadow** øyenskygge *m*
eyebrow ['aibrau] *n* øyenbryn *nt*
eyelash ['ailæʃ] *n* øyenvippe *m*
eyelid ['ailid] *n* øyenlokk *nt*
eyewitness ['aiˌwitnəs] *n* øyenvitne *nt*

F

fable ['feibəl] *n* fabel *m*; sagn *nt*
fabric ['fæbrik] *n* stoff *nt*; struktur *m*
façade [fə'sɑːd] *n* fasade *m*
face [feis] *n* ansikt *nt*; *v* konfrontere; **~ cream** ansiktskrem *m*
facilities [fə'silətis] *pl* innretning(er) *pl*; **cooking ~** mulighet til å lage mat
facing overfor
fact [fækt] *n* kjensgjerning *c*, faktum *nt*; **in ~** faktisk
factor ['fæktə] *n* faktor *m*
factory ['fæktəri] *n* fabrikk *m*
factual ['fæktʃuəl] *adj* faktisk
faculty ['fækəlti] *n* evne *c*; begavelse *m*, anlegg *nt*; fakultet *nt*
fade [feid] *v* blekne, falme
fail [feil] *v* mislykkes; mangle; forsømme; dumpe, *stryke; **without ~** helt sikkert
failure ['feiljə] *n* fiasko *m*
faint [feint] *v* besvime; *adj* svak, vag
fair [fɛə] *n* basar *m*; varemesse *c*; *adj* rettferdig; lyshåret, blond; vakker
fairly ['fɛəli] *adv* nokså, temmelig, ganske
fairy ['fɛəri] *n* fe *m*
fairytale ['fɛəriteil] *n* eventyr *nt*
faith [feiθ] *n* tro *c*; tillit *m*
faithful ['feiθful] *adj* trofast
fake [feik] *n* forfalskning *m*
fall [fɔːl] *n* fall *nt*; høst *m*
***fall** [fɔːl] *v* *falle
false [fɔːls] *adj* falsk; gal, uekte; **~ teeth** gebiss *nt*
falter ['fɔːltə] *v* vakle; stamme
fame [feim] *n* berømmelse *m*; rykte *nt*
familiar [fə'miljə] *adj* velkjent; fortrolig
family ['fæməli] *n* familie *m*; slekt *c*; **~ name** etternavn *nt*
famous ['feiməs] *adj* berømt
fan [fæn] *n* vifte *c*; beundrer *m*; **~ belt** vifterem *c*
fanatical [fə'nætikəl] *adj* fanatisk
fancy ['fænsi] *v* *ha lyst til, like; tenke seg, forestille seg; *n* lune *nt*; fantasi *m*
fantastic [fæn'tæstik] *adj* fantastisk
fantasy ['fæntəzi] *n* fantasi *m*
far [fɑː] *adj* fjern; *adv* meget; **by ~** uten sammenligning; **so ~** hittil; **~ away** langt borte
fare [fɛə] *n* billettpris *m*;

kost *m*
farm [fɑːm] *n* bondegård *m*
farmer ['fɑːmə] *n* bonde *m*
farmhouse ['fɑːmhaus] *n* våningshus *nt*
far-off ['fɑːrɔf] *adj* fjern
farther ['fɑːðə] *adj* videre
fascinate ['fæsineit] *v* fengsle, fjetre
fascism ['fæʃizəm] *n* fascisme *m*
fascist ['fæʃist] *adj* fascistisk; *n* fascist *m*
fashion ['fæʃən] *n* mote *m*; måte *m*
fashionable ['fæʃənəbəl] *adj* moderne
fast [fɑːst] *adj* rask, hurtig; fast
fasten ['fɑːsən] *v* feste; stenge
fastener ['fɑːsənə] *n* festeinnretning *m*
fat [fæt] *adj* tykk, fet; *n* fett *nt*; **~ free** *adj* fettfri
fatal ['feitəl] *adj* dødelig, skjebnesvanger, fatal
fate [feit] *n* skjebne *m*
father ['fɑːðə] *n* far *m*; pater *m*
father-in-law ['fɑːðərinlɔː] *n* (pl fathers-) svigerfar *m*
fatigue [fətiːg] *n* utmattelse *m*, tretthet *c*
fatty ['fæti] *adj* fettholdig
faucet ['fɔːsit] *nAm* vannkran *c*
fault [fɔːlt] *n* feil *m*, defekt *m*
faultless ['fɔːltləs] *adj* feilfri; perfekt
faulty ['fɔːlti] *adj* defekt, mangelfull
favo(u)r ['feivə] *n* tjeneste *m*; *v* privilegere, begunstige
favo(u)rable ['feivərəbəl] *adj* gunstig
favo(u)rite ['feivərit] *n* favoritt *m*, yndling *m*; *adj* yndlings-
fax [fæks] *n* telefaks *m*, faks *m*; **send a ~** sende en faks
fear [fiə] *n* frykt *m*, engstelse *m*; *v* frykte
feasible ['fiːzəbəl] *adj* mulig, gjennomførbart
feast [fiːst] *n* fest *m*
feat [fiːt] *n* prestasjon *m*
feather ['feðə] *n* fjær *c*
feature ['fiːtʃə] *n* kjennemerke *nt*; ansiktstrekk *nt*
February ['februəri] februar
federal ['fedərəl] *adj* forbunds-
federation [ˌfedə'reiʃən] *n* forbundsstat *m*
fee [fiː] *n* honorar *nt*; gebyr *nt*
feeble ['fiːbəl] *adj* svak
***feed** [fiːd] *v* mate; **fed up with** lei av
***feel** [fiːl] *v* føle; **~ like** *ha lyst til
feeling ['fiːliŋ] *n* følelse *m*
feet (pl foot)
fell [fel] *v* (p fall)
fellow ['felou] *n* fyr *m*
felt[1] [felt] *n* filt *m*

felt² [felt] *v* (p, pp feel)
female ['fi:meil] *adj* hunn-
feminine ['feminin] *adj* feminin
fence [fens] *n* gjerde *nt*; stakitt *nt*; *v* fekte
ferment [fə:'ment] *v* gjære
ferry-boat ['feribout] *n* ferge *c*; ferje *c*
fertile ['fə:tail] *adj* fruktbar
festival ['festivəl] *n* festival *m*
festive ['festiv] *adj* festlig
fetch [fetʃ] *v* hente *innbringe
feudal ['fju:dəl] *adj* føydal
fever ['fi:və] *n* feber *m*
feverish ['fi:vəriʃ] *adj* feberaktig
few [fju:] *adj* få
fiancé [fi'ɑ̃:sei] *n* forlovede *m*
fiancée [fi'ɑ̃:sei] *n* forlovede *m*
fibre ['faibə] *n* fiber *m*
fiction ['fikʃən] *n* skjønnlitteratur *m*, oppdiktning *m*
field [fi:ld] *n* mark *c*, åker *m*; felt *nt*; **~ glasses** feltkikkert *m*
fierce [fiəs] *adj* vill; heftig
fifteen [ˌfif'ti:n] *num* femten
fifteenth [ˌfif'ti:nθ] *num* femtende
fifth [fifθ] *num* femte
fifty ['fifti] *num* femti
fig [fig] *n* fiken *m*
fight [fait] *n* strid *m*, kamp *m*
***fight** [fait] *v* kjempe, *slåss
figure ['figə] *n* skikkelse *m*, figur *m*; tall *nt*
file [fail] *n* kartotek *nt*, fil *m*; dokumentsamling *c*; rekke *c*
fill [fil] *v* fylle; **~ in** fylle ut; **~ out** *Am* fylle ut; **~ up** fylle opp; **filling station** bensinstasjon *m*
filling ['filiŋ] *n* plombe *m*; fyll *nt*
film [film] *n* film *m*; *v* filme
filter ['filtə] *n* filter *nt*
filthy ['filθi] *adj* skitten
final ['fainəl] *adj* endelig
finally ['fainəli] *adv* endelig, til slutt
finance [fai'næns] *v* finansiere
finances [fai'nænsiz] *pl* finanser *pl*
financial [fai'nænʃəl] *adj* finansiell
finch [fintʃ] *n* finke *m*
***find** [faind] *v* *finne
fine [fain] *n* mulkt *c*; *adj* fin; pen; skjønn, utmerket; **~ arts** skjønne kunster
finger ['fiŋgə] *n* finger *m*; **little ~** lillefinger *m*
fingerprint ['fiŋgəprint] *n* fingeravtrykk *nt*
finish ['finiʃ] *v* fullende, avslutte, slutte; opphøre; *n* slutt *m*; mållinje *c*; **finished** ferdig
Finland ['finlənd] Finland
Finn [fin] *n* finne *m*
Finnish ['finiʃ] *adj* finsk

fire [faiə] *n* ild *m*; brann *m*; *v* *skyte; avskjedige; **~ alarm** brannalarm *m*; **~ brigade** brannvesen *nt*; **~ escape** branntrapp *c*; **~ extinguisher** brannslokker *m*
firefighter ['faiə,faitə] *n* brannmannskap *nt*
fireplace ['faiəpleis] *n* peis *m*
fireproof ['faiəpru:f] *adj* brannsikker; ildfast
firewall ['faiə‿,wɔ:l] *n* brannmur *c*
firm [fə:m] *adj* fast; solid; *n* firma *nt*
first [fə:st] *num* første; **at ~** først; i begynnelsen; **~ name** fornavn *nt*
first aid [,fə:st'eid] *n* førstehjelp *c*; **~ kit** førstehjelpsutstyr *nt*; **~ post** førstehjelpsstasjon *m*
first-class [,fə:st'klɑ:s] *adj* førsteklasses
first-rate [,fə:st'reit] *adj* førsteklasses, førsterangs
fir tree ['fə:tri:] *n* nåletre *nt*, gran *c*
fish¹ [fiʃ] *n* (pl ~, ~es) fisk *m*; **~ shop** fiskeforretning *c*
fish² [fiʃ] *v* fiske; **fishing gear** fiskeutstyr *nt*; **fishing hook** fiskekrok *m*; **fishing industry** fiskeri *nt*; **fishing license** *Am*, **fishing licence** fiskekort *nt*; **fishing line** fiskesnøre *nt*; **fishing net** fiskegarn *nt*; **fishing rod** fiskestang *c*; **fishing tackle** fiskeredskap *nt*
fishbone ['fiʃboun] *n* fiskebein *nt*
fisherman ['fiʃəmən] *n* (pl -men) fisker *m*
fist [fist] *n* knyttneve *m*
fit [fit] *adj* egnet; *n* anfall *nt*; *v* passe; **fitting room** prøverom *nt*
five [faiv] *num* fem
fix [fiks] *v* reparere, ordne
fixed [fikst] *adj* fast
fizz [fiz] *n* brusing *c*
fjord [fjɔ:d] *n* fjord
flag [flæg] *n* flagg *nt*
flame [fleim] *n* flamme *m*
flamingo [flə'miŋgou] *n* (pl ~s, ~es) flamingo *m*
flannel ['flænəl] *n* flanell *m*
flash [flæʃ] *n* glimt *nt*; **~ bulb** blitzlampe *c*
flashlight ['flæʃlait] *n* lommelykt *c*
flask [flɑ:sk] *n* flaske *c*; **thermos ~** termosflaske *c*
flat [flæt] *adj* flat, plan; *n* leilighet *c*; **~ tyre** punktering *c*
flavo(u)r ['fleivə] *n* smak *m*; *v* *sette smak på
flaw [flɔ:] *n* sprekk *m*; svakhet *c*
flee [fli:] *v* flykte, rømme
fleet [fli:t] *n* flåte *m*
flesh [fleʃ] *n* kjøtt *nt*
flew [flu:] *v* (p fly)
flex [fleks] *n* ledning *m*; *v* bøye

flexible ['fleksibəl] *adj* bøyelig
flight [flait] *n* flytur *m*; **charter ~** chartertur *m*
flint [flint] *n* flintstein *m*
float [flout] *v* *flyte; *n* flottør *m*
flock [flɔk] *n* flokk *m*
flood [flʌd] *n* oversvømmelse *m*; flo *m*
floor [flɔː] *n* gulv *nt*; etasje *m*; **first ~** annen etasje; *Am* første etasje; **~ show** floor-show *nt*
florist ['flɔrist] *n* blomsterhandler *m*
flour [flauə] *n* mel *nt*
flow [flou] *v* strømme, *flyte
flower [flauə] *n* blomst *m*; **~ shop** blomsterforretning *c*
flowerbed ['flauəbed] *n* blomsterbed *nt*
flown [floun] *v* (pp fly)
flu [fluː] *n* influensa *m*
fluent ['fluːənt] *adj* flytende
fluid ['fluːid] *adj* flytende; *n* væske *c*
flute [fluːt] *n* fløyte *c*
fly [flai] *n* flue *c*; buksesmekk *m*
***fly** [flai] *v* *fly
foam [foum] *n* skum *nt*; *v* skumme; **~ rubber** skumgummi *m*
focus ['foukəs] *n* brennpunkt *nt*
fog [fɔg] *n* tåke *c*
foggy ['fɔgi] *adj* tåket
foglamp ['fɔglæmp] *n* tåkelykt *c*
fold [fould] *v* brette, folde; folde sammen; *n* fold *m*
folk [fouk] *n* folk *nt*; **~ dance** folkedans *m*; **~ song** folkevise *c*
folklore ['fouklɔː] *n* folklore *m*
follow ['fɔlou] *v* *følge; **following** *adj* neste, følgende
fond: *be ~ of [biː fɔnd ɔv] like
food [fuːd] *n* mat *m*; føde *c*; **~ poisoning** matforgiftning *m*
foodstuffs ['fuːdstʌfs] *pl* matvarer *pl*
fool [fuːl] *n* tosk *m*; *v* narre
foolish ['fuːliʃ] *adj* fjollet, tåpelig; dum
foot [fut] *n* (pl feet) fot *m*; **on ~** til fots
football ['futbɔːl] *n* fotball *m*; **~ match** fotballkamp *m*
foot brake ['futbreik] *n* fotbrems *m*
footpath ['futpɑːθ] *n* gangsti *m*
footwear ['futwɛə] *n* skotøy *nt*
for [fɔː, fə] *prep* til; i; på grunn av, av, for; *conj* for
***forbid** [fə'bid] *v* *forby
force [fɔːs] *v* *tvinge; forsere; *n* kraft *c*, styrke *m*; vold *m*; **by ~** nødtvunget; **driving ~** drivkraft *c*
forecast ['fɔːkɑːst] *n* varsel *nt*; *v* *forutsi, varsle
foreground ['fɔːgraund] *n*

forgrunn *m*
forehead ['fɔred] *n* panne *c*
foreign ['fɔrin] *adj* utenlandsk; fremmed
foreigner ['fɔrinə] *n* utlending *m*
foreman ['fɔːmən] *n* (pl -men) formann *m*
foremost ['fɔːmoust] *adj* fremst, forrest
forest ['fɔrist] *n* skog *m*
forester ['fɔristə] *n* forstmann *m*
forever, **for ever** [fɔ'revə] *adv* for alltid; stadig
forge [fɔːdʒ] *v* forfalske
***forget** [fə'get] *v* glemme
forgetful [fə'getfəl] *adj* glemsom
***forgive** [fə'giv] *v* *tilgi
fork [fɔːk] *n* gaffel *m*; skillevei *m*; *v* dele seg
form [fɔːm] *n* form *c*; blankett *m*; skjema *nt*; klasse *c*; *v* forme
formal ['fɔːməl] *adj* formell
formality [fɔː'mæləti] *n* formalitet *m*
former ['fɔːmə] *adj* forhenværende; tidligere; **formerly** før i tiden
formula ['fɔːmjulə] *n* (pl ~e, ~s) formel *m*
fortnight ['fɔːtnait] *n* fjorten dager
fortress ['fɔːtris] *n* festning *m*
fortunate ['fɔːtʃənət] *adj* heldig
fortunately ['fɔːtʃənətli] *adv* heldigvis
fortune ['fɔːtʃuːn] *n* formue *m*; skjebne *m*, lykke *c*
forty ['fɔːti] *num* førti
forward ['fɔːwəd] *adv* frem, fremad; *v* ettersende
foster parents ['fɔstəˌpɛərənts] *pl* pleieforeldre *pl*
fought [fɔːt] *v* (p, pp fight)
foul [faul] *adj* skitten; gemen
found[1] [faund] *v* (p, pp find)
found[2] [faund] *v* *grunnlegge, opprette, stifte
foundation [faun'deiʃən] *n* grunnlag *nt*; stiftelse *m*
fountain ['fauntin] *n* springvann *nt*; kilde *m*
fountain pen ['fauntinpen] *n* fyllepenn *m*
four [fɔː] *num* fire
fourteen [ˌfɔː'tiːn] *num* fjorten
fourteenth [ˌfɔː'tiːnθ] *num* fjortende
fourth [fɔːθ] *num* fjerde
fowl [faul] *n* (pl ~s, ~) fjærkre *nt*
fox [fɔks] *n* rev *m*
foyer ['fɔiei] *n* foajé *m*
fraction ['frækʃən] *n* brøkdel *m*
fracture ['fræktʃə] *v* *brekke; *n* brudd *nt*
fragile ['frædʒail] *adj* skjør; skrøpelig
fragment ['frægmənt] *n*

bruddstykke *nt*; stykke *nt*
frame [freim] *n* ramme *c*; innfatning *m*
France [frɑːns] Frankrike
franchise ['fræntʃaiz] *n* stemmerett *m*
frank [fræŋk] *adj* oppriktig
fraternity [frə'təːnəti] *n* brorskap *m / nt*
fraud [frɔːd] *n* bedrageri *nt*
fray [frei] *v* trevle opp
free [friː] *adj* fri; gratis; **~ of charge** gratis; **~ ticket** fribillett *m*
freedom ['friːdəm] *n* frihet *c*
***freeze** [friːz] *v* *fryse; fryse
freezer [friːzə] *n* fryser *m*, fryseboks *m*
freezing ['friːziŋ] *adj* iskald
freezing point ['friːziŋpɔint] *n* frysepunkt *nt*
freight [freit] *n* last *c*, frakt *c*
freight train ['freittrein] *nAm* godstog *nt*
French [frentʃ] *adj* fransk; **the ~** *pl* franskmennene; **~ fries** *pl* pommes frites
Frenchman ['frentʃmən] *n* (pl -men) franskmann *m*
frequency ['friːkwənsi] *n* frekvens *m*; hyppighet *c*
frequent ['friːkwənt] *adj* stadig, hyppig; **frequently** ofte
fresh [freʃ] *adj* fersk; forfriskende; **~ water** ferskvann *nt*
friction ['frikʃən] *n* friksjon *m*
Friday ['fraidi] fredag *m*
fridge [fridʒ] *n* kjøleskap *nt*
friend [frend] *n* venn *m*; venninne *c*
friendly ['frendli] *adj* vennlig; vennskapelig
friendship ['frendʃip] *n* vennskap *nt*
fright [frait] *n* skrekk *m*, angst *m*
frighten ['fraitən] *v* forskrekke
frightened ['fraitənd] *adj* skremt; ***be ~** *bli forskrekket
frightful ['fraitfəl] *adj* forferdelig, forskrekkelig
fringe [frindʒ] *n* frynse *c*
frock [frɔk] *n* kjole *m*
frog [frɔg] *n* frosk *m*
from [frɔm] *prep* fra; av; fra og med
front [frʌnt] *n* forside *c*; **in ~ of** foran
frontier ['frʌntiə] *n* grense *c*
frost [frɔst] *n* frost *m*
frozen ['frouzən] *adj* frossen; **~ food** dypfryst mat
fruit [fruːt] *n* frukt *c*
fry [frai] *v* steke
frying pan ['fraiiŋpæn] *n* stekepanne *c*
fuck [fʌk] *v vulgar* knulle, pule
fuel ['fjuːəl] *n* brensel *nt*; bensin *m*; **~ pump** *Am* bensinpumpe *c*
full [ful] *adj* full; **~ board** helpensjon *m*; **~ stop**

punktum *nt*; ~ **up** fullsatt
fun [fʌn] *n* moro *c*, gøy *m* / *nt*
function ['fʌŋkʃən] *n* funksjon *m*
fund [fʌnd] *n* fond *nt*
fundamental [ˌfʌndə'mentəl] *adj* fundamental
funeral ['fju:nərəl] *n* begravelse *m*
funnel ['fʌnəl] *n* trakt *c*
funny ['fʌni] *adj* pussig, komisk; merkelig
fur [fə:] *n* pels *m*; ~ **coat** pelskåpe *c*
furious ['fjuəriəs] *adj* rasende
furnace ['fə:nis] *n* ovn *m*
furnish ['fə:niʃ] *v* forsyne, skaffe; møblere, innrette; ~ **with** forsyne med
furniture ['fə:nitʃə] *n* møbler *pl*
furrier ['fʌriə] *n* buntmaker *m*
further ['fə:ðə] *adj* videre; ytterligere
furthermore ['fə:ðəmɔ:] *adv* dessuten
furthest ['fə:ðist] *adj* fjernest; lengst
fuse [fju:z] *n* sikring *c*; lunte *c*
fuss [fʌs] *n* bråk *nt*; oppstyr *nt*, mas *nt*
future ['fju:tʃə] *n* fremtid *c*; *adj* fremtidig

G

gable ['geibəl] *n* gavl *m*
gadget ['gædʒit] *n* innretning *m*, apparat *nt*
gain [gein] *v* *vinne; *n* fortjeneste *m*
gale [geil] *n* storm *m*
gall [gɔ:l] *n* galle *m*; ~ **bladder** galleblære *c*
gallery ['gæləri] *n* galleri *nt*; kunstgalleri *nt*
gallon ['gælən] *n* gallon *m* (Brit 4,55 l; Am 3,79 l)
gallop ['gæləp] *n* galopp *m*
gallows ['gælouz] *pl* galge *m*
gallstone ['gɔ:lstoun] *n* gallestein *m*
game [geim] *n* spill *nt*; vilt *nt*
gang [gæŋ] *n* bande *m*; gjeng *m*
gangway ['gæŋwei] *n* landgang *m*
gap [gæp] *n* åpning *c*
garage ['gærɑ:ʒ] *n* garasje *m*; *v* *sette i garasje
garbage ['gɑ:bidʒ] *n* avfall *nt*, søppel *nt*
garden ['gɑ:dən] *n* hage *m*; **public** ~ offentlig parkanlegg; **zoological gardens** zoologisk hage
gardener ['gɑ:dənə] *n* gartner *m*

gargle ['gɑ:gəl] *v* gurgle
garlic ['gɑ:lik] *n* hvitløk *m*
garment [ˌgɑ:mənt] *n* klesplagg *nt*
gas [gæs] *n* gass *m*; bensin *m*; ~ **cooker** gasskomfyr *m*; ~ **pump** *Am* bensinpumpe *c*; ~ **station** bensinstasjon *m*; ~ **stove** gasovn *m*
gasoline ['gæsəli:n] *nAm* bensin *m*
gastric ['gæstrik] *adj* mage-; ~ **ulcer** magesår *nt*
gasworks ['gæswə:ks] *n* gassverk *nt*
gate [geit] *n* port *m*; grind *c*
gather ['gæðə] *v* samle; samles; høste
gauge [geidʒ] *n* måleinstrument *nt*
gave [geiv] *v* (p give)
gay [gei] *adj* munter; fargerik; *colloquial* homofil
gaze [geiz] *v* stirre
gear [giə] *n* gir *nt*; utstyr *nt*; **change** ~ skifte gir; ~ **lever** girstang *c*
gearbox ['giəbɔks] *n* girkasse *c*
geese [dʒi:z] *n* (pl goose) gjess *pl*
gem [dʒem] *n* edelstein *m*, juvel *m*; klenodie *nt*
gender ['dʒendə] *n* kjønn *nt*
general ['dʒenərəl] *adj* generell; *n* general *m*; ~ **practitioner** allmennpraktiserende lege; **in** ~ som regel
generate ['dʒenəreit] *v* *frembringe
generation [ˌdʒenə'reiʃən] *n* generasjon *m*
generator ['dʒenəreitər] *n* generator *m*
generosity [ˌdʒenə'rɔsəti] *n* gavmildhet *c*
generous ['dʒenərəs] *adj* gavmild
genital ['dʒenitəl] *adj* kjønns-
genius ['dʒi:niəs] *n* geni *nt*
gentle ['dʒentəl] *adj* mild; lett, øm; forsiktig
gentleman ['dʒentəlmən] *n* (pl -men) herre *m*
genuine ['dʒenjuin] *adj* ekte
geography [dʒi'ɔgrəfi] *n* geografi *m*
geology [dʒi'ɔlədʒi] *n* geologi *m*
geometry [dʒi'ɔmətri] *n* geometri *m*
germ [dʒə:m] *n* basill *m*; kim *m*
German ['dʒə:mən] *adj* tysk; *n* tysker *m*
Germany ['dʒə:məni] Tyskland
gesticulate [dʒi'stikjuleit] *v* gestikulere
get-together sammenkomst *m*
***get** [get] *v* *få; hente; *bli; ~ **back** *gå tilbake; ~ **off** *stige av; ~ **on** *stige på; *gjøre fremskritt; ~ **up** *stå opp

ghost [goust] *n* spøkelse *nt*; ånd *m*
giant ['dʒaiənt] *n* kjempe *m*
giddiness ['gidinəs] *n* svimmelhet *c*
giddy ['gidi] *adj* svimmel
gift [gift] *n* presang *m*, gave *c*; evne *c*; **~ card** *n* gavekort *nt*
gifted ['giftid] *adj* begavet
gigantic [dʒai'gæntik] *adj* enorm
giggle ['gigəl] *v* fnise
gill [gil] *n* gjelle *c*
gilt [gilt] *adj* forgylt
ginger ['dʒindʒə] *n* ingefær *m*
girl [gə:l] *n* pike *m*
girlfriend ['gə:lfrend] *n* kjæreste *m*
***give** [giv] *v* *gi; *overrekke; **~ away** røpe; **~ in** *gi seg, *gi etter; **~ up** *oppgi, *gi opp
glacier ['glæsiə] *n* isbre *m*
glad [glæd] *adj* fornøyd, glad; **gladly** med glede, gjerne
gladness ['glædnəs] *n* glede *c*
glamorous ['glæmərəs] *adj* betagende, fortryllende
glamour ['glæmə] *n* sjarm *m*
glance [glɑ:ns] *n* blikk *nt*; *v* kaste et blikk
gland [glænd] *n* kjertel *m*
glare [glɛə] *n* skarpt lys; skinn *nt*
glaring ['glɛəriŋ] *adj* blendende
glass [glɑ:s] *n* glass *nt*; glass-; **glasses** briller *pl*; **magnifying ~** forstørrelsesglass *nt*
glaze [gleiz] *v* glasere
glide [glaid] *v* *gli
glider ['glaidə] *n* glidefly *nt*
glimpse [glimps] *n* glimt *nt*; *v* skimte
global ['gloubəl] *adj* verdensomfattende; **~ warming** *n* global oppvarming *c*
globalization [,gloubəli'zeiʃən] *n* globalisering *c*
globalize ['gloubə,laiz] *v* globalisere
globe [gloub] *n* globus *m*, jordklode *m*
gloom [glu:m] *n* mørke *nt*
gloomy ['glu:mi] *adj* dyster
glorious ['glɔ:riəs] *adj* strålende
glory ['glɔ:ri] *n* ære *c*, berømmelse *m*; ros *m*, heder *m*
gloss [glɔs] *n* glans *m*
glossy ['glɔsi] *adj* blank
glove [glʌv] *n* hanske *m*
glow [glou] *v* gløde; *n* glød *m*
glue [glu:] *n* lim *nt*
***go** [gou] *v* *gå; reise; **~ ahead** *fortsette; **~ away** reise bort; **~ back** vende tilbake; **~ home** *gå hjem; **~ in** *gå inn; **~ on** *fortsette, *gå videre; **~ out**

*gå ut; ~ **through** *gjennomgå, *gå igjennom
goal [goul] *n* mål *nt*
goalkeeper ['goul,ki:pə] *n* målmann *m*
goat [gout] *n* geit *c*
god [gɔd] *n* gud *m*
goddess ['gɔdis] *n* gudinne *c*
godmother ['gɔd,mʌðə] *n* gudmor *c*; fadder *m*
godfather ['gɔd,fɑ:ðə] *n* gudfar *m*; fadder *m*
goggles ['gɔgəlz] *pl* dykkerbriller *pl*, snøbriller *pl*
gold [gould] *n* gull *nt*; ~ **leaf** bladgull *nt*
golden ['gouldən] *adj* gyllen
goldsmith ['gouldsmiθ] *n* gullsmed *m*
golf [gɔlf] *n* golf *m*; ~ **course** golfbane *m*; ~ **links** golfbane *m*
golfclub ['gɔlfklʌb] *n* golfkølle *c*; golfklubb *m*
gondola ['gɔndələ] *n* gondol *m*
gone [gɔn] *adv* (pp go) borte
good [gud] *adj* bra, god; snill
goodbye [,gud'bai] adjø
good-humo(u)red [,gud'hju:məd] *adj* godlynt
good-looking [,gud'lukiŋ] *adj* pen
good-natured [,gud'neitʃəd] *adj* godmodig
goods [gudz] *pl* varer *pl*; ~ **train** godstog *nt*
good-tempered [,gud'tempəd] *adj* godmodig
goodwill [,gud'wil] *n* godvilje *m*
goose [gu:s] *n* (pl geese) gås *c*; ~ **flesh** gåsehud *c*
gooseberry ['guzbəri] *n* stikkelsbær *nt*
gorge [gɔ:dʒ] *n* kløft *c*; *v* proppe seg
gorgeous ['gɔ:dʒəs] *adj* praktfull
gospel ['gɔspəl] *n* evangelium *nt*
gossip ['gɔsip] *n* sladder *m*; *v* sladre
got [gɔt] *v* (p, pp get)
gout [gaut] *n* gikt *c*
govern ['gʌvən] *v* regjere
government ['gʌvənmənt] *n* styre *nt*, regjering *c*
governor ['gʌvənə] *n* guvernør *m*
gown [gaun] *n* kjole *m*
GPS ['dʒi:pi:'es], **global positioning system** *n* GPS *nt*, globalt posisjonsystem *nt*
grace [greis] *n* ynde *m*; nåde *m*
graceful ['greisfəl] *adj* yndig, grasiøs
grade [greid] *n* grad *m*; klasse *c*, *v* klassifisere; gradere
gradient ['greidiənt] *n* helling *c*

gradual ['grædʒuəl] *adj* gradvis
graduate ['grædʒueit] *v* *ta avsluttende eksamen
grain [grein] *n* korn *nt*
gram [græm] *n* gram *nt*
grammar ['græmə] *n* grammatikk *m*; **~ book** grammatikk *m*
grammatical [grə'mætikəl] *adj* grammatisk
grand [grænd] *adj* storartet
grandchild ['græn,tʃaild] *n* barnebarn *nt*
granddad ['grændæd], **grandfather** ['græn,fɑːðə] *n* farfar *m*; morfar *m*; bestefar *m*
grandma ['grænmɑ], **grandmother** ['græn,mʌðə] *n* farmor *c*; mormor *c*; bestemor *c*
grandparents ['græn,pɛərənts] *pl* besteforeldre *pl*
granite ['grænit] *n* granitt *m*
grant [grɑːnt] *v* bevilge; innvilge; *n* stipend *nt*, tilskudd *nt*
grapefruit ['greipfruːt] *n* grapefrukt *c*
grapes [greips] *pl* druer *pl*
graph [græf] *n* diagram *nt*
graphic ['græfik] *adj* grafisk
grasp [grɑːsp] *v* *gripe; *n* grep *nt*
grass [grɑːs] *n* gress *nt*
grasshopper ['grɑːs,hɔpə] *n* gresshoppe *c*
grate [greit] *n* rist *c*; *v* raspe
grateful ['greitfəl] *adj* takknemlig
grater ['greitə] *n* rivjern *nt*; rasp *c*
gratis ['grætis] *adj* gratis
gratitude ['grætitjuːd] *n* takknemlighet *c*
gratuity [grə'tjuːəti] *n* drikkepenger *pl*
grave [greiv] *n* grav *c*; *adj* alvorlig
gravel ['grævəl] *n* grus *m*
gravestone ['greivstoun] *n* gravstein *m*
graveyard ['greivjɑːd] *n* kirkegård *m*
gravity ['grævəti] *n* tyngdekraft *c*; alvor *nt*
gravy ['greivi] *n* saus *m*
graze [greiz] *v* beite; *n* skrubbsår *nt*
grease [griːs] *n* fett *nt*; *v* *smøre
greasy ['griːsi] *adj* fettet
great [greit] *adj* stor; **Great Britain** Storbritannia
Greece [griːs] Hellas
greed [griːd] *n* griskhet *c*
greedy ['griːdi] *adj* grisk; grådig
Greek [griːk] *adj* gresk; *n* greker *m*
green [griːn] *adj* grønn; **~ card** grønt kort
greengrocer ['griːn,grousə] *n* grønnsakhandler *m*
greenhouse ['griːnhaus] *n* drivhus *nt*
greens [griːnz] *pl* grønnsaker *pl*

greet [griːt] *v* hilse
greeting ['griːtiŋ] *n* hilsen *m*
grey [grei] *adj* grå
greyhound ['greihaund] *n* mynde *m*
grief [griːf] *n* sorg *c*; smerte *m*
grieve [griːv] *v* sørge
grill [gril] *n* grill *m*; *v* grille
grim [grim] *adj* grusom, skrekkelig
grin [grin] *v* glise, smile bredt; *n* glis *nt*
***grind** [graind] *v* male; finmale
grip [grip] *v* *gripe; *n* grep *nt*, tak *nt*
grit [grit] *n* grus *m*; fasthet *c*
groan [groun] *v* stønne
grocer ['grousə] *n* matvarehandler *m*; **grocer's** matvareforretning *c*
groceries ['grousəriz] *pl* matvarer *pl*
groin [grɔin] *n* lyske *m*
groom [gruːm] *n* hestepleier *m*, stallkar *m*; brudgom *m*; *v* pleie
groove [gruːv] *n* fure *m*
gross [grous] *adj* grov; brutto
grotto ['grɔtou] *n* (pl ~es, ~s) grotte *c*
ground[1] [graund] *n* jord *c*, grunn *m*; **~ floor** første etasje; **grounds** tomt *m*
ground[2] [graund] *v* (p, pp grind)
group [gruːp] *n* gruppe *c*
grouse [graus] *n* (pl ~) rype *c*
grove [grouv] *n* lund *m*
***grow** [grou] *v* vokse; dyrke; *bli
growl [graul] *v* brumme
grown-up ['grounʌp] *adj* voksen; *n* voksen *m*
growth [grouθ] *n* vekst *m*; svulst *m*
grudge [grʌdʒ] *v* misunne
grumble ['grʌmbəl] *v* knurre, klage
guarantee [ˌgærən'tiː] *n* garanti *m*; kausjon *m*; *v* garantere
guard [gɑːd] *n* vakt *c*; *v* bevokte
guardian ['gɑːdiən] *n* formynder *m*
guess [ges] *v* gjette; *anta; *n* formodning *m*
guest [gest] *n* gjest *m*; **~ room** gjesteværelse *nt*
guesthouse ['gesthaus] *n* pensjonat *nt*
guide [gaid] *n* guide *m*; *v* vise vei
guidebook ['gaidbuk] *n* reisehåndbok *c*
guide dog ['gaiddɔg] *n* førerhund *m*
guideline ['gaidlain] *n* retningslinje *c*
guilt [gilt] *n* skyld *c*
guilty ['gilti] *adj* skyldig
guinea pig ['ginipig] *n* marsvin *nt*; forsøksdyr *nt*
guitar [gi'tɑː] *n* gitar *m*

gulf [gʌlf] *n* golf *m*; vik *c*
gull [gʌl] *n* måke *c*
gum [gʌm] *n* tannkjøtt *nt*; gummi *m*; lim *nt*
gun [gʌn] *n* revolver *m*, gevær *nt*; kanon *m*
gunpowder ['gʌnˌpaudə] *n* krutt *nt*
gust [gʌst] *n* vindkast *nt*
gusty ['gʌsti] *adj* blåsende
gut [gʌt] *n* tarm *m*; **guts** vågemot *nt*
gutter ['gʌtə] *n* rennestein *m*
guy [gai] *n* kar *m*
gymnasium [dʒim'neiziəm] *n* (pl ~s, -sia) gymnastikksal *m*
gymnast ['dʒimnæst] *n* turner *m*
gymnastics [dʒim'næstiks] *pl* gymnastikk *m*
gynaecologist [ˌgainə'kɔlədʒist] *n* kvinnelege *m*, gynekolog *m*

H

habit ['hæbit] *n* vane *m*
habitable ['hæbitəbəl] *adj* beboelig
habitual [hə'bitʃuəl] *adj* vanemessig
had [hæd] *v* (p, pp have)
haddock ['hædək] *n* (pl ~) kolje *c*
h(a)emorrhage ['hemərid3] *n* blødning *m*
haemorrhoids ['hemərɔidz] *pl* hemorroider *pl*
hail [heil] *n* hagl *nt*
hair [hɛə] *n* hår *nt*; ~ **gel** hårgelé
hairbrush ['hɛəbrʌʃ] *n* hårbørste *m*
haircut ['hɛəkʌt] *n* hårklipp *m*
hairdo ['hɛədu:] *n* frisyre *m*
hairdresser ['hɛəˌdresə] *n* frisør *m*
hairdrier, **hairdryer** ['hɛədraiə] *n* hårtørrer *m*
hairpin ['hɛəpin] *n* hårspenne *c*
hair spray ['hɛəsprei] *n* hårlakk *m*
hairy ['hɛəri] *adj* håret
half[1] [hɑ:f] *adj* halv
half[2] [hɑ:f] *n* (pl halves) halvdel *m*
half time [ˌhɑ:f'taim] *n* halvtid *c*
halfway [ˌhɑ:f'wei] *adv* halvveis
halibut ['hælibət] *n* (pl ~) kveite *c*
hall [hɔ:l] *n* vestibyle *m*; sal *m*
halt [hɔ:lt] *v* stanse
halve [hɑ:v] *v* halvere
ham [hæm] *n* skinke *c*
hamlet ['hæmlət] *n* liten landsby
hammer ['hæmə] *n* hammer

m
hammock ['hæmək] *n* hengekøye *c*
hamper ['hæmpə] *n* kurv *m*
hand [hænd] *n* hånd *c*; *v* *overrekke; **~ cream** håndkrem *m*
handbag ['hændbæg] *n* håndveske *c*
handbook ['hændbuk] *n* håndbok *c*
handbrake ['hændbreik] *n* håndbrems *m*
handcuffs ['hændkʌfs] *pl* håndjern *pl*
handful ['hændful] *n* håndfull *m*
handheld ['hand,held] *adj* håndholdt
handicraft ['hændikrɑːft] *n* håndverk *nt*; kunsthåndverk *nt*
handicap ['hændikæp] *n* handikap *nt*; funksjonshemming *c*
handkerchief ['hæŋkətʃif] *n* lommetørkle *nt*
handle ['hændəl] *n* skaft *nt*, håndtak *nt*; *v* håndtere; behandle
hand-made [ˌhænd'meid] *adj* håndlaget
handshake ['hændʃeik] *n* håndtrykk *nt*
handsome ['hænsəm] *adj* pen
handwork ['hændwəːk] *n* håndarbeid *nt*
handwriting ['hændˌraitiŋ] *n* håndskrift *c*
handy ['hændi] *adj* hendig
***hang** [hæŋ] *v* *henge
hanger ['hæŋə] *n* henger *m*
hangover ['hæŋˌouvə] *n* bakrus *m*, tømmermenn *pl*
happen ['hæpən] *v* hende, skje
happening ['hæpəniŋ] *n* hendelse *m*, begivenhet *c*
happiness ['hæpinəs] *n* lykke *c*
happy ['hæpi] *adj* lykkelig, glad
harbour ['hɑːbə] *n* havn *c*
hard [hɑːd] *adj* hard; vanskelig; **~ disk** harddisk; **hardly** neppe
hardware ['hɑːdwɛə] *n* jernvarer *pl*; **~ store** jernvarehandel *m*
hare [hɛə] *n* hare *m*
harm [hɑːm] *n* skade *m*; fortred *m*; *v* skade
harmful ['hɑːmfəl] *adj* skadelig
harmless ['hɑːmləs] *adj* uskadelig; harmløs
harmony ['hɑːməni] *n* harmoni *m*
harp [hɑːp] *n* harpe *c*
harpsichord ['hɑːpsikɔːd] *n* cembalo *m*
harsh [hɑːʃ] *adj* streng; grusom
harvest ['hɑːvist] *n* avling *c*
has [hæz] *v* (pr have)
haste [heist] *n* hast *m*
hasten ['heisən] *v* skynde seg
hasty ['heisti] *adj* hurtig;

forhastet
hat [hæt] *n* hatt *m*
hatch [hætʃ] *n* luke *c*; *v* ruge ut
hate [heit] *v* avsky; hate; *n* hat *nt*
hatred ['heitrid] *n* hat *nt*
haughty ['hɔːti] *adj* hovmodig
haul [hɔːl] *v* slepe
***have** [hæv] *v* *ha; *få; **~ to** *måtte
hawk [hɔːk] *n* hauk *m*; falk *m*
hay [hei] *n* høy *nt*; **~ fever** høysnue *m*
hazard ['hæzəd] *n* risiko *m*
haze [heiz] *n* dis *m*
hazelnut ['heizəlnʌt] *n* hasselnøtt *c*
hazy ['heizi] *adj* disig
he [hiː] *pron* han
head [hed] *n* hode *nt*; *v* lede; **~ of state** statsoverhode *nt*; **~ teacher** overlærer *m*; **~ waiter** hovmester *m*
headache ['hedeik] *n* hodepine *c*
heading ['hediŋ] *n* overskrift *c*
headlamp ['hedlæmp] *n* frontlys *nt*
headlight ['hedlait] *n* frontlys *nt*
headline ['hedlain] *n* overskrift *c*
headmaster [ˌhed'mɑːstə] *n* overlærer *m*; rektor *m*
headquarters [ˌhed'kwɔːtəz] *pl* hovedkvarter *nt*
headrest ['hedrest] *n* nakkestøtte *c*
head-strong ['hedstrɔŋ] *adj* sta
heal [hiːl] *v* hele, lege
health [helθ] *n* helse *c*; **~ certificate** helseattest *m*
healthy ['helθi] *adj* sunn
heap [hiːp] *n* hop *m*, haug *m*
***hear** [hiə] *v* høre
hearing ['hiəriŋ] *n* hørsel *m*
heart [hɑːt] *n* hjerte *nt*; kjerne *m*; **by ~** utenat; **~ attack** hjerteanfall *nt*
heartburn ['hɑːtbəːn] *n* halsbrann *m*
hearth [hɑːθ] *n* ildsted *nt*
heartless ['hɑːtləs] *adj* hjerteløs
hearty ['hɑːti] *adj* hjertelig
heat [hiːt] *n* hete *m*, varme *m*; *v* varme opp; **heating pad** varmepute *c*
heater ['hiːtə] *n* varmeovn *m*
heath [hiːθ] *n* hei *c*
heathen ['hiːðən] *n* hedning *m*; *adj* hedensk
heather ['heðə] *n* lyng *m*
heating ['hiːtiŋ] *n* fyring *c*
heaven ['hevən] *n* himmel *m*
heavy ['hevi] *adj* tung
Hebrew ['hiːbruː] *n* hebraisk *nt*
hedge [hedʒ] *n* hekk *m*
hedgehog ['hedʒhɔg] *n* pinnsvin *nt*

heel [hiːl] *n* hæl *m*
height [hait] *n* høyde *m*; høydepunkt *nt*
heir [ɛə] *n* arving *m*
heiress [ɛəres] *n* kvinnelig arving *m*
helicopter ['helikʌptə] *n* helikopter *nt*
hell [hel] *n* helvete *nt*
hello! [he'lou] hei!, hallo!; **say hello to** hilse på
helm [helm] *n* ror *nt*
helmet ['helmit] *n* hjelm *m*
helmsman ['helmzmən] *n* rormann *m*
help [help] *v* *hjelpe; *n* hjelp *c*
helper ['helpə] *n* hjelper *m*
helpful ['helpfəl] *adj* hjelpsom
helping ['helpiŋ] *n* porsjon *m*
hem [hem] *n* fald *m*; søm *m*
hemp [hemp] *n* hamp *m*
hen [hen] *n* høne *c*
her [həː] *pron* henne; hennes
herb [həːb] *n* urt *c*
herd [həːd] *n* flokk *m*; bøling *m*
here [hiə] *adv* her; **~ you are!** vær så god!
hereditary [hi'reditəri] *adj* arvelig
hernia ['həːniə] *n* brokk *m* / *nt*
hero ['hiərou] *n* (pl ~es) helt *m*
heron ['herən] *n* hegre *m*
herring ['heriŋ] *n* (pl ~, ~s) sild *c*
herself [həː'self] *pron* seg; selv
hesitate ['heziteit] *v* nøle
heterosexual [ˌhetərə'sekʃuəl] *adj* heteroseksuell
hiccup ['hikʌp] *n* hikke *m*
hide [haid] *n* skinn *nt*
***hide** [haid] *v* gjemme; skjule
hideous ['hidiəs] *adj* avskyelig
hierarchy ['haiərɑːki] *n* hierarki *nt*
high [hai] *adj* høy
highway ['haiwei] *n* riksvei *m*; motorvei *m*
hijack ['haidʒæk] *v* kapre
hijacker ['haidʒækə] *n* kaprer *m*
hike [haik] *v* *gå fottur
hill [hil] *n* bakke *m*
hillside ['hilsaid] *n* li *c*; bakke *m*
hilltop ['hiltɔp] *n* bakketopp *m*
hilly ['hili] *adj* kupert
him [him] *pron* han, ham
himself [him'self] *pron* seg; selv
hinder ['hində] *v* hindre
hinge [hindʒ] *n* hengsel *nt*
hint [hint] *n* hint; antydning
hip [hip] *n* hofte *c*
hip-hop ['hipˌhɔp] *n* hiphop *c*
hire [haiə] *v* leie; **for ~** til leie
hire purchase

[,haiə'pə:tʃəs] *n* avbetalingskjøp *nt*
his [hiz] *adj* hans
historian [hi'stɔ:riən] *n* historiker *m*
historic [hi'stɔrik] *adj* historisk
historical [hi'stɔrikəl] *adj* historisk
history ['histəri] *n* historie *c*
hit [hit] *n* suksess *m*; slag *nt*; treff *nt*
***hit** [hit] *v* *slå; ramme, *treffe
hitchhike ['hitʃhaik] *v* haike
hitchhiker ['hitʃ,haikə] *n* haiker *m*
hoarse [hɔ:s] *adj* hes
hobby ['hɔbi] *n* hobby *m*
hobbyhorse ['hɔbihɔ:s] *n* kjepphest *m*
hockey ['hɔki] *n* hockey *m*
hoist [hɔist] *v* heise
hold [hould] *n* lasterom *nt*
***hold** [hould] *v* *holde, *holde på; *beholde; **~ on** *holde seg fast; **~ up** *holde oppe, støtte
hold-up ['houldʌp] *n* overfall *nt*
hole [houl] *n* hull *nt*
holiday ['hɔlədi] *n* ferie *m*; helligdag *m*; **~ camp** ferieleir *m*; **~ resort** feriested *nt*; **on ~** på ferie
Holland ['hɔlənd] Holland
hollow ['hɔlou] *adj* hul
holy ['houli] *adj* hellig
homage ['hɔmidʒ] *n* hyllest *m*
home [houm] *n* hjem *nt*; pleiehjem *nt*; *adv* hjemover, hjemme; **at ~** hjemme
homework ['houmwə:k] *n* hjemmelekser *pl*, lekser *pl*
home-made [,houm'meid] *adj* hjemmelaget
homesickness ['houm,siknəs] *n* hjemlengsel *m*
homosexual [,houmə'sekʃuəl] *adj* homoseksuell; homofil
honest ['ɔnist] *adj* ærlig; oppriktig
honesty ['ɔnisti] *n* ærlighet *c*
honey ['hʌni] *n* honning *m*
honeymoon ['hʌnimu:n] *n* hvetebrødsdager *pl*, bryllupsreise *c*
honk [hʌŋk] *vAm* tute
honour ['ɔnə] *n* ære *c*; *v* hedre, ære
honourable ['ɔnərəbəl] *adj* ærefull, hederlig; rettskaffen
hood [hud] *n* hette *c*; motorpanser *nt*
hoof [hu:f] *n* hov *m*
hook [huk] *n* krok *m*
hoot [hu:t] *v* tute
hooter ['hu:tə] *n* bilhorn *nt*
hop[1] [hɔp] *v* hoppe; *n* hopp *nt*
hop[2] [hɔp] *n* humle *m*
hope [houp] *n* håp *nt*; *v* håpe
hopeful ['houpfəl] *adj*

håpefull
hopeless ['houpləs] *adj* håpløs
horizon [hə'raizən] *n* horisont *m*
horizontal [ˌhɔri'zɔntəl] *adj* horisontal
horn [hɔːn] *n* horn *nt*; signalhorn *nt*
horrible ['hɔribəl] *adj* redselsfull; grusom, avskyelig, skrekkelig
horror ['hɔrə] *n* gru *m*, redsel *m*
hors d'œuvre [ɔː'dəːvr] *n* forrett *m*
horse [hɔːs] *n* hest *m*
horseman ['hɔːsmən] *n* (pl -men) rytter *m*
horsepower ['hɔːsˌpauə] *n* hestekraft *c*
horserace ['hɔːsreis] *n* hesteveddeløp *nt*
horseradish ['hɔːsˌrædiʃ] *n* pepperrot *c*
horseshoe ['hɔːsʃuː] *n* hestesko *m*
hospitable ['hɔspitəbəl] *adj* gjestfri
hospital ['hɔspitəl] *n* sykehus *nt*, hospital *nt*
hospitality [ˌhɔspi'tæləti] *n* gjestfrihet *c*
host [houst] *n* vert *m*
hostage ['hɔstidʒ] *n* gissel *nt*
hostess ['houstis] *n* vertinne *c*
hostile ['hɔstail] *adj* fiendtlig
hot [hɔt] *adj* het, varm
hotel [hou'tel] *n* hotell *nt*
hotspot ['hɔtˌspɔt] *n* (*internet*) trådløs sone *c*
hot-tempered [ˌhɔt'tempəd] *adj* hissig
hour [auə] *n* time *m*
hourly ['auəli] *adj* hver time
house [haus] *n* hus *nt*; bolig *m*; ~ **agent** eiendomsmegler *m*; ~ **block** *Am* kvartal *nt*; **public** ~ vertshus *nt*
houseboat ['hausbout] *n* husbåt *m*
household ['haushould] *n* husstand *m*
housekeeper ['hausˌkiːpə] *n* husholderske *c*
housekeeping ['hausˌkiːpiŋ] *n* husholdning *m*
housemaid ['hausmeid] *n* hushjelp *c*
housewife ['hauswaif] *n* husmor *c*
housework ['hauswəːk] *n* husarbeid *nt*
how [hau] *adv* hvordan; hvor; ~ **many** hvor mange; ~ **much** hvor mye
however [hau'evə] *conj* likevel
hug [hʌg] *v* omfavne; klemme; *n* klem *m*
huge [hjuːdʒ] *adj* svær, veldig, enorm
hum [hʌm] *v* nynne
human ['hjuːmən] *adj* menneskelig; ~ **being**

menneske *nt*
humanity [hju'mænəti] *n* menneskehet *c*
humble ['hʌmbəl] *adj* ydmyk
humid ['hju:mid] *adj* fuktig
humidity [hju'midəti] *n* fuktighet *c*
humorous ['hju:mərəs] *adj* vittig, morsom, humoristisk
humo(u)r ['hju:mə] *n* humor *m*
hundred ['hʌndrəd] *n* hundre
Hungarian [hʌŋ'geəriən] *adj* ungarsk; *n* ungarer *m*
Hungary ['hʌŋgəri] Ungarn
hunger ['hʌŋgə] *n* sult *m*
hungry ['hʌŋgri] *adj* sulten
hunt [hʌnt] *v* jakte; *n* jakt *c*; **~ for** lete etter
hunter ['hʌntə] *n* jeger *m*
hurricane ['hʌrikən] *n* orkan *m*; **~ lamp** stormlykt *c*
hurry ['hʌri] *v* forte seg, skynde seg; *n* hastverk *nt*; **in a ~** i full fart
***hurt** [hə:t] *v* *gjøre vondt, skade; såre
hurtful ['hə:tfəl] *adj* skadelig
husband ['hʌzbənd] *n* ektemann *m*; mann *m*
hut [hʌt] *n* hytte *c*
hygiene ['haidʒi:n] *n* hygiene *m*
hygienic [hai'dʒi:nik] *adj* hygienisk
hymn [him] *n* hymne *m*, salme *m*
hyphen ['haifən] *n* bindestrek *m*
hypocrisy [hi'pɔkrəsi] *n* hykleri *nt*
hypocrite ['hipəkrit] *n* hykler *m*
hypocritical [,hipə'kritikəl] *adj* hyklersk, skinnhellig
hysterical [hi'sterikəl] *adj* hysterisk

I

I [ai] *pron* jeg
ice [ais] *n* is *m*; **~ cream** iskrem *m*
Iceland ['aislənd] Island
Icelander ['aisləndə] *n* islending *m*
Icelandic [ais'lændik] *adj* islandsk
icon ['aikɔn] *n* ikon *m / nt*
ID [ai'di:] *n* identitetskort *nt*
idea [ai'diə] *n* idé *m*; tanke *m*, innfall *nt*; begrep *nt*, forestilling *c*
ideal [ai'diəl] *adj* ideell; *n* ideal *nt*
identical [ai'dentikəl] *adj* identisk
identification [ai,dentifi'keiʃən] *n* identifisering *c*

identify [ai'dentifai] *v* identifisere
identity [ai'dentəti] *n* identitet *m*; ~ **card** identitetskort *nt*
idiom ['idiəm] *n* idiom *nt*
idiomatic [ˌidiə'mætik] *adj* idiomatisk
idiot ['idiət] *n* idiot *m*
idiotic [ˌidi'ɔtik] *adj* idiotisk
idle ['aidəl] *adj* uvirksom; lat; nytteløs
idol ['aidəl] *n* avgud *m*; idol *nt*
if [if] *conj* hvis; om
ignition [ig'niʃən] *n* tenning *c*; ~ **coil** tennspole *m*
ignorant ['ignərənt] *adj* uvitende
ignore [ig'nɔː] *v* ignorere
ill [il] *adj* syk; dårlig
illegal [i'liːgəl] *adj* illegal, ulovlig
illegible [i'ledʒəbəl] *adj* uleselig
illiterate [i'litərət] *n* analfabet *m*
illness ['ilnəs] *n* sykdom *m*
illuminate [i'luːmineit] *v* opplyse, belyse
illumination [iˌluːmi'neiʃən] *n* belysning *m*
illusion [i'luːʒən] *n* illusjon *m*; fantasifoster *nt*
illustrate ['iləstreit] *v* illustrere
illustration [ˌilə'streiʃən] *n* illustrasjon *m*
image ['imidʒ] *n* bilde *nt*
imaginary [i'mædʒinəri] *adj* innbilt
imagination [iˌmædʒi'neiʃən] *n* fantasi *m*
imagine [i'mædʒin] *v* forestille seg; innbille seg; tenke seg
imitate ['imiteit] *v* imitere, etterligne
imitation [ˌimi'teiʃən] *n* imitasjon *m*, etterligning *c*
immediate [i'miːdjət] *adj* øyeblikkelig
immediately [i'miːdjətli] *adv* straks, øyeblikkelig, umiddelbart
immense [i'mens] *adj* enorm, veldig, umåtelig
immigrant ['imigrənt] *n* innvandrer *m*
immigrate ['imigreit] *v* immigrere
immigration [ˌimi'greiʃən] *n* immigrasjon *m*
immodest [i'mɔdist] *adj* ubeskjeden
immunity [i'mjuːnəti] *n* immunitet *m*
immunize ['imjunaiz] *v* *gjøre immun
impartial [im'pɑːʃəl] *adj* upartisk
impassable [im'pɑːsəbəl] *adj* ufremkommelig
impatient [im'peiʃənt] *adj* utålmodig
impede [im'piːd] *v* hindre, sinke
impediment [im'pedimənt] *n* hindring *c*

imperfect [im'pəːfikt] *adj* ufullkommen
imperial [im'piəriəl] *adj* keiserlig; riks-
impersonal [im'pəːsənəl] *adj* upersonlig
impertinence [im'pəːtinəns] *n* frekkhet *c*
impertinent [im'pəːtinənt] *adj* uforskammet, nesevis
implement[1] ['implimənt] *n* verktøy *nt*
implement[2] ['impliment] *v* iverksette, implementere
imply [im'plai] *v* antyde; *innebære
impolite [ˌimpə'lait] *adj* uhøflig
import[1] [im'pɔːt] *v* importere, innføre
import[2] ['impɔːt] *n* innførsel *m*, importvarer *pl*, import *m*; ~ **duty** importavgift *c*
importance [im'pɔːtəns] *n* viktighet *c*, betydning *m*
important [im'pɔːtənt] *adj* betydningsfull, viktig
importer [im'pɔːtə] *n* importør *m*
imposing [im'pouziŋ] *adj* imponerende
impossible [im'pɔsəbəl] *adj* umulig
impotence ['impətəns] *n* impotens *m*
impotent ['impətənt] *adj* impotent; avmektig
impress [im'pres] *v* *gjøre inntrykk på, imponere
impression [im'preʃən] *n* inntrykk *nt*
impressive [im'presiv] *adj* imponerende
imprison [im'prizən] *v* fengsle
imprisonment [im'prizənmənt] *n* fangenskap *nt*
improbable [im'prɔbəbəl] *adj* usannsynlig
improper [im'prɔpə] *adj* upassende
improve [im'pruːv] *v* forbedre
improvement [im'pruːvmənt] *n* forbedring *c*
improvise ['imprəvaiz] *v* improvisere
impudent ['impjudənt] *adj* uforskammet
impulse ['impʌls] *n* impuls *m*; innskytelse *m*
impulsive [im'pʌlsiv] *adj* impulsiv
in [in] *prep* i; om; *adv* inn
inaccessible [iˌnæk'sesəbəl] *adj* utilgjengelig
inaccurate [i'nækjurət] *adj* unøyaktig
inadequate [i'nædikwət] *adj* utilstrekkelig
incapable [iŋ'keipəbəl] *adj* udugelig
incense ['insens] *n* røkelse *m*
inch ['intʃ] *n* tomme *m* (2,54 cm)
incident ['insidənt] *n*

hendelse *m*
incidental [ˌinsi'dentəl] *adj* tilfeldig
incite [in'sait] *v* anspore, egge
inclination [ˌiŋkli'neiʃən] *n* tilbøyelighet *c*
incline [iŋ'klain] *n* skråning *m*
inclined [iŋ'klaind] *adj* tilbøyelig
include [iŋ'klu:d] *v* innbefatte, omfatte; **included** inkludert
inclusive [iŋ'klu:siv] *adj* inklusive
income ['iŋkəm] *n* inntekt *c*; **~ tax** inntektsskatt *m*
incompetent [iŋ'kɔmpətənt] *adj* inkompetent; udugelig
incomplete [ˌinkəm'pli:t] *adj* ufullstendig
inconceivable [ˌiŋkən'si:vəbəl] *adj* utenkelig
inconspicuous [ˌiŋkən'spikjuəs] *adj* uanselig
inconvenience [ˌiŋkən'vi:njəns] *n* ubeleilighet *c*, besvær *nt*
inconvenient [ˌiŋkən'vi:njənt] *adj* ubeleilig; besværlig
incorrect [ˌiŋkə'rekt] *adj* uriktig, feil
increase[1] [iŋ'kri:s] *v* øke; forsterke, *tilta
increase[2] ['iŋkri:s] *n* vekst *m*; stigning *m*
incredible [iŋ'kredəbəl] *adj* utrolig
incurable [iŋ'kjuərəbəl] *adj* uhelbredelig
indecent [in'di:sənt] *adj* uanstendig
indeed [in'di:d] *adv* virkelig
indefinite [in'definit] *adj* ubestemt; uklar
indemnity [in'demnəti] *n* skadeserstatning *m*; erstatning *m*
independence [ˌindi'pendəns] *n* uavhengighet *c*
independent [ˌindi'pendənt] *adj* uavhengig; selvstendig
index ['indeks] *n* fortegnelse *m*, register *nt*; **~ finger** pekefinger *m*
India ['indiə] India
Indian ['indiən] *adj* indisk; indiansk; *n* inder *m*; indianer *m*
indicate ['indikeit] *v* antyde, anvise, *angi
indication [ˌindi'keiʃən] *n* tegn *nt*
indicator ['indikeitə] *n* blinklys *nt*
indifferent [in'difərənt] *adj* likegyldig
indigestion [ˌindi'dʒestʃən] *n* dårlig fordøyelse
indignation [ˌindig'neiʃən] *n* forargelse *m*
indirect [ˌindi'rekt] *adj* indirekte

individual [ˌindi'vidʒuəl] *adj* individuell, enkelt; *n* enkeltperson *m*, individ *nt*
Indonesia [ˌində'ni:ziə] Indonesia
Indonesian [ˌində'ni:ziən] *adj* indonesisk; *n* indonesier *m*
indoor ['indɔ:] *adj* innendørs
indoors [ˌin'dɔ:z] *adv* inne
indulge [in'dʌldʒ] *v* *gi etter; *hengi seg til
industrial [in'dʌstriəl] *adj* industriell; **~ area** industriområde *nt*
industrious [in'dʌstriəs] *adj* flittig
industry ['indəstri] *n* industri *m*; næring *c*
inedible [i'nedibəl] *adj* uspiselig
inefficient [ˌini'fiʃənt] *adj* udugelig; ineffektiv
inevitable [i'nevitəbəl] *adj* uunngåelig
inexpensive [ˌinik'spensiv] *adj* billig
inexperienced [ˌinik'spiəriənst] *adj* uerfaren
infant ['infənt] *n* spedbarn *nt*
infantry ['infəntri] *n* infanteri *nt*
infect [in'fekt] *v* infisere, smitte
infection [in'fekʃən] *n* smitte *m*
infectious [in'fekʃəs] *adj* smittsom
infer [in'fə:] *v* utlede
inferior [in'fiəriə] *adj* dårligere, underlegen; mindreverdig; nedre
infinite ['infinət] *adj* uendelig
infinitive [in'finitiv] *n* infinitiv *m*
inflammable [in'flæməbəl] *adj* ildsfarlig
inflammation [ˌinflə'meiʃən] *n* betennelse *m*
inflatable [in'fleitəbəl] *adj* oppblåsbar
inflate [in'fleit] *v* blåse opp
inflation [in'fleiʃən] *n* inflasjon *m*
inflict [in'flikt] *v* tilføye
influence ['influəns] *n* innflytelse *m*; *v* påvirke
influential [ˌinflu'enʃəl] *adj* innflytelsesrik
influenza [ˌinflu'enzə] *n* influensa *m*
inform [in'fɔ:m] *v* opplyse, informere; underrette, meddele
informal [in'fɔ:məl] *adj* uformell
information [ˌinfə'meiʃən] *n* informasjon *m*; meddelelse *m*, opplysning *m*; **~ bureau** informasjonskontor *nt*
infra-red [ˌinfrə'red] *adj* infrarød
infrequent [in'fri:kwənt] *adj* sjelden

ingredient [iŋ'griːdiənt] *n* bestanddel *m*, ingrediens *m*
inhabit [in'hæbit] *v* bebo
inhabitable [in'hæbitəbəl] *adj* beboelig
inhabitant [in'hæbitənt] *n* innbygger *m*; beboer *m*
inhale [in'heil] *v* innånde
inherit [in'herit] *v* arve
inheritance [in'heritəns] *n* arv *m*
inhibit [in'hibit] *v* hemme; forhindre
initial [i'niʃəl] *adj* opprinnelig, begynnelses-; *n* forbokstav *m*; *v* merke med initialer
initiate [i'niʃieit] *v* innføre; *ta initiativet til
initiative [i'niʃətiv] *n* initiativ *nt*
inject [in'dʒekt] *v* innsprøyte
injection [in'dʒekʃən] *n* injeksjon *m*
injure ['indʒə] *v* skade, kveste; krenke
injury ['indʒəri] *n* skade *m*; krenkelse *m*
injustice [in'dʒʌstis] *n* urett *m*
ink [iŋk] *n* blekk *nt*
inlet ['inlet] *n* vik *c*
inn [in] *n* vertshus *nt*
inner ['inə] *adj* indre
innkeeper ['in,kiːpə] *n* vertshusholder *m*
innocence ['inəsəns] *n* uskyld *c*
innocent ['inəsənt] *adj* uskyldig
inoculate [i'nɔkjuleit] *v* vaksinere
inoculation [i,nɔkju'leiʃən] *n* vaksinasjon *m*
inquire [iŋ'kwaiə] *v* *forespørre, forhøre seg
inquiry [iŋ'kwaiəri] *n* forespørsel *m*; etterforskning *m*; **~ office** informasjonskontor *nt*
inquisitive [iŋ'kwizətiv] *adj* nysgjerrig
insane [in'sein] *adj* sinnssyk
inscription [in'skripʃən] *n* inskripsjon *m*
insect ['insekt] *n* insekt *nt*; **~ repellent** insektmiddel *nt*
insecticide [in'sektisaid] *n* insektmiddel *nt*
insensitive [in'sensətiv] *adj* ufølsom
insert [in'səːt] *v* *sette inn, *innskyte
inside [,in'said] *n* innside *c*; *adj* indre; *adv* inne; inni; *prep* innen, innenfor; **~ out** vrengt; **insides** innvoller *pl*
insight ['insait] *n* innsikt *m*
insignificant [,insig'nifikənt] *adj* ubetydelig; intetsigende, uanselig; uvesentlig
insist [in'sist] *v* insistere; *fastholde
insolence ['insələns] *n* uforskammethet *c*
insolent ['insələnt] *adj* uforskammet, frekk

insomnia [in'sɔmniə] *n* søvnløshet *c*
inspect [in'spekt] *v* inspisere
inspection [in'spekʃən] *n* inspeksjon *m*; kontroll *m*
inspector [in'spektə] *n* inspektør *m*
inspire [in'spaiə] *v* inspirere
install [in'stɔ:l] *v* installere
installation [ˌinstə'leiʃən] *n* installasjon *m*
instal(l)ment [in'stɔ:lmənt] *n* avdrag *nt*; **installment plan** *Am* avbetalingskjøp *nt*
instance ['instəns] *n* eksempel *nt*; tilfelle *nt*; **for ~** for eksempel
instant ['instənt] *n* øyeblikk *nt*
instant message ['instənt‿'mesədʒ] *n* lynmelding *c*
instantly ['instəntli] *adv* øyeblikkelig, straks, umiddelbart
instead of [in'sted ɔv] istedenfor
instinct ['instiŋkt] *n* instinkt *nt*
institute ['institju:t] *n* institutt *nt*; forordning *m*; *v* opprette, stifte
institution [ˌinsti'tju:ʃən] *n* institusjon *m*, stiftelse *m*
instruct [in'strʌkt] *v* undervise
instruction [in'strʌkʃən] *n* undervisning *c*; veiledning *m*
instructive [in'strʌktiv] *adj* lærerik
instructor [in'strʌktə] *n* instruktør *m*
instrument ['instrumənt] *n* instrument *nt*; **musical ~** musikkinstrument *nt*
insufficient [ˌinsə'fiʃənt] *adj* utilstrekkelig
insulate ['insjuleit] *v* isolere
insulation [ˌinsju'leiʃən] *n* isolasjon *m*
insulator ['insjuleitə] *n* isolator *m*
insult[1] [in'sʌlt] *v* fornærme
insult[2] ['insʌlt] *n* fornærmelse *m*
insurance [in'ʃuərəns] *n* forsikring *c*; **~ policy** forsikringspolise *m*
insure [in'ʃuə] *v* forsikre
intact [in'tækt] *adj* intakt
integrate ['intəgreit] integrere; innlemme
intellect ['intəlekt] *n* intellekt *nt*, forstand *m*
intellectual [ˌintə'lektʃuəl] *adj* intellektuell
intelligence [in'telidʒəns] *n* intelligens *m*
intelligent [in'telidʒənt] *adj* intelligent
intend [in'tend] *v* *ha til hensikt
intense [in'tens] *adj* intens
intention [in'tenʃən] *n* hensikt *m*
intentional [in'tenʃənəl] *adj* tilsiktet

intercourse ['intəkɔːs] *n* omgang *m*
interest ['intrəst] *n* interesse *m*; rente *c*; *v* interessere
interested ['intristid] *adj* interessert
interesting ['intrəstiŋ] *adj* interessant
interfere [ˌintə'fiə] *v* *gripe inn; **~ with** blande seg inn i
interference [ˌintə'fiərəns] *n* innblanding *c*
interim ['intərim] *n* mellomtid *c*; *adj* foreløpig
interior [in'tiəriə] *n* innside *c*
interlude ['intəluːd] *n* mellomspill *nt*
intermediary [ˌintə'miːdjəri] *n* mellommann *m*
intermission [ˌintə'miʃən] *n* pause *m*
internal [in'təːnəl] *adj* indre
international [ˌintə'næʃənəl] *adj* internasjonal
Internet [in'tənet] *n* Internett *nt*, nett *nt*
interpret [in'təːprit] *v* tolke
interpreter [in'təːpritə] *n* tolk *m*
interrogate [in'terəgeit] *v* forhøre
interrogation [inˌterə'geiʃən] *n* forhør *nt*
interrupt [ˌintə'rʌpt] *v* *avbryte
interruption [ˌintə'rʌpʃən] *n* avbrytelse *m*
intersection [ˌintə'sekʃən] *n* veikryss *nt*
interval ['intəvəl] *n* pause *m*; intervall *nt*
intervene [ˌintə'viːn] *v* *gripe inn
interview ['intəvjuː] *n* intervju *nt*
intestine [in'testin] *n* tarm *m*; **intestines** tarmer
intimate ['intimət] *adj* intim
into ['intu] *prep* inn i
intolerable [in'tɔlərəbəl] *adj* utålelig
intoxicated [in'tɔksikeitid] *adj* beruset
intrigue [in'triːg] *n* intrige *m*
introduce [ˌintrə'djuːs] *v* introdusere, presentere, innføre
introduction [ˌintrə'dʌkʃən] *n* presentasjon *m*; innledning *m*
invade [in'veid] *v* trenge inn
invalid[1] ['invəliːd] *n* funksjonshemmet *m*, ufør *m*; *adj* funksjonshemmet, ufør
invalid[2] [in'vælid] *adj* ugyldig
invasion [in'veiʒən] *n* invasjon *m*
invent [in'vent] *v* *oppfinne; oppdikte
invention [in'venʃən] *n* oppfinnelse *m*
inventive [in'ventiv] *adj* oppfinnsom

inventor [in'ventə] *n* oppfinner *m*
inventory ['invəntri] *n* inventar *nt*; inventarliste *c*
invert [in'vəːt] *v* snu om
invest [in'vest] *v* investere
investigate [in'vestigeit] *v* etterforske
investigation [inˌvesti'geiʃən] *n* undersøkelse *m*; etterforskning *m*
investment [in'vestmənt] *n* investering *c*; kapitalanbringelse *m*, pengeanbringelse *m*
invisible [in'vizəbəl] *adj* usynlig
invitation [ˌinvi'teiʃən] *n* innbydelse *m*
invite [in'vait] *v* *innby, invitere
invoice ['invɔis] *n* faktura *m*
involve [in'vɔlv] *v* innblande
inwards ['inwədz] *adv* innover
iodine ['aiədiːn] *n* jod *m*
Iran [i'rɑːn] Iran
Iranian [i'reiniən] *adj* iransk; *n* iraner *m*
Iraq [i'rɑːk] Irak
Iraqi [i'rɑːki] *adj* irakisk; *n* iraker *m*
Ireland ['aiələnd] Irland
Irish ['aiəriʃ] *adj* irsk
iron ['aiən] *n* jern *nt*; strykejern *nt*; jern-; *v* *stryke
ironical [ai'rɔnikəl] *adj* ironisk
irony ['aiərəni] *n* ironi *m*
irregular [i'regjulə] *adj* uregelmessig
irreparable [i'repərəbəl] *adj* ubotelig
irrevocable [i'revəkəbəl] *adj* ugjenkallelig
irritable ['iritəbəl] *adj* irritabel
irritate ['iriteit] *v* irritere, ergre
is [iz] *v* (pr be)
island ['ailənd] *n* øy *c*
isolate ['aisəleit] *v* isolere
isolation [ˌaisə'leiʃən] *n* isolasjon *m*
Israel ['izreil] Israel
Israeli [iz'reili] *adj* israelsk; *n* israeler *m*
issue ['iʃuː] *v* utstede; *utgi; *n* utstedelse *m*; utgivelse *m*; spørsmål *nt*, sak *c*; utgang *m*, resultat *nt*, følge *m*, sluttresultat *nt*; utvei *m*
it [it] *pron* det
Italian [i'tæljən] *adj* italiensk; *n* italiener *m*
Italy ['itəli] Italia
itch [itʃ] *n* kløe *m*; *v* klø
item ['aitəm] *n* post *m*; punkt *nt*
itinerary [ai'tinərəri] *n* reiserute *c*, reiseplan *m*
its [its] *pron* dens, dets
itself [it'self] *pron* seg; seg selv; selv; **by ~** alene; av seg selv
ivory ['aivəri] *n* elfenbein *nt*
ivy ['aivi] *n* eføy *m*

J

jack [dʒæk] *n* jekk *m*
jacket ['dʒækit] *n* dressjakke *c*, jakke *c*; omslag *nt*
jade [dʒeid] *n* jade *m*
jail [dʒeil] *n* fengsel *nt*
jam [dʒæm] *n* syltetøy *nt*; trafikkkork *m*
janitor ['dʒænitə] *n* vaktmester *m*
January ['dʒænjuəri] januar
Japan [dʒə'pæn] Japan
Japanese [ˌdʒæpə'ni:z] *adj* japansk; *n* japaner *m*
jar [dʒɑ:] *n* krukke *c*
jargon [dʒɑ:gən] *n* sjargong *m*
jaundice ['dʒɔ:ndis] *n* gulsott *m*
jaw [dʒɔ:] *n* kjeve *m*
jealous ['dʒeləs] *adj* sjalu
jealousy ['dʒeləsi] *n* sjalusi *m*
jeans [dʒi:nz] *pl* dongeribukse *c*, jeans *m*, olabukse *c*
jelly ['dʒeli] *n* gelé *m*
jellyfish ['dʒelifiʃ] *n* manet *m*
jersey ['dʒə:zi] *n* jersey *m*; genser *m*
jet [dʒet] *n* stråle *m*; jetfly *nt*
jet lag ['jet‿ˌlæg] *n* jetlag *c*
jetty ['dʒeti] *n* molo *m*
Jew [dʒu:] *n* jøde *m*
jewel ['dʒu:əl] *n* smykke *nt*
jewelry ['dʒu:əlri] *nAm* smykker *pl*
jeweller ['dʒu:ələ] *n* gullsmed *m*
jewellery ['dʒu:əlri] *n* smykker *pl*
Jewish ['dʒu:iʃ] *adj* jødisk
job [dʒɔb] *n* jobb *m*; stilling *c*
jobless ['dʒɔbles] *adj* arbeidsløs
jockey ['dʒɔki] *n* jockey *m*
join [dʒɔin] *v* *forbinde; slutte seg til; forene, sammenføye
joint [dʒɔint] *n* ledd *nt*; *adj* felles, forent; **~ venture** fellesprosjekt *nt*
jointly ['dʒɔintli] *adv* i fellesskap
joke [dʒouk] *n* vits *m*, spøk *m*
jolly ['dʒɔli] *adj* lystig
Jordan ['dʒɔ:dən] Jordan
Jordanian [dʒɔ:'deiniən] *adj* jordansk; *n* jordaner *m*
journal ['dʒə:nəl] *n* tidsskrift *nt*
journalism ['dʒə:nəlizəm] *n* journalistikk *m*
journalist ['dʒə:nəlist] *n* journalist *m*
journey ['dʒə:ni] *n* reise *c*
joy [dʒɔi] *n* glede *c*, fryd *m*
joyful ['dʒɔifəl] *adj* glad
jubilee ['dʒu:bili:] *n*

jubileum *nt*
judge [dʒʌdʒ] *n* dommer *m*; *v* dømme; bedømme
judgment ['dʒʌdʒmənt] *n* dom *m*
jug [dʒʌg] *n* mugge *c*
juice [dʒu:s] *n* saft *m*
juicy ['dʒu:si] *adj* saftig
July [dʒu'lai] juli
jump [dʒʌmp] *v* hoppe; *n* hopp *nt*, sprang *nt*
junction ['dʒʌŋkʃən] *n* veikryss *nt*; knutepunkt *nt*
June [dʒu:n] juni
jungle ['dʒʌŋgəl] *n* urskog *m*, jungel *m*
junior ['dʒu:njə] *adj* junior
junk [dʒʌŋk] *n* skrap *nt*
jurisdiction [dʒuərisdikʃən] *n* jurisdiksjon *m*
jury ['dʒuəri] *n* jury *m*
just [dʒʌst] *adj* rettferdig, passende; riktig; *adv* nettopp; akkurat
justice ['dʒʌstis] *n* rett *m*; rettferdighet *c*
justify ['dʒʌstifai] *v* rettferdiggjøre
juvenile ['dʒu:vənail] *adj* ungdoms-

K

kangaroo [ˌkæŋgə'ru:] *n* kenguru *m*
kayak ['kaijæk] *n* kajakk *m*
keel [ki:l] *n* kjøl *m*
keen [ki:n] *adj* begeistret; skarp
***keep** [ki:p] *v* *holde; bevare; *holde på med; **~ away from** mmholde seg borte fra; **~ off** *la være; **~ on** *fortsette; **~ quiet** tie; **~ up** *holde ut; **~ up with** *holde følge med
kennel ['kenəl] *n* hundehus *nt*; kennel *m*
Kenya ['kenjə] Kenya
kerosene ['kerəsi:n] *n* petroleum *m*; kerosin *m*, flybensin *m*
kettle ['ketəl] *n* kjele *m*
key [ki:] *n* nøkkel *m*
keyhole ['ki:houl] *n* nøkkelhull *nt*
khaki ['kɑ:ki] *n* kaki *m*
kick [kik] *v* sparke; *n* spark *nt*
kickoff [ˌki'kɔf] *n* avspark *nt*
kid [kid] *n* barn *nt*, unge *m*; *v* skrøne
kidney ['kidni] *n* nyre *c*
kill [kil] *v* drepe, *slå i hjel
kilogram ['kiləgræm] *n* kilo *m* / *nt*
kilometer *Am*, **kilometre** ['kiləˌmi:tə] *n* kilometer *m*
kind [kaind] *adj* snill, vennlig; god; *n* sort *m*
kindergarten ['kindəˌgɑ:tən] *n* barnehage *m*, førskole *m*
king [kiŋ] *n* konge *m*
kingdom ['kiŋdəm] *n*

kongerike *nt*; rike *nt*
kiosk ['ki:ɔsk] *n* kiosk *m*
kiss [kis] *n* kyss *nt*; *v* kysse
kit [kit] *n* utstyr *nt*
kitchen ['kitʃin] *n* kjøkken *nt*; **~ garden** kjøkkenhage *m*; **~ towel** kjøkkenhåndkle *nt*
knapsack ['næpsæk] *n* ryggsekk *m*; ransel *m*
knave [neiv] *n* knekt *m*
knee [ni:] *n* kne *nt*
kneecap ['ni:kæp] *n* kneskål *c*
***kneel** [ni:l] *v* knele
knew [nju:] *v* (p know)
knife [naif] *n* (pl knives) kniv *m*
knight [nait] *n* ridder *m*
***knit** [nit] *v* strikke; **knitting wool** garn *nt*
knob [nɔb] *n* knott *m*
knock [nɔk] *v* banke; *n* bank *nt*; **~ against** støte på; **~ down** *slå ned
knot [nɔt] *n* knute *m*; *v* knytte
***know** [nou] *v* *vite; *kunne, kjenne
knowledge ['nɔlidʒ] *n* kjennskap *nt*; kunnskap *m*
knuckle ['nʌkəl] *n* knoke *m*

L

label ['leibəl] *n* etikett *m*; *v* *sette merkelapp på
laboratory [lə'bɔrətəri] *n* laboratorium *nt*
labo(u)r ['leibə] *n* arbeid *nt*; fødselsveer *pl*; *v* *slite, anstrenge seg; **labor permit** *Am* arbeidstillatelse *m*
labo(u)rer ['leibərə] *n* arbeider *m*
labo(u)r-saving ['leibə,seiviŋ] *adj* arbeidsbesparende
labyrinth ['læbərinθ] *n* labyrint *m*
lace [leis] *n* kniplinger *pl*; lisse *c*
lack [læk] *n* savn *nt*, mangel *m*; *v* mangle
lacquer ['lækə] *n* lakk *m*
lactose ['læktous] *n* laktose *c*
lactose intolerant ['læktous‿in'tɔlərənt] *adj* laktoseintolerant
lad [læd] *n* gutt *m*
ladder ['lædə] *n* stige *m*
lady ['leidi] *n* dame *c*; **ladies' room** dametoalett *nt*
lagoon [lə'gu:n] *n* lagune *m*
lake [leik] *n* innsjø *m*
lamb [læm] *n* lam *nt*; lammekjøtt *nt*
lame [leim] *adj* lam, halt
lamentable ['læməntəbəl] *adj* beklagelig
lamp [læmp] *n* lampe *c*
lampshade ['læmpʃeid] *n*

lampeskjerm *m*
land [lænd] *n* land *nt*; *v* lande; *gå i land
landlady ['lænd,leidi] *n* vertinne *c*
landlord ['lændlɔ:d] *n* vert *m*, huseier *m*; husvert *m*
landmark ['lændmɑ:k] *n* landemerke *nt*
landscape ['lændskeip] *n* landskap *nt*
lane [lein] *n* smug *nt*, smal vei; fil *m*
language ['læŋgwidʒ] *n* språk *nt*
lantern ['læntən] *n* lykt *c*
lap [læp] *n* fang *nt*; runde *m*; *v* slikke
lapel [lə'pel] *n* jakkeslag *nt*
laptop ['læp,tɔp] *n* bærbar PC *c*
large [lɑ:dʒ] *adj* stor; rommelig
lark [lɑ:k] *n* lerke *c*
laryngitis [,lærin'dʒaitis] *n* strupekatarr *m*
last [lɑ:st] *adj* sist; forrige; *v* vare; **at ~** til slutt
lasting ['lɑ:stiŋ] *adj* varig
latchkey ['lætʃki:] *n* entrénøkkel *m*
late [leit] *adj* sen; for sent
lately ['leitli] *adv* i det siste, nylig
lather ['lɑ:ðə] *n* skum *nt*
Latin America ['lætin ə'merikə] Latin-Amerika
Latin-American [,lætinə'merikən] *adj* latinamerikansk
latitude ['lætitju:d] *n* breddegrad *m*
laugh [lɑ:f] *v* *le; *n* latter *m*
laughter ['lɑ:ftə] *n* latter *m*
launch [lɔ:ntʃ] *v* *sette i gang; *skyte opp; *n* motorbåt *m*
launching ['lɔ:ntʃiŋ] *n* sjøsetning *m*
launderette [,lɔ:ndə'ret] *n* selvbetjeningsvaskeri *nt*
laundry ['lɔ:ndri] *n* vaskeri *nt*; vask *m*
lavatory ['lævətəri] *n* toalett *nt*
lavish ['læviʃ] *adj* ødsel
law [lɔ:] *n* lov *m*; rett *m*; **~ court** domstol *m*
lawful ['lɔ:fəl] *adj* lovlig
lawn [lɔ:n] *n* gressplen *m*
lawsuit ['lɔ:su:t] *n* rettssak *c*
lawyer ['lɔ:jə] *n* advokat *m*; jurist *m*
laxative ['læksətiv] *n* avføringsmiddel *nt*
***lay** [lei] *v* plassere, *legge, *sette; **~ bricks** mure
layer [leiə] *n* lag *nt*
layman ['leimən] *n* lekmann *m*
lazy ['leizi] *adj* doven; lat
***lead** [li:d] *v* lede
lead[1] [li:d] *n* forsprang *nt*; ledelse *m*; hunderem *c*
lead[2] [led] *n* bly *nt*
leader ['li:də] *n* fører *m*, anfører *m*
leadership ['li:dəʃip] *n* ledelse *m*; lederskap *nt*
leading ['li:diŋ] *adj* ledende

leaf [liːf] *n* (pl leaves) blad *nt*
league [liːg] *n* forbund *nt*; liga *m*
leak [liːk] *v* lekke; *n* lekkasje *m*
leaky ['liːki] *adj* lekk
lean [liːn] *adj* mager
***lean** [liːn] *v* lene seg
leap [liːp] *n* hopp *nt*
***leap** [liːp] *v* hoppe
leap year ['liːpjiə] *n* skuddår *nt*
***learn** [ləːn] *v* lære
learner ['ləːnə] *n* nybegynner *m*
lease [liːs] *n* leiekontrakt *m*; forpaktning *m*; *v* forpakte bort, leie ut; leie; lease
leash [liːʃ] *n* koppel *nt*, bånd *nt*
least [liːst] *adj* minst; **at ~** i det minste; minst
leather ['leðə] *n* lær *nt*; skinn-, lær-
leave [liːv] *n* permisjon *m*
***leave** [liːv] *v* *forlate, *gå bort; *legge igjen, *etterlate; **~ behind** *etterlate; **~ out** *utelate
Lebanese [ˌlebə'niːz] *adj* libanesisk; *n* libaneser *m*
Lebanon ['lebənən] Libanon
lecture ['lektʃə] *n* foredrag *nt*, forelesning *m*
left[1] [left] *adj* venstre
left[2] [left] *v* (p, pp leave)
left-hand ['lefthænd] *adj* venstre
left-handed [ˌleft'hændid] *adj* keivhendt
leg [leg] *n* bein *nt*
legacy ['legəsi] *n* legat *nt*
legal ['liːgəl] *adj* legal; rettslig; juridisk
legalization [ˌliːgəlai'zeiʃən] *n* legalisering *c*
legation [li'geiʃən] *n* legasjon *m*
legible ['ledʒibəl] *adj* leselig
legitimate [li'dʒitimət] *adj* lovlig
leisure ['leʒə] *n* fritid *c*; ro og mak
lemon ['lemən] *n* sitron *m*
lemonade [ˌlemə'neid] *n* limonade *m*; brus *m*
***lend** [lend] *v* låne bort
length [leŋθ] *n* lengde *c*
lengthen ['leŋθən] *v* forlenge
lengthways ['leŋθweiz] *adv* på langs
lens [lenz] *n* linse *c*; **telephoto ~** teleobjektiv *nt*; **zoom ~** zoomlinse *c*
leprosy ['leprəsi] *n* spedalskhet *c*
lesbian ['lesbiən] *adj* lesbisk
less [les] *adv* mindre
lessen ['lesən] *v* minske, forminske
lesson ['lesən] *n* leksjon *m*, time *m*
***let** [let] *v* *la; leie ut; **~ down** svikte
lethal ['liːðəl] *adj* dødelig
letter ['letə] *n* brev *nt*;

bokstav *m*; ~ **of credit** akkreditiv *nt*; ~ **of recommendation** anbefalingsbrev *nt*
letterbox ['letəbɔks] *n* postkasse *c*
lettuce ['letis] *n* bladsalat *m*
level ['levəl] *adj* jevn; plan; *n* plan *nt*, nivå *nt*; *v* nivellere, utligne; ~ **crossing** planovergang *m*
lever ['liːvə] *n* vektstang *c*
liability [ˌlaiə'biləti] *n* ansvar *nt*; forpliktelse *m*
liable ['laiəbəl] *adj* ansvarlig; ~ **to** utsatt for
liar ['laiə] *n* løgner *m*
liberal ['libərəl] *adj* liberal; rundhåndet, gavmild
liberation [ˌlibə'reiʃən] *n* befrielse *m*
Liberia [lai'biəriə] Liberia
Liberian [lai'biəriən] *adj* liberisk; *n* liberier *m*
liberty ['libəti] *n* frihet *c*
library ['laibrəri] *n* bibliotek *nt*
licence ['laisəns] *n*, **license** *nAm* bevilling *c*; tillatelse *m*; **driving** ~, **driver's** ~ *Am* førerkort *nt*; ~ **number** *Am* registreringsnummer *nt*; ~ **plate** nummerskilt *nt*
license ['laisəns] *v* *gi tillatelse
lick [lik] *v* slikke
lid [lid] *n* lokk *nt*
lie [lai] *v* lyve; *n* løgn *c*
***lie** [lai] *v* *ligge; ~ **down** *legge seg ned
life [laif] *n* (pl lives) liv *nt*; ~ **insurance** livsforsikring *c*; ~ **jacket** svømmevest *m*
lifebelt ['laifbelt] *n* livbelte *nt*
lifetime ['laiftaim] *n* levetid *c*
lift [lift] *v* løfte; *n* heis *m*
light [lait] *n* lys *nt*; *adj* lett; lys; ~ **bulb** lyspære *c*
***light** [lait] *v* tenne
lighter ['laitə] *n* lighter *m*
lighthouse ['laithaus] *n* fyrtårn *nt*
lighting ['laitiŋ] *n* belysning *m*
lightning ['laitniŋ] *n* lyn *nt*
like [laik] *v* like; *adj* lik; *conj* liksom; *prep* liksom
likely ['laikli] *adj* sannsynlig
like-minded [ˌlaik'maindid] *adj* likesinnet
likewise ['laikwaiz] *adv* likeså, likeledes
lily ['lili] *n* lilje *c*
limb [lim] *n* lem *nt*; gren *c*
lime [laim] *n* kalk *m*; lind *m*; limett *m*
limetree ['laimtriː] *n* lindetre *nt*
limit ['limit] *n* grense *c*; *v* begrense
limp [limp] *v* halte; *adj* slapp
line [lain] *n* linje *c*; strek *m*; line *c*; kø *m*; **stand in** ~ *Am* stå i kø
linen ['linin] *n* lin *nt*, lintøy *nt*
liner ['lainə] *n* passasjerbåt *m*

lingerie ['lɔ̃ʒəri:] *n* dameundertøy *nt*
lining ['lainiŋ] *n* fôr *nt*
link [liŋk] *v* *forbinde; *n* (*computer*) lenke *m*; ledd *nt*; link *m*
lion ['laiən] *n* løve *m*
lip [lip] *n* leppe *c*; ~ **balm** leppepomade *m*
liposuction ['lipou,sʌkʃən] *n* fettsuging *c*
lipstick ['lipstik] *n* leppestift *m*
liqueur [li'kjuə] *n* likør *m*
liquid ['likwid] *adj* flytende; *n* væske *c*
liquor ['likə] *n* sprit *m*; brennevin *nt*; ~ **store** *Am* alkoholutsalg *nt*
liquorice ['likəris] *n* lakris *m*
list [list] *n* liste *c*; *v* *innskrive, regne opp
listen ['lisən] *v* lytte
listener ['lisnə] *n* lytter *m*
liter ['li:tə] *nAm* liter *m*
literary ['litrəri] *adj* litterær
literature ['litrətʃə] *n* litteratur *m*
litre ['li:tə] *n* liter *m*
litter ['litə] *n* avfall *nt*, søppel *nt*; kull *nt*
little ['litəl] *adj* liten; lite
live[1] [liv] *v* leve; bo
live[2] [laiv] *adj* levende; direkte
livelihood ['laivlihud] *n* levebrød *nt*
lively ['laivli] *adj* livlig
liver ['livə] *n* lever *c*
living ['liviŋ] *n* liv *nt*; levebrød *nt*; *adj* levende; ~ **room** dagligstue *c*; stue *c*
lizard ['lizəd] *n* firfisle *c*
load [loud] *n* last *c*; bør *c*; *v* laste
loaf [louf] *n* (pl loaves) brød *nt*
loan [loun] *n* lån *nt*
lobby ['lɔbi] *n* vestibyle *m*; foajé *m*; lobby *m*
lobster ['lɔbstə] *n* hummer *m*
local ['loukəl] *adj* lokal, stedlig; ~ **call** lokalsamtale *m*; ~ **train** lokaltog *nt*
locality [lou'kæləti] *n* sted *nt*
locate [lou'keit] *v* lokalisere
location [lou'keiʃən] *n* beliggenhet *c*
lock [lɔk] *v* låse; *n* lås *m*; sluse *c*; ~ **up** låse opp, sperre inne
locker ['lɔkə] *n* skap *nt*
locomotive [,loukə'moutiv] *n* lokomotiv *nt*
lodge [lɔdʒ] *v* huse; *n* hytte *c*
lodger ['lɔdʒə] *n* leieboer *m*
lodgings ['lɔdʒiŋz] *pl* losji *nt*
log [lɔg] *n* kubbe *m*; ~ **in** *v* logge inn; ~ **off** *v* logge ut
logic ['lɔdʒik] *n* logikk *m*
logical ['lɔdʒikəl] *adj* logisk
lonely ['lounli] *adj* ensom
long [lɔŋ] *adj* lang; langvarig; ~ **for** lengte etter; **no longer** ikke

lenger
longing ['lɔŋiŋ] *n* lengsel *m*
longitude ['lɔndʒitju:d] *n* lengdegrad *m*
look [luk] *v* *se; synes, *se ut; *n* blikk *nt*; utseende *nt*; ~ **after** sørge for, passe; ~ **at** *se på; ~ **for** lete etter; ~ **out** *se opp, passe seg for; ~ **up** *slå opp
looking-glass ['lukiŋgla:s] *n* speil *nt*
loop [lu:p] *n* løkke *c*
loose [lu:s] *adj* løs
loosen ['lu:sən] *v* løsne
lord [lɔ:d] *n* lord *m*; herre *m*
lorry ['lɔri] *n* lastebil *m*
***lose** [lu:z] *v* tape, miste
loser ['lu:z ə] *n* taper *m*
loss [lɔs] *n* tap *nt*
lost [lɔst] *adj* gått vill; forsvunnet; ~ **and found** hittegods *nt*; ~ **property office** hittegodskontor *nt*
lot [lɔt] *n* lodd *m*; mengde *m*, hop *m*
lotion ['louʃən] *n* hudkrem *m*; **aftershave** ~ barbervann *nt*
lottery ['lɔtəri] *n* lotteri *nt*
loud [laud] *adj* høylydt, høy
loudspeaker [,laud'spi:kə] *n* høyttaler *m*
lounge [laundʒ] *n* salong *m*; vestibyle *m*
louse [laus] *n* (pl lice) lus *c*
love [lʌv] *v* elske, *være glad i; *n* kjærlighet *c*; **in** ~ forelsket
lovely ['lʌvli] *adj* yndig, herlig, skjønn
lover ['lʌvə] *n* elsker *m*
love story ['lʌv,stɔ:ri] *n* kjærlighetshistorie *c*
low [lou] *adj* lav; dyp; nedstemt; ~ **tide** fjære *c*
lower ['louə] *v* senke; *adj* lavere
lowlands ['louləndz] *pl* lavland *nt*
loyal ['lɔiəl] *adj* lojal
lubricate ['lu:brikeit] *v* *smøre
lubrication [,lu:bri'keiʃən] *n* smøring *c*; ~ **oil** smøreolje *c*
luck [lʌk] *n* hell *nt*; tilfeldighet *c*; **bad** ~ uflaks *m*; **good** ~! lykke til!
lucky ['lʌki] *adj* heldig; ~ **charm** amulett *m*
ludicrous ['lu:dikrəs] *adj* latterlig
luggage ['lʌgidʒ] *n* bagasje *m*; **hand** ~ håndbagasje *m*; **left** ~ **office** bagasjeoppbevaring *c*; ~ **rack** bagasjehylle *c*; ~ **van** bagasjevogn *c*
lukewarm ['lu:kwɔ:m] *adj* lunken
lumbago [lʌm'beigou] *n* lumbago *m*
luminous ['lu:minəs] *adj* lysende
lump [lʌmp] *n* klump *m*, stykke *nt*; kul *m*; ~ **of sugar** sukkerbit *m*; ~ **sum** rund sum
lumpy ['lʌmpi] *adj* klumpet

lunch [lʌntʃ] *n* formiddagsmat *m*, lunsj *m*
luncheon ['lʌntʃən] *n* lunsj *m*
lung [lʌŋ] *n* lunge *c*
lust [lʌst] *n* begjær *nt*
luxurious [lʌg'ʒuəriəs] *adj* luksuriøs
luxury ['lʌkʃəri] *n* luksus *m*

M

machine [mə'ʃi:n] *n* maskin *m*, apparat *nt*
machinery [mə'ʃi:nəri] *n* maskineri *nt*
mackerel ['mækrəl] *n* (pl ~) makrell *m*
mackintosh ['mækintɔʃ] *n* regnfrakk *m*
mad [mæd] *adj* gal, vanvittig, rasende
madam ['mædəm] *n* frue *c*
madness ['mædnəs] *n* galskap *m*
magazine [,mægə'zi:n] *n* tidsskrift *nt*
magic ['mædʒik] *n* magi *m*, trolldom *m*; *adj* magisk
magician [mə'dʒiʃən] *n* tryllekunstner *m*
magistrate ['mædʒistreit] *n* dommer *m*
magnetic [mæg'netik] *adj* magnetisk
magnificent [mæg'nifisənt] *adj* praktfull, storslått
magnify [mæg'nifai] *v* forstørre, overdrive
maid [meid] *n* hushjelp *c*
maiden name ['meidən neim] pikenavn *nt*
mail [meil] *n* post *m*; *v* poste; ~ **order** *Am* postanvisning *m*
mailbox ['meilbɔks] *nAm* postkasse *c*
main [mein] *adj* hoved-; størst; ~ **deck** øverste dekk *nt*; ~ **road** hovedvei *m*; ~ **street** hovedgate *c*
mainland ['meinlənd] *n* fastland *nt*
mainly ['meinli] *adv* hovedsakelig
mains [meinz] *pl* hovedledning *m*
maintain [mein'tein] *v* *opprettholde
maintenance ['meintənəns] *n* vedlikehold *nt*
maize [meiz] *n* mais *m*
major ['meidʒə] *adj* større; eldre; *n* major *m*; dur *m*
majority [mə'dʒɔrəti] *n* flertall *nt*
***make** [meik] *v* lage; tjene; nå; ~ **do with** nøye seg med; ~ **good** *godtgjøre; ~ **up** *sette opp
make-up ['meikʌp] *n* sminke *c*
malaria [mə'lεəriə] *n* malaria *m*

Malay [mə'lei] *n* malaysier *m*
Malaysia [mə'leiziə] Malaysia
Malaysian [mə'leiziən] *adj* malaysisk
male [meil] *adj* hann-
malicious [mə'liʃəs] *adj* ondskapsfull
malignant [mə'lignənt] *adj* ondartet
mall [mɔːl] *nAm* kjøpesenter *nt*
mallet ['mælit] *n* kølle *c*
malnutrition [ˌmælnju'triʃən] *n* underernæring *c*
mammal ['mæməl] *n* pattedyr *nt*
man [mæn] *n* (pl men) mann *m*; menneske *nt*; **men's room** herretoalett *nt*
manage ['mænidʒ] *v* bestyre; lykkes
manageable ['mænidʒəbəl] *adj* håndterlig
management ['mænidʒmənt] *n* ledelse *m*; administrasjon *m*
manager ['mænidʒə] *n* sjef *m*, direktør *m*
mandarin ['mændərin] *n* mandarin *m*
mandate ['mændeit] *n* mandat *nt*
manger ['meindʒə] *n* krybbe *c*
manicure ['mænikjuə] *n* manikyr *m*
mankind [mæn'kaind] *n* menneskehet *c*
mannequin ['mænəkin] *n* utstillingsdukke *c*
manner ['mænə] *n* måte *m*, vis *nt*; **manners** *pl* manerer *pl*
man-of-war [ˌmænəv'wɔː] *n* krigsskip *nt*
manor house ['mænəhaus] *n* herregård *m*
mansion ['mænʃən] *n* herregård *m*
manual ['mænjuəl] *adj* hånd-, manuell
manufacture [ˌmænju'fæktʃə] *v* fabrikkere
manufacturer [ˌmænju'fæktʃərə] *n* fabrikant *m*
manure [mə'njuə] *n* gjødsel *c*
manuscript ['mænjuskript] *n* manuskript *nt*
many ['meni] *adj* mange
map [mæp] *n* kart *nt*
maple ['meipəl] *n* lønn *c*
marble ['mɑːbəl] *n* marmor *m*; klinkekule *c*
March [mɑːtʃ] mars
march [mɑːtʃ] *v* marsjere; *n* marsj *m*
mare [mɛə] *n* hoppe *c*
margarine [ˌmɑːdʒə'riːn] *n* margarin *m*
margin ['mɑːdʒin] *n* marg *m*
maritime ['mæritaim] *adj* maritim
mark [mɑːk] *v* markere; merke; kjennetegne; *n*

merke *nt*; karakter *m*; skyteskive *c*
market ['mɑ:kit] *n* marked *nt*
marketplace ['mɑ:kitpleis] *n* torg *nt*
marmalade ['mɑ:məleid] *n* marmelade *m*
marriage ['mæridʒ] *n* ekteskap *nt*
marrow ['mærou] *n* marg *m*
marry ['mæri] *v* gifte seg; **married couple** ektepar *nt*
marsh [mɑ:ʃ] *n* sump *m*
martyr ['mɑ:tə] *n* martyr *m*
marvel ['mɑ:vəl] *n* vidunder *nt*; *v* undre seg
marvel(l)ous ['mɑ:vələs] *adj* vidunderlig
mascara [mæ'skɑ:rə] *n* øyensverte *c*
masculine ['mæskjulin] *adj* maskulin
mash [mæʃ] *v* mose; **mashed potatoes** *npl* potetstappe *c*
mask [mɑ:sk] *n* maske *c*
Mass [mæs] *n* messe *m*
mass [mæs] *n* mengde *m*; **~ production** masseproduksjon *m*
massage ['mæsɑ:ʒ] *n* massasje *m*; *v* massere
masseur [mæ'sə:] *n* massør *m*
massive ['mæsiv] *adj* massiv
mast [mɑ:st] *n* mast *c*
master ['mɑ:stə] *n* mester *m*; lektor *m*, lærer *m*; *v* mestre, beherske
masterpiece ['mɑ:stəpi:s] *n* mesterverk *nt*
mat [mæt] *n* matte *c*; *adj* glansløs, matt
match [mætʃ] *n* fyrstikk *m*; kamp *m*; *v* passe til
matchbox ['mætʃbɔks] *n* fyrstikkeske *c*
material [mə'tiəriəl] *n* materiale *nt*; stoff *nt*; *adj* materiell
mathematical [,mæθə'mætikəl] *adj* matematisk
mathematics [,mæθə'mætiks] *n* matematikk *m*
matrimony ['mætriməni] *n* ekteskap *nt*
matter ['mætə] *n* stoff *nt*; spørsmål *nt*, sak *c*; *v* *være av betydning; **as a ~ of fact** faktisk, i virkeligheten
matter-of-fact [,mætərəv'fækt] *adj* realistisk
mattress ['mætrəs] *n* madrass *m*
mature [mə'tjuə] *adj* moden
maturity [mə'tjuərəti] *n* modenhet *c*
mausoleum [,mɔ:sə'li:əm] *n* mausoleum *nt*
mauve [mouv] *adj* lilla
May [mei] mai
***may** [mei] *v* *kunne
maybe ['meibi:] *adv* kanskje
mayor [mɛə] *n* borgermester *m*

maze [meiz] *n* labyrint *m*
me [miː] *pron* meg
meadow ['medou] *n* eng *c*
meal [miːl] *n* måltid *nt*
mean [miːn] *adj* sjofel; *n* gjennomsnitt *nt*
***mean** [miːn] *v* bety; mene
meaning ['miːniŋ] *n* mening *m*
meaningless ['miːniŋləs] *adj* meningsløs
means [miːnz] *n* middel *nt*; **by no ~** på ingen måte
meantime: in the ~ [in ðə 'miːntaim] i mellomtiden, imens
meanwhile ['miːnwail] *adv* i mellomtiden, imens
measles ['miːzəlz] *n* meslinger *pl*
measure ['meʒə] *v* måle; *n* mål *nt*; foranstaltning *m*
meat [miːt] *n* kjøtt *nt*
mechanic [mi'kænik] *n* mekaniker *m*
mechanical [mi'kænikəl] *adj* mekanisk
mechanism ['mekənizəm] *n* mekanisme *m*
medal ['medəl] *n* medalje *m*
media ['miːdiə] *pl* media *pl*
mediaeval [ˌmedi'iːvəl] *adj* middelaldersk
mediate ['miːdieit] *v* megle
mediator ['miːdieitə] *n* megler *m*
medical ['medikəl] *adj* medisinsk
medicine ['medsin] *n* medisin *m*; legevitenskap *m*
meditate ['mediteit] *v* meditere
Mediterranean [ˌmeditə'reiniən] Middelhavet
medium ['miːdiəm] *adj* gjennomsnittlig, middels
***meet** [miːt] *v* møte; *treffe
meeting ['miːtiŋ] *n* møte *nt*, sammenkomst *m*
meeting place ['miːtiŋpleis] *n* møtested *nt*
melancholy ['meləŋkəli] *n* melankoli *m*
mellow ['melou] *adj* bløt; moden
melodrama ['meləˌdrɑːmə] *n* melodrama *nt*
melody ['melədi] *n* melodi *m*
melon ['melən] *n* melon *m*
melt [melt] *v* smelte
member ['membə] *n* medlem *nt*; **Member of Parliament** parlamentsrepresentant *m*
membership ['membəʃip] *n* medlemskap *nt*
memo ['memou] *n* (pl ~s) memorandum *nt*
memorable ['memərəbəl] *adj* minneverdig
memorial [mə'mɔːriəl] *n* minnestein *m*
memorize ['memәraiz] *v* lære utenat
memory ['meməri] *n* hukommelse *m*; minne *nt*
mend [mend] *v* reparere,

*gjøre i stand
menstruation [ˌmenstru'eiʃən] *n* menstruasjon *m*
mental ['mentəl] *adj* mental
mention ['menʃən] *v* nevne; *n* omtale *m*
menu ['menju:] *n* spisekart *nt*, meny *m*
merchandise ['mə:tʃəndaiz] *n* varer *pl*, handelsvare *m*
merchant ['mə:tʃənt] *n* kjøpmann *m*
merciful ['mə:sifəl] *adj* barmhjertig
mercury ['mə:kjuri] *n* kvikksølv *nt*
mercy ['mə:si] *n* barmhjertighet *c*, nåde *m*
merely ['miəli] *adv* bare
merge ['mə:dʒ] *v* sammensmelte; fusjonere
merger ['mə:dʒə] *n* sammensmeltning *m*; fusjon *m*
merit ['merit] *v* fortjene; *n* fortjeneste *m*
merry ['meri] *adj* munter
merry-go-round ['merigouˌraund] *n* karusell *m*
mesh [meʃ] *n* nett *nt*, maske *c*
mess [mes] *n* rot *nt*; **~ up** rote til
message ['mesidʒ] *n* beskjed *m*
message board ['mesədʒ‿ˌbɔ:d] *n* oppslagstavle *c*
messenger ['mesindʒə] *n* budbringer *m*
metal ['metəl] *n* metall *nt*; metall-
meter ['mi:tə] *n* måler *m*
method ['meθəd] *n* metode *m*, fremgangsmåte *m*; ordning *c*
methodical [mə'θɔdikəl] *adj* metodisk
metre ['mi:tə] *n* meter *m*
metric ['metrik] *adj* metrisk
Mexican ['meksikən] *adj* meksikansk; *n* meksikaner *m*
Mexico ['meksikou] Mexico
mice (pl mouse)
microphone ['maikrəfoun] *n* mikrofon *m*
microwave oven ['maikrəweiv 'ʌvən] *n* mikrobølgeovn *m*
midday ['middei] *n* middag *m*; midt på dagen
middle ['midəl] *n* midte *m*; *adj* mellomste; **Middle Ages** middelalderen; **~ class** middelklasse *c*; **middle-class** *adj* borgerlig
midnight ['midnait] *n* midnatt *c*
midst [midst] *n* midte *m*
midsummer ['midˌsʌmə] *n* midtsommer *m*
midwife ['midwaif] *n* (pl -wives) jordmor *c*
might [mait] *n* makt *c*
***might** [mait] *v* *kunne
mighty ['maiti] *adj* mektig

migraine ['migrein] *n* migrene *m*
mild [maild] *adj* mild
mildew ['mildju] *n* mugg *m*
mile [mail] *n* engelsk mil
milage ['mailidʒ] *n* distanse *m*
milepost ['mailpoust] *n* veiskilt *nt*
milestone ['mailstoun] *n* milestein *m*
milieu ['mi:ljə:] *n* miljø *nt*
military ['militəri] *adj* militær-; **~ force** krigsmakt *c*
milk [milk] *n* melk *c*
milkshake ['milkʃeik] *n* milkshake *m*
milky ['milki] *adj* melkaktig
mill [mil] *n* mølle *c*; fabrikk *m*
million ['miljən] *n* million *m*
millionaire [ˌmiljə'nɛə] *n* millionær *m*
mince [mins] *v* finhakke
mind [maind] *n* sinn *nt*; *v* *ha noe imot; passe på, passe seg for, bry seg om
mine [main] *n* gruve *c*
miner ['mainə] *n* gruvearbeider *m*
mineral ['minərəl] *n* mineral *nt*; **~ water** naturlig mineralvann *nt*
mingle ['mingl] *v* blande (seg) med; blande seg inn
miniature ['minjətʃə] *n* miniatyr *m*
minimum ['minimәm] *n* minimum *nt*
mining ['mainiŋ] *n* gruvedrift *c*
minister ['ministə] *n* statsråd *m*; prest *m*; **Prime Minister** statsminister *m*
ministry ['ministri] *n* departement *nt*; prestegjerning *c*
mink [miŋk] *n* mink *m*
minor ['mainə] *adj* mindre, liten; underordnet; *n* mindreårig *m*; moll *m*
minority [mai'nɔrəti] *n* mindretall *nt*
mint [mint] *n* mynte *c*
minus ['mainəs] *prep* minus
minute[1] ['minit] *n* minutt *nt*; **minutes** referat *nt*
minute[2] [mai'nju:t] *adj* bitte liten
miracle ['mirəkəl] *n* mirakel *nt*
miraculous [mi'rækjuləs] *adj* mirakuløs
mirror ['mirə] *n* speil *nt*
misbehave [ˌmisbi'heiv] *v* oppføre seg dårlig
miscarriage [mis'kæridʒ] *n* spontan abort *m*
miscellaneous [ˌmisə'leiniəs] *adj* diverse
mischief ['mistʃif] *n* spillopper *pl*; ugagn *m*, skade *m*
mischievous ['mistʃivəs] *adj* skøyeraktig
miserable ['mizərəbəl] *adj* elendig, ulykkelig
misery ['mizəri] *n* elendighet *c*, ulykke *c*; nød

c
misfortune [mis'fɔːtʃen] *n* ulykke *c*, uhell *nt*
mishap ['mishæp] *n* ulykke *c*, uhell *nt*
***mislay** [mis'lei] *v* *forlegge
misplaced [mis'pleist] *adj* malplassert; mistet
mispronounce [ˌmisprə'nauns] *v* uttale galt
miss [mis] *v* miste
missing ['misiŋ] *adj* manglende; **~ person** savnet person
mist [mist] *n* dis *m*, tåke *c*
mistake [mi'steik] *n* feiltakelse *m*, feil *m*
***mistake** [mi'steik] *v* forveksle
mistaken [mi'steikən] *adj* feilaktig; ***be ~** *ta feil
mister ['mistə] herr, herre *m* (*obsolete*)
mistress ['mistrəs] *n* frue *c*; bestyrer *m*; elskerinne *c*
mistrust [mis'trʌst] *v* mistro
misty ['misti] *adj* disig
***misunderstand** [ˌmisʌndə'stænd] *v* *misforstå
misunderstanding [ˌmisʌndə'stændiŋ] *n* misforståelse *m*
misuse [mis'juːs] *n* misbruk *nt*
mitten ['mitən] *n* vott *m*
mix [miks] *v* blande; **~ with** *omgås med
mixed [mikst] *adj* blandet
mixer ['miksə] *n* mikser *m*
mixture ['mikstʃə] *n* blanding *c*
moan [moun] *v* jamre
moat [mout] *n* vollgrav *c*
mobile ['moubail] *adj* bevegelig, mobil; **~ (phone)** mobil(telefon) *m*
mock [mɔk] *v* håne
mockery ['mɔkəri] *n* hån *m*
model ['mɔdəl] *n* modell *m*; manneken*g m*; *v* modellere, forme
modem ['moudem] *n* modem *nt*
moderate ['mɔdərət] *adj* moderat; middelmådig
modern ['mɔdən] *adj* moderne
modest ['mɔdist] *adj* beskjeden
modesty ['mɔdisti] *n* beskjedenhet *c*
modify ['mɔdifai] *v* modifisere, endre
moist [mɔist] *adj* fuktig, våt
moisten ['mɔisən] *v* fukte
moisture ['mɔistʃə] *n* fuktighet *c*; **moisturizing cream** fuktighetskrem *m*
molar ['moulə] *n* jeksel *m*
mom ['mɔm], **mommy** ['mɔmi] mamma *m*
moment ['moumənt] *n* øyeblikk *nt*
momentary ['mouməntəri] *adj* kortvarig
monarch ['mɔnək] *n* monark *m*

monarchy ['mɔnəki] *n* monarki *nt*
monastery ['mɔnəstri] *n* kloster *nt*
Monday ['mʌndi] mandag *m*
monetary ['mʌnitəri] *adj* penge-; ~ **unit** myntenhet *m*
money ['mʌni] *n* penger *pl*; ~ **exchange** vekslingskontor *nt*; ~ **order** postanvisning *m*
monk [mʌŋk] *n* munk *m*
monkey ['mʌŋki] *n* ape *c*
monologue ['mɔnəlɔg] *n* monolog *m*
monopoly [mə'nɔpəli] *n* monopol *nt*
monotonous [mə'nɔtənəs] *adj* monoton
month [mʌnθ] *n* måned *m*
monthly ['mʌnθli] *adj* månedlig
monument ['mɔnjumənt] *n* monument *nt*, minnesmerke *nt*
mood [mu:d] *n* humør *nt*, stemning *m*
moon [mu:n] *n* måne *m*
moonlight ['mu:nlait] *n* måneskinn *nt*
moose [mu:s] *n* (pl ~, ~s) elg *m*
moped ['mouped] *n* moped *m*
moral ['mɔrəl] *n* moral *m*; *adj* moralsk, sedelig
morality [mə'ræləti] *n* moral *m*
more [mɔ:] *adj* mer; **once** ~ en gang til
moreover [mɔ:'rouvə] *adv* dessuten, for øvrig
morning ['mɔ:niŋ] *n* morgen *m*, formiddag *m*; ~ **paper** morgenavis *c*; **this** ~ i morges
Moroccan [mə'rɔkən] *adj* marokkansk; *n* marokkaner *m*
Morocco [mə'rɔkou] Marokko
morphine ['mɔ:fi:n] *n* morfin *m*
morsel ['mɔ:səl] *n* bit *m*
mortal ['mɔ:təl] *adj* dødelig
mortgage ['mɔ:gidʒ] *n* pantelån *nt*
mosaic [mə'zeiik] *n* mosaikk *m*
mosque [mɔsk] *n* moské *m*
mosquito [mə'ski:tou] *n* (pl ~es) mygg *m*; moskito *m*; ~ **net** myggnett *nt*
moss [mɔs] *n* mose *m*
most [moust] *adj* flest; **at** ~ høyst; ~ **of all** mest
mostly ['moustli] *adv* for det meste
motel [mou'tel] *n* motell *nt*
moth [mɔθ] *n* møll *m*; nattsvermer *m*
mother ['mʌðə] *n* mor *c*; ~ **of pearl** perlemor *m*; ~ **tongue** morsmål *nt*
mother-in-law ['mʌðərinlɔ:] *n* (pl mothers-) svigermor *c*
motion ['mouʃən] *n* bevegelse *m*; forslag *nt*
motive ['moutiv] *n* motiv *nt*

motivate ['moutiveit] *v* motivere
motor ['moutə] *n* motor *m*; *v* bile; ~ **body** *nAm* karosseri *nt*; **starter** ~ starter *m*
motorbike ['moutəbaik] *nAm* moped *m*
motorboat ['moutəbout] *n* motorbåt *m*
motorcycle ['moutə,saikəl] *n* motorsykkel *m*
motoring ['moutəriŋ] *n* bilkjøring *c*
motorist ['moutərist] *n* bilist *m*
motorway ['moutəwei] *n* motorvei *m*
motto ['mɔtou] *n* (pl ~es, ~s) motto *nt*
mouldy ['mouldi] *adj* muggen
mound [maund] *n* haug *m*
mount [maunt] *v* *bestige; *n* berg *nt*
mountain ['mauntin] *n* fjell *nt*; ~ **pass** pass *nt*; ~ **range** fjellkjede *m*
mountaineering [,maunti'niəriŋ] *n* fjellklatring *c*
mountainous ['mauntinəs] *adj* fjellendt
mourning ['mɔːniŋ] *n* sorg *c*
mouse [maus] *n* (pl mice) mus *c*; ~ **pad** musmatte *c*
moustache [mə'stɑːʃ] *n* bart *m*
mouth [mauθ] *n* munn *m*; kjeft *m*, gap *nt*; munning *m*
mouthwash ['mauθwɔʃ] *n* munnvann *nt*
movable ['muːvəbəl] *adj* flyttbar
move [muːv] *v* bevege; flytte; røre seg; *n* trekk *nt*, skritt *nt*; flytting *c*
movement ['muːvmənt] *n* bevegelse *m*; sats *m*
movie ['muːvi] *n* film *m*; **movies** *plAm* kino *m*; ~ **theater** kino *m*
much [mʌtʃ] *adj* mange, mye; *adv* mye; **as** ~ like mye; så vidt
mud [mʌd] *n* søle *c*
muddle ['mʌdəl] *n* forvirring *c*, rot *nt*, virvar *nt*; *v* rote
muddy ['mʌdi] *adj* sølet
muffler ['mʌflə] *nAm* lydpotte *c*
mug [mʌg] *n* krus *nt*
mule [mjuːl] *n* mulesel *nt*, muldyr *nt*
multicultural [,mʌlti'kʌltʃərəl] *adj* multikulturell
multiplex ['mʌlti,pleks] *n* multiplex *nt*
multiplication [,mʌltipli'keiʃən] *n* multiplikasjon *m*
multiply ['mʌltiplai] *v* multiplisere
mumps [mʌmps] *n* kusma *m*
municipal [mjuː'nisipəl] *adj* kommunal, by-
municipality

[mjuː,nisi'pæləti] *n* kommune *m*
murder ['məːdə] *n* mord *nt*; *v* myrde
murderer ['məːdərə] *n* morder *m*
muscle ['mʌsəl] *n* muskel *m*
muscular ['mʌskjulə] *adj* muskuløs
museum [mjuː'ziːəm] *n* museum *nt*
mushroom ['mʌʃruːm] *n* sjampinjong *m*; sopp *m*
music ['mjuːzik] *n* musikk *m*; **~ academy** konservatorium *nt*; **~ hall** revyteater *nt*
musical ['mjuːzikəl] *adj* musikalsk; *n* musikal *m*
musician [mjuː'ziʃən] *n* musiker *m*
mussel ['mʌsəl] *n* blåskjell *nt*
Muslim ['mʌslim] *n* muslim *m*
***must** [mʌst] *v* *måtte
mustard ['mʌstəd] *n* sennep *m*
mute [mjuːt] *adj* stum
mutiny ['mjuːtini] *n* mytteri *nt*
mutton ['mʌtən] *n* fårekjøtt *nt*
mutual ['mjuːtʃuəl] *adj* gjensidig
my [mai] *adj* min
myself [mai'self] *pron* meg; selv
mysterious [mi'stiəriəs] *adj* gåtefull, mystisk
mystery ['mistəri] *n* mysterium *nt*
myth [miθ] *n* myte *m*

N

nail [neil] *n* negl *m*; spiker *m*; **~ file** neglefil *c*; **~ polish** neglelakk *m*; **~ scissors** *pl* neglesaks *c*
naïve [nɑː'iːv] *adj* naiv
naked ['neikid] *adj* naken; bar
name [neim] *n* navn *nt*; *v* oppkalle, kalle; **in the ~ of** i …s navn
namely ['neimli] *adv* nemlig
nap [næp] *n* lur *m*
napkin ['næpkin] *n* serviett *m*
nappy ['næpi] *n* bleie *c*
narcosis [nɑː'kousis] *n* (pl -ses) narkose *m*
narcotic [nɑː'kɔtik] *n* narkotisk middel
narrow ['nærou] *adj* trang, smal, snever
narrow-minded [,nærou'maindid] *adj* sneversynt
nasty ['nɑːsti] *adj* ubehagelig, vemmelig; ekkel
nation ['neiʃən] *n* nasjon *m*;

folk *nt*
national ['næʃənəl] *adj* nasjonal; folke-; stats-; **~ anthem** nasjonalsang *m*; **~ dress** nasjonaldrakt *c*; bunad *m*; **~ park** nasjonalpark *m*
nationality [ˌnæʃə'næləti] *n* nasjonalitet *m*
nationalize ['næʃənəlaiz] *v* nasjonalisere
native ['neitiv] *n* innfødt *m*; *adj* født; **~ country** fedreland *nt*; hjemland *nt*; **~ language** morsmål *nt*
natural ['nætʃərəl] *adj* naturlig; medfødt
naturally ['nætʃərəli] *adv* selvfølgelig, naturligvis
nature ['neitʃə] *n* natur *m*
naughty ['nɔːti] *adj* uskikkelig, slem
nausea ['nɔːsiə] *n* kvalme *m*
naval ['neivəl] *adj* marine-
navel ['neivəl] *n* navle *m*
navigable ['nævigəbəl] *adj* seilbar
navigate ['nævigeit] *v* navigere
navigation [ˌnævi'geiʃən] *n* navigasjon *m*; seilas *m*
navy ['neivi] *n* flåte *m*
near [niə] *prep* nær; *adj* nær
nearby ['niəbai] *adj* nærliggende, tilstøtende
nearly ['niəli] *adv* nesten
neat [niːt] *adj* nett, ordentlig
necessary ['nesəsəri] *adj* nødvendig
necessity [nə'sesəti] *n* nødvendighet *c*
neck [nek] *n* hals *m*; **nape of the ~** nakke *m*
necklace ['nekləs] *n* halskjede *nt*
necktie ['nektai] *n* slips *nt*
need [niːd] *v* behøve, trenge; *n* behov *nt*; nødvendighet *c*; **~ to** *måtte
needle ['niːdəl] *n* nål *c*
needlework ['niːdəlwəːk] *n* håndarbeid *nt*
negative ['negətiv] *adj* negativ, benektende; *n* negativ *nt*
neglect [ni'glekt] *v* forsømme; *n* forsømmelse *m*
negligee ['negliʒei] *n* neglisjé *m / nt*
negotiate [ni'gouʃieit] *v* forhandle
negotiation [niˌgouʃi'eiʃən] *n* forhandling *c*
neighbo(u)r ['neibə] *n* granne *m*, nabo *m*
neighbo(u)rhood ['neibəhud] *n* nabolag *nt*
neighbo(u)ring ['neibəriŋ] *adj* tilstøtende, nærliggende
neither ['naiðə] *pron* ingen av dem; **neither … nor** verken … eller
nephew ['nefjuː] *n* nevø *m*
nerve [nəːv] *n* nerve *m*; dristighet *c*
nervous ['nəːvəs] *adj* nervøs

nest [nest] *n* rede *nt*
net [net] *n* nett *nt*; *adj* netto
Netherlands: the ~ ['neðələndz] Nederland
network ['netwə:k] *n* nettverk *nt*
networking ['net,wə:kiŋ] *n* nettverksbygging *c*
neuralgia [njuə'rældʒə] *n* nevralgi *m*
neurosis [njuə'rousis] *n* nevrose *m*
neuter ['nju:tə] *adj* intetkjønns-
neutral ['nju:trəl] *adj* nøytral
never ['nevə] *adv* aldri
nevertheless [,nevəðə'les] *adv* ikke desto mindre
new [nju:] *adj* ny; **New Year** nyttår *nt*
news [nju:z] *n* nyheter *pl*, nyhet *c*
newspaper ['nju:z,peipə] *n* avis *c*
newsstand ['nju:zstænd] *n* aviskiosk *m*
New Zealand [nju: 'zi:lənd] Ny-Zealand
next [nekst] *adj* neste; **~ to** ved siden av
next-door [,nekst'dɔ:] *adv* ved siden av, nabo-
nice [nais] *adj* koselig, snill, pen; lekker; sympatisk
nickel ['nikəl] *n* nikkel *m*; 5-cent-mynt
nickname ['nikneim] *n* kjælenavn *nt*
nicotine ['nikəti:n] *n* nikotin *m*
niece [ni:s] *n* niese *c*
Nigeria [nai'dʒiəriə] Nigeria
Nigerian [nai'dʒiəriən] *adj* nigeriansk; *n* nigerianer *m*
night [nait] *n* natt *c*; kveld *m*; **by ~** om natten; **~ rate** natt-takst *m*; **~ train** natt--tog *nt*
nightclub ['naitklʌb] *n* nattklubb *m*
night cream ['naitkri:m] *n* nattkrem *m*
nightingale ['naitiŋgeil] *n* nattergal *m*
nightly ['naitli] *adj* nattlig
nil [nil] ingenting; null
nine [nain] *num* ni
nineteen [,nain'ti:n] *num* nitten
nineteenth [,nain'ti:nθ] *num* nittende
ninety ['nainti] *num* nitti
ninth [nainθ] *num* niende
nitrogen ['naitrədʒən] *n* kvelstoff *nt*
no [nou] nei; *adj* ingen; **~ one** ingen
nobility [nou'biləti] *n* adel *m*
noble ['noubəl] *adj* adelig; edel
nobody ['noubɔdi] *pron* ingen
nod [nɔd] *n* nikk *nt*; *v* nikke
noise [nɔiz] *n* lyd *m*; bulder *nt*, larm *m*, støy *m*
noisy ['nɔizi] *adj* støyende
nominal ['nɔminəl] *adj* nominell

nominate ['nɔmineit] *v* nominere
nomination [ˌnɔmi'neiʃən] *n* nominasjon *m*; utnevnelse *m*
none [nʌn] *pron* ingen
nonsense ['nɔnsəns] *n* nonsens *nt*
non-smoker [ˌnɔn'smoukə] *n* ikke-røyker *m*
noodles [nu:dəls] *pl* nudler *pl*, pasta *m*
noon [nu:n] *n* klokken (klokka) tolv
normal ['nɔ:məl] *adj* normal
north [nɔ:θ] *n* nord *m*; *adj* nordlig; **North Pole** Nordpolen
north-east [ˌnɔ:θ'i:st] *n* nordøst *m*
northern ['nɔ:ðən] *adj* nordlig
north-west [ˌnɔ:θ'west] *n* nordvest *m*
Norway ['nɔ:wei] Norge
Norwegian [nɔ:'wi:dʒən] *adj* norsk; *n* nordmann (pl –menn) *m*
nose [nouz] *n* nese *c*
nosebleed ['nouzbli:d] *n* neseblod *nt*
nostril ['nɔstril] *n* nesebor *nt*
nosy ['nouzi] *adj colloquial* nysgjerrig
not [nɔt] *adv* ikke
notary ['noutəri] *n* notar *m*
note [nout] *n* merknad *m*, notis *m*; notat *nt*; tone *m*; *v* notere; bemerke, konstatere
notebook ['noutbuk] *n* notisbok *c*
noted ['noutid] *adj* kjent
notepaper ['nout,peipə] *n* brevpapir *nt*
nothing ['nʌθiŋ] *n* ingenting, intet *nt*
notice ['noutis] *v* merke, bemerke, *legge merke til, oppdage; *se; *n* underretning *m*, kunngjøring *c*; oppmerksomhet *c*
noticeable ['noutisəbəl] *adj* merkbar; bemerkelsesverdig
notify ['noutifai] *v* meddele; underrette; varsle
notion ['nouʃən] *n* anelse *m*, begrep *nt*
notorious [nou'tɔ:riəs] *adj* beryktet
nought [nɔ:t] *n* null *m* / *nt*
noun [naun] *n* substantiv *nt*
nourishing ['nʌriʃiŋ] *adj* nærende
nourishment ['nʌriʃment] *n* næring *c*
novel ['nɔvəl] *n* roman *m*
novelist ['nɔvəlist] *n* romanforfatter *m*
November [nou'vembə] november
now [nau] *adv* nå; **from ~ on** heretter; **~ and then** nå og da
nowadays ['nauədeiz] *adv* nåtildags
nowhere ['nouwɛə] *adv*

ingensteds, ingen steder
nozzle ['nɔzəl] *n* tut *m*
nuance [nju:'ɑ̃:s] *n* nyanse *m*
nuclear ['nju:kliə] *adj* kjerne-; **~ energy** kjernekraft *c*
nucleus ['nju:kliəs] *n* kjerne *m*
nude [nju:d] *adj* naken; *n* akt *m*
nuisance ['nju:səns] *n* plage *m*
numb [nʌm] *adj* følelsesløs; valen
number ['nʌmbə] *n* nummer *nt*; tall *nt*, antall *nt*
numeral ['nju:mərəl] *n* tallord *nt*
numerous ['nju:mərəs] *adj* tallrik
nun [nʌn] *n* nonne *c*
nurse [nə:s] *n* sykepleier *m*; barnepike *m*; *v* pleie; amme
nursery ['nə:səri] *n* barneværelse *nt*; planteskole *m*
nut [nʌt] *n* nøtt *c*; mutter *m*
nutcrackers ['nʌt,krækəz] *pl* nøtteknekker *m*
nutmeg ['nʌtmeg] *n* muskatnøtt *c*
nutritious [nju:'triʃəs] *adj* nærende
nutshell ['nʌtʃel] *n* nøtteskall *nt*

O

oak [ouk] *n* eik *c*
oar [ɔ:] *n* åre *c*
oasis [ou'eisis] *n* (pl oases) oase *m*
oath [ouθ] *n* ed *m*
oats [outs] *pl* havre *m*
obedience [ə'bi:diəns] *n* lydighet *c*
obedient [ə'bi:diənt] *adj* lydig
obese [ou'bi:s] *adj* fet
obesity [ou'bi:siti] *n* fedme *m*
obey [ə'bei] *v* *adlyde
object[1] ['ɔbdʒikt] *n* objekt *nt*; gjenstand *m*; formål *nt*
object[2] [əb'dʒekt] *v* protestere, innvende
objection [əb'dʒekʃən] *n* innvending *c*
objective [əb'dʒektiv] *adj* objektiv; *n* formål *nt*
obligatory [ə'bligətəri] *adj* obligatorisk
oblige [ə'blaidʒ] *v* forplikte; ***be obliged to** *være forpliktet til; *være nødt til
obliging [ə'blaidʒiŋ] *adj* imøtekommende
oblong ['ɔblɔŋ] *adj* avlang; *n* rektangel *nt*
obscene [əb'si:n] *adj* uanstendig; obskøn
obscure [əb'skjuə] *adj*

uklar, mørk
observation [ˌɔbzəˈveiʃən] *n* iakttakelse *m*, observasjon *m*
observatory [əbˈzəːvətri] *n* observatorium *nt*
observe [əbˈzəːv] *v* *iaktta, observere
obsession [əbˈseʃən] *n* besettelse *m*
obstacle [ˈɔbstəkəl] *n* hindring *c*
obstinate [ˈɔbstinət] *adj* sta; hardnakket
obtain [əbˈtein] *v* erverve, *få
obtainable [əbˈteinəbəl] *adj* oppnåelig
obvious [ˈɔbviəs] *adj* innlysende
occasion [əˈkeiʒən] *n* tilfelle *nt*; foranledning *m*
occasionally [əˈkeiʒənəli] *adv* av og til, nå og da
occupant [ˈɔkjupənt] *n* beboer *m*
occupation [ˌɔkjuˈpeiʃən] *n* beskjeftigelse *m*; okkupasjon *m*
occupy [ˈɔkjupai] *v* *besette; beskjeftige; **occupied** *adj* opptatt
occur [əˈkəː] *v* hende, *forekomme, skje
occurrence [əˈkʌrəns] *n* hendelse *m*
ocean [ˈouʃən] *n* hav *nt*
October [ɔkˈtoubə] oktober
octopus [ˈɔktəpəs] *n* blekksprut *m*
oculist [ˈɔkjulist] *n* øyenlege *m*
odd [ɔd] *adj* underlig, rar; ulike
odo(u)r [ˈoudə] *n* lukt *c*
of [ɔv, əv] *prep* av; fra; i
off [ɔf] *adv* av; vekk; *prep* av
offence [əˈfens] *n* forseelse *m*; krenkelse *m*; anstøt *nt*, fornærmelse *m*
offend [əˈfend] *v* krenke, fornærme; *forgå seg
offense [əˈfens] *nAm* forseelse *m*; krenkelse *m*; anstøt *nt*, fornærmelse *m*
offensive [əˈfensiv] *adj* offensiv; støtende, krenkende
offer [ˈɔfə] *v* *tilby; yte; *n* tilbud *nt*
office [ˈɔfis] *n* kontor *nt*; embete *nt*; **~ hours** kontortid *c*
officer [ˈɔfisə] *n* offiser *m*
official [əˈfiʃəl] *adj* offisiell
off-licence [ˈɔfˌlaisəns] *n* alkoholutsalg *nt*
often [ˈɔfən] *adv* ofte
oil [ɔil] *n* olje *c*; **fuel ~** brenselolje *c*; **~ drilling platform** boreplattform *nt*; **~ filter** oljefilter *nt*; **~ painting** oljemaleri *nt*; **~ pressure** oljetrykk *nt*; **~ refinery** oljeraffineri *nt*; **~ well** oljebrønn *m*
oily [ˈɔili] *adj* oljet; glatt
ointment [ˈɔintmənt] *n* salve *c*
okay!, **OK!** [ˌouˈkei] greit!

ok!
old [ould] *adj* gammel; **~ age** alderdom *m*
old-fashioned [ˌould'fæʃənd] *adj* gammeldags
olive ['ɔliv] *n* oliven *m*; **~ oil** olivenolje *c*
omelette ['ɔmlət] *n* omelett *m*
ominous ['ɔminəs] *adj* illevarslende
omit [ə'mit] *v* *utelate
omnipotent [ɔm'nipətənt] *adj* allmektig
on [ɔn] *prep* på; ved
once [wʌns] *adv* en gang; **at ~** straks; **for ~** for en gangs skyld; **~ more** en gang til
oncoming ['ɔnˌkʌmiŋ] *adj* kommende; møtende
one [wʌn] *num* en; *pron* man
oneself [wʌn'self] *pron* selv
one-way ['wʌn-wei] *adj* enkel
only ['ounli] *adj* eneste; *adv* bare, alene, kun; *conj* men
onwards ['ɔnwədz] *adv* fremover
onyx ['ɔniks] *n* onyks *m*
opal ['oupəl] *n* opal *m*
open ['oupən] *v* åpne; *adj* åpen; åpenhjertig
opener ['oupənə] *n* (flaske-)åpner *m*; åpningsnummer *nt*
opening ['oupəniŋ] *n* åpning *c*
opera ['ɔpərə] *n* opera *m*; **~ house** opera *m*
operate ['ɔpəreit] *v* virke, *drive; operere
operation [ˌɔpə'reiʃən] *n* virksomhet *c*; operasjon *m*
operator ['ɔpəreitə] *n* operatør *m*
opinion [ə'pinjən] *n* oppfatning *m*, mening *m*
opponent [ə'pounənt] *n* motstander *m*
opportunity [ˌɔpə'tju:nəti] *n* leilighet *c*, anledning *m*
oppose [ə'pouz] *v* *motsette seg, opponere
opposite ['ɔpəzit] *prep* overfor; *adj* motsatt
opposition [ˌɔpə'ziʃən] *n* opposisjon *m*
oppress [ə'pres] *v* undertrykke, knuge
optician [ɔp'tiʃən] *n* optiker *m*
optimism ['ɔptimizəm] *n* optimisme *m*
optimist ['ɔptimist] *n* optimist *m*
optimistic [ˌɔpti'mistik] *adj* optimistisk
optional ['ɔpʃənəl] *adj* valgfri
or [ɔ:] *conj* eller
oral ['ɔ:rəl] *adj* muntlig
orange ['ɔrindʒ] *n* appelsin *m*; *adj* oransje
orbit ['ɔ:bit] *n* omløp *nt*
orchard ['ɔ:tʃəd] *n* frukthage *m*
orchestra ['ɔ:kistrə] *n* orkester *nt*; **~ seat** *Am*

orkesterplass *m*
order ['ɔːdə] *v* beordre; bestille; *n* rekkefølge *m*, orden *m*; ordre *m*, befaling *c*; bestilling *c*; **in ~** i orden; **in ~ to** for å; **made to ~** laget på bestilling; **out of ~** i uorden
ordinary ['ɔːdənri] *adj* vanlig, dagligdags
ore [ɔː] *n* malm *m*
organ ['ɔːgən] *n* organ *nt*; orgel *nt*
organic [ɔː'gænik] *adj* organisk
organization [ˌɔːgənai'zeiʃən] *n* organisasjon *m*
organize ['ɔːgənaiz] *v* organisere
Orient ['ɔːriənt] *n* Orienten
oriental [ˌɔːri'entəl] *adj* orientalsk
orientate ['ɔːriənteit] *v* orientere seg
origin ['ɔridʒin] *n* avstamning *m*, opphav *nt*; herkomst *m*
original [ə'ridʒinəl] *adj* original, opprinnelig
originally [ə'ridʒinəli] *adv* i begynnelsen
ornament ['ɔːnəmənt] *n* utsmykning *m*
ornamental [ˌɔːnə'mentəl] *adj* dekorativ
orphan ['ɔːfən] *n* foreldreløst barn
orthodox ['ɔːθədɔks] *adj* ortodoks
ostrich ['ɔstritʃ] *n* struts *m*
other ['ʌðə] *adj* annen
otherwise ['ʌðəwaiz] *conj* ellers; *adv* annerledes
***ought to** [ɔːt] *burde
ounce ['auns] *n* vektenhet, ca 30 g
our, ours [auə] *adj* vår
ourselves [auə'selvz] *pron* oss; selv
out [aut] *adv* ute, ut; **~ of** sluppet opp for
outbreak ['autbreik] *n* utbrudd *nt*
outcome ['autkʌm] *n* resultat *nt*
***outdo** [ˌaut'duː] *v* *overgå
outdoors [ˌaut'dɔːz] *adv* utendørs
outer ['autə] *adj* ytre
outfit ['autfit] *n* utrustning *m*; klesdrakt *c*
outing ['autiŋ] *n* utflukt *c*
outline ['autlain] *n* kontur *m*, omriss *nt*; *v* gi et omriss av
outlook ['autluk] *n* utsikt *m*; syn *nt*
output ['autput] *n* produksjon *m*
outrage ['autreidʒ] *n* fornærmelse *m*; krenkelse *m*
outside [ˌaut'said] *adv* utenfor; *prep* utenfor; *n* utside *c*, ytterside *c*
outsize ['autsaiz] *n* stor størrelse
outskirts ['autskəːts] *pl* utkant *m*

outstanding [ˌaut'stændiŋ] *adj* fremtredende, fremragende
outward ['autwəd] *adj* utvendig
outwards ['autwədz] *adv* utad
oval ['ouvəl] *adj* oval
oven ['ʌvən] *n* stekeovn *m*
over ['ouvə] *prep* over, ovenfor; *adv* over; over ende; ~ **there** der borte
overall ['ouvərɔ:l] *adj* total
overalls ['ouvərɔ:lz] *pl* overall *m*
overcast ['ouvəkɑ:st] *adj* overskyet
overcoat ['ouvəkout] *n* frakk *m*
***overcome** [ˌouvə'kʌm] *v* *overvinne
overdo [ˌouvə'du:] *v* overdrive
overdraft ['ouvədrɑ:ft] *n* overtrekk *nt*
overdue [ˌouvə'dju:] *adj* forsinket; forfalt
overgrown [ˌouvə'groun] *adj* overgrodd
overhaul [ˌouvə'hɔ:l] *v* overhale
overhead [ˌouvə'hed] *adv* ovenfor
overlook [ˌouvə'luk] *v* *overse
overnight [ˌouvə'nait] *adv* natten over
overseas [ˌouvə'si:z] *adj* oversjøisk
oversight ['ouvəsait] *n* forglemmelse *m*
***oversleep** [ˌouvə'sli:p] *v* *forsove seg
overstrung [ˌouvə'strʌŋ] *adj* overspent
***overtake** [ˌouvə'teik] *v* kjøre forbi; **no overtaking** forbikjøring forbudt
over-tired [ˌouvə'taiəd] *adj* overtrett
overture ['ouvətʃə] *n* ouverture *m*
overweight ['ouvəweit] *n* overvekt *c*; *adj* overvektig
overwhelm [ˌouvə'welm] *v* overvelde
overwork [ˌouvə'wə:k] *v* overanstrenge seg
owe [ou] *v* *være skyldig, skylde; *ha å takke for; **owing to** på grunn av
owl [aul] *n* ugle *c*
own [oun] *v* eie; *adj* egen
owner ['ounə] *n* eier *m*, innehaver *m*
ox [ɔks] *n* (pl oxen) okse *m*
oxygen ['ɔksidʒən] *n* surstoff *nt*
oyster ['ɔistə] *n* østers *m*
ozone ['ouzoun] *n* ozon *nt*

P

pace [peis] *n* skritt *nt*; tempo *nt*
Pacific Ocean [pə'sifik 'ouʃən] Stillehavet
pacifism ['pæsifizəm] *n* pasifisme *m*
pacifist ['pæsifist] *n* pasifist *m*; pasifistisk
pack [pæk] *v* pakke; *nAm* kortstokk *m*; ~ **up** pakke ned
package ['pækidʒ] *n* pakke *c*
packet ['pækit] *n* liten pakke, småpakke *c*
packing ['pækiŋ] *n* innpakning *m*
pact [pækt] *n* pakt *c*; kontrakt *m*
pad [pæd] *n* pute *m*; notisblokk *c*
paddle ['pædəl] *n* padleåre *c*
padlock ['pædlɔk] *n* hengelås *m* / *nt*
pagan ['peigən] *adj* hedensk; *n* hedning *m*
page [peidʒ] *n* side *c*
pail [peil] *n* spann *nt*
pain [pein] *n* smerte *m*; **pains** umake *m*
painful ['peinfəl] *adj* smertefull
painkiller ['peinkilə] *n* smertestillende middel *nt*
painless ['peinləs] *adj* smertefri
paint [peint] *n* maling *c*; *v* male
paintbox ['peintbɔks] *n* malerskrin *nt*
paintbrush ['peintbrʌʃ] *n* pensel *m*
painter ['peintə] *n* maler *m*
painting ['peintiŋ] *n* maleri *nt*
pair [pɛə] *n* par *nt*
Pakistan [ˌpɑːki'stɑːn] Pakistan
Pakistani [ˌpɑːki'stɑːni] *adj* pakistansk; *n* pakistaner *m*
palace ['pæləs] *n* palass *nt*
pale [peil] *adj* blek; lyse-
palm [pɑːm] *n* palme *m*; håndflate *c*
palpable ['pælpəbəl] *adj* følelig, merkbar
palpitation [ˌpælpi'teiʃən] *n* hjerteklapp *m*
pan [pæn] *n* panne *c*; kasserolle *m*
pane [pein] *n* vindusrute *c*
panel ['pænəl] *n* panel *nt*
panelling ['pænəliŋ] *n* panelverk *nt*
panic ['pænik] *n* panikk *m*
pant [pænt] *v* pese
panties ['pæntiz] *pl* underbukse *c*, truse *c*
pants [pænts] *pl* underbukse *c*; bukse *c*
pant suit ['pæntsuːt] *n* buksedrakt *c*, buksedress

m

panty hose ['pæntihouz] *n* strømpebukse *c*

paper ['peipə] *n* papir *nt*; avis *c*; papir-; **~ bag** papirpose *m*; **~ knife** papirkniv *m*; **~ napkin** papirserviett *m*; **wrapping ~** innpakningspapir *nt*

paperback ['peipəbæk] *n* billigbok *c*

parade [pə'reid] *n* parade *m*; tog *nt*

paradise [pærədais] *n* paradis *nt*

paraffin ['pærəfin] *n* parafin *m m*

paragraph ['pærəgrɑ:f] *n* avsnitt *nt*; paragraf *m*

parakeet ['pærəki:t] *n* papegøye *m*

parallel ['pærəlel] *adj* parallell; *n* parallell *m*

paralyse ['pærəlaiz] *v* lamme

parcel ['pɑ:səl] *n* pakke *c*

pardon ['pɑ:dən] *n* tilgivelse *m*; benådning *m*

parent ['pɛərənt] *n* forelder *m*

parents ['pɛərənts] *pl* foreldre *pl*

parents-in-law ['pɛərəntsinlɔ:] *pl* svigerforeldre *pl*

parish ['pæriʃ] *n* sogn *nt*

park [pɑ:k] *n* park *m*; *v* parkere

parking ['pɑ:kiŋ] *n* parkering *c*; **no ~** parkering forbudt; **~ fee** parkeringsavgift *c*; **~ light** parkeringslys *nt*; **~ lot** *Am* parkeringsplass *m*; **~ meter** parkometer *nt*; **~ zone** parkeringssone *c*

parliament ['pɑ:ləmənt] *n* parlament *nt*

parliamentary [ˌpɑ:lə'mentəri] *adj* parlamentarisk

parrot ['pærət] *n* papegøye *m*

parsley ['pɑ:sli] *n* persille *c*

parson ['pɑ:sən] *n* prest *m*

parsonage ['pɑ:sənidʒ] *n* prestegård *m*

part [pɑ:t] *n* del *m*; stykke *nt*; *v* skille; **spare ~** reservedel *m*

partial ['pɑ:ʃəl] *adj* delvis; partisk

participant [pɑ:'tisipənt] *n* deltaker *m*

participate [pɑ:'tisipeit] *v* *delta

particular [pə'tikjulə] *adj* spesiell, særegen; kresen; **in ~** i særdeleshet

parting ['pɑ:tiŋ] *n* avskjed *m*; hårskill *m*

partition [pɑ:'tiʃən] *n* skillevegg *m*

partly ['pɑ:tli] *adv* delvis

partner ['pɑ:tnə] *n* partner *m*; kompanjong *m*

partridge ['pɑ:tridʒ] *n* rapphøne *c*

party ['pɑ:ti] *n* parti *nt*; selskap *nt*; gruppe *c*

pass [pɑːs] *v* *forløpe, passere; *rekke; *bestå; **no passing** *Am* forbikjøring forbudt; **~ by** *gå forbi; **~ through** *gå gjennom
passage ['pæsidʒ] *n* passasje *m*; overfart *m*; avsnitt *nt*; gjennomreise *c*
passenger ['pæsəndʒə] *n* passasjer *m*; **~ train** persontog *nt*
passer-by [ˌpɑːsə'bai] *n* forbipasserende *m*
passion ['pæʃən] *n* lidenskap *m*
passionate ['pæʃənət] *adj* lidenskapelig
passive ['pæsiv] *adj* passiv
passport ['pɑːspɔːt] *n* pass *nt*; **~ control** passkontroll *m*; **~ photograph** passfoto *nt*
password ['pɑːswəːd] *n* passord *nt*
past [pɑːst] *n* fortid *c*; *adj* forrige, tidligere; *prep* forbi, langs
paste [peist] *n* lim *nt*; *v* klistre
pastime ['pɑːstaim] *n* tidsfordriv *nt*
pastry ['peistri] *n* finere bakverk *nt*; **~ shop** konditori *nt*
pasture ['pɑːstʃə] *n* beite *nt*
pasty ['peisti] *n* postei *m*
patch [pætʃ] *n* lapp *m*
patent ['peitənt] *n* patent *nt*
path [pɑːθ] *n* sti *m*
patience ['peiʃəns] *n* tålmodighet *c*
patient ['peiʃənt] *adj* tålmodig; *n* pasient *m*
patriot ['peitriət] *n* patriot *m*
patrol [pə'troul] *n* patrulje *m*; *v* patruljere; overvåke
pattern ['pætən] *n* mønster *nt*, motiv *nt*
pause [pɔːz] *n* pause *m*; *v* *holde pause
pave [peiv] *v* *legge veidekke; *brolegge
pavement ['peivmənt] *n* fortau *nt*; veidekke *nt*
pavilion [pə'viljən] *n* paviljong *m*
paw [pɔː] *n* pote *m*
pawn [pɔːn] *v* *pantsette; *n* sjakkbonde *m*
pawnbroker ['pɔːnˌbroukə] *n* pantelåner *m*
pay [pei] *n* gasje *m*, lønn *c*
***pay** [pei] *v* betale; lønne seg; **~ attention to** *være oppmerksom på; **~ off** nedbetale; **~ on account** avbetale; **paying** lønnsom
pay desk ['peidesk] *n* kasse *c*
payment ['peimənt] *n* betaling *c*
pea [piː] *n* ert *c*
peace [piːs] *n* fred *m*
peaceful ['piːsfəl] *adj* fredelig
peach [piːtʃ] *n* fersken *m*
peacock ['piːkɔk] *n* påfugl *m*
peak [piːk] *n* tind *m*; topp

m; ~ **hour** rushtid *c*; ~ **season** høysesong *m*
peanut ['pi:nʌt] *n* peanøtt *m c*
pear [pɛə] *n* pære *c*
pearl [pə:l] *n* perle *c*
peasant ['pezənt] *n* bonde *m*
pebble ['pebəl] *n* småstein *m*
peculiar [pi'kju:ljə] *adj* underlig; eiendommelig
peculiarity [pi,kju:li'ærəti] *n* eiendommelighet *c*
pedal ['pedəl] *n* pedal *m*
pedestrian [pi'destriən] *n* fotgjenger *m*; ~ **crossing** fotgjengerovergang *m*; **no pedestrians** ikke for fotgjengere
peel [pi:l] *v* skrelle; *n* skrell *nt*
peep [pi:p] *v* kikke
peg [peg] *n* knagg *m*
pelican ['pelikən] *n* pelikan *m*
pelvis ['pelvis] *n* bekken *nt*
pen [pen] *n* penn *m*
penalty ['penəlti] *n* bot *c*; straff *m*; ~ **kick** straffespark *nt*
pencil ['pensəl] *n* blyant *m*; ~ **sharpener** blyantspisser *m*
penetrate ['penitreit] *v* trenge gjennom
penguin ['peŋgwin] *n* pingvin *m*
penicillin [,peni'silin] *n* penicillin *nt*
peninsula [pə'ninsjulə] *n* halvøy *c*
penknife ['pennaif] *n* (pl -knives) lommekniv *m*
penny ['peni] *n* (pl pennies, pence) penny *m*
pension[1] ['pɑ̃:siɔ̃:] *n* pensjonat *nt*
pension[2] ['penʃən] *n* pensjon *m*
Pentecost ['pentikast] *n* pinse *c*
people ['pi:pəl] *pl* folk *pl*; *n* folk *nt*, folkeslag *nt*
pepper ['pepə] *n* pepper *m*
peppermint ['pepəmint] *n* peppermynte *c*
per [pə:] *prep* per, pr.; ~ **cent** prosent
perceive [pə'si:v] *v* fornemme
percent [pə'sent] *n* prosent *m*
percentage [pə'sentidʒ] *n* prosentsats *m*
perceptible [pə'septibəl] *adj* merkbar
perception [pə'sepʃən] *n* fornemmelse *m*
perch [pə:tʃ] (pl ~) åbor *m*
percolator ['pə:kəleitə] *n* kaffetrakter *m*
perfect ['pə:fikt] *adj* fullkommen, perfekt
perfection [pə'fekʃən] *n* perfeksjon *m*, fullkommenhet *c*
perform [pə'fɔ:m] *v* utføre; *opptre; utøve
performance [pə'fɔ:məns]

n forestilling *c*
perfume ['pəːfjuːm] *n* parfyme *m*
perhaps [pə'hæps] *adv* kanskje; muligens
peril ['peril] *n* fare *m*
perilous ['periləs] *adj* livsfarlig
period ['piəriəd] *n* periode *m*, tid *c*; punktum *nt*
periodical [ˌpiəri'ɔdikəl] *n* tidsskrift *nt*; *adj* periodevis
perish ['periʃ] *v* *omkomme; *forgå
perishable ['periʃəbəl] *adj* bedervelig
perjury ['pəːdʒəri] *n* mened *m*
permanent ['pəːmənənt] *adj* varig, permanent, vedvarende, fast
permission [pə'miʃən] *n* tillatelse *m*; lov *m*
permit[1] [pə'mit] *v* *tillate
permit[2] ['pəːmit] *n* tillatelse *m*, permisjon *m*
peroxide [pə'rɔksaid] *n* vannstoff hyperoksyd
perpendicular [ˌpəːpən'dikjulə] *adj* loddrett
persecute ['pəːsikjuːt] *v* *forfølge, plage
Persia ['pəːʃə] Persia
Persian ['pəːʃən] *adj* persisk; *n* perser *m*
person ['pəːsən] *n* person *m*; **per ~** per person
personal ['pəːsənəl] *adj* personlig
personality [ˌpəːsə'næləti] *n* personlighet *c*
personnel [ˌpəːsə'nel] *n* personale *nt*
perspective [pə'spektiv] *n* perspektiv *nt*
perspiration [ˌpəːspə'reiʃən] *n* svette *m*
perspire [pə'spaiə] *v* transpirere, svette
persuade [pə'sweid] *v* overtale; overbevise
persuasion [pə'sweiʒən] *n* overbevisning *m*; overtaling *c*
pessimism ['pesimizəm] *n* pessimisme *m*
pessimist ['pesimist] *n* pessimist *m*
pessimistic [ˌpesi'mistik] *adj* pessimistisk
pet [pet] *n* kjæledyr *nt*; kjæledegge *m*; *adj* yndlings-
petal ['petəl] *n* kronblad *nt*
petition [pi'tiʃən] *n* bønn *m*; petisjon *m*
petrol ['petrəl] *n* bensin *m*; **unleaded ~** blyfri bensin; **~ pump** bensinpumpe *c*; **~ station** bensinstasjon *m*; **~ tank** bensintank *m*
petroleum [pi'trouliəm] *n* petroleum *m*
petty ['peti] *adj* smålig, ubetydelig, liten; **~ cash** småpenger *pl*
phantom ['fæntəm] *n* fantasibilde *nt*; gjenferd *nt*
pharmacology

[ˌfɑːmə'kɔlədʒi] *n* farmakologi *m*
pharmacy ['fɑːməsi] *n* apotek *nt*
phase [feiz] *n* fase *m*
Philippine ['filipain] *adj* filippinsk
Philippines ['filipiːnz] *pl* Filippinene
philosopher [fi'lɔsəfə] *n* filosof *m*
philosophy [fi'lɔsəfi] *n* filosofi *m*
phone [foun] *n* telefon *m*; *v* telefonere, ringe; **~ card** telefonkort *nt*
phonetic [fə'netik] *adj* fonetisk
phoney ['founi] *adj* falsk; *n* bløffmaker *m*
photo ['foutou] *n* (pl ~s) fotografi *nt*
photo message ['foutou‿ˌmesədʒ] *n* bildemelding *c*
photocopy ['foutəkɔpi] *n* fotokopi *m*; *v* (foto)kopiere
photograph ['foutəgrɑːf] *n* fotografi *nt*; *v* fotografere
photographer [fə'tɔgrəfə] *n* fotograf *m*
photography [fə'tɔgrəfi] *n* fotografering *c*
phrase [freiz] *n* uttrykk *nt*
phrase book ['freizbuk] *n* parlør *m*
physical ['fizikəl] *adj* fysisk
physician [fi'ziʃən] *n* lege *m*
physicist ['fizisist] *n* fysiker *m*
physics ['fiziks] *n* fysikk *m*
physiology [ˌfizi'ɔlədʒi] *n* fysiologi *m*
pianist ['piːənist] *n* pianist *m*
piano [pi'ænou] *n* piano *nt*; **grand ~** flygel *nt*
pick [pik] *v* plukke; *velge; *n* valg *nt*; **~ up** *ta opp; hente; **pick-up van** varebil *m*
picnic ['piknik] *n* piknik *m*; *v* *dra på piknik
picture ['piktʃə] *n* maleri *nt*; illustrasjon *m*, stikk *nt*; bilde *nt*; **~ postcard** prospektkort *nt*; **pictures** kino *m*
picturesque [ˌpiktʃə'resk] *adj* pittoresk, malerisk
piece [piːs] *n* stykke *nt*, bit *m*; brikke *c*
pier [piə] *n* utstikker *m*
pierce [piəs] *v* gjennombore
pig [pig] *n* gris *m*
pigeon ['pidʒən] *n* due *c*
piggy bank ['pigibæŋk] *n* sparegris *m*
pig-headed [ˌpig'hedid] *adj* sta
piglet ['piglət] *n* smågris *m*
pigskin ['pigskin] *n* svinelær *nt*
pike [paik] (pl ~) gjedde *c*
pile [pail] *n* haug *m*; *v* stable; **piles** *pl* hemorroider *pl*
pilgrim ['pilgrim] *n* pilegrim *m*

pilgrimage ['pilgrimidʒ] *n* pilegrimsreise *c*
pill [pil] *n* pille *c*
pillar ['pilə] *n* søyle *c*
pillar-box ['piləbɔks] *n* postkasse *c*
pillow ['pilou] *n* pute *c*, hodepute *c*
pillowcase ['piloukeis] *n* putevar *nt*
pilot ['pailət] *n* pilot *m*; los *m*
pimple ['pimpəl] *n* kvise *c*
pin [pin] *n* knappenål *c*; *v* feste med nål; **bobby ~** *Am* hårspenne *c*
PIN [pin], **personal identification number** *n* PIN, kode *c*
pincers ['pinsəz] *pl* knipetang *c*
pinch [pintʃ] *v* *klype
pineapple ['pai,næpəl] *n* ananas *m*
ping-pong ['piŋpɔŋ] *n* bordtennis *m*
pink [piŋk] *adj* lyserød, rosa
pioneer [,paiə'niə] *n* nybygger *m*; pioner *m*
pious ['paiəs] *adj* from
pip [pip] *n* kjerne *m*
pipe [paip] *n* pipe *c*; rør *nt*; **~ cleaner** piperenser *m*; **~ tobacco** pipetobakk *m*
pirate ['paiərət] *n* sjørøver *m*
pistol ['pistəl] *n* pistol *m*
piston ['pistən] *n* stempel *nt*
pit [pit] *n* grop *c*; gruve *c*
pitcher ['pitʃə] *n* krukke *c*
pity ['piti] *n* medlidenhet *c*; *v* synes synd på, *ha medlidenhet med; **what a pity!** så synd!
placard ['plækɑːd] *n* plakat *m*
place [pleis] *n* sted *nt*; *v* *sette, stille; **~ of birth** fødested *nt*; ***take ~** *finne sted
plague [pleig] *n* plage *c*; pest *m*
plaice [pleis] (pl **~**) rødspette *c*
plain [plein] *adj* tydelig; alminnelig, enkel; *n* slette *c*
plan [plæn] *n* plan *m*; *v* *planlegge
plane [plein] *adj* flat; *n* fly *nt*; **~ crash** flyulykke *c*
planet ['plænit] *n* planet *m*
planetarium [,plæni'tɛəriəm] *n* planetarium *nt*
plank [plæŋk] *n* planke *m*
plant [plɑːnt] *n* plante *c*; fabrikk *m*; *v* plante
plantation [plæn'teiʃən] *n* plantasje *m*
plaster ['plɑːstə] *n* murpuss *m*, gips *m*; plaster *nt*
plastic ['plæstik] *adj* plastikk-; *n* plastikk *m*
plate [pleit] *n* tallerken *m*; plate *c*
plateau ['plætou] *n* (pl **~x**, **~s**) vidde *c*; høyslette *c*
platform ['plætfɔːm] *n* perrong *m*
platinum ['plætinəm] *n*

platina *m*
play [plei] *n* lek *m*; teaterstykke *nt*; *v* leke; spille; **one-act ~** enakter *m*; **~ truant** skulke
player [pleiə] *n* spiller *m*
playground ['pleigraund] *n* lekeplass *m*
playing card ['pleiiŋkɑ:d] *n* spillkort *nt*
playwright ['pleirait] *n* skuespillforfatter *m*
plea [pli:] *n* påstand *m*; bønn *m*
plead [pli:d] *v* føre en sak; trygle
pleasant ['plezənt] *adj* hyggelig, deilig
please [pli:z] vennligst; *v* glede; **pleased** fornøyd; **pleasing** behagelig
pleasure ['pleʒə] *n* behag *nt*, fornøyelse *m*
plentiful ['plentifəl] *adj* rikelig
plenty ['plenti] *n* rikelighet *c*; overflod *m*
pliers [plaiəz] *pl* tang *c*
plot [plɔt] *n* komplott *nt*, sammensvergelse *m*; handling *c*; tomt *c*
plough [plau] *n* plog *m*; *v* pløye
plucky ['plʌki] *adj* modig
plug [plʌg] *n* stikkontakt *m*; **~ in** sette i kontakten, plugge inn
plum [plʌm] *n* plomme *c*
plumber ['plʌmə] *n* rørlegger *m*
plump [plʌmp] *adj* lubben
plural ['pluərəl] *n* flertall *nt*
plus [plʌs] *prep* pluss
pneumatic [nju:'mætik] *adj* luft..., pneumatisk
pneumonia [nju:'mouniə] *n* lungebetennelse *m*
poach [poutʃ] *v* **~ed eggs** pocherte egg
pocket ['pɔkit] *n* lomme *c*
pocketbook ['pɔkitbuk] *nAm* lommebok *c*
pocketknife ['pɔkitnaif] *n* (pl -knives) lommekniv *m*
poem ['pouim] *n* dikt *nt*
poet ['pouit] *n* dikter *m*
poetry ['pouitri] *n* poesi *m*
point [pɔint] *n* punkt *nt*; spiss *m*; *v* peke; **~ of view** synspunkt *nt*; **~ out** vise
pointed ['pɔintid] *adj* spiss
poison ['pɔizən] *n* gift *c*; *v* forgifte
poisonous ['pɔizənəs] *adj* giftig
Poland ['poulənd] Polen
pole [poul] *n* stang *c*
police [pə'li:s] *pl* politi *nt*; **~ station** politistasjon *m*
policeman [pə'li:smən] *n* (pl -men) politibetjent *m*
policewoman [pə'li:swumən] *n* (pl -women) politibetjent *m*
policy ['pɔlisi] *n* politikk *m*; polise *m*
Polish ['pouliʃ] *adj* polsk
polish ['pɔliʃ] *v* pusse, polere
polite [pə'lait] *adj* høflig

political [pə'litikəl] *adj* politisk
politician [ˌpɔli'tiʃən] *n* politiker *m*
politics ['pɔlitiks] *n* politikk *m*
poll [poul] *n* meningsmåling *c*; valg; **go to the polls** velge
pollute [pə'lu:t] *v* forurense
pollution [pə'lu:ʃən] *n* forurensning *m*
pond [pɔnd] *n* dam *m*
pony ['pouni] *n* ponni *m*
pool [pu:l] *n* dam *m*; svømmebasseng *nt*; **~ attendant** badevakt *c*
poor [puə] *adj* fattig; fattigslig; dårlig
pope [poup] *n* pave *m*
pop music [pɔp 'mju:zik] popmusikk *m*
poppy ['pɔpi] *n* valmue *m*
popular ['pɔpjulə] *adj* populær; folke-
population [ˌpɔpju'leiʃən] *n* befolkning *m*
populous ['pɔpjuləs] *adj* folkerik
porcelain ['pɔ:səlin] *n* porselen *nt*
porcupine ['pɔ:kjupain] *n* pinnsvin *nt*
pork [pɔ:k] *n* svinekjøtt *nt*
port [pɔ:t] *n* havn *c*; babord
portable ['pɔ:təbəl] *adj* transportabel
porter ['pɔ:tə] *n* bærer *m*; portier *m*
porthole ['pɔ:thoul] *n* kuøye *nt*
portion ['pɔ:ʃən] *n* porsjon *m*
portrait ['pɔ:trit] *n* portrett *nt*
Portugal ['pɔ:tjugəl] Portugal
Portuguese [ˌpɔ:tju'gi:z] *adj* portugisisk; *n* portugiser *m*
position [pə'ziʃən] *n* posisjon *m*; situasjon *m*; holdning *m*; stilling *c*
positive ['pɔzətiv] *adj* positiv; *n* positivt bilde
possess [pə'zes] *v* eie; **possessed** *adj* besatt
possession [pə'zeʃən] *n* besittelse *m*; **possessions** eiendeler *pl*
possibility [ˌpɔsə'biləti] *n* mulighet *c*
possible ['pɔsəbəl] *adj* mulig; eventuell
post [poust] *n* stolpe *m*; post *m*; *v* poste; **post--office** postkontor *nt*
postage ['poustidʒ] *n* porto *m*; **~ paid** portofri; **~ stamp** frimerke *nt*
postcard ['poustkɑ:d] *n* postkort *nt*; prospektkort *nt*
poster ['poustə] *n* plakat *m*
poste restante [poust re'stɑ̃:t] poste restante
postman ['poustmən] *n* (pl -men) postbud *nt*
post-paid [ˌpoust'peid] *adj* frankert

postpone [pə'spoun] *v* *utsette
pot [pɔt] *n* gryte *c*
potato [pə'teitou] *n* (pl ~es) potet *m*
pottery ['pɔtəri] *n* keramikk *m*; steintøy *nt*
pouch [pautʃ] *n* pung *m*
poultry ['poultri] *n* fjærkre *nt*
pound [paund] *n* pund *nt*
pour [pɔː] *v* helle, skjenke
poverty ['pɔvəti] *n* fattigdom *m*
powder ['paudə] *n* pudder *nt*
power [pauə] *n* kraft *c*, styrke *m*; energi *m*; makt *c*; ~ **station** kraftverk *nt*
powerful ['pauəfəl] *adj* mektig; sterk
powerless ['pauələs] *adj* maktesløs
practical ['præktikəl] *adj* praktisk
practically ['præktikli] *adv* praktisk talt
practice ['præktis] *n* praksis *m*
practise ['præktis] *v* praktisere; øve seg
praise [preiz] *v* rose; *n* ros *m*
pram [præm] *n* barnevogn *c*
prawn [prɔːn] *n* reke *c*
pray [prei] *v* *be
prayer [prɛə] *n* bønn *m*
preach [priːtʃ] *v* preke
precarious [pri'kɛəriəs] *adj* risikabel; utrygg
precaution [pri'kɔːʃən] *n* forsiktighet *c*; sikkerhetstiltak *nt*
precede [pri'siːd] *v* *gå forut for
preceding [pri'siːdiŋ] *adj* foregående
precious ['preʃəs] *adj* kostbar; dyrebar; ~ **stone** edelstein *m*
precipice ['presipis] *n* stup *nt*
precipitation [priˌsipi'teiʃən] *n* nedbør *m*
precise [pri'sais] *adj* presis, nøyaktig; pertentlig
predecessor ['priːdisesə] *n* forgjenger *m*
predict [pri'dikt] *v* spå
prefer [pri'fəː] *v* *foretrekke
preferable ['prefərəbəl] *adj* til å foretrekke
preference ['prefərəns] *n* forkjærlighet *c*
prefix ['priːfiks] *n* forstavelse *m*
pregnant ['pregnənt] *adj* gravid
pregnancy ['pregnənsi] *n* svangerskap *nt*
prejudice ['predʒədis] *n* fordom *m*
preliminary [pri'liminəri] *adj* innledende; forberedende
premature ['premətʃuə] *adj* forhastet; for tidlig
premier ['premiə] *n* statsminister *m*

premises ['premisiz] *pl* eiendom *m*
premium ['pri:miəm] *n* forsikringspremie *m*
prepaid [ˌpri:'peid] *adj* forhåndsbetalt
preparation [ˌprepə'reiʃən] *n* forberedelse *m*
prepare [pri'pɛə] *v* forberede; tilberede
prepared [pri'pɛəd] *adj* beredt
preposition [ˌprepə'ziʃən] *n* preposisjon *m*
prescribe [pri'skraib] *v* *foreskrive
prescription [pri'skripʃən] *n* resept *m*
presence ['prezəns] *n* nærvær *nt*; tilstedeværelse *m*
present[1] ['prezənt] *n* presang *m*, gave *c*; nåtid *c*; *adj* nåværende; tilstedeværende
present[2] [pri'zent] *v* presentere; *forelegge
presentation [pri'zent'eiʃən] *v* presentasjon
presently ['prezəntli] *adv* snart
preservation [ˌprezə'veiʃən] *n* konservering *c*
preserve [pri'zə:v] *v* konservere; hermetisere
president ['prezidənt] *n* president *m*; formann *m*
press [pres] *n* presse *m*; *v* trykke på, trykke; presse; **~ conference** pressekonferanse *m*
pressing ['presiŋ] *adj* presserende, inntrengende
pressure ['preʃə] *n* trykk *nt*; press *nt*; **atmospheric ~** lufttrykk *nt*; **~ cooker** trykkoker *m*
prestige [pre'sti:ʒ] *n* prestisje *m*
presumable [pri'zju:məbəl] *adj* antakelig
presumptuous [pri'zʌmpʃəs] *adj* overmodig; anmassende
pretence [pri'tens] *n* påskudd *nt*
pretend [pri'tend] *v* *foregi, *late som
pretext ['pri:tekst] *n* påskudd *nt*
pretty ['priti] *adj* pen; *adv* ganske, temmelig
prevent [pri'vent] *v* avverge, forhindre; forebygge
preventive [pri'ventiv] *adj* forebyggende
preview ['privju:] *n* forhåndsvisning *m*
previous ['pri:viəs] *adj* foregående, tidligere, forrige
price [prais] *n* pris *m*; *v* prise
priceless ['praisləs] *adj* uvurderlig
price list ['praisˌlist] *n* prisliste *c*
pride [praid] *n* stolthet *c*

priest [pri:st] *n* katolsk prest
primary ['praiməri] *adj* primær; hoved-, første; elementær
primeval forest [praim'i:vəl 'fɔrist] *n* urskog *m*
prince [prins] *n* prins *m*
princess [prin'ses] *n* prinsesse *c*
principal ['prinsəpəl] *adj* hoved-; *n* rektor *m*, skolebestyrer *m*
principle ['prinsəpəl] *n* prinsipp *nt*, grunnsetning *m*
print [print] *v* trykke; *n* avtrykk *nt*; trykk *nt*
printer ['printə] *n* printer *m*, skriver *m*
printout ['printaut] *n* utskrift *c*
prior ['praiə] *adj* forutgående
priority [prai'ɔrəti] *n* fortrinnsrett *m*, prioritet *m*
prison ['prizən] *n* fengsel *nt*
prisoner ['prizənə] *n* fange *m*, innsatt *m*; ~ **of war** krigsfange *m*
privacy ['praivəsi] *n* privatliv *nt*
private ['praivit] *adj* privat; personlig
privilege ['privilidʒ] *n* privilegium *nt*
prize [praiz] *n* premie *m*; belønning *c*
probable ['prɔbəbəl] *adj* sannsynlig
probably ['prɔbəbli] *adv* sannsynligvis
problem ['prɔbləm] *n* problem *nt*; spørsmål *nt*
procedure [prə'si:dʒə] *n* fremgangsmåte *m*
proceed [prə'si:d] *v* *fortsette; *gå til verks
process ['prouses] *n* prosess *m*, fremgangsmåte *m*; rettergang *m*
procession [prə'seʃən] *n* opptog *nt*, prosesjon *m*
proclaim [prə'kleim] *v* *kunngjøre
produce[1] [prə'dju:s] *v* fremstille, produsere
produce[2] ['prɔdju:s] *n* landbruksprodukter *pl*; avling *c*
producer [prə'dju:sə] *n* produsent *m*
product ['prɔdʌkt] *n* produkt *nt*
production [prə'dʌkʃən] *n* produksjon *m*
profession [prə'feʃən] *n* yrke *nt*; fag *nt*
professional [prə'feʃənəl] *adj* profesjonell
professor [prə'fesə] *n* professor *m*
profit ['prɔfit] *n* fortjeneste *c*, fordel *m*; *v* *ha utbytte av
profitable ['prɔfitəbəl] *adj* innbringende
profound [prə'faund] *adj* dypsindig; grundig
programme ['prougræm] *n*

program *nt*
progress[1] ['prougres] *n* fremskritt *nt*
progress[2] [prə'gres] *v* *gjøre fremskritt
progressive [prə'gresiv] *adj* progressiv, fremadstrebende; tiltagende
prohibit [prə'hibit] *v* *forby
prohibition [,proui'biʃən] *n* forbud *nt*
prohibitive [prə'hibitiv] *adj* uoverkommelig
project ['prɔdʒekt] *n* plan *m*, prosjekt *nt*
promenade [,prɔmə'nɑːd] *n* promenade *m*
promise ['prɔmis] *n* løfte *nt*; *v* love
promote [prə'mout] *v* forfremme, fremme
promotion [prə'mouʃən] *n* forfremmelse *m*
prompt [prɔmpt] *adj* omgående, straks
pronoun ['prounaun] *n* pronomen *nt*
pronounce [prə'nauns] *v* uttale
pronunciation [,prənʌnsi'eiʃən] *n* uttale *m*
proof [pruːf] *n* bevis *nt*
propaganda [,prɔpə'gændə] *n* propaganda *m*
propel [prə'pel] *v* *drive frem
propeller [prə'pelə] *n* propell *m*
proper ['prɔpə] *adj* passende; sømmelig, riktig
property ['prɔpəti] *n* eiendeler *pl*, eiendom *m*; egenskap *m*
prophet ['prɔfit] *n* profet *m*
proportion [prə'pɔːʃən] *n* proporsjon *m*
proportional [prə'pɔːʃənəl] *adj* forholdsmessig
proposal [prə'pouzəl] *n* forslag *nt*
propose [prə'pouz] *v* *foreslå
proposition [,prɔpə'ziʃən] *n* forslag *nt*
proprietor [prə'praiətə] *n* eier *m*
prosecute ['prɔsikjuːt] *v* saksøke, anklage
prospect ['prɔspekt] *n* utsikt *m*
prosperity [prɔ'sperəti] *n* fremgang *m*, velstand *m*
prosperous ['prɔspərəs] *adj* velstående
prostitute ['prɔstitjuːt] *n* prostituert *m*
protect [prə'tekt] *v* beskytte
protection [prə'tekʃən] *n* beskyttelse *m*
protein ['proutiːn] *n* protein *nt*
protest[1] ['proutest] *n* protest *m*
protest[2] [prə'test] *v* protestere
Protestant ['prɔtistənt] *adj* protestantisk
proud [praud] *adj* stolt;

hovmodig
prove [pruːv] *v* bevise; vise seg
proverb ['prɔvəːb] *n* ordspråk *nt*
provide [prə'vaid] *v* forsyne, skaffe; **provided that** forutsatt at
province ['prɔvins] *n* fylke *nt*; provins *m*
provincial [prə'vinʃəl] *adj* provinsiell
provisional [prə'viʒənəl] *adj* foreløpig
provisions [prə'viʒənz] *pl* proviant *m*
prudent ['pruːdənt] *adj* klok; varsom
prune [pruːn] *n* sviske *c*
psychiatrist [sai'kaiətrist] *n* psykiater *m*
psychic ['saikik] *adj* psykisk
psychoanalyst [ˌsaikou'ænəlist] *n* psykoanalytiker *m*
psychological [ˌsaikɔ'lɔdʒikəl] *adj* psykologisk
psychologist [sai'kɔlədʒist] *n* psykolog *m*
psychology [sai'kɔlədʒi] *n* psykologi *m*
pub [pʌb] *n* kro *c*, kneipe *c*, pub *m*
public ['pʌblik] *adj* offentlig; allmenn; *n* publikum *nt*; **~ garden** offentlig parkanlegg; **~ house** vertshus *nt*
publication [ˌpʌbli'keiʃən] *n* offentliggjørelse *m*
publicity [pʌ'blisəti] *n* publisitet *m*
publish ['pʌbliʃ] *v* *utgi, *offentliggjøre
publisher ['pʌbliʃə] *n* forlegger *m*
puddle ['pʌdəl] *n* pytt *m*
pull [pul] *v* *trekke; **~ out** *trekke seg; *dra av sted; **~ up** stanse
pulley ['puli] *n* (pl ~s) trinse *c*
Pullman ['pulmən] *n* sovevogn *c*
pullover ['puˌlouvə] *n* genser *m*
pulpit ['pulpit] *n* prekestol *m*, talerstol *m*
pulse [pʌls] *n* puls *m*
pump [pʌmp] *n* pumpe *c*; *v* pumpe
pun [pʌn] *n* ordspill *nt*
punch [pʌntʃ] *v* *slå; *n* knyttneveslag *nt*; punsj *m*
punctual ['pʌŋktʃuəl] *adj* punktlig, presis
puncture ['pʌŋktʃə] *n* punktering *c*
punctured ['pʌŋktʃəd] *adj* punktert
punish ['pʌniʃ] *v* straffe
punishment ['pʌniʃmənt] *n* straff *m*
pupil ['pjuːpəl] *n* elev *m*
puppet-show ['pʌpitʃou] *n* dukketeater *nt*
purchase ['pəːtʃəs] *v* kjøpe; *n* kjøp *nt*, anskaffelse *m*; **~ price** kjøpesum *m*; **~ tax**

moms *m*
purchaser ['pə:tʃəsə] *n* kjøper *m*
pure [pjuə] *adj* ren
purple ['pə:pəl] *adj* purpurfarget, lilla
purpose ['pə:pəs] *n* hensikt *m*, formål *nt*; **on ~** med vilje
purse [pə:s] *n* pengepung *m*, håndveske *c*
pursue [pə'sju:] *v* *forfølge; strebe etter
pus [pʌs] *n* verk *m*; materie *m*
push [puʃ] *n* dytt *m*, støt *nt*; *v* *skyve; trenge seg frem
push button ['puʃ,bʌtən] *n* trykknapp *m*
***put** [put] *v* stille, *legge, plassere; putte; **~ away** rydde vekk; **~ off** *utsette; **~ on** *ta på; **~ out** slokke
puzzle ['pʌzəl] *n* puslespill *nt*; gåte *c*; *v* volde hodebry; **jigsaw ~** puslespill *nt*
puzzling ['pʌzliŋ] *adj* uforståelig
pyjamas [pə'dʒɑ:məz] *pl* pyjamas *m*

Q

quack [kwæk] *n* sjarlatan *m*, kvakksalver *m*
quail [kweil] *n* (pl ~, ~s) vaktel *m*
quaint [kweint] *adj* eiendommelig; gammeldags
qualification [,kwɔlifi'keiʃən] *n* kvalifikasjon *m*; forbehold *nt*, innskrenkning *m*
qualified ['kwɔlifaid] *adj* kvalifisert; kompetent
qualify ['kwɔlifai] *v* kvalifisere seg
quality ['kwɔləti] *n* kvalitet *m*; egenskap *m*
quantity ['kwɔntəti] *n* kvantitet *m*; antall *nt*
quarantine ['kwɔrənti:n] *n* karantene *m*
quarrel ['kwɔrəl] *v* trette, krangle; *n* krangel *m* / *nt*, trette *c*
quarry ['kwɔri] *n* steinbrudd *nt*
quarter ['kwɔ:tə] *n* kvart; kvartal *nt*; kvarter *nt*; *Am* 25-cent-mynt; **~ of an hour** kvarter *nt*
quarterly ['kwɔ:təli] *adj* kvartals-
quay [ki:] *n* kai *c*
queen [kwi:n] *n* dronning *c*
queer [kwiə] *adj* merkelig, underlig; sær
query ['kwiəri] *n* forespørsel *m*; *v* *forespørre; betvile
question ['kwestʃən] *n* spørsmål *nt*, problem *nt*; *v* *spørre ut; *dra i tvil; **~ mark** spørsmålstegn *nt*

queue [kjuː] *n* kø *m*; *v* *stå i kø
quick [kwik] *adj* hurtig
quick-tempered [ˌkwik'tempəd] *adj* hissig
quiet ['kwaiət] *adj* stille, rolig, stillferdig; *n* stillhet *c*, ro *m*
quilt [kwilt] *n* vatt-teppe *nt*
quit [kwit] *v* slutte, stoppe
quite [kwait] *adv* helt; ganske, temmelig, særdeles
quiz [kwiz] *n* (pl ~zes) spørrelek *m*; prøve *c*
quota ['kwoutə] *n* kvote *m*
quotation [kwou'teiʃən] *n* sitat *nt*; **~ marks** anførselstegn *pl*
quote [kwout] *v* sitere

R

rabbit ['ræbit] *n* kanin *m*
rabies ['reibiz] *n* hundegalskap *m*, rabies *m*
race [reis] *n* kappløp *nt*, veddeløp *nt*; rase *m*
racecourse ['reiskɔːs] *n* veddeløpsbane *m*
racehorse ['reishɔːs] *n* veddeløpshest *m*
racetrack ['reistræk] *n* veddeløpsbane *m*
racial ['reiʃəl] *adj* rase-
racket ['rækit] *n* rabalder *nt*; racket *m*
radiator ['reidieitə] *n* radiator *m*
radical ['rædikəl] *adj* radikal
radio ['reidiou] *n* radio *m*
radish ['rædiʃ] *n* reddik *m*
radius ['reidiəs] *n* (pl radii) radius *m*
raft [rɑːft] *n* flåte *m*
rag [ræg] *n* fille *c*
rage [reidʒ] *n* raseri *nt*; *v* rase
raid [reid] *n* angrep *nt*
rail [reil] *n* gelender *nt*, rekkverk *nt*
railing ['reiliŋ] *n* gelender *nt*
railroad ['reilroud] *nAm* jernbane *m*
railway ['reilwei] *n* jernbane *m*; skinnegang *m*
rain [rein] *n* regn *nt*; *v* regne
rainbow ['reinbou] *n* regnbue *m*
raincoat ['reinkout] *n* regnfrakk *m*
rainy ['reini] *adj* regnfull
raise [reiz] *v* heve; øke; dyrke, *oppdra, ale opp; *pålegge; *nAm* lønnstillegg *nt*
raisin ['reizən] *n* rosin *c*
rake [reik] *n* rake *m*
rally ['ræli] *n* rally *nt*; opptog *nt*; *v* samle seg
ramp [ræmp] *n* rampe *c*
ramshackle ['ræmˌʃækəl] *adj* falleferdig
rancid ['rænsid] *adj* harsk
rang [ræŋ] *v* (p ring)

range [reindʒ] *n* rekkevidde *c*; ~ **finder** avstandsmåler *m*
rank [ræŋk] *n* rang *m*; rekke *c*
ransom ['rænsəm] *n* løsepenger *pl*
rap [ræp] *n* rap *c*
rape [reip] *v* *voldta; *n* voldtekt *c*
rapid ['ræpid] *adj* hurtig
rapids ['ræpidz] *pl* elvestryk *nt*
rare [rɛə] *adj* sjelden; lettstekt, blodig
rarely ['rɛəli] *adv* sjelden
rascal ['rɑːskəl] *n* skurk *m*, slyngel *m*
rash [ræʃ] *n* utslett *nt*; *adj* forhastet, ubesindig
raspberry ['rɑːzbəri] *n* bringebær *nt*
rat [ræt] *n* rotte *c*
rate [reit] *n* tariff *m*, pris *m*; fart *m*; **at any** ~ i alle fall, i hvert fall; ~ **of exchange** valutakurs *m*
rather ['rɑːðə] *adv* temmelig, ganske, riktig; heller
ration ['ræʃən] *n* rasjon *m*
raven ['reivən] *n* ravn *m*
raw [rɔː] *adj* rå; ~ **material** råmateriale *nt*
ray [rei] *n* stråle *m*
razor ['reizə] *n* barberhøvel *m*; ~ **blade** barberblad *nt*
reach [riːtʃ] *v* nå; *n* rekkevidde *c*
react [ri'ækt] *v* reagere
reaction [ri'ækʃən] *n* reaksjon *m*
***read** [riːd] *v* lese
reading ['riːdiŋ] *n* lesning *m*
reading lamp ['riːdiŋlæmp] *n* leselampe *c*
reading room ['riːdiŋruːm] *n* lesesal *m*
ready ['redi] *adj* klar, parat; ferdig
real [riəl] *adj* virkelig
reality [ri'æləti] *n* virkelighet *c*
realizable ['riəlaizəbəl] *adj* mulig
realize ['riəlaiz] *v* *innse, *ha klart for seg; realisere
really ['riəli] *adv* virkelig, faktisk; egentlig
rear [riə] *n* bakside *c*; *v* *oppdra; heve; ~ **light** baklykt *c*
reason ['riːzən] *n* årsak *c*, grunn *m*; fornuft *m*, forstand *m*; *v* resonnere
reasonable ['riːzənəbəl] *adj* fornuftig; rimelig
reassure [ˌriːə'ʃuə] *v* berolige
rebate ['riːbeit] *n* fradrag *nt*, rabatt *m*
rebellion [ri'beljən] *n* oppstand *m*, opprør *nt*
recall [ri'kɔːl] *v* erindre, minnes; tilbakekalle; annullere
receipt [ri'siːt] *n* kvittering *c*; mottakelse *m*
receive [ri'siːv] *v* *få, *motta

receiver [ri'si:və] *n* telefonrør *nt*
recent ['ri:sənt] *adj* ny
recently ['ri:səntli] *adv* forleden, nylig
reception [ri'sepʃən] *n* mottakelse *m*; ~ **office** resepsjon *m*
receptionist [ri'sepʃənist] *n* resepsjonist *m*
recession [ri'seʃən] *n* tilbakegang *m*
recipe ['resipi] *n* oppskrift *c*
recital [ri'saitəl] *n* solistkonsert *m*
reckon ['rekən] *v* regne; tro
recognition [ˌrekəg'niʃən] *n* anerkjennelse *m*; gjenkjennelse *m*
recognize ['rekəgnaiz] *v* kjenne igjen; anerkjenne
recollect [ˌrekə'lekt] *v* huske
recommend [ˌrekə'mend] *v* anbefale; tilråde
recommendation [ˌrekəmen'deiʃən] *n* anbefaling *c*
reconciliation [ˌrekənsili'eiʃən] *n* forsoning *c*
record[1] ['rekɔ:d] *n* plate *c*; rekord *m*; protokoll *m*
record[2] [ri'kɔ:d] *v* registrere
recorder [ri'kɔ:də] *n* kassettspiller *m*
recording [ri'kɔ:diŋ] *n* opptak *nt*
recover [ri'kʌvə] *v* *finne igjen; bli frisk, *komme seg
recovery [ri'kʌvəri] *n* helbredelse *m*, bedring *c*
recreation [ˌrekri'eiʃən] *n* atspredelse *m*, rekreasjon *m*; ~ **center** *Am*, ~ **centre** rekreasjonssenter *nt*
recruit [ri'kru:t] *n* rekrutt *m*
rectangle ['rektæŋgəl] *n* rektangel *nt*
rectangular [rek'tæŋgjulə] *adj* rektangulær
rector ['rektə] *n* sogneprest *m*
rectum ['rektəm] *n* endetarm *m*
recyclable [ri'saikləbəl] *adj* resirkulerbar
recycle [ri'saikəl] *v* resirkulere
red [red] *adj* rød; **red tape** papirmølle *c*, byråkrati *nt*
redeem [ri'di:m] *v* frelse
reduce [ri'dju:s] *v* redusere, minske
reduction [ri'dʌkʃən] *n* reduksjon *m*, avslag *nt*
redundant [ri'dʌndənt] *adj* overflødig
reed [ri:d] *n* siv *nt*
reef [ri:f] *n* rev *nt*
reference ['refrəns] *n* referanse *m*, henvisning *m*; forbindelse *m*; **with ~ to** vedrørende
refer to [ri'fə:] henvise til
referee [ˌrefə'ri:] *n* dommer *m*
refill ['ri:fil] *n* refill *m*
refinery [ri'fainəri] *n*

raffineri *nt*
reflect [ri'flekt] *v* reflektere; gjenspeile
reflection [ri'flekʃən] *n* refleks *m*; speilbilde *nt*
reflector [ri'flektə] *n* reflektor *m*
refresh [ri'freʃ] *v* forfriske
refreshment [ri'freʃmənt] *n* forfriskning *m*
refrigerator [ri'fridʒəreitə] *n* kjøleskap *nt*
refugee [ˌrefju'dʒiː] *n* flyktning *m*
refund[1] [ri'fʌnd] *v* refundere
refund[2] ['riːfʌnd] *n* tilbakebetaling *c*
refusal [ri'fjuːzəl] *n* avslag *nt*
refuse[1] [ri'fjuːz] *v* *avslå
refuse[2] ['refjuːs] *n* avfall *nt*
regard [ri'gɑːd] *v* *anse; betrakte; *n* respekt *m*; **as regards** angående, med hensyn til; **best ~** med vennlig hilsen, mvh
regarding [ri'gɑːdiŋ] *prep* med hensyn til; angående
regatta [ri'gætə] *n* regatta *m*
régime [rei'ʒiːm] *n* regime *nt*
region ['riːdʒən] *n* egn *m*; område *nt*
regional ['riːdʒənəl] *adj* regional
register ['redʒistə] *v* *innskrive seg; bokføre; **registered letter** rekommandert brev
registration [ˌredʒi'streiʃən] *n* registrering *c*; **~ number** registreringsnummer *nt*; **~ plate** nummerskilt *nt*
regret [ri'gret] *v* beklage; *n* beklagelse *m*
regular ['regjulə] *adj* regelmessig; normal, vanlig
regulate ['regjuleit] *v* regulere
regulation [ˌregju'leiʃən] *n* regel *m*, bestemmelse *m*; regulering *c*
rehabilitation [ˌriːhəˌbili'teiʃən] *n* rehabilitering *c*
rehearsal [ri'həːsəl] *n* prøve *c*; øvelse *m*
rehearse [ri'həːs] *v* prøve; øve
reign [rein] *n* regjeringstid *c*; *v* herske
reimburse [ˌriːim'bəːs] *v* tilbakebetale
reindeer ['reindiə] *n* (pl ~) reinsdyr *nt*
reject [ri'dʒekt] *v* tilbakevise, avvise; forkaste
relate [ri'leit] *v* *fortelle
related [ri'leitid] *adj* beslektet
relation [ri'leiʃən] *n* forhold *nt*, forbindelse *m*; slektning *m*
relative ['relətiv] *n* slektning *m*; *adj* relativ
relax [ri'læks] *v* slappe av
relaxation [ˌrilæk'seiʃən] *n* avslapning *m*

reliable [ri'laiəbəl] *adj* pålitelig
relic ['relik] *n* relikvie *m*
relief [ri'li:f] *n* lindring *c*, lettelse *m*; hjelp *c*; relieff *nt*
relieve [ri'li:v] *v* lindre; avløse
religion [ri'lidʒən] *n* religion *m*
religious [ri'lidʒəs] *adj* religiøs
rely on [ri'lai] stole på
remain [ri'mein] *v* *forbli; *bli igjen
remainder [ri'meində] *n* rest *m*
remaining [ri'meiniŋ] *adj* resterende
remark [ri'mɑ:k] *n* bemerkning *m*; *v* bemerke
remarkable [ri'mɑ:kəbəl] *adj* bemerkelsesverdig
remedy ['remədi] *n* legemiddel *nt*; botemiddel *nt*
remember [ri'membə] *v* huske
remembrance [ri'membrəns] *n* erindring *c*, minne *nt*
remind [ri'maind] *v* minne
remit [ri'mit] *v* overføre
remittance [ri'mitəns] *n* remisse *m*
remnant ['remnənt] *n* rest *m*, levning *m*
remote [ri'mout] *adj* fjern, avsides
remote control [ri'mout‿kən'troul] *n* fjernkontroll *c*
removal [ri'mu:vəl] *n* fjerning *c*
remove [ri'mu:v] *v* fjerne
remuneration [ri,mju:nə'reiʃən] *n* godtgjørelse *m*
renew [ri'nju:] *v* fornye
renewable [ri'nju:əbəl] *adj* fornybar
rent [rent] *v* leie; *n* leie *c*
repair [ri'pɛə] *v* reparere; *n* reparasjon *m*
reparation [,repə'reiʃən] *n* reparasjon *m*
***repay** [ri'pei] *v* tilbakebetale
repayment [ri'peimənt] *n* tilbakebetaling *c*
repeat [ri'pi:t] *v* *gjenta
repellent [ri'pelənt] *adj* frastøtende
repentance [ri'pentəns] *n* anger *m*
repertory ['repətəri] *n* repertoar *nt*
repetition [,repə'tiʃən] *n* gjentakelse *m*
replace [ri'pleis] *v* erstatte
reply [ri'plai] *v* svare; *n* svar *nt*; **in ~** som svar
report [ri'pɔ:t] *v* rapportere; melde; melde seg; *n* rapport *m*, melding *c*
reporter [ri'pɔ:tə] *n* reporter *m*
represent [,repri'zent] *v* representere; forestille
representation

[ˌreprizen'teiʃən] *n* representasjon *m*
representative [ˌrepri'zentətiv] *adj* representativ
reprimand ['reprimɑːnd] *v* *irettesette
reproach [ri'proutʃ] *n* bebreidelse *m*; *v* bebreide
reproduce [ˌriːprə'djuːs] *v* reprodusere
reproduction [ˌriːprə'dʌkʃən] *n* reproduksjon *m*
reptile ['reptail] *n* krypdyr *nt*
republic [ri'pʌblik] *n* republikk *m*
republican [ri'pʌblikən] *adj* republikansk
repulsive [ri'pʌlsiv] *adj* frastøtende
reputation [ˌrepju'teiʃən] *n* rykte *nt*; anseelse *m*
request [ri'kwest] *n* anmodning, bønn *m*; *v* anmode, be*
require [ri'kwaiə] *v* kreve; behøve
requirement [ri'kwaiəmənt] *n* krav *nt*
requisite ['rekwizit] *adj* påkrevd
rescue ['reskjuː] *v* redde; *n* redning *m*
research [ri'səːtʃ] *n* forskning *m*
resemblance [ri'zembləns] *n* likhet *c*
resemble [ri'zembəl] *v* likne
resent [ri'zent] *v* *ta ille opp
reservation [ˌrezə'veiʃən] *n* reservasjon *m*; forbehold *nt*
reserve [ri'zəːv] *v* reservere; bestille; *n* reserve *m*
reserved [ri'zəːvd] *adj* reservert
reservoir ['rezəvwɑː] *n* reservoar *nt*
reside [ri'zaid] *v* bo
residence ['rezidəns] *n* bolig *m*; **~ permit** oppholdstillatelse *m*
resident ['rezidənt] *n* fastboende *m*; *adj* bosatt; stedlig
resign [ri'zain] *v* *fratre; *gå av
resignation [ˌrezig'neiʃən] *n* avskjedssøknad *m*; avskjed *m*
resist [ri'zist] *v* *gjøre motstand mot
resistance [ri'zistəns] *n* motstand *m*
resolute ['rezəluːt] *adj* bestemt, besluttsom
respect [ri'spekt] *n* respekt *m*; ærbødighet *c*, aktelse *m*; *v* respektere
respectable [ri'spektəbəl] *adj* respektabel
respectful [ri'spektfəl] *adj* ærbødig
respective [ri'spektiv] *adj* respektiv
respiration [ˌrespə'reiʃən] *n* åndedrett *nt*
respite ['respait] *n* henstand

m
responsibility [ri,spɔnsə'biləti] *n* ansvar *nt*
responsible [ri'spɔnsəbəl] *adj* ansvarlig
rest [rest] *n* hvile *m*; rest *m*; *v* hvile
restaurant ['restərɔ̃:] *n* restaurant *m*
restful ['restfəl] *adj* beroligende
rest home ['resthoum] *n* hvilehjem *nt*
restless ['restləs] *adj* urolig; rastløs
restrain [ri'strein] *v* tøyle
restriction [ri'strikʃən] *n* innskrenkning *m*
rest room ['restru:m] *nAm* toalett *nt*
result [ri'zʌlt] *n* resultat *nt*; følge *m*; *v* resultere
resume [ri'zju:m] *v* *gjenoppta
résumé ['rezjumei] *n* resymé *nt*
retail ['ri:teil] *n* ~ **trade** detaljhandel *m*
retina ['retinə] *n* netthinne *c*
retire [ri'taiə] *v* trekke seg tilbake; gå av med pensjon
retired [ri'taiəd] *adj* pensjonert
retirement [ri'taiəment] *n* pensjon *m*
return [ri'tə:n] *v* vende tilbake, *komme tilbake; *n* tilbakekomst *m*; ~ **flight** tilbaketur *m*; ~ **journey** hjemreise *m*, tilbakereise *c*
reunite [,ri:ju:'nait] *v* gjenforene
reveal [ri'vi:l] *v* åpenbare, avsløre
revelation [,revə'leiʃən] *n* avsløring *c*
revenge [ri'vendʒ] *n* hevn *m*
revenue ['revənju:] *n* inntekter *pl*, toll *m*
reverse [ri'və:s] *n* motsetning *m*; bakside *c*; revers *m*; motgang *m*; omslag *nt*; *adj* motsatt; *v* rygge
review [ri'vju:] *n* anmeldelse *m*; tidsskrift *nt*
revise [ri'vaiz] *v* revidere
revision [ri'viʒən] *n* revisjon *m*
revival [ri'vaivəl] *n* gjenopplivelse *m*
revolt [ri'voult] *v* *gjøre opprør; *n* oppstand *m*, opprør *nt*
revolting [ri'voultiŋ] *adj* motbydelig, frastøtende, opprørende
revolution [,revə'lu:ʃən] *n* revolusjon *m*; omdreining *m*
revolutionary [,revə'lu:ʃənəri] *adj* revolusjonær
revolver [ri'vɔlvə] *n* revolver *m*
revue [ri'vju:] *n* revy *m*
reward [ri'wɔ:d] *n* belønning *c*; *v* belønne
rheumatism ['ru:mətizəm]

n reumatisme *m*
rhinoceros [rai'nɔsərəs] *n* (pl ~, ~es) neshorn *nt*
rhubarb ['ru:bɑ:b] *n* rabarbra *m*
rhyme [raim] *n* rim *nt*
rhythm ['riðəm] *n* rytme *m*
rib [rib] *n* ribbein *nt*
ribbon ['ribən] *n* bånd *nt*
rice [rais] *n* ris *m*
rich [ritʃ] *adj* rik
riches ['ritʃiz] *pl* rikdom *m*
rid [rid] *v* befri (of fra); **get ~ of** bli kvitt
riddle ['ridəl] *n* gåte *c*
ride [raid] *n* tur *m*
***ride** [raid] *v* kjøre; *ride
rider ['raidə] *n* rytter *m*
ridge [ridʒ] *n* høydedrag *nt*
ridicule ['ridikju:l] *v* *latterliggjøre
ridiculous [ri'dikjuləs] *adj* latterlig
riding ['raidiŋ] *n* ridning *m*; **~ school** rideskole *m*
rifle ['raifəl] *v* gevær *nt*
right [rait] *n* rettighet *c*; *adj* rett, riktig; høyre; rettferdig; **all right!** bra!; ***be ~** *ha rett; **~ of way** forkjørsrett *m*
righteous ['raitʃəs] *adj* rettskaffen
right-hand ['raithænd] *adj* på høyre side, høyre
rightly ['raitli] *adv* med rette
rim [rim] *n* felg *m*; kant *m*
ring [riŋ] *n* ring *m*; krets *m*; manesje *m*
***ring** [riŋ] *v* ringe; **~ up** ringe opp
rinse [rins] *v* skylle; *n* skylling *c*
riot ['raiət] *n* oppløp *nt*
rip [rip] *v* *rive i stykker
ripe [raip] *adj* moden
rise [raiz] *n* pålegg *nt*, høyde *m*; oppstigning *m*; opprinnelse *m*
***rise** [raiz] *v* reise seg; *stå opp; *stige
rising ['raiziŋ] *n* oppstand *m*
risk [risk] *n* risiko *m*; fare *m*; *v* risikere
risky ['riski] *adj* risikabel, dristig
rival ['raivəl] *n* rival *m*; konkurrent *m*; *v* rivalisere
rivalry ['raivəlri] *n* rivalitet *m*; konkurranse *m*
river ['rivə] *n* elv *m*; **~ bank** elvebredd *m*
riverside ['rivəsaid] *n* elvebredd *m*
roach [routʃ] *n* (pl ~) mort *m*
road [roud] *n* gate *c*, vei *m*; **~ fork** veiskille *m*; **~ map** veikart *nt*; **~ system** veinett *nt*; **~ up** veiarbeid *nt*
roadhouse ['roudhaus] *n* veikro *c*
roadrage ['roud,reidʒ] *n* trafikkraseri *nt*
roadside ['roudsaid] *n* veikant *m*; **~ restaurant** vertshus *m*
roadway ['roudwei] *nAm*

kjørebane *m*
roam [roum] *v* streife omkring
roar [rɔː] *v* brøle, bruse; *n* dur *m*, brøl *nt*
roast [roust] *v* steke, riste; *n* stek *c*
rob [rɔb] *v* rane
robber ['rɔbə] *n* ransmann *m*
robbery ['rɔbəri] *n* plyndring *c*, ran *nt*, tyveri *nt*; overfall *nt*
robe [roub] *n* lang kjole; embetsdrakt *c*
robin ['rɔbin] *n* rødstrupe *m*
robust [rou'bʌst] *adj* robust
rock [rɔk] *n* klippe *m*; *v* gynge
rocket ['rɔkit] *n* rakett *m*
rocky ['rɔki] *adj* steinet
rod [rɔd] *n* stang *c*
roe [rou] *n* rogn *c*
roll [roul] *v* rulle; *n* rull *m*; rundstykke *nt*
Rollerblade® ['roulə,bleid] *n* (inline) rulleskøyter *c*
roller-skating ['roulə,skeitiŋ] *n* rulleskøyteløping *c*
Roman Catholic ['roumən 'kæθəlik] romersk-katolsk
romance [rə'mæns] *n* romanse *m*
romantic [rə'mæntik] *adj* romantisk
roof [ruːf] *n* tak *nt*; **thatched ~** halmtak *nt*
room [ruːm] *n* rom *nt*, værelse *nt*; plass *m*; **~ and board** kost og losji; **~ service** værelsesbetjening *c*; **~ temperature** værelsestemperatur *m*
roomy ['ruːmi] *adj* rommelig
root [ruːt] *n* rot *c*
rope [roup] *n* rep *nt*
rosary ['rouzəri] *n* rosenkrans *m*
rose [rouz] *n* rose *c*; *adj* rosa
rotten ['rɔtən] *adj* råtten
rouge [ruːʒ] *n* rouge *m*
rough [rʌf] *adj* ru
roulette [ruː'let] *n* rulett *m*
round [raund] *adj* rund; *prep* om, omkring; *n* runde *m*; **~ trip** *Am* tur-retur
roundabout ['raundəbaut] *n* rundkjøring *c*
rounded ['raundid] *adj* avrundet
route [ruːt] *n* rute *c*
routine [ruː'tiːn] *n* rutine *m*
row¹ [rou] *n* rad *m*; *v* ro
row² [rau] *n* krangel *m / nt*
rowdy ['raudi] *adj* ståkende, voldsom
rowing boat ['rouiŋbout] *n* robåt *m*
royal ['rɔiəl] *adj* kongelig
rub [rʌb] *v* *gni
rubber ['rʌbə] *n* gummi *m*; viskelær *nt*; **~ band** strikk *m*
rubbish ['rʌbiʃ] *n* avfall *nt*; tull *nt*, sludder *nt*; **talk ~** vrøvle; **~ bin** søppelbøtte *c*
ruby ['ruːbi] *n* rubin *m*
rucksack ['rʌksæk] *n*

ryggsekk *m*
rudder ['rʌdə] *n* ror *nt*
rude [ru:d] *adj* uforskammet
rug [rʌg] *n* rye *m*
ruin ['ru:in] *v* *ødelegge; *n* undergang *m*; **ruins** ruin *m*
rule [ru:l] *n* regel *m*; styre *nt*, makt *c*, regjering *c*; *v* regjere, herske; **as a ~** som regel, vanligvis
ruler ['ru:lə] *n* regent *m*, monark *m*; linjal *m*
Rumania [ru:'meiniə] Romania
Rumanian [ru:'meiniən] *adj* rumensk; *n* rumener *m*
rumour ['ru:mə] *n* rykte *nt*
***run** [rʌn] *v* *løpe; *renne; **~ into** støte på
runaway ['rʌnəwei] *n* rømling *m*
rung [rʌŋ] *v* (pp ring)
runner ['rʌnə] *n* løper *m*
runway ['rʌnwei] *n* startbane *m*
rural ['ruərəl] *adj* landlig
ruse [ru:z] *n* list *c*
rush [rʌʃ] *v* styrte; *n* siv *nt*
rush hour ['rʌʃauə] *n* rushtid *c*
Russia ['rʌʃə] Russland
Russian ['rʌʃən] *adj* russisk; *n* russer *m*
rust [rʌst] *n* rust *m*
rustic ['rʌstik] *adj* landsens, rustikal
rusty ['rʌsti] *adj* rusten

S

sack [sæk] *n* sekk *m*
sacred ['seikrid] *adj* hellig
sacrifice ['sækrifais] *n* offer *nt*; *v* ofre
sacrilege ['sækrilidʒ] *n* helligbrøde *m*
sad [sæd] *adj* bedrøvet; vemodig, bedrøvelig, trist
saddle ['sædəl] *n* sal *m*
sadness ['sædnəs] *n* vemod *nt*
safe [seif] *adj* sikker; *n* safe *m*, pengeskap *nt*
safety ['seifti] *n* sikkerhet *c*; **~ belt** sikkerhetsbelte *nt*; bilbelte *nt*; **~ pin** sikkerhetsnål *c*; **~ razor** barberhøvel *m*
sail [seil] *v* seile; *n* seil *nt*
sailing boat ['seiliŋbout] *n* seilbåt *m*
sailor ['seilə] *n* sjømann *m*
saint [seint] *n* helgen *m*
salad ['sæləd] *n* salat *m*
salad-oil ['sælədɔil] *n* matolje *c*
salary ['sæləri] *n* gasje *m*, lønn *c*
sale [seil] *n* salg *nt*; **for ~** til salgs; **sales** utsalg *nt*; **sales tax** moms *m*
saleable ['seiləbəl] *adj* salgbar
salesman ['seilzmən] *n* (pl

-men) ekspeditør *m*, butikkselger *m*
salmon ['sæmən] *n* (pl ~) laks *m*
salon ['sælɔ-:] *n* salong *m*
saloon [sə'lu:n] *n* bar *m*
salt [sɔ:lt] *n* salt *nt*; ~ **cellar**, *Am* ~ **shaker** *n* saltkar *nt*
salty ['sɔ:lti] *adj* salt
salute [sə'lu:t] *v* hilse
same [seim] *adj* samme
sample ['sɑ:mpəl] *n* vareprøve *c*
sanatorium [,sænə'tɔ:riəm] *n* (pl ~s, -ria) sanatorium *nt*
sand [sænd] *n* sand *m*
sandal ['sændəl] *n* sandal *m*
sandpaper ['sænd,peipə] *n* sandpapir *nt*
sandy ['sændi] *adj* sandet
sanitary ['sænitəri] *adj* sanitær; ~ **towel**, *Am* ~ **napkin** (sanitets)bind *nt*
sapphire ['sæfaiə] *n* safir *m*
sardine [sɑ:'di:n] *n* sardin *m*
satchel ['sætʃəl] *n* ransel *m*
satellite ['sætəlait] *n* satellitt *m*; ~ **dish** parabolantenne *c*; ~ **radio** *n* satelittradio *c*; ~ **tv** satellittoverføring *c*, satellitt-TV *m*
satin ['sætin] *n* sateng *m*
satisfaction [,sætis'fækʃən] *n* tilfredsstillelse *m*, tilfredshet *c*
satisfactory [,sætis'fæktəri] *adj* tilfredsstillende
satisfy ['sætisfai] *v* tilfredsstille; **satisfied** tilfreds, tilfredsstilt
Saturday ['sætədi] lørdag *m*
sauce [sɔ:s] *n* saus *m*
saucepan ['sɔ:spən] *n* kasserolle *m*, gryte *c*
saucer ['sɔ:sə] *n* skål *c*
Saudi Arabia [,saudiə'reibiə] Saudi-Arabia
Saudi Arabian [,saudiə'reibiən] *adj* saudiarabisk
sauna ['sɔ:nə] *n* badstue *c*
sausage ['sɔsidʒ] *n* pølse *c*
savage ['sævidʒ] *adj* vill
save [seiv] *v* redde; spare
savings ['seiviŋz] *pl* sparepenger *pl*; ~ **bank** sparebank *m*
saviour ['seivjə] *n* frelser *m*
savo(u)ry ['seivəri] *adj* velsmakende; pikant
saw[1] [sɔ:] *v* (p see)
saw[2] [sɔ:] *n* sag *c*
sawdust ['sɔ:dʌst] *n* sagflis *c*
sawmill ['sɔ:mil] *n* sagbruk *nt*
***say** [sei] *v* *si
scaffolding ['skæfəldiŋ] *n* stillas *nt*
scale [skeil] *n* målestokk *m*; skala *m*; skjell *nt*; **scales** *pl* vekt *c*
scan [skæn] *v* skanne
scandal ['skændəl] *n* skandale *m*
Scandinavia [,skændi'neiviə]

Skandinavia
Scandinavian [ˌskændi'neiviən] *adj* skandinavisk; *n* skandinav *m*
scanner ['skænə] *n* skanner *c*
scapegoat ['skeipgout] *n* syndebukk *m*
scar [skɑː] *n* arr *nt*
scarce [skɛəs] *adj* knapp
scarcely ['skɛəsli] *adv* knapt
scarcity ['skɛəsəti] *n* knapphet *c*
scare [skɛə] *v* skremme; *n* panikk *m*
scarf [skɑːf] *n* (pl ~s, scarves) skjerf *nt*
scarlet ['skɑːlət] *adj* skarlagenrød
scary ['skɛəri] *adj* foruroligende; nifs
scatter ['skætə] *v* spre
scene [siːn] *n* scene *m*
scenery ['siːnəri] *n* landskap *nt*
scenic ['siːnik] *adj* naturskjønn
scent [sent] *n* duft *m*
schedule ['ʃedjuːl] *n* ruteplan *m*, timeplan *m*
scheme [skiːm] *n* skjema *nt*; plan *m*
scholar ['skɔlə] *n* akademiker; student *m*; elev *m*
scholarship ['skɔləʃip] *n* stipend *nt*
school [skuːl] *n* skole *m*
schoolboy ['skuːlbɔi] *n* skolegutt *m*
schoolgirl ['skuːlgəːl] *n* skolepike *m*
schoolmaster ['skuːlˌmɑːstə] *n* lærer *m*
schoolteacher ['skuːlˌtiːtʃə] *n* lærer *m*
science ['saiəns] *n* (natur)vitenskap *m*
scientific [ˌsaiən'tifik] *adj* vitenskapelig
scientist ['saiəntist] *n* vitenskapskvinne *c*; vitenskapsmann (pl –menn) *m*
scissors ['sizəz] *pl* saks *c*
scold [skould] *v* skjenne på; skjelle
scooter ['skuːtə] *n* scooter *m*; sparksykkel *m*
score [skɔː] *n* poengsum *m*; *v* markere
scorn [skɔːn] *n* hån *m*, forakt *m*; *v* forakte
Scotland ['skɔtlənd] Skottland
Scottish ['skɔtiʃ] *adj* skotsk
scout [skaut] *n* speider *m*
scrap [skræp] *n* bit *m*
scrape [skreip] *v* skrape
scratch [skrætʃ] *v* skrape, rispe; *n* risp *nt*, skramme *c*
scream [skriːm] *v* *skrike, hyle; *n* hyl *nt*, skrik *nt*
screen [skriːn] *n* skjermbrett *nt*; skjerm *m*, filmlerret *nt*
screw [skruː] *n* skrue *m*; *v* skru

screwdriver ['skru:ˌdraivə] *n* skrujern *nt*
scrub [skrʌb] *v* skrubbe; *n* kratt *nt*
sculptor ['skʌlptə] *n* billedhogger *m*
sculpture ['skʌlptʃə] *n* skulptur *m*
sea [si:] *n* sjø *m*; ~ **urchin** sjøpinnsvin *nt*; ~ **water** sjøvann *nt*
seabird ['si:bə:d] *n* sjøfugl *m*
seacoast ['si:koust] *n* kyst *m*
seagull ['si:gʌl] *n* havmåke *c*
seal [si:l] *n* segl *nt*; sel *m*, kobbe *m*
seam [si:m] *n* søm *m*
seaman ['si:mən] *n* (pl -men) sjømann *m*
seaport ['si:pɔ:t] *n* havneby *m*
search [sə:tʃ] *v* lete etter; ransake; *n* leting *c*
searchlight ['sə:tʃlait] *n* lyskaster *m*
seascape ['si:skeip] *n* bilde med maritimt motiv
seashell ['si:ʃel] *n* skjell *nt*
seashore ['si:ʃɔ:] *n* strand *c*; kyst *m*
seasick ['si:sik] *adj* sjøsyk
seasickness ['si:ˌsiknəs] *n* sjøsyke *m*
seaside ['si:said] *n* kyst *m*; ~ **resort** badested *nt*
season ['si:zən] *n* sesong *m*, årstid *c*; **high** ~ høysesong *m*; **low** ~ lavsesong *m*; **off** ~ utenfor sesongen; ~ **ticket** sesongkort *nt*
seat [si:t] *n* sete *nt*; plass *m*, sitteplass *m*; ~ **belt** sikkerhetsbelte *nt*
second ['sekənd] *num* annen; *n* sekund *nt*; øyeblikk *nt*
secondary ['sekəndəri] *adj* sekundær, underordnet; ~ **school** høyere skole
second-hand [ˌsekənd'hænd] *adj* brukt
secret ['si:krət] *n* hemmelighet *c*; *adj* hemmelig
secretary ['sekrətri] *n* sekretær *m*
section ['sekʃən] *n* seksjon *m*, avdeling *c*
secure [si'kjuə] *adj* sikker; *v* sikre seg
security [si'kjuərəti] *n* sikkerhet *c*; kausjon *m*
sedative ['sedətiv] *n* beroligende middel
seduce [si'dju:s] *v* forføre
***see** [si:] *v* *se; *innse, *begripe, *forstå; ~ **to** sørge for
seed [si:d] *n* frø *nt*
***seek** [si:k] *v* søke
seem [si:m] *v* *late til, synes
seen [si:n] *v* (pp see)
seesaw ['si:sɔ:] *n* vippe *c*
seize [si:z] *v* *gripe
seldom ['seldəm] *adv* sjelden
select [si'lekt] *v* *utvelge,

*velge ut; *adj* utsøkt, utvalgt
selection [si'lekʃən] *n* utvalg *nt*
self [self] selves; *n* selv, jeg; selv…
self-centered *Am*, **self--centred** [ˌself'sentəd] *adj* selvopptatt
self-employed [ˌselfim'plɔid] *adj* selvstendig næringsdrivende
self-evident [ˌsel'fevidənt] *adj* opplagt
self-government [ˌself'gʌvəmənt] *n* selvstyre *nt*
selfish ['selfiʃ] *adj* selvisk
selfishness ['selfiʃnəs] *n* egoisme *m*
self-service [ˌself'sə:vis] *n* selvbetjening *c*; **~ restaurant** kafeteria *m*
***sell** [sel] *v* *selge
semblance ['sembləns] *n* utseende *nt*; likhet *c*
semi- ['semi] halv-
semicircle ['semiˌsə:kəl] *n* halvsirkel *m*
semicolon [ˌsemi'koulən] *n* semikolon *nt*
senate ['senət] *n* senat *nt*
senator ['senətə] *n* senator *m*
***send** [send] *v* sende; **~ back** sende tilbake, returnere; **~ for** sende bud etter; **~ off** sende av sted
sender ['sendə] *n* sender *m*; avsender *m*
senile ['si:nail] *adj* senil
sensation [sen'seiʃən] *n* sensasjon *m*; fornemmelse *m*, følelse *m*
sensational [sen'seiʃənəl] *adj* sensasjonell, oppsiktsvekkende
sense [sens] *n* sans *m*; fornuft *m*; mening *m*, betydning *m*; *v* merke; **~ of honour** æresfølelse *m*
senseless ['sensləs] *adj* meningsløs
sensible ['sensəbəl] *adj* fornuftig
sensitive ['sensitiv] *adj* følsom
sentence ['sentəns] *n* setning *m*; dom *m*; *v* dømme
sentimental [ˌsenti'mentəl] *adj* sentimental
separate[1] ['sepəreit] *v* skille, separere
separate[2] ['sepərət] *adj* særskilt, atskilt
separately ['sepərətli] *adv* separat
September [sep'tembə] september
septic ['septik] *adj* septisk; ***become ~** *gå betennelse i
sequel ['si:kwəl] *n* fortsettelse *m*
sequence ['si:kwəns] *n* rekkefølge *m*; serie *m*
serene [sə'ri:n] *adj* rolig; klar

series ['siəri:z] *n* (pl ~) serie *m*
serious ['siəriəs] *adj* seriøs, alvorlig
seriousness ['siəriəsnəs] *n* alvor *nt*
sermon ['sə:mən] *n* preken *m*
servant ['sə:vənt] *n* tjener *m*
serve [sə:v] *v* servere
service ['sə:vis] *n* tjeneste *m*; betjening *c*; ~ **charge** serveringsavgift *c*; ~ **station** bensinstasjon *m*
serviette [ˌsə:vi'et] *n* serviett *m*
session ['seʃən] *n* sesjon *m*
set [set] *n* klikk *m*; sett *nt*
***set** [set] *v* *sette; ~ **menu** fast meny; ~ **out** *dra av sted
setting ['setiŋ] *n* omgivelser *pl*
settle ['setəl] *v* ordne, avslutte; ~ **down** *slå seg ned
settlement ['setəlmənt] *n* ordning *c*, overenskomst *m*
seven ['sevən] *num* sju, syv
seventeen [ˌsevən'ti:n] *num* sytten
seventeenth [ˌsevən'ti:nθ] *num* syttende
seventh ['sevənθ] *num* sjuende, syvende
seventy ['sevənti] *num* sytti
several ['sevərəl] *adj* atskillige, flere
severe [si'viə] *adj* heftig, streng
***sew** [sou] *v* sy; ~ **up** sy sammen
sewer ['su:ə] *n* kloakk *m*
sewing machine ['souiŋməˌʃi:n] *n* symaskin *m*
sex [seks] *n* kjønn *nt*; sex *m*
sexual ['sekʃuəl] *adj* seksuell
sexuality [ˌsekʃu'æləti] *n* seksualitet *m*
shade [ʃeid] *n* skygge *m*; nyanse *m*
shadow ['ʃædou] *n* skygge *m*
shady ['ʃeidi] *adj* skyggefull
***shake** [ʃeik] *v* riste, ryste
shaky ['ʃeiki] *adj* vaklende
***shall** [ʃæl] *v* *skal
shallow ['ʃælou] *adj* grunn
shame [ʃeim] *n* skam *c*; **shame!** fy!
shampoo [ʃæm'pu:] *n* sjampo *m*
shape [ʃeip] *n* form *c*; *v* forme
share [ʃɛə] *v* dele; *n* del *m*; aksje *m*
shark [ʃɑ:k] *n* hai *m*
sharp [ʃɑ:p] *adj* spiss
sharpen ['ʃɑ:pən] *v* spisse
shave [ʃeiv] *v* barbere seg
shaver ['ʃeivə] *n* barbermaskin *m*
shaving brush ['ʃeiviŋbrʌʃ] *n* barberkost *m*
shaving foam ['ʃeiviŋfoum] *n* barberskum *nt*
shawl [ʃɔ:l] *n* sjal *nt*

she [ʃiː] *pron* hun
shed [ʃed] *n* skur *nt*
***shed** [ʃed] *v* *utgyte; spre
sheep [ʃiːp] *n* (pl ~) sau *m*
sheer [ʃiə] *adj* pur, absolutt; skjær, gjennomsiktig, tynn
sheet [ʃiːt] *n* laken *nt*; ark *nt*; plate *c*
shelf [ʃelf] *n* (pl shelves) hylle *c*
shell [ʃel] *n* skjell *nt*; skall *nt*
shellfish ['ʃelfiʃ] *n* skalldyr *nt*
shelter ['ʃeltə] *n* ly *nt*, tilfluktssted *nt*; *v* *gi ly
shepherd ['ʃepəd] *n* gjeter *m*
shift [ʃift] *n* skift *nt*
***shine** [ʃain] *v* skinne; glinse, stråle
ship [ʃip] *n* skip *nt*; *v* skipe
shipowner ['ʃi,pounə] *n* skipsreder *m*
shipyard ['ʃipjɑːd] *n* skipsverft *nt*
shirt [ʃəːt] *n* skjorte *c*
shiver ['ʃivə] *v* *skjelve, hutre; *n* skjelven *m*
shock [ʃɔk] *n* sjokk *nt*; *v* sjokkere; **~ absorber** støtdemper *m*
shocking ['ʃɔkiŋ] *adj* sjokkerende
shoe [ʃuː] *n* sko *m*; **~ polish** skokrem *m*; **~ shop** skotøyforretning *c*; **gym shoes** turnsko *pl*
shoelace ['ʃuːleis] *n* skolisse *c*
shoemaker ['ʃuː,meikə] *n* skomaker *m*
shook [ʃuk] *v* (p shake)
***shoot** [ʃuːt] *v* *skyte
shop [ʃɔp] *n* forretning *c*; *v* handle; **~ assistant** ekspeditør *m*, butikkselger *m*; **shopping bag** handlebag *m*; **shopping centre** kjøpesenter *nt*
shopkeeper ['ʃɔp,kiːpə] *n* kjøpmann *m*
shopwindow [,ʃɔp'windou] *n* utstillingsvindu *nt*
shore [ʃɔː] *n* bredd *m*, kyst *m*
short [ʃɔːt] *adj* kort; liten; **~ circuit** kortslutning *m*
shortage ['ʃɔːtidʒ] *n* knapphet *c*, mangel *m*
shorten ['ʃɔːtən] *v* forkorte
shortly ['ʃɔːtli] *adv* snart, i nær fremtid
shorts [ʃɔːts] *pl* shorts *m*; underbukse *c*
short-sighted [,ʃɔːt'saitid] *adj* nærsynt
shot [ʃɔt] *n* skudd *nt*; sprøyte *c*; scene *m*
***should** [ʃud] *v* *skulle
shoulder ['ʃouldə] *n* skulder *c*
shout [ʃaut] *v* *skrike, rope; *n* rop *nt*
shovel ['ʃʌvəl] *n* skuffe *c*
show [ʃou] *n* oppførelse *m*, forestilling *c*; utstilling *c*
***show** [ʃou] *v* vise; utstille, vise frem; bevise
showcase ['ʃoukeis] *n* monter *m*

shower [ʃauə] *n* dusj *m*; regnskur *m*, skur *m*
showroom ['ʃouru:m] *n* utstillingslokale *nt*
shriek [ʃri:k] *v* *skrike; *n* hvin *nt*
shrimp [ʃrimp] *n* reke *c*
shrine [ʃrain] *n* helgenskrin *nt*, helligdom *m*
***shrink** [ʃriŋk] *v* krympe
shrinkproof ['ʃriŋkpru:f] *adj* krympefri
shrub [ʃrʌb] *n* busk *m*
shudder ['ʃʌdə] *n* gys *nt*
shuffle ['ʃʌfəl] *v* stokke
***shut** [ʃʌt] *v* lukke; **shut** stengt, lukket; **~ in** stenge inne
shutter ['ʃʌtə] *n* vinduslem *m*, skodde *m*
shy [ʃai] *adj* sjenert, sky
shyness ['ʃainəs] *n* skyhet *c*
Siamese [ˌsaiə'mi:z] *adj* siamesisk
sick [sik] *adj* syk; kvalm
sickness ['siknəs] *n* sykdom *m*; kvalme *m*
side [said] *n* side *c*; parti *nt*; **one-sided** *adj* ensidig
sideburns ['saidbə:nz] *pl* kinnskjegg *nt*
side street ['saidstri:t] *n* sidegate *c*
sidewalk ['saidwɔ:k] *nAm* fortau *nt*
sideways ['saidweiz] *adv* til siden
siege [si:dʒ] *n* beleiring *c*
sieve [siv] *n* sil *m*; *v* sikte, sile
sight [sait] *n* syne *nt*; skue *nt*, syn; severdighet *c*
sign [sain] *n* tegn *nt*; vink *nt*, gest *m*; *v* undertegne
signal ['signəl] *n* signal *nt*; tegn *nt*; *v* signalisere
signature ['signətʃə] *n* underskrift *c*, signatur *m*
significant [sig'nifikənt] *adj* betydningsfull
signpost ['sainpoust] *n* veiviser *m*
silence ['sailəns] *n* stillhet *c*; *v* få til å tie
silencer ['sailənsə] *n* lydpotte *c*
silent ['sailənt] *adj* stille, taus; ***be ~** tie
silk [silk] *n* silke *m*
silly ['sili] *adj* dum, tåpelig
silver ['silvə] *n* sølv *nt*; sølv-
silversmith ['silvəsmiθ] *n* sølvsmed *m*
silverware ['silvəwɛə] *n* sølvtøy *nt*
similar ['similə] *adj* liknende
similarity [ˌsimi'lærəti] *n* likhet *c*
simple ['simpəl] *adj* likefrem, enkel; vanlig
simply ['simpli] *adv* simpelthen
simulate ['simjuleit] *v* etterligne
simultaneous [ˌsiməl'teiniəs] *adj* samtidig
sin [sin] *n* synd *c*
since [sins] *prep* siden; *adv*

siden; *conj* siden; fordi
sincere [sin'siə] *adj* oppriktig; **yours sincerely** med vennlig hilsen, mvh
sinew ['sinju:] *n* sene *c*
***sing** [siŋ] *v* *synge
singer ['siŋə] *n* sanger *m*; sangerinne *c*
single ['siŋgəl] *adj* enkel; ugift; **~ room** enkeltrom *nt*
singular ['siŋgjulə] *n* entall *nt*; *adj* enestående
sinister ['sinistə] *adj* illevarslende
sink [siŋk] *n* vask *m*
***sink** [siŋk] *v* *synke
sip [sip] *n* slurk *m*
sir [sə:] min herre
siren ['saiərən] *n* sirene *c*
sister ['sistə] *n* søster *c*
sister-in-law ['sistərinlɔ:] *n* (pl sisters-) svigerinne *c*
***sit** [sit] *v* *sitte; **~ down** *sette seg
site [sait] *n* sted *nt*; beliggenhet *c*
sitting room ['sitiŋru:m] *n* stue *c*
situated ['sitʃueitid] *adj* beliggende
situation [ˌsitʃu'eiʃən] *n* situasjon *m*; stilling *c*
six [siks] *num* seks
sixteen [ˌsiks'ti:n] *num* seksten
sixteenth [ˌsiks'ti:nθ] *num* sekstende
sixth [siksθ] *num* sjette
sixty ['siksti] *num* seksti
size [saiz] *n* størrelse *m*, dimensjon *m*; format *nt*
skate [skeit] *v* *gå på skøyter; *n* skøyte *c*
skating ['skeitiŋ] *n* skøyteløping *c*; **~ rink** skøytebane *m*
skeleton ['skelitən] *n* skjelett *nt*
sketch [sketʃ] *n* skisse *c*, utkast *nt*; *v* tegne, skissere
ski[1] [ski:] *v* *gå på ski
ski[2] [ski:] *n* (pl ~, ~s) ski *c*; **~ boots** skistøvler *pl*; **~ jump** skihopp *nt*; hoppbakke *m*; **~ lift** skiheis *m*; **~ pants** skibukse *c*; **~ poles** *Am* skistaver *pl*; **~ sticks** skistaver *pl*
skid [skid] *v* *gli
skier ['ski:ə] *n* skiløper *m*
skiing ['ski:iŋ] *n* skiløping *c*
skil(l)ful ['skilfəl] *adj* kyndig, flink, dyktig
skill [skil] *n* dyktighet *c*
skilled [skild] *adj* kyndig, dreven; faglært
skin [skin] *n* hud *c*, skinn *nt*; skall *nt*
skip [skip] *v* hoppe; hoppe over
skirt [skə:t] *n* skjørt *nt*
skull [skʌl] *n* skalle *m*
sky [skai] *n* himmel *m*; luft *c*
skyscraper ['skaiˌskreipə] *n* skyskraper *m*
slack [slæk] *adj* treg; slapp
slacks [slæks] *pl* bukse *c*, bukser *pl*
slam [slæm] *v* *slå igjen
slander ['sla:ndə] *n*

bakvaskelse *m*
slang [slæŋ] *n* slang *m*; sjargong *m*
slant [slɑ:nt] *v* skråne
slanting ['slɑ:ntiŋ] *adj* skjev, skrånende, skrå
slap [slæp] *v* fike; *n* fik *m*
slate [sleit] *n* skifer *m*
slave [sleiv] *n* slave *m*
sledge [sledʒ] *n* slede *m*, kjelke *m*
sleep [sli:p] *n* søvn *m*
***sleep** [sli:p] *v* *sove
sleeping bag ['sli:piŋbæg] *n* sovepose *m*
sleeping car ['sli:piŋka:] *n* sovevogn *c*
sleeping pill ['sli:piŋpil] *n* sovepille *c*
sleepless ['sli:pləs] *adj* søvnløs
sleepy ['sli:pi] *adj* søvnig
sleet [sli:t] *n* sludd *nt*
sleeve [sli:v] *n* erme *nt*; omslag *nt*
sleigh [slei] *n* kjelke *m*, slede *m*
slender ['slendə] *adj* slank
slice [slais] *n* skive *c*
slide [slaid] *n* rutsjebane *m*; lysbilde *nt*
***slide** [slaid] *v* *gli
slight [slait] *adj* ubetydelig; svak
slim [slim] *adj* slank; *v* slanke seg
slip [slip] *v* *gli, skli; *smette; *n* feiltrinn *nt*
slipper ['slipə] *n* tøffel *m*
slippery ['slipəri] *adj* glatt, sleip
slogan ['slougən] *n* slagord *nt*, valgspråk *nt*
slope [sloup] *n* skråning *m*; *v* helle
sloping ['sloupiŋ] *adj* skrånende
sloppy ['slɔpi] *adj* slurvet
slot [slɔt] *n* myntsprekk *m*; åpning *c*; **~ machine** automat *m*
slovenly ['slʌvənli] *adj* sjusket
slow [slou] *adj* tungnem, langsom, sakte; **~ down** *sette ned farten, saktne farten; bremse
slum [slʌm] *n* slum *m*
slump [slʌmp] *n* prisfall *nt*
slush [slʌʃ] *n* snøslaps *nt*
sly [slai] *adj* slu
smack [smæk] *v* smekke; *n* dask *m*
small [smɔ:l] *adj* liten; ringe
smallpox ['smɔ:lpɔks] *n* kopper *pl*
smart [smɑ:t] *adj* fiks; smart, flink, lur
smash [smɑʃ] *n* hardt slag *m*; *v* knuse; ødelegge
smell [smel] *n* lukt *c*
***smell** [smel] *v* lukte; *stinke
smelly ['smeli] *adj* illeluktende
smile [smail] *v* smile; *n* smil *nt*
smith [smiθ] *n* smed *m*
smoke [smouk] *v* røyke; *n* røyk *m*; **no smoking**

røyking forbudt
smoke-free ['smouk,fri:] *adj* røykfri
smoker ['smoukə] *n* røyker *m*; røykekupé *m*
smoking compartment ['smoukiŋkəm,pa:tmənt] *n* røykekupé *m*
smooth [smu:ð] *adj* jevn, smul, glatt; myk
smuggle ['smʌgəl] *v* smugle
snack [snæk] *n* matbit *m*
snail [sneil] *n* snegl *m*
snake [sneik] *n* slange *m*
snapshot ['snæpʃɔt] *n* øyeblikksfotografi *nt*, snapshot *nt*
sneakers ['sni:kəz] *plAm* tennissko *pl*, joggesko *pl*
sneeze [sni:z] *v* *nyse
sniper ['snaipə] *n* snikskytter *m*
snooty ['snu:ti] *adj* hoven
snore [snɔ:] *v* snorke
snorkel ['snɔ:kəl] *n* snorkel *m*
snout [snaut] *n* snute *c*
snow [snou] *n* snø *m*; *v* snø
snowstorm ['snoustɔ:m] *n* snøstorm *m*
so [sou] *conj* så; *adv* slik; så, i den grad; **and ~ on** og så videre; **~ far** hittil; **~ that** så, slik at
soak [souk] *v* gjennombløte, bløte
soap [soup] *n* såpe *c*
sober ['soubə] *adj* edru; nøktern
so-called [,sou'kɔ:ld] *adj* såkalt
soccer ['sɔkə] *n* fotball *m*; **~ team** fotball-lag *nt*
social ['souʃəl] *adj* samfunns-, sosial
socialism ['souʃəlizəm] *n* sosialisme *m*
socialist ['souʃəlist] *adj* sosialistisk; *n* sosialist *m*
society [sə'saiəti] *n* samfunn *nt*; selskap *nt*, forening *c*
sock [sɔk] *n* sokk *m*
socket ['sɔkit] *n* pæreholder *m*; stikkontakt *m*
soda ['soudə]: **~ pop** *nAm colloquial* brus *m*; **~ water** soda *m*, selters *m*; naturlig mineralvann *m*
sofa ['soufə] *n* sofa *m*
soft ['sɔft] *adj* myk; **~ drink** alkoholfri drikk
soften ['sɔfən] *v* *bløtgjøre
software ['sɔftweə] *n* programvare *m*
soil [sɔil] *n* jord *m*; jordbunn *m*; jordsmonn *nt*
soiled [sɔild] *adj* skitten
solar ['soulə] *adj* sol…; **~ system** solsystem *nt*
sold [sould] *v* (p, pp sell); **~ out** utsolgt
soldier ['souldʒə] *n* soldat *m*
sole[1] [soul] *adj* eneste
sole[2] [soul] *n* såle *m*; flyndre *c*
solely ['soulli] *adv* utelukkende
solemn ['sɔləm] *adj*

høytidelig
solicitor [sə'lisitə] *n* sakfører *m*, advokat *m*
solid ['sɔlid] *adj* solid; massiv; *n* fast stoff
soluble ['sɔljubəl] *adj* oppløselig
solution [sə'lu:ʃən] *n* løsning *c*; oppløsning *c*
solve [sɔlv] *v* løse
somber *Am*, **sombre** ['sɔmbə] *adj* dyster
some [sʌm] *adj* noen; *pron* visse, enkelte; litt; **~ day** en gang; **~ more** litt mer; **~ time** en gang
somebody ['sʌmbədi] *pron* noen
somehow ['sʌmhau] *adv* på en eller annen måte
someone ['sʌmwʌn] *pron* noen
something ['sʌmθiŋ] *pron* noe
sometimes ['sʌmtaimz] *adv* av og til
somewhat ['sʌmwɔt] *adv* nokså
somewhere ['sʌmwɛə] *adv* etsteds
son [sʌn] *n* sønn *m*
song [sɔŋ] *n* sang *m*
son-in-law ['sʌninlɔ:] *n* (pl sons-) svigersønn *m*
soon [su:n] *adv* fort, snart; **as ~ as** så snart som
sooner ['su:nə] *adv* heller
sore [sɔ:] *adj* sår, øm; *n* ømt sted; sår *nt*; **~ throat** halsesyke *m*
sorrow ['sɔrou] *n* sorg *c*
sorry ['sɔri] *adj* lei for; **sorry!** unnskyld!, beklager!
sort [sɔ:t] *v* ordne, sortere; *n* sort *m*, slags *m* / *nt*; **all sorts of** alle slags
soul [soul] *n* sjel *c*
sound [saund] *n* klang *m*, lyd *m*; *v* *lyde; *adj* sunn; pålitelig
soundproof ['saundpru:f] *adj* lydtett
soup [su:p] *n* suppe *c*; **~ plate** suppetallerken *m*; **~ spoon** suppeskje *c*
sour [sauə] *adj* sur
source [sɔ:s] *n* kilde *m*
south [sauθ] *n* syd *m*, sør *m*; **South Pole** Sydpolen
South Africa [sauθ 'æfrikə] Sør-Afrika
South America [sauθ ə'merikə] Sør-Amerika
southeast [ˌsauθ'i:st] *n* sørøst *m*
southerly ['sʌðəli] *adj* sørlig
southern ['sʌðən] *adj* sørlig
southwest [ˌsauθ'west] *n* sørvest *m*
souvenir ['su:vəniə] *n* suvenir *m*
sovereign ['sɔvrin] *n* hersker *m*
***sow** [sou] *v* så
spa [spɑ:] *n* kursted *nt*
space [speis] *n* rom *nt*; verdensrom *nt*; avstand *m*, mellomrom *nt*; *v* sette mellomrom; **~ shuttle** romferge *c*

spacious ['speiʃəs] *adj* rommelig
spade [speid] *n* spade *m*
Spain [spein] Spania
Spaniard ['spænjəd] *n* spanjol *m*, spanier *m*
Spanish ['spæniʃ] *adj* spansk
spanking ['spæŋkiŋ] *n* juling *c*; ris *nt*
spare [speə] *adj* reserve-, ekstra; *v* *unnvære; **~ part** reservedel *m*; **~ room** gjesteværelse *nt*; **~ time** fritid *c*; **~ tyre** reservedekk *nt*; **~ wheel** reservehjul *nt*
spark [spɑːk] *n* gnist *m*
spark(ing) plug ['spaːkiŋplʌg] *n* tennplugg *m*
sparkling ['spaːkliŋ] *adj* funklende; musserende
sparrow ['spærou] *n* spurv *m*
***speak** [spiːk] *v* snakke
speaker phone ['spiːkə‿ˌfoun] *n* høytalertelefon *c*
spear [spiə] *n* spyd *nt*
special ['speʃəl] *adj* spesiell; **~ delivery** ekspress
specialist ['speʃəlist] *n* spesialist *m*
speciality [ˌspeʃi'æləti] *n* spesialitet *m*
specialize ['speʃəlaiz] *v* spesialisere seg
specially ['speʃəli] *adv* i særdeleshet
species ['spiːʃiːz] *n* (pl **~**) art *m*
specific [spə'sifik] *adj* spesifikk
specimen ['spesimən] *n* prøve *c*, eksemplar *nt*
speck [spek] *n* flekk *m*
spectacle ['spektəkəl] *n* skue *nt*, syn *nt*; **spectacles** briller *pl*
spectator [spek'teitə] *n* tilskuer *m*
speculate ['spekjuleit] *v* spekulere
speech [spiːtʃ] *n* tale *m*
speechless ['spiːtʃləs] *adj* målløs
speed [spiːd] *n* hastighet *c*; fart *m*; **cruising ~** marsjfart *m*; **~ dial(ing)** *n* hurtigtaster *c*; **~ limit** fartsgrense *c*
***speed** [spiːd] *v* kjøre fort; kjøre for fort
speeding ['spiːdiŋ] *n* råkjøring *c*
speedometer [spiː'dɔmitə] *n* fartsmåler *m*
spell [spel] *n* fortryllelse *m*
***spell** [spel] *v* stave
spelling ['speliŋ] *n* stavemåte *m*
***spend** [spend] *v* bruke, spandere; *tilbringe
sphere [sfiə] *n* kule *c*; område *nt*
spice [spais] *n* krydder *nt*; **spices** krydderier *pl*
spiced [spaist] *adj* krydret
spicy ['spaisi] *adj* krydret

spider ['spaidə] *n* edderkopp *m*; **spider's web** spindelvev *m*
***spill** [spil] *v* søle
***spin** [spin] *v* *spinne; snurre
spinach ['spinidʒ] *n* spinat *m*
spine [spain] *n* ryggrad *m*
spire [spaiə] *n* spir *nt*
spirit ['spirit] *n* ånd *m*; spøkelse *nt*; **~ stove** spritapparat *nt*; **spirits** spirituosa *pl*, alkoholholdige drikker; humør *nt*
spiritual ['spiritʃuəl] *adj* åndelig
spit [spit] *n* spytt *nt*; spidd *nt*
***spit** [spit] *v* spytte
spite [spait] *n* ondskapsfullhet *c*; *v* være ekkel mot; **in ~ of** til tross for
spiteful ['spaitfəl] *adj* ondskapsfull
splash [splæʃ] *v* skvette
splendid ['splendid] *adj* praktfull, glimrende
splendo(u)r ['splendə] *n* prakt *m*
splint [splint] *n* beinskinne *c*
splinter ['splintə] *n* splint *m*
***split** [split] *v* kløyve
***spoil** [spɔil] *v* *ødelegge; skjemme bort
spoke[1] [spouk] *v* (p speak)
spoke[2] [spouk] *n* eike *c*
sponge [spʌndʒ] *n* svamp *m*
spool [spu:l] *n* spole *m*
spoon [spu:n] *n* skje *c*
spoonful ['spu:nful] *n* skjefull *m*
sport [spɔ:t] *n* sport *m*
sports car ['spɔ:tska:] *n* sportsbil *m*
sportsman ['spɔ:tsmən] *n* (pl -men) idrettsmann *m*
sportswear ['spɔ:tswɛə] *n* sportsklær *pl*
sportswoman ['spɔ:tswumən] *n* (pl -women) idrettskvinne *c*
spot [spɔt] *n* flekk *m*; sted *nt*
spotless ['spɔtləs] *adj* plettfri
spotlight ['spɔtlait] *n* prosjektør *m*
spotted ['spɔtid] *adj* flekket
spout [spaut] *n* tut *m*
sprain [sprein] *v* forstue; *n* forstuing *c*
spray [sprei] *n* sprut *m*; spray *m*; *v* sprøyte (planter), sprute; spraye
***spread** [spred] *v* spre
spring [spriŋ] *n* vår *m*; fjær *c*; kilde *m*
springtime ['spriŋtaim] *n* vår *m*
sprouts [sprauts] *pl* rosenkål *m*
spy [spai] *n* spion *m*
square [skwɛə] *adj* kvadratisk; *n* kvadrat *nt*; plass *m*
squash [skwɔʃ] *n* fruktsaft

c; squash *m*; *v* kryste
squeeze [skwi:z] *v* presse (saft); trykke
squirrel ['skwirəl] *n* ekorn *nt*
squirt [skwə:t] *n* sprut *m*
stable ['steibəl] *adj* stabil; *n* stall *m*
stack [stæk] *n* stabel *m*
stadium ['steidiəm] *n* stadion *nt*
staff [stɑ:f] *n* personale *nt*
stage [steidʒ] *n* scene *m*; stadium *nt*, fase *m*; etappe *m*
stain [stein] *v* flekke; *n* flekk *m*; **stained glass window** glassmaleri *nt*; **~ remover** flekkfjerner *m*
stainless ['steinləs] *adj* plettfri; **~ steel** rustfritt stål
staircase ['stɛəkeis] *n* trapp *c*
stairs [stɛəz] *pl* trapp *c*
stale [steil] *adj* **~ bread** gammelt brød; **~ air** dårlig luft
stall [stɔ:l] *n* utsalgsbord *nt*; orkesterplass *m*
stamp [stæmp] *n* frimerke *nt*; stempel *nt*; *v* frankere; trampe; **~ machine** frimerkeautomat *m*
stand [stænd] *n* stand *m*; tribune *m*
***stand** [stænd] *v* *stå
standard ['stændəd] *n* norm *m*; standard-; **~ of living** levestandard *m*
stanza ['stænzə] *n* strofe *m*; vers *nt*
staple ['steipəl] *n* stift *m*
star [stɑ:] *n* stjerne *c*
starboard ['stɑ:bəd] *n* styrbord
stare [stɛə] *v* stirre
starling ['stɑ:liŋ] *n* stær *m*
start [stɑ:t] *v* begynne; *n* start *m*
starting point ['stɑ:tiŋpɔint] *n* utgangspunkt *nt*
state [steit] *n* stat *m*; stand *m*; *v* erklære; **the States** [ðə steits] De forente stater
statement ['steitmənt] *n* erklæring *c*
station ['steiʃən] *n* stasjon *m*; posisjon *m*
stationary ['steiʃənəri] *adj* stillestående
stationer's ['steiʃənəz] *n* papirhandel *m*
stationery ['steiʃənəri] *n* papirvarer *pl*
statistics [stə'tistiks] *pl* statistikk *m*
statue ['stætʃu:] *n* statue *m*
stay [stei] *v* *bli; *oppholde seg, *ta inn; *n* opphold *nt*
steadfast ['stedfɑ:st] *adj* standhaftig
steady ['stedi] *adj* stø
steak [steik] *n* biff *m*
***steal** [sti:l] *v* *stjele
steam [sti:m] *n* damp *m*
steamer ['sti:mə] *n* dampskip *nt*
steel [sti:l] *n* stål *nt*

steep [sti:p] *adj* bratt, steil
steeple ['sti:pəl] *n* kirketårn *nt*
steer [sti:ə] *v* styre
steering column ['stiəriŋ,kɔləm] *n* rattstamme *m*
steering wheel ['stiəriŋwi:l] *n* ratt *nt*
steersman ['stiəzmən] *n* (pl -men) rorgjenger *m*
stem [stem] *n* stilk *m*
stem cell ['stem‿,sel] *n* stamcelle *c*
step [step] *n* skritt *nt*, steg *nt*; trinn *nt*; *v* *tre, trå
stepchild ['stept∫aild] *n* (pl -children) stebarn *nt*
stepfather ['step,fa:ðə] *n* stefar *m*
stepmother ['step,mʌðə] *n* stemor *c*
stereo [steriou] *n* stereo *m*; *colloquial* stereoanlegg *nt*
sterile ['sterail] *adj* steril
sterilize ['sterilaiz] *v* sterilisere
steward ['stju:əd] *n* stuert *m*; flyvert *m*
stewardess ['stju:ədes] *n* flyvertinne *c*
stick [stik] *n* stokk *m*
***stick** [stik] *v* klebe
sticker [stikə] *n* klistremerke *nt*
sticky ['stiki] *adj* klebrig
stiff [stif] *adj* stiv
still [stil] *adv* fremdeles; likevel; *adj* stille
stimulant ['stimjulənt] *n* stimulans *m*
stimulate ['stimjuleit] *v* stimulere
sting [stiŋ] *n* stikk *nt*
***sting** [stiŋ] *v* *stikke
stingy ['stindʒi] *adj* gjerrig; smålig
***stink** [stiŋk] *v* *stinke
stipulate ['stipjuleit] *v* *fastsette
stipulation [,stipju'lei∫ən] *n* betingelse *m*
stir [stə:] *v* røre
stitch [stit∫] *n* sting *nt*; hold *nt*
stock [stɔk] *n* forsyning *c*; *v* lagre; ~ **exchange** fondsbørs *m*, børs *m*; ~ **market** fondsmarked *nt*; **stocks and shares** verdipapirer *pl*
stocking ['stɔkiŋ] *n* strømpe *c*
stole[1] [stoul] *v* (p steal)
stole[2] [stoul] *n* stola *m*
stomach ['stʌmək] *n* mage *m*; ~ **ache** magesmerter *pl*
stone [stoun] *n* stein *m*; edelstein *m*; stein-; **pumice** ~ pimpstein *m*
stood [stud] *v* (p, pp stand)
stop [stɔp] *v* stoppe; avslutte, *holde opp med; *n* holdeplass *m*; **stop!** stopp!
stopper ['stɔpə] *n* kork *m*
storage ['stɔ:ridʒ] *n* lagring *c*
store [stɔ:] *n* lagerbeholdning *m*;

forretning *c*; *v* lagre; **~ house** lagerbygning *m*
stor(e)y ['stɔːri] *n* etasje *m*
stork [stɔːk] *n* stork *m*
storm [stɔːm] *n* storm *m*
stormy ['stɔːmi] *adj* stormfull
story ['stɔːri] *n* fortelling *c*
stout [staut] *adj* korpulent, tykkfallen
stove [stouv] *n* ovn *m*; komfyr *m*
straight [streit] *adj* rak; ærlig; *adv* rett; **~ ahead** rett frem; **~ away** med en gang; **~ on** rett frem
strain [strein] *n* anstrengelse *m*; anspennelse *m*; *v* overanstrenge; sile
strainer ['streinə] *n* sil *m*; dørslag *nt*
strange [streindʒ] *adj* fremmed; underlig
stranger ['streindʒə] *n* fremmed *m*
strangle ['stræŋgəl] *v* kvele
strap [stræp] *n* rem *c*
straw [strɔː] *n* halm *m*
strawberry ['strɔːbəri] *n* jordbær *nt*
stream [striːm] *n* bekk *m*; strøm *m*; *v* strømme
street [striːt] *n* gate *c*
streetcar ['striːtkɑː] *nAm* trikk *m*
strength [streŋθ] *n* styrke *m*
stress [stres] *n* stress *nt*; trykk *nt*; *v* belaste, *legge vekt på
stretch [stretʃ] *v* tøye; *n* strekning *m*
strict [strikt] *adj* streng
strike [straik] *n* streik *m*
***strike** [straik] *v* *slå; *slå til; streike; *stryke
striking ['straikiŋ] *adj* påfallende, oppsiktsvekkende, slående
string [striŋ] *n* snor *c*; streng *m*
strip [strip] *n* strimmel *m*
stripe [straip] *n* stripe *c*
striped [straipt] *adj* stripet
stroke [strouk] *n* slaganfall *nt*
stroll [stroul] *v* slentre; *n* spasertur *m*
strong [strɔŋ] *adj* sterk; kraftig
stronghold ['strɔŋhould] *n* tilfluktssted *nt*; høyborg *c*
structure ['strʌktʃə] *n* struktur *m*
struggle ['strʌgəl] *n* strid *m*, kamp *m*; *v* *slåss, kjempe
stubborn ['stʌbən] *adj* sta
student ['stjuːdənt] *n* student *m*; elev *m*
studies ['stʌdiz] *pl* studium *nt*
study ['stʌdi] *v* studere; *n* studium *nt*; arbeidsværelse *nt*
stuff [stʌf] *n* materiale *nt*; saker *pl*
stuffed [stʌft] *adj* fylt
stuffing ['stʌfiŋ] *n* fyll *nt*
stuffy ['stʌfi] *adj* trykkende;

snerpet
stumble ['stʌmbəl] *v* snuble
stung [stʌŋ] *v* (p, pp sting)
stupid ['stju:pid] *adj* dum
style [stail] *n* stil *m*
subject[1] ['sʌbdʒikt] *n* subjekt *nt*; undersått *m*; gjenstand *m*; emne *nt*; **~ to** utsatt for
subject[2] [səb'dʒekt] *v* underkue
sublet [ˌsub'let] *v* fremleie
submarine ['sʌbməri:n] *n* ubåt *m*
submit [səb'mit] *v* underkaste seg
subordinate [sə'bɔ:dinət] *adj* underordnet; sekundær
subscriber [səb'skraibə] *n* abonnent *m*
subscription [səb'skripʃən] *n* abonnement *nt*
subsequent ['sʌbsikwənt] *adj* følgende
subsidy ['sʌbsidi] *n* tilskudd *nt*
substance ['sʌbstəns] *n* substans *m*
substantial [səb'stænʃəl] *adj* substansiell; virkelig; anselig
substitute ['sʌbstitju:t] *v* erstatte; *n* erstatning *m*; stedfortreder *m*
subtitle ['sʌbˌtaitəl] *n* undertekst *m*
subtle ['sʌtəl] *adj* subtil
subtract [səb'trækt] *v* *trekke fra
suburb ['sʌbə:b] *n* forstad *m*
suburban [sə'bə:bən] *adj* forstads-
subway ['sʌbwei] *nAm* undergrunnsbane *m*
succeed [sək'si:d] *v* lykkes; *etterfølge
success [sək'ses] *n* suksess *m*
successful [sək'sesfəl] *adj* vellykket
succumb [sə'kʌm] *v* bukke under
such [sʌtʃ] *adj* sånn, slik; *adv* slik; **~ as** slik som
suck [sʌk] *v* suge
sudden ['sʌdən] *adj* plutselig
suddenly ['sʌdənli] *adv* plutselig
suede [sweid] *n* semsket skinn
suffer ['sʌfə] *v* *lide; *gjennomgå
suffering ['sʌfəriŋ] *n* lidelse *m*
suffice [sə'fais] *v* *være tilstrekkelig
sufficient [sə'fiʃənt] *adj* tilstrekkelig
suffrage ['sʌfridʒ] *n* stemmerett *m*
sugar ['ʃugə] *n* sukker *nt*
suggest [sə'dʒest] *v* *foreslå
suggestion [sə'dʒestʃən] *n* forslag *nt*
suicide ['su:isaid] *n* selvmord *nt*; **~ attack** *n* selvmordangrep *nt*; **~**

bomber *n* selvmordsbomber *c*
suit [su:t] *v* passe; tilpasse; kle; *n* dress *m*
suitable ['su:təbəl] *adj* egnet
suitcase ['su:tkeis] *n* koffert *m*
suite [swi:t] *n* suite *m*
sum [sʌm] *n* sum *m*
summary ['sʌməri] *n* sammendrag *nt*
summer ['sʌmə] *n* sommer *m*; **~ time** sommertid *c*
summit ['sʌmit] *n* topp *m*
sun [sʌn] *n* sol *c*
sunbathe ['sʌnbeið] *v* sole seg
sunburn ['sʌnbə:n] *n* solbrenthet *c*
Sunday ['sʌndi] søndag *m*
sunglasses ['sʌn,glɑ:siz] *pl* solbriller *pl*
sunlight ['sʌnlait] *n* sollys *nt*
sunny ['sʌni] *adj* solrik
sunrise ['sʌnraiz] *n* soloppgang *m*
sunset ['sʌnset] *n* solnedgang *m*
sunshade ['sʌnʃeid] *n* parasoll *m*
sunshine ['sʌnʃain] *n* solskinn *nt*
sunstroke ['sʌnstrouk] *n* solstikk *nt*
suntan ['sʌntæn] brunfarge *m*
suntan oil ['sʌntænɔil] sololje *c*
super ['sjupə] *adj colloquial* flott, bra; kul, kult
superb [su'pə:b] *adj* storartet
superficial [,su:pə'fiʃəl] *adj* overfladisk
superfluous [su'pə:fluəs] *adj* overflødig
superior [su'piəriə] *adj* høyere, overlegen, bedre, større
supermarket ['su:pə,ma:kit] *n* supermarked *nt*
superstition [,su:pə'stiʃən] *n* overtro *c*
supervise ['su:pəvaiz] *v* overvåke
supervision [,su:pə'viʒən] *n* overoppsyn *nt*, oppsyn *nt*
supervisor ['su:pəvaizə] *n* kontrollør *m*
supper ['sʌpə] *n* aftensmat *m*
supple ['sʌpəl] *adj* bøyelig, smidig, myk
supplement ['sʌplimənt] *n* tillegg *nt*
supply [sə'plai] *n* tilførsel *m*, levering *c*; forråd *nt*; tilbud *nt*; *v* forsyne
support [sə'pɔ:t] *v* *bære, *hjelpe; *n* støtte *m*
supporter [sə'pɔ:tə] *n* tilhenger *m*; forsørger *m*
suppose [sə'pouz] *v* *anta; **supposing that** forutsatt at
suppository [sə'pɔzitəri] *n* stikkpille *c*

suppress [sə'pres] *v* undertrykke
surcharge ['sə:tʃɑ:dʒ] *n* ekstragebyr *nt*
sure [ʃuə] *adj* sikker
surely ['ʃuəli] *adv* sikkert
surface ['sə:fis] *n* overflate *c*
surf (the Net) [sə:f] *v* surfe
surfboard ['sə:fbɔ:d] *n* surfingbrett *nt*
surgeon ['sə:dʒən] *n* kirurg *m*; **veterinary ~** veterinær *m*
surgery ['sə:dʒəri] *n* operasjon *m*; legekontor *nt*; **reconstructive ~** rekonstruktiv kirurgi *c*
surname ['sə:neim] *n* etternavn *nt*
surplus ['sə:pləs] *n* overskudd *nt*
surprise [sə'praiz] *n* overraskelse *m*; *v* overraske; forbause
surrender [sə'rendə] *v* *overgi seg; *n* overgivelse *m*
surround [sə'raund] *v* *omgi, omringe
surrounding [sə'raundiŋ] *adj* omkringliggende
surroundings [sə'raundiŋz] *pl* omegn *m*
survey ['sə:vei] *n* oversikt *m*
surveillance [sə:'veiəns] *n* overvåking *c*
survival [sə'vaivəl] *n* overleving *c*
survive [sə'vaiv] *v* overleve
suspect[1] [sə'spekt] *v* mistenke; ane
suspect[2] ['sʌspekt] *n* mistenkt *m*
suspend [sə'spend] *v* suspendere
suspenders [sə'spendəz] *plAm* bukseseler *pl*
suspension [sə'spenʃən] *n* fjæring *c*; **~ bridge** hengebro *c*
suspicion [sə'spiʃən] *n* mistanke *m*; mistenksomhet *c*; anelse *m*
suspicious [sə'spiʃəs] *adj* mistenkelig; mistenksom, mistroisk
sustain [sə'stein] *v* orke; *opprettholde
SUV ['esyu:'vi:], **sport utility vehicle** *n* SUV *nt*, sports og nyttekjøretøy
Swahili [swə'hi:li] *n* swahili *m*
swallow ['swɔlou] *v* svelge, sluke; *n* svale *c*
swam [swæm] *v* (p swim)
swamp [swɔmp] *n* myr *c*
swan [swɔn] *n* svane *c*
swap [swɔp] *v* bytte
***swear** [swɛə] *v* *sverge; banne
sweat [swet] *n* svette *m*; *v* svette
sweater ['swetə] *n* ulljakke *c*; genser *m*
sweatshirt ['swetʃə:t] *n* (bomulls)genser
Swede [swi:d] *n* svenske *m*

Sweden ['swi:dən] Sverige
Swedish ['swi:diʃ] *adj* svensk
***sweep** [swi:p] *v* feie
sweet [swi:t] *adj* søt; *n* sukkertøy *nt*; dessert *m*; **sweets** sukkertøy *pl*; godter *pl*
sweeten ['swi:tən] *v* sukre
sweetheart ['swi:thɑ:t] *n* elskling *m*
swell [swel] *adj* flott
***swell** [swel] *v* svelle
swelling ['sweliŋ] *n* hevelse *m*
swift [swift] *adj* rask
***swim** [swim] *v* svømme
swimmer ['swimə] *n* svømmer *m*
swimming ['swimiŋ] *n* svømming *c*; **~ pool** svømmebasseng *nt*
swimmingtrunks ['swimiŋtrʌŋks] *pl* badebukse *c*
swimsuit ['swimsu:t], *n* **swimming suit** *nAm* badedrakt *c*
swindle ['swindəl] *v* svindle; *n* svindel *m*
swindler ['swindlə] *n* svindler *m*
swing [swiŋ] *n* huske *c*
***swing** [swiŋ] *v* svinge; huske
Swiss [swis] *adj* sveitsisk; *n* sveitser *m*
switch [switʃ] *n* bryter *m*; *v* skifte; **~ off** *slå av; **~ on** *slå på
switchboard ['switʃbɔ:d] *n* sentralbord *nt*
Switzerland ['switsələnd] Sveits
sword [sɔ:d] *n* sverd *nt*
swum [swʌm] *v* (pp swim)
syllable ['siləbəl] *n* stavelse *m*
symbol ['simbəl] *n* symbol *nt*
sympathetic [ˌsimpə'θetik] *adj* deltakende, medfølende
sympathy ['simpəθi] *n* sympati *m*; medfølelse *m*
symphony ['simfəni] *n* symfoni *m*
symptom ['simtəm] *n* symptom *nt*
synagogue ['sinəgɔg] *n* synagoge *m*
synonym ['sinənim] *n* synonym *nt*
synthetic [sin'θetik] *adj* syntetisk
Syria ['siriə] Syria
Syrian ['siriən] *adj* syrisk; *n* syrer *m*
syringe [si'rindʒ] *n* sprøyte *c*
syrup ['sirəp] *n* sirup *m*
system ['sistəm] *n* system *nt*; **decimal ~** desimalsystem *nt*
systematic [ˌsistə'mætik] *adj* systematisk

T

table ['teibəl] *n* bord *nt*; tabell *m*; **~ of contents** innholdsfortegnelse *m*; **~ tennis** bordtennis *m*
tablecloth ['teibəlkloθ] *n* duk *m*
tablespoon ['teibəlspu:n] *n* spiseskje *c*
tablet ['tæblit] *n* tablett *m*; plate *c*
taboo [tə'bu:] *n* tabu *nt*
tactics ['tæktiks] *pl* taktikk *m*
tag [tæg] *n* merkelapp *m*
tail [teil] *n* hale *m*
taillight ['teillait] *n* baklys *nt*
tailor ['teilə] *n* skredder *m*
tailor-made ['teiləmeid] *adj* skreddersydd
***take** [teik] *v* *ta; *gripe; *følge; skjønne, *forstå, *begripe; **~ away** *ta med seg; fjerne, *ta vekk; **~ off** lette; **~ out** *ta bort; **~ over** *overta; **~ place** *finne sted; **~ up** *oppta
take-off ['teikof] *n* start *m*
tale [teil] *n* fortelling *m*, eventyr *nt*
talent ['tælənt] *n* begavelse *m*, talent *nt*
talented ['tæləntid] *adj* begavet
talk [tɔ:k] *v* snakke; *n* samtale *m*
talkative ['tɔ:kətiv] *adj* snakkesalig
tall [tɔ:l] *adj* høy, lang
tame [teim] *adj* tam; *v* temme
tampon ['tæmpən] *n* tampong *m*
tangerine [,tændʒə'ri:n] *n* mandarin *m*
tangible ['tændʒibəl] *adj* følbar
tank [tæŋk] *n* tank *m*
tanker ['tæŋkə] *n* tankbåt *m*
tanned [tænd] *adj* brun
tap [tæp] *n* kran *c*; lett slag; *v* banke
tape [teip] *n* lydbånd *nt*; bånd *nt*; **adhesive ~** limbånd *nt*, tape *m*; heftplaster *nt*; **~ measure** målebånd *nt*; **~ recorder** båndopptaker *m*
tar [ta:] *n* tjære *c*
target ['ta:git] *n* skyteskive *c*, mål *nt*
tariff ['tærif] *n* tariff *m*
task [ta:sk] *n* oppgave *c*
taste [teist] *n* smak *m*; *v* smake; smake på
tasteless ['teistləs] *adj* smakløs
tasty ['teisti] *adj* velsmakende
taught [tɔ:t] *v* (p, pp teach)
tavern ['tævən] *n* kro *c*
tax [tæks] *n* skatt *m*; *v* *skattlegge

taxation [tæk'seiʃən] *n* beskatning *m*
tax-free ['tæksfriː] *adj* skattefri
taxi ['tæksi] *n* taxi *m*, drosje *c*; ~ **driver** drosjesjåfør *m*; ~ **rank** drosjeholdeplass *m*; ~ **stand** *nAm* drosjeholdeplass *m*
taximeter ['tæksi,miːtə] *n* taksameter *nt*
tea [tiː] *n* te *m*; ~ **set** teservise *nt*
***teach** [tiːtʃ] *v* lære, undervise
teacher ['tiːtʃə] *n* lærer *m*, lektor *m*
teachings ['tiːtʃiŋz] *pl* lære *c*
tea cloth ['tiːklɔθ] *n* kjøkkenhåndkle *nt*
teacup ['tiːkʌp] *n* tekopp *m*
team [tiːm] *n* lag *nt*
teapot ['tiːpɔt] *n* tekanne *c*
***tear** [tɛə] *v* *rive
tear[1] [tiə] *n* tåre *c*
tear[2] [tɛə] *n* rift *c*
tease [tiːz] *v* erte
tea-shop ['tiːʃɔp] *n* tesalong *m*
teaspoon ['tiːspuːn] *n* teskje *c*
technical ['teknikəl] *adj* teknisk; ~ **support** teknisk støtte
technician [tek'niʃən] *n* tekniker *m*
technique [tek'niːk] *n* teknikk *m*
technological [,teknə'lɔdʒikəl] *adj* teknologisk
technology [tek'nɔlədʒi] *n* teknologi *m*
teenager ['tiː,neidʒə] *n* tenåring *m*
telecommunications [,telikəmjuːni'keiʃənz] *n* telekommunikasjon *c*
telepathy [ti'lepəθi] *n* telepati *m*
telephone ['telifoun] *n* telefon *m*; ~ **book** *Am* telefonkatalog *m*; ~ **booth** telefonkiosk *m*; ~ **call** telefon *m*, telefonsamtale *m*; ~ **directory** telefonkatalog *m*; ~ **exchange** telefonsentral *m*
television ['teliviʒən] *n* fjernsyn *nt*; ~ **set** fjernsynsapparat *nt*
***tell** [tel] *v* *si; *fortelle
telly ['teli] *n colloquial* fjernsyn *nt*, TV *m*
temper ['tempə] *n* sinne *nt*
temperature ['temprətʃə] *n* temperatur *m*
tempest ['tempist] *n* storm *m*
temple ['tempəl] *n* tempel *nt*; tinning *m*
temporary ['tempərəri] *adj* midlertidig, foreløpig
tempt [tempt] *v* friste
temptation [temp'teiʃən] *n* fristelse *m*
ten [ten] *num* ti
tenant ['tenənt] *n* leieboer *m*

tend [tend] *v* *ha tendens til; passe; **~ to** *være tilbøyelig til
tendency ['tendənsi] *n* tendens *m*, tilbøyelighet *c*
tender ['tendə] *adj* øm, myk; mør
tendon ['tendən] *n* sene *c*
tennis ['tenis] *n* tennis *m*; **~ court** tennisbane *m*; **~ shoes** tennissko *pl*; joggesko *pl*
tense [tens] *adj* anspent
tension ['tenʃən] *n* spenning *m*
tent [tent] *n* telt *nt*
tenth [tenθ] *num* tiende
tepid ['tepid] *adj* lunken
term [təːm] *n* uttrykk *nt*; frist *m*, termin *m*; betingelse *m*
terminal ['təːminəl] *n* endestasjon *m*; terminal *m*
terrace ['terəs] *n* terrasse *m*
terrain [te'rein] *n* terreng *nt*
terrible ['teribəl] *adj* fryktelig, forferdelig, grusom
terrific [tə'rifik] *adj* storartet
terrify ['terifai] *v* skremme; **terrifying** skremmende
territory ['teritəri] *n* område *nt*
terror ['terə] *n* redsel *m*
terrorism ['terərizəm] *n* terror *m*, terrorisme *m*
terrorist ['terərist] *n* terrorist *m*
terry(cloth) ['teri(klɔθ)] frotté *m*
test [test] *n* prøve *c*, test *m*; *v* teste
testify ['testifai] *v* vitne
text [tekst] *n* tekst *m*
textbook ['teksbuk] *n* lærebok *c*
textile ['tekstail] *n* tekstil *m* / *nt*
texture ['tekstʃə] *n* struktur *m*
Thai [tai] *adj* thailandsk; *n* thailender *m*
Thailand ['tailænd] Thailand
than [ðæn] *conj* enn
thank [θæŋk] *v* takke; **~ you!** takk !
thankful ['θæŋkfəl] *adj* takknemlig
that [ðæt] *pron* den, det; som; *conj* at
thaw [θɔː] *v* tine, smelte; *n* tøvær *nt*
the [ðə,ði] *art* -en, -a; -et; **the ... the** jo ... jo
theater *Am*, **theatre** ['θiətə] *n* teater *nt*
theft [θeft] *n* tyveri *nt*
their [ðɛə] *adj* deres
them [ðem] *pron* dem
theme [θiːm] *n* tema *nt*, emne *nt*
themselves [ðəm'selvz] *pron* seg; selv
then [ðen] *adv* da; deretter, så
theology [θi'ɔlədʒi] *n* teologi *m*
theoretical [θiə'retikəl] *adj* teoretisk

theory ['θiəri] *n* teori *m*
therapy ['θerəpi] *n* terapi *m*
there [ðεə] *adv* der; dit
therefore ['ðεəfɔː] *conj* derfor
thermometer [θə'mɔmitə] *n* termometer *nt*
thermostat ['θəːməstæt] *n* termostat *m*
these [ðiːz] *adj* disse
thesis ['θiːsis] *n* (pl theses) tese *m*; avhandling *c*
they [ðei] *pron* de
thick [θik] *adj* tykk; tett
thicken ['θikən] *v* tykne
thickness ['θiknəs] *n* tykkelse *m*
thief [θiːf] *n* (pl thieves) tyv *m*
thigh [θai] *n* lår *nt*
thimble ['θimbəl] *n* fingerbøl *nt*
thin [θin] *adj* tynn; mager
thing [θiŋ] *n* ting *m*
***think** [θiŋk] *v* tenke; tenke etter; ~ **of** tenke på; *komme på; ~ **over** tenke over
thinker ['θiŋkə] *n* tenker *m*
third [θəːd] *num* tredje
thirst [θəːst] *n* tørst *m*
thirsty ['θəːsti] *adj* tørst
thirteen [ˌθəː'tiːn] *num* tretten
thirteenth [ˌθəː'tiːnθ] *num* trettende
thirtieth ['θəːtiəθ] *num* trettiende
thirty ['θəːti] *num* tretti
this [ðis] *adj* denne; *pron* denne
thistle ['θisəl] *n* tistel *m*
thorn [θɔːn] *n* torn *m*
thorough ['θʌrə] *adj* omhyggelig, grundig
thoroughfare ['θʌrəfεə] *n* ferdselsåre *c*, hovedvei *m*
those [ðouz] *pron* de
though [ðou] *conj* selv om, skjønt; *adv* imidlertid
thought[1] [θɔːt] *v* (p, pp think)
thought[2] [θɔːt] *n* tanke *m*
thoughtful ['θɔːtfəl] *adj* tankefull; omtenksom
thousand ['θauzənd] *num* tusen
thread [θred] *n* tråd *m*; *v* *tre
threadbare ['θredbεə] *adj* loslitt
threat [θret] *n* trussel *m*
threaten ['θretən] *v* true
three [θriː] *num* tre
three-quarter [ˌθriː'kwɔːtə] *adj* tre fjerdedels
threshold ['θreʃould] *n* terskel *m*
threw [θruː] *v* (p throw)
thrifty ['θrifti] *adj* sparsommelig
throat [θrout] *n* hals *m*; strupe *m*
throne [θroun] *n* trone *c*
throttle ['ðrɔtəl] *n* choke *m*
through [θruː] *prep* gjennom
throughout [θruː'aut] *adv* overalt; heltigjennom
throw [θrou] *n* kast *nt*

***throw** [θrou] *v* slenge, kaste
thrush [θrʌʃ] *n* trost *m*
thumb [θʌm] *n* tommelfinger *m*
thumbtack ['θʌmtæk] *nAm* tegnestift *m*
thump [θʌmp] *v* dunke
thunder ['θʌndə] *n* torden *m*; *v* tordne
thunderstorm ['θʌndəstɔːm] *n* tordenvær *nt*
Thursday ['θəːzdi] torsdag *m*
thus [ðʌs] *adv* slik
thyme [taim] *n* timian *m*
tick [tik] *n* merke *nt*; **~ off** krysse av
ticket ['tikit] *n* billett *m*; lapp *m*; **~ machine** billettautomat *m*
tickle ['tikəl] *v* kile
tide [taid] *n* tidevann *nt*; **high ~** høyvann *nt*; **low ~** lavvann *nt*
tidy ['taidi] *adj* ordentlig; **~ up** rydde opp
tie [tai] *v* *binde, knytte; *n* slips *nt*
tiger ['taigə] *n* tiger *m*
tight [tait] *adj* stram; trang; *adv* fast
tighten ['taitən] *v* stramme; strammes
tights [taits] *pl* strømpebukse *c*
tile [tail] *n* gulvflis *c*; takstein *m*
till [til] *prep* inntil, til; *conj* inntil
timber ['timbə] *n* tømmer *nt*
time [taim] *n* tid *c*; gang *m*; takt *m*; **all the ~** hele tiden; **in ~** i tide; **~ of arrival** ankomsttid *c*; **~ of departure** avgangstid *c*
time-saving ['taim,seiviŋ] *adj* tidsbesparende
timetable ['taim,teibəl] *n* ruteplan *m*
timid ['timid] *adj* blyg
timidity [ti'midəti] *n* sjenerthet *c*
tin [tin] *n* tinn *nt*; boks *m*, hermetikkboks *m*; **tinned food** hermetikk *m*; **~ opener** hermetikkåpner *m*
tiny ['taini] *adj* bitte liten
tip [tip] *n* spiss *m*; drikkepenger *pl*
tire[1] [taiə] *n* dekk *nt*
tire[2] [taiə] *v* *bli trett
tired [taiəd] *adj* utmattet, trett; **~ of** lei av
tiring ['taiəriŋ] *adj* trettende
tissue ['tiʃuː] *n* vev *nt*; papirlommetørkle *nt*
title ['taitəl] *n* tittel *m*
to [tuː] *prep* til, på; for å
toad [toud] *n* padde *c*
toadstool ['toudstuːl] *n* fluesopp *m*; giftig sopp
toast [toust] *n* ristet brød; skål *m*; *v* riste
tobacco [tə'bækou] *n* (pl ~s) tobakk *m*
tobacconist's tobakksforretning *c*
today [tə'dei] *adv* i dag
toddler ['tɔdlə] *n* småbarn

nt
toe [tou] *n* tå *c*
toffee ['tɔfi] *n* en slags karamell
together [tə'geðə] *adv* sammen
toilet ['tɔilət] *n* toalett *nt*, *colloquial* do *m* / *nt*; ~ **case** toalettveske *c*; ~ **paper** toalettpapir *nt*
toiletry ['tɔilətri] *n* toalettsaker *pl*
token ['toukən] *n* tegn *nt*; bevis *nt*; sjetong *m*
told [tould] *v* (p, pp tell)
tolerable ['tɔlərəbəl] *adj* utholdelig
toll [toul] *n* bompenger *pl*; gebyr *nt*
tomato [tə'mɑ:tou] *n* (pl ~es) tomat *m*
tomb [tu:m] *n* grav *c*
tombstone ['tu:mstoun] *n* gravstein *m*
tomorrow [tə'mɔrou] *adv* i morgen
ton [tʌn] *n* tonn *nt*
tone [toun] *n* tone *m*; klang *m*
tongs [tɔŋz] *pl* tang *c*
tongue [tʌŋ] *n* tunge *c*
tonight [tə'nait] *adv* i kveld, i natt
tonsilitis [,tɔnsə'laitis] *n* betente mandler
tonsils ['tɔnsəlz] *pl* mandler *pl*
too [tu:] *adv* altfor; også
took [tuk] *v* (p take)
tool [tu:l] *n* verktøy *nt*, redskap *nt*
toot [tu:t] *vAm* tute
tooth [tu:θ] *n* (pl teeth) tann *c*
toothache ['tu:θeik] *n* tannverk *m*; tannpine *c*
toothbrush ['tu:θbrʌʃ] *n* tannbørste *m*
toothpaste ['tu:θpeist] *n* tannkrem *m*
toothpick ['tu:θpik] *n* tannpirker *m*
top [tɔp] *n* topp *m*; overside *c*; lokk *nt*; øverst; **on ~ of** oppå; **~ side** overside *c*
topic ['tɔpik] *n* emne *nt*
topical ['tɔpikəl] *adj* aktuell
torch [tɔ:tʃ] *n* fakkel *m*; lommelykt *c*
torment[1] [tɔ:'ment] *v* pine
torment[2] ['tɔ:ment] *n* pine *c*
torture ['tɔ:tʃə] *n* tortur *m*; *v* torturere
toss [tɔs] *v* kaste
tot [tɔt] *n* lite barn
total ['toutəl] *adj* total; fullstendig; *n* totalsum *m*
totalitarian [,toutæli'tɛəriən] *adj* totalitær
touch [tʌtʃ] *v* røre, berøre; *n* kontakt *m*, berøring *c*; følesans *m*
touching ['tʌtʃiŋ] *adj* rørende
tough [tʌf] *adj* seig
tour [tuə] *n* rundreise *c*, tur *m*
tourism ['tuərizəm] *n* turisttrafikk *m*

tourist ['tuərist] *n* turist *m*; ~ **class** turistklasse *c*; ~ **office** turistkontor *nt*
tournament ['tuənəmənt] *n* turnering *c*
tow [tou] *v* taue
towards [tə'wɔːdz] *prep* mot; overfor
towel [tauəl] *n* håndkle *nt*
towel(l)ing ['tauəliŋ] *n* frotté *m*
tower [tauə] *n* tårn *nt*
town [taun] *n* by *m*; ~ **center** *Am*, ~ **centre** sentrum *nt*; ~ **hall** rådhus *nt*
townspeople ['taunz,piːpəl] *pl* byfolk *pl*
toxic ['tɔksik] *adj* giftig
toy [tɔi] *n* leketøy *nt*
toyshop ['tɔiʃɔp] *n* leketøysforretning *c*
trace [treis] *n* spor *nt*; *v* etterspore, oppspore
track [træk] *n* spor *nt*; bane *m*
tracksuit [træksuːt] *n* treningsdrakt *c*
tractor ['træktə] *n* traktor *m*
trade [treid] *n* handel *m*; yrke *nt*; *v* *drive handel
trademark ['treidmaːk] *n* varemerke *nt*
trader ['treidə] *n* kjøpmann *m*
tradesman ['treidzmən], **tradeswoman** [,treidz'wumən], *n* (pl -men, -women) butikkeier *m*
trade union [,treid'juːnjən] *n* fagforening *c*
tradition [trə'diʃən] *n* tradisjon *m*
traditional [trə'diʃənəl] *adj* tradisjonell
traffic ['træfik] *n* trafikk *m*; ~ **jam** trafikk-kork *m*; ~ **light** trafikklys *nt*
tragedy ['trædʒədi] *n* tragedie *m*
tragic ['trædʒik] *adj* tragisk
trail [treil] *n* sti *m*, spor *nt*
trailer ['treilə] *n* tilhenger *m*; campingvogn *c*
train [trein] *n* tog *nt*; *v* dressere, trene; **stopping** ~ somletog *nt*; **through** ~ hurtigtog *nt*; ~ **ferry** jernbaneferje *c*
trainee [trei'niː] *n* lærling; trainee
trainer ['treinə] *n* trener *m*
training ['treiniŋ] *n* trening *c*
trait [treit] *n* trekk *nt*
traitor ['treitə] *n* forræder *m*
tram [træm] *n* trikk *m*
tramp [træmp] *n* landstryker *m*; **go for a** ~ gå på tur
tranquil ['træŋkwil] *adj* rolig
tranquillizer ['træŋkwilaizə] *n* beroligende middel
transaction [træn'zækʃən] *n* transaksjon *m*
transatlantic [,trænzət'læntik] *adj* transatlantisk
transfer [træns'fəː] *v* overføre

transform [træns'fɔːm] *v* forvandle, omdanne
transformer [træns'fɔːmə] *n* transformator *m*
transition [træn'siʃən] *n* overgang *m*
translate [træns'leit] *v* *oversette
translation [træns'leiʃən] *n* oversettelse *m*
translator [træns'leitə] *n* oversetter *m*
transmission [trænz'miʃən] *n* sending *c*
transmit [trænz'mit] *v* sende
transmitter [trænz'mitə] *n* sender *m*
transparent [træn'spɛərənt] *adj* gjennomsiktig
transport[1] ['trænspɔːt] *n* transport *m*
transport[2] [træn'spɔːt] *v* transportere
transportation [ˌtrænspɔː'teiʃən] *n* transport *m*
trap [træp] *n* felle *c*
trash [træʃ] *n* rask *nt*, skrap *nt*; **~ can** *Am* søppelkasse *c*
travel ['trævəl] *v* reise; **~ agency**, **~ agent** reisebyrå *nt*; **~ insurance** reiseforsikring *c*; **travelling expenses** reiseutgifter *pl*
travel(l)er ['trævələ] *n* reisende *m*; **travel(l)er's cheque** reisesjekk *m*
tray [trei] *n* brett *nt*
treason ['triːzən] *n* forræderi *nt*
treasure ['treʒə] *n* skatt *m*
treasurer ['treʒərə] *n* kasserer *m*
treasury ['treʒəri] *n* statskasse *c*
treat [triːt] *v* behandle
treatment ['triːtmənt] *n* behandling *c*
treaty ['triːti] *n* traktat *m*
tree [triː] *n* tre *nt*
tremble ['trembəl] *v* *skjelve; dirre
tremendous [tri'mendəs] *adj* kolossal
trendy ['trendi] *adj* *colloquial* moderne
trespass ['trespəs] *v* krenke annens eiendom
trespasser ['trespəsə] *n* uvedkommende *m*
trial [traiəl] *n* rettssak *c*; forsøk *nt*
triangle ['traiæŋgəl] *n* trekant *m*
triangular [trai'æŋgjulə] *adj* trekantet
tribe [traib] *n* stamme *m*
tributary ['tribjutəri] *n* bielv *c*
tribute ['tribjuːt] *n* hyllest *m*
trick [trik] *n* knep *nt*; trick *nt*
trigger ['trigə] *n* avtrekker *m*
trim [trim] *v* klippe, stusse
trip [trip] *n* reise *c*, utflukt *c*, tur *m*
triumph ['traiəmf] *n* triumf *m*; *v* triumfere

triumphant [trai'ʌmfənt] *adj* triumferende
troops [tru:ps] *pl* tropper *pl*
tropical ['trɔpikəl] *adj* tropisk
tropics ['trɔpiks] *pl* tropene *pl*
trouble ['trʌbəl] *n* trøbbel *nt*, uleilighet *c*, besvær *nt*; *v* bry
troublesome ['trʌbəlsəm] *adj* brysom
trousers ['trauzəz] *pl* bukse *c*; **trouser...** bukse...
trout [traut] *n* (pl ~) ørret *m*
truck [trʌk] *nAm* lastebil *m*
true [tru:] *adj* sann; ekte, virkelig; trofast, tro
trumpet ['trʌmpit] *n* trompet *m*
trunk [trʌŋk] *n* koffert *m*; stamme *m*; bagasjerom *nt*
trust [trʌst] *v* stole på; *n* tillit *m*
trustworthy ['trʌst,wə:ði] *adj* pålitelig
truth [tru:θ] *n* sannhet *c*
truthful ['tru:θfəl] *adj* sannferdig
try [trai] *v* prøve, forsøke, anstrenge seg; *n* forsøk *nt*; **~ on** prøve
tube [tju:b] *n* rør *nt*; tube *m*
tuberculosis [tju:,bə:kju'lousis] *n* tuberkulose *m*
Tuesday ['tju:zdi] tirsdag *m*
tug [tʌg] *v* taue; *n* slepebåt *m*; rykk *nt*
tuition [tju:'iʃən] *n* undervisning *c*; skolepenger *pl*
tulip ['tju:lip] *n* tulipan *m*
tumo(u)r ['tju:mə] *n* svulst *m*
tuna ['tju:nə] *n* (pl ~, ~s) tunfisk *m*
tune [tju:n] *n* melodi *m*; **~ in** stille inn
tuneful ['tju:nfəl] *adj* melodisk
tunic ['tju:nik] *n* tunika *m*
Tunisia [tju:'niziə] Tunisia
Tunisian [tju:'niziən] *adj* tunisisk; *n* tunisier *m*
tunnel ['tʌnəl] *n* tunnel *m*
turbine ['tə:bain] *n* turbin *m*
turbojet [,tə:bou'dʒet] *n* turbojet *m*
Turkey ['tə:ki] Tyrkia
turkey ['tə:ki] *n* kalkun *m*
Turkish ['tə:kiʃ] *adj* tyrkisk; **~ bath** romerbad *nt*
turn [tə:n] *v* dreie; vende, svinge, *vri om; *n* dreining *m*, vending *c*; sving *m*; tur *m*; **~ back** vende tilbake; **~ down** forkaste; **~ into** forvandles til; **~ off** stenge av; **~ on** *sette på; skru på; **~ over** vende om; **~ round** snu; snu seg
turning ['tə:niŋ] *n* sving *m*
turning point ['tə:niŋpɔint] *n* vendepunkt *nt*
turnover ['tə:,nouvə] *n* omsetning *m*; **~ tax** moms *m*
turnpike ['tə:npaik] *nAm* bomvei *m*

turpentine ['tə:pəntain] *n* terpentin *m*
turtle ['tə:təl] *n* skilpadde *c*
tutor ['tju:tə] *n* huslærer *m*
tuxedo [tʌk'si:dou] *nAm* (pl ~s, ~es) smoking *m*
TV [ˌti'vi:] *n colloquial* TV *m*; **on ~** på TV
tweed [twi:d] *n* tweed *m*
tweezers ['twi:zəz] *pl* pinsett *m*
twelfth [twelfθ] *num* tolvte
twelve [twelv] *num* tolv
twentieth ['twentiəθ] *num* tyvende
twenty ['twenti] *num* tyve
twice [twais] *adv* to ganger
twig [twig] *n* kvist *m*
twilight ['twailait] *n* skumring *c*
twine [twain] *n* hyssing *m*
twins [twinz] *pl* tvillinger *pl*
twist [twist] *v* sno; *vri; *n* vridning *m*
two [tu:] *num* to
two-piece [ˌtu:'pi:s] *adj* todelt
type [taip] *v* *skrive på data; taste; *n* type *m*
typhoid ['taifɔid] *n* tyfus *m*
typical ['tipikəl] *adj* typisk
tyrant ['taiərənt] *n* tyrann *m*
tyre [taiə] *n* dekk *nt*; **~ pressure** lufttrykk *nt*

U

ugly ['ʌgli] *adj* stygg
ulcer ['ʌlsə] *n* magesår *nt*
ultimate ['ʌltimət] *adj* siste
ultraviolet [ˌʌltrə'vaiələt] *adj* ultrafiolett
umbrella [ʌm'brelə] *n* paraply *m*
umpire ['ʌmpaiə] *n* dommer *m*
unable [ʌ'neibəl] *adj* ute av stand til
unacceptable [ˌʌnək'septəbəl] *adj* uakseptabel
unaccountable [ˌʌnə'kauntəbəl] *adj* uforklarlig; uansvarlig
unaccustomed [ˌʌnə'kʌstəmd] *adj* uvant
unanimous [ju:'næniməs] *adj* enstemmig
unanswered [ˌʌ'nɑ:nsəd] *adj* ubesvart
unauthorized [ˌʌ'nɔ:θəraizd] *adj* uten fullmakt
unavoidable [ˌʌnə'vɔidəbəl] *adj* uunngåelig
unaware [ˌʌnə'wɛə] *adj* ubevisst
unbearable [ʌn'bɛərəbəl] *adj* uutholdelig
unbreakable [ˌʌn'breikəbəl] *adj* uknuselig
unbroken [ˌʌn'broukən] *adj* intakt
unbutton [ˌʌn'bʌtən] *v*

knappe opp
uncertain [ʌn'səːtən] *adj* uviss, usikker
uncle ['ʌŋkəl] *n* onkel *m*
uncomfortable [ʌn'kʌmfətəbəl] *adj* ubekvem
uncommon [ʌn'kɔmən] *adj* usedvanlig, sjelden
unconditional [ˌʌnkən'diʃənəl] *adj* betingelsesløs
unconscious [ʌn'kɔnʃəs] *adj* bevisstløs
uncork [ˌʌn'kɔːk] *v* *trekke opp
uncover [ʌn'kʌvə] *v* avdekke
uncultivated [ˌʌn'kʌltiveitid] *adj* udyrket
under ['ʌndə] *prep* under, nedenfor
undercurrent ['ʌndəˌkʌrənt] *n* understrøm *m*
underestimate [ˌʌndə'restimeit] *v* undervurdere
underground ['ʌndəgraund] *adj* underjordisk; *n* undergrunnsbane *m*
underline [ˌʌndə'lain] *v* understreke
underneath [ˌʌndə'niːθ] *adv* nedenunder
underpants ['ʌndəpænts] *plAm* truse *c*
***understand** [ˌʌndə'stænd] *v* *forstå, fatte
understanding [ˌʌndə'stændiŋ] *n* forståelse *m*
understate [ˌʌndə'steit] *v* underdrive
understatement [ˌʌndə'steitmənt] *n* underdrivelse *m*
***undertake** [ˌʌndə'teik] *v* *gå i gang med
undertaking [ˌʌndə'teikiŋ] *n* foretak *nt*
underwater ['ʌndəˌwɔːtə] *adj* undervanns-
underwear ['ʌndəwɛə] *n* undertøy *pl*
undesirable [ˌʌndi'zaiərəbəl] *adj* uønsket
***undo** [ˌʌn'duː] *v* åpne, løse opp
undoubtedly [ʌn'dautidli] *adv* utvilsomt
undress [ˌʌn'dres] *v* kle av seg
unearned [ˌʌ'nəːnd] *adj* ufortjent
uneasy [ʌ'niːzi] *adj* urolig
uneducated [ˌʌ'nedjukeitid] *adj* uten utdannelse
unemployed [ˌʌnim'plɔid] *adj* arbeidsløs; arbeidsledig
unemployment [ˌʌnim'plɔimənt] *n* arbeidsløshet *c*; arbeidsledighet *c*
unequal [ˌʌ'niːkwəl] *adj* ulik

uneven [ˌʌ'niːvən] *adj* ulik, ujevn
unexpected [ˌʌnik'spektid] *adj* uventet
unfair [ˌʌn'fɛə] *adj* urettferdig
unfaithful [ˌʌn'feiθfəl] *adj* utro
unfamiliar [ˌʌnfə'miljə] *adj* ukjent
unfasten [ˌʌn'fɑːsən] *v* løse, løsne
unfavo(u)rable [ˌʌn'feivərəbəl] *adj* ugunstig
unfit [ˌʌn'fit] *adj* uegnet
unfold [ʌn'fould] *v* brette ut, folde ut
unfortunate [ʌn'fɔːtʃənət] *adj* uheldig
unfortunately [ʌn'fɔːtʃənətli] *adv* uheldigvis, dessverre
unfriendly [ˌʌn'frendli] *adj* uvennlig
ungrateful [ʌn'greitfəl] *adj* utakknemlig
unhappy [ʌn'hæpi] *adj* ulykkelig
unhealthy [ʌn'helθi] *adj* usunn
unhurt [ˌʌn'həːt] *adj* uskadd
uniform ['juːnifɔːm] *n* uniform *c*; *adj* ensartet
unimportant [ˌʌnim'pɔːtənt] *adj* uviktig
uninhabitable [ˌʌnin'hæbitəbəl] *adj* ubeboelig
uninhabited [ˌʌnin'hæbitid] *adj* ubebodd
unintentional [ˌʌnin'tenʃənəl] *adj* utilsiktet
union ['juːnjən] *n* fagforening *c*; union *m*, forbund *nt*
unique [juː'niːk] *adj* enestående
unit ['juːnit] *n* enhet *m*
unite [juː'nait] *v* forene; **united** *adj* forent
United States [juː'naitid steits] De forente stater
unity ['juːnəti] *n* enhet *m*
universal [ˌjuːni'vəːsəl] *adj* universell, generell
universe ['juːnivəːs] *n* univers *nt*
university [ˌjuːni'vəːsəti] *n* universitet *nt*
unjust [ˌʌn'dʒʌst] *adj* urettferdig
unkind [ʌn'kaind] *adj* uvennlig; ukjærlig
unknown [ˌʌn'noun] *adj* ukjent
unlawful [ˌʌn'lɔːfəl] *adj* ulovlig
unless [ən'les] *conj* med mindre
unlike [ˌʌn'laik] *adj* forskjellig
unlikely [ʌn'laikli] *adj* usannsynlig
unlimited [ʌn'limitid] *adj* grenseløs, ubegrenset
unload [ˌʌn'loud] *v* lesse av
unlock [ˌʌn'lɔk] *v* lukke opp; låse opp

unlucky [ʌn'lʌki] *adj* uheldig
unnecessary [ʌn'nesəsəri] *adj* unødvendig
unoccupied [ˌʌ'nɔkjupaid] *adj* ledig
unofficial [ˌʌnə'fiʃəl] *adj* uoffisiell
unpack [ˌʌn'pæk] *v* pakke opp
unpleasant [ʌn'plezənt] *adj* utrivelig, ubehagelig; usympatisk, utiltalende
unpopular [ˌʌn'pɔpjulə] *adj* upopulær
unprotected [ˌʌnprə'tektid] *adj* ubeskyttet
unqualified [ˌʌn'kwɔlifaid] *adj* ukvalifisert
unreal [ˌʌn'riəl] *adj* uvirkelig
unreasonable [ʌn'ri:zənəbəl] *adj* urimelig
unreliable [ˌʌnri'laiəbəl] *adj* upålitelig
unrest [ˌʌn'rest] *n* uro *m*; rastløshet *c*
unsafe [ˌʌn'seif] *adj* usikker, utrygg
unsatisfactory [ˌʌnsætis'fæktəri] *adj* utilfredsstillende
unscrew [ˌʌn'skru:] *v* skru løs
unselfish [ˌʌn'selfiʃ] *adj* uselvisk
unskilled [ˌʌn'skild] *adj* ufaglært
unsound [ˌʌn'saund] *adj* usunn
unstable [ˌʌn'steibəl] *adj* ustabil
unsteady [ˌʌn'stedi] *adj* ustø; ustadig
unsuccessful [ˌʌnsək'sesfəl] *adj* mislykket
unsuitable [ˌʌn'su:təbəl] *adj* uegnet
unsurpassed [ˌʌnsə'pɑ:st] *adj* uovertruffen
untidy [ʌn'taidi] *adj* uordentlig
untie [ˌʌn'tai] *v* knytte opp
until [ən'til] *prep* inntil, til
untrue [ˌʌn'tru:] *adj* usann
untrustworthy [ˌʌn'trʌstˌwə:ði] *adj* upålitelig
unusual [ʌn'ju:ʒuəl] *adj* uvanlig, ualminnelig
unwell [ˌʌn'wel] *adj* uvel
unwilling [ˌʌn'wiliŋ] *adj* uvillig
unwise [ˌʌn'waiz] *adj* uklok
unwrap [ˌʌn'ræp] *v* pakke opp
up [ʌp] *adv* opp, oppover
upholster [ʌp'houlstə] *v* *trekke, polstre
upkeep ['ʌpki:p] *n* vedlikehold *nt*
uplands ['ʌpləndz] *pl* høyland *nt*
upload ['ʌpˌloud] *v* laste opp
upon [ə'pɔn] *prep* på
upper ['ʌpə] *adj* øvre, over-
upright ['ʌprait] *adj* rank; rett; loddrett

***upset** [ʌp'set] *v* forstyrre; *adj* opprørt
upside down [ˌʌpsaid'daun] *adv* på hodet; opp ned
upstairs [ˌʌp'stɛəz] *adv* ovenpå
upstream [ˌʌp'stri:m] *adv* mot strømmen
upwards ['ʌpwədz] *adv* oppover
urban ['ə:bən] *adj* by-
urge [ə:dʒ] *v* formane; *n* trang *m*
urgency ['ə:dʒənsi] *n* innstendighet *c*; viktighet *c*
urgent ['ə:dʒənt] *adj* presserende
urine ['juərin] *n* urin *m*
Uruguay ['juərəgwai] Uruguay
Uruguayan [ˌjuərə'gwaiən] *adj* uruguayansk; *n* uruguayaner *m*
us [ʌs] *pron* oss
usable ['ju:zəbəl] *adj* anvendelig
usage ['ju:zidʒ] *n* sedvane *m*; bruk *m*
use¹ [ju:z] *v* bruke; ***be used to** *være vant til; **~ up** bruke opp
use² [ju:s] *n* bruk *m*; nytte *c*; ***be of ~** *være til nytte
useful ['ju:sfəl] *adj* nyttig, brukbar
useless ['ju:sləs] *adj* unyttig
user ['ju:zə] *n* bruker *m*
usher ['ʌʃə] *v* vise veien
usual ['ju:ʒuəl] *adj* vanlig
usually ['ju:ʒuəli] *adv* vanligvis
utensil [ju:'tensəl] *n* redskap *nt*; kjøkkenredskap *nt*
utility [ju:'tiləti] *n* nytte *c*
utilize ['ju:tilaiz] *v* anvende
utmost ['ʌtmoust] *adj* ytterst
utter ['ʌtə] *adj* total, fullstendig; *v* ytre

V

vacancy ['veikənsi] *n* ledig stilling
vacant ['veikənt] *adj* ledig
vacation [və'keiʃən] *n* ferie *m*
vaccinate ['væksineit] *v* vaksinere
vaccination [ˌvæksi'neiʃən] *n* vaksinering *c*
vacuum ['vækjuəm] *n* vakuum *nt*; *vAm* støvsuge; **~ cleaner** støvsuger *m*
vague [veig] *adj* vag
vain [vein] *adj* forfengelig; forgjeves; **in ~** forgjeves
valid ['vælid] *adj* gyldig
valley ['væli] *n* dal *m*
valuable ['væljubəl] *adj* verdifull; **valuables** *pl* verdisaker *pl*

value ['vælju:] *n* verdi *m*; *v* taksere, vurdere
valve [vælv] *n* ventil *m*
van [væn] *n* varebil *m*
vanilla [və'nilə] *n* vanilje *m*
vanish ['væniʃ] *v* *forsvinne
vapo(u)r ['veipə] *n* damp *m*
variable ['vɛəriəbəl] *adj* variabel
variation [,vɛəri'eiʃən] *n* avveksling *c*; forandring *c*
variety [və'raiəti] *n* utvalg *nt*
various ['vɛəriəs] *adj* forskjellige, diverse
varnish ['vɑ:niʃ] *n* lakk *m*; *v* lakkere
vary ['vɛəri] *v* variere; forandre; *være forskjellig
vase [vɑ:z] *n* vase *m*
vast [vɑ:st] *adj* vidstrakt, umåtelig
vault [vɔ:lt] *n* hvelving *m*; bankhvelv *nt*
veal [vi:l] *n* kalvekjøtt *nt*
vegetable ['vedʒətəbəl] *n* grønnsak *c*; ~ **merchant** grønnsakshandler *m*
vegetarian [,vedʒi'tɛəriən] *n* vegetarianer *m*
vegetation [,vedʒi'teiʃən] *n* vegetasjon *m*
vehicle ['vi:əkəl] *n* kjøretøy *nt*
veil [veil] *n* slør *nt*
vein [vein] *n* åre *c*; **varicose** ~ åreknute *m*
velvet ['velvit] *n* fløyel *m*
velveteen [,velvi'ti:n] *n* bomullsfløyel *m*
venerable ['venərəbəl] *adj* ærverdig
venereal disease [vi'niəriəl di'zi:z] kjønnssykdom *m*
Venezuela [,veni'zweilə] Venezuela
Venezuelan [,veni'zweilən] *adj* venezuelansk; *n* venezuelaner *m*
ventilate ['ventileit] *v* ventilere; lufte, lufte ut
ventilation [,venti'leiʃən] *n* ventilasjon *m*; utluftning *m*
ventilator ['ventileitə] *n* ventilator *m*
venture ['ventʃə] *v* våge
veranda [və'rændə] *n* veranda *m*
verb [və:b] *n* verb *nt*
verbal ['və:bəl] *adj* muntlig
verdict ['və:dikt] *n* kjennelse *m*, dom *m*
verify ['verifai] *v* kontrollere
verse [və:s] *n* vers *nt*
version ['və:ʃən] *n* versjon *m*
versus ['və:səs] *prep* kontra
vertical ['və:tikəl] *adj* vertikal
very ['veri] *adv* svært, meget; *adj* eksakt, virkelig; absolutt
vessel ['vesəl] *n* fartøy *nt*; kar *nt*
vest [vest] *n* undertrøye *c*; vest *m*
veterinary surgeon ['vetrinəri 'sə:dʒən] dyrlege *m*
via [vaiə] *prep* via
vibrate [vai'breit] *v* vibrere

vibration [vai'breiʃən] *n* vibrasjon *m*
vicar ['vikə] *n* sogneprest *m*
vicarage ['vikəridʒ] *n* prestegård *m*
vice president [ˌvais'prezidənt] *n* visepresident *m*
vicinity [vi'sinəti] *n* nabolag *nt*, nærhet *c*
vicious ['viʃəs] *adj* ondskapsfull
victim ['viktim] *n* offer *nt*
victory ['viktəri] *n* seier *m*
video camera ['vidiou'kæmərə] *n* video-kamera *nt*
video cassette ['vidiou'kæset] *n* videokassett *m*
video recorder ['vidiou ri'kɔːdə] *n* video-spiller *m*
view [vjuː] *n* utsikt *m*; oppfatning *m*, syn; *v* betrakte
viewfinder ['vjuːˌfaində] *n* søker *m*
vigilant ['vidʒilənt] *adj* årvåken
villa ['vilə] *n* villa *m*
village ['vilidʒ] *n* landsby *m*; bygd *c*
villain ['vilən] *n* skurk *m*
vine [vain] *n* vinranke *m*
vinegar ['vinigə] *n* eddik *m*
vintage ['vintidʒ] *n* vinhøst *m*; årgang *m*
violation [vaiə'leiʃən] *n* krenkelse *m*
violence ['vaiələns] *n* vold *m*
violent ['vaiələnt] *adj* voldsom, heftig
violet ['vaiələt] *n* fiol *m*; *adj* fiolett, lilla
violin [vaiə'lin] *n* fiolin *m*
virgin ['vəːdʒin] *n* jomfru *c*
virtue ['vəːtʃuː] *n* dyd *m*
virus ['vairəs] *n* virus *nt*
visa ['viːzə] *n* visum *nt*
visibility [ˌvizə'biləti] *n* sikt *m*
visible ['vizəbəl] *adj* synlig
vision ['viʒən] *n* syn
visit ['vizit] *v* besøke; *n* besøk *nt*, visitt *m*; **visiting hours** besøkstid *c*
visitor ['vizitə] *n* besøkende *m*
vital ['vaitəl] *adj* vesentlig
vitamin ['vitəmin] *n* vitamin *nt*
vivid ['vivid] *adj* livfull
vocabulary [və'kæbjuləri] *n* ordforråd *nt*; ordliste *c*
vocal ['voukəl] *adj* vokal
vocalist ['voukəlist] *n* sanger *m*
voice [vɔis] *n* stemme *m*
voice mail ['vois‿ˌmeil] *n* voicemail *c*
void [vɔid] *adj* ugyldig
volcano [vɔl'keinou] *n* (pl ~es, ~s) vulkan *m*
volt [voult] *n* volt *m*
voltage ['voultidʒ] *n* spenning *m*
volume ['vɔljum] *n* volum *nt*; bind *nt*
voluntary ['vɔləntəri] *adj*

frivillig
volunteer [ˌvɔlən'tiə] *n* frivillig *m*
vomit ['vɔmit] *v* kaste opp, *brekke seg
vote [vout] *v* stemme; *n* stemme *m*; avstemning *m*
voucher ['vautʃə] *n* bong *m*
vow [vau] *n* løfte *nt*, ed *m*; *v* *sverge
vowel [vauəl] *n* vokal *m*
voyage ['vɔiidʒ] *n* reise *c*
vulgar ['vʌlgə] *adj* vulgær; simpel, ordinær
vulnerable ['vʌlnərəbəl] *adj* sårbar
vulture ['vʌltʃə] *n* gribb *m*

W

wade [weid] *v* vasse
waffle ['wɔfəl] *n* vaffel *m*
wages ['weidʒiz] *pl* lønn *c*
wag(g)on ['wægən] *n* godsvogn *c*; vogn *c*
waist [weist] *n* midje *c*
waistcoat ['weiskout] *n* vest *m*
wait [weit] *v* vente; **~ on** oppvarte
waiter ['weitə] *n* kelner *m*, servitør *m*
waiting ['weitiŋ] *n* venting *c*; **~ list** venteliste *c*; **~ room** venteværelse *nt*
waitress ['weitris] *n* (kvinnelig) servitør *m*
***wake** [weik] *v* vekke; **~ up** våkne
walk [wɔːk] *v* *gå; spasere; *n* spasertur *m*; gange *m*; **walking** til fots
walker ['wɔːkə] *n* turgjenger *m*
walking stick ['wɔːkiŋstik] *n* spaserstokk *m*
wall [wɔːl] *n* mur *m*; vegg *m*
wallet ['wɔlit] *n* lommebok *c*
wallpaper ['wɔːlˌpeipə] *n* tapet *nt*
walnut ['wɔːlnʌt] *n* valnøtt *c*
waltz [wɔːls] *n* vals *m*
wander ['wɔndə] *v* flakke, vandre
want [wɔnt] *v* *ville; ønske; *n* behov *nt*; mangel *m*
war [wɔː] *n* krig *m*
wardrobe ['wɔːdroub] *n* klesskap *nt*, garderobe *m*
warehouse ['wɛəhaus] *n* pakkhus *nt*, lagerbygning *m*
wares [wɛəz] *pl* varer *pl*
warm [wɔːm] *adj* varm; *v* varme
warmth [wɔːmθ] *n* varme *m*
warn [wɔːn] *v* advare
warning ['wɔːniŋ] *n* advarsel *m*
wary ['wɛəri] *adj* forsiktig
was [wɔz] *v* (p be)
wash [wɔʃ] *v* vaske; **~ and wear** strykefri; **~ up** vaske

opp
washable ['wɔʃəbəl] *adj* vaskbar
washbasin ['wɔʃˌbeisən] *n* håndvask *m*
washing ['wɔʃiŋ] *n* vask *m*; **~ machine** vaskemaskin *m*; **~ powder** vaskepulver *nt*
washroom ['wɔʃru:m] *nAm* toalett *nt*
wasp [wɔsp] *n* veps *m*
waste [weist] *v* sløse bort; *n* sløseri *nt*; *adj* øde; **~ separation** kildesortering *c*
wasteful ['weistfəl] *adj* ødsel
wastepaper basket [weist'peipəˌbɑ:skit] *n* papirkurv *m*
watch [wɔtʃ] *v* betrakte, *iaktta; bevokte; *n* ur *nt*; **~ for** *holde utkikk etter; **~ out** *være forsiktig
watchmaker ['wɔtʃˌmeikə] *n* urmaker *m*
watchstrap ['wɔtʃstræp] *n* klokkerem *c*
water ['wɔ:tə] *n* vann *nt*; **iced ~** isvann *nt*; **running ~** innlagt vann; **~ ski** vannski *c*
watercolo(u)r ['wɔ:təˌkʌlə] *n* vannfarge *m*; akvarell *m*
waterfall ['wɔ:təfɔ:l] *n* foss *m*
watermelon ['wɔ:təˌmelən] *n* vannmelon *m*
waterproof ['wɔ:təpru:f] *adj* vanntett
watt [wɔt] *n* watt *m*
wave [weiv] *n* bølge *c*; *v* vinke
wavelength ['weivleŋθ] *n* bølgelengde *m*
wavy ['weivi] *adj* bølget
wax [wæks] *n* voks *m*
waxworks ['wækswə:ks] *pl* vokskabinett *nt*
way [wei] *n* vis *nt*, måte *m*; vei *m*; retning *m*; avstand *m*; **any ~** på hvilken som helst måte; **by the ~** forresten; **out of the ~** avsides; **the other ~ round** tvert om; **~ back** fjern fortid; **~ in** inngang *m*; **~ out** utgang *m*; **one-way traffic** enveiskjøring *c*
wayside ['weisaid] *n* veikant *m*
we [wi:] *pron* vi
weak [wi:k] *adj* svak; tynn
weakness ['wi:knəs] *n* svakhet *c*
wealth [welθ] *n* rikdom *m*
wealthy ['welθi] *adj* rik
weapon ['wepən] *n* våpen *nt*
***wear** [wεə] *v* *ha på seg; **~ out** *slite ut
weary ['wiəri] *adj* trett, sliten
weather ['weðə] *n* vær *nt*; **~ forecast** værmelding *c*
***weave** [wi:v] *v* veve
website ['webˌsait] *n* nettsted *nt*
wedding ['wediŋ] *n* vielse *m*, bryllup *nt*; **~ ring** vielsesring *m*
wedge [wedʒ] *n* kile *m*
Wednesday ['wenzdi] onsdag *m*

weed [wi:d] *n* ugress *nt*
week [wi:k] *n* uke *c*
weekday ['wi:kdei] *n* hverdag *m*
weekend ['wi:kend] *n* helg *c*
weekly ['wi:kli] *adj* ukentlig
***weep** [wi:p] *v* *gråte
weigh [wei] *v* veie
weight [weit] *n* vekt *c*
Welch [welʃ] *adj* walisisk
welcome ['welkəm] *adj* velkommen; *n* velkomst *m*; *v* hilse velkommen
weld [weld] *v* sveise
welfare ['welfεə] *n* velferd *m*
well[1] [wel] *adv* godt; *adj* frisk; **as ~** også; **as ~ as** så vel som; **well!** ja vel!
well[2] [wel] *n* kilde *m*; brønn *m*
well-founded [ˌwel'faundid] *adj* velbegrunnet
well-known ['welnoun] *adj* velkjent
well-to-do [ˌweltə'du:] *adj* velhavende
went [went] *v* (p go)
were [wə:] *v* (p be)
west [west] *n* vest *m*
westerly ['westəli] *adj* vestlig
western ['westən] *adj* vestlig
wet [wet] *adj* våt; fuktig
whale [weil] *n* hval *m*
wharf [wɔ:f] *n* (pl ~s, wharves) kai *c*
what [wɔt] *pron* hva; **~ for** hvorfor
whatever [wɔ'tevə] *pron* hva enn
wheat [wi:t] *n* hvete *m*
wheel [wi:l] *n* hjul *nt*
wheelbarrow ['wi:lˌbærou] *n* trillebår *c*
wheelchair ['wi:ltʃεə] *n* rullestol *m*
when [wen] *adv* når; *conj* når, da
whenever [we'nevə] *conj* når enn; alltid når
where [wεə] *adv* hvor; *conj* hvor
wherever [wεə'revə] *conj* hvor enn
whether ['weðə] *conj* om; **whether … or** om … eller
which [witʃ] *pron* hvilken; som
whichever [wi'tʃevə] *adj* hvilken som helst
while [wail] *conj* mens; *n* stund *c*
whim [wim] *n* innfall *nt*, nykke *nt*
whip [wip] *n* pisk *m*; *v* vispe
whiskers ['wiskəz] *pl* kinnskjegg *nt*
whisper ['wispə] *v* hviske; *n* hvisking *c*
whistle ['wisəl] *v* plystre; *n* fløyte *c*
white [wait] *adj* hvit
whiting ['waitiŋ] *n* (pl ~) hvitting *m*
wit [wit] *n* vidd *nt*
who [hu:] *pron* hvem; som
whoever [hu:'evə] *pron* hvem (som) enn
whole [houl] *adj* fullstendig,

hel; uskadd; *n* hele *nt*
wholesale ['houlseil] *n* engroshandel *m*; **~ dealer** grosserer *m*
wholesome ['houlsəm] *adj* sunn
wholly ['houlli] *adv* helt
whom [hu:m] *pron* til hvem
whore [hɔ:] *n* hore *c*
whose [hu:z] *pron* hvis
why [wai] *adv* hvorfor
wicked ['wikid] *adj* ond
wide [waid] *adj* bred, vid
widen ['waidən] *v* utvide
widow ['widou] *n* enke *c*
widower ['widouə] *n* enkemann *m*
width [widθ] *n* bredde *m*
wife [waif] *n* (pl wives) kone *c*
wig [wig] *n* parykk *m*
wild [waild] *adj* vill
will [wil] *n* vilje *m*; testamente *nt*
***will** [wil] *v* *vil
willing ['wiliŋ] *adj* villig
willow ['wilou] *n* pil *c*
willpower ['wilpauə] *n* viljestyrke *m*
***win** [win] *v* *vinne
wind [wind] *n* vind *m*
***wind** [waind] *v* sno seg; *trekke opp, vikle
winding ['waindiŋ] *adj* buktet
windmill ['windmil] *n* vindmølle *c*
window ['windou] *n* vindu *nt*
windowsill ['windousil] *n* vinduskarm *m*
windscreen ['windskri:n] *n* frontrute *c*; **~ wiper** vindusvisker *m*
windshield ['windʃi:ld] *nAm* frontrute *c*; **~ wiper** *Am* vindusvisker *m*
windy ['windi] *adj* vindhard
wine [wain] *n* vin *m*; **~ cellar** vinkjeller *m*; **~ list** vinkart *nt*
wing [wiŋ] *n* vinge *m*
winner ['winə] *n* vinner *m*
winning ['winiŋ] *adj* vinnende; **winnings** *pl* gevinst *m*
winter ['wintə] *n* vinter *m*; **~ sports** vintersport *m*
wipe [waip] *v* tørke, tørke bort; tørke av
wire [waiə] *n* wire *m*, vaier *m*; ståltråd *m*
wireless ['waiələs] *adj* trådløs
wisdom ['wizdəm] *n* visdom *m*
wise [waiz] *adj* vis
wish [wiʃ] *v* lenges etter, ønske; *n* ønske *nt*, lengsel *m*
witch [witʃ] *n* heks *c*
with [wið] *prep* med; hos; av
***withdraw** [wið'drɔ:] *v* *trekke tilbake
***withhold** [wið'hould] *v* *holde tilbake
within [wi'ðin] *prep* innenfor; *adv* innvendig; innen
without [wi'ðaut] *prep* uten
witness ['witnəs] *n* vitne *nt*

wits [wits] *pl* forstand *m*
witty ['witi] *adj* vittig; spirituell
WMD ['dʌbəlju:'em'di:] *n*, **weapons of mass destruction** masseødeleggelsesvåpen *nt*
wolf [wulf] *n* (pl wolves) ulv *m*
woman ['wumən] *n* (pl women) kvinne *c*
womb [wu:m] *n* livmor *c*
won [wʌn] *v* (p, pp win)
wonder ['wʌndə] *n* under *nt*; forundring *c*; *v* undre seg
wonderful ['wʌndəfəl] *adj* skjønn, vidunderlig; herlig
wood [wud] *n* trevirke *nt*; skog *m*; **~ carving** treskjærerarbeid *nt*
wooded ['wudid] *adj* skogkledd
wooden ['wudən] *adj* tre-; **~ shoe** tresko *m*
woodland ['wudlənd] *n* skogsområde *nt*
wool [wul] *n* ull *c*
wool(l)en ['wulən] *adj* ull-
word [wə:d] *n* ord *nt*
wore [wɔ:] *v* (p wear)
work [wə:k] *n* arbeid *nt*; *v* arbeide; virke, fungere; **working day** arbeidsdag *m*; **~ of art** kunstverk *nt*; **~ permit** arbeidstillatelse *m*
workaholic [ˌwə:kə'hɔlik] *n* arbeidsnarkoman *c*
worker ['wə:kə] *n* arbeider *m*
workman ['wə:kmən] *n* (pl -men) arbeider *m*
works [wə:ks] *pl* fabrikk *m*
workshop ['wə:kʃɔp] *n* verksted *nt*
world [wə:ld] *n* verden *m*; **~ war** verdenskrig *m*
world-famous [ˌwə:ld'feiməs] *adj* verdensberømt
world-wide ['wə:ldwaid] *adj* verdensomspennende
worm [wə:m] *n* mark *m*
worn [wɔ:n] *adj* (pp wear) slitt
worn-out [ˌwɔ:n'aut] *adj* utslitt
worried ['wʌrid] *adj* bekymret
worry ['wʌri] *v* bekymre seg; *n* bekymring *c*
worse [wə:s] *adj* verre; *adv* verre
worship ['wə:ʃip] *v* *tilbe; *n* gudstjeneste *m*
worst [wə:st] *adj* verst; *adv* verst
worth [wə:θ] *n* verd *nt*; ***be ~** *være verd; ***be worth-while** *være umaken verd
worthless ['wə:θləs] *adj* verdiløs
worthy of ['wə:ði əv] verdig
would [wud] *v* (p will)
wound[1] [wu:nd] *n* sår *nt*; *v* såre
wound[2] [waund] *v* (p, pp wind)
wrap [ræp] *v* pakke inn
wreck [rek] *n* vrak *nt*; *v*

*ødelegge
wrench [rentʃ] *n* skrunøkkel *m*; rykk *nt*; *v* *vri
wrinkle ['riŋkəl] *n* rynke *c*
wrist [rist] *n* håndledd *nt*
wristwatch ['ristwɔtʃ] *n* armbåndsur *nt*
***write** [rait] *v* *skrive; **in writing** skriftlig; **~ down** *skrive ned
writer ['raitə] *n* forfatter *m*
writing pad ['raitiŋpæd] *n* skriveblokk *c*
writing paper ['raitiŋ,peipə] *n* skrivepapir *nt*
written ['ritən] *adj* (pp write) skriftlig
wrong [rɔŋ] *adj* gal, uriktig; *n* urett *m*; *v* *gjøre urett; ***be ~** *ta feil
wrote [rout] *v* (p write)

X

Xmas ['krisməs] jul *c*
X-ray ['eksrei] *n* røntgenbilde *nt*; *v* røntgenfotografere

Y

yacht [jɔt] *n* lystbåt *m*; **~ club** seilforening *c*
yachting ['jɔtiŋ] *n* seilsport *m*
yard [jɑːd] *n* gårdsplass *m*; hage *m*
yarn [jɑːn] *n* garn *nt*
yawn [jɔːn] *v* gjespe
year [jiə] *n* år *nt*
yearly ['jiəli] *adj* årlig
yeast [jiːst] *n* gjær *m*
yell [jel] *v* hyle; *n* hyl *nt*
yellow ['jelou] *adj* gul
yes [jes] ja
yesterday ['jestədi] *adv* i går
yet [jet] *adv* ennå; *conj* likevel, allikevel
yield [jiːld] *v* yte; *vike
yoghurt ['jɔgət] *n* yoghurt, jogurt *m*
yoke [jouk] *n* åk *nt*
yolk [jouk] *n* eggeplomme *c*
you [juː] *pron* du; deg; dere
young [jʌŋ] *adj* ung
your [jɔː] *pron* din; dine, deres
yours [jɔːz] *pron* din; dine, deres
yourself [jɔː'self] *pron* deg; selv
yourselves [jɔː'selvz] *pron* dere; selv
youth [juːθ] *n* ungdom *m*; **~ hostel** ungdomsherberge *nt*; vandrerhjem *nt*
yuppie ['jʌpi] *n* japp *c*

Z

zeal [ziːl] *n* iver *m*
zealous ['zeləs] *adj* ivrig
zebra ['ziːbrə] *n* sebra *m*
zenith ['zeniθ] *n* senit *nt*; høydepunkt *nt*
zero ['ziərou] *n* (pl ~s) null *nt*
zest [zest] *n* lyst *c*; iver *m*
zinc [ziŋk] *n* sink *m*
zip [zip] *n* glidelås *m*; ~ **code** *Am* postnummer *nt*
zipper ['zipə] *n* glidelås *m*
zodiac ['zoudiæk] *n* dyrekretsen
zone [zoun] *n* sone *c*; område
zoo [zuː] *n* (pl ~s) dyrehage *m*
zoology [zou'ɔlədʒi] *n* zoologi *m*

Some Basic Phrases	Noen vanlige uttrykk
Hello!	Hei!
Please.	Vær så snill.
Thank you very much.	Tusen takk.
Don't mention it.	Ingen årsak.
Good morning.	God morgen.
Good afternoon.	God dag.
Good evening.	God kveld.
Good night.	God natt.
Good-bye.	Ha det (bra)!
See you later.	Vi ses!
Where is/Where are…?	Hvor er…?
What do you call this?	Hva heter (kalles) dette?
What does that mean?	Hva betyr det?
Do you speak English?	Snakker du engelsk?
Do you speak German?	Snakker du tysk?
Do you speak French?	Snakker du fransk?
Do you speak Spanish?	Snakker du spansk?
Do you speak Italian?	Snakker du italiensk?
Could you speak more slowly, please?	Kunne du snakke litt langsommere?
I don't understand.	Jeg forstår ikke.
Can I have…?	Kan jeg få…?
Can you show me…?	Kan du vise meg…?
Can you tell me…?	Kan du si meg…?
Can you help me, please?	Kan du være så vennlig å hjelpe meg?
I'd like…	Jeg ville gjerne ha…
We'd like…	Vi ville gjerne ha…
Please give me…	Vær så snill å gi meg…
Please bring me…	Vær så snill å la meg få…
I'm hungry.	Jeg er sulten.
I'm thirsty.	Jeg er tørst.
I'm lost.	Jeg har gått meg vill.
Hurry up!	Skynd deg!
There is/There are…	Det finnes…
There isn't/There aren't…	Det finnes ikke…

Arrival	Ankomst
Your passport, please.	Passet, takk.
Have you anything to declare?	Har du noe å fortolle?
No, nothing at all.	Nei, ingenting.
Can you help me with my luggage, please?	Kan du hjelpe meg med bagasjen?
Where's the bus to the centre of town, please?	Hvor tar man bussen til sentrum?
This way, please.	Denne veien.
Where can I get a taxi?	Hvor kan jeg få tak i en drosje?
What's the fare to…?	Hva koster det til…?
Take me to this address, please.	Vær så snill å kjøre meg til denne adressen.
I'm in a hurry.	Jeg har det travelt.

Hotel	Hotell
My name is…	Mitt navn er…
Have you a reservation?	Har du bestilt?
I'd like a room with a bath.	Jeg vil gjerne ha et rom med bad.
What's the price per night?	Hva koster det for en natt?
May I see the room?	Kan jeg få se rommet?
What's my room number, please?	Hvilket værelsesnummer har jeg?
There's no hot water.	Det er ikke noe varmt vann.
May I see the manager, please?	Kan jeg få snakke med direktøren?
Did anyone telephone me?	Har det vært noen telefon til meg?
Is there any mail for me?	Er det noe post til meg?
May I have my bill (check), please?	Kan jeg få regningen, takk.

Eating out	Restaurant
Do you have a fixed-price menu?	Har dere en fast meny?

May I see the menu?	Kan jeg få se spisekartet?
May we have an ashtray, please?	Kan vi få et askebeger, takk?
Where's the toilet, please?	Hvor er toalettet?
I'd like an hors d'œuvre (starter).	Jeg vil gjerne ha en forrett.
Have you any soup?	Har dere suppe?
I'd like some fish.	Jeg vil gjerne ha fisk.
What kind of fish do you have?	Hva slags fisk har dere?
I'd like a steak.	Jeg vil gjerne ha en biff.
What vegetables have you got?	Hvilke grønnsaker har dere?
Nothing more, thanks.	Takk, jeg er forsynt.
What would you like to drink?	Hva vil du ha å drikke?
I'll have a beer, please.	Jeg vil gjerne ha en øl, takk.
I'd like a bottle of wine.	Jeg vil gjerne ha en flaske vin.
May I have the bill (check), please?	Regningen, takk!
Is service included?	Er service inkludert?
Thank you, that was a very good meal.	Takk. Det smakte utmerket.

Travelling	**På reise**
Where's the railway station, please?	Hvor er jernbanestasjonen?
Where's the ticket office, please?	Unnskyld, kan du si meg hvor billettluken er?
I'd like a ticket to…	Jeg vil gjerne ha en billett til…
First or second class?	Første eller annen klasse?
First class, please.	Første, takk.
Single or return (one way or roundtrip)?	Enkeltbillett eller tur-retur?
Do I have to change trains?	Må jeg bytte tog?
What platform does the train for… leave from?	Fra hvilken plattform går toget til…?

Where's the nearest underground (subway) station?	Hvor er nærmeste undergrunnsstasjon?
Where's the bus station, please?	Hvor er buss-stasjonen?
When's the first bus to…?	Når går den første bussen til…?
Please let me off at the next stop.	Kan du slippe meg av på neste holdeplass?

Meeting people	Bekjentskap
How do you do.	God dag.
How are you?	Hvordan står det til?
Very well, thank you. And you?	Bare bra, takk. Og med deg?
May I introduce…?	Kan jeg få presentere…?
My name is…	Mitt navn er…
I'm very pleased to meet you.	Gleder meg (å treffe deg).
How long have you been here?	Hvor lenge har du vært her?
It was nice meeting you.	Det var hyggelig å treffe deg.
Do you mind if I smoke?	Har du noe imot at jeg røyker?
Do you have a light, please?	Unnskyld, kan du gi meg fyr?
May I get you a drink?	Kan jeg by deg på en drink?
May I invite you for dinner tonight?	Vil du spise middag med meg i kveld?
Where shall we meet?	Hvor skal vi møtes?

Emergencies	Ulykker
Call a doctor quickly.	Tilkall en lege – fort.
Call an ambulance.	Ring etter en sykebil.
Please call the police.	Tilkall politiet.

Norwegian Abbreviations

adm.dir.	*administrerende direktør*	managing director
alm.	*alminnelig(het)*	general(ly)
A/S	*aksjeselskap*	Ltd., Inc.
dvs.	*det vil si*	i.e.
e.Kr.	*etter Kristi fødsel*	A.D.
el.	*eller*	or
EU	*Den europeiske union*	European Union
f.eks.	*for eksempel*	e.g.
fj.	*fjord*	fjord
f.Kr.	*før Kristi fødsel*	B.C.
flt.	*flertall*	plural
FN	*De forente nasjoner*	UN, United Nations
gen.sekr.	*generalsekretær*	secretary general
...gt.	*gate*	street
iflg.	*ifølge*	according to
KFUK	*Kristelig Forening av Unge Kvinner*	YWCA, Young Women's Christian Association
KFUM	*Kristelig Forening av Unge Menn*	YMCA, Young Men's Christian Association
kl.	*klokken*	hour, o'clock
KNM	*Den Kongelige Norske Marine*	Royal Norwegian Navy
kr	*krone*	crown (currency)
LO	*Landsorganisasjonen i Norge*	Association of Norwegian Trade Unions
mht.	*med hensyn til*	concerning
moms	*meromsetningsskatt*	VAT, value added tax
mots.	*motsatt*	contrary
N	*Norge*	Norway
nr.	*nummer*	number
NRK	*Norsk Rikskringkasting*	Norwegian Broadcasting Service
NSB	*Norges Statsbaner*	Norwegian National Railways
NTB	*Norsk Telegrambyrå*	Norwegian News Agency

NUH	*Norske ungdomsherberger*	Norwegian Youth Hostels
o.a.	*og annet, og andre*	etc., and others
osv.	*og så videre*	etc., and so on
stk.	*stykke(r)*	piece(s)
tlf.	*telefon*	telephone
...vn.	*veien, vegen*	road
årh.	*århundre*	century

Engelske forkortelser

A.D.	*anno Domini*	e.Kr.
Am.	*America; American*	Amerika; amerikansk
a.m.	*ante meridiem (before noon)*	mellom kl. 00.00 og 12.00
Amtrak	*American railroad corporation*	sammenslutning av private amerikanske jernbaneselskaper
Ave.	*avenue*	aveny
B.C.	*before Christ*	f.Kr.
Blvd.	*boulevard*	boulevard
B.R.	*British Rail*	Britiske statsbaner
Brit.	*Britain; British*	Storbritannia; britisk
Bros.	*brothers*	brødrene (i firmanavn)
¢	*cent*	1/100 dollar
Can.	*Canada; Canadian*	Canada; kanadisk
CID	*Criminal Investigation Department*	Det britiske kriminalpoliti
CNR	*Canadian National Railway*	Kanadiske statsbaner
c/o	*(in) care of*	adressert
Co.	*company*	kompani
Corp.	*corporation*	aksjeselskap *Am*
CPR	*Canadian Pacific Railways*	et privat kanadisk jernbaneselskap
D.C.	*District of Columbia*	Columbia-distriktet (Washington, D.C.)

DDS	*Doctor of Dental Science*	tannlege
e.g.	*for instance*	f.eks.
Eng.	*England; English*	England; engelsk
EU	*European Union*	Den europeiske union
ft.	*foot/feet*	fot (30,5 cm)
GB	*Great Britain*	Storbritannia
H.H.	*His Holiness*	Hans Hellighet
H.M.	*His/her Majesty*	Hans/Hennes Majestet
H.M.S.	*Her Majesty's ship*	britisk marineskip
hp	*horsepower*	hestekraft
i.e.	*that is to say*	dvs.
in.	*inch*	tomme (2,54 cm)
Inc.	*incorporated*	A/S
£	*pound sterling*	engelsk pund
L.A.	*Los Angeles*	Los Angeles
Ltd.	*limited*	A/S
M.D.	*Doctor of Medicine*	lege
M.P.	*Member of Parliament*	medlem av Det britisk parlament
mph	*miles per hour*	eng. mil i timen
Mr.	*Mister*	herr
Mrs.	*Missis*	fru
Ms.	*Missis/Miss*	fru/frk.
nat.	*national*	nasjonal
No.	*number*	nr.
N.Y.C.	*New York City*	byen New York
p.	*page; penny/pence*	side; $^{1}/_{100}$ pund
p.a.	*per annum*	pr. år
Ph.D.	*Doctor of Philosophy*	dr. philos.
p.m.	*post meridiem (after noon)*	mellom kl. 12.00 og 24.00
PO	*Post Office*	postkontor
P.T.O.	*please turn over*	vennligst bla om
RCMP	*Royal Canadian Mounted Police*	Det kongelige kanadiske ridende politi
Rd.	*road*	vei, veg
ref.	*reference*	referanse
Rev.	*reverend*	pastor
RFD	*rural free delivery*	postboks (på landsbygda)

RR	*railroad*	jernbane
RSVP	*please reply*	vennligst svar
$	*dollar*	dollar
Soc.	*society*	selskap
St.	*saint; street*	sankt; gate
STD	*Subscriber Trunk Dialling*	automattelefon
UN	*United Nations*	FN
US	*United States*	USA
USS	*United States Ship*	amerikansk marineskip
VAT	*value added tax*	med moms
VIP	*very important person*	betydningsfull person
Xmas	*Christmas*	jul
yd.	*yard*	yard (91,44 cm)
YMCA	*Young Men's Christian Association*	KFUM
YWCA	*Young Women's Christian Association*	KFUK
ZIP	*ZIP code*	postnummer

Mini Norwegian Grammar

Articles

Norwegian nouns are either masculine, feminine or neuter. The majority of feminine nouns also have a masculine form, so we have chosen to use the denotations *m* (masculine), *c* (common) and *n* (neuter). In this way, you will have to learn only two sets of articles, as masculine and common words can have the same article:

1. Indefinite article (a/an)

masculine:	***en* bil**	*a* car
common*:	***en* dør**	*a* door
neuter:	***et* eple**	*an* apple

2. Definite article (the)

Where we, in English, say "the house" Norwegians tag the definite article onto the end of the noun and say "house-the". In masculine and common nouns "the" is **-(e)n**, in neuter nouns **-(e)t**.

masculine:	**bil*en***	*the* car
common*:	**dør*en***	*the* door
neuter:	**eple*t***	*the* apple

Nouns

The plural of most nouns is formed by an **-(e)r** ending (indefinite plural) and an **-(e)ne** ending (definite plural).

masculine:	**bile*r***	car*s*	**bil*ene***	*the* cars
common*:	**døre*r***	doors	**dør*ene***	*the* doors
neuter:	**eple*r***	apple*s*	**eple*ne***	*the* apples

Many monosyllabic nouns have irregular plurals.

en mann	a man	**menn**	men	**mennene**	the men
en sko	a shoe	**sko**	shoes	**skoene**	the shoes

* In the feminine form "a door, the door" would be *ei* dør, dør*a*; the common form is *en* dør, dør*en*. In plural there is no difference.

Adjectives

1. Adjectives agree with the noun in gender and number. For the indefinite form, the neuter is generally formed by adding **-t**, the plural by adding **-e**.

(en) stor hund	(a) big dog	**store hunder**	big dogs
(et) stor*t* hus	(a) big house	**store hus**	big houses

2. The ending **-e** (masculine, common, neuter and plural) is used when the adjective is preceded by **den, det, de** (the definite article used with adjectives) or by a demonstrative or a possessive adjective.

den store hunden	the big dog	**det store huset**	the big house
de store hundene	the big dogs	**de store husene**	the big houses

3. Comparative and superlative

The comparative and superlative are normally formed either by adding the endings **-(e)re** and **-(e)st**, respectively, to the adjective or by putting **mer** (more) and **mest** (most) before the adjective.

stor/stør*re*/stør*st*	big/bigger/biggest
lett/lett*ere*/lett*est*	easy/easier/easiest
imponerende/*mer* imponerende/*mest* imponerende	impressive/more impressive/the most impressive

4. Possessive adjectives agree in number and gender with the noun they modify, i.e. with the thing possessed and not the possessor.

	common	neuter	plural
my	**min**	**mitt**	**mine**
your	**din**	**ditt**	**dine**
his	**sin, hans**	**sitt, hans**	**sine, hans**
her	**sin, hennes**	**sitt, hennes**	**sine, hennes**
its	**sin, dens/dets***	**sitt, dens/dets**	**sine, dens/dets**
our	**vår**	**vårt**	**våre**
their	**sin, deres**	**sitt, deres**	**sine, deres**

* Use **dens** if "it" is of common gender and **dets** if "it" is neuter.

Personal pronouns

	subject	object	genitive
I	**jeg**	**meg**	–
you	**du**	**deg**	–
he	**han**	**ham/han**	**hans**
she	**hun**	**henne**	**hennes**
it	**den/det**	**den/det**	**dens/dets**
we	**vi**	**oss**	–
you (plural)	**dere**	**dere**	–
they	**de**	**dem**	**deres**

Verbs

The present tense is simple, because it has the same form for all persons.

	to ask	to buy	to go	to do
Infinitive	**å spørre**	**å kjøpe**	**å gå**	**å gjøre**
Present tense	**spør**	**kjøper**	**går**	**gjør**
Imperative	**spør**	**kjøp**	**gå**	**gjør**

There is no equivalent to the English present continuous tense. Thus:

Jeg reiser. I travel/I am travelling.

Negation is expressed by using the adverb **ikke** (not). It is usually placed immediately after the verb in a main clause. In compound tenses, **ikke** appears between the auxiliary and the main verb.

Jeg snakker norsk. I speak Norwegian.
Jeg snakker ikke norsk. I do not speak Norwegian.

Irregular Verbs

There is a large number of prefixes in Norwegian, like *an-*, *av-*, *be-*, *etter-*, *for-*, *fra-*, *frem-*, *inn-*, *med-*, *ned-*, *om-*, *opp-*, *over-*, *på-*, *til-*, *under-*, *unn-*, *unna-*, *ut-*, *ved-*, etc. A prefixed verb is conjugated in the same way as the stem verb.

Infinitive	*Preterite*	*Past participle*	
be	ba	bedt	*ask, pray*
binde	bandt	bundet	*bind, tie*
bite	bet	bitt	*bite*
bli	ble	blitt	*become, remain*
brekke	brakk	brukket	*break*
brenne	brant/brente*	brent	*burn*
bringe	brakte	brakt	*bring*
briste	brast	bristet	*burst*
bryte	brøt	brutt	*break*
by	bydde/bød	budt	*offer; command*
bære	bar	båret	*bear*
dra	dro(g)	dradd/dratt	*pull; go, travel*
drikke	drakk	drukket	*drink*
drive	drev	drevet	*lead, manage; drift*
ete	åt	ett	*eat (animals)*
falle	falt	falt	*fall*
fare	fór	faret/fart	*go away, leave*
finne	fant	funnet	*find*
fly	fløy	fløyet	*fly*
flyte	fløt	flytt	*flow, float*
forstå	forsto(d)	forstått	*understand*
forsvinne	forsvant	forsvunnet	*disappear*
fortelle	fortalte	fortalt	*tell, relate*
fryse	frøs	frosset	*be cold, freeze*
følge	fulgte	fulgt	*follow*
få	fikk	fått	*get*

* These verbs are regular when used transitively, i.e. when they take an object.

gi	ga(v)	gitt	*give*
gjelde	gjaldt	gjeldt	*concern; be valid*
gjøre	gjorde	gjort	*do, make*
gli	gled	glidd	*slide, glide*
gnage	gnagde/gnog	gnagd	*gnaw*
gni	gnidde/gned	gnidd	*rub*
grave	gravde/grov	gravd	*dig*
gripe	grep	grepet	*catch, seize*
gråte	gråt	grått	*weep, cry*
gyte	gytte/gjøt	gytt	*spawn*
gå	gikk	gått	*walk, go*
ha	hadde	hatt	*have*
henge	hang/hengte*	hengt	*hang*
hete	het/hette	hett	*be called*
hive	hev	hevet	*throw*
hjelpe	hjalp	hjulpet	*help*
holde	holdt	holdt	*hold*
klinge	klang	kling(e)t	*ring*
klype	klypte/kløp	klypt/kløpet	*pinch*
klyve	kløv	kløvet	*climb*
knekke	knakk/knekte*	knekt/knekket	*crack, break*
knipe	knep	knepet	*pinch*
komme	kom	kommet	*come*
krype	krøp	krøpet	*creep, crawl*
kunne (kan)	kunne	kunnet	*can*
kveppe	kvapp	kveppet	*startle*
la(te)	lot	latt	*let*
le	lo	ledd	*laugh*
legge	la	lagt	*lay, put*
lide	led	lidd	*suffer*
ligge	lå	ligget	*lie*
lyde	lød	lydt	*sound*
lyge	løy	løyet	*tell a lie*
løpe	løp	løpt	*run*
måtte (må)	måtte	måttet	*must*
nyse	nyste/nøs	nyst	*sneeze*

* These verbs are regular when used transitively, i.e. when they take an object.

nyte	nøt	nytt	*enjoy*
pipe	pep	pepet	*chirp*
rekke	rakte/rakk	rakt/rukket	*reach; hand*
renne	rant/rente*	rent	*run, flow*
ri(de)	red	ridd	*ride*
rive	rev	revet	*tear*
ryke	røk	røket	*smoke*
se	så	sett	*see*
selge	solgte	solgt	*sell*
sette	satte	satt	*set*
si	sa	sagt	*say*
sitte	satt	sittet	*sit*
skjelve	skalv	skjelvet	*tremble*
skjære	skar	skåret	*cut*
skri(de)	skred	skredet/skridd	*stride, stalk*
skrike	skrek	skreket	*scream*
skrive	skrev	skrevet	*write*
skryte	skrøt	skrytt	*boast*
skulle (skal)	skulle	skullet	*shall*
skvette	skvatt/skvettet*	skvettet	*startle; splash*
skyte	skjøt	skutt	*shoot*
skyve	skjøv	skjøvet	*push, shove*
slenge	slang/slengte*	slengt	*throw, fling*
slippe	slapp	sluppet	*let go, drop*
slite	slet	slitt	*pull, tear*
slå	slo	slått	*strike, beat*
slåss	sloss	slåss	*fight*
smelle	smalt/smelte*	smelt	*smack, slam*
smette	smatt	smettet	*slip away*
smøre	smurte	smurt	*smear*
snike	snek	sneket	*sneak*
snyte (seg)	snøt	snytt	*blow one's nose; cheat*
sove	sov	sovet	*sleep*
spinne	spant	spunnet	*spin; purr*
sprekke	sprakk	sprukket	*burst*
sprette	spratt	sprettet	*bound*

* These verbs are regular when used transitively, i.e. when they take an object.

springe	sprang	sprunget	*run; jump*
spørre	spurte	spurt	*ask*
stige	steg	steget	*rise, climb*
stikke	stakk	stukket	*sting*
stjele	stjal	stjålet	*steal*
strekke	strakk	strukket	*stretch*
stri(de)	stridde/stred	stridd	*quarrel*
stryke	strøk	strøket	*iron; cross out*
stå	sto	stått	*stand*
sverge	sverget/svor	sverget/svoret	*swear*
svi	sved/svidde*	svidd	*singe*
svike	svek	sveket	*betray, disappoint*
svinge	svang	sving(e)t/ svunget	*swing*
synge	sang	sunget	*sing*
synke	sank	sunket	*sink*
ta	tok	tatt	*take*
telle	talte/telte	talt/telt	*count*
tie	tidde	tidd	*be/keep silent*
tigge	tigget/tagg	tigget/tigd	*beg*
tre	trådte	trådt	*tread, step*
treffe	traff	truffet	*meet; hit*
trekke	trakk	trukket	*pull*
tvinge	tvang	tvunget	*force*
tygge	tygde	tygd	*chew*
vekke	vakte	vakt	*wake*
velge	valgte	valgt	*choose, elect*
vike	vek	veket	*yield*
ville (vil)	ville	villet	*will*
vinde	vandt	vundet	*wind*
vinne	vant	vunnet	*win*
vite	visste	visst	*know*
vri	vred	vridd	*wrench, twist*
være	var	vært	*be*

Engelsk minigrammatikk

Artikler

Den **bestemte** artikkel har samme form i entall og flertall: **the.**

the room – the rooms	rommet – rommene

Den **ubestemte** artikkel har to former: **a**, som brukes foran ord som begynner med en konsonant, og **an**, som brukes foran vokal eller stum **h**.

a coat	en kåpe/frakk
an umbrella	en paraply
an hour	en time

Some angir en ubestemt mengde eller et ubestemt antall. Det anvendes foran substantiv i både entall og flertall, og tilsvarer på norsk «noen», «noe», «litt».

I'd like some tea, please.	Jeg vil gjerne ha litt te.
Give me some stamps, please.	Gi meg noen frimerker, er du snill.

Any betyr «noen»/«hvilken som helst», og brukes ofte i nektende og spørrende setninger.

There isn't any soap.	Det er ikke noe såpe her.
Do you have any stamps?	Har du frimerker?
Is there any mail for me?	Er det kommet noe post til meg?

Substantiver

Flertall dannes som regel ved å føye **-(e)s** til entallsformen.

cup – cups	kopp – kopper
dress – dresses	kjole – kjoler

Obs! Hvis et substantiv slutter på **-y** i entall, endres stavemåten til **-ies** i flertall hvis **y** kommer etter en konsonant. Kommer den etter en vokal, anvendes den normale flertallsendelsen **-s.**

lady – ladies	dame – damer
day – days	dag – dager

Men ingen regel unten unntak…

man – men	mann – menn
woman – women	kvinne – kvinner
child – children	barn – barn
foot – feet	fot – føtter
knife – knives	kniv – kniver

Genitiv

1. Når eieren er et levende vesen og når substantivet ikke slutter på **-s**, føyer man til **'s.**

the boy's room	guttens rom
Anne's dress	Annes kjole

Hvis substantivet slutter på **-s**, føyer man kun til apostrofen (').

the boy's room	guttenes rom

2. Hvis eieren ikke er et levende vesen, brukes preposisjonen **of.**

the end of the journey	reisens slutt (slutten på reisen)

Adjektiver

Adjektivet forblir uendret både foran substantivet og når det står alene.

a large brown suitcase	en stor brun koffert
Komparativ og **superlativ**	kan dannes på to måter.

1. Adjektiver med én stavelse og de fleste adjektiver med to stavelser får endelsen **-(e)r** og **-(e)st.**

small – smaller – smallest	liten – mindre – minst
pretty – prettier – prettiest	søt – søtere – søtest

Obs! **-y** etter konsonant endres til **i** foran **-er** og **-est.**

2. Adjektiver med flere enn to stavelser og enkelte adjektiver med to stavelser (f.eks. de som slutter på **-ful** eller **-less**) danner komparativ og superlativ ved hjelp av **more** og **most.**

expensive (dyr) – **more expensive – most expensive**
careful (forsiktig) – **more careful – most careful**

Følgende adjektiver er uregelmessige:

good (bra) – **better** – **best**
bad (dårlig) – **worse** – **worst**
little (lite) – **less** – **least**
much (mye) } – **more** – **most**
many (mange) } – **more** – **most**

Pronomener

	personlige nominativ	pronomer akkusativ	eiendomspronomener 1)	2)
jeg	**I**	**me**	**my**	**mine**
du	**you**	**you**	**your**	**yours**
han	**he**	**him**	**his**	**his**
hun	**she**	**her**	**her**	**hers**
den/det	**it**	**it**	**its**	–
vi	**we**	**us**	**our**	**ours**
dere	**you**	**you**	**your**	**yours**
de	**they**	**them**	**their**	**theirs**

Verb

Tre viktige **hjelpeverb** i presens:

to be (å være)

	sammentrukket form	sammentrukket nektende form	
I am	**I'm**	**I'm not**	–
you are	**you're**	**you're not**	**you aren't**
he is	**he's**	**he's not**	**he isn't**
she is	**she's**	**she's not**	**she isn't**
it is	**it's**	**it's not**	**it isn't**
we are	**we're**	**we're not**	**we aren't**
you are	**you're**	**you're not**	**you aren't**
they are	**they're**	**they're not**	**they aren't**

Spørreform: **Am I? – Is he? – Are they?**
Obs! I dagligtale brukes så å si bare de sammentrukne formene.

to have (å ha)

	sammentrukket form	sammentrukket nektende form
I have	**I've**	**I haven't**
you have	**you've**	**you haven't**
he/she/it has	**he's/she's/it's**	**he/she/it hasn't**
we have	**we've**	**we haven't**
you have	**you've**	**you haven't**
they have	**they've**	**they haven't**

Spørrende: **Have you? – Has he?**

to do (å gjøre)

I do, you, he/she/it does, we do, you do, they do

Nektende: **I do not (I don't) – He does not (He doesn't)**
Spørrende: **Do you? – Does she?**

For alle hjelpeverb gjelder:

1. Nektende form dannes med **not** (ikke).
2. Spørrende form dannes ved å sette verbet foran subjektet.

Andre verb

Engelske verb beholder samme form i alle personer i **presens,** med unntak av 3. person entall der man legger til **-(e)s.**

	to speak (å snakke)	**to ask** (å spørre)	**to go** (å gå)
I	**speak**	**ask**	**go**
you	**speak**	**ask**	**go**
he/she/it	**speaks**	**asks**	**goes**
we/you/they	**speak**	**ask**	**go**

Imperfektum og **perfektum partisipp** dannes for regelmessige verb ved å føye til endelsen **-d** eller **-ed.**

Presens partisipp dannes ved å føye endelsen **-ing** til infinitivsformen.

Nektende form dannes med hjelpeverbet **do** + **not** + infinitiv:
I do not (don't) like this hotel. Jeg liker ikke dette hotellet.

Spørrende form dannes med hjelpeverbet **do** + subjekt + infinitiv:
Do you drink wine? Drikker du vin?

Progressiv (pågående) form
Denne formen finnes ikke på norsk, men motsvarer «holder på med å», og dannes med hjelpeverbet **to be** fulgt av presens partisipp av verbet.

infinitiv	presens partisipp	progressiv form
to read	**reading**	**I'm reading.**
to sing	**singing**	**She's singing.**

What are you doing? Hva er det du holder på med (å gjøre)?
I'm writing a letter. Jeg holder på (med) å skrive et brev.

Uregelmessige verb

Her er en liste over uregelmessige engelske verb. Sammensatte verb, eller verb som har prefiks, bøyes etter samme mønster som det enkle verbet; eks.: *overdrive* bøyes som *drive*, *mistake* som *take*.

Infinitiv	*Imperfektum*	*Perfektum partisipp*	
arise	arose	arisen	*stå opp*
awake	awoke	awoken/ awaked	*vekke; våkne*
be	was	been	*være*
bear	bore	borne	*bære*
beat	beat	beaten	*slå*
become	became	become	*bli*
begin	began	begun	*begynne*
bend	bent	bent	*bøye*
bet	bet	bet	*vedde*
bid	bade/bid	bidden/bid	*by (befale)*
bind	bound	bound	*binde*
bite	bit	bitten	*bite*
bleed	bled	bled	*blø*
blow	blew	blown	*blåse*
break	broke	broken	*brekke*
breed	bred	bred	*ale opp*
bring	brought	brought	*bringe*
build	built	built	*bygge*
burn	burnt/burned	burnt/burned	*brenne*
burst	burst	burst	*briste*
buy	bought	bought	*kjøpe*
can*	could	–	*kunne*
cast	cast	cast	*kaste*
catch	caught	caught	*gripe*
choose	chose	chosen	*velge*
cling	clung	clung	*klamre seg til*
clothe	clothed/clad	clothed/clad	*kle på*
come	came	come	*komme*
cost	cost	cost	*koste*

* presens indikativ

creep	crept	crept	*krype*
cut	cut	cut	*skjære*
deal	dealt	dealt	*handle*
dig	dug	dug	*grave*
do (he does*)	did	done	*gjøre*
draw	drew	drawn	*trekke*
dream	dreamt/ dreamed	dreamt/ dreamed	*drømme*
drink	drank	drunk	*drikke*
drive	drove	driven	*kjøre*
dwell	dwelt	dwelt	*bo*
eat	ate	eaten	*spise*
fall	fell	fallen	*falle*
feed	fed	fed	*fôre*
feel	felt	felt	*føle*
fight	fought	fought	*slåss*
find	found	found	*finne*
flee	fled	fled	*flykte*
fling	flung	flung	*kaste*
fly	flew	flown	*fly*
forsake	forsook	forsaken	*svikte*
freeze	froze	frozen	*fryse*
get	got	got	*få*
give	gave	given	*gi*
go (he goes*)	went	gone	*gå*
grind	ground	ground	*male, knuse*
grow	grew	grown	*gro*
hang	hung	hung	*henge*
have (he has*)	had	had	*ha*
hear	heard	heard	*høre*
hew	hewed	hewed/hewn	*hugge*
hide	hid	hidden	*gjemme*
hit	hit	hit	*slå*
hold	held	held	*holde*
hurt	hurt	hurt	*såre*
keep	kept	kept	*beholde*
kneel	knelt	knelt	*knele*
knit	knitted/knit	knitted/knit	*strikke*

* presens indikativ

know	knew	known	*vite*
lay	laid	laid	*legge*
lead	led	led	*lede*
lean	leant/leaned	leant/leaned	*lene*
leap	leapt/leaped	leapt/leaped	*hoppe*
learn	learnt/learned	learnt/learned	*lære*
leave	left	left	*forlate*
lend	lent	lent	*låne* (*ut*)
let	let	let	*la; leie ut*
lie	lay	lain	*ligge*
light	lit/lighted	lit/lighted	*tenne*
lose	lost	lost	*miste*
make	made	made	*lage*
may*	might	–	*kunne* (*få lov*)
mean	meant	meant	*mene*
meet	met	met	*møte*
mow	mowed	mowed/mown	*slå* (*gress*)
must*	must	–	*måtte*
ought* **(to)**	ought	–	*burde*
pay	paid	paid	*betale*
put	put	put	*legge*
read	read	read	*lese*
rid	rid	rid	*befri*
ride	rode	ridden	*ride*
ring	rang	rung	*ringe*
rise	rose	risen	*reise seg*
run	ran	run	*løpe*
saw	sawed	sawn	*sage*
say	said	said	*si*
see	saw	seen	*se*
seek	sought	sought	*søke*
sell	sold	sold	*selge*
send	sent	sent	*sende*
set	set	set	*sette*
sew	sewed	sewed/sewn	*sy*
shake	shook	shaken	*riste*
shall*	should	–	*skulle*
shed	shed	shed	*felle*

* presens indikativ

shine	shone	shone	*skinne*
shoot	shot	shot	*skyte*
show	showed	shown	*vise*
shrink	shrank	shrunk	*krympe*
shut	shut	shut	*lukke*
sing	sang	sung	*synge*
sink	sank	sunk	*synke*
sit	sat	sat	*sitte*
sleep	slept	slept	*sove*
slide	slid	slid	*gli*
sling	slung	slung	*kaste*
slink	slunk	slunk	*luske*
slit	slit	slit	*flenge*
smell	smelled/smelt	smelled/smelt	*lukte*
sow	sowed	sown/sowed	*så*
speak	spoke	spoken	*snakke*
speed	sped/speeded	sped/speeded	*haste*
spell	spelt/spelled	spelt/spelled	*stave*
spend	spent	spent	*gi ut; tilbringe*
spill	spilt/spilled	spilt/spilled	*søle, spille*
spin	spun	spun	*spinne*
spit	spat	spat	*spytte*
split	split	split	*splitte*
spoil	spoilt/spoiled	spoilt/spoiled	*ødelegge; skjemme bort*
spread	spread	spread	*spre*
spring	sprang	sprung	*hoppe opp*
stand	stood	stood	*stå*
steal	stole	stolen	*stjele*
stick	stuck	stuck	*klebe*
sting	stung	stung	*stikke*
stink	stank/stunk	stunk	*stinke*
strew	strewed	strewed/strewn	*strø*
stride	strode	stridden	*skride*
strike	struck	struck/stricken	*slå*
string	strung	strung	*tre på snor*
strive	strove	striven	*streve*
swear	swore	sworn	*banne; sverge*
sweep	swept	swept	*feie*

swell	swelled	swollen/ swelled	*hovne*
swim	swam	swum	*svømme*
swing	swung	swung	*svinge*
take	took	taken	*ta*
teach	taught	taught	*undervise*
tear	tore	torn	*rive*
tell	told	told	*fortelle*
think	thought	thought	*tenke*
throw	threw	thrown	*kaste*
thrust	thrust	thrust	*støte*
tread	trod	trodden	*trå*
wake	woke/waked	woken/waked	*våkne; vekke*
wear	wore	worn	*ha på seg*
weave	wove	woven	*veve*
weep	wept	wept	*gråte*
will*	would	–	*ville*
win	won	won	*vinne*
wind	wound	wound	*sno*
wring	wrung	wrung	*vri*
write	wrote	written	*skrive*

* presens indikativ

Numerals

Cardinal numbers		Ordinal numbers	
0	null	1.	første
1	en	2.	annen
2	to	3.	tredje
3	tre	4.	fjerde
4	fire	5.	femte
5	fem	6.	sjette
6	seks	7.	syvende/sjuende
7	syv/sju	8.	åttende
8	åtte	9.	niende
9	ni	10.	tiende
10	ti	11.	ellevte
11	elleve	12.	tolvte
12	tolv	13.	trettende
13	tretten	14.	fjortende
14	fjorten	15.	femtende
15	femten	16.	sekstende
16	seksten	17.	syttende
17	sytten	18.	attende
18	atten	19.	nittende
19	nitten	20.	tyvende/tjuende
20	tyve/tjue	21.	enogtyvende/ tjueførste
21	enogtyve/tjueen	22.	toogtyvende/tjueandre
30	tredve/tretti	23.	treogtyvende/ tjuetredje
31	enogtredve/trettien	24.	firogtyvende/ tjuefjerde
40	førti	25.	femogtyvende/ tjuefemte
41	enogførti/førtien	26.	seksogtyvende/ tjuesjette
50	femti	27.	syvogtyvende/ tjuesjuende
51	enogfemti/femtien		
60	seksti	28.	åtteogtyvende/ tjueåttende
61	enogseksti/sekstien		
70	sytti	29.	niogtyvende/ tjueniende
71	enogsytti/syttien	30.	tredevte/trettiende
80	åtti	40.	førtiende
81	enogåtti/åttien	50.	femtiende
90	nitti	60.	sekstiende
91	enognitti/nittien	70.	syttiende
100	hundre	80.	åttiende
101	hundre og en	90.	nittiende
1 000	tusen	100.	hundrede
1 000 000	en million	1 000.	tusende

Tall

Grunntall

0	zero
1	one
2	two
3	three
4	four
5	five
6	six
7	seven
8	eight
9	nine
10	ten
11	eleven
12	twelve
13	thirteen
14	fourteen
15	fifteen
16	sixteen
17	seventeen
18	eighteen
19	nineteen
20	twenty
21	twenty-one
22	twenty-two
23	twenty-three
24	twenty-four
25	twenty-five
30	thirty
40	forty
50	fifty
60	sixty
70	seventy
80	eighty
90	ninety
100	a/one hundred
230	two hundred and thirty
1,000	a/one thousand
10,000	ten thousand
100,000	a/one hundred thousand
1,000,000	a/one million

Ordenstall

1st	first
2nd	second
3rd	third
4th	fourth
5th	fifth
6th	sixth
7th	seventh
8th	eighth
9th	ninth
10th	tenth
11th	eleventh
12th	twelfth
13th	thirteenth
14th	fourteenth
15th	fifteenth
16th	sixteenth
17th	seventeenth
18th	eighteenth
19th	nineteenth
20th	twentieth
21st	twenty-first
22nd	twenty-second
23rd	twenty-third
24th	twenty-fourth
25th	twenty-fifth
26th	twenty-sixth
27th	twenty-seventh
28th	twenty-eighth
29th	twenty-ninth
30th	thirtieth
40th	fortieth
50th	fiftieth
60th	sixtieth
70th	seventieth
80th	eightieth
90th	ninetieth
100th	hundredth
230th	two hundred and thirtieth
1,000th	thousandth

Time

Although official time in Norway is based on the 24-hour clock, the 12-hour system is used in conversation.

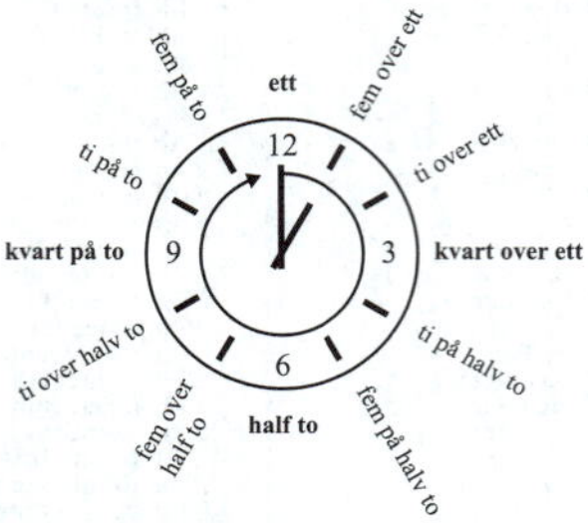

If you have to indicate that it is a.m. or p.m., add *om morgenen*, *om formiddagen*, *om ettermiddagen*, *om kvelden*, *om natten*.

Thus:

klokken syv om morgenen	7 a.m.
klokken elleve om formiddagen	11 a.m.
klokken to om ettermiddagen	2 p.m.
klokken åtte om kvelden	8 p.m.
klokken to om natten	2 a.m.

Days of the week

søndag	Sunday	*torsdag*	Thursday
mandag	Monday	*fredag*	Friday
tirsdag	Tuesday	*lørdag*	Saturday
onsdag	Wednesday		

Klokken

Både engelskmennene og amerikanerne anvender uttrykkene a.m. (ante meridiem) om tiden etter midnatt frem til kl. 12, og p.m. (post meridiem) om tiden etter kl. 12 frem til midnatt. I England går man imidlertid mer og mer over til å bruke 24-timerssystemet.

Eksempler:

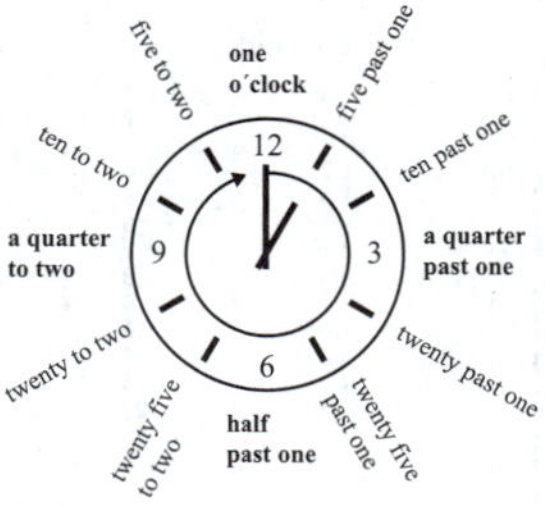

I'll come at seven a.m. Jeg kommer kl. 7 om morgenen.
I'll come at two p.m. Jeg kommer kl. 2 om ettermiddagen.
I'll come at eight p.m. Jeg kommer kl. 8 om kvelden.

Dagene

Sunday	søndag	*Thursday*	torsdag
Monday	mandag	*Friday*	fredag
Tuesday	tirsdag	*Saturday*	lørdag
Wednesday	onsdag		

Conversion tables/Omregningstabeller

Metres and feet

The figure in the middle stands for both metres and feet, e.g. 1 metre = 3.281 ft. and 1 foot = 0.30 m.

Meter og fot

Tallene i midten gjelder både for meter og fot, dvs. 1 meter = 3,281 fot, og 1 fot = 0,30 meter.

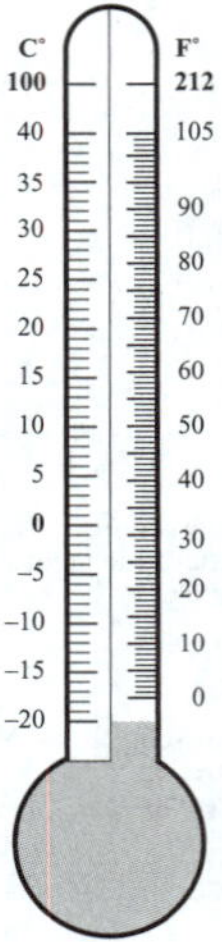

Metres/Meter		Feet/Fot
0.30	**1**	3.281
0.61	**2**	6.563
0.91	**3**	9.843
1.22	**4**	13.124
1.52	**5**	16.403
1.83	**6**	19.686
2.13	**7**	22.967
2.44	**8**	26.248
2.74	**9**	29.529
3.05	**10**	32.810
3.66	**12**	39.372
4.27	**14**	45.934
6.10	**20**	65.620
7.62	**25**	82.023
15.24	**50**	164.046
22.86	**75**	246.069
30.48	**100**	328.092

Temperature

To convert Centigrade to Fahrenheit, multiply by 1.8 and add 32.
To convert Fahrenheit to Centigrade, subtract 32 from Fahrenheit and divide by 1.8.

Temperatur

For å regne om fra celsius- til fahrenheitgrader, ganger en med 1,8 og legger til 32. Omvendt – for å regne om fra fahrenheit- til celsiusgrader – trekker en fra 32 og deler med 1,8.